The Politics of Sustainable Development

Citizens, Unions and the Corporations

Laurie E. Adkin

Montréal/New York
London

To the activists leading the way.

Copyright © 1998 BLACK ROSE BOOKS

No part of this book may be reproduced or transmitted in any form, by any means electronic or mechanical, including photocopying and recording, or by any information storage or retrieval system—without written permission from the publisher, or, in the case of photocopying or other reprographic copying, a license from the Canadian Reprography Collective, with the exception of brief passages quoted by a reviewer in a newspaper or magazine.

Black Rose Books No. AA247
Hardcover ISBN: 1-55164-081-3 (bound)
Paperback ISBN: 1-55164-080-5 (pbk.)
Library of Congress Catalog Card Number: 96-79518

Cover Design by Associés libres, Montréal

Canadian Cataloguing in Publication Data

Adkin, Laurie Elizabeth, 1958-
Politics of sustainable development : citizens, unions and the corporations

ISBN 1-55164-081-3 (bound).—
ISBN 1-55164-080-5 (pbk.)

1. Political participation. 2. Sustainable development—Political aspects.
I. Title.

HD75.6.A35 1996   333.7   C96-900777-9

C.P. 1258	250 Sonwil Drive	99 Wallis Road
Succ. Place du Parc	Buffalo, New York	London, E9 5LN
Montréal, Québec	14225 USA	England
H2W 2R3 Canada		

To order books in North America: (phone) 1-800-565-9523 (fax) 1-800-221-9985
In Europe: (phone) 44-081-986-4854 (fax) 44-081-533-5821

Our Web Site address: http://www.web.net/blackrosebooks

A publication of the Institute of Policy Alternatives of Montréal (IPAM)
Printed in Canada

Table of Contents

List of Tables and Figures	vi
List of Abbreviations	vii
Preface	x
Introduction	xii

PART I: SOCIAL MOVEMENTS AND SOCIAL CHANGE

1.	New Social Movements, Labour, and Theories of Social Change	1

PART II: DEFINING THE STAKES OF ENVIRONMENTAL POLITICS: CITIZEN, UNION, AND CORPORATE ACTORS

2.	Environmental Crisis: The Context for Citizen Mobilization in the 1980s	28
3.	The Ontario "Spills Bill"	39
4.	The Canadian Environmental Protection Act	50
5.	The Ontario Municipal-Industrial Strategy for Abatement	73
6.	The Great Lakes Water Quality Agreement Review	86
7.	Brush-fires of Democratization: The Remedial Action Plans	99

PART III: CORPORATE UNIONISM AND SOCIAL MOVEMENTS: THE ENERGY AND CHEMICAL WORKERS

8.	The Political Economy and Culture of a Union: The Energy and Chemical Workers Union in the 1980s	117
9.	Collective Bargaining and Union-Employer Relations	146
10.	Chemical Workers and Toxic Pollution Issues	160
11.	Toxic Chemical Pollution of the Chemical Valley in the 1980s	188

PART IV: SOCIAL UNIONISM AND SOCIAL MOVEMENTS: THE CANADIAN AUTOWORKERS

12.	The CAW Environmental Policy	226
13.	Two Strategies of Social Unionism	256
14.	Union-Environmental Movement Convergence	281

Conclusion	315
Appendix	332
Bibliography	337

List of Tables

1. Environmental organizations and citizens' groups active in Ontario in the 1980s (a partial list)
2. Partial list of conferences on Great Lakes Basin environmental issues, 1986-88
3. MISA schedules for monitoring and abatement regulations, 1986, 1989
4. Representation of social actors in government review processes for environmental legislation
5. Participation in GLWQA public consultation processes
6. Public participation processes in 17 Areas of Concern
7. St. Clair River RAP Bi-national Public Advisory Committee membership, May 1988
8. Environmental campaigns affecting the energy and petrochemical industries
9. Structure and membership of the ECWU, 1985
10. Average weekly earnings (hourly wage-earners only) for ECWU-related sectors, 1980, 1987
11. Wage differentials for selected sectors, 1980-87
12. The "Top Ten" United States Chemical companies, 1984-86
13. Leading chemical companies in Canada, 1988
14. Leading integrated oil companies, 1988
15. Work force categories, Polysar, 1986-88
16. Chemical company employment in Canada, 1983-86
17. Plant closings affecting ECWU members, 1982-88
18. Percentage of adults reporting occupational exposure to risk factors
19. Percentage of adults reporting residential exposure to risk factors
20. Position in union hierarchy vs. future participation in a union environment committee
21. Priorities for allocation of union resources (five locals)
22. Union priorities vs. occupational groups (five locals)
23. Reasons for non-participation in environment committees
24. Proposed changes to encourage participation
25. Environmental issues mentioned vs. CAW local
26. Means of information about committees listed by respondents
27. Awareness of environmental issues among CAW locals
28. Willingness to participate in a local environment committee
29. Willingness to participate in a non-union environment group
30. CAW local by ability to name one environmental issue
31. Support for union strategies (five locals)
32. Highest union position held by choice of union strategy
33. CAW Mergers, 1985-95
34. Data on Survey Distribution and Response (Appendix 1)

FIGURES

1. Remedial Action Plan Process, Canadian Jurisdictions
2. Map of the Chemical Valley
3. Sectoral and Geographical Distribution of CAW membership, 1996

Abbreviations

ACCs	advanced capitalist countries
AECL	Atomic Energy of Canada Ltd.
AIA	Access to Information Act
AOCs	Areas of Concern
ASMAC	Adhesives and Sealants Manufacturers Association of Canada
BADT	best available demonstrated technology
BAT-EA	best available technology, economically attainable
BCFL	British Columbia Federation of Labour
BPAC	binational public advisory committee
CAC	Community Awareness Committee of the companies in Lambton County
CAC(s)	Citizens' Advisory Committee(s)
CADIS	Centre d'Analyse et d'Intervention sociologiques, Paris
CAER	Community Awareness and Emergency Response (initiative of the CCPA)
CAIMAW	Canadian Association of Industrial, Mechanical and Allied Workers
CARE	Citizens Advocating Responsibility for the Environment
CAW	Canadian Auto Workers
CBC	Canadian Broadcasting Corporation
CCCW	Citizens' Coalition for Clean Water (Wallaceburg)
CCPA	Canadian Chemical Producers Association
CCW	Canadian Chemical Workers
CDP	continuing dialogue program
CEA	Citizens' Environmental Alliance (Windsor)
CEBR	Canadian Environmental Bill of Rights
CELA	Canadian Environmental Law Association
CEP	Communications, Energy, and Paperworkers Union, 1992-
CEPA	Canadian Environmental Protection Act
CFDT	Confédération Française Démocratique du Travail
CIO	Congress of Industrial Organizations
CLC	Canadian Labour Congress
CMA	Canadian Manufacturers Association
COACH	Citizens Organized Against Chemical Hazards
CPPA	Canadian Pulp and Paper Association
CPU	Canadian Paperworkers Union
CROP	Centre de Recherche sur l'Opinion Publique
CSD	Confédération des Syndicats Démocratiques (Québec)
CSN	Confédération des Syndicats Nationaux (Québec)
CUPE	Canadian Union of Public Employees
CWA	Clean Water Alliance (Windsor)
DDT	Dichlorodiphenyl trichlorethane

DNR	Michigan Department of Natural Resources
DNT	dinitrotolulene
DOE	Department of the Environment (Canada)
EA	economically attainable
EC	environment committee
ECA	Environmental Contaminants Act
ECAAC	Environmental Contaminants Act Amendments Consultation (Committee)
ECC	Environmental Control Commission
ECPC	Energy, Conservation, and Pollution Control (Committee of the OFL)
ECWU	Energy and Chemical Workers Union
EPA or USEPA	Environmental Protection Agency (United States)
FOE	Friends of the Earth
GATT	General Agreement on Tariffs and Trade
GLI	Great Lakes Institute, Windsor
GLU	Great Lakes United
GLWQA	Great Lakes Water Quality Agreement
GWA	Green Work Alliance
HCB	hexachlorobenzene
HCBD	hexachlorobutadiene
HCE	hexachloroethane
HMIRA	Hazardous Materials Information Resources Act
IAOFGWRWA	International Association of Oil Field, Gas Well, and Refinery Workers of America
ICW	International Chemical Workers
IDRC	International Development Research Centre (Canada)
IJC	International Joint Commission
INCO	International Nickel Company
JPR	job performance report
JT	Junction Triangle (area of Toronto)
JTC	Joint Technical Committee
KWS	Keynesian Welfare State
LAPA	Lambton Anti-Pollution Association
LIS	Lambton Industrial Society
LOON	Lake Ontario Organizing Network
LSCAC	Lake St. Clair Advisory Committee
MAC	Mining Association of Canada
MBTE	methyl tertiary butyl ether
MISA	Municipal-Industrial Strategy of Abatement (Ontario)
MMT	methylcyclopentadienyl manganese tricarbonyl
MNCs	multinational corporations
MOE	Ministry of the Environment (Ontario)
MOEE	Ontario Ministry of the Environment and Energy
MOL	Ministry of Labour (Ontario)
MP	Member of Parliament (Canada)
MPP	Member of Provincial Parliament of Ontario
NAFTA	North American Free Trade Agreement
NDP	New Democratic Party
NEB	National Executive Board (ECWU)
NEP	National Energy Programme

List of Abbreviations

NGO	non-governmental organization
NSM(s)	new social movement(s)
NUPGE	National Union of Provincial Government Employees
OCAWIU or OCAW	Oil, Chemical, and Atomic Workers International Union
OCS	octachlorostyrene
OECD	Organization for Economic Co-operation and Development
OEN	Ontario Environmental Network
OFA	Ontario Federation of Agriculture
OFL	Ontario Federation of Labour
OPSEU	Ontario Public Service Employees Union
ORF	Ontario Research Foundation
OWIU	Oil Workers International Union
OWMC	Ontario Waste Management Corporation
OWRA	Ontario Water Resources Act
OWRC	Ontario Water Resources Commission
PACE	Petroleum Association for Conservation of the Canadian Environment
PAC(s)	public advisory committee(s)
PC	Progressive Conservative Party
PCBs	polychlorinated biphenols
PCE	perchloroethylene
PCI	Italian Communist Party
PEL	Paid Education Leave
ppt	parts per trillion
PSAC	Public Service Alliance of Canada
QCB	pentachlorobenzene
QWL	quality of work life
RAP(s)	remedial action plan(s)
SCRICN	St. Clair River International Citizens' Network
SCRRC	St. Clair River Research Committee
SEEDS	Society, Environment and Energy Development Studies Foundation
SEMCOG	Southeast Michigan Council of Governments
SRCHC	South Riverdale Community Health Centre (Toronto)
STP(s)	sewage treatment plant(s)
TCDD	tetrachlorodibenzo-para-dioxin
TDI	toluene di-isocyanate
THMs	trihalomethanes
UAW	United Automobile, Aerospace, and Agricultural Implement Workers of America
ug/dl	micrograms/decilitre
USWA	United Steelworkers of America
WACSJ	Windsor & Area Coalition for Social Justice
WCWC	Wallaceburg Clean Water Committee
WHMIS	Workplace Hazardous Materials Information System
WQB	Water Quality Board
WREC	CAW Windsor Regional Environmental Council

Preface

The problems addressed in this book first took shape in the form of the jobs-versus-health/environment "trade-offs" faced by so many working people and their dependants. In 1984 the Canadian Broadcasting Corporation (CBC) aired a documentary about the dilemma confronting steel and coke oven workers and their families in Sydney, Nova Scotia. Despite the very high rates of cancer and other diseases related to exposure to coke oven and open hearth furnace gases and smoke, and the high incidence of such diseases among the working-class community living downwind of the plant, the Steelworkers' union in Sydney was opposing the permanent closure of the coke ovens. The pressure was coming mainly from Environment Canada. The official unemployment rate in Sydney at the time was 25 percent, and the unofficial rate, 40 percent. Steel was the only industry in town. The wife of a steelworker, interviewed by a CBC journalist, said that although her father—also a steelworker—was dying of cancer, and although she knew the risks for her husband and for her family, she could see no alternative to continuing production on the same terms. This woman's statement (albeit perhaps half-hearted) that there was no other way, focused my attention on the problems of explaining this perception, and of demonstrating that there is another way.

In October 1987 I had the opportunity to travel to Cape Breton, and to interview steelworkers, coke oven workers, some of their family members (including the woman mentioned above), various researchers, public officials, and others, about the situation at the Sydney Steel Corporation (SYSCO). The research included about thirty-five interviews, many of them in-depth, wide-ranging discussions about the past and present conditions of struggle, beliefs in change, analyses of causes.[1]

Meanwhile, through a friend who was working as a political analyst at the Great Lakes Institute in Windsor, I became aware of the struggles unfolding in southwestern Ontario around toxic chemical pollution. The August 1985 discovery of a major pollution disaster—the "toxic blob" in the St. Clair River, created by a Dow Chemical Canada spill of perchloroethylene—triggered the formation of a number of citizens' organizations. This incident marked a turning point not only for the citizens' environmental movement, but also for the chemical companies (still reeling from the Bhopal disaster), which began to see their environmental images—and new environmental regulation—as a priority concern. It occurred to me in the midst of this, to ask how the chemical workers' union, the Energy and Chemical Workers Union (ECWU), was dealing with the growing pressure on their industry from environmentalists.

Toxic chemicals became a major pollution issue in Canada in the 1980s, eclipsing even nuclear reactors in the ranking of public environmental concerns. In addition, the demands which the citizens' groups and environmentalists were beginning to advance regarding popular participation in the making of economic and environmental policy, made this a fertile area for research on the counter-hegemonic character of new social movements.

While I was in Windsor in 1986, the Canadian Auto Workers Union (CAW) decided to implement environmental committees in all of its local unions, as part of a new environmental initiative. The first committees to be formed were in Windsor and St. Catharines. This presented an opportunity to study a "strong case" of union social activism, and to see

Preface

what might be concluded about the potential for labour-environmental convergence. Moreover, upon becoming more familiar with the history of chemical industry development and unionism in Sarnia, I began to perceive significant differences between the strategies being pursued by the two unions. In Sarnia, the bases for a citizens-workers alliance seemed less hopeful. This was the mixture of theoretical preoccupations and fortuitous events which shaped a good part of the research presented in this book.

Shortly after the 1986-1989 period of research was completed, I took up a post-doctoral position in France, where I began a study of the anti-nuclear and ecology movements, hoping to pick up the story where Alain Touraine's group had left off at the end of the 1970s. While this work was still in the formative stages, I was offered a position at the University of Alberta, in 1991. During this time I have kept in touch with developments in the Ontario labour and environmental movements, and in 1996 the occasion arose to update the earlier work and to extend the analysis of the CAW's social unionism strategy. In light of the significant changes in the social, political, and economic environment of Ontario since the end of the 1980s, an interesting opportunity was presented to examine arguments about the effects of such periods of crisis on union strategies.

The individuals to whom I am indebted intellectually and personally cannot possibly be fully acknowledged here. I shall ever be thankful for the intellectual comradeship and stimulation of the individuals who constituted the Programme of Studies in National and International Development and the Women's Studies Programme at Queen's University during my years there, and in particular, the rigorous intellectual example and friendship of Colin Leys. I received invaluable assistance with the processing of the survey data from Mustafa Kaya, who, in addition, has been a most patient and supportive companion throughout the writing of this book. Indeed, without friends and family many obstacles to its completion might not have been overcome.

Catherine Alpaugh and Rick Coronado introduced me to Windsor and the Chemical Valley, and assisted me in developing a network of research contacts. The interview and survey research were made possible by the co-operation of officials and members of the ECWU in Sarnia and the CAW in the Windsor-Toronto region. Cathy Walker of the CAW National Office helped put me in touch with environmental committee members interviewed in 1996.

Financial support in 1986-89 was provided by the Social Sciences and Humanities Research Council of Canada and by the Skelton-Clark Graduate Research Fund Committee of the Department of Political Studies at Queen's. A grant from the Social Sciences Research Fund of the University of Alberta assisted with the preparation of the manuscript. I would also like to thank Pam Ouimet and Donna Maskell for their work formatting the manuscript, and Michael Wagner for his excellent research assistance in 1996.

Most of all, I wish to express my deep gratitude and respect to the individuals who shared their knowledge and experiences with me, who provided documentation or first-hand accounts, agreed to be interviewed, and who read and commented on drafts of this work. In Sydney, Toronto, Sarnia, Windsor, Detroit, and places in between, you shared your stories with me, and inspired me by your commitments to social change. The interpretation of the struggles recounted in this book is of course my own, but it has been informed in a multitude of ways by your insights. It is my hope that this work will contribute to our shared efforts to interpret and to change the world.

NOTES

1. Although details of the SYSCO case and of these interviews could not be included in this study, they played an important part in its motivation.

Introduction

Environmental politics lead us to some of the central conflicts of our times. Ultimately they are about choices among alternatives—choices which determine the path of societal development and the conditions within which future generations will struggle to realize their visions of the good and sustainable life for humans and other species. Struggles around conceptions of sustainable and desirable development are therefore struggles about who makes the decisions, which interests are defeated, marginalized, or never represented, and which interests predominate.

These questions are at the core of political and historical sociology, which, as one observer has said, ask: "To what extent does the world have to be the way it is?"[1] What are the historically inherited, institutional norms (economic, political-legal, and social) which shape the efforts of individuals and groups to make history? How are these institutions and relationships themselves changed by actors? What transforms individuals and their experiences into agents of collective projects to change the world, sharing a common understanding of what needs to be changed, and how? What roles do organisations play in creating collective actors, or in obstructing their formation? These are the dynamic, dialectical relationships which this study of environmental politics in Canada tries to illuminate. In attempting to better understand "the puzzle of human agency...in terms of the process of social structuring,"[2] I make use of the tools of political economy, discourse analysis, feminist theory, and participant-observer sociological method.

The problem which motivates—or rather, haunts—this work is the prophesy of an emancipatory social movement, and the question of its discursive elements and its social agents. Since the 1970s, Marxists have been debating with feminists, ecologists, the black liberation movement, and other subjects of the new social movements about the relationship of all these forms of oppression to the struggle against capitalism. Political struggles about the desired ends of a society's path of development are at the heart of both socialism and ecology as social movements. Historically, socialism has been the radical project of industrial workers and their middle-class allies to transform capitalism's inefficient, inhumane, and inegalitarian organisation of production and social relations. Ecology encompasses the radical critiques of modernization associated with the new middle classes. These include counter-cultural perspectives rooted in the destruction of pre-industrial social relations and human-nature relations, modern critiques of capitalism drawing on Marxism and humanism, as well as "postmodern" critiques of the modes of rationality and domination which characterize modern thought, including Marxism.

Thus, while there is no simple opposition between socialism and ecology (and, indeed, "social ecology" may be viewed as a synthesis of their radical perspectives), the relationship is often ambivalent and sometimes conflictual. The widely observed differences in the compositions of their social bases of support, the relative numerical decline of the industrial working class in the West, the crisis of the social democratic paradigm and the decline of political support for socialist discourse, the dissolution of the traditional party systems in the West, and other phenomena have given rise to some very broad generalizations about the passage from one historical era to another, from one social movement to another, and so on. All of these theories choose to focus on differences and ruptures, rather than similarities and continuities in the historical projects of socialism and ecology.

Introduction xiii

A reader of the "orthodox Marxist" versus "post-Marxist" interpretations of the relationship of trade unions to radical social change, or of the historical meaning of the new social movements, cannot but be struck by the general absence of analyses of *actually existing social movements*. New social movements and unions have been much theorized about, but little studied from "ground level." This study seeks to examine questions about the agency and discourse of a counter-hegemonic social movement in a historically contextualised and comparative manner. Moreover, the participant-observer approach captures the complexity of the competing discursive tendencies and practices within actual social movements.

I do not attempt, in this work, to address all aspects of new social movement or union politics in Canada, but instead focus on the ways in which two industrial unions (representing different strategic orientations) as well as citizens' groups and environmental organisations have engaged issues related to the central conflicts of societal development. These are located in the environment-economy nexus which necessarily shapes, and is shaped by, the strategic perceptions and choices made by union and environmental movement actors. More specifically, this book investigates the obstacles to, and the potential for, a "convergence" of the projects of socialism and ecology, along with other alternative movements,[3] in the form of a new counter-hegemonic social movement. The term "convergence" is used intentionally to signal that what is at stake is not an ecological socialism, but a new project which will be profoundly transformative of pre-existing identities. The key to advancing counter-hegemonic politics today, in my view, is a discourse which links human needs and conceptions of the good life to egalitarian, participatory, and pluralist democratic demands. The subject of such a discourse may turn out to be, simply, the citizen.

THE CASES

The environmental movement in Canada is highly differentiated by sector and region, as well as ideologically. The segment of the movement studied in this work is the citizens' groups and environmental organisations which mobilized around questions of toxic chemical pollution in the 1980s, and which are located mainly in highly urbanized, southern Ontario. Documentation and observation of the struggles to determine the outcomes of governmental regulatory initiatives allows us to analyse the discursive strategies of corporations, unions, and environmental and citizens' groups. How do the elements of these discourses serve either to defend, or to call into question, the hegemonic model of development? The existing processes of decision making? How successful are these various interests in shaping the economic-environmental regulatory framework? Analyses of the roles of actors such as citizens' groups and unions in the formation of public policy have been notably lacking in Canada. The regulatory battles studied here include the amendment to the Ontario Environmental Protection Act which became known as the "Spills Bill"; Ontario's Municipal-Industrial Strategy of Abatement for pollution entering waterways; the introduction of the Canadian Environmental Protection Act; the public review of the Great Lakes Water Quality Agreement; and the public participation process for the Remedial Action Plans for the "areas of concern" in the Great Lakes Basin.

In addition, this work compares the responses of two industrial trade unions to environmental regulation of industry and the growing influence of the environmental movement. These are the Energy and Chemical Workers Union (ECWU) and the Canadian Auto Workers Union (CAW). The ECWU's responses to environmental issues affecting its membership are studied in the context of the union's relations with petrochemical industry employers during expansionary and recession eras. Among the issues affecting chemical workers, this work examines air pollution in Sarnia in the 1950s and 1960s; mercury contamination of the St. Clair River; leaded gasoline and lead smelting; and toxic chemical pollution. The ECWU provides a case study of a union which has maintained a largely passive, and at times hostile, stance toward the initiatives of the environmental movement. The political economy of the petrochemical sector, as well as corporate management approaches, the ideological perspectives of union leaders and rank-and-file members, and the views of unions adopted by environmentalists, are among the factors examined in order to explain this union's orientation.

The CAW has adopted a more activist and alliance-oriented approach to the environmental movement, including the creation of local environmental committees in the mid-1980s. The development of the environmental committees is examined in depth in the cases of six CAW locals in Essex county. The CAW case study focuses on the limitations and possibilities suggested by the "social unionism" strategy. The factors outlined in the ECWU case are also examined with regard to the CAW in order to explain the differences between the two cases. The ECWU merged with other unions in 1992 to form the Communications, Energy, and Paper Workers union (CEP), and the research on the ECWU ends at this point (although some observations are made of subsequent CEP interventions). Developments in CAW strategy, however, are traced to 1996, and thus permit an analysis to be made of that union's transition from social unionism to "movement unionism" in the 1990s, and the implications of these changes for theoretical claims regarding the potential of trade unions to provide counter-hegemonic leadership.

Deriving general theoretical conclusions from the empirical evidence and interpretations of these cases is a complex task indeed, not to mention one fraught with risks. In my view, the contributions of this study lie mainly in the questions it raises about the limitations of structuralist approaches such as traditional political economy, or theorizations of historical stages (e.g., "post-industrial society"), for helping us to understand the processes of social change. In a sense, I have tried to bring the actors back in, to listen to the many layers of their constructions of "the way the world is," and to understand how these perceptions change through interaction with other subjects, and in the context of the processes of social structuring. Admittedly, this approach stems from an obstinate optimism of the will, which, for Gramsci, never meant faith in the inevitable collapse of the hegemonic order, but rather belief in the capacity of humans to change the way the world is.

NOTES

1. Philip Abrams, *Historical Sociology* (Somerset, England: Open Books Publishing, 1982), p. 5.
2. Ibid., pp. x-xi.
3. The counter-hegemonic movement envisaged certainly includes other struggles, as I have tried to indicate throughout the text. The interfaces between unions and other social movements have to some extent been examined by others (e.g., anti-nuclear and peace movements, the women's movement, anti-racism and anti-poverty organisations, unions of the unemployed). It is an overwhelming project to attempt to identify the intersections of all of these subject positions on the web of articulated struggles, and I have not attempted to do so in this book. The connections between other subject positions and ecological goals and principles may, however, be investigated using the methodology of this study. For example, in a recent essay I have sketched some of the themes of equivalence among struggles to end the oppressive sexual division of labour, material insecurity for the unemployed and partially employed, excessive work, and the destruction of nature, among others. See "Ecological Politics in Canada: Elements of a Strategy of Collective Action," in D. Bell et al., eds. *Political Ecology: Global and Local Perspectives* (New York and London: Routledge, forthcoming).

PART I

SOCIAL MOVEMENTS AND SOCIAL CHANGE

New Social Movements, Labour, and Theories of Social Change

INTRODUCTION

New social movements (NSMs) have been the subjects of considerable debate among social theorists in recent years. The term refers to the somewhat amorphous, mass extra-parliamentary movements that mobilized in the late 1960s around such issues as sexual equality and freedom, civil liberties, anti-racism, peace, ecology, health, and international solidarity with anti-imperialist and democratic struggles in the Third World. The NSMs are distinguished from the "traditional" social movement, the labour movement, which encompasses not only the unions, but the cultural traditions and institutions created to advance the interests of workers (educational, recreational, health, credit unions, co-operatives, etc.). The NSMs are also distinguished from the earlier women's, peace, environmental, and human rights/anti-slavery movements of the nineteenth and early twentieth centuries on the grounds that the discourses of the 1960s-1980s movements—while embodying significant continuities with the traditions of the earlier movements—are also a specific response to the contradictions of the post-war Fordist model of development in the Western industrialized societies.[1]

They are, moreover, seen by some authors to be "new" insofar as they go beyond liberal-democratic or socialist critiques of dominant social norms and institutions, to a rejection of some of the shared assumptions linking liberalism, Marxism, and social democracy as "modern" discourses or developmental models. Since the discourses of contemporary social movements typically incorporate "pre-modern" (e.g., romantic, organicist, spiritual) and modern (e.g., Freudian, Marxist, liberal-democratic) elements as well as "post-modern" conceptions of politics (e.g., the obsolescence of the right-left ideological spectrum, local- and global- as well as nation–state-centred practices), they may be understood as the cultural expressions of a particular historical conjuncture—that of the crisis not only of capitalism, or of Marxism, but of the foundations of modernity. This view was reinforced by events in Eastern and Central Europe leading to the collapse of the state-socialist regimes. It became apparent that "new social movements" were not unique to the Western industrialized countries, but had played an important part in mobilizing grass-roots opposition to the model of development in the East, as well. This recognition focused attention on the similarities between, for example, the productivism inherent in these developmental models, rather than on the political differences which had been the bases of their categorization by western political theorists. Since the qualifier "new" tends to obscure important continuities and similarities, some theorists have preferred to use the term "alternative social movements." "Alternative" signals a *transformative*, critical, and counter-hegemonic social function, distinguishing such movements as those for women's equality, peace, and ecology, from contemporary movements which are *reactive*, that is, based on social groups whose interests are threatened by change or whose identities are in dissolution. "NSM," however, remains a widely-used label for a body of European and North American literature dealing with the historical origins and meanings of the postwar women's, environmental, anti-racist, and other oppositional, change-oriented movements, and it is in this sense that it is used in this work.

Liberal theorists have viewed NSMs essentially as interest groups pursuing "quality of life" goals. Such groups have arisen outside the traditional political party systems because these parties have ceased to reflect the predominant social cleavages. Traditional class cleavages, they argue—which emerged with the development of industrial capitalism—have gradually dissolved in an era of post-industrial capitalism. In this view, capitalist development in the West has succeeded in creating sufficient material affluence for the majority of citizens to render "material" concerns (economic security, basic welfare, etc.) secondary to "quality of life" goals (e.g., a clean environment, more leisure, recreational and cultural activities, self-development, demand for higher quality and more differentiated consumer products). Since traditional political parties have been slow to accommodate "post-materialist" priorities, interest groups have proliferated.[2] Ronald Inglehart, in his well-known studies of comparative data on sociological variables and "value" choices, coined the terms "materialist society" and "post-materialist society," and characterized the watershed of the late 1960s in the West as a "silent revolution" (in cultural values), and later, as a "culture shift."[3]

While liberal theorists have explained the phenomena of the NSMs and the values which seem to underpin their concerns in terms of the "embourgeoisement of the working class," some Marxists have argued that these movements reflect the demands of a growing "new middle class" associated with the expansion of the public sector, services, and in general white-collar employment. Jane Jenson and George Ross, adopting Nicos Poulantzas' conceptualization of these strata as elements of a "new petite bourgeoisie" (rather than as sectors of the working class), interpreted the social movements of the 1970s as "a distinctive form of middle strata politics," motivated by individualist socialization and goals, privileged social and cultural experience, and the frustration of certain lifestyle expectations.[4]

This argument is taken up from a historical-cultural perspective by the German sociologist Klaus Eder, who, in *The New Politics of Class: Social Movements and Cultural Dynamics in Advanced Societies*, views the new middle class as the bearer of a counter-cultural tradition which combines both modern and pre-modern elements.[5] However, rather than advancing the Marxist view that the "new politics" are secondary or tangential to the "core" class struggle between industrial workers and capitalists, Eder asserts the importance of granting a key social agency role to the new middle class. His thesis is that the new social movements are "the mechanism creating a new class structure in modern societies, giving these middle classes a central role in the restructuring of class relationships" (pp. 165-166). The NSMs are the collective practices expressing a redefinition of class conflict in which the new middle class opposes modernization because it obstructs or prevents the good life. Marxist treatments of the petite bourgeoisie have emphasized the ambiguous class position of such strata or their anti-modern or reactionary roles (e.g., in analyses of fascism), while downplaying their radical *cultural* discourses (the enlightenment, the romantics, the communitarians).

Eder proposes that instead of defining social classes solely by their positions in the relations of production of the dominant mode of production, we can conceptualise classes on the basis of these criteria: (1) Is there a social opportunity structure for collective action? (2) Do the cultural orientations of mobilized groups manifest specific interests, normative belief systems, and value orientations? That is, can we identify "mutually exclusive ways of defining social reality," or "cultural dichotomies at stake in collective mobilizations"? He argues that the social opportunity structure of middle-class radicalism is these individuals' involvement in "qualified production and service occupations, i.e., those based on educational training which distinguishes them from working class culture," and in the production and reproduction of "the cultural resources in modern societies" (p. 180). Second, they are preoccupied with the problem of identity, and they are the carriers of traditional notions of "a good life and consensual social relations." For Eder, "the concept of good life is more than a philosophical idea: it is the expression of a class-specific life-form" (p. 181). The idea of consensual social relations "fosters the idea of an authentic life-form where people interact as equals and free persons," and whose central feature is *communication*. Bringing together the social opportunity structure and the "life-world" of the new middle class allows us to explain why these strata are "prone to engage in issues beyond traditional class issues," and how they have access to the means to actually redefine social reality. Eder's analysis suggests, therefore, that the futures of the new social movements (which draw so predominantly on these strata for their activists) are closely related to the fate of the social opportunity structure for middle-class radicalism.

Eder's conception of social movements draws on a tradition established by the group of sociologists at the Centre d'analyse et d'intervention sociologiques (CADIS, Paris), led by Alain Touraine. Their analyses of the workers' movement, the students' movement, and of the discourse of the anti-nuclear movement, led them to argue that what was occurring was a transition to a "post-industrial society," in which the central conflict is no longer between industrial workers and capitalists, but between citizens and technocrats.[6] The "stakes" of this struggle are not merely control of the *means* of production and of the *appropriation* of its product. The stakes are the *telos* of production, and hence, control over social decision-making. This struggle brings citizens of industrialized societies into conflict with those elites and institutions which dominate decision making—whose rationale, means of coercion, prestige, etc., allow them to determine the direction of social development.

For Touraine, the French anti-nuclear movement expressed the elements of this emerging social conflict, its terrain, and its stakes. Its militants identified the enemy as the technocratic State, committed to a productivist, instrumental logic, and prepared to use any means of control of information, or repression, to defend these interests. They questioned the necessity—the reason—of each decision to which the technocratic apparatus commits the society; these were reconstructed as *choices among alternatives*, and reinterpreted as struggles for the control of *historicity* (struggles over the orientation of societal development). Because the anti-nuclear movement activists articulated these critiques of the anti-democratic and technocratic nature of the State (and vis-à-vis perhaps the archetypal case in the West!), and of the productivist, capitalist logic of the economy and of social relations, Touraine's group viewed this movement as the incipient social movement of the new historical era, albeit in fragmentary and inconsistent form. What the labour movement had been to industrial capitalism in the nineteenth and early twentieth centuries, the anti-nuclear movement could become to a system of domination rooted in the control of information and technocratic decision-making. This was the *prophétie anti-nucléaire*.

Touraine's approach shifts the terrain of struggle from the sphere of production to the universe of discourse, and from a structuralist analysis to an actor-centred analysis. There are, of course, a number of problems with Touraine's theory. These include an overly schematic, evolutionary view of stages of development, since the "old" social movements drop out of the story, except insofar as they remain attached to the "old" stakes of the industrial era. As Eder puts it, there is "a logical sequence" of "changing universes of discourse" which parallel the societal types (historically defined by Touraine as commercial, industrial, and postindustrial). Analysis of the socio-structural interests common to the technocratic elites within the State, political parties, and private sector of production is lacking (e.g., how are such values and orientations reproduced within these institutions?).

Nevertheless, the post-Marxist theorizations of new social movements were greatly influenced by the interpretation of NSMs as radical critics of modernization, and carriers of (at least elements of) a new societal paradigm. This is summed up by Klaus Eder in these terms:

> Attacks on modern culture based on its rationalism have always been commonplace. But something has changed. The protest has gained a political dimension that disturbs the institutional reproduction of modern societies through its attacks on the model of social development particular to advanced Western industrial societies. There is a general tendency leading to a central conflict in the modern world much more pervasive than that of the nineteenth century (p. 119).

Another German sociologist, Claus Offe, also differentiates between "old" and "new" paradigms of social conflict, and suggests that some synthesis of their social movements is a prerequisite for posing real challenges to neoliberal restructuring.[7] Offe also views the NSMs as being at least in part an outcome of the contradictions of the modern welfare State.[8] The State was compelled to intervene in the economy in order to mediate class conflict. However, State intervention also impeded capitalist accumulation and allowed non-market processes and principles to challenge the normative and legal bases of the dominant principle of exchange (capitalist commodity relations). The NSMs have, in effect, exploited this contradiction to assert the rights of "citizens," to expand the spheres of decommodification (those areas of social life not ruled by the principle of exchange), and to democratize the political decision-making structures of the State itself.

Conservatives have been less concerned with identifying the social bases of the proliferating social movements of the 1970s and 1980s than with their implications for the restricted democracy which underpins capitalism in the West. In their 1975 report to the Trilateral Commission, Samuel Huntington, Michel Crozier et al. warned of the consequences of such "excessive" democracy.[9] Yet liberal, conservative, and socialist theorists often agree that the concomitant of the growth in numbers and political efficacy of the new middle strata is the decline of the traditional manual or industrial working class. The reduction in the traditional industrial workforce relative to other sectors of the economies of the advanced capitalist countries, and the growing isolation of the unionized workforce in declining industries, have led some socialists to rethink their strategic assumptions—most saliently, the centrality of the traditional working class in the struggle against capitalism.[10]

The period of international capitalist restructuring following the crisis of Fordism has confronted socialists, trade unionists, and activists in the new social movements with the necessity to develop a coherent alternative to the social democratic model of development. Debates within Marxism in the 1980s about the agents of socialist change have revolved around contending conceptions of the working class and the changes in its composition and culture since the Second World War. Interpretations of the new social movements reflect very different assumptions about their social bases and ideological tendencies.[11] Moreover, the debates about labour and the new social movements brought into sharp focus the significant differences among socialists regarding their visions of socialism. As a result, socialist theorists have drawn quite divergent conclusions about the significance of the NSMs for socialist strategy in the West. The more traditional Marxist view argues that these movements are middle class by virtue of their social bases and their quality of life goals, downplaying their bases of support, and reaffirming the centrality of the traditional working class in its conception of socialist strategy.

In neo-Gramscian terms, however, the problem became to theorize counter-hegemonic struggle anew.[12] The project of creating "working class" identity and consciousness, which would form the core of a new historical bloc was replaced by a project to identify the themes or principles which might articulate to one another all of these contestatory movements. Their struggles encompassed many more relationships of oppression than those of wage-labour, and the "enemy," therefore, had to be grasped as multiple forms of domination. However, the continuing assumption that these multiple subject positions and struggles *had to be articulated to unifying principles, values, or themes* expressed the continuing desire to fulfill the prophesy of the new social movement—the prophesy of emancipation.[13]

The "post-Marxist" approach of Chantal Mouffe and Ernesto Laclau rejected any attempt to predict the politico-ideological behaviour of social subjects in relation to their economic positions. In their 1985 book, *Hegemony and Socialist Strategy: Towards a Radical Democratic Politics*, Mouffe and Laclau rejected even Gramsci's concepts of class-based hegemony and counter-hegemonic struggle as being economic reductionist,[14] provoking a series of responses from defenders of traditional Marxism, which are briefly summarized below. Mouffe went on to develop her argument for radical and plural democracy as a counter-hegemonic strategy for the left, addressing many of the criticisms that were made of the 1985 work. The "radical democratization" approach is a central theme of this book.

Despite their significant differences, all of the approaches sketched above recognize that we have been experiencing, since the 1970s, a period of profound crisis and restructuring of capitalism internationally. This transitional era—which the French "school of regulation" has called the crisis of Fordism—is the context in which major structural changes are taking place in the economies of the West, affecting the composition of social classes.[15] New opportunities as well as limitations have been posed for both ruling elites and subordinate groups, as the terms of restructuring are contested. The predominant capitalist response to the crisis has been neoliberalism. In North America, the left, the unions, and the NSMs (especially the women's and environmental movements) have faced, on the one hand, the challenge of defending past gains from neoliberal and neoconservative[16] campaigns for their dismantlement, and, on the other hand, the inadequacy of social democratic responses to the social and ecological conflicts of the late twentieth century. It is for the purposes of constructing a new vision of society—one based not on the imperatives of capital accumulation, patriarchy, racism, and the domination of nature, but on humanist, egalitarian, and ecological principles—as well as a strategy to move towards this society, that an understanding of the struggles of citizens and workers in the new social movements and the labour movements is so crucial.

SOCIALIST APPROACHES TO SOCIAL MOVEMENTS

An era of capitalist crisis and restructuring has resulted in the advanced capitalist countries (ACCs) in the usurpation of social democratic modes of (capitalist) regulation by neoliberal and neoconservative regimes. Rapid deindustrialization of the traditional industrial sectors (accelerated in Canada by the Free Trade Agreement, negotiated with the United States and implemented in 1988), combined with monetarist and supply-side economic policies have, since the late 1970s, created high levels of long-term unemployment, gradually polarizing workforces between relatively privileged, full-time workers, and growing numbers of part-time or "marginal" workers and the unemployed. Recession conditions for labour have contributed to the increasing isolation of the "permanent" core workforce from the unorganised majorities, and in some cases to what has been called the "sectionalism" and economism of the trade unions.[17] The development of the welfare state in the postwar era, entailing an expansion of public-service employment, has also been reversed by neoliberal governments in the name of eliminating debts and deficits. The new information technology has provided some growth in certain areas of services employment, and is changing the nature of the labour process in many industries.

The crisis of social democracy and the Western Marxist critique of "existing socialism" provide the context in which a number of socialist theorists advanced "revisionist" analyses of the prospects for radical change and the social agents likely to bring it about. A predominant aspect of the "new revisionism" is the displacement of the working class from its traditional position in Marxist theory as the central revolutionary subject. Writers such as André Gorz, Chantal Mouffe and Ernesto Laclau share the view that the working class is not, by virtue of its position in the social relations of capitalist production, any more likely to develop revolutionary consciousness than any other social group. In other words, they see no reason why citizens-as-workers should be a privileged subject relative to other potential bearers of the project of socialist transformation. Mouffe and Laclau argued, in addition, that Marx's predictions that the proletariat would become more homogeneous and united have been invalidated by the apparent dissolution of working class culture and solidarity.

Mouffe and Laclau also made a lengthy critique of classical and recent Marxist thought, arguing that all approaches share the error of economic reductionism. While they seemed in their 1985 work to approve of Gramsci's conceptualization of politics as a war of position, they rejected his view that society can be understood in terms of a struggle between the hegemonic projects of two fundamentally antagonistic classes (or what Mouffe and Laclau call "hegemonic cores"). They also rejected Gramsci's assumption that—except during periods of organic crisis when the "common sense" of the era is fundamentally discredited along with the legitimacy of the ruling elite—society is hegemonized by one of the fundamental classes (in Mouffe and Laclau's terminology, by a "single hegemonic centre"). Instead, they argued that there exists a plurality of political spaces in which the fundamental antagonism is not class, but democratic versus elite, or popular struggle. Therefore, the poles of social conflict (and their political subjects) may be constituted on the terrain of democratic struggle, rather than that of class. They viewed hegemony as "a type of political relation" which cannot "be conceived as an irradiation of effects from a privileged point." They did accept that "loci of power," or "nodal points" exist within every social formation, but they explained these as merely "contingent" and conjunctural phenomena. They rejected a conception of these relations of power as being in any way "fixed" by social factors such as the relations of production.

The "new revisionism" provoked numerous responses ranging from the rejection of certain aspects to trenchant defences of Marxist orthodoxy, as in the 1980s work of Ellen Meiksins-Wood and Peter Meiksins.[18] Wood minimized the potential of a democratic discourse to provide the "glue" for an anti-capitalist hegemonic bloc. Instead, she conflated the strategies of progressive democratization and popular frontism. She essentially equated progressive democratization with the right variant of Eurocommunism, and specifically, with the "advanced democracy" (popular front) strategy of the Italian Communist Party (PCI). Although her critical assessment of the PCI's version of a gradualist strategy was warranted, Wood made the mistake of rejecting any form of gradualism which aims at transforming the State from within and through struggles in civil society. While Mouffe and Laclau's 1985 formulation of counter-hegemonic strategy was certainly vague and open to various interpretations, they did not intend that the counter-hegemonic ideology of "radical democracy" remain within the parameters of liberal-democratic discourse. Rather, their approach implied an implosion of the tensions and contradictions inherent in this discourse, particularly, the limits on egalitarian and participatory principles required for capitalist accumulation and other forms of domination to be sustained.

Radical democratization, in other words, involves demonstrating the limitations of democracy required by capitalism, patriarchy, racism, and other forms of oppression.

These differing evaluations of progressive democratization as a socialist strategy have important consequences for the ways in which both sides of the debate view the political significance of the labour and new social movements. Wood conceived of democracy not as a means, or strategy of socialist struggle, but as a goal to be attained after the abolition of classes. The implications of this are profound. First, the meaning of "socialism" is thereby narrowly confined to struggle for control of the means of production. The working class is "central" to this struggle for tactical reasons, and "working class interests" are defined as those relating to wages, conditions of work—i.e., to conflicts located at the point of production. Wood claimed a privileged position in anti-capitalist struggle for what she called the "people who are the direct objects of class exploitation." This assumed a rank-ordering of experiences of exploitation, which is then translated into the political sphere in the form of "priority" struggles. Thus it is not surprising to find Wood repeatedly making the unsupported assumption that there are given (*a priori*) "working class interests" distinct from (and more integral to socialism than) what she called the "universal human goals" of the NSMs. The problem with the "New True Socialists" [or post-Marxists], she asserted, was that they were trying to shift strategic priorities away from "class-bound material interests to universal 'human' goals." Her argument rested upon the assumption that class interests are determined solely in the sphere of production and pertain primarily to struggles around the allocation of surplus-value. "Working class interests," therefore, are those represented by trade unions (and so-called workers' parties). The "other" goals of the NSMs, on the other hand, do not have an anti-capitalist character because they are abstracted from the level of the class nature of society to the level of general human interests. Thus, such concerns as women's emancipation are, presumably, for somewhere down the road—for after the "class" struggle. They are not integral to socialism, but are among its "ultimate objectives."

The strategy which corresponds to these assumptions is also familiar: the task of socialists is to keep pushing the economic struggles of workers into confrontation with capital because this will create crisis which will eventually (and with the leadership of a revolutionary vanguard) "spill over into the political arena." Hegemony is understood in a tactical sense, as either a necessary deception of allied groups and classes in the first stage of anti-capitalist struggle (e.g., isolating monopoly capital), in which themes such as nationalism, anti-dictatorship struggle, or anti-fascism are utilized by the progressive forces, or as a subordination of the working class in a populist project led by other social forces (e.g., the petite bourgeoisie or national bourgeoisie). In either case, the bases for alliance are viewed as merely tactical; the actors are in no way transformed by unifying principles, and the latter are little more than a cleverly rigged disguise for a particular class project. Hence the implicit equation of "democracy" in Wood's thinking with liberal or "bourgeois" democracy, and the stages conception of transition to socialism found in Wood's writing. The conception of revolutionary strategy implicit in Wood's analysis reflects an old dichotomous way of thinking on the left, in which all practice is labelled either "social democratic reformist" or "revolutionary." This dichotomy sheds little light on problems of short and medium-term practice—of transitional strategy. It provides no space for a gradualist strategy with revolutionary vision and objectives, or for what Miliband and Liebman called "revolutionary reformism."[19]

Most striking about this 1980s debate was that neither the "new revisionist" nor "old left" position grounded its arguments in analyses of actual social movements. The constitutive principles of Mouffe and Laclau's conception of socialist hegemony were obscure and highly abstract. *Hegemony and Socialist Strategy* failed to demonstrate the ways in which anti-capitalist struggles could be articulated to other struggles—or reinterpreted as popular democratic struggles—by means of a radical democratization discourse. The book was therefore interpreted by some as advocating a kind of "utter relativism" regarding the starting points for counter-hegemonic struggle.[20] Wood's arguments, on the other hand, merely reproduced familiar economic reductionist strategic prescriptions, again without analysis of the practice of contemporary union and other social movements. Consequently, the debate presented a false dichotomy of strategic choices for the left.

Although Mouffe and Laclau claimed in *Hegemony and Socialist Strategy* to reject historical materialist method, they in fact utilized this method in their analysis of the crisis of Fordism, of the Keynesian Welfare State, of contradictions in the labour process, and of the origins of the new social movements. Their analysis drew on the work of the French school of regulation, and on Claus Offe's work on the crisis of the Keynesian Welfare State (KWS). Morever, their conception of radical democracy was implicitly assumed to be anti-capitalist.[21] However, the NSMs were seen to be more effective—and more promising—as agents of a "rapid diffusion of social conflictuality to more and more numerous relations" than the "working class" organisations (trade unions, social democratic parties). The former, they claimed, had called into question new forms of subordination "derived from the implanting and expansion of capitalist relations of production and the growing intervention of the State" (e.g., the State's role in the production and consumption of weapons, nuclear power). In addition, while Mouffe and Laclau argued that Gramsci's theory of hegemony is fundamentally reductionist, and claimed to have transcended this error in their own theory, their outline of a "democratic hegemonic practice" remains in essence Gramscian, entailing a dualistic construction of social conflict, only one based on a democratic/anti-democratic antagonism, rather than a class cleavage. They argued, for example, that the democratic "imaginary" could displace the (liberal-bourgeois) discourse which legitimates relations of domination/subordination, and might transform the latter into relations of antagonism.

Many points of ambiguity and controversy arose from Mouffe and Laclau's assertions that there are no "objective," or *a priori* "interests," i.e., prior to the construction of such interests by political discourses, and that no inherent relationships exist between material or economic and political positions. The first position, in particular, appeared to allow no ethical grounds for the legitimation of any kind of social project. Moreover, the two assertions were conflated by both Mouffe and Laclau and their critics, thereby closing any space for a theoretical approach which would permit one to accept that the economic and other positions which people occupy do subject them to certain common *experiences* (e.g., of authority/privilege or oppression/subordination), but would not require one to assume that these experiences will in themselves generate predictable political expressions. Yet Mouffe and Laclau themselves assumed that the experience of exclusion from decision-making authority (oppression by elites) will lead to demands for democratization—for the rights of "the people" or particular oppressed groups. It was not until some years later that Mouffe addressed the problem of establishing interests and rights in relation to emancipatory discourse. In her 1993 essay "Radical Democracy: Modern or Postmodern?" Mouffe argued for a postmodern political philosophy

> in which judgement plays a fundamental role that must be conceptualized appropriately so as to avoid the false dilemmas between, on the one hand, the existence of some universal criterion and, on the other, the rule of arbitrariness. That a question remains unanswerable by science or that it does not attain the status of a truth that can be demonstrated does not mean that a reasonable opinion cannot be formed about it or that it cannot be an opportunity for a rational choice...

> To assert that one cannot provide an ultimate rational foundation for any given system of values does not imply that one considers all views to be equal... It is always possible to distinguish between the just and the unjust, the legitimate and the illegitimate, but this can only be done from within a given tradition, with the help of the standards that this tradition provides.[22]

She is concerned here with rearticulating existing elements of the liberal democratic tradition, "no longer viewing rights in an individualist framework but rather conceiving of 'democratic rights,'" which, "while belonging to the individual, can only be exercised collectively and which presuppose the existence of equal rights for others" (p. 18-19). The linking of diverse democratic struggles "requires the creation of new subject positions that would allow the common articulation, for example, of antiracism, antisexism and anticapitalism" (p. 18).

In effect, Mouffe and Laclau were in 1985 making the rather unoriginal observation that political interests are constructed in the politico-ideological sphere. The importance of comprehending "objective interests"—conceived of as experiential knowledge—is to be able to determine in some measure which political projects might be, at a given historical conjuncture, discursively constructed, and how specific social forces might lead, or be attached to them. It is, indeed, this understanding of politics which preoccupied Gramsci. A more accurate distinction between Mouffe and Laclau and the Marxists whose theories they criticised in *Hegemony and Socialist Strategy* might be that, while the latter (including Gramsci) saw the fundamental task of hegemony as being the construction of *class* identity, Mouffe and Laclau argue that the bonds of common cause uniting the majority of the population against hegemonic elites—in the context of late-twentieth-century Western capitalism—might be articulated in terms of *democratic struggle*, i.e., struggles for equality, autonomy, and freedom. In this way, multiple forms of oppression (some associated with capitalist relations of production, some not, e.g., aspects of patriarchy, racism) could be encompassed within a counter-hegemonic, historical bloc. Intrinsic to this project, however (including for Mouffe and Laclau), is an anti-capitalist struggle. Contrary to Wood's characterisation of radical democratization as no more than a bourgeois-reformist or populist (petit bourgeois) project, Mouffe and Laclau's hegemonic strategy envisages a profound social transformation which will encompass all forms of oppression, including those specifically experienced by workers at the point of production, and those stemming from commodity relations in general.

The label "post-Marxist" for the radical democratization approach is, however, warranted, since this approach moves us beyond both socialist strategy as traditionally conceived and a political discourse which attempts to construct the identity of a mass social movement around the category of class. A counter-hegemonic politics of radical and pluralist democracy is not, however, "post" in the sense of denying the continuing existence of capitalism as a system of institutions and relationships which profoundly organise human societies as well as their relationships to nature. Rather, the "post" signals an ongoing connection with, and utilization of, Marxism's unique insights into the capitalist nature of society and social conflict.

A Post-Gramscian View of Contemporary Counter-Hegemonic Politics

The New Social Movements

It is true that Gramsci, in the context of post-First World War Italy, viewed class identity as the necessary hegemonic core of a new historical bloc. Yet he was also aware that a hegemonic bloc is constituted around much more than the wage relation, and that a movement for socialism must define class interests in universal terms. The key point of the theorists of the NSMs is that the "class identity" and culture of a previous era no longer encompass enough of the experiences of enough persons to constitute the core identity of a mass movement for profound social change. They belong, rather, to an era before the welfare state and the institutionalization of industrial relations, before the penetration of commodity relations into nearly every area of private life, and before the dissolution of homogeneous working-class communities. What has supplanted an intense but relatively narrow struggle around the allocation of surplus-value and the management of the productive apparatus is a more diffuse and generalized struggle against many forms of power. The socialist call (not necessarily that of the trade unions) for control over the means of production has become an increasingly inadequate programme to generate the cultural values and solidarities necessary to oppose not only the nature of capitalism and states at the end of the twentieth century, but also the domination of nature, racial and sexual oppression, and the enormously destructive forces threatening the planet. The themes necessary to link these struggles must also reflect a transformative, rather than a merely tactical, conceptualisation of alliance-building. In other words, the problem is not simply to cultivate class consciousness among industrial workers because of tactical advantages stemming from their location in the sphere of production. Apart from other considerations, workers' occupation of workplaces would achieve little in the absence of a broad social mobilization in support of their goals. Nor is the problem one of forming tactical coalitions between groups with fixed, one-dimensional identities, such as "workers," "environmentalists," "women," "blacks," and so on, since such boundaries are ultimately untenable and may obstruct—rather than inform—the politics of solidarity. As Mouffe argues:

> [I]t is not a matter of establishing a mere alliance between given interests but of actually modifying the very identity of these forces. In order that the defence of workers' interests is not pursued at the cost of the rights of women, immigrants, or consumers, it is necessary to establish an equivalence between these different struggles. It is only under these circumstances that struggles against power become truly democratic.[23]

Moreover, what is often referred to today as the "politics of difference" (or sometimes as "identity politics"), is, as Canadian sociologist Himani Bannerji argues, merely an evasion of the actuality of *relationships* which we may not wish to acknowledge.[24] This question has certainly arisen within the North American women's movements, which have been riven by debates among women of colour, white women, straight women, lesbians, native and "third world" women, not to mention working-class and middle-class women's different priorities. Bannerji observes that one of the responses of middle-class white feminists to critiques of their praxis has been to say to women of colour: "Well, being a white woman I can only speak for myself—I'll stand back from 'your' issues (i.e., racism) and let you speak for yourself." The problem with this is that racism is not a "black" issue. This is an example of the way in which a discourse about "differences" obscures a relationship. In North America, racism is about white supremacy, and therefore about white *privileges* as well as black subordination. The problem is not simply one of "difference," but one of a relationship of domination/subordination. Thus, forming a "rainbow coalition" or a common front for the organisation of an event may bring different social subjects together, but it may not result in their actually engaging in a discussion about both their conflicts and their commonalities, and hence, in the modification of their particular identities.

On the other hand, to create—as socialist discourse does—a hierarchy of counter-hegemonic struggles, with production/economic conflicts at the top and other social

New Social Movements, Labour, and Theories of Social Change

conflicts ranked somewhere below, is not only to define social conflict in narrow and exclusive terms, but to reinforce a bourgeois conception of social reality. Those who are dependent upon a wage for subsistence are uniquely vulnerable to the vagaries of capitalist accumulation. But even if we were to accept Wood's assertion that, for this reason, workers (at the point of production) have "the most direct objective interest in bringing about the transition to socialism," this is not in itself sufficient basis to conclude that workplace-centred conflict is the necessary or sole starting point of counter-hegemonic struggle. It is not evident that, as Wood insists, "an appropriate [socialist] politics" will "grow out of" the economic struggles of workers, first, because this is to ignore the crucial interpretive function of political discourse and leadership, and second, because ultimately, counter-hegemonic goals can only be posed at a societal level of discourse. "Working class interests," in other words, are neither limited to nor fulfilled by, economic struggles alone, any more than "workers" are one-dimensional social beings. Which sectors of the population initiate counter-hegemonic struggles (industrial workers, public sector or service sector workers, women's organisations, ethnic or racial groups, etc.) and whether—and how—these struggles are articulated to one another, are not outcomes predetermined by a hierarchy of "objective interests," but ones shaped by struggles in the politico-ideological sphere.

The oppressive nature of capitalism is experienced through the commodification of all spheres of life—through the opposition between profit imperatives and human needs. This "class struggle" encompasses all aspects of the reproduction of capitalist relations of production and the conditions of existence of the working class. To accept the separation of "working class" or "material" goals from "universalistic" or so-called "post-materialist" goals—to accept a prioritization of struggles and a stages conception of social change—is to lose sight of the only real bases upon which to construct a counter-hegemonic historical bloc. Building a democratic, mass movement for an alternative society requires first rejecting bourgeois conceptual boundaries such as those between the economic and the political, the worker and the consumer, the worker and the citizen, and the private and the public.

If, like Wood, we hold that socialization of the means of production is the "real core" of radical change, while participatory democracy, peace, a healthy environment, and so on, are somehow "secondary," we cannot effectively demonstrate the necessity and desirability of socializing the means of production. Unless we identify the equivalences which can cement an organic unity of diverse social struggles, we will reproduce the failed strategies of the past, reinforcing only corporative consciousness and interest group politics.

This argument was also made by Raymond Williams, in his book *Towards 2000*:

> [T]he isolation of economic bonding…permits its incorporation within non-socialist or anti-socialist economic forms, which can meet it, at least temporarily, on isolated economic grounds…
>
> What then most needs to be emphasized is that it is capitalism which proposes and tries to enforce the isolation of economic bonding: "the cash-nexus between man and man" [sic]. To reproduce this as a principle or model of socialism is to move, step by step, into the capitalist consciousness which is now a majority force in the old industrial societies… The sources of a different ethos are then primarily in those other social bonds, those ultimately deeper attachments and purposes, which capitalism tries to push into a lower importance, or where necessary to cancel. It is then in what happens or can happen in these other practices and relationships that the resources of a wider socialism have to be developed. It is a matter of what happens in the primary care of people, in families and neighbourhoods and communities. It is a matter of what happens in the organised services of health

and education; in protection and enhancement of our physical environment; in the quality of our public information and entertainment.[25]

Williams argued further that, although the new social movements—which have taken up issues left unaddressed by unions and social democratic parties—have been considered "beyond class politics":

> there is not one of these issues which, followed through, fails to lead us into the central systems of the industrial-capitalist mode of production and...into its system of classes. These movements and the needs and feelings which nourish them are now our major positive resources, but their whole problem is how they relate or can relate to the apparently more important institutions which derive from the isolation of employment and wage-labour.[26]

There are both obstacles to and potential for a counter-hegemonic strategy which seeks to articulate[27] the struggles of the NSMs to the fundamentally exploitative and oppressive relations of capitalist society. One of the objectives of this book is to identify some of the obstacles as well as the opportunities for this kind of movement-building, through an analysis of actual social movements engaged in struggles around industrial pollution, environmental regulation, and strategies of economic development.

THE TRADE UNIONS

The new social movement theorists have tended to view industrial workers as a group closely attached to the "old paradigm" of social change. This view is supported by the typical sociological profiles of adherents of the alternative movements. The activists of the NSMs are drawn predominantly from the so-called "new middle class," especially people who work in the human service professions and/or the public sector, and are relatively educated, being thus in positions to experience first-hand, and to bring a critical analysis to, issues of control over decision making (at the level of the State and the economy), of social priorities, and of the rationality of the system. They also tend to be young, and to have higher female participation than the activist bases or official ranks of political parties and industrial unions. Another important component of the NSMs is made up of what Offe calls "decommodified groups"—people who are outside of the labour market, such as unemployed workers, students, housewives, and retired persons. At certain conjunctures— particularly in environmental struggles—the issues of the alternative movements have attracted support from the traditional middle class (farmers, shop owners, artisans-producers) whose interests are threatened by proposed developments. The one group the alternative movements have typically *not* included is the predominantly male, industrial workforce—the so-called traditional working class. Certain French theorists (writing in the context of a society with relatively strong workers' parties and union organisations attached to the Fordist paradigm, it must be noted), have suggested that there is an objective, historical conflict of interests between this class—seen to be deeply committed to the institutional rules and ethics of the industrial capitalist era—and the interests represented by the alternative movements.[28] Others, like Offe, have stopped short of such a claim, while observing that "the classes, strata, and groups that are penetrated least easily by the concerns, demands, and forms of action of the 'new' paradigm are exactly the 'principal' classes of capitalist societies, namely, the industrial working class and the holders and agents of economic and administrative power."[29]

Relations between industrial and resource-sector workers and environmentalists, given the "jobs-versus-the-environment" construction of trade-offs in a capitalist economy, are often conflictual. Short-term material security is also typically pitted against occupational or public health and safety concerns. At the same time it is evident that these conflicts stem from *a particular construction of the choices available to citizens-as-workers*, one which imposes the costs of harmful industrial practices on wage earners either in the form of economic deprivation and insecurity, or in the form of the degradation of health and the quality of life. This trade-off, although experienced by many as "a fact of life," is the outcome of existing relationships of power. Objectively, it is workers in the most polluting industries who have most to gain from the success of environmental demands. Thus, rather than posit an objective or historical conflict between certain strata of workers and the alternative movements, it is more useful to examine the factors which allow these trade-offs to be reproduced, and which prevent alternatives from being considered.

Among these factors is the question of union leadership. Classical Marxists, including Gramsci, advanced various explanations of what they viewed as the bureaucratic conservatism of the trade unions. In *Farewell to the Working Class*, André Gorz preferred an explanation which emphasized unions' "institutionalization as negotiating and bargaining forums." Gorz argued that:

> Unions possess power as institutions that are relatively autonomous from their mandators. They become autonomous as a result of the mediatory power conferred upon them by their institutional role. There is no point in reproving individual trade unionists for this fact. They sometimes experience the contradiction as a source of anguish or misery. Not they individually are at fault but the technical and social division of labour, the mode and relations of production, the size and inertia of the industrial machine which, because they rigidly predetermine both the results and the phases of the work process, leave no more than marginal space for workers' control in and over production.[30]

For Gorz, real workers' control over production will arise only when the entire social, economic, and ideological context within which production is organised, enters into crisis—when people question the system, rather than seeking explanations for oppression in personal characteristics (corrupt leaders, co-opted union officials, etc.).

In *Trade Unions and Socialist Politics*, John Kelly reviews classical Marxist theses regarding the revolutionary potential of trade unions, and examines some of the evidence for these theses. In particular, he looks at the explanations that have been offered for union bureaucrats' conservatism, including: (1) material interests (Engels, Lenin); (2) a lack of structures of accountability; (3) isolation from the rank and file; and (4) the bargaining function and the maintenance of the organisation (Lenin, Trotsky, Gramsci). The fourth factor has the least to do with the corruptible nature of human beings and the most to do with the interaction between individual actors and social structures. R. Hyman, quoted by Kelly, describes the institutional reasons for union bureaucratic conservatism:

> Collective bargaining undertaken by "specialist" negotiators on behalf of the broader membership consolidates a representative hierarchy functionally oriented towards accommodation and compromise with capital and its agents; committed to what has been called an "industrial legality" which may permit some improvement in workers' conditions yet simultaneously endorses the legitimacy and security of the employer. Representation becomes detached from mobilization; the preservation of the bargaining relationship with the employer bespeaks a containment of 'unofficial' exercises in class struggle.[31]

This view of the union's institutional role was expressed by Gramsci in blunter terms in his 1921 essay, "Masses and Leaders":

> *Objectively*, the trade union is nothing other than a commercial company, of a purely capitalistic type, which aims to secure, in the interests of the proletariat, the maximum price for the commodity labour, and to establish a monopoly over this commodity in the national and international fields. The trade union is distinguished from capitalist mercantilism only *subjectively*.[32]

The managers of the trade unions, Gramsci observed, often lose their interest in activities which may potentially destabilize the bases of their own power as mediators, or negotiators, between workers and bosses:

> These men no longer live for the class struggle, no longer feel the same passions, the same desires, the same hopes as the masses. Between them and the masses an unbridgeable gap has opened up. The only contact between them and the masses is the account ledger and the membership file. These men no longer see the enemy in the bourgeoisie, they see him in the communists. They are afraid of competition; instead of leaders they have become bankers of men in a monopoly situation…[33]

Some of the theses prepared for the Rome congress of the Italian Communist Party (PCI) (March 20-24, 1922) also dealt with the question of the unions. "Function and Development of Unions," attributed to Gramsci,[34] reasserted the views developed in Gramsci's 1921 writings.[35] For example, Gramsci argued that, for the majority of workers, to be organized meant "not to participate in the life of their own community, to exercise and to develop their own intellectual gifts and morals, but only…to enjoy formal liberties … which the citizen enjoys under the rule of the parliamentary State."[36] (The analogy between the union and the State, both hegemonized by bourgeois, parliamentary governments, is a recurring theme in Gramsci's writing on unions.) The union organisation was described as institutionally embedded in capitalism, its corporative functions limiting its political role.

> By reason of its very origins and the paths of its development, the union organization has limits which cannot be surpassed organically, by an automatic expansion of the initial movement. The Union was born and developed, not by virtue of an autonomous force, but as a reaction to the evils which the development of the capitalist system engenders to the detriment of the working class. The union organisation moves in a fashion parallel to the movement of capitalist organisation, as a reflection of this movement; side by side with the process of monopolization of the material instruments of production and of exchange there develops the process of monopolization of the labour force. It is always a question of a phenomenon which does not differentiate itself objectively from the capitalist phenomenon, and reality has demonstrated the total absurdity of the prediction which announced that, in the competition the monopoly of the labour force would prevail, and simple corporative resistance would cause the industrial power, and consequently the political power of capitalists to collapse.[37]

Gramsci suggested that the trade unions would be superseded by new organisational forms in a context of deepening organic crisis. The transformation would involve changes in working-class organisation that would "facilitate hegemonic consciousness: it must embrace workers as members of a class, not a trade or occupation; it must operate at the level of the workplace so that workers could intervene in the labour process; and it must aspire to the complete control of the labour process and not rest content with negotiation over the terms and conditions of labour's exploitation by capital."[38] In "Unions and Councils," written in October 1919, Gramsci envisaged the spirit of the factory councils spreading throughout the trade unions.

> The workers will carry this new consciousness into the trade unions, which in place of the simple activity of the class struggle will dedicate themselves to the fundamental task of stamping economic life and work techniques with a new pattern; they will elaborate the form of economic life and professional technique proper to communist civilization. In this sense the unions, who are made up of the best and most conscious workers, will realize the highest moment of the class struggle and the dictatorship of the proletariat: they will create the objective conditions in which classes will no longer be able to exist or re-emerge.[39]

While such transformation could occur to some extent within the traditional union structure, and Gramsci supported the agitational role of communist cadre within the unions, the latter's institutional *raison d'être* presented certain limits to the assumption of a counter-hegemonic role by its leaders. In Gramsci's view, the primary, or "specific" task of the Communist Party should be to promote the development of workplace councils, and to work to assert politico-ideological leadership within these bodies.[40] The factory councils were to be the Party's direct link with the working class, autonomous from the union "officialdom."[41] In the midst of an experience in which the union and Socialist Party leaders had failed to organise resistance to fascist violence, or to call for a general insurrection, but had instead opted for a corporatist strategy mediated by the Liberal leader, Giolitti, and drawing as well on contemporary English, Hungarian, and other experiences, Gramsci argued that, in the face of bourgeois offensives, the union organisation had typically proved to be "a pure phantom without substance."[42] In such situations:

> The organization continues to exist, the proletariat does not lose its *esprit de classe*, but the organization and the spirit are no longer expressed within the Union, which often is then deserted; it is expressed on the contrary in the multiple manifestations which gravitate around the political party that the working class recognizes as its party: from the simply corporative level, the resistance passes to the political level.[43]

Kelly criticises the above explanations of union bureaucratic conservatism for their ahistorical generality, pointing out that:
a. collective bargaining is not always usefully understood as a compromise by the subordinate class, but may in fact achieve significant victories for workers; moreover, underlying the accusation of compromise is often an unfounded assumption that a greater, or complete victory was possible in the circumstances;
b. there is "no convincing evidence that union officials, on the whole, are more 'conservative' than their memberships... Clearly there are 'conservative' officials and militant workers, but there are also militant officials and conservative workers, and the precise balance between these groups is likely to vary with circumstances."

Kelly prefers an explanation which he attributes to Claus Offe and Hans Wiesenthal, which emphasizes a dynamic formation and dissolution of worker solidarity and militancy, linked to profitability cycles in the economy, and changing State policies toward the legal framework of union functions.[44] These authors assume not a "collectivization" of workers with the development of capitalist relations of production, but workers' atomization. Most of the time—at least in economic growth periods—the reinforcement of collective consciousness is not a primary concern of the union; but in periods of crisis, "unions are forced to rely on their members, and to try and mobilize them in the struggle to defend both their procedural and substantive gains."[45] In this interpretation, we move away from a view of "trade union bureaucracy" as an inevitably conservative and immutable feature of worker organisation under capitalism, and toward a more dialectical view of the constantly changing conjunctures of social forces and events which shape the strategies of union leaders.

Kelly also takes issue with Gramsci's emphasis on the importance of the development of class consciousness as a precondition of the "highest moment" of the class struggle, which Kelly summarizes as follows:

> [R]evolutionary action by the working class would require as a precondition the attainment of revolutionary, or hegemonic, consciousness by many of its members. Revolutionary action could not successfully proceed on the basis of sectional or corporate consciousness: the conventional trade union demands corresponding to these levels of consciousness could not facilitate the overthrow of capitalism because they did not embody the constructive aspect of revolution, the creation of the elementary forms of 'the new order'.[46]

Instead, Kelly argues that the corporate demands of workers may, "in the context of widespread industrial and political class conflict and profound economic crisis," contribute to the creation of "a revolutionary situation in which workers engage in radical actions such as factory occupations (a view associated with Rosa Luxemburg)."[47]

> There are circumstances in which worker mobilization rises rapidly, where periodic strike waves throw the balance of power and the orderliness of industrial relations into flux. As workers' confidence increases and their horizons expand, the role of union leadership becomes critical in retarding or advancing such struggles. All the evidence…suggests that union officials are much more likely to be advancing such struggles and promoting radical demands than they have been in the past.[48]

This view downplays the ideological conditions for revolutionary action at the centre of Gramsci's analysis, i.e., the transcendence of a corporate level of consciousness, and the growth of counter-hegemonic consciousness among broad sectors of the population. The presence of such conditions implies a much more profound crisis, one in which unions—like other institutions—may dissolve and new forms may arise. Gramsci's approach also implies a greater likelihood that what will emerge is the foundations of a democratic socialist society. (Indeed, it is not evident that the conditions described by Kelly would necessarily promote socialist consciousness at all.)

Moreover, this argument leaves unexplained the origins of the "widespread" and "profound" crisis Kelly describes, or its relationship to the "radical" actions taken by workers. Indeed, Kelly's qualifying context amounts to the organic crisis described by Gramsci, in which old forms are in dissolution. Nor does the argument that corporate demands may be generalized or radicalized into an insurrectionary movement explain why, during periods of relative stability in industrial relations, union leaders do not assume ideological tasks. It assumes that the primary determinant of workers' behaviour is the economic policies of the bourgeoisie, and gives no reason to expect that workers' consciousness—even in periods of crisis—will transcend a corporate level. Workers' actions are thus viewed as revolutionary effects, rather than causes; their demands have accidental, rather than intended consequences. Indeed, Kelly's argument is rather functionalist, omitting explanatory factors at the levels of ideology and political leadership.

Offe and Wiesenthal's theory of union behaviour in fact suggests that the historical institutionalization of collective-bargaining relations represents a progression of stages which makes it increasingly unlikely that unions will be able to assume radical political leadership in the absence of external social mobilization. The historical experience of most industrial capitalist societies is that the union gradually loses the basis of its initial power, that is, an active, militant, and class-conscious membership. Even when the union leadership reverts to a strategy of mobilizing its members, the objectives of the fight are likely to be the defence of the status quo ante, rather than an agenda of radical social reform. The militant sector of the workers is likely to be smaller and more associated with the bureaucracy. Offe and Wiesenthal conclude that there is no way out of the union's institutional logic in the absence of an external, social "politicization" or crisis.

What the Gramscian, Luxemburg, Offe and Weisenthal, and Kelly analyses all seem to suggest is that it is possible for unions to undergo certain transformations in ways which reflect much broader societal changes. In "ordinary times" the conservative functions of unions as mediating bureaucracies inserted between management and workers are least subject to radical challenges. But even in "ordinary times," the status quo represents a rough *modus vivendi* of social forces, one subject to constant testing and struggle. When employers refuse to accede to wage demands, or bargain for concessions, union leaders may behave more confrontationally, but in any case must respond in such a way as to maintain their credibility with members. In periods of crisis, when the old bases of bourgeois hegemony have been eroded, and the outlines of the emerging order are widely contested, the functions and structures of workers' organisation are called into question; new demands are made on leaders, and parallel or alternative forms of organisation and struggle may arise. Long-established organisational forms may outlast the historical conditions which gave rise to them; a situation may develop in which rapid changes in workers' organisation emerge within the unions, but, as a period of organic crisis intensifies, they implode the old structure. The new forms of organisation may dissolve the boundaries not only among groups of workers, but those between workers and citizens, factories and communities.

Gramsci's critique of trade unions is predominantly about what trade unions are in normal times, especially their internalization of a "narrow, petty-and-middle-bourgeois mentality."[49] This "mentality," however, also makes them incapable of assuming leadership in periods of organic crisis. His argument that "trade union action, within its own sphere and using its own methods, stands revealed as being utterly incapable of overthrowing capitalist society,"[50] leaves open the possibility that, in a context in which the "sphere" and the "methods" are compelled to interact with other social forces undergoing profound change, the forms and objectives of workers' organisation might also be transformed (e.g., in Gramsci's view, as, in the formation of the factory councils, or the soviets). Gramsci did not relinquish the view that workplace organisation would be crucial in the revolutionary process; rather, he argued that it must become the locus of counter-hegemonic class consciousness prior to the decisive confrontations with the bourgeoisie.[51]

Even in "normal" times, a significant radicalization of union leadership and a democratization of the internal practices of unions may occur as consequences of the work of organic intellectuals of the working class within workplace-centred organisations. However, the political culture of a workforce is not determined in isolation from changes in the external environment (e.g., the character, absence, or presence, of political leadership; the social mobilization of other groups; the strategies of the bourgeoisie, etc.). In a situation where—as in Canada—most union leaders adhere to a predominantly social democratic ideology, we must ask under what circumstances these changes in consciousness and in union priorities could occur.

I would, like Gramsci, attribute greater importance than Kelly does to factors which may engender the formation of counter-hegemonic consciousness. Among these I would include the task of building coalitions among social actors sharing counter-hegemonic interests. For it is also in the context of alliances with other subordinate groups that union leaders and members come to develop more radical critiques of capitalism and other forms of oppression, as well as more coherent visions of a different world. As Raymond Williams said, it is necessary to resist the isolation of economic relationships from all of the other social relationships which give meaning to our lives as whole human beings, and are therefore the greatest "resources of hope" for social change. I would also place greater emphasis on measures to develop union research and educational capabilities, to enhance workers' self-confidence and competence to participate in economic and social planning. This is a key element of Gavin Kitching's "pre-emptive unionism." [52] Kitching's conceptualization of union practice as one aspect of a broader war of position, grounded in a project to democratize decision-making, seems to me a useful contribution to a theory of social change. In other words, it addresses the problem of how we may envisage unions moving toward a leadership role in counter-hegemonic struggles.

The politicization of many relations of domination/subordination—particularly by the women's movement, but increasingly by other political subjects as well—has contributed to the broadening of union organisations' discourse to make reference to forms of domination which intersect the subject position "worker." This increasingly poses a problem for an understanding of the union's counter-hegemonic role as one of cultivating *working-class* identity and consciousness. Either all of the diverse experiences of individuals (as gendered, raced, nationalized, etc., subjects) are to be subsumed under the identity "worker"—as variants of hyphenated socialist discourse attempt to do, linking every form of domination back, in the end, to capitalist relations of production—or, equivalences must be established among these different subject positions which acknowledge what is unique about each experience while demonstrating their common stakes in a counter-hegemonic project. At least implicitly, many campaigns around sexual harassment, racism, or the environment in the workplace make appeals to humanist values, democratic rights, and social responsibility as the principles making possible (as well as necessary) working-class solidarity.

It might still be argued, however, that the union's special task in the broader war of position is to raise consciousness among its members about the exploitative and oppressive nature of wage labour, and about the ways in which the organisation of production and exchange around the maximization of surplus value for the owners of capital determines social priorities and explains social ills. (Indeed such a discourse is crucial to mobilize workers around collective bargaining and workplace-related issues, and to counter the corporatist, neoliberal, or other discourses of employers and states with regard to industrial relations.) With respect to the creation of a counter-hegemonic project, the problem is not the function of the union in defining a unique (working-class) subject position, but the way in which the relationships among this subject position and others are understood. The subject position of worker (defined in relation to experiences of exploitation and subordination) may be privileged (as in Marxist discourse) as the central axis of social conflict, in which case other subject positions are necessarily of secondary, tangential, or tactical importance. This interpretation, when couched in terms of a radical (transformative) political project, means that the labour movement must be "hegemonic" vis-à-vis its allies, and that the capital-labour conflict must have strategic priority.

The subject position of worker may also be privileged, however, within a social democratic discourse whose aims are primarily to "manage" the existing institutions of a capitalist and productivist society. This has been the predominant ideological discourse of the leaders of the Canadian labour movement. However, as I have already noted, the privileging of the identity and interests of the "worker" (what union officials often describe as their "bottom line") is increasingly being challenged by the identities and interests defended by the alternative movements. Union officials try to avoid "choosing sides" in conflicts which pit their members' job security against the environment, health, gender or racial equality, peace, or the aspirations of "third world" peoples. They may do this by downplaying or minimizing the costs to "the other side" (public health, the environment, gender or racial equality) of an outcome which favours the immediate interests of profit and job security. They thereby attempt to ward off accusations of having narrowly and short-sightedly defined the interests of their members, or of having "sacrificed" the interests of other social groups.

However, this response (which I characterize as "corporate unionism" in part 3) is usually adopted only when an appeal to the State to intervene in a conflict between the interests of workers' economic security, environmental protection or health, and the conditions of profitability for corporations has failed, and the union believes itself to be in too weak a position to confront employers in the sphere of collective bargaining. Many union leaders and members view the appropriate role of the State to be the facilitating of both economic growth and the fulfillment of an array of other goals, including the redistribution of wealth, environmental protection, the safeguarding of civil and political rights, and so on. Since it is the social democratic party—in Canada, the New Democratic Party (NDP)—whose election is viewed as necessary to secure these State functions, to "resolve" these kinds of conflicts, much of the "political" strategy and resources of the Canadian labour movement have been directed to supporting the NDP.

Another important aspect of the social democratic orientation of union leadership is that the articulation of the equivalences among social movements (among subject positions) is seen to be primarily a responsibility of the political party—the NDP. Apart from large unions, which have considerable financial resources, most labour organisations function as "service agents," assisting members in the interpretation of legal rights, mediating during collective bargaining, and monitoring agreements. Rank-and-file education and grass-roots coalition-building are activities outside of these institutional priorities. The bureaucratic organisation created to carry out these functions is characterized by hierarchical and representative, rather than by inclusive and participatory, structures. "Mobilization" increasingly comes to refer to recruiting picketers during strikes, rather than to an ongoing process of education, skill-developing, analysis, and empowerment. This is not to say, however, that union priorities are locked into a linear progression of historical stages which can not be transformed in response to changes in leadership or in the external environment of union practice. There are, nevertheless, limits to the challenges to capital that unions can pose within the state-regulated framework of collective bargaining—hence the division of labour with a social democratic political party. The current direction of capitalist restructuring (greater freedom/mobility for multinational capital, structural unemployment, erosion of social security, etc.) makes the achievement of social gains through collective bargaining even more difficult. However, the most important constraint upon the potential of the union to function as a political party is its institutional *raison d'être*, which is to represent and defend—with limited resources—the particular interests of its membership. Stretching the definition of those interests requires continual efforts of education and mobilization linked to a multi-faceted social movement.

The counter-hegemonic functions of the union, therefore, are not only to develop a political class identity among workers, but to do so in a way which continually demonstrates how the identity and experience of the worker is informed or shaped by racial, gender, ethnic and other subject positions, and which does not claim for the subject position "worker" a fixed, privileged status in a hierarchy of struggles or experiences. The discourse which can link these struggles or subject positions to one another is radical and pluralist democracy. By this I mean a discourse which interprets the meaning of diverse struggles as struggles for equality, understood as freedom from unwarranted discrimination; for autonomy, understood as respect for difference, or freedom from unwarranted assumptions of sameness in relation to some pseudo-universal norm; and for deepened and broadened participation in decision making at all levels of society.

Once the union assumes such counter-hegemonic functions, the potential is created for participation in coalitions to move beyond merely tactical alliances, toward a convergence with other social actors which is transformative and radicalizing. Thus it is possible to envisage counter-hegemonic leadership emerging from the trade unions. What so many Marxist and NSM theorists have observed, however, is that this kind of leadership has not tended, historically, to emerge from the industrial trade unions. For Marxist theorists, the problem is that the unions have not been in the vanguard of anti-capitalist struggles. For the NSM theorists, the problem is that the unions have at best remained attached to social democratic or socialist praxis, instead of making a broader and more radical critique of modernization (its productivist, rationalist, patriarchal, and other aspects). Both positions are, of course, critical of those unions which defend the status quo (whether identified as capitalism or modernization processes). An important question addressed by this study, therefore, is: under what circumstances are unions likely to adopt counter-hegemonic roles in the sense outlined above (i.e., continual efforts of education and mobilization, including the agenda of collective bargaining, linked to a multifaceted social movement)? The case of the CAW's transition from "social unionism" to "movement unionism" in the 1990s offers some insights into this question, and is examined in part 4.

There is one more aspect of the discussion of unions and counter-hegemonic politics which needs to be addressed here. This concerns the relationship between the union and the political party. The analysis of union politics and strategy in this work places considerable emphasis on the roles of the union organisations, rather than those of political parties. It is not my intention to argue that the union organisation alone may provide politico-ideological leadership at the point of production; indeed, it is possible to conceive of other organisations which could perform these tasks (e.g., factory councils, party cells, workers' study groups). However, in Canada at the present time, politico-ideological activities in the workplace (apart from those of employers) are largely the domain of union committees, rather than, say, autonomous rank-and-file workers' organisations linked to one or more political parties.[53] Moreover, in many cases—certainly in those of the two unions studied in this work—the political affiliation of the unions has been (until recently) with the social democratic NDP. The two organisations (party and union) have operated with a certain division of labour, discussed in parts 3 and 4, which leaves workplace mobilization primarily in the hands of the union organisations.

Gramsci's thinking on the question of union-party relations, and on the potential politico-ideological role of the union organisation, assumed the existence of a revolutionary political party dedicated to "reconstruct the unitary consciousness and the capacity for action of the union movement."[54] In this context, Gramsci wrote:

> The mass organization is to the Communist Party what, in the traditional historical development, the State is to the government: the specific end of the Communist Party is in effect to promote...the birth of a state organization of workers' resistance and to make itself the preponderant element of government within it...[55]

If the NDP or another group of intellectuals were to assume the role of Gramsci's Modern Prince, undertaking to create class identity among workers (as producers) and to promote counter-hegemonic consciousness, would the function of the union organisation as a school for the creation of "organic intellectuals"[56] (of counter-hegemonic struggle) then be so important? Presumably, union relationships with such a party would be very different from the social democratic, parliamentarist relationship which has predominated until now. More radical union leaderships would find their educational and organising efforts reinforced, and the boundaries between economic and political actions would become blurred. More conservative leaderships might contest the "governing" ambitions of the Modern Prince. In the latter case, workers might be mobilized through alternative workplace-based organisations or outside of the workplace. Needless to say, such developments would entail very radical changes in the prevailing political culture as well as the norms of employer-worker relations (including management and owners' prerogatives).

The situation of unions in Canada today—but also in Europe and in North America as a whole—is that neoliberal, neo-Taylorist economic restructuring has occurred in large part *as a result of* a vacuum in political leadership from the left. Opposition to the corporations' agenda has come mainly from the alternative movements, along with more militant sectors of the union movement. In the absence of a Modern Prince, unions are faced with essentially two choices: to defend corporate, or sectoral interests, or, to engage in social-movement building which is, in effect, to assume the functions which the social democratic division of labour had reserved for the political party.

NOTES

1. On the relation of the NSMs to the contradictions of Fordism, see Joachim Hirsch, "The Crisis of Fordism, Transformations of the 'Keynesian' Security State, and New Social Movements," *Research in Social Movements, Conflicts and Change* vol. 10 (1988). "Fordism" here refers to the type of capitalist development which took shape in the United States after World War Two, and whose characteristics were then generalized to the other industrialized countries. Fordism entailed a rapid expansion of industrial output thanks to the introduction of assembly-line mass production and the gradual elimination of skilled workers whose knowledge was incorporated into the production process through the techniques of scientific time management (or Taylorism). Markets for these mass-produced goods had to be created, however, and this was accomplished in two ways. The first was the creation of an international trade and financial system which promoted free trade (and in which the United States played a predominant role). The second was creation of domestic demand through the institutionalisation of the Keynesian welfare state and of collective-bargaining relations between workers and employers. National economic management sought to maintain high and stable levels of demand, while collective bargaining allowed workers' wages to keep pace with increases in productivity and prices. The postwar "social democratic consensus" represented a victory for egalitarian and solidarity values which was hard-fought by workers' movements. The extent of such changes, however, varied significantly from one country to another, as the differences between the welfare states of the United States and Sweden suggest. The aspect of Fordism which is particularly relevant to analyses of the political role of labour movements is summarized by Andrew Gamble in this way: "Organised labour was successfully incorporated as a support for the modern industrial order and there followed an era of exceptional growth in output, living standards and the public sector throughout the advanced capitalist countries" (*The Free Economy and the Strong State: The Politics of Thatcherism*, 2nd ed. (London: Macmillan, 1994), p. 17).
2 For one of the early liberal-pluralist explanations of working-class integration into western political systems in terms of an "era of de-ideologization," see O. Kirchheimer, "The Transformation of the Western European Party Systems," in J. Lapalombara and M. Weiner, eds., *Political Parties and Political Development* (Princeton, NJ: Princeton Univ. Press, 1966). The argument that rising levels of material affluence have led to an "embourgeoisement" of the

working class, and therefore a superseding of industrial-era social cleavages along class lines, is used by S. Flanagan and R. Dalton in "Parties under Stress: Realignment and Dealignment in Advanced Industrial Societies," *Western European Politics* vol. 7, no. 1 (1984), and to some extent by Samuel Beer in *Britain Against Itself* (London: Faber and Faber, 1982).

3. See Ronald Inglehart, *The Silent Revolution* (Princeton, NJ: Princeton Univ. Press, 1977), and *Culture Shift* (Princeton, NJ: Princeton Univ. Press, 1990).
4. See Jane Jenson and George Ross, "Post-War Class Struggles and the Crisis of Left Politics," *Socialist Register* 1985/86, pp. 37-38, and Nicos Poulantzas, *Classes in Contemporary Capitalism*, trans. by David Fernbach (London: New Left Books, 1978).
5. Klaus Eder, *The New Politics of Class: Social Movements and Cultural Dynamics in Advanced Societies* (London: Sage, 1993).
6. See Alain Touraine, *The Voice and the Eye: An Analysis of Social Movements* (Cambridge: Cambridge Univ. Press/Editions de La Maison des Sciences de l'Homme, 1981) [trans. from the original *La Voix et le Regard* (Paris: Editions du Seuil, 1978)]; Alain Touraine et al., *Anti-Nuclear Protest: The opposition to nuclear energy in France* (Cambridge: Cambridge Univ. Press, 1983) [first published as *La Prophétie Anti-Nucléaire* (Paris: Editions du Seuil, 1980)].
7. Claus Offe, "New Social Movements: Challenging the Boundaries of Institutional Politics," *Social Research* vol. 52, no. 4 (Winter 1985). The term neoliberalism refers to the revival of the nineteenth-century economics theory that, shorn of all State regulation of economic activities, such as corporate taxation, tariffs, subsidies to producers, labour legislation (minimum wages, legalization of trade unions), State ownership of productive capacity, etc., markets would be "freed" to achieve their "equilibrium" levels of wages, employment, prices, etc., on the bases of the laws of supply and demand. Market laws would result in the most efficient and productive use of both capital investment and labour. Ultimately, both capitalists and workers would benefit from a "laissez-faire" approach to the role of the State in the economy. In the late 1970s, this ideology took a strong hold on the British Conservative Party, led by Margaret Thatcher. In this "neoliberal" view, strong trade unions were seen to be a major cause of the poor productivity rates and non-competitiveness of British manufacturing. Neoliberalism is also a key component of the Republican Party agenda in the United States since the Reagan presidency, and has become predominant in international trade and financial institutions such as the World Bank and the International Monetary Fund.
8. Claus Offe, *Contradictions of the Welfare State*, John Keane, ed. (Cambridge, MA: MIT Press, 1984).
9. M. Crozier, S. Huntington et al., *The Crisis of Democracy* (Report on the Governability of Democracies to the Trilateral Commission) (New York: New York University Press,1975).
10. See, for example, Martin Jacques and Francis Mulhern, eds., *The Forward March of Labour Halted?* (London: NLB, in association with *Marxism Today*, 1981); Gavin Kitching, *Rethinking Socialism* (London and New York: Methuen, 1983); André Gorz, *Farewell to the Working Class: An Essay on Post-industrial Socialism*, trans. by Michael Sonenscher (London: Pluto Press, 1982); Alain Touraine, Michel Wieviorka and François Dubet, *The Workers' Movement*, trans. by Ian Patterson (Cambridge: Cambridge Univ. Press, 1987). A substantial literature has focused on the question of the role of the working class, and of trade unions, in contemporary socialist praxis. For some replies to the "decline of the working class" view, see Leo Panitch, "The Impasse of Social Democratic Politics," *Socialist Register* 1985/86, pp. 50-97; Mateo Alaluf, "Work and the Working Class," *Socialist Register* 1985/86, pp. 455-475; John Kelly, *Trade Unions and Socialist Politics* (London: Verso Books, 1988); Raymond Williams, "The Forward March of Labour Halted," *Resources of Hope: Culture, Democracy, Socialism*, Robin Gable, ed. (London: Verso Books, 1989).
11. Analyses of the new social movements have for the most part been constructed with very little reference to any empirical investigation on the part of the authors, leading to widely differing takes on their significance. Leo Panitch in a 1985 article, "Founding the UAW in Canada: Reflections on the Working Class," described the NSMs as having "slender social bases" compared with the labour movement (*Canadian Dimension* vol. 19, no. 5, p. 46). Raymond Williams, on the other hand, said in 1983 that "if one undertakes the political arithmetic of adding together the people involved (in the new social movements) here is a natural in-built majority... You've got the lack of fit between these active movements which are not mere minorities (however one

might quantitatively assess them) and the weakest political situation the Left has been in since the mid-thirties" (*Towards 2000* (London: Hogarth Press, 1983), p. 14).
12. A number of terms used in this book, including "counter-hegemony," "historical compromise," and "war of position," are derived from the theoretical writings of the Italian Marxist Antonio Gramsci (particularly, the *Prison Notebooks*, written during his long imprisonment under Mussolini's fascist regime). In simplified terms, hegemony refers to the relatively stable exercise of social, political, and economic power by the dominant, ruling group. The two key elements of hegemony are consent (the internalization by the masses of the philosophy of the ruling group, which thereby becomes the "common wisdom" of the period), which is backed up when necessary by *coercion* (military force). In the Western capitalist societies, Gramsci argued, capitalist hegemony typically relies more on consent (the widely accepted legitimacy of the assumptions of bourgeois ideology) than on naked repression (dictatorship). In Gramsci's view, rule which is highly reliant upon force is a *fragile* form of hegemony. In order to maintain its positions of hegemony, the ruling group must attach to its philosophy other "allied" or "subordinate" groups in society. In this way it forms a "popular-historical bloc." Normally this entails certain compromises, or concessions, to the interests of these other groups. The resulting—relatively stable—period of dominance of a particular hegemonic order, while characterized by fundamental conflicts and contradictions, may be referred to in these terms as an "historical compromise." The period most often referred to in these terms is the postwar era of unprecedented economic growth in the West which is known as "Fordism." The *political* compromise which underpinned this era was the social democratic, Keynesian Welfare State.

    For Gramsci, the "core" of a hegemonic historical bloc was identified in class terms (a fraction of the bourgeoisie). The core of the "counter-hegemonic" bloc was the working-class, and the task of the political leadership of the working-class (the Modern Prince or workers' party) was to develop the revolutionary consciousness of this class, while "attaching" to it other social strata. Thus politics is understood as a "war of position" in all social spheres (above all, cultural) between the core antagonists to maintain or construct a hegemonic historical bloc. The subordinate class, however, must first "deconstruct" the "common wisdom" of the day—demonstrate that it is not "natural" or inevitable—and so weaken the ideological hegemony of the ruling group. In the liberal-democratic systems of the West, the project of the subordinate group(s) is to decisively shift the majority of the population towards its values and its alternative vision of society.
13. I took this position in "Labour, Ecology, and the Politics of Convergence in Canada," *Socialist Studies Annual No. 4: Social Movements/Social Change*, Frank C. Cunningham et al., eds. (Toronto: Socialist Studies Society/Between the Lines, 1988), co-authored with C. Alpaugh; and in "Ecology and Labour: Towards a New Societal Paradigm," *Culture and Social Change*, Colin Leys and Marguerite Mendell, eds. (Montréal: Black Rose Books, 1992). The key work with regard to Antonio Gramsci is *Selections from the Prison Notebooks*, edited and trans. by Quintin Hoare and G. N. Smith (New York: International Publishers, 1971). For expositions of Gramsci, see Chantal Mouffe, "Hegemony and Ideology in Gramsci," in *Gramsci and Marxist Theory*, Chantal Mouffe, ed. (London: Routledge & Kegan Paul, 1979); Carl Boggs, *Gramsci's Marxism* (London: Pluto Press, 1976), and *The Two Revolutions: Gramsci and the Dilemmas of Western Marxism* (Boston: South End Press, 1984).
14. Chantal Mouffe and Ernesto Laclau, *Hegemony and Socialist Strategy: Towards a Radical Democratic Politics* (London: Verso Books, 1985), p. 4.
15. The core body of work in the regulation school (in English) includes: Christian Palloix, "The Labour Process: From Fordism to neo-Fordism," in *The Labour Process and Class Strategies* (London: CSE Books, 1976); Michel Aglietta, *A Theory of Capitalist Regulation: The U.S. Experience* (London: New Left Books, 1979); Alain Lipietz, "Towards Global Fordism?," *New Left Review* 132 (March-April 1982); Alain Lipietz, "How Monetarism Choked Third World Industrialization," *New Left Review* 145 (May-June 1984); Alain Lipietz, *Mirages and Miracles: The Crisis of Global Fordism*, trans. by David Macey (London: Verso Books, 1987); Alain Lipietz, "Reflections on a Tale: The Marxist Foundations of the Concepts of Regulation and Accumulation," trans. by Jane Jenson and Marguerite Mendell, *Studies in Political Economy* 26 (Summer 1988); Alain Lipietz, *Towards a New Economic Order: Postfordism, Ecology, and Democracy* (Oxford: Polity Press, 1992).

16. I follow the practice of differentiating between neoliberalism, as a primarily economic strategy and ideology appealing to bourgeois views of human nature and society, and neoconservatism, which refers to a set of patriarchal and authoritarian beliefs about law and order, the family, and social morality in general. Thatcherism and Reaganism may be viewed as somewhat unstable articulations of both types of discourse.
17. See, for example, E. Hobsbawm's argument in *The Forward March of Labour Halted?*
18. Ellen Meiksins-Wood, "Marxism Without Class Struggle?," *Socialist Register* 1983, and *Retreat from Class* (London: Verso Books, 1986); E. M. Wood and Peter Meiksins, "Beyond Class? A Reply to Chantal Mouffe," *Studies in Political Economy* 17 (Summer 1985). A number of other authors have taken positions somewhere in between the orthodox and post-Marxist poles; in addition to Leo Panitch, and Jenson and Ross, see Norman Geras, "Post-Marxism?" *New Left Review* 163 (May/June 1987). These authors have tended to focus their criticisms on the "discourse theorists," rather than on the orthodox responses.
19. Ralph Miliband and Marcel Liebman, "Beyond Social Democracy," *Socialist Register* 1985/86, pp. 485-486.
20. Leo Panitch, "The Impasse of Social Democratic Politics," *Socialist Register* 1985/86, p.63.
21. At one point Laclau and Mouffe explicitly acknowledge that radical democracy is inseparable from the project of socializing the means of production (*Hegemony and Socialist Strategy*, chap. 4). This point recalls Gramsci's comment: "It often happens that people combat historical economism in the belief that they are attacking historical materialism." ("The Modern Prince," *Selections from the Prison Notebooks*, p. 163).
22. Chantal Mouffe, *The Return of the Political* (London: Verso, 1993), pp. 14-15.
23. Ibid., p. 19.
24. Himani Bannerji, "But Who Speaks for Us? Experience and Agency in Conventional Feminist paradigms," in H. Bannerji et al., *Unsettling Relations: The University as a Site of Feminist Struggles* (Toronto: The Women's Press, 1991), pp. 67-107.
25. Williams, *Towards 2000*, pp. 168-171.
26. Ibid., pp. 173-76. In "Problems of the Coming Period," Williams identified "as the most important radical politics the peace movement, the women's movement, the ecology movement, the movements of anti-imperialism and of solidarity with particular struggles in the Third World, and the alternative culture which is still very resilient" (*New Left Review* 140 (July-August, 1983), p. 13).
27. The term "articulation" and the verb "to articulate" are used here in the French sense of the joining together of discrete parts in such a way as to transform their meanings or functions, and to create a new ensemble. For example, when the upper femur and the shin bone are joined together the result is the knee—a complex joint which permits a range of motions for the organism it supports. (One meaning of *articulation* in French is, indeed, "joint.") In more figurative terms, to articulate means to organise distinct elements in such a way that they function as an ensemble. The more common meaning of "articulation" in English usage is "to express" or "to enunciate" a thought or idea. To avoid confusion, I have not used "articulate" in this latter sense.
28. In *La Prophétie anti-nucléaire*, Touraine et al., argue that the "real meaning" of political ecology is a conflict with "working class ideology":

> [P]olitical ecology takes shape in response to a working-class movement which has lost itself to communist power, social-democratic influence or the devout belief in a technical and scientific revolution bringing social progress with it. It criticises the working-class ideology as the working-class movement criticised the bourgeois liberties. Its intention is to be both the successor and the adversary of the working-class movement just as the latter both opposed and continued the work of the bourgeois revolutions (p. 185).

"The working-class movement" here refers to the French Communist Party and the Confédération Générale du Travail. The Confédération Française Démocratique du Travail [CFDT], on the other hand, was viewed (at the end of the 1970s) as an exception because it had capitulated neither to reformism, nor to the domination of the CGT, and was still open to struggles in the name of *auto-gestion* (self-management).
29. Claus Offe, "New Social Movements," p. 835.

New Social Movements, Labour, and Theories of Social Change 25

30. Gorz, *Farewell to the Working Class*, pp. 49-52.
31. R. Hyman, *Strikes*, 3rd ed. (London: Fontana, 1984), pp. 229-30, quoted by J. Kelly in *Trade Unions and Socialist Politics*, p. 173.
32. A. Gramsci, "Masses and Leaders," in *Selections from Political Writings, 1921-1926* (London: Lawrence and Wishart, 1978), p. 76, quoted by Kelly in *Trade Unions and Socialist Politics*, p. 55.
33. A. Gramsci, "Officialdom," March 4, 1921, in *Selections, 1921-1926*, pp. 17-18.
34. Various sources argue that Gramsci was primarily responsible for the sections dealing with union-party relations and the factory councils. See A. De Clementi, "La politica del Partito Comunista d'Italia nel 1921-1922 e il rapporto Bordiga-Gramsci," in *Rivista Storica del Socialismo* (1966), pp. 74f., cited by Robert Paris, and Paris' notes to *Ecrits Politiques* Vol. II (1921-1922), edited by Robert Paris and trans. by M. Martin-Gistucci, G. Moget, and R. Paris (Paris: Editions Gallimard, 1975), p. 339.
35. See, for example, "La Confédération Générale du Travail," and "Contrôle Ouvrier," in *Ecrits Politiques* Vol. II.
36. "Fonction et développement des syndicats," *Ecrits Politiques* Vol. II, p. 207, my translation.
37. Ibid., p. 206, my translation.
38. Kelly, *Trade Unions and Socialist Politics*, p. 67.
39. A. Gramsci (unsigned), in *L'Ordine Nuovo* October 11, 1919, vol. 1, no. 21, reproduced in translation in A. Gramsci, *Selections from the Political Writings, 1910-1920* (New York: International Publishers, 1977), p. 101.
40. The strategy of working "from within" the union while simultaneously building up parallel structures of "government" within the workplace, is also elaborated in "Notre Ligne Syndicale," *Lo Stato Operaio*, in *Ecrits Politiques* Vol. III (1923-1926), pp. 84-90.
41. See "La Confédération générale du travail," February 25, 1921, in *Ecrits Politiques* Vol. II, p. 83.
42. "Fonction et développement des syndicats," p. 206.
43. Ibid., p. 206 (my translation).
44. Offe and Wiesenthal's argument is found in the essay "Two logics of collective action," in M. Zeitlin, ed. *Political Power and Social Theory* vol. 1 (Greenwich, CT: JAI Press, 1980), and reprinted in C. Offe, *Disorganized Capitalism* (Oxford: Polity Press, 1985).
45. Kelly's summary, in *Trade Unions and Socialist Politics*, p. 153.
46. Ibid., p. 68.
47. Ibid., p. 69.
48. Ibid., p. 183.
49. A. Gramsci, "Syndicalism and the Councils," in *Selections, 1910-1920*, p. 109. See also the Rome theses of 1922, in *Ecrits Politiques* Vol. II, p. 207.
50. "Trade Unions and the Dictatorship," in *Selections, 1910-1920*, p. 105.
51. In his analysis of the conservatism of trade unions in revolutionary Hungary, Gramsci stated:

    For if the masses must be persuaded that the trade union is perhaps the most important proletarian organism of the communist revolution, since the socialization of industry must be based upon it and since it must create the conditions in which private enterprise will disappear never to re-emerge, so too must they be persuaded of the need to create, prior to the revolution, subjective and objective conditions under which there could not possibly be any conflict or power dualism between the various organs in which the proletarian class struggle against capitalism is embodied. ("Trade Unions and the Dictatorship," in *Selections, 1910-1920*, p. 103.)

52. Gavin Kitching, *Rethinking Socialism* (London and New York: Methuen, 1983).
53. Revolutionary groupings like the Revolutionary Workers League have attempted to create bases in industrial workplaces, but with limited and very local success.
54. "Le Parti communiste et les Syndicats," in *Ecrits Politiques*, Vol. II, p. 208, my translation.
55. Ibid., my translation.
56. This term was used by Gramsci to refer to those individuals who are "the thinking and organizing element of a particular fundamental social class" (by which he meant, either the bourgeoisie or the proletariat). The hallmark of the organic intellectual of the working class is not his/her profession or occupation, but his/her function in directing the ideas and aspirations of

the working class. Workers become "organic intellectuals" by assuming conscious responsibility for the organisation of production and for political leadership. The bourgeoisie, of course, also has its "organic intellectuals," who in different ways (e.g., as entrepreneurs, managers, marketers, technicians, economists, lawyers, and various "experts") practice, reproduce, and make coherent the elements of the dominant "common sense." Gramsci distinguished organic intellectuals from "traditional" intellectuals, who are less directly associated with either of the principal classes (e.g., clergy, professional intellectuals like philosophers and university professors), and who are in a sense carry-overs from previous historical eras when they were attached to the aristocracy, the church, the landed gentry, and so on. It is possible, of course, for individuals in such occupations to become organic intellectuals. The key passages in the *Prison Notebooks* touching on the organic intellectuals are: "The Intellectuals," "On Education," "Socialism and Culture," and "Men or Machines?" There is also a detailed discussion of these terms in Anne Showstack Sassoon, *Gramsci's Politics* (Minneapolis, MN: University of Minnesota Press, 1987).

Part II

Defining the Stakes of Environmental Politics: Citizen, Union and Corporate Actors

[2]

Environmental Crisis: The Context for Citizen Mobilization in the 1980s

The extent of environmental mobilization stemmed first from widespread public concern about pollution and health. The media devoted considerable attention in the 1980s to issues such as acid rain, the breakdown of stratospheric ozone, climatic change (Greenhouse effect, desertification, water levels, etc.), and the more spectacular nuclear and chemical accidents. The Brundtland Commission of the United Nations, the Toronto Conference on World Climate Change (June 1988), and statements about environmental problems by the Organization for Economic Co-operation and Development (OECD) leaders at the annual summits all received significant media coverage. Incidents of chemical spills, government bans or limits on fish harvest, and reports of toxic contamination of soil, water, air, and food, became linked in the public mind with effects on human health.

Reports which received high-profile media coverage in the southern Ontario region began emerging in the 1980s. First came a report in November, 1980 that the most deadly chemical known, 2,3,7,8-tetrachlorodibenzo-para-dioxin (TCDD dioxin), had been found in herring gull eggs from around the Great Lakes, especially in Lake Ontario.[1] Since the 1980 discovery, dioxin has been found in many fish species, including Lake Ontario salmon and trout, and pike in Rainy River, in a chemical dump at Elmira in southern Ontario, and in the sediment of the St. Clair River, among other places. It has also been detected in human tissues and in women's breast milk. By the late 1980s dioxin and furans, among other chemicals, had been traced to the effluents of pulp and paper mills as well as other (particularly chemical) industrial sources.

In addition to these reports, studies have been publicized regarding the chemicals and other pollutants to which urban residents are exposed through their drinking water, air, and food. In 1981 Pollution Probe released *Toxics on Tap*, and in 1983, *Drinking Water: Make it Safe*. The City of Toronto's Health Department was compelled to initiate its own studies, which turned up more evidence of the presence of eighty-three compounds, only twenty-eight of which were subject to government safety guidelines, and seven of which were known human carcinogens.[2] Scientists admitted that they could not predict the health effects of these quantities or substances. A particular concern is trihalomethanes (THMs), compounds produced when chlorine reacts with organic matter in the water. One THM, chloroform, causes cancer in laboratory animals and is a suspected carcinogen in humans. A study in 1977-82 of drinking water from 138 Ontario communities found that almost all had THMs at or below Canadian Government-accepted levels. However, as Michael Keating points out in his book, *To the Last Drop*, the Canadian standard for THMs is "more than three times as high as the U.S. maximum and 350 times higher than West Germany's."[3]

Various other studies in 1985 reported concerns about drinking water quality in sites all around the Great Lakes Basin, including Toronto, Hamilton harbours, Niagara River, Bay of Quinte, Buffalo River, Rochester, the Welland Canal, and the St. Clair River. Studies by the Environmental Protection Agency (EPA) of the United States, released in May 1986, showed that dioxin had been detected in carp from twenty-nine of fifty areas sampled: most of these were areas of industrial chemical discharges. The single highest level of dioxin was found at Midland, Michigan, the home of Dow Chemical, where Tittabawassee River carp containing 525 parts per trillion (ppt) of dioxin were tested. The EPA estimated that human health may be threatened at concentrations of 1 ppt. Lake Ontario contained the highest levels of dioxin-contaminated carp, followed by Lakes Huron and Michigan, then Erie and Superior.[4]

A study by Dr. Katherine Davies of the Toronto Department of Public Health released in May 1986, found thirty-two chemicals, including dioxin, in samples of fresh meat, milk, vegetables, and fruit grown in southern Ontario. The study contended that about 86 percent of the toxic chemicals people are exposed to come from ingestion of fresh food, while less than 10 percent are from drinking water, and 4.5 percent from inhaling air. This is because of bioaccumulation of toxins in the food chain. Crops are exposed not only to pesticides and herbicides directly applied, but also to "toxic precipitation." Areas downwind of incinerators are depositories of airborne emissions; the Niagara Peninsula, where much of southern Ontario's fresh produce is grown, is affected by fallout from Niagara Falls' "toxic mist." Dr. Davies' findings were widely cited by the press. Late in 1985, a study of the toxic burden of Great Lakes citizens was completed by the Royal Society of Canada and the U.S. National Research Council. The report included a statement which subsequently has often been quoted, and has heightened the concerns of many citizens: "The human population living in the Great Lakes basin is exposed to, and accumulates, appreciably more toxic chemical burden than other human populations in similarly large regions of North America for which data are available."[5]

A follow-up to Davies' study was done by the Ontario ministries for Agriculture and the Environment. They reported, in September 1988, that a wide variety of foods consumed in Ontario (meats, fish, eggs, fruits, vegetables, dairy products) contain low levels of dioxins, dibenzofurans, and other toxic chemicals. However, the public was assured that "the food eaten by an average person in Ontario is likely to contain less than 20 percent of the maximum exposure to chemicals allowed under current federal or provincial health regulations."[6] This finding sparked a controversy over the appropriate government response. Government officials suggested that the Food and Drugs Act regulation banning dioxin in food should be changed to allow "acceptable" levels. The regulation had been implemented in the 1970s, when testing technology could not detect the toxic chemicals at the levels now detectable. The finding that almost all food consumed in Ontario contains dioxins meant, in effect, that the food was being sold illegally and could be recalled or prohibited. A spokesperson for Health and Welfare Canada said that if the law were enforced, "there would be nothing to eat."[7] Government scientists suggested, therefore, that the regulatory goal should be to "assess what level is acceptable and take action...over that amount."[8] Other scientists and environmentalists, however, including Dr. Davies, insisted that there is no scientifically proven "safe level." These chemicals are suspected of increasing the likelihood of cancer, inhibiting the immune system, and altering hormones. Colin Isaacs of Pollution Probe responded to the government suggestion in this way: "It's absolutely absurd. If dioxin is in food, then we should find ways of eliminating dioxin from food, rather than changing [government] regulations in order to accommodate the level of environmental pollution that we have."[9]

One result of toxic contamination which has affected individuals particularly directly is the discovery of harmful chemicals in human milk. Davies' study estimated that the average total exposure (in 1985) of an infant to polychlorinated biphenols (PCBs) over three months' breastfeeding was 1.08 mg. Most women tested since the mid-seventies have had PCB levels high enough to raise concern about breastfeeding. A 1988 story in *The Globe and Mail* focused on the experience of a nursing mother living in Toronto. She had recently learned that her milk contained 14 ppb PCBs and 17 ppb DDT. The federal health department advises women not to breastfeed if their milk has levels of 50 ppb or more of PCBs, but admits that the effects of smaller doses are not known. The anxiety among parents about milk contamination was expressed by this woman:

> It's horrifying... That has got to be a denial of one of the most basic of human functions, which is that as a mother I should be nurturing my child with this breast milk. To think that instead of nurturing I could be poisoning her... I've always been concerned that my children are not going to be able to enjoy the canoeing and the fishing and sailing that I've loved and enjoyed. So I've always felt that I was a fairly strong environmentalist, but that was nothing compared to the way I feel now, because the profound implication is that this is the suicide of the species.
>
> If we are passing on toxins in such great accumulated levels to our small children, will they survive?[10]

Considerable press attention was paid also to a report by two Environment Canada researchers—an economist and a sociologist—which raised concerns about the correlations between chemical exposures and health effects. The Ministry decided that the report was "unscientific," because it did not demonstrate causality, and refused to authorize or distribute it. In the end it was released by the authors themselves, to mixed reviews.[11]

Books documenting the environmental crisis facing North Americans, and focusing on industrial and toxic pollution, proliferated in the 1980s. Among the best known are Michael Brown's *Laying Waste: The Poisoning of America by Toxic Chemicals* (1981), Jackson and Weller's *Chemical Nightmare* (1982), William Ashworth's *The Late, Great Lakes* (1986), and *To the Last Drop: Canada and the World's Water Crisis* (1986), by Michael Keating, former environmental reporter for *The Globe and Mail*. This growing literature, aimed at a not technically versed readership, has helped to raise public awareness of the prevalence of chemical products in the advanced capitalist countries. Environment Canada estimated that by the 1980s there were more than 30,000 chemical substances in common commercial use, and about 1,000 entering the market each year.[12] By 1985, about 1,200 of these were considered dangerous. The most disturbing fact is that only a small percentage of chemicals in use have actually been tested for health and environmental effects. The onus has been on victims to prove harmful effect, rather than on companies to prove safety before marketing. In addition, very little is known about the synergistic effects of all these chemicals.

Various polls have been commissioned by governments, newspapers, the chemical companies, and others, to determine the nature of public concern about environmental issues. In an Environment Canada survey of 1981, 53.2 percent of all respondents said they were dissatisfied with water quality in the Great Lakes. Forty-nine percent thought pollution of the lakes was getting worse, 22 percent thought it was getting better, and the rest saw no change or had no opinion.[13] A 1981-82 poll by the Centre de Recherche sur l'Opinion Publique (CROP) asked respondents whether there was enough government regulation to protect the environment from toxic materials. More than 75 percent said that existing regulations were inadequate.[14] Canadian attitudes towards nuclear power shifted significantly over the period 1976 to 1982, according to Gallop polls.[15] The accident at the Three Mile Island nuclear reactor, Harrisburg, Pennsylvania, March 1979, is thought to have been a factor in making people more cautious about nuclear power. "Support for increasing nuclear power generation declined from 41 percent in 1976 to 20 percent in 1982. The percentage favouring no further development of nuclear power increased from 20 percent in 1976 to 35 percent in 1982. The portion of respondents that would stop generation of nuclear power increased from 14 percent in 1976 to 31 percent in 1982." A Decima Research poll taken in June 1982 found that—even during one of the worst periods of recession—62 percent of Canadians polled said they were willing "to protect the environment even if it cost jobs."[16]

Decima Research found that, in the summer of 1984, over 80 percent of Canadians were "unconvinced that environmental laws should be relaxed in order to achieve economic growth." A year later, Decima reported that about 60 percent of Canadians agreed that "more should be done to protect the environment even if jobs are lost in the process."[17] A CROP survey of June 1985 showed that 82 percent of respondents agreed that the Canadian economy is "highly dependent on the state of the environment." Ninety-four percent agreed, strongly (64 percent) or somewhat (30 percent), that "every major economic project should be proven environmentally sound before it can go ahead."[18]

In 1986, following media reporting of the disastrous "blob" incident affecting the St. Clair River downstream of Sarnia, Ontario, the Canadian Chemical Producers' Association (CCPA) commissioned Decima Research to carry out another survey, this time on the public's image of the chemical industry. The results, reported by the Canadian Press Agency in November, 1986, may be summarized as follows:

1. Sixty-five percent of those polled were "willing to back moves to protect the environment even if those measures affected employment";
2. "Most Canadians believe the risks of pollution are not worth the benefits to society or the economy";
3. "While Canadians think the nuclear industry poses greater risks than do chemicals, one third…believed the risks associated with the chemical industry are growing quickly";
4. "About three quarters indicated an accident like the one…at Bhopal, India, is likely to occur in Canada";
5. Seventy-five percent said "chemical companies get away with too much" and 65 percent favoured jail for executives of companies that pollute the environment.

A poll conducted by *The Environmental Monitor* in the fall of 1987 was reported by *The Globe and Mail,* April 23, 1988. The survey showed that:

1. Nine out of ten persons believe human health has already been affected by environmental pollution.
2. Eighty-eight percent believe that a clean environment is technologically possible.
3. Eighty-seven percent are upset at the "lack of action being taken to protect the environment."
4. Sixty-six percent reject the argument of jobs versus health, i.e., that "environmental clean-up will cost jobs." Indeed, 69 percent believe that "major spending on environmental protection will have a positive effect on the economy."
5. Seventy-eight percent are willing to pay higher prices or taxes to improve environmental protection.
6. Ninety-two percent believe corporate executives should be held personally responsible if their company "repeatedly pollutes the environment at unsafe levels." Nineteen percent would like to see such executives imprisoned.
7. Eight in ten respondents said they are "very concerned about the possible effects of pollution on human health and safety," and about the effects of pollution on future generations.[19]

In 1988, Angus Reid polled 1,501 Canadians on environmental attitudes. Seventy-seven percent said they would pay 10 percent more for a product if it were labelled environmentally safe. Fifty-six percent said they would pay a two-cent tax on a litre of milk or gasoline to "help improve the environment." Eighty-four percent said they thought Canadian governments should be doing more to protect the environment, while only 14 percent thought governments were doing enough.[20]

These data indicate that concern about the environment rose to a high point by the mid-1980s. According to *Canadian Trend Report*, there was also a shift in public priorities from remedial actions to *preventive control by governments*. Moreover, there was increasing awareness of the relationships between environmental and personal health.[21] It became common wisdom—promoted not only by the popular health movement and the health products industry, but by the experiences and observations of countless individuals—that our exposure to multiple pollutants is a major cause of high cancer rates, allergic reactions, and other immune-system-related health problems. This knowledge comes not only through the media and the experience of "consumers," but also from workplace exposure to pollutants. Although unions have faced tremendous obstacles in winning legal and scientific acceptance of their occupational health concerns, and in some cases have not even taken up these struggles, individual workers exposed to harmful substances have made the connections for themselves.

In North America and Western Europe the emphasis on particular environmental problems varies according to economic, demographic, and geographic factors. Nationally recognized environmental organisations like Greenpeace and Pollution Probe have significant bases in the heavily industrialized regions, for obvious reasons. In agricultural and other resource-based areas, a more dispersed, rural network of environmentalists exists—sometimes in alliance with Canadian native peoples—and focuses on such issues as the use of pesticides, herbicides, organic methods of farming, on ecological silviculture, preservation of wilderness areas, wildlife protection, and opposition to ecologically destructive development projects.

Southwestern Ontario is one of the most heavily industrialized areas of Canada (also affected by pollution from the United States). Consequently, its environment suffers the accumulated abuses of decades of industrial and urban pollution.[22] Approximately 7 million people live around Lake Ontario. The population of the Great Lakes Basin is estimated at 42 million. The concentration of population has meant, among other things, loss of green areas to the transportation web and construction, car pollution, and massive waste production and disposal problems. Some of the worst polluters in the region are publicly owned utilities (hydro and nuclear power), and inadequate sewage treatment systems.[23] The millions of people who live in this area experience daily the effects of crowding, noise pollution, and various health effects of air pollution. In addition to fears about exposure to radiation (heightened by the accidents at Three-Mile Island, Chernobyl, problems at Pickering, Port Hope, Fermi II near Amherstburg, criticisms of Darlington, etc.), they are anxious about the long-term effects of cumulative exposure to toxic chemicals in their air, water, and food. Table 1 contains a list of environmental organisations and citizens groups active in southern Ontario in the mid-1980s. Table 2 provides a partial list of conferences that were held around the Great Lakes Basin on environmental issues and citizens' mobilization.

Citizens around Lake Ontario have heard about the toxic dumps seeping into the Niagara River, which provides 83 percent of the inflow of water to the Lake. They have heard about dioxins in the drinking water and PCBs in human milk. Most people have heard about the Love Canal, or the St. Clair River "Blob." Many are worried about eating fish from the Great Lakes, or local produce, sprayed with pesticides and watered with "toxic rain." The Niagara, St. Clair, and Detroit rivers are already considered too contaminated to be safe sources of drinking water. The St. Lawrence has been called "a sewer leading to the sea," where the rare Beluga whales are dying from PCB and Mirex poisoning.

Table 1
Environmental Organizations and Citizens' Groups Active in Ontario in the 1980s: A Partial List

Action for Social Change, Kingston
Bay of Quinte Environmental Group, Picton
Bay Residents Association, Hamilton
Better Understanding Committee, Thorold
Binbrook Anti-Dump Committee, Binbrook
Breslube Citizens Committee, Waterloo
Canadian Coalition on Acid Rain, Toronto
Canadian Environmental Law Association, Toronto
Canadian Environmental Network, Toronto
Canadian Nature Federation, Ottawa
Canadians for a Clean Environment, Niagara Falls
CAW Local 444 Environment Committee, Windsor
CAW Local 199 Environment Committee, St. Catharines
CAW Local 1973 Environment Committee, Windsor
CAW Canada Council Environment Committee, Toronto
Chippawa Watershed Association, Wellandport
Citizens' Coalition for Clean Water, Wallaceburg
Citizens' Coalition to Maintain the Environment, London
Citizens' Environmental Advisory Committee, Elmira
Citizens for Modern Waste Management, Vineland
Citizens' Network on Waste Management, Kitchener
Citizens Reacting Against Pollution Organization, Lucan
Citizens Rebelling Against Waste, Merlin
Concerned Citizens of Georgina, Willow Beach
Concerned Citizens of Whitchurch-Stouffville, Stouffville
Conservation Council of Ontario, Toronto
Conserver Society of Hamilton and District, Hamilton
Decisions for the Great Lakes, Kingston
Ducks Unlimited
Embro Citizens Group, Embro
Energy Probe, Toronto
Essex County Citizens Against Fermi II, Amherstburg
Federation of Ontario Naturalists
Friends of the Earth, Ottawa
Friends of the Spit, Toronto
Glenburnie Residents Association, Glenburnie
Great Lakes United
Greenpeace Foundation, Toronto
Haldimand-Norfolk Organization for a Pure Environment, Dunnville
Kingston Environmental Action Project, Kingston
Kingston Field Naturalists
Lambton Anti-Pollution Association, Mooretown
Little Cataraqui Environmental Association, Kingston
Lake Ontario Organizing Network
Maidstone Against Dumping, Essex
National Capital Pollution Probe, Ottawa
Niagara Ecosystem Taskforce, St. Catharines
Niagara Neighbourhood Association, Lead Pollution Committee, Toronto
Ontario Environmental Action
Ontario Environmental Network
Ontario Public Interest Research Groups
    (Guelph, Ottawa, Hamilton, Toronto, Peterborough, Waterloo, and Windsor)

Ontario Recycling Information Service, Toronto
Operation Clean Niagara, Niagara-on-the-Lake
Pollution Probe Foundation, Toronto
Project for Environmental Priorities
Recycling Council of Ontario, Toronto
Save Our Streams, Inc., Willowdale
Save the Rouge Valley System, Scarborough
Sierra Club of Ontario, Toronto
South Riverdale Community Health Centre, Toronto
Springvale Citizens' Group, Hagersville
St. Clair River International Citizens' Network
St. Marys River Water Quality Task Force
Stop Contaminating our Waterfront, Toronto
Temagami Wilderness Society
Temiskaming Environmental Action Committee, New Liskeard
Tiny Ratepayers Against Pollution, Perkinsfield
Toronto Waterfront Remedial Action Plan Committee
Toxic Waste Research Coalition, St. Catharines
Tremain Britannia Group, Milton
Upper Ottawa Street Residents Association, Hamilton
Wallaceburg Clean Water Committee, Wallaceburg
Windsor and District Clean Water Alliance, Windsor

TABLE 2
PARTIAL LIST OF CONFERENCES ON GREAT LAKES BASIN ENVIRONMENTAL ISSUES,
1986-1988

April 1986: Conference on Pesticides, Your Right to Know (organized by the Sierra Club Northeast Ohio Group, the League of Women Voters, and the Northeast Ohio Coalition against the misuse of pesticides), John Carroll University, OH.
May 1986: Great Lakes United [GLU] 4th annual meeting, Mackinac City, MI.
May 1986: Midwest Conference on Environmental Dispute Resolution, Champaign, IL.
June to September, 1986: Public information hearings organized by Michigan's Office of the Great Lakes (10 locations).
July 19, 1986: People Power Rally Against Toxic Waste Dumps, West Lincoln, Niagara region (5,000 people).
July-October 1986: GLU public hearings on the Great Lakes Water Quality Agreement, 19 locations, from Duluth, Minnesota to Montréal, QC.
October 1986: Globescope II. An international forum on long-term trends in global environment, development, resources, and population, Tufts University, Mass.
October 1986: Conference on rural groundwater contamination: assessment of needs, strategies for action, Michigan State University, Institute of Water Research.
November 1986: Ontario Labour-Environment Conference, Hamilton, Ontario, organized by the Ontario Environmental Network.
November 1986: Center for the Great Lakes (Chicago) Water Quality Summit meeting, Detroit, MI
November 29, 1986: People Power Convention, St. Catharines, ON.
March 1987: Week of lobbying in Washington, D.C., around theme: "Toxic Air Pollution in the Great Lakes Basin: A Call for Action."
April 1987: Midwestern Groundwater Conference, Indianapolis, IN.
April 1987: Annual conference of the National Association of Environmental Professionals, "Managing the Environment: National Issues, Regional Approaches", Chicago May 1987 "Toxics in the Harbour: The Milwaukee Remedial Action Plan — A Call to Action," meeting organized by Citizens for a Better Environment and the Sierra Club chapter, Milwaukee, WI.
May 1987: International meeting on the St. Lawrence River, Montréal (organized by the Société pour vaincre la pollution).

July 19-26, 1987: Great Lakes Week.
September 1987: Workshop on "Cleaning up Great Lakes Toxic Hot Spots Through Citizen Involvement in Remedial Action Plans," Buffalo, NY.
October 1987: "Air Toxics and the Great Lakes," conference organized by Michigan's Office of the Great Lakes and the Center for Environmental Study, Grand Rapids.
October 1987: "Women, Peace, and the Environment," conference organized by the Great Lakes Women's Network, Windsor, ON.
October 1987: National conference for coastal environment activists: "Saving our Bays, Sounds, and the Great Lakes," Warwick, RI (delegates represented 8 million members).
November 1987: Week of meetings on the Great Lakes, to coincide with the International Joint Commission's Biennial Meeting on Great Lakes Water Quality — Forum II for RAP coordinators.
November 1987: GLU Lake Ontario Regional Meeting, Niagara Falls, NY.
December 1987: Formation of the Lake Ontario Organizing Network [LOON], Steering Committee includes: Great Lakes United, the Canadian Environmental Law Association, the Ecumenical Taskforce, Energy Probe, Centre for the Great Lakes, Citizens' Action for New York, Atlantic States Legal Foundation, and Pollution Probe. The Network's first project was to develop the "Citizens' Agenda for the Restoration of Lake Ontario," which was released in July 1988, and has formed the basis of subsequent meetings and campaigns.
Citizens' Action for New York, Atlantic States Legal Foundation, and Pollution Probe. The Network's first project was to develop the "Citizens' Agenda for the Restoration of Lake Ontario," which was released in July 1988, and has formed the basis of subsequent meetings and campaigns.
February 29-March 4, 1988: Third Annual Great Lakes lobbying week in Washington (GLU, Sierra Club).
Winter 1987-1988: Wisconsin State public hearings on water quality.
March 1988: Conference on Environmental Dispute Resolution in the Great Lakes Region: A Critical Appraisal (sponsored by the Great Lakes Program at SUNY, Buffalo), SUNY, Buffalo.
April 1988: Summit for Lake Michigan activists, Michigan City, IN.
May 1988: Binational Conference on Societal Impact of International Water Management, co-sponsored by the Centre for Canadian- American Studies, Univ. of Windsor, and the Canadian Studies Center, Eastern Michigan Univ., Ypsilanti, MI.
May 1988: GLU sixth annual meeting, Cleveland, OH.
May 1988: Evergreen Alliance — four days of meetings and protests around the Detroit incinerator and recycling issues, Detroit, MI.
May 1988: "Recycling: the solution to Western New York's Solid Waste Crisis," sponsored by the Recycling Coalition of Western New York and the Erie County Dept. of Environment and Planning, Erie County, NY.
May 1988: "Environment '88" forums in Buffalo, Jamestown, and Albany, New York, sponsored by the Environmental Protection Bureau of the NY. State Attorney General's Office and 25 environmental groups, including the GLU.
May-August 1988: Greenpeace tour of Great Lakes toxic hot spots, in the Beluga lab-boat
June 1988: Public consultation workshop, including coalition building strategies, organized by the OEN, Scarborough, Ontario.
June 1988: The Summit Citizens Conference — one day devoted to environmental crisis: "Building an economy that sustains the environment," Toronto, ON.
June 1988: Conference on "The changing atmosphere, implications for global security," organized by Environment Canada, Toronto, ON.
September 1988: LOON meeting in Kingston, ON to discuss priority projects
September 9, 1989: Regional LOON meeting in Syracuse, NY.
September 18, 1989: Forum on Progress in Great Lakes Research, Syracuse, NY.
September 30, 1989: Regional meeting of LOON, Hamilton, on the "Political dynamics of Great Lakes environmental issues."

Lake Ontario has been labelled "the worst toxic lake in the world," because of the chemical dumps leaking into its main tributary, and the industrial and municipal effluents discharged into it.[24]

Chemicals, indeed, became the focus of public fear and of government regulation in the 1980s. For many, the petrochemical industry—although by no means the sole source of chemical discharges into our air and water—came to symbolize the problem: how to prevent industries from damaging the environment (and consequently, human health) as a result of their production practices and the drive to increase the sales of their products. Since the end of the decade, environmental and health movement campaigns focusing on toxic chemicals (especially dioxins, furans, and pesticides) and on industrial pollution emissions have intensified and have made use of a growing body of scientific research on the health and ecosystem effects of chemicals as ubiquitous as chlorine.[25] The campaign spearheaded by Greenpeace since the beginning of the 1990s (but adopted by most environmental organisations and even the International Joint Commission which monitors pollution in the Great Lakes Basin) for the phasing out of chlorine as an industrial feedstock, as well as many chlorine-based products, would make an excellent subject for the further analysis of citizens', environmental organisations', unions', and corporations' discourses about what is at stake in the development of our society. Moreover, the chlorine-ban campaign may be the decade's most salient example of what some authors are calling environmental regulation-led modernization, and the battles surrounding such regulatory changes. Part 2 examines the struggles which determined the nature of the regulatory framework established by the end of the 1980s, including the key environmental legislation of the province of Ontario and the Government of Canada.

NOTES

1. Dioxin is the name for a family of seventy-five related isomers, all of which behave differently and have different toxicity. Less than one-millionth of a gram of TCDD dioxin kills a guinea-pig. In test animals it causes cancer, cell mutations, and birth defects, kills embryos and suppresses the immune system. It is a by-product formed when certain substances, particularly those containing chlorine, are burned. Dioxin is a component of certain herbicides, and of Agent Orange, used by the United States military in Vietnam. See Michael Keating, *To the Last Drop* (Toronto: Macmillan of Canada, 1986), pp. 45-47 and *passim*; Cathy Trost, *Elements of Risk* (New York: Times Books, 1984), pp. 293-297.
2. Keating, *To the Last Drop*, p. 114.
3. Ibid., pp. 111, 114. In April 1988 a toxicologist at the Québec Environment Department announced the results of a three-year study of treated drinking water in eighteen Québec municipalities. THMs, including chloroform, were found "in almost all the samples." THMs and chlorinated water have been linked to cancer of the pancreas, liver, brain, bladder, kidney, intestine, rectum, esophagus, and other sites. Ayotte noted that even higher levels had been found in Ontario municipalities' water, and suggested that this is the most serious health threat posed by our drinking water. See Dennis Bueckert, "Chlorine in drinking water harmful, scientist warns," *The Globe and Mail*, April 8, 1988.
4. See Dudley K. Pierson, "Dioxin levels high in some Lakes fish," *The Detroit News*, May 13, 1986, p. 9A; Bob Campbell, "Dioxin findings cause warning on state fish," *Detroit Free Press*, May 13, 1986. Research by the Ontario Cancer Treatment and Research Foundation has found correlations between certain chemicals and associated health effects, including forms of cancer. See Robert F. Spengler, Sc.D., "Water contamination by toxic chemicals a challenge to cancer registries in assessing population risks," *Focus on Great Lakes Water Quality* vol. 7, no. 2 (IJC Great Lakes Regional Office, Windsor, Ont.).
5. The National Research Council of the United States and the Royal Society of Canada, *The Great Lakes Water Quality Agreement: An Evolving Instrument for Ecosystem Management* (Washington,

The Politics of Sustainable Development 37

DC: National Academy Press, 1985), p. 9. This claim was repeated by Dr. W. Swain, former head of the US Environmental Protection Agency's Great Lakes Research Center, at a Center for the Great Lakes Conference in November 1986. See Martin Stuart-Harle, "Dirty Pool," *Canadian Research* vol. 20, no. 2 (February 1987), p. 52.

6. "Small amounts of toxins found in Ontario foods," *The Globe and Mail*, September 16, 1988.
7. Bonnie Fox, quoted by Christie McLaren, "Most food eaten in Ontario illegal under obsolete law banning dioxin," *The Globe and Mail*, September 17, 1988.
8. Dr. Bev Houston, quoted in ibid.
9. Ibid.
10. Lyndsay Green, quoted by Craig McInnes, "Chemical pollution a motherhood issue," *The Globe and Mail*, April 23, 1988, p. D4. Doctors at the State University of New York in Binghamton released the results of a study of human milk in December 1987. They found that dioxin in human milk was 4.5 ppt, and that "nursing infants exposed to such concentrations absorb twenty-seven times more dioxin in a year than the EPA regards as acceptable" in a lifetime. Nevertheless, they said "there was no need for mothers to stop nursing." See "Dioxin in mothers' milk said to exceed life limits," *Chemical Marketing Reporter* December 21, 1987, p. 7.
11. Thomas Muir and Anne Sudar, "Toxic Chemicals in the Great Lakes Basin Ecosystem: Some Observations," November 1987. See *Great Lakes United*, Winter 1988.
12. P. Mineau et al., "Using the herring gull to monitor levels and effects of organo chlorine contamination in the Canadian Great Lakes," in *Toxic Contaminants in the Great Lakes*, Jerome O. Nriagu and Milagros S. Simmons, eds. (New York: John Wiley & Sons, 1984), p. 426.
13. Environment Canada, "Public Perceptions of Water Quality in the Great Lakes." (Ottawa: Inland Waters Directorate, 1981).
14. CROP Survey Reports, 81-1, 82-2, 83-2, cited in Environment Canada, *State of the Environment Report for Canada*, May 1986, pp. 259-60.
15. Data summarized in *State of the Environment Report*, pp. 257, 260.
16. Canadian Press report, November 21, 1986.
17. Data cited in *State of the Environment Report*, p. 262.
18. Ibid.
19. A study of public opinion polls on environment attitudes in the United States, covering the period 1973 to 1986, concluded that, while public concern with environmental quality was consistently high—i.e., ranked highly as a priority as against economic or other concerns—this "consensus" had not translated into a clear identification with particular political parties, as measured by electoral results. Analysts argued that environmental concern has been a "permissive consensus," which must be blatantly and repeatedly violated by a party or government before the public will associate electoral choices with this issue. This, they argued, had been the trend during the Reagan Administration, which made major blunders on environmental questions, and was actively opposed by organised environmentalists. Thus, a growing percentage of the electorate was supporting more government regulation of environmental standards, rather than accepting the application of free-market logic to this area of concern. Both Republicans and Democrats took this public concern into account during their campaigning for the 1988 presidential election.

    However, what the empirical analysts did not consider was the role of the parties themselves as interpreters of discrete issues or concerns. The environmental consensus was so permissive not only for the reasons given above, but because neither the mainstream media nor the Democrats had succeeded (one might say, tried) to explain the Reagan Administration's anti-environmental policies as the necessary consequence of its socioeconomic project—the removal of obstacles to increasing capitalist profits. No clear identification was made between a profit-driven system of production and consumption, the parties which seek to administer and renovate it, and the inevitable degradation of human health and the global ecosystem. See Riley E. Dunlap, "Polls, Pollution, and Politics Revisited: Public Opinion on the Environment in the Reagan Era," *Environment* vol. 29, no. 6 (July/August 1987).
20. *Toronto Star*, August 6, 1988.
21. 1984 and 1985 trends reported in *Canadian Trend Report* are summarized in *State of the Environment Report*, May 1986, p. 262.

22. Keating reports that there are 11,000 industries discharging into the basin. In 1985, of ninety-nine "significant industries," forty-three—or 43.4 percent—were not in compliance with government regulations. *To the Last Drop*, p. 63.
23. It is estimated that 400,000 tonnes a year of hazardous waste enters the Great Lakes from sewer systems. There are 302 Canadian municipalities discharging pollution into the Great Lakes or their tributary rivers. Ibid.
24. See, for example, reports in *Kingston Whig-Standard*, June 4, 1985, and *Kingston This Week*, March 27, 1985.
25. The most disturbing connection established so far is the effect of dioxins on the endocrinal system, and in particular the thyroid gland. The hypothesis is that dioxins induce disruptions of the regulatory functions of the thyroid gland, thereby threatening normal psychomotor development and the maturation of the central nervous system. A link has also been established between chlorinated drinking water and increased risk of human bladder and rectal cancers, although the precise agent responsible is still in question (THMs are suspected).

[3]

The Spills Bill

INTRODUCTION

By the time of the 1985 provincial election campaign in Ontario, media reports of incidents involving hazardous chemicals had generated considerable public concern. These events drew attention to the Conservative government's "cozy relationship" with private sector polluters, and provided a key issue for the Liberal and New Democratic Party (NDP) campaigns. *The Globe and Mail* revealed in April 1985 that the Ontario Ministry of the Environment (MOE) had banned the release of information on environmental problems in order to avoid further embarrassments during the election campaign. Scientists in the federal Department of the Environment (DOE) and the International Joint Commission (IJC) complained about the withholding of information, including a drinking water study of Niagara River, completed in December 1984; data on Ontario industrial and municipal polluters of the Great Lakes; data on 1983 discharges into Lake Superior from four Ontario pulp and paper mills.[1]

The public perception that the Conservative Government was not protecting the general interest, but the private interests of polluters, was reinforced by information emerging about the Ministry's lax policies regarding polychlorinated biphenols (PCBs). In June 1984 it was revealed that the MOE had had evidence of serious PCB contamination of the Pottersburg Creek in London, Ontario, since 1980, but had neither acted on this information nor informed the public. In the ensuing months, the provincial health and environment ministries downplayed the risks associated with exposure. The suspected source of the PCBs, Westinghouse Canada, also insisted that there was no danger to human health, while denying responsibility. By December, when "hot spots" with PCB levels as high as 2,256 ppm had been identified,[2] the government was promising a clean-up. The City of London put fences around the hotspots, and Westinghouse agreed to build a special vault to contain its PCB waste. A Pottersburg Creek Pollution Committee formed, which was vocally critical of city and provincial authorities for failing to protect public health.[3]

Then, just before the May 1985 election, two events occurred which contributed to the Conservatives' defeat. First, a truck carrying old PCB transformers from Ontario to Winnipeg for disposal spilled PCB-contaminated oil over a stretch of the Trans-Canada Highway near Kenora, Ontario. Several persons suffered acute exposure. The incident received high-profile television and press coverage, including stories in *The Globe and Mail*, *Maclean's*, and *Saturday Night*. Government officials, instead of acknowledging that chemical spills pose a risk to the public, suggested that the degree of concern was unwarranted. A third incident occurred when *The Globe and Mail* reported that, although a sample of southern Ontario milk tested by the MOE in 1983 had contained 3,200 ppb of PCBs, the government had made no attempt to stop the sale of the milk.[4] Public concern was further heightened at this time when the results of a three-year Environment Canada/Northwest Territories Government study were released. Government scientists had found agricultural and industrial chemicals —in particular PCBs—in the tissues of

[39]

polar bears. Environment minister Suzanne Blais-Grenier announced $1 million for research into toxic chemicals.

Researchers at the Great Lakes Institute, examining the political implications of a series of PCBs-related incidents, concluded that there was a pattern of government response, in which government authorities first denied the existence of the problem, and then, as evidence mounted and citizens mobilized, promised some remedial measures. But in the process, the Conservative Government's credibility was eroded; the public increasingly came to view it as too closely tied to the interests of the polluters.[5] Both the Liberals and the NDP recognized the electoral value of a strong pro-environment stance in the 1985 election campaign. David Peterson promised the electorate that a Liberal government would immediately proclaim a bill amending the Environmental Protection Act [Part IX], which the media had labelled the "Spills Bill." Proclamation of the bill also became an article of the Liberal-NDP Accord. The Spills Bill meant that the onus would no longer be on the victims of a spill to prove that the owner or shipper was negligent. The owners, handlers, and transporters of hazardous chemicals would be responsible for the immediate clean-up of any spill, or accident, with compensation to be sorted out later. The bill had passed third reading in the legislature under the Davis Conservative Government in 1979, but had never been proclaimed because of industry opposition.[6]

PRIVATE SECTOR AND CITIZENS' MOBILIZATION

Industry associations immediately began lobbying the Liberals to amend the bill, to reduce what they called its "absolute liability requirement." The Canadian Manufacturers Association (CMA) and the Canadian Chemical Producers Association (CCPA) succeeded in making alliances with the Ontario Trucking Association and the Ontario Federation of Agriculture (OFA) to oppose the bill. Indeed, the "small guys" became the public relations front of the private sector's opposition. The key threat was that the liability provisions of the law would make it impossible for small firms and farmers to obtain accident insurance.

The new environment minister, James Bradley, agreed to a brief consultation period during which industry and insurance company representatives could make submissions to a panel of environmental experts appointed by the minister. This review would end in August; changes to regulations would be ready by late September, and the bill would be proclaimed November 29, 1985. Bradley also changed the bill to allow the Environmental Compensation Corporation "to provide immediate compensation instead of acting only after all other legal processes had been tried. That corporation—which would spend money out of the Government's consolidated revenue fund—would then pursue the polluters for repayment."[7] Unlike his predecessors,[8] who had accepted the private sector's claims, Bradley rejected the argument that insurance would be impossible to obtain. Instead, he reminded the public that the affected firms had six years to work out insurance arrangements and to improve handling and shipping standards. More importantly, he questioned the motive for their opposition. "The resistance," he stated, "is to the *principle* of the bill [emphasis added]."[9] Bradley focused on the theme of *responsibility* for the harmful consequences of private sector activities; this was the beginning of his efforts, as environment minister, to reduce the social costs of pollution and transfer them back to the private polluters. Despite concerted opposition, Bradley told the legislature in October that: "There is no free ride. People whose business creates risk, whether they are truckers, farmers, or businessmen, should be expected to bear the costs which result from their activities." This rule, if applied to other aspects of private sector activities—such as the environmentally harmful aspects of the production process itself—would greatly increase the costs of production. It represented a rude shock to a private sector which had grown accustomed to a "live and let live" relationship with the ruling Conservatives.[10]

In the following months, the public hearings on the bill became the forum for these two conflicting "principles." Industry representatives' strategy was not, of course, to engage the debate at the level of the costs of doing business, i.e., who pays? Instead, they used the themes of protecting small firms which would be unable to compete at the predicted insurance rates, or would be forced into bankruptcy by compensation claims; they pointed out the costs to workers of lost jobs and to "consumers" of higher prices, as insurance and compensation costs were transferred. As in subsequent legislative review processes, the pattern became that local presenters at each stop on the panel's itinerary were primed with similar points of criticism of the bill. For example, farmers testified that they were afraid they would be held responsible for spills involving chemicals they had purchased, even though they had no control over their handling and transportation.[11] Farm representatives tried to win the support of consumers, by arguing that higher costs for fuel and pesticides would increase food prices. Their fear was that "suppliers will use the bill to insist on up-front payments for fuel and pesticides, which would make farmers legal owners of loads even before delivery."[12]

At a hearing in St. Catharines in August, the executive vice-president of the Petroleum Marketers Association of Canada, representing small and medium-sized independent petroleum marketers, voiced the fear that the smaller petrol and waste haulers would be driven out of business: "If the result of this legislation is that only a few, very large trucking companies are able to obtain environmental protection insurance, then the effect is to destroy competition from small and medium-sized...marketers."[13] The president of the Canadian Manufacturers' Association (CMA), Laurent Thibault, was careful to couch his criticisms of the bill in expressions of support for its intent—"to clean up the environment." He predicted that the bill's provisions would be "ineffective," that victims would be worse off, caught up in "endless litigation" for compensation.[14] The themes of bankruptcy and "endless litigation" were also taken up by the Ontario Trucking Association.[15] The business organisations attempted to shift the focus from private sector producers and transporters of chemical products, to public utilities and municipal sewage treatment plants, arguing that these, too, should be included in the new regulation. At the same time, they tried to mobilize municipal councils to join them in opposing the bill, by claiming that municipalities would be liable for incidents such as sewer back-ups, and would face horrendous compensation charges. Andy Brandt, Conservative member of the Ontario provincial parliament (MPP) for Sarnia, sent a letter in October to "council members of municipalities throughout Ontario, presenting a list of horrific examples of liabilities which municipalities might incur."[16] This tactic was meant to obscure the difference between the public paying for the costs of public sector operations, and the public paying for the costs of private sector operations. Representatives of the insurance industry testified before the panel that they would not be able to cover companies for potentially huge costs of environmental clean-ups. The president of the Insurance Bureau of Canada called the Spills Bill "the most God-awful set of regulations I have ever seen."[17]

Executives from Polysar and Dow Chemical implied that the "financial viability of Ontario's industries" was at stake (a claim which is repeated again and again in environmental regulatory struggles). They proposed that the government consider instead the creation of an agency to purchase spill insurance. This insurance would be financed by fees charged to industries, truckers, farmers, and municipalities.[18] Although the large corporations argued that everyone would thereby be protected from having to pay crushing sums for environmental cleanups, such an arrangement would essentially redistribute the costs of liability away from the most serious and frequent polluters, to a larger number of "small guys" who would probably not have had such high risks—and therefore premiums—in the first place.

Although the CMA/CCPA-led coalition tried to take the hearings by storm, environmental groups rallied to the bill's defence. Spokespersons for the Niagara Ecosystem Taskforce, Operation Clean Niagara, and others urged quick implementation of the bill. A number of lawyers argued at the hearings that the industry groups were "exaggerating the worst-case scenario."[19] First, most of the 1,000 spills that occur yearly in Ontario cost relatively little, with the average cost of cleaning up a hazardous spill around $10,000. Second, trucking companies already have liability clauses in their motor-vehicle insurance policies that cover damages caused by spills. Moreover, industry representatives' complaint that the new law is unfair, "because it makes the owner or hauler of a substance absolutely liable for the costs of cleaning up spills, whether they are at fault or not," was said to be nothing more than "a red herring." According to lawyers defending the bill:

> Under common law, owners of spilled substances are already liable for the costs of clean-up... The only difference is that now, companies can go to court to argue over who will pay. Under the spills bill, they would have to pay for the clean-up first. Firms with assets of less than $1 million would be liable for $400,000 of the cost or 40 percent of their assets; the maximum that large firms would be required to pay is $1 million.[20]

Toby Vigod, of the Canadian Environmental Law Association (CELA), told the panel that "statistics compiled by the provincial government show that larger industries and hazardous material-hauling companies are responsible for the majority of spills in Ontario and that smaller businesses and farmers are more often the *victims* of spills where a hazardous substance has done damage to property [emphasis added]." Statistics from 1983 showed that "the vast majority of the 592 spills reported were caused by large companies, only four percent by individuals, and only 1.8 percent by farmers."[21] In fact, Vigod's analysis was borne out by counsellors for the large manufacturers and chemical companies, in their capacity as spokespersons for the opposition. A director of the CMA, Gordon Lloyd, and a lawyer for DuPont Canada spelled out rather bluntly the basis for the alliance between small and large firms. This is summed up in an interview reported by Doug Draper in *The Standard* (St. Catharines, Ontario):

> Mr. Lloyd and Mr. Wood added that if the spills bill is enacted in its present form, some manufacturers of hazardous substances are already considering taking legal steps to transfer ownership of the material to shippers and purchasers before it leaves their gates in order to avoid any liability associated with a spill. "That's not a tack that we want to take," said Mr. Lloyd but "politicians should realize what choice they are forcing companies to make." "Companies have obligations to their shareholders to try and minimize their risk and their exposure...
>
> Smaller companies, which make up the bulk of CMA members, don't want larger companies to face that choice because *[the smaller firms] are going to end up bearing the brunt [of the liability]* and are not well equipped to do that," said Mr. Lloyd.
>
> Mr. Wood stressed that the CMA and other corporate associations are not recommending their members disavow ownership of hazardous substances but are only trying to make the general public aware of one of the possible consequences if the spills bill is enacted.[22]

Moreover, the bill's opponents had not been able to come up with a single case of a spill which would have forced the responsible firm out of business (from 1980 to 1985).

The Spills Bill

Vigod emphasized that the necessity to place more liability on handlers of hazardous wastes stemmed from the fact that "they are the parties engaging in a risky operation *for the purpose of making money*." CELA's research director, Frank Giorno, also pointed out that the bill did not establish "absolute liability" as former environment minister Andy Brandt and others were asserting. Section 87 of the bill states that the owners or persons who have control of the spilled pollutant are not liable to compensate victims if they took reasonable care or if the spill was caused by something beyond their control. Absolute liability applies only to the containment, cleanup and restoration costs. "Even at that a company that spills is only responsible for paying to the extent that it is practicable. When determining what is practicable regard shall be had to the technical, physical and financial resources that can be reasonably made available. In addition, a company which spills may be eligible for compensation costs for undertaking a cleanup under certain circumstances."[23]

As August drew to a close, the private sector alliance shifted the emphasis of its opposition to the bill, asserting that their "bottom line" was protection of the environment, and that their key concern was that the bill would not be effective in punishing the "real" polluters.[24] Underlying this argument, was the repeated warning, or threat, that the regulation would harm the economy of the province. MPP Brandt fuelled this campaign, describing the bill as "a disaster for the economy" and potentially detrimental to the environment. He proposed delaying implementation of the regulations by terminating the advisory panel and tabling the bill with a committee of the legislature.[25] Instead of liability for clean-up, Brandt argued, the government should emphasize better inspections of "potential polluters" and "encourage" them to use modern technology. This approach—self-policing with friendly advice—is consistently promoted by the chemical industry in its relations with government, as subsequent regulatory cases will show.

The chemical-industry-led coalition also argued that the government's legislation made no "distinction between good actors and bad actors," another theme which invariably appears in their strategy to deal with regulation. This meshes with the "incentives-preferred-to-punishment" and the "unfairness of one bad apple spoiling the barrel" themes which are also employed. In other words, the basic line is that most corporations are good corporate citizens, responsive to positive incentives (like tax credits) for pollution abatement, and willing to co-operate as equal partners with government in efforts to protect the environment. Stiff penalties for pollution offences (usually called accidents) do not result in better behaviour, since companies are already doing everything within their means to avoid such incidents.

The Liberal government of David Peterson, however, maintained that the bill would be implemented, as scheduled, November 29. Changes to its regulations would be made following the report of the advisory panel. Meanwhile, the MOE appointed a Toronto lawyer as a "special liaison" with the insurance industry, to discuss means of providing coverage. In a last-ditch effort to stop the bill, private sector opponents formed a coalition called Citizens Advocating Responsibility for the Environment (CARE). It comprised the CCPA, the CMA, the Ontario Federation of Agriculture (OFA), the Ontario Trucking Association, DuPont Canada, and C-I-L. A spokesperson for the CMA told the media that: "The whole idea of absolute liability is an affront to our legal system and *as citizens* we can't live with that [emphasis added]." Defense of legal concepts, when they are compatible with the interests of the private corporations, is another approach adopted by the chemical industry in various regulatory conflicts. This is a key strategy of their later opposition to elements of the draft Canadian Environmental Protection Act. In this case, in addition to protecting the rights of "citizens," the industry associations repeated—as is implied by the name CARE—their concern for environmental protection.

This concern was backed up by a lobbying budget, a "glossy brochure," and a Toronto Dominion Centre mailing address. Lawyers from Stelco, DuPont Canada, and the CCPA were assigned to represent CARE's objectives to MPPs and the media at events scheduled by a Toronto public relations firm. Between October 16 and November 4, $20,000 to $25,000 was spent, according to a CARE spokesperson.[26] Environmental organisations (CELA, Pollution Probe) immediately responded, describing the coalition as "the same people who've been trying to prevent adequate spills legislation since 1979," and motivated by *economic* interests, not health or environmental concerns. Frank Giorno of CELA said: "Calling CARE a citizens' group is a complete misnomer. It's really a group of corporations trying to scare farmers and consumers into aligning themselves with the Canadian Manufacturers' Association against the spills bill. The CMA has really done nothing but fight the bill for years."[27]

At the end of October, Bradley announced changes to the regulations. A pool of twenty-four Ontario licensed insurers would provide coverage of up to $1 million for all claims from any one "sudden and accidental" spill. Should damage surpass $1 million, the Environmental Compensation Corp. would pay a percentage of further costs based on the size of the company at fault, and then try to recoup money from the polluter through the courts. A maximum liability of $500,000 was set for farmers.[28] Bradley described the implementation of the Spills Bill, on schedule, as a victory for the principle of holding private corporations accountable for any environmental degradation resulting from their activities. The government was praised by one Niagara newspaper for standing up to the coalition led by the chemical companies. The issue was clearly defined as one of public welfare versus private profits.[29]

Throughout the battle over the Spills Bill, the environmental organisations CELA and Pollution Probe were crucial actors in articulating the "principled" defence of the legislation, i.e., the necessity of protecting public welfare and the environment from private polluters whose guiding motive is profit. They provided research expertise, replies to the arguments of the private sector representatives, and acted as well-known contacts for media reporters. The Liberal government seems to have been sustained by two key factors: the commitment of the environment minister to the project, and his ability to persuade cabinet of the popularity of the government's position (backed up by the fear that the NDP would seize the issue if the Liberals failed). The citizens' groups played an important part, appearing at the Advisory Panel hearings and lobbying government officials in support of the bill.

In this case, the chemical producers were successful in forming an alliance with small and medium capital in the manufacturing and transportation sectors, as well as farmers, to oppose any additional cost of production. In a sense, the Spills Bill fight was a test run for subsequent regulatory battles. The companies seem to have learned from it:
1. that economic blackmail threats would not be sufficient to get the government to back down;
2. that they could not win the battle of principles in the media—people would not accept the necessity of profit over environmental quality. Indeed, this was a dangerous terrain. (The doctors' strike and the struggle around the banning of tobacco advertising—where attempts were made to mobilize popular support by appealing to professional and individual rights/freedoms—have pointed to the same conclusion.);
3. there was a new relationship between citizens and government; the old industry-government closeness could no longer be taken for granted.

In future battles, corporate relations would (*a*) stress the responsibility and concern of the corporations for the environment, and pay attention to the citizens' groups; (*b*) try to influence government policy through the "consultation" process, promising

The Spills Bill

co-operation in return for access to the Ministry; and (c) try to work behind doors, and not in the public realm.

LABOUR RESPONSE

The connections between public and work-place safety and health were not emphasized by legislators, environmentalists, or union leaders. Unions in general remained aloof from the 1985 Spills Bill conflict, in some cases because of job blackmail by employers.[30] The latter argued that additional regulations and stiffer penalties might lead to plant closures or lay-offs. The Pottersburg Creek clean-up cost Westinghouse millions. Editorials in the *Sarnia Observer* criticised "idealistic" environmentalists for endangering jobs in the Chemical Valley.[31]

Officials in the Energy and Chemical Workers Union (ECWU) were concerned that the Environmental Protection Act (EPA) would be used to prosecute their members. Rather than perceiving the Spills Bill as another weapon in the fight to improve workplace standards for storage and handling of hazardous substances, the legislation was viewed by the union as a threat to the security of employees. The ECWU's director of legislation and health and safety co-ordinator said in an interview in May 1988 that he thought a number of ECWU members had already been prosecuted under the EPA.[32] ECWU members interviewed in 1986 and 1988 emphasized the liability of employees to prosecution under the EPA, and observed that employees' right to refuse work which pollutes the environment is not well defined, and is seldom defended successfully.[33] There is an analogy here with the right to refuse unsafe work, provided by the Occupational Health and Safety Act. Workers who grieve a disciplinary measure arising from such an incident find that the costs usually outweigh even a favourable outcome. Similarly, workers do not feel adequately protected to report the polluting activities of their employers. It seemed that chemical companies' managers had played on these fears in order to neutralize possible union support for the Act during the consultation process and public debate.

The MOE and the Ministry of Labour (MOL) might have attempted to emphasize the advantages of the legislation for union members, and to allay some of their fears. First, the detailed regulations provided under the Spills Bill for the safe handling and transportation of hazardous materials could serve to support workplace advocates of more stringent health and safety practices. They could strengthen the hands of union occupational health and safety committees, and of activists in small, non-union firms. Second, Section 134b of the EPA does provide some protection to workers who refuse to pollute. The MOE and the MOL might have considered ways to strengthen this section in consultation with the unions. However, it does not appear that the MOL involved itself in the 1985 Spills Bill debate.[34] As for the MOE, its view was that the provisions for protection of employees from job blackmail conflicts were adequate. When asked to comment on the apparent weakness in the legislation, an official at the Legal Services Branch of the MOE said:

> Section 134b makes it clear, in law, that an employee has the right to refuse work that would make him or her liable to prosecution under our environmental laws; and it provides the Ontario Labour Relations Board with the power to prevent any employer from taking action against an employee who asserts this right...
>
> The position of the worker whose employer orders him or her to perform an illegal act is always going to be a difficult one, no matter what the law says, simply because the employee has so much at stake. But it is the Ministry's understanding that the law has now been made clear and strong on this point,

resulting in a significant betterment of the position of an employee who is forced into this sort of a situation.[35]

However, there is no evidence of consultation with unions on this question, or of official reassurance about the effectiveness of protection for workers.

The increasing public attention being directed toward hazardous chemical threats by the late 1970s was heightening workers' concern about the effects of chemical exposures. Many workers were (are) affected in particular by exposure to PCBs—the chemical at the centre of the Spills Bill controversy. PCBs have been banned from industrial use in Canada since 1978, but the problem of disposing of existing sources and wastes was not resolved by the prohibition. Workers at plants like Westinghouse—where PCBs were used as a transformer coolant—"were heavily exposed to the substance, often having skin or clothing soaked by the solution day after day, sometimes for years."[36] However, their official union representatives were reluctant to challenge the employers' argument that more stringent regulation would cost jobs. In the infamous Westinghouse (Hamilton) case, a shop-floor health and safety representative who had investigated PCB exposure in his plant, was told by his union president to "back off the PCB issue because 'blackening the name of Westinghouse' would do nobody any good."[37]

In July 1984, workers at the Westinghouse transformer plant in Hamilton complained about trace levels of PCBs. *Three months later*, the Ministry of Labour conducted tests. The workers had to wait until February 1985 to be told the results. The Ministry at that time ordered the company to clean up the PCBs "forthwith." In mid-March 1985, although the PCBs were still present, a Ministry inspector "gave the plant a clean bill of health and praised its internal responsibility system."[38] Stan Gray accused Westinghouse of negligence in allowing exposures to PCBs to continue, despite the evidence of high contamination levels. The workers were convinced that a number of cancer deaths among long-term employees were related to PCB exposure.[39] Then, in April 1985, the Kenora PCB spill happened. Intensive media coverage focused on the health risks associated with PCB exposure. Workers who had been exposed to PCBs for years were naturally alarmed. Ed Dent, an employee at an electrical transformer manufacturing plant in St. Catharines, told a reporter:

> They told us we had nothing to worry about when we worked in PCB oils up to our armpits, and the company still says there's nothing to worry about... But then they ban it. And then a little bit spills on the road in Kenora and they tear up half the Trans-Canada Highway.[40]

In May, Toronto sewage plant workers stopped work when they learned that PCBs had deliberately been dumped into the sewer system on forty-four different occasions in the previous few months.[41] About a dozen Westinghouse workers in Hamilton stopped work, demanding guarantees that the floor of their plant was free of contamination. Stan Gray protested the government's apparent unwillingness to enforce its health and safety laws: "If that kind of thing existed at the cottage or on the highway they'd be screaming blue murder. They have a different standard for workers."[42] Only at this time did the Westinghouse workers get any support from their union officials for an investigation. It was also revealed in April 1985 that the provincial Ministry of Labour, officers of the United Electrical Workers Union, and Westinghouse management had agreed on a long range clean-up plan for the Hamilton plant, but "the legally responsible shop floor representative was not informed of the plan," and did not approve of it when he did learn of it.[43] A second inspection was carried out at Westinghouse, which uncovered 540 gallons of PCB-contaminated oil in a trench under the factory floor. PCBs were at 21,000 ppm, or 420 times the legal guideline. The trench was drained and filled with concrete in August 1985, but efforts

The Spills Bill

to seal the floor continued until December 1985. On March 7, 1986, nearly two years after the initial complaint, a ministry inspector finally recommended that Westinghouse be prosecuted for violating the Occupational Health and Safety Act, and for non-compliance with the orders issued by the Ministry. The company was not prosecuted.

As the Westinghouse case illustrates, labour support for stricter regulation of hazardous substances comes mainly from rank-and-file efforts to improve health and safety in the workplace. Stan Gray has observed that:

> the most rank-and-file oriented movements in labour have been for women's rights and for health and safety. To some extent, neither of them has been 'tamed' by the companies or by the labour hierarchy—the movements have retained their independence and their militancy.[44]

Although workers are threatened with the loss of economic security by certain demands of the environmental movement, they cannot extricate themselves from the health consequences of environmental pollution and workplace contamination. Environmental activists in the unions have already recognized that occupational health and safety struggles (pitting, as they do, human/health priorities against the imperatives of profit and management control) are a key potential bridge from the shop floor to the broader sphere of social conflict outside the plant gate.

NOTES

1. Jock Ferguson, "Environment Ministry blocking data flow, scientists say," *The Globe and Mail*, April 10, 1985, p. 24.
2. M. Cathy Alpaugh and Lynn Sabean, "The Politics of PCBs in the 1980s: Part II," *International Journal of Environmental Studies* (1987). For comparison, Canadian federal limits for PCBs in drinking water were 3.0 ppb in 1985, and 50.0 ppm by weight in liquid waste (Ibid., Part I, table 1, pp. 19-21).
3. R. Platiel, "Families worried about PCBs in creek where children play," *The Globe and Mail*, September 5, 1984.
4. A. Corelli, "Milk tainted by PCBs sold two years ago," *The Globe and Mail*, April 29, 1985, p. 23; J. Ferguson, "Provincial blitz will seek PCBs in Niagara Milk," *The Globe and Mail*, April 30, 1985, p. 23.
5. See Alpaugh and Sabean, "The Politics of PCBs."
6. According to one environmental law expert, the reason the Ontario Conservatives allowed passage of the bill was the necessity of appearing to do something, following the infamous derailment in Mississauga of a CP train carrying chlorine gas in 1979. See Frank Giorno, "The Spills Bill: The criticisms have been met," *Toronto Star*, November 12, 1985. In 1979 the Conservatives held only a minority of seats in the legislature. After they regained a majority in the March 1981 election, the Spills Bill was shelved.
7. Duncan McMonagle, "Ontario 'spills bill' to take effect in November," *The Globe and Mail*, July 6, 1985, p. 1.
8. The previous environment minister (1983-85), Andy Brandt, was the Progressive Conservative Party member from Sarnia, in Ontario's "Chemical Valley." From 1971 to 1974 Brandt was a Sarnia alderperson, associated with business interests. He was Sarnia's mayor from 1975-80, before being elected to the Ontario Legislature in 1981. (See chapters 10 and 11, which look at the politico-ideological influence of the chemical industry in Sarnia.) During the public hearings on the Spills Bill, Brandt made statements in support of the bill's opponents, reinforcing the conception that the bill places "unlimited" liability on owners and transporters to compensate victims. He called on the Liberal government to find some way of providing insurance to companies before implementing the regulations. (See "New spills bill needs change, Brandt warns," *Toronto Star*, August 15, 1985; "Spills bill now includes insurance, Bradley says," *Toronto Star*, October 29, 1985.)

9. Quoted by Duncan McMonagle, "Ontario 'spills bill' to take effect in November," p. 1.
10. The manager of the DuPont plant in Kingston complained to panel members that the regulations were "arbitrary, complicated, and costly." When asked by the panel why his company had not tried to come up with alternatives, or made arrangements to adjust to the law since 1979, Norman said: "[It] sat on the shelf since 1979, I never thought it would see the light of day." He added that they had no interest in adjusting to the regulations, and that their goal was to make the government "take it back to the drawing board." See "Task force faces critical audience," *The Standard* (St. Catharines), August 22, 1985, p. 16.
11. See, e.g., *The Standard* (St. Catharines), August 14, 1985, pp. 1, 2 (St. Catharines hearing); *The Standard* (St. Catharines), August 22, 1985, p. 16 (Kingston hearing).
12. Bill Walker, "Spills bill will mean dearer food, farmers say," *Toronto Star*, August 27, 1985. This fear was created by the petrochemical producers and transporters; see the interview quoted below.
13. *The Standard* (St. Catharines), August 14, 1985, p. 2.
14. "Victims to be hurt more," *The Standard* (St. Catharines), August 17, 1985.
15. "Difficulties with spills bill, truckers say," *The Globe and Mail*, August 24, 1985.
16. This fact was revealed by Donald MacDonald, former Ontario NDP leader, in an article in the *Toronto Star*, December 1, 1985.
17. Bill Walker, "Spills law will leave firms uninsured, MPPs told," *Toronto Star*, August 16, 1985, p. A3.
18. Chemical companies warn about insurance problems," *The Globe and Mail*, August 20, 1985.
19. Christie McLaren, "Insurance fears over 'spills bill' unfounded, lawyers say," *The Globe and Mail*, August 17, 1985, p. 16.
20. Ibid.
21. Doug Draper, "Spills bill opposition tactics rapped," *The Standard* (St. Catharines), August 21, 1985; Frank Giorno, "Spills Bill: the criticisms have been met," *Toronto Star*, November 12, 1985.
22. See "Chemical spills bill faced with mounting opposition," *The Standard* (St. Catharines), November 4, 1985.
23. Frank Giorno, "Spills Bill not unfair to polluters, association says," *Toronto Star*, August 24, 1985.
24. See, for example, "Spills bill won't punish polluters," *The Standard* (St. Catharines), August 24, 1985; Bill Walker, "Ontario's Spills Bill: Boon to environment or blow to business?," *Toronto Star*, August 26, 1985, p. 2.
25. Bill Walker, "Spills bill spells disaster, MPP warns," *Toronto Star*, August 28, 1985, p. A23.
26. See, "Farmers, industry fighting spills bill," *The Standard* (St. Catharines), October 17, 1985; "Farmers join with industry to fight chemical spills bill," *The Globe and Mail*, October 17, 1985; Peter Rickwood, "Coalition won't hamper spills bill, aide vows," *Toronto Star*, October 17, 1985; Doug Draper, "Chemical spills bill faced with mounting opposition," *The Standard* (St. Catharines), November 4, 1985, p. 1; Dale Ferns (spokesperson for CARE) "The Spills Bill: guilty until proven innocent," *Toronto Star*, November 11, 1985.
27. Quoted in Doug Draper, "Chemical spills bill faced with mounting opposition," *The Standard* (St. Catherines), November 4, 1985, p. 2.
28. Bill Walker, "Spills Bill now includes insurance, Bradley says," *Toronto Star*, October 29, 1985.
29. Denise Harrington, "New spills law example to all, minister says," *Toronto Star*, November 30, 1985; Doug Draper, "Spills bill puts public's welfare ahead of profits," *The Standard* (St. Catharines), November 16, 1985.
30. According to an MOE official, union briefs were received by the legislative standing committee reviewing Bill 209 in 1978 and 1979. The only evidence of such presentations I was able to locate was a reference to a sessional paper, "Background material relative to Bill 209, an Act to amend the Environmental Protection Act, 1977" (No. 278), *The Journals of the Legislative Assembly of Ontario* vol. CXII (1978), 31st Parliament, 2nd Session, p. 277. This document, however, was not published.
31. See, for example, "Warning issued for Greenpeace," [editorial] *Sarnia Observer*, August 19, 1985 (published just after the "blob" discovery).
32. Dan Ublansky mentioned cases associated with the Cassidy Works (Hamilton); Shell Canada Products (Sarnia); DuPont (Maitland); and a rendering plant near Guelph. I sought confirmation of this from the MOE. The Legal Services Branch was able to provide only records of prosecutions of firms and individuals (sometimes identified as co-accused); no information was

The Spills Bill

available about union involvement. However, a survey of these cases indicates that even before the amending bill was passed, employees of firms were prosecuted for offences under the EPA and Ontario Water Resources Act (OWRA). Between February 1985 and August 1987, charges were laid under the EPA against Shell Canada Products, DuPont Canada, and a rendering plant called Elmira Refiners, as well as employees of these firms. (These may be among the cases referred to by Ublansky.)

In the first two cases, charges against the employees were withdrawn. Shell paid $24,000 in fines and DuPont paid $5,000. (Information in the International Joint Commission, Water Quality Board, *Report on the Great Lakes Water Quality Agreement* (1987), Appendix A, p. 196, suggests that Ublansky's recollection of charges against a DuPont (Maitland) employee were related to lead discharges into Blue Church Bay. DuPont produced tetraethyl lead from 1965 to 1985, when it closed the plant. In 1985 the MOE issued a fish consumption advisory based on lead levels detected in Blue Church Bay in 1983 and 1984.) In the Elmira case, an individual—possibly an employee—was fined $14,000. The company was fined $30,975. Other cases in which employees were charged under the EPA include Domtar (October 1985), C-I-L (March 1985), Celanese Canada (May 1985), Courtaulds Canada (April 1987), Clearmount Plastics (March 1988), PetroCanada (December 1986). Individuals have also been charged under the OWRA in the cases of: Canada Packers (September 1987); Shell Canada (February and September 1985); Courtaulds Canada (April 1987); Domtar (September-December 1987). Some of these cases may have involved members of the ECWU. (Source: *Prosecution Activity Reports*, Toronto: MOE, Legal Services Branch, April 1, 1977 to October 3, 1988.)

33. Interviews with Dave Pretty, national staff of ECWU, Sarnia Office, in December 1986, and with Dan Ublansky, legislative director and health and safety co-ordinator for the ECWU, London, May 1988 (see chapter 11).
34. I wrote to Minister Bradley to ask whether he recalled any Ministry of Labour involvement in the Spills Bill political debate, or in the development of Section 134b. An official from his department replied that: "Whenever a Ministry develops a piece of legislation, all other Ministries are invited to offer comments. The Ministry of Labour was closely involved in the development of S.134b." (Letter to the author, c. 1987, from Peter Van Den Bergh, Legal Services Branch, MOE.) While this question could be pursued further with the MOL, the key issue seems to be that the MOL did not participate in the *public* debate in 1985, to counter the claims of employers, and to reassure workers of their rights.
35. Letter to the author from Peter Van Den Bergh, c. 1987.
36. *WOSH News* (Windsor), Fall 1985, p. 12.
37. Incident involving United Electrical Workers member, Stan Gray, in 1977, reported by J. Deverell, "PCB scandal lurking, expert says," *Toronto Star*, April 26, 1985.
38. Elie Martel, *Still Not Healthy, Still Not Safe: Report of the Ontario New Democrat Caucus Second Task Force on Occupational Health and Safety* (Toronto: Ontario New Democratic Party, July 1986), p. 6.
39. The Workers' Compensation Board does not recognize a link between cancer and workplace PCB exposure, and has turned down all claims. In 1985 the Hamilton Workers Health Clinic began trying to document all cases of employee illness or death suffered after PCB exposure. According to Elie Martel's report, doctors at the Ontario Workers' Health Centre in Hamilton had, by fall 1986, "diagnosed 24 PCB cancer-related victims from a group of 450 workers. Ten of the victims worked for Ferranti-Packard; 14 for Westinghouse Canada in Hamilton." Ibid.
40. Quoted by J. Deverell, "Workers distrust government study on PCB exposure," *Toronto Star*, June 7, 1985, p. A7.
41. B. Clark, "Sewage workers force meeting over PCBs," *Toronto Star*, May 5, 1985.
42. M. Pettapiece and K. Von Appen, "Workers fear PCB contamination," *Hamilton Spectator*, April 27, 1985.
43. Ibid.
44. Quoted by D. Field, "Beyond male bias in occupational health," *Healthsharing* (Summer 1985), p. 22.

[4]

The Canadian Environmental Protection Act

INTRODUCTION

The Canadian Environmental Protection Act (CEPA) was introduced in December 1986 as the Mulroney Conservative government's response to mounting environmental concerns in the industrialized provinces of Québec and Ontario. The federal government was under pressure to demonstrate that its policy of "closer relations" with the United States would not lead to loss of ground on binational environmental issues, nor to a declining interest in environmental regulation and enforcement (which characterised the Reagan Administration). The focus of the CEPA is greater regulation of chemicals. Ministry material accompanying release of the draft bill asserted that the government was concerned with protecting the health of Canadians and their environment from chemical pollution, and that this would entail "a comprehensive framework assisting governments to control toxic chemicals throughout their life cycle—namely from their development, through their manufacture, transport, distribution, use, storage, right up to their ultimate disposal as waste."

The draft was based in part on reports produced by two government-appointed task forces. In 1985 Environment Canada and Health and Welfare Canada convened two task forces, whose members included representatives of "industries,"[1] environmental groups, federal and provincial governments, labour, and other concerned groups and individuals.[2] The first task force was, according to Environment Minister Tom McMillan, "designed to find a solution to the toxic chemicals issue that would minimize the risks to human health and the environment, *while supporting industrial productivity and competitiveness* (emphasis added)."[3] This group produced the report "From Cradle-to-Grave: A Management Approach to Chemicals" in September 1986. The Task Force on the Management of Chemicals included representatives from Dow Chemical Canada, Petrosar Ltd., the Petroleum Association for Conservation of the Canadian Environment (PACE), Imperial Oil, the Canadian Chemical Producers' Association (CCPA), the Insurance Bureau of Canada, six government officials, three environmental organisations, one "participant at large," and one official of the Energy and Chemical Workers' Union (ECWU). The second task force reviewed proposals to change the Environmental Contaminants Act (ECA). Participants included "industry and labour" representatives. This group released its final report in October 1986.

The draft CEPA, which repealed and incorporated the Environmental Contaminants Act, the Clean Air Act, Part III of the Canada Water Act, and part of the Department of the Environment Act, and was subject to the Access to Information Act (AIA), was introduced by the Ministers of the Environment and Health and Welfare in December 1986. A public consultation period lasted until March 31, 1987. The Act was then revised and passed second reading in the House of Commons in October 1987. The next stage was legislative committee hearings, from November 25, 1987 to February 8, 1988. Thirty witnesses testified before the committee, including citizens' group and labour representatives.

The Canadian Environmental Protection Act

After committee examination of the Bill (C-74) ended in March, the legislation was returned to the House of Commons, where it passed third reading May 5, 1988. It was proclaimed June 30, 1988. While the Act sets out objectives and principles of environmental protection, its effective enforcement relies very much on accompanying regulations. Both the private sector and citizens'/environmental groups were concerned with having a part in the drafting of such regulations. One goal of the CEPA was to establish a "Priority Substances List" requiring monitoring and/or regulation. The ministers created an Advisory Panel of academic, community, labour, and environment experts to draw up such a list. The Panel included four well-known environmental advocates, two of whom are also academics, two other scientists, a Ministry of Labour advisor, and two representatives from the CCPA and the International Nickel Company (INCO).

The CEPA was intended to expand the powers of the federal government to regulate chemicals. The Act also proposed to shift the burden of responsibility for ensuring the safety of chemicals to the producers and marketers. Under the Environmental Contaminants Act, the government had to demonstrate "reason to believe" that a substance already on the market was harmful, before it could require the producer or seller to do tests. This meant the government had to do prior testing. The CEPA would require companies to notify the Ministry of the Environment before introducing a chemical into Canada, and to submit a "data package" with information on its use and environmental and health impacts. The Ministry could then ban the chemical, permit entry of the chemical (subject to conditions), or require further testing. The Act also gave inspectors enhanced powers of enforcement, including the right to search premises without a warrant, if the delay necessary to get one "would result in danger to human life or the environment or the loss or destruction of evidence" (Section 44, clause 4). The Minister was also given authority to recall "chemicals or products distributed in contravention of the Act" (Section 24), and to order clean-ups, to take remedial action, and to recover costs from the polluter (Sections 22, 23). Section 25 of the proposed CEPA required that an exporter of a substance which is banned or restricted in Canada must notify a national authority in the country of destination.

CEPA introduced new offences and penalties. Among the former are: failure to provide the Minister with requested or required information; failure to notify the Minister when a chemical is first found to be dangerous; failure to perform tests or take measurements; and fraudulent testing or reporting of results. Penalties were significantly increased, reflecting the view of many environmental law experts that previous fines were "almost trivial."[4] The ECA had allowed fines of up to $100,000 and two years' imprisonment, and the Clean Air Act had specified a maximum fine of $200,000. CEPA set a new maximum penalty of $1,000,000 and five years' imprisonment. In addition, Section 71 of the proposed Act provided for civil action against polluters. In a civil suit, the polluter's previous conviction for an offence (under CEPA), would be considered sufficient to establish guilt.

Private Sector Response to the Draft CEPA

Dozens of presentations and written briefs were prepared by firms in the mining, petrochemical and other manufacturing sectors. This time, instead of attempting a public campaign, which would provoke critical media attention and mobilize organised environmental groups, the industry associations concentrated on developing a co-operative relationship with other "stakeholders," and ensuring themselves representation within the consultative and amending processes. They were careful to preface all their proposals with statements of commitment to the principles of the Act. Of nearly 400 written submissions received by Environment Canada on the draft Act, the majority were from the private sector. Out of approximately 258 consultation attendees, roughly eighty-four were from private industry. (Other categories include citizens groups, environmental organisations, individuals, consultants, academics or university institutes, governmental representatives, municipalities, non-governmental organisations (NGOs), and labour.) At the legislative committee hearings, nine out of 30 non-governmental witnesses were representatives of the private sector. The chemical and manufacturing industry organisations formed a united set of positions throughout the consultative process. Their briefs were virtually identical, a fact which did not go unnoticed by members of the CEPA legislative committee.[5] Indeed, the brief of the Adhesives and Sealants Manufacturers Association of Canada (ASMAC) reveals that an "industry coordination group" was formed to prepare positions for the ECA Amendments Consultative Committee.[6] private-sector briefs all urge that the recommendations of that committee be adopted in CEPA. They are like fenceposts, marking a boundary, beyond which the interests of the private sector begin to be outweighed by the demands of environmental and citizens' groups. The Canadian Manufacturers' Association (CMA) had created an "environmental committee" representing eighty companies, which had prepared that body's government submissions. At the hearing in December, 1987, the Chairperson of the CMA admitted that the CCPA, PACE, and CMA had "got together" to deal with new government regulations.[7]

The overall strategy of the industry associations was to limit the extension of new government powers over their operations as much as possible, while at the same time avoiding the appearance that their economic interests were taking precedence over their environmental concern. The main tactics used were appeal to the existing legal framework; support for provincial rights in the environmental field (as against additional federal powers in this jurisdiction); insistence that a voluntary and co-operative framework of regulation would be more effective in preventing environmental degradation than "punitive" and "rigid" laws (backed up by the threat of non-co-operation); efforts to ensure that private-sector representatives would be included in "multipartite" consultations to draw up regulations; and measures to restrict public access to information, intervenor funds, and consultation. To make these arguments, they used the language of "balance, co-operation, flexibility, pragmatism, and realism" which was contrasted with the "imbalance, confrontation, adversarial, rigid, and punitive" approach of government regulation. Specific areas of private-sector concern can be divided into the following categories.

Confidentiality of Business Information

The draft CEPA proposed that the regulations, guidelines, and objectives of the Access to Information Act be transferred to the CEPA, i.e., that the conditions for access to any information required to fulfil the objectives of CEPA would be the same as for information requested under the Access to Information Act. Private-sector representatives sought instead to make the grounds for access to information about new chemicals similar to those provided for in the Workplace Hazardous Materials Information System (WHMIS). WHMIS provides for "trade secret screening" and appeal by a firm. This path had been approved by the ECA Amendments Consultative Committee, and the CCPA, CMA, and other representatives referred to environmental and labour participation in the ECA amendment process to establish the legitimacy and reasonableness of such proposals.

The private sector preferred regulations which would allow the Minister to waive certain requirements from the information package (on a new chemical), and allow companies to withhold information considered crucial "intellectual property," pending an appeal. The manager of "environmental affairs" for the CMA summed up the corporations' concern: "[T]he current bill...has *unbalanced* rights of appeal for the public and for the owner of the information [emphasis added]."[8] In their submission to Environment Canada, the CCPA provided alternative wording for Section 10, setting out specific criteria for non-disclosure of certain information. The CCPA's preferred version included several additional hoops for the Minister to jump through before obtaining information considered confidential by the company: the Minister could ask for justification of the supplier's claims; if that was not satisfactory, the minister could refer the claim to an *independent third party agency...for a final decision.* If the Minister "lost," there could be an appeal.[9] In effect, this wording would have considerably weakened the minister's power to obtain information from private firms.

The environmental representatives on the ECA Amendments Consultative Committee had not been involved in the drafting of the Hazardous Materials Information Resources Act. They viewed the WHMIS as primarily a labelling system for chemicals used in the workplace. Their expectations for environmental contaminants regulation went far beyond the mandate of WHMIS. They wanted access to workplace environmental and health studies, the raw data, and full data packages on chemicals, and were concerned that the parameters of WHMIS would be too restrictive for the CEPA.

In the end, CEPA Sections 20 and 21 represented a compromise between these interests. Section 20 added classes of information (to be accessible to the public) which were not covered in the AIA. In this respect CEPA broadened public access to information. However, Section 21 allowed an exemption: information will be disclosed as required by the AIA except when a request for confidentiality has been made under the Hazardous Materials Information Resources Act, and the claim meets HMIRA requirements. Environmentalists therefore viewed the CEPA provisions on disclosure of information as ambiguous.[10]

Powers of Inspectors

The CEPA proposed greater powers for inspectors to enter company premises and to carry out investigations, specifying, in addition, conditions under which a warrant could be waived. The Act proposed that, in the course of an investigation, an inspector could make a decision that there were grounds to prosecute, and could then seize any materials considered evidence. The companies argued that this violated their rights to due process under criminal law. They said an inspector should have to leave the premises and inform her/his superiors about the situation. The government could then send an enforcement officer, with a warrant specifying the materials to be rendered. The two functions, they said—inspection (monitoring for compliance) and enforcement—should not be combined. The companies did not get their way on this point, however. The right of an inspector to seize anything as evidence, without first obtaining a warrant, was retained in Section 104 (1).

Company presentations suggested as well that their personnel would not co-operate with inspectors if there were a possibility that prosecution would result. In fact, they appealed to the Charter of Rights. The chemical companies, in particular, raised the possibility that employees might be expected to give verbal or other information to inspectors which might lead to their being charged with a criminal offence, and thus they might be compelled, under the Act, to incriminate themselves. (See Union Carbide's brief to Environment Canada.) This "concern" was no doubt transmitted to the Energy and Chemical Workers' Union. As was the case during the Spills Bill battle, the industry associations played a double game here, to create the bases for an alliance with the union. While warning employees of the danger of prosecution, management was recommending to Environment Canada that evidence of violation of the Act be tied to "the identification of the offending employee or agent...as an essential ingredient of the offence."[11]

The final CEPA, however, stated that corporate executives could be held liable whether or not an employee is identified or prosecuted for the offence (Section 124). Also with regard to inspection and enforcement, the companies wanted the Ministry to make environmental audit reports inadmissible evidence for prosecution on the grounds that otherwise, companies would be reluctant to carry them out.[12]

Ministerial Discretion

The companies recommended amendments to various sections which would have the effect of making action by the Minister discretionary, rather than mandatory (Sections 8 and 9).[13] Certain discretionary clauses were retained in the final version.

Burden of Proof

Amendments were requested which would place greater onus on the Ministers to show scientific reason to require further testing or more information regarding a substance, e.g., changing "may be harmful" to "is likely to be harmful" (Section 11).[14] This recommendation was not incorporated in the final CEPA.

Costs

The companies questioned the necessity of testing all new substances, arguing that tests and standards in other countries could be sufficient. The leeway that was allowed in the final version of the Act for ministerial discretion seems to permit the relaxation of testing requirements. Section 16 allows the minister to extend the deadlines for provision of requested information. Section 26 says that, with respect to information requested on substances being newly introduced to Canada, the minister may "*waive* any of the requirements for prescribed information" if the substance is deemed to be: (i) non-toxic; (ii) not a threat to the environment or human life under the circumstances of its intended use; or if deemed "not practicable or feasible to obtain the test data necessary."

There were also suggestions that the costs of compliance with the Act would be too onerous for smaller firms, and would therefore affect decisions about new investment and threaten existing jobs. According to Environment Canada's summary of the written submissions on the draft CEPA, several firms argued that: "Development of new chemicals may be discouraged and it was anticipated that industries producing small quantities of chemicals will move to other countries or that insurance may make it prohibitive for some companies to operate"(p. 14). This argument was similar to that used by the large companies during the Spills Bill debate, to mobilize small firms against the legislation. The threat of industry disinvestment had earlier been voiced by the CCPA in its "Position Paper on Confidentiality,"at the Roundtable Discussion on Toxic Chemicals Law and Policy in Canada:

> It is a fact that if unnecessary or excessive costs, delays, or uncertainty are introduced unilaterally by any country (or province), innovation and development will simply cease or be transferred to jurisdictions with a more favourable business climate. Should this happen in Canada, it could very quickly (be) reduced to a warehouse economy for chemicals.[15]

Civil Actions

Section 71 (2) of the draft CEPA gave individuals the right to launch a civil suit for damages against a polluter, and to use as evidence a conviction against the polluter in a criminal court. The corporate response to this was that it encouraged more civil actions and "double indemnification." They attempted to appeal to nationalist sentiment here, arguing that such civil litigation was an "American" style of resolving conflicts, and that a more corporatist approach better suits private sector-government-public relations *in Canada*. The CMA recommended deletion of Section 71, arguing that it would make it harder for manufacturers to get insurance, and would prejudice the defendant's case in a civil action.[16] In the final Act, however, Section 71 remained unchanged (now Section 136).

"Criminalization" of Environmental Offences and Severity of the Penalties

Section 54 of the draft CEPA made it a criminal offence to "knowingly or recklessly cause a disaster that results in a loss of the use of the environment," or to "knowingly, recklessly or negligently cause serious damage to the environment that results in (i) a risk

The Canadian Environmental Protection Act

of death or serious harm to another person, or (ii) the death of a person or serious harm to another person." The CMA wanted "disaster" to be defined, and suggested the first phrase be replaced with: "conduct which results *in a loss of livelihood for an entire community*." In this way, the prosecution would have to show not only that the polluting act degraded the environment, and thus affected all its potential uses, but that it resulted in direct economic loss for some group.

Chemical company briefs to Environment Canada argued that criminal offences related to the environment should be added to the Criminal Code, instead of incorporated in the regulations of CEPA. The Criminal Code would deal with "flagrant contravention of environmental laws," while the CEPA would deal with negligence. The belief of the corporations is that, in most cases, they could make a defense of "due diligence," or "reasonable care," which would prevent their conviction under CEPA. The most serious penalties would come under the Criminal Code, where it would be very difficult to prove that a company deliberately, knowingly, and repeatedly violated the law.

In the final version of the Act, the wording of the environmental damage offence was changed from: (*a*) "knowingly or recklessly," to "intentionally or recklessly" and from (*b*) "knowingly, recklessly or negligently causes serious damage" to: "shows wanton or reckless disregard for the lives or safety of other persons." The new wording therefore required the establishment of intent or certain knowledge of the consequences by the prosecution.

Defence

The companies claimed entitlement to a due diligence defence, which would lessen their liability for spills. The CCPA, DuPont, and other briefs to Environment Canada asked that the requirement for industries to take "all necessary measures" to comply with regulations be changed to "all reasonable measures" (Section 60). This would, of course, make it more difficult to obtain a conviction. The Ontario MOE raised the concern that this might conflict with the stronger liability provisions in the Ontario Environmental Protection Act (Spills section). There was confusion about which legislation would take precedence, for an incident in Ontario. In the final version, a due diligence defence was made available(Section 125). Liability became less absolute than the "all necessary measures" condition in the first draft.

Consultation

Companies were concerned to prevent any further erosion of their position of influence within the State. In virtually every brief, companies congratulated the government for its "multi-stakeholder approach" to the drafting of regulations. Within a consultative or advisory body, where "industry" is one of three sectors represented, along with the "public/environmentalists" and "labour," the corporations have certain advantages. First, of course, are their immensely superior research and legal resources. Second, there is the likelihood that union representatives will adopt many of the perspectives of management, and the possibility that citizens' groups' representatives can be co-opted or manipulated. Third, by insisting on "consensus" decision-making, the private sector can establish the limits of reforms. The "stakeholder" language preserves the ideological myth that all parties in the negotiation are equal in power and influence. The CCPA even goes so far as to describe its members as mere "citizens," as we saw in the industry campaign against the Ontario Spills Bill. There is a real fear among corporate executives that unless they can use this "consensus" language and process to manage the pace and direction of change, they may be excluded from the regulatory and enforcement process altogether.

Corporatist language is prevalent in much of the management response; it reflects an ideological effort to prevent the question being raised: "What if environmental goals *cannot be made compatible* with the pursuit of profit?" This explains the private sector representatives' repeated praise for the consensus recommendations of the ECA Amendments

Consultative Committee, which included labour and public membership. In its presentation before the legislative committee reviewing the CEPA, CCPA executives commended Environment Canada for "using multi-stakeholder consultation to resolve complex social issues," and said: "*We believe it is the best process devised to date* to provide workable solutions to environmental problems." With regard to the establishment of a Ministers' Advisory Committee on the Act, the CCPA recommended "*equal representation* from labour, environmental groups and industry."[17] Note, however, that management wanted to be made responsible for the development of codes of practice.[18] In this instance, they claimed more *expertise*, which, it appears, overrides "consensus" as a criterion of participation. MP Charles Caccia, a member of the CEPA legislative committee, objected to management's wish to be the sole, or primary drafters of the codes.

Management was worried about the change in the nature of its relationship with the government, given participation by public interest groups in the regulatory process, and "get tough" legislation emanating from Queen's Park and Ottawa. Underlying the *pro forma* statements of environmental concern was the carefully-phrased threat of economic (i.e., capital investment) repercussions. For example, the Fiberglass Canada brief to Environment Canada warned:

> The shift from a co-operative to an adversarial approach is clearly demonstrated in both the penalty sections of the proposed Act, and in the stated need for an enforcement policy. Adoption of an adversarial system *in a field where the regulators and the regulated face constant resource constraints must be counter-productive* [emphasis added].[19]

A letter from the managing director of the Mining Association of Canada to the Minister of the Environment, concerning CEPA, provides one of the least subtle statements of the private sector's interests.

> In common with other industry groups, the mining industry is concerned about an increasingly "legalistic" tendency in proposed environmental legislation. In past submissions The Mining Association of Canada (MAC) has always stressed that the environment benefits most when government, industry, and the public reach a *reasoned accommodation*, rather than entering into a litigious system such as exists in the U.S. In this way, efforts and resources are not wasted on sterile confrontation.
>
> Virtually all human (including industrial) activity has an effect on the environment. But different means of arriving at necessary trade-offs can have different impacts on the wealth-producing portion of society. This being the case, we believe that every project should be evaluated on a cost-benefit analysis and that its environmental elements can be managed through the full life of the project and improved as technology evolves.
>
> Bearing the above in mind, you may understand that we in the mining industry are distressed by *the punitive and litigious aspects* of the proposed Environmental Protection Act...
>
> We believe that you will be asked from many sides, both now and in future years, to give individual citizens and groups the right to legal action under this Act. We believe that these members of the public should have their input at the time of environmental hearings as opposed to recourse to litigation. Unfortunately, every project bringing economic benefit to this nation has some detractor who, it seems, would condemn the industry for its very existence.
>
> If such objections are encouraged and carried to the full extent of the law,

The Canadian Environmental Protection Act

worthwhile projects could be drastically delayed. In the mining area, it is even possible that being tied up in court for a period of time could threaten the life of some major mine. *Much more certain is that new projects would be thwarted* [emphasis added].[20]

The British Columbia Forest Products Ltd. complained in a letter to McMillan, dated April 27, 1987, that the proposed CEPA "presents a wish list of some environmental groups and...the needs of the manufacturing industry in Canada are not properly recognized."[21]

The Lambton Industrial Society (LIS), an industry-funded organisation which commissions research and handles environmental public relations for the Chemical Valley (see chapters 10, 11), stressed the need to avoid "over-politicizing" the task of environmental protection.[22] The LIS said that Sarnia "stands to gain or lose so much as a consequence of changes to the Environmental Protection Act," but did not elaborate on this.

The CMA stressed that "co-operative approaches towards abatement should always be the preferred option, with prosecution as the last and least preferred option."[23] The organisation also called for government regulations to be subject to cost-benefit analysis (countering environmental impact assessment), to "take account of the economic realities which affect the competitive position of Canadian industry." They went further, recommending that environmental regulations be based not on the best technology available, but on "demonstrated need for such measures in Canada."

In summary, private-sector lobbying around the CEPA was geared to preserving the pattern of business-State relations described by Ted Schrecker, in which "industry (large industrial firms, in particular) occupies a uniquely favored position in terms both of gaining access to decision-makers and of articulating its policy priorities."[24] Schrecker has observed that Canadian environmental law has always consisted "mainly of enabling legislation, which merely provides regulatory officials with the authority to make and implement regulations under specific conditions. A corollary is that administrators may (and often do) fail to regulate environmental hazards, or to enforce existing laws, even when a clear legal basis exists for doing so."[25] Large firms in Canada have had a privileged role in shaping environmental policy, and have succeeded in substituting "co-operative" processes for formal-legal ones in many cases. Schrecker gives the following examples:

> Federal effluent guidelines for the pulp and paper industry, for example, were drafted by a government-industry task force, whose recommendations were the product of a process of private negotiation among the representatives of industry, provincial and federal governments (Parlour, 1981; Victor and Burrell, 1981). This process appears routine at the federal level, at least (Castrilli and Lax, 1981, p. 339). Industry representatives were consulted on at least two drafts of the federal *Environmental Contaminants Act*, supposedly "our (the federal government's) main approach" to the problem of toxic substances in the environment, before the legislation was introduced in Parliament, and expressed general satisfaction with the results. In 1977, representatives of Amax of Canada Ltd., a subsidiary of a transnational mining corporation, requested permission to dump 10,800 tonnes a day of heavy metal-laden tailing from a reactivated B.C. molybdenum mine into the ocean, although such dumping was expressly prohibited by regulations under the federal *Fisheries Act*. Discussions of the approval included a private meeting among departmental officials, Amax's lawyers and two Cabinet ministers in September 1978. When Environment Canada decided to grant permission for the dumping, the needed regulations were developed on the basis of letters and drafts exchanged by Environment Canada and the law firm acting for the corporation, and enacted by Order-in-Council.[26]

Citizens, on the other hand, have sought to implant more popular content in legislation—specific measures guaranteeing public participation and environmental rights—to counter the historical bias of the State. Thus the extent of industry-State consultation and of administrative and political discretion has been the object of struggles between citizens' groups and private firms with regard to the CEPA, as well as other legislation.

Citizen and Environmentalist Response to CEPA

At the public consultation meetings held in Sarnia, Sudbury, Ottawa, Toronto and Windsor (January 23-February 27, 1987), and in briefs submitted to Environment Canada and the Legislative Committee on CEPA, citizens' groups and environmental organisations lobbied for their objectives. The general thrust of these was to open the decision-making processes to the public as much as possible. They also manifested considerable skepticism about not only the motives of the private sector, but also the intention of the government to produce an effective Act and to rigorously enforce it.

Mandate of the Act

Most groups argued that the CEPA was not, in fact, what the name implies, but only an Act to regulate toxic substances. Many had advocated that an Environmental Bill of Rights be incorporated into the CEPA, or drafted separately. The final version did not include a bill of rights; indeed, the preamble was considerably shortened.[27] The preventative purpose of the law was emphasized, however, and the need to make environmentally acceptable socioeconomic choices was stated as a commitment.

Citizens' and environmental groups wanted the mandate of CEPA broadened, to include such areas as radioactivity (discharges and emissions), noise, factors affecting climatic changes, biological agents (e.g., viral or bacterial pathogens used in biotechnology), pesticides and herbicides, vehicle emissions, habitat protection, incinerator emissions, wastes from recycling, and the operation of landfills. It was also proposed that petroleum and natural gas pipelines, high tension electrical lines, and sources of electromagnetic diffusion should be added to the list of federal installations and works to be regulated under the Act. The Canadian Environmental Law Association (CELA) and Pollution Probe advocated defining "toxic" as "a substance which causes a deleterious effect," thereby broadening its scope. These groups, along with Friends of the Earth (FOE), Energy Probe, and Canadian Auto Workers (CAW) Local 444 also recommended adding lead, asbestos, vinyl chloride, and mercury to the schedule of substances to be regulated under the Act. Another area where the Act was found wanting was its lack of a mandate to regulate chemical substances already in use. The CEPA incorporates the former Environmental Contaminants Act, but the latter had developed regulations for only five chemicals. In addition, CELA and two CAW locals proposed the creation of a "superfund" like that in the United States, to clean up abandoned waste sites. This fund would be created by taxing chemical feed stocks and waste disposal operators—the private-sector firms believed to be responsible for the problem. This proposal was not incorporated in the final version of the law.

The socioeconomic consequences of expanding the Act's regulatory powers in these ways were to some extent addressed by organisations such as Energy Probe, the Canadian Organic Growers, the Nova Scotia Coalition for Alternatives to Pesticides, and Canadians for Responsible Northern Development. At a general level, the theme of "sustainable development" underpinned arguments about long-term social and economic costs of environmental degradation. The message was that the private sector would have to adapt to the social priorities of a clean environment and public health and safety. The extent to which this is possible was not dealt with explicitly; private-sector submissions tended to raise the likelihood of conflict, whereas the issue was evaded by the environmental organisations. Some of the trade union briefs attempted to address specific aspects of the problem.

View of Government and Private-Sector Relationship

While private-sector representatives had urged the government to increase the Ministers' powers of discretion, the citizens and environmental groups sought to change "may" to "will" throughout the Act. Their reasoning was that governments have repeatedly, in the past, relaxed the rules for polluters, extending permits for discharges, or agreeing to amend or not to enforce control orders. Any room for ministerial discretion—for example in requiring information on the safety of new chemicals—would more likely be used to protect the investments and profits of polluters, than to protect the environment. Officials of the Canadian Labour Congress (CLC), testifying before the CEPA legislative committee, pointed out that, while the Act refers to "ministerial" discretion, the people who administer the Act are ministry employees.

The brief from the Citizens' Coalition for Clean Water (Wallaceburg) to Environment Canada, regarding the CEPA, states:

> The reprehensible pollution record of Chemical Valley is sad testimony to the environmental compromises and co-operations established in the past between the petrochemical industries and various levels of government... Chemical Valley industries do not believe they should be held financially liable for our pipe-line project because, aside from spills, the contamination they supply to the St. Clair is entirely legal under existing provincial law and licensing, and drinking water quality falls within provincial guidelines. They are collectively quite willing and obviously able to accept the consequences of Ontario's Spills Bill which has done nothing to deter the frequency of spills into our water sources.[28]

Moreover, citizens were concerned that the Ministers might not act quickly enough, or at all, to investigate violations and to prosecute. They therefore supported strongly the civil action provisions which were so anathema to companies like Union Carbide and the Mining Association. They went further, asking that citizens be permitted to request ministry action, and that the Minister be required to respond according to procedures set out in the Act. In effect, they were seeking ways to oblige the government to be their advocate against polluters, as expressed by this representative of the CCCW, Wallaceburg:

> We also feel that there should be something in [this law] where individuals such as us... there is no way that we could take litigation against C-I-L or Dow or any other one. They would tie us up in the court for dozens of years and we would end up with no homes or anything else... (W)e should have something in there where we can go to our government and get court action, maybe have an injunction put against places like C-I-L or Dow Chemical.[29]

The final version of CEPA included Section 108, "Investigation of Offences," which allows two persons to request a Ministry investigation of a suspected violation of the Act, and sets out the procedures which must be followed by the Ministry upon receiving such a request. Initiation and termination of an investigation, however, remain ministerial decisions. The Minister is obliged only to report findings and decisions to the applicants.

The government was repeatedly urged to enforce the Act rigorously, and people said that public pressure would be necessary to prevent the government from slipping back into its usual *modus operandi* of secrecy and "compromise" with corporate polluters. The proposed Environmental Bill of Rights was to include: (i) personal right to action, (ii) provisions for public involvement in decisions, and (iii) right to a judicial review at the insistence of the public.[30] In addition, environment and CAW groups recommended measures to ensure public participation in the regulatory process (these are discussed under the heading "Citizens and the State").

The citizens' and environmentalists' fears that polluting activities would not be regulated effectively enough, and their belief that the private sector was not likely to regulate itself to their satisfaction, were expressed in demands that "guidelines, objectives and codes of practice," which are not enforceable, be replaced by regulations, which are. For example, the Minister should be able to set regulations for ambient water quality, and national drinking water standards that would be legally enforceable. The final version, however, retained the section enabling the Ministers to establish objectives and guidelines which are not enforceable.

The citizens' groups and environmental organisations were also rejecting self-policing for industry, and supporting greater enforcement powers for the government. While on one hand, industries were protesting further powers for inspectors, environmentalists (and even the Ontario Ministry of the Environment, MOE) were concerned that these powers were too narrow.[31] There was also pressure for more public funding for research into health and environmental problems, and the synergistic effects of chemicals, to help citizens make the case for environmental protection.[32] Citizens' and environmental groups called for "independent" testing by government, rather than reliance on private-sector testing and reporting. Even government testing, moreover, should be subject to public scrutiny, by means of an advisory committee to select testing requirements, evaluation criteria, and methods of control.[33]

While the private sector was challenging the federal government's jurisdictional rights to set national standards, and insisting on developing its own sectoral codes of practice, citizens', environmental and union organisations were supporting a strong federal role in environmental regulation. The CAW representative at the legislative hearings referred to a "Meech Lake mentality" that was being used by the Conservative government as a front for deregulation of the economy, including in the area of environmental protection.[34] The final CEPA did not allay these fears, as the phrase "shall endeavour to act in cooperation with the governments" was added to the Administrative Duties section. Moreover, Section 6 commits the federal Environment Minister to establish a federal-provincial advisory committee to advise the Minister on (a) regulations pertaining to toxic substances, and (b) "other environmental matters that are of mutual interest to the federal and provincial governments and pertain to this Act."[35] Section 34 allows the Governor in Council to make regulations for toxic substances "after the federal-provincial advisory committee is provided an opportunity to render its advice under Section 6."

Given these clauses, some environmentalists have concluded that the federal Conservative government was trying to avoid involvement in environmental regulation, preferring to leave this area under provincial jurisdiction. CELA lawyer Toby Vigod, argues that Sections 34 (5) and (6), which "essentially provide that the regulation can be made inapplicable to a province where the Minister and the province agree in writing that the province has an 'equivalent' regulation, and that the province's investigation provisions are 'similar' to s.108-110 of CEPA" are vague, and that they

> give the indirect, but nonetheless apparent message that the federal government does not intend to aggressively regulate existing chemicals in Canada. These sections undermine the federal government's ability to implement a comprehensive nationwide toxics program. Clearly, extensive use of the equivalency provisions may result in a patchwork of inconsistent regulations and enforcement practices across Canada. Different penalties and enforcement capabilities presently exist across the country, which may result in the development of so-called 'pollution havens.' This stands in stark contrast to the Brundtland Report which calls for strong national regulatory standards.[36]

The greatest weakness of the CEPA may be that it applies almost exclusively to areas under federal jurisdiction; in reality, it is the provinces which are still mainly responsible for setting and enforcing environmental regulations.[37] This fact was demonstrated in August 1988, when a fire at a PCB storage site at St. Basile-le-Grande, Québec, caused clouds of contaminated smoke to settle over neighbourhoods surrounding the site. On a Canadian Broadcasting Corporation (CBC) radio broadcast, August 28, Minister McMillan admitted that the CEPA would probably not apply to this case—that the site's negligent owners would be prosecuted under Québec's environmental legislation. This confirmed environmentalists' fears that, so long as provincial environmental legislation is not made equivalent to the most stringent national standards, firms may exploit "pollution ghettos." (Herein lies one reason for the private sector's support for "provincial rights" over "expansionist" federal regulation during the CEPA debate.) Under considerable pressure from opposition parties and environmentalists, and with a federal election approaching (in which the environment was expected to play a large role), McMillan subsequently announced a "special interim order" requiring all depots for PCBs to meet federal or equivalent provincial standards within thirty days, or face fines of up to $1 million for failure to comply. Previously, federal standards were only guidelines, with which—in the spirit of federal-provincial consultation—provinces were invited to some day comply. The new order made these standards legally-enforceable requirements. This was exactly what the environmental and citizens' groups had earlier urged the federal government to do for all areas covered by the CEPA.[38] However, by mid-October, 1988, all provinces except Prince Edward Island had claimed exemption from the federal government's new standards for PCB storage on the grounds that they already had "legally enforceable requirements with comparable effect" (i.e., "equivalency").[39] Environmental groups, especially FOE and CELA, argued that the problem was that provinces were not *enforcing* the standards, and that the federal government decision to let the provinces continue to have primary jurisdiction in this area would change nothing.[40]

Federal regulatory and enforcement power were indeed challenged in another case related to PCB regulation, described here by Graham Reynolds:

> On August 6, 1992, Judge André Trotier of the Québec Superior Court determined in the case of *R. v. Hydro-Québec* that the PCB interim order dated February 23, 1989 made pursuant to the emergency interim order provisions of section 35 (1) [of CEPA] was of no force or effect, holding that the section is *ultra vires* the Parliament of Canada. The Crown, relying upon *Friends of the Oldman River Society v. Canada (Minister of Transport)* and *R. v. Crown Zellerbach Canada Ltd.* urged that the environment was an area of shared jurisdiction, and that Parliament's "national concern" over peace, order, and good government, together with the criminal law power under section 91(27) of the *Constitution Act*, was supportive of Parliament's power to enact the provisions of section 35(1).
>
> The Court rejected the Crown's position, holding that Parliament's national concern could apply only where the subject of the legislation had real consequences outside provincial boundaries. According to Judge Trotier, the regulatory power contained in the section was overly broad and would improperly entitle regulation over [areas] entirely within province undertakings...
>
> The effect of the decision is to eliminate CEPA's regulatory scheme in cases where the pollution event does not have an effect beyond the borders of a province. The decision of Trotier, J., is under further appeal by the Crown to the Quebec Court of Appeal.[41]

CELA argues that the federal government has fewer regulatory powers under CEPA than existed in some of the preceding legislation, such as the Clean Air Act, which permitted the federal government to "unilaterally enact national air emission standards, as well as national air quality objectives with no 'equivalency' roadblock."[42] In seeking explanations for this "backward step," Vigod suggests:

> One is that the federal government, driven largely by an agenda of de-regulation, privatization, free trade and devolution of responsibility to the provinces, would rather appear to be protecting the environment than be actually regulating. The other explanation is that the federal government continues to be plagued by conservative constitutional advice in relation to environmental matters.

CELA takes the position that existing constitutional powers do allow for a much stronger federal role, particularly with regard to toxic substances.

> These heads of power include the criminal law power, trade and commerce power, and the 'peace, order and good government' power which the Supreme Court of Canada in *Crown Zellerbach* [1988] held can be invoked to support legislation in the area of marine pollution. Other Supreme Court of Canada decisions have confirmed that the federal government also enjoys concurrent jurisdiction with respect to "health." A number of commentators have written that the *Crown Zellerbach* decision provides a basis for upholding the "toxic substances" regulatory provisions. These substances are persistent and cross provincial boundaries. The definition of toxic substances as outlined above may sufficiently distinguish them from the class of less damaging, less persistent substances that may be regulated effectively at the local level.[43]

Citizens and the State

From the point of view of the citizens' and environmental groups, they need the authority and resources of the State to help them pare away the prerogatives of the private sector to pollute the environment. But the State has proved to be a treacherous ally at best; often, governmental agencies, politicians, laws, and the judiciary are part of the "enemy's" defences. The struggle of the citizens' and environmental groups is to demonstrate sufficient moral and political authority to win over the State at crucial moments, and to gradually democratize its institutions.

The first demand, given these objectives, is to be consulted about environmental policy at its early stages of development. Consultation around the CEPA was unusually extensive, in that Ministry officials attended public meetings in different regions of the country and reviewed written submissions before second reading. Nevertheless, the government's agenda was to introduce the draft for public discussion in late December 1986, and have it ready for parliamentary debate by late spring, 1987. This was not sufficient time for many public groups to analyse the draft, consult with one another, and prepare their briefs. The length of the consultation period is a contested issue in almost every regulatory process, and was the subject of criticism and complaint in the case of CEPA as well. The significance is that the citizens' and environmental groups view an inadequate period for study and consultation as a government tactic to limit their input, as well as their ability to mobilize public opinion.

They are seriously disadvantaged, moreover, in relation to the private sector's ability to deploy research departments, consultants, and lawyers in response to a new legislative initiative. Those who have the most difficulty preparing responses are the citizens' groups. They are dependent, to some extent, on the research and analysis prepared by the national or regional environmental organisations with full-time staff, and on university-based

The Canadian Environmental Protection Act

researchers. Government ministries have relatively close contacts with environmental organisations like Pollution Probe, Great Lakes United (GLU), and the Canadian Environmental Law Association, and rely upon these groups to organise grass-roots response. For example, CELA organised the governments' public hearings on the Great Lakes Water Quality Agreement (GLWQA) in 1988. GLU, the Ontario Environmental Network (OEN), and the Lake Ontario Organizing Network (LOON), which have considerable overlap of personnel, and have regular channels of contact with the environment ministries of Canada and Ontario, have organised public responses to initiatives like the 1987-88 review of the GLWQA, MISA, and the Lake Ontario Toxics Management Plan. The citizens' groups tend to rely on the expertise of these organisations to help them interpret and assess the government initiatives, and this process of intra-movement consultation takes some time, especially for groups not located in the metropoles.

The second demand is for participation in advisory bodies created to oversee development of regulations and to make recommendations to the ministers. As we saw in the last section, private sector associations are very concerned to have representation in these relatively new appendages of the State. The citizens' and environmental groups view these bodies as a crucial terrain in the battle for representation within the State. Their objectives range from attempting to neutralize or modify the influence of the private sector, to restructuring the agenda of reforms. In the case of CEPA, these groups advocated the creation of the Advisory Council mentioned above, which would have representation from the public, as well private sectors.

There were also a number of recommendations having to do with the conditions for citizen participation: access to information; funding for intervenors in law suits; funding for citizens' representatives to participate in advisory committees; and more money for government-sponsored research, the results of which would be accessible to the public. CELA, Energy Probe, Pollution Probe, and the National Research Council were concerned that information from corporations be at least as accessible under CEPA as under the Access to Information Act; they proposed including CEPA in the Act's schedule. Moreover, they realized that the AIA does not apply to ad hoc boards or tribunals, so they recommended that any Boards of Review established under the CEPA should be specifically scheduled under the AIA. This would allow such boards to release information on toxicology and health to the public. This was also recommended for the Advisory Committees.

LABOUR RESPONSE TO CEPA

There were only six written briefs submitted to Environment Canada, and four of these were by national union offices or provincial federations: Canadian Association of Industrial, Mechanical and Allied Workers (CAIMAW), the British Columbia Federation of Labour, the Saskatchewan Federation of Labour, and the Confédération des Syndicats Nationaux (CSN). One came from the Public Service Alliance of Canada (National Dept. of Health and Welfare), and one from CAW local 1973's environment committee. The most substantial of these was the submission from the CSN, which is examined at some length in this section. Only two union organisations were represented at the public hearings, and these were both CAW locals with active environmental committees: 199 (General Motors, St. Catharines), and 1973 (GM, Windsor). At the legislative committee hearings, there were presentations from CAW Local 444—one of the most influential locals in the union, with an active environmental committee—and the Canadian Labour Congress (CLC). The CLC presentation, discussed in this section, emphasized tripartite consultation.

The unions endorsed most of the public participation proposals already discussed in relation to the environmental and citizens' groups. They called for an Environmental Bill of

Rights (which they also support for Ontario); they opposed more ministerial discretion; they emphasized the need for enforcement; and they supported stiffer penalties and the civil action clause. In addition, the CAIMAW brief urged the government not to submit to economic blackmail, and to use environmental and health legislation to transfer these social costs back to the private sector. The CAIMAW brief stated its position very succinctly:

> From a trade union perspective we are very clearly and very directly interested in job creation. However, we want to say, and this is a perspective generally shared by labour, that we are not interested in jobs at any costs. We are not just workers. We are at one and the same time environmentalists and we are parents. We are committed to do our best to ensure that the future we leave to our children and our grandchildren is a future worth having. We will have failed our children if we fail to adequately protect our environment. We are also voters.[44]

The CSN submitted an eloquent and thoughtful brief, which—in addition to supporting measures to broaden the scope and strengthen the enforcement powers of the Act—maintained considerable consistency about its objectives and its socioeconomic implications. The CSN stressed that the Act should have a *preventative* and long-term focus. They recommended deleting the phrase "may also harm biological processes on which the survival of humankind depends" from the preamble, on the grounds that such an effect can be proven only after the damage is done. The onus on citizens to show evidence of such effects is too great; instead, the Act should seek to eliminate the necessity of such risks to health and environment.

> *En fait, et en poussant l'argument jusqu'aux limites de l'absurde, un "écocide" seul menacèrait "la survie de l'homme." La Suisse, la France, l'Allemagne fédérale et les Pays-Bas pourraient "in extremis" survivre à la pollution catastrophique du Rhin comme ce fut récemment le cas; et notre société pourrait survivre très longtemps avec les traces dangereuses de dioxines; et de bi-phènyles polychlorés dans le lait maternel.*[45]

The above phrase was, in the end, deleted from the preamble of the Act.

The CSN also proposed that *minimum* penalties be set for offences as a deterrent to polluters. Their argument was that, too often, polluters calculate relatively small fines into the costs of their operations. The certainty that a conviction would bring a stiff minimal penalty would provide a better deterrent to the crime. This idea was not adopted by the government, however. Sections 111 to 116 of the final Act contain no minimum penalties.

On the export of hazardous substances, the CSN recommended, along with other groups, that it be forbidden to export any substance whose manufacture or use in Canada is proscribed. The CSN went further than other groups, however, in recommending also that exports of any regulated substances should be accompanied by complete instructions regarding safe use and disposal. This would assist Third World countries, in particular, where resources for scientific research are scarce, and access to information may be inadequate. This recommendation was accepted by the government, insofar as the final Act prohibits the export of substances banned in Canada, and allows the export of *regulated* substances subject to notification of the receiving country. The category of hazardous wastes was also added to the substances covered by this clause.

Recognizing that the loss of export markets could affect some jobs, the CSN proposed: (*a*) that Canada use its influence within the OECD to bring about a common policy on the export of proscribed substances; and (*b*) that the government develop a policy of aid to help firms to restructure production away from dangerous products and toward environmentally-benign ones. The first point needed to be made in response to the chemical industry's lobbying against export restrictions. The latter's reasons were the paperwork involved, and that Canada should not adopt such a policy unilaterally, but only when an international agreement was in place. Otherwise, Canadian exporters would be "unfairly" disadvantaged. A similar argument was made, however, by people in the Energy and Chemical Workers Union, who said that banning production of certain products in Canada is unfair, and does no one any good, if companies can simply relocate production elsewhere.[46] It is interesting that this point was not addressed by the ECWU during the public consultation process; as far as I can determine, it was raised only by the CSN.

Another point of concern, which one might have expected the ECWU to raise, is protection for workers from reprisals by employers, for reporting offences. Given the direct involvement of chemical workers in actions to either commit or prevent acts of pollution, this seems to be an important area for intervention. According to David Bennett, National Workplace Health and Safety Representative for the CLC, and a member of the Environmental Contaminants Act Amendments Consultation (ECAAC) multipartite Committee, the ECWU "was strongly involved in...areas such as Environmental Reporting," referring, it seems, to the area which became Section 36 of the CEPA.[47] (Section 36 of the final Act states that informers may request confidentiality. Only federal government employees are specifically protected from harassment or dismissal for reporting an offence [Section 37, 4].) The ECWU's concerns about employee liability were, apparently, raised within the CLC structures dealing with the ECA, and subsequently, the CEPA reviews. The only union organisation to call for protection of workers at the public hearings was the CAW's Local 444 environmental committee. No ECWU submissions were made to Environment Canada, at the public hearings, or at the legislative committee hearings.

Regarding the liability of employees to prosecution, it may have been possible for the unions to negotiate a section guaranteeing a worker's right to refuse to perform a job which s/he believes may pollute the environment. There is a parallel for this in the Occupational Health and Safety Act, which recognizes a worker's right to refuse potentially unsafe work. Rather than endorsing the ECAAC Committee's recommendations *carte blanche*, the CLC and other organisations could have withheld support for the Act until they received a guarantee that this right would be entrenched in the CEPA and/or an Environmental Bill of Rights. This would have cut off the CCPA's strategy to neutralize chemical workers' potential support for the environmentalists with the threat of employee prosecution.

The CLC was represented on the ECAAC Committee by David Bennett, National Representative on Workplace Health and Safety Issues. Bennett also participated in the socioeconomic evaluation working group of the Committee. (The other labour representative on the Committee was Stewart Skinner of the Public Service Alliance of Canada [PSAC].) Labour's interest in the Act stemmed mainly from workplace occupational health and safety concerns; the Hazardous Materials Information Review Act had recently been drafted, and the consensus method of "stakeholder" consultation, as well as some of its provisions regarding access to information, served as models for the work of the Consultation Committee.[48] Stuart Sullivan, in 1988 the Ontario Region Co-ordinator of the ECWU, claimed that his union was closely involved in the work of the Consultation Committee, through the participation of himself and two other ECWU members.[49] Sullivan was at that time a member of the Ontario Federation of Labour (OFL) Committee on Energy, Conservation, and Pollution Control (ECPC), and participated in his capacity as an OFL representative. Yet the ECWU was not one of the unions consulted about the CLC's brief to the government concerning the CEPA; nor did the OFL committee make a separate presentation during the CEPA consultation process.[50]

According to David Bennett, the ECWU was "not especially" involved in preparing the CLC response to the CEPA. The composition of the CLC environment committee (formed after the ECA consultation process, in July 1987) during the CEPA review period included: Canadian Union of Public Employees (CUPE), Canadian Paperworkers Union (CPU), Public Service Alliance of Canada (PSAC), CAW, and National Union of Provincial Government Employees (NUPGE) representatives, as well as CLC staff representatives, but not the ECWU. A letter from David Bennett of the CLC, with appended comments on the CEPA, and dated July 17, 1987, was sent for review to nine union people working in the area of occupational health and environment, but not to anyone in the ECWU, or the OFL's ECPC committee.

If in fact members of the ECWU were key participants in the ECA consultative process, this involvement seems to have waned after the final report in October 1986. During the January to April 1987 period of public review of the CEPA, it seems that the ECWU chose to work through OFL and CLC structures, rather than participate directly. Nor did the union become involved in the legislative hearings on the CEPA later that year. At a December 15, 1987 meeting of the Ontario Labour-Environment Co-ordinating Committee, Sullivan said that the OFL's ECPC Committee had been "relatively quiet for the last six months."[51] The CLC environment committee assumed the responsibility of representing labour in consultations around a national legislative initiative.

The CLC and PSAC representatives on the ECAAC Committee strongly endorsed the multi-partite consultation process and were more prepared to accommodate employers' concerns about trade secret confidentiality and other points than were the environmentalists.[52] The latter appended a lengthy statement on the shortcomings of the final recommendations, which was not endorsed by the labour representatives. The environmentalists had organised a "caucus" with representatives from eleven organisations across the country, which worked with the two representatives appointed to the Committee. When asked about the apparent differences among the CLC and environmental positions, and the extent to which the two constituencies worked together in the ECAAC Committee, David Bennett said:

> The CLC has a clearly defined constituency and mandate. We are also used to negotiating and compromising—where the compromise is clearly useful to workers. You cannot have effective consultation and agreements unless all parties push for the implementation of the agreement and not something else, e.g., bureaucratic fantasies about what is needed in the area concerned. By contrast, the environmental groups are used to protest, crusading and Agitprop, "all-or-nothing." Their mandate to negotiate is not always clear. That is why they (quite understandably) wanted their cake (the agreement) and to eat it—in order to seem pure with their constituency. Also, that this was not to be the end of the story over the ECA amendments.
>
> Despite these differences, the CLC worked very well with FOE and CELA. They took our lead over mutagenicity testing and ecotoxicity; we followed them over the general requirements of effective environmental regulation. Another difference: we have a full employment policy as well as environmental concerns; the environmental movements are not primarily concerned with employment.[53]

In this response we see several themes which arise repeatedly in environmentalist-labour relations, and which are examined further in this work:
1. the tendency of union officials to deal with environmental issues within the collective bargaining mode of practice applied to other issues, i.e., to avoid politicizing their relations with employers;

2. a perception of environmental organizations as lacking a legitimate, identifiable social base (which is linked to their "protest" tactics);
3. a perception that, in a situation where trade-offs between jobs and the environment are imposed, unions and environmentalists confront each other in a zero-sum game.

Were one to ask the environmental representatives on the ECAAC Committee what they thought about the unions' role, they would likely point to their own structure for soliciting input from groups across the country, and question the democratic representativeness of the CLC officials. They would also be likely to complain that the unions had been too quick to accept employers' assertions about the necessary conditions for investment and employment.

Review of the draft CEPA was the first task taken up by the nascent CLC environment committee in the summer of 1987.[54] The CLC brief to the legislative committee supported a number of the environmental and citizens' groups demands, including the need for a national environmental bill of rights; the desirability of national standards, "with consultation with the provinces, labour, the environmental movement, and business"; and the need for diligent and mandatory enforcement of the Act. The CLC supported the "multi-partite" method of consultation, and urged that the Advisory Committee proposed by the ECA Consultative Committee be written into the Act and not left to ministerial discretion. The Advisory Committee, however, was left optional in the final wording of the Act.

The CLC's conception of "multi-partism" was rather ambiguous. It seemed to be based on the model of consultation developed for the occupational safety and health programme, WHMIS. This process, however, included labour, business, and government. The alliances foreseen by organised labour within the government-business-labour-*environmental* negotiating process were not made explicit, reflecting, perhaps, the ambivalent and pivotal position of labour. The unions seemed to be trying to work out a *modus vivendi* with capital which avoided insofar as possible economic consequences unfavourable for workers, given the existing structure of choices. At the same time, pressures from other social movements to improve occupational health and safety, and to support progressive demands in the environmental and other spheres (peace, women's equality, employment, international solidarity), place unions in a mediating role vis-à-vis employers.

Unions may thus act either as "insulation" between radical social demands and private capital, or, attempt to shift employers in the direction of reforms. Depending upon where workers see the greatest likelihood of success, as well as the union's ideological motivations, the union may intervene in the parliamentary process with the objective either to push the government to socialize the costs of production (government-funded clean-ups, subsidies; tax credits, etc.), or to apply State coercion to private firms to assume such costs. In the 1980s the unions were working to bring about the election of the NDP, as the party expected to deliver social democratic solutions to the conflicts between social movement demands and capitalist accumulation. Mediating between the alternative social movements and private employers, so as not to endanger their members' economic interests on one hand, or lose credibility as a progressive social force, on the other, is a very difficult game to play. In many cases, the unions have "talked radical" about general commitments to ecology, peace, and feminism, but at crucial conjunctures sided with employers. This behaviour is evident in the history of the ECWU (see part 3). It is not, however, so much a question of hypocrisy, or bad faith, as it is one of real conflict, given the way union leaders perceive their choices.

The Five-Year-Point Review of CEPA

While there is not space here to develop a detailed analysis of the 1994-95 review of CEPA, undertaken by the House of Commons Standing Committee on the Environment and Sustainable Development, it should be mentioned that the Standing Committee's report responded favorably to many of the concerns of citizens, environmentalists, and unions, as described above.[55] The Committee was chaired by Liberal MP Charles Caccia, a long-time advocate of environmental regulation at the federal level. The intense lobbying that surrounded the review and the report's recommendations provides a wealth of material for further analysis of the roles of citizen, environmental organisation, union, and corporate actors. One significant feature of this consultation process was the extensive participation of aboriginal peoples' representatives. The Canadian Environmental Network Caucus, encompassing fifty-three non-governmental groups, submitted a barrage of detailed position papers on all aspects of the CEPA. Labour organisations which testified or submitted written briefs included: the Canadian Labour Congress, the Ontario Federation of Labour, and United Fisherman and Allied Workers. The large manufacturing and resource industry associations were, of course, represented, along with individual firms.

Briefly, the Committee proposed measures to improve public participation and "citizens' rights" (devoting an entire chapter of its 357-page report to this subject), as well as measures for more effective enforcement of the existing law. It also advocated a strong federal role in the creation and enforcement of national standards for environmental regulation, much to the chagrin of the Bloc Québecois members of the Committee, who wrote a lengthy dissenting opinion.

The report criticized the Department of Environment's reluctance to prosecute, citing these figures:

> ...since CEPA came into force in 1988, approximately 13,500 industry inspections had been carried out, 1,000 warnings and 29 inspectors' directions were issued, 600 suspected offences were investigated, and 66 prosecutions were instituted, 51 of which resulted in a conviction... If one reviews the enforcement data from other Canadian jurisdictions, particularly those known for their 'hard line' approach, Environment Canada's enforcement record pales by comparison... Since 1987/1988, Ontario has instituted more than two hundred prosecutions *per year*—with a very high conviction rate—for violations of its environmental laws. In 1994, close to 300 prosecutions were initiated. During the peak years of 1991 and 1992, the totals were even higher...
>
> In contrast, enforcement under CEPA for fiscal year 1993-1994 resulted in only three prosecutions (pp. 238-241)...

The Committee also supported the *centralization* of enforcement functions, an approach resisted by Regional Directors and by Environment Canada submissions.

The report was very well-received by environmentalists. Mark Winfield of the Canadian Institute for Environmental Law and Policy called it "the most important federal environmental policy document in over twenty years," while Paul Muldoon of the Canadian Environmental Law Association said that "the proposed changes really show an understanding of how the old ways have failed." These views were shared by the president of the binational environmental organisation, Great Lakes United, who applauded the report's support for "pollution prevention" and "the precautionary principle" in the licensing of chemicals.[56] The government's response to the Committee's report, however, was received as a major disappointment.[57] Muldoon attributed the watering-down of the Committee's proposals to "intense lobbying by some of Canada's biggest industrial associations," as well as pressure from the federal Departments of Industry, Agriculture, and Natural Resources. Winfield expressed the concern that the government's proposals might weaken the existing law.[58]

The Canadian Environmental Protection Act

Indeed, the entire thrust of the Committee's report diverged from the predominantly neoliberal direction of the Liberal Government, which was opting for "voluntary pollution agreements" with polluters rather than enforcement. As environmentalists have observed, a serious commitment to sustainable development is not compatible with cuts to Environment Canada's budget of the order of 30 percent (announced in the February 1995 budget), meaning a reduction from $737 million to $503 million over three years. Over the same period, staffing will be reduced from 5,700 to 4,300 persons, or by 24 percent. Many goals and target-dates for environmental remediation or regulation have been postponed or dropped. The regulatory gains made in the 1980s are under siege in the 1990s.

NOTES

1. "Industry representatives" is used in most of the literature, whether from government, management, or unions, to mean the equivalent of "corporate management." This is significant because very often there is no union representation in the consultation process, implying that "industry" is represented by management alone. Union participation is usually referred to as "labour representatives."
2. Tom McMillan, Minister of the Environment, "The Right to a Healthy Environment: An Overview of the Proposed Environmental Protection Act," Government media release, June 1987, p. 10.
3. Ibid., p. 10 (emphasis added).
4. This was the conclusion of the Peat Marwick Consulting firm, regarding the penalties for violations of Ontario environmental legislation, but is echoed by others regarding federal law. The federal Law Reform Commission and the Canadian Environmental Law Association have recommended stiffer penalties for crimes against the environment.
5. Following the presentation of the CMA at the hearing of December 15, 1987, Charles Caccia remarked in exasperation: "I am increasingly baffled by the mirror representations being made by CCPA, by PACE, and today by CMA. It is rather peculiar that each of them would come up with exactly the same type of observations on this bill." Government of Canada, *Minutes and Proceedings and Evidence of the Legislative Committee on Bill C-74, an Act respecting the protection of the environment and human life and health,* issue no. 6, (December 15, 1987) p. 48.
6. M. Duval, President, Polycol Ltée., "Comments of the ASMAC on the Proposed Environmental Protection Act" (February 18, 1987). Obtained from Environment Canada, Ontario Region office, Toronto.
7. CMA, "Submission to the Legislative Committee on Bill C-74," in Government of Canada, *Minutes and Proceedings and Evidence of the Legislative Committee on Bill C-74,* issue no. 6 (December 15, 1987), pp. 49-50.
8. Ibid., p. 47.
9. CCPA, "Submission to Environment Canada on the Proposed Enviromental Protection Act," March 1987, pp. 12-13. Obtained from Environment Canada.
10. This summary is based in part on a discussion with Toby Vigod, legal counsel and clinic director at the Canadian Environmental Law Association, who sat on the ECAACC and co-authored the CELA's submission to Environment Canada on the proposed federal Environmental Protection Act (March 1987).
11. CMA, "Submission to the Minister of the Environment, The Hon. Thomas McMillan, on the Draft Environmental Protection Act," March 1987, p. 12. Copy obtained from Environment Canada and in possession of author. Note that Union Carbide would be particularly keen on this condition, following its Bhopal experience. The Bhopal gas disaster of December 1984 left more than 3,300 persons dead and 200,000 injured. (500,000 damage claims were filed.) The Indian government filed a US$3.3 billioncompensation suit against Union Carbide, based in Danbury, CT, on behalf of the victims. In December 1987, the government laid criminal charges against nine individuals, including the former chairperson of Union Carbide, Warren Anderson. In 1988 an Indian court ordered Union Carbide to pay about $US190 million in interim compensation, but the company appealed the ruling. (Union

Carbide's profit reached $720 million in 1988.) Many victims began filing for out-of-court settlements. In February 1989, Union Carbide and the Indian Government reached an out-of-court settlement in which Union Carbide agreed to pay US$470 million to the Government of India as full and final compensation for "all claims, rights, and liabilities related to...the Bhopal gas disaster" (ruling by Judge Pathak, Indian Supreme Court, February 14, 1989). All criminal charges were dismissed. Union Carbide stock rose sharply on the NYSE, since the settlement was much lower than investors had expected. See "Bhopal victims want settlement now," *The Globe and Mail*, July 18, 1988; "Carbide to pay $470 million as compensation for Bhopal," *The Globe and Mail*, February 15, 1989, p. A2; and "Smaller more vulnerable Union Carbide tries to leave Bhopal behind," *The Globe and Mail*, February 16, 1989, p. B21.

12. See CMA, "Submission to the Minister of the Environment," p. 13, and letter from DuPont Canada's vice-president of corporate affairs to "Tom" (the Minister for the Environment), dated March 2, 1987, p. 4 (in author's possession).
13. CCPA, "Submission to the Legislative Committee on Bill C-74," in Government of Canada, Minutes and Proceedings and Evidence of the Legislative Committee on Bill C-74," issue no. 6 (December 15, 1987), p. 8.
14. CMA, "Submission to the Legislative Committee on Bill C-74.
15. The CCPA's position paper is reproduced in Appendix C of the proceedings of the Round-Table Discussion on Toxic Chemicals Law and Policy in Canada (Toronto: Canadian Environmental Law Research Foundation, 1981). This paragraph is quoted by Ted Schrecker in "Resisting Regulation: Environmental Policy and Corporate Power," *Alternatives* vol. 13, no. 1 (December 1985).
16. CMA, "Submission to the Minister of the Environment," pp. 17-18; Union Carbide, "Submission to Environment Canada on the Proposed Environmental Protection Act," February 19, 1987, p. 3; CCPA, "Submission to the Minister of the Environment," *passim.*; and other chemical company briefs to Environment Canada regarding the proposed CEPA (available from Environment Canada).
17. *Minutes and Proceedings* issue no. 6 (1987), p. 6 (emphasis added). Note that when the Advisory Committee was appointed, there were only two industry representatives, compared to the environmentalists' four. Workers were represented by a Ministry of Labour official.
18. PACE, "PACE Submissions on the Proposed Environmental Protection Act," March 2, 1987. Obtained from Environment Canada; in possession of the author. Also CCPA, "Submissions to the Legislative Committee on Bill C-74."
19. Fiberglass Canada, brief to Environment Canada on the draft CEPA, March 18, 1987, p. 2. Copy in the author's possession. Available from Environment Canada.
20. Letter from C. George Miller to the Hon. Thomas McMillan, Minister of the Environment, regarding the proposed Environmental Protection Act (Ottawa, April 3, 1987), p. 2. The Mining Association brief may reflect the strongly "free enterprise" and "anti-communist" positions taken for many years by one of its leaders, the late Steven Roman, owner of Dennison Mines.
21. British Columbia Forest Products Ltd., letter to the Hon. Thomas McMillan, Minister of the Environment, on the draft CEPA; in posssssion of the author.
22. Lambton Industrial Society, brief to Environment Canada, February 16, 1987, p. 4. In author's possession.
23. CMA, "Submission to the Minister of the Environment," p. 5.
24. "The Mobilization of Bias in Closed Systems: Environmental Regulation in Canada," *Journal of Business Administration* vol. 15 (1984/85), p. 48.
25. Ted Schrecker, "Resisting Regulation," p. 18.
26. Ted Schrecker, "The Mobilization of Bias," pp. 45-46.
27. Elaine L. Hughes describes the attempts since the 1970s to obtain a Canadian Environmental Bill of Rights (CEBR), as well as provincial environmental bills of rights and the inclusion of environmental provisions in the Canadian constitution, in "Civil Rights to Environmental Quality," E. Hughes, A. Lucas, and W. Tilleman II, eds., *Environmental Law and Policy* (Toronto: Emond Montgomery Publications, 1993), pp. 409-439. A bill which would have included (albeit weak) environmental rights in the Constitution (Bill C-60) was defeated in 1978. *The Constitution Act* (1982) "contained no reference to environmental rights whatsoever" (ibid., p. 424). In the absence of such constitutional provisions, subsequent federal governments have taken the position that a

The Canadian Environmental Protection Act 71

CEBR would be ineffective. W. Andrews, quoted by Hughes, said that this was the advice which led Minister McMillan to drop the CBER from the CEPA. See W. Andrews, "The environment and the Canadian Charter of Rights and Freedoms," in N. Duplé, ed., *Le droit à la qualité de l'environnement* (Montréal: Québec Amérique, 1988), p. 264. Nevertheless, environmentalists continue to lobby for a statutory bill of rights.

28. Citizens' Coalition for Clean Water, Wallaceburg, Ont., "Submission to the Minister of the Environment, The Hon. Thomas McMillan, on the Draft Environmental Protection Act," March 1987, pp. 4-5, in the author's possession.
29. Don Laprise, testimony before the legislative committee on Bill C-74, January 21, 1988, in *Minutes and Proceedings*, issue 11, p. 7.
30. See the CELA, Energy Probe, Pollution Probe, CAW local 444 presentations at public meetings held by Environment Canada. Thes are summarized in Summary of Public Hearings on the Proposed Environmental Protection Act (Ottawa: Government of Canada, Department of the Environment, March 31, 1987).
31. In a presentation at a public meeting on the CEPA, the MOE stated its view that inspectors' powers were too restricted, because they limited entry without a warrant to emergencies and to situations where evidence may be destroyed. The latter case, obviously, could never be proved. (Ibid., p. 8.)
32. See the submissions to Environment Canada on the proposed CEPA from the Canadian Cancer Society, the Environmentally Sensitive, and the International Institute for Public Health. Obtained from Environment Canada.
33. See the Wallaceburg Clean Water Committee, CELA, MOE, Local 444, Canadian Cancer Society, Environmentally Sensitive, Learning Disabilities Association, and Save the Rouge Valley submissions to Environment Canada regarding Bill C-74. Obtained from Environment Canada.
34. Rick Coronado, representing CAW Local 44, in *Minutes and Proceedings*. The CLC also supported "strong federal environmental provision" (quotation from written comments on the CLC role in the CEPA review, provided to the author by David Bennett, National Representative for Workplace Health and Safety, CLC, October 1988).
35. One such "other matter" is the production of CFCs. Under the auspices of the Federal-Provincial Advisory Committee a working group was created to study controls for ozone layer depleting substances, which reports to the Canadian Council of Ministers of the Environment. The federal government's efforts to obtain provincial co-operation in the regulation (reduction) of such substances illustrate the limitations of the "national guidelines" approach. The government of Alberta, for example, supports the companies' preference for voluntary action and self-monitoring, and has refused to commit itself to a federal-provincial agreement to reduce greenhouse emissions by 2000. See "Alberta says no way to anti-pollution plan," *Edmonton Journal*, November 8, 1994.
36. Toby Vigod, "Overview of federal law, regulation and policy," The Canadian Institute, *The Fundamentals of Environmental Law and Regulation* (proceedings of a conference held July 18, 1994) (Toronto: The Canadian Institute, 1994), pp. 24-26.
37. In his review of the constitutional bases for federal jurisdiction in environmental matters, lawyer D. D. Graham Reynolds refers to federal criminal law power; sea coast and inland fisheries power under section 91 (2) of the *Constitution Act*; the authority to make environmental protection regulations in respect of federal departments, agencies, Crown corporations, works, undertakings, and lands (section 92 and subsection 92 (1) of the *Constitution Act*); and international obligations relating to air pollution and ocean dumping. See "Overview of federal law, regulation and policy," *The Fundamentals of Environmental Law and Regulation*, pp. 3-25.
38. Ross Howard, "Ottawa to enforce PCB safety standard if provinces do not," *The Globe and Mail*, September 20, 1988, p. A3.
39. Craig McInnes, "All provinces but PEI want PCB rule waiver," *The Globe and Mail*, October 14, 1988, pp. A1, A3. See Craig McInnes, "PCB rule is called a farce," *The Globe and Mail*, October 15, 1988. Following the St. Basile accident, the Québec Ministry of Environment carried out a "mass inspection" of the fifty-two largest PCB storage sites in the province, and found only two that met government requirements. See "St.-Basile pronounced 'unique' after Québec PCB inspection," *Kingston Whig-Standard*, November 4, 1988.

40. I asked a CELA staff member why environmentalists feel that the federal government would or could enforce environmental standards more rigorously than the provinces, and was told that the federal government can be viewed as a single pressure-point for lobbying. The belief is that the federal government may be held more politically accountable by organised environmentalists than twelve provincial and territorial governments. Moreover, CEPA's Enforcement and Compliance Policy (May 1988) is considered very stringent, at least on paper.
41. Reynolds, *The Fundamentals of Environmental Law*, p. 10.
42. Vigod, "Overview," p. 26.
43. Ibid., pp. 27-28.
44. Jeff Keighley, CAIMAW, brief no. 206 to Environment Canada on Bill C-74. Obtained from Environment Canada.
45. *Memoire de la Confédération des syndicats nationaux*, présenté au Ministère de l'environnement du Canada, sur l'avant-projet de Loi sur la protection de l'environnement, Montréal, March 10, 1987, p. 5.
46. When I raised the implications of environmental pressure to ban products like styrofoam and non-biodegradable plastics with members of the ECWU in Sarnia, this was the typical response.
47. Written comments to the author, October 1989.
48. See, for example, the references to the WHMIS consultation procedure in the CLC "Submission on Proposals for Amendments to the Environmental Contaminants Act," (Ottawa: CLC, August 1985).
49. Sullivan was interviewed in Sarnia, May 5, 1988. He subsequently became a vice-president of the OFL. Ken Rodgers and Dan Ublansky were the other ECWU participants mentioned by Sullivan. Rodgers was at that time the Ontario Region Co-ordinator for the ECWU. Dan Ublansky was the ECWU's legislative director and co-ordinator for health and safety policy. The latter's participation in the Consultative Committee must have been fairly marginal, because when I interviewed him in May, 1988, he could not remember any specific examples of ECWU contributions to the CEPA process, or any other environmental policy process.
50. A letter from David Bennett of the CLC, with appended comments on the CEPA, dated July 17, 1987, was sent for review to nine union people working in the area of occupational health and environment, but not to anyone in the ECWU, or the OFL's ECPC committee.
51. Minutes of the meeting in the author's possession.
52. A brief CLC statement appended to the Final Report of the Committee stated: "While the ECAA Consultation Committee does not go as far as the CLC's submission of August 1985, it represents major advances and the CLC representatives on the project strongly recommend its acceptance by the officers of the CLC." See Government of Canada, Environmental Contaminants Act Amendments Consultative Committee, *Final Report* (Ottawa, October 1986).
53. Written comments to the author, received in October 1988.
54. A number of union officials with interests in the health and safety and environmental areas received a letter dated July 17, 1987, informing them that an environmental committee of the CLC was being created. The Chairperson would be Dick Martin, an executive vice-president of the CLC, and the joint secretaries were to be David Bennett and Guy Adam, National Representative in Social and Community Programmes. According to Bennett, members of the CLC environment committee are selected by "invitation"; some request participation. Written comments to the author, received in October 1988.
55. The report of the Standing Committee on the Environment and Sustainable Development was entitled *It's About Our Health! Towards Pollution Prevention: CEPA Revisited* (Canada Communication Group, Publishing, Public Works, and Government Services Canada, Ottawa, June 1995).
56. These spokespersons are quoted in "CEPA review surprisingly bold, thoroughgoing," *Great Lakes United* (Summer 1995), p. 19.
57. See the coverage in *Great Lakes United* (Spring 1996), p. 27.
58. Muldoon and Winfield quoted in "Government CEPA response 'disappointing'," *Great Lakes United* (Spring 1996), p. 27.

[5]

The Ontario Municipal-Industrial Strategy for Abatement

INTRODUCTION

Having attained office in the provincial election of June 1985, the Liberal minority government proceeded to announce a series of environmental measures intended to fulfil some of the expectations raised by their campaign. This project was made more urgent by the discovery of the St. Clair River "Blob" in August 1985. By this time at least 362 chemical compounds had been detected in the Great Lakes basin. In June 1986, environment minister James Bradley introduced a white paper outlining a Municipal-Industrial Strategy of Abatement (MISA) aimed at reducing the discharge of persistent toxic substances into Ontario's waterways.[1] There followed a sixty-day review period for public and private sector responses. Previous regulations placed controls only on the concentration of chemicals in waste water discharges, not on the total loadings. Thus, companies could dilute waste until acceptable concentrations were reached, with no limits on the total quantities of chemicals actually entering the waterway. MISA proposed to "cap" the total amount of each toxic contaminant from each polluter. The effluent limits would be set at levels attainable using "best available technology, economically attainable" (BAT-EA). If these levels were not low enough to protect receiving water quality, then the thresholds would be lowered further.

In addition to reducing pollution from direct dischargers, MISA would aim to reduce pollution going into municipal sewer systems from industrial sources (indirect discharges). The municipal sector includes 400 sewage treatment plants (STPs) taking waste from about 12,000 industries. Dischargers would be periodically reexamined to see if standards could be improved, using developments in abatement technology. This process would "drive MISA toward the goal of the virtual elimination of persistent toxic pollution from our waterways"—the stated objective of the programme . As John Swaigen and Mark Winfield point out:

> All of this marked a major departure from the ministry's previous approaches to the development and implementation of water-related standards. The non-enforceable "blue" and "green" book objectives for water quality and the control of industrial discharges, which had been used to provide the basis for the contents of certificates of approval, control orders, and program approvals, were to be replaced by enforceable regulatory requirements.[2]

Moreover, under the MISA "the process of negotiating the allowable effluent levels was to occur on a province-wide basis, rather than being left in the hands of regional officials," indicating that the Liberal Government had taken a lesson from the revelations of collusion between Ministry of the Environment (MOE) officials and the companies in the Chemical Valley (see chapter 11).

MISA would be implemented in a series of steps. First, there would be a pre-regulation phase, during which draft monitoring regulations would be prepared, in consultation with the public and with industries and municipalities. Then monitoring regulations would be released for public review. These would stipulate the conditions for company monitoring of effluents. Self-monitoring would be "policed" by random testing by the MOE. Abatement regulations were scheduled for introduction nine to twelve months after the monitoring regulations had come into effect. They were to be based on "best available technology" (BAT) for each of eight industrial sectors and the municipal sector, and would be enforceable under the Ontario Environmental Protection and Water Resources Acts (EPA and OWRA). Finally, there would be periodic reviews of the adequacy of these effluent standards, to determine whether or not they might be further improved. Initially, early 1989 was targeted as the date for having the complete abatement programme for the eight industrial sectors in place; the first sector to be regulated would be petroleum refining, and the second would be organic chemicals. For these sectors, the target date was early 1988.

As of October 1988, the revised schedule for MISA regulations had shifted the deadlines further into the future (see table 3). In fact, effluent *monitoring* regulations for all of the nine sectors were not completed until December 1990. The promulgation of *effluent limits* has been held up by conflicts over the definition of terms such as "virtual elimination," "zero discharge," and "economic achievability."[3] Limits regulations for the Petroleum Refining and Pulp and Paper sectors had been promulgated by May 1994. Draft regulations for the Metal Mining, Industrial Minerals, and Metal Castings sectors had been released for public comment, and regulations for the remaining four sectors were still being drafted.

The MISA regulations would be enforced by three means: (i) self-monitoring by companies and reporting of violations; (ii) MOE staff screening of the monitoring data submitted by dischargers; (iii) MOE staff evaluating data collected during inspections. The Ministry could respond to violations by: (i) issuing a "notification of violation" with a request for a remedy; or (ii) issuing a control order (by authority granted under the EPA and OWRA). Failure to comply with a control order could lead to prosecution. The Ministry promised stiffer penalties for violations. As of June 1986, the maximum fine for conviction of the first offence under the OWRA and the EPA was $5,000 and $10,000 for each subsequent conviction for each day the offence continues. Contravention of the Municipal Act (Sewers-Use By-law) was punishable by the rather insignificant fine of $2,000.[4]

The "public participation" process for the MISA immediately became contested terrain. The sixty days initially announced for public review of the draft MISA was extended to seventy days, by the end of which, 110 written briefs had been submitted. Nineteen of these were from industry associations or individual firms, nine were from citizens' or environmental groups, and about half came from various individuals. As in the case of the 1985 Spills Bill review process, there were no briefs from labour organisations.[5]

One of the first battles fought by the citizens' and environmental groups was for positions on the Joint Technical Committees (JTCs) which would draft the regulations for each sector. These Committees were meant to include representatives from the MOE, Environment Canada, and the private sector only. They would employ consultants who would be paid by the companies or their associations. The rationale for this was the technical nature of the work, and the Ministry's concern to win co-operation from the private sector. Public "interest groups" (firms are not considered to be "interest groups") would have an opportunity to criticize and propose changes to the regulations in review periods, and through an Advisory Committee. These groups' briefs on the draft MISA (see, e.g., the St. Clair River citizens' network response) pushed for public representatives on the *technical* committees, and for government funding for interest groups to retain technical experts. The Ministry accepted the first of these demands, and requested the MISA Advisory

TABLE 3
MISA SCHEDULES

Sector	June 1986 schedule		1989 (revised) schedule	
	Monitoring phase	Abatement phase	Monitoring phase	Abatement phase
Petroleum refining+	Spring 1987	Early 1988	Available	Sept. 1990
Organic chemicals	Spring 1988	Early 1989	Available	June 1991
Electrical power generators	End of 1988	Early 1989	March 1989	Nov. 1991
Industrial minerals*	Summer 1988	Early 1989	July 1989	March 1992
Inorganic chemicals manuf.	Fall 1988	Early 1989	February 1989	Sept. 1991
Iron and steel	Fall 1988	Early 1989	Oct.-Nov. 1988	June 1991
Metal mining refining	Summer 1988	Early 1989	—	—
Pulp and paper	Summer 1988	Early 1989	Nov. 1989	June 1991
Metal casting*	Fall 1988	Early 1989	March 1989	October 1991
Municipal STPs (and indirect discharges)	End of 1988	End of 1989	April 1989	Nov. 1991

* Industrial minerals was amalgamated with metal casting (which was added after the review process), and 17 subsectors were created under the new category.

+ The draft monitoring regulation for petroleum refining sector was released in July 1987. The draft monitoring regulation for the Priority Pollutants List was issued for public review in August 1987.

Sources: MOE, Municipal - Industrial Strategy for Abatement (M.I.S.A.), June 1986. The October 1989 schedule was obtained from the Ministry of the Environment, Legal Services Branch.

Committee to recommend individuals for such positions. However, no remuneration for the expenses of citizens' representatives would be provided. This was an important handicap, since the citizens would have to travel from their homes to Toronto for most of the Committee meetings. In addition, no money would be provided directly to the citizens' or environmental groups. The MOE would provide some funds to the Advisory Committee for professional services, and would make all technical reports available to the public. This did not address the concern of these groups, however, which was their need of technical advisors who could help them interpret the technical reports.

The Advisory Committee was to be the public's voice in the Minister's ear—a kind of watchdog for the MISA process. Environmental groups asked, therefore, that no industry representatives be appointed to the Advisory Committee. The Ministry's response was that the Committee would have one industry or municipal representative, nominated by the sectoral technical committees, according to the regulations being examined. The permanent membership would include:

- Douglas Hallet, Chairperson (former Environment Canada research scientist and an environmental biologist, biochemist, and analytical chemist)
- Toby Vigod, Vice-chairperson, CELA
- Monica Campbell, toxicologist, University of Toronto
- Harvey Claire, retired environmental protection co-ordinator for Imperial Oil
- Paul Hebert, biologist, Great Lakes Institute
- Donald McKay, chemistry professor, University of Toronto
- James McLaren, environmental engineering and policy management consultant
- Kai Millyard, researcher for Pollution Probe

MANAGEMENT RESPONSES TO MISA

The briefs submitted to the MOE on the MISA by corporate management revealed the following concerns:

1. *BAT-EA criteria:* Corporate representatives wanted effluent limits to be based not on BAT-EA, but on the "environmental impact that can be scientifically established with adequate cause/effect relationships."[6] This would mean, in effect, no change from the old practice of diluting effluent in order to meet receiving water quality criteria. Given the MISA's goals of reduction and virtual elimination of toxic contaminants, this was rejected by the Ministry.

2. The petroleum industry asked that, in the interests of "equity," their firms not be required to comply with new MISA regulations until regulations were in place for all sectors. The Ministry said no.

3. "The majority of industrial sectors expressed concern over the application of future load reductions beyond BAT-EA." They perceived that the more stringent limits "may require expenditures that could significantly impact on the competitive positions of Ontario firms, to the point of leading to plant closures." In effect, this was an attempt to define BAT-EA to mean changes which do not affect profitability.[7] They wanted a ten-year interval between reviews. The Ministry response was that a reasonable time period for dischargers to absorb the costs of new standards would be allowed, and that economic factors would be taken into account in setting the timing of reviews. Socioeconomic studies of each sector were being prepared, and would be part of the considerations in setting regulations.

4. The private-sector briefs called for more time to comply with Ministry abatement requests—more than the 180 days stipulated by the draft MISA. In reply, the Ministry assured the companies that the 180 days did not constitute a deadline for completion of

The Ontario Municipal-Industrial Strategy for Abatement

compliance measures, but only for reaching an agreement with the MOE (legally binding) on an abatement program.

5. Management briefs complained that the MISA schedule was, overall, "highly optimistic and unrealistic," and that a "more realistic" schedule should be worked out for each sector *at the technical committee level.*[8] This point suggests the potential strategic usefulness of private-sector representation on the technical committees. Not only could regulations be watered-down (like their preferred method for treating effluents!), but the schedule of implementation could be delayed by industry arguments about what technology and expenditures are "realistic." The Ministry response addressed subtly, this veiled threat of obstructionism: "The Ministry believes that with the full co-operation of industries and municipalities the MISA timetable...can be substantially achieved."

The Ministry also raised its strong suit in any confrontation, noting that environmental and citizens' groups were pushing the government to move faster, and that the Ministry's schedule was, in fact, moderate and accommodating. The desire of corporate management to keep decision-making about new regulation in the technocratic realm—to avoid its "politicization"—and to claim a monopoly of expertise within this realm, is a crucial dimension of the whole struggle around democratization. There is considerable sympathy for this elite, technocratic management of social/environmental problems among State technocrats and bureaucrats, who have been socialized through the same educational/professional institutions.[9]

6. *Data confidentiality:* Private sector briefs wanted "assurance that safeguards for protection of proprietory and process information will be put in place...and that Government will minimize the information required from industry, and that interagency release of information will require prior owners' consent by agreement."[10] A model for such an agreement was worked out in the organic chemicals sector technical committee. It set out the terms under which the provincial Ministry could give certain information to the federal department, and what kind of information would be released to the public. Significantly, the public would have the right to any information relating to the compliance records of firms. Public scrutiny and censure were recognized by the Ministry to be strengths crucial to the successful implementation and enforcement of the new rules.

CITIZEN AND ENVIRONMENTALIST RESPONSE

This outline of some of the key points in the citizens' and environmental groups' briefs illustrates the same kinds of concerns that were raised with regard to the Canadian Environmental Protection Act (CEPA). But since MISA offers a framework for long-term *regulation* of polluters, apparently "technical" matters begin to be examined, such as the definition of "best available technology economically attainable," where there is potential for conflicts between environmentalists and the private sector.

1. *BAT-EA*: These groups pointed out that, in the US, BAT-EA has ended up being the average of treatment technologies used in a given sector. They wanted instead, a requirement for dischargers to comply with the "best available demonstrated technology" (BADT). The Ministry response was that BAT-EA would be determined by the technical committees (where citizens' groups are under-represented). The Minister's decision will be based on this recommendation, as well as the socioeconomic studies and the advice received from the MISA Advisory Committee and the public review of draft regulations. In some cases, BADT might be the result. Moreover, the Ministry may decide that new plants will be required to use BADT, while existing plants may comply with BAT-EA.

Environmental groups wanted BAT-EA to be generically defined in the Ontario EPA, so that companies cannot delay implementation of new technology through court challenges, as has happened in the US. Also, the technical committees and the public should have a clear idea about what BAT-EA is supposed to be. The Ministry replied that a generic definition would be considered. It would also compile economic data on sectors and firms to help assess their ability to absorb increasing environmental costs.

2. *Industry self-monitoring*: Here the citizens' and environmental groups pointed quite explicitly to a conflict of interest. The Ministry response was that self-monitoring is a way of getting industry to bear the costs, under government supervision. If companies prove themselves untrustworthy, the measures will be changed. But the environmental groups argued that the enforcement methods proposed by MISA are "essentially no different from the method presently used by the Ministry," and therefore already proven inadequate.

Ted Schrecker has shown that the Canadian government has typically relied on firms to provide data about their own operations, because of inadequate government expertise, staff, and resources. He quotes a senior environment official who expressed fear that "more extensive public consultation on regulatory decisions might break down that relationship with the industry that has served us very well in providing us with technical information."[11] The same kind of relationship was revealed during the inquiry into Dow Chemical's mercury contamination of the St. Clair River in the 1970s (see chapter 10). In the MISA review process, the Ministry's answer (above) begged the following question: "If the purpose of self-monitoring is to force capitalists to pay the costs, why not have the government do the work of monitoring, but send the bill to the firm in the form of fees or taxes?" The citizens-versus-corporations conflict over monitoring terms reflects the larger battle for strategic positions within the legal-bureaucratic institutions of the State.

3. While management had asked for a ten-year review period, environmental groups recommended a mandatory five-year review for each sector. The Ministry said this might be too frequent, and the government would have to study the question further.

4. Environmental and citizens' groups asked for sixty-day periods for public response to regulations. This time is necessary, as pointed out in relation to the CEPA, because of the greater difficulty citizens' groups have in obtaining technical and legal advice. The Ministry, however, granted thirty days, with possible exceptions, giving as the reason the timetable's requirements. It added that the Advisory Committee would have a chance to review draft regulations before they are released to the public. This did not, however, redress the imbalance: details of the regulations would be confidential until their public release, so members of the Advisory Committee would not be able to feed information to their organisations. The companies, on the other hand, would have had a key role in the actual drafting of the regulations, and would have done much of their consulting at this stage.

By 1993, however, citizens had succeeded in obtaining a ninety-day public review period following the release of each draft regulation developed by the JTCs and the MISA Advisory Committee. This was a considerable achievement, since, as Winfield and Swaigen observe: "In the past, there had been no formal mechanism for public involvement in the Ministry's standard-setting procedures."[12]

5. Environmental and citizens' groups, and some municipalities wanted better controls over industrial discharges into municipal sewers, which constitute the worst pollution problem. These controls included:

i. pre-treatment regulations and standards;
ii. stricter enforcement of STP compliance and making STPs liable to prosecution; and
iii. a long-term goal of "completely phasing out the use of Ontario's municipal sewer systems for any toxic discharges because municipal STPs were not designed to treat toxic wastes successfully."

These points are important because municipal authorities are the most vulnerable to corporate influence and blackmail. Thus, municipal officials have to be compelled to enforce the laws by threat of legal sanction. On the other hand, the province must give the municipalities more money and technical assistance if they are to implement the regulations effectively.

The Ministry response was to point out that municipalities will, in fact, become liable to prosecution under the Act Respecting Enforcement of Statutes related to the Environment (which received Royal Assent on December 18, 1986). The phasing-out of all industry discharges to municipal sewers would be considered as a long-term goal.

6. Environmental groups viewed the control order process as ineffective in stopping discharges. Companies simply negotiate extensions and exemptions with Ministry officials.[13] The Ministry, however, defended the need for "flexibility," and suggested that the conditions for control orders would be subject to public review.

7. Greenpeace recommended an Environmental Control Commission (ECC) to oversee all aspects of MISA. It would comprise members of the public and would—among other functions—be empowered to: hire or fire any member of the bureaucracy involved in abatement processes; ensure that the overall goal of each technical committee is zero discharge, or no detectable quantities. The Ministry responded that the Advisory Committee was public watchdog enough, and that the Minister's conscience would be guided by her/his ultimate accountability to the electorate.

8. On the socioeconomic aspects, environmental and citizens' groups recommended that: studies should include the long-term economic benefits of controlling toxics; economic factors should not override health considerations; a definition of "economically achievable" should include a consideration of the costs associated with continued/increased pollution.

Interestingly, the Ministry stated its agreement with all of these points, simply choosing to ignore the conflict inherent in the second objective—to place health priorities above those of capitalist accumulation.

The democratization themes of the citizens' groups are illustrated as well by the lobbying of the St. Clair River International Citizens' Network (SCRICN) around the MISA, which is examined below. (The SCRICN's relations with chemical industry management and workers is studied in detail in chapter 11.)

St. Clair River International Citizens' Network

The SCRICN includes Citizens Organized Against Chemical Hazards (Algonac, MI.), Lambton Anti-Pollution Association (Moore Township, Ont.), League of Women Voters (Port Huron area), Southeastern Michigan Conservation Club, Wallaceburg Clean Water Committee, and the Windsor and District Clean Water Alliance. These groups, together with representatives of the Great Lakes Institute, Great Lakes United, Greenpeace, and the Lake St. Clair Advisory Committee (St. Clair Shores, Michigan), formed the network in June 1986. The Walpole Island Indian Band Council sent an observer to the SCRICN meetings, to represent the band's concerns about the toxic contamination of their main source of food. (A research centre on the island studies consumption of wild game and fish.)

The immediate impetus for the formation of the SCRICN was the discovery of the blob in August 1985 (chapter 11) and the subsequent proliferation of government studies and media reports documenting the extent of contamination of the river. The initial demands of the SCRICN included standardization of water testing on both sides of the international boundary, and testing of the St. Clair River delta near Walpole Island (Lake St. Clair). With the release by the MOE of the MISA white paper in June 1986, and by the State of Michigan's Office of the Great Lakes of the *St. Clair River Situation Report* in July, these citizens' groups had a set of recommendations to digest and the task of formulating responses. In this process, they drew upon the expertise of organisers and researchers from Great Lakes United, the Great Lakes Institute, and the Canadian Environmental Law Association.

They chose not to put their concerns to their parliamentary or congressional representatives (as a primary mode of action), but to lobby the MOE and Environment Canada directly (on the Canadian side), and to secure the greatest possible media attention for their demands. There are several reasons for this. First, the citizens had become skeptical about the willingness of their elected Conservative and Liberal members of parliament to act on their concerns. In the Sarnia area there was a long history of collusion between Conservative members of parliament and members of the Ontario legislature, and the chemical companies. Second, the political party which some may have seen as having a closer link to their interests—the New Democratic Party—seemed to be perpetually in opposition, both in Ontario and federally. Thus, citizens perceived few options but to lobby agencies of the State directly, and to try to increase their own participation in the decision-making processes. The idea of direct participation in the process is central to the citizens' groups' conception of democratization.

By September 1986, SCRICN had prepared a detailed response to the MISA paper, which was submitted as a brief to the Ontario Minister of the Environment.[14] The positions outlined in this brief indicated a significant advance beyond the immediate concerns and solutions proposed by the SCRICN at the time of its formation. The MISA brief contained an analysis of some of the systemic roots of the water pollution problems faced by the St. Clair River communities, in particular, the inherently "anti-environment" and "anti-health" nature of industry's fundamental interests, and the State's anti-popular bias insofar as it gives priority to industry's interests over those of citizens. For example, the SCRICN brief argued that:

> the development and implementation of MISA rests much too heavily with industrial polluters—the source of the problem. In monitoring, in assessing best available technologies economically achievable and in developing regulations, industry is depended upon as the driving force. Experience indicates that when it comes to pollution controls, industry is a follower, responding to pressures exerted by the public's demands for stricter controls and stiffer penalties.
>
> We are convinced, therefore, that achievement of the virtual elimination of toxic discharges will be heavily dependent upon the extent to which the immediately affected public, such as those living in the St. Clair River area, *are directly involved* in all stages of developing and implementing the MISA program [emphasis added].

The brief made specific proposals for broadening public participation in establishing environmental priorities, goals, and methods of implementation. These included: (i) representation of citizens' and environmental organisations on the technical committees; (ii) funding so that citizens' groups could hire independent technical experts; (iii) extensions of the time period for citizen response to government draft regulations; (iv) preparation and distribution of a list of interested groups to whom regulations would automatically be sent.

The Windsor and District Clean Water Alliance (CWA) brief to the government on MISA stated these demands forcefully:

> The Windsor and District Clean Water Alliance welcomes this opportunity to comment on the proposed program but this is not a substitute for the role it is entitled to play in the abatement policy. Public involvement in monitoring, setting of standards, implementation and enforcement of regulations—in MISA and in environmental protection in general—*must be immediate, permanent, and continuous*.[15]

Second, the SCRICN brief pointed to the conflict between the goal of optimal environmental protection (best available technology) and the profit concerns of companies. (The government has allowed industry to define "best available technology" accepting the condition, "economically affordable" by which the companies understand, "profitable.") The brief urged the Ministry to give priority to the goal of "the virtual elimination of the discharge of toxic substances." In addition, the SCRICN argued the need for *public access to the financial books of private industry*, in order to determine what capital resources are in fact available for investment in environmental improvement.

A further challenge to the traditional prerogatives of private industry and to the industry-State status quo took the form of the demand that *the burden of proof should be placed on the dischargers to prove that emissions will not have deleterious impacts*. The citizens' groups accepted the view that: "In the absence of precise evidence, we must assume that all man-made chemicals are poisons with the power to modify, often irreversibly, the growth and life of all organisms." They adopted the uncompromising goal of zero-discharge of toxins. At the same time, they urged the government to undertake extensive studies of health and environmental impacts of pollution.[16]

The opposition "private industry/public welfare" was posed most sharply in the brief's discussion of MISA's development and implementation. The citizens were concerned that Ministry control orders, negotiated on a company-by-company basis, give individual firms too much leeway in prolonging deadlines for compliance. Moreover, they claimed that government reliance on private companies to monitor and report their own discharges is an inadequate means to enforce regulations. "Past records prove that industry cannot be relied upon to monitor itself. The provincial government must allocate sufficient resources to undertake extensive monitoring programs." The brief also urged measures to facilitate greater public involvement in monitoring industry's performance. These included: (i) public education about environmental regulations; (ii) a 24-hour hotline for reporting violations; (iii) legislation to protect workers who report pollution by their employers; (iv) a rewards system to encourage reporting of contamination.

Finally, the SCRICN advocated the rigorous prosecution of pollution offenders, noting the poor government record on enforcement of regulations. The assumption was very clear: unless compelled, by a committed government with the backing of a vigilant public, private industry will continue to put profit ahead of environmental and health concerns.

The above principles were reasserted in the SCRICN's response to the *St. Clair River Situation Report's* recommendations. SCRICN asked the Great Lakes Office that the Network be included on the committee to review implementation of the recommendations. In addition, they asked that all meetings and information regarding the work of the committee be publicly accessible.

Labour Response to MISA

Given that the first target of regulation under the MISA was the petroleum refining sector, followed by the organic chemicals sector, and given that the petrochemical industry was raising the spectre of environmental costs as a threat to jobs in the industry, the involvement of the Energy and Chemical Workers Union (ECWU) at the "drafting" stage of the regulation might have shifted the outcome further towards one position or the other (environmentalist or corporate management objectives). Union representation on the sectoral technical committees, moreover, would be a valuable source of information about the use and potential dangers of toxic substances. Nevertheless, it seems that neither the citizens' groups nor the union itself made a case for union participation in the technical committees. The equation "industry = management" went unchallenged.

TABLE 4
REPRESENTATION OF SOCIAL ACTORS IN GOVERNMENT REVIEW PROCESSES FOR ENVIRONMENTAL LEGISLATION

Government Process	Private Sector Management	Labour	Environmental/ Citizens	Academics	Private Consultants
Neilson Task Force on Program Review, Study Team to review DOE (1985)	Team leader (Stelco) (2)	CLC (1)	(1)	(1)	(1)
Neilson Task Force Review of Natural Resources, Study Team	(3)	(1)	none	(1)	(2)
MISA Public Review (Ont.MOE) (Briefs submitted to MOE)	(19)	none	(9)	(2)	none
MISA Advisory Committee membership (appointed by Bradley)	one per sector, as required	none	(2)	(3)	(3)
Joint Technical Committees for each industrial sector to be regulated Under MISA	representation but members unspecified	none	admitted after lobbying, nos. unspecified	(3)	(3)
Canadian Environmental Protection Act Review (briefs submitted to DOE	(76)	(6)	(71)	N/A	N/A
National Task Force on Environment and Economy (membership)	Chair, from Dow Chemical (6)	none	(2)	(1)	none
Review Board Workshop on the GLWQA (participants)	(3)	(2)	(8)	(6)	none
Review Board Public Hearings on GLWQA (presentations)	(1)	(1)	(9)	(3)	N/A
Lake Ontario Toxics Management Plan Consultation Workshop (participants)	(4)	(3)	(12)	(6)	(2+)

Moreover, the ECWU made no formal submission to the MOE, and did not participate in the efforts of the SCRICN to prepare a response. Table 4 shows how marginal labour representation has been in government consultation processes. In every case studied in part 2, the main polarization occurred between corporate management and environmentalists; the affected workforces were left out of the equation almost entirely.

Some initiatives had been taken by citizens' groups towards incorporating union concerns in their briefs to government. Mainly because of the involvement of CAW activists, the Windsor and District Clean Water Alliance and Windsor-Essex Water Quality Liaison Committee comments on MISA included such proposals. For example, the Clean Water Alliance recommended:

> Laws which parallel those covering worker reporting of violations in occupational health and safety practices should be developed so that employees are compelled to report suspected pollution problems and when they do so, are protected from retribution by employers.[17]

The Liaison Committee—whose chairperson was at the time the CAW's key environmental activist—made a similar proposal in its report on MISA to the Mayor and City Council of Windsor.[18]

A few employees of the chemical companies (along with CAW representatives from Windsor) did attend the network's meetings, and may have influenced the inclusion in the SCRICN brief of the recommendation concerning protection for "whistle-blowers." However, the chemical workers, while providing valuable expertise to the citizens' groups, did not officially represent any level of the ECWU. Nor were they acting as liaisons with the union, but solely as concerned citizens. While they were not opposed by ECWU officials in Sarnia, there were no attempts by the union to back them up, or to endorse their efforts. Indeed, some union officials seemed to view these individuals' activities as verging on the fanatical.[19] The strategic positioning of the ECWU leadership vis-à-vis the environmental movement is examined in detail in chapters 10 and 11.

NOTES

1. M. Keating, "Great Lakes Cleanup accord will widen pollution search," *The Globe and Mail,* November 19, 1987, p. 2.
2. Mark Winfield and John Swaigen, "Water," in David Estrin and John Swaigen, eds., *Environment on Trial: A Guide to Ontario Environmental Law and Policy,* 3rd ed. (Toronto: Emond Montgomery Publications, 1993), p. 546.
3. See the Ontario Ministry of the Environment reports: *MISA Issues Resolution Process: Background* (Toronto: MOE, February 1990); *MISA Issues Resolution Process: Issue Resolution Committee Reports* (Toronto: MOE, June 1990); *MISA—Issue Resolution Process—Final Report* (Toronto: MOE, September 1991).
4. 1986 and 1990 amendments to the Environmental Protection Act significantly increased fines for both first and second convictions. For section 14 offences (section 14 makes it an offence for a person to discharge a contaminant into the natural environment that causes or is likely to cause an adverse effect), maximum fines for individuals increased from $10,000 per day to $25,000 and up to one year in jail. Corporations may be fined up to $200,000 per day and $400,000 for subsequent convictions. See Estrin and Swaigen, *Environment on Trial,* p. 455; and David Hunter and Michael W. Bader, Q.C., "The defence begins the day the discharge occurs—environmental prosecutions in Ontario," in The Canadian Institute, *The Fundamentals of Environmental Law and Regulation* (Toronto: The Canadian Institute, 1994), p. 37.
5. James Bradley, foreword to the *MISA White Paper, Municipal-Industrial Strategy of Abatement (MISA). A Policy and Program Statement of the Government of Ontario on Controlling Municipal and Industrial Discharges into Surface Waters* (Toronto: MOE, June 1986), p. ii.

6. MOE, *The Public Review of the MISA White Paper* and the MOE's Response to It (Toronto: MOE, January 1987), p. 8.
7. Ibid., p. 13.
8. Ibid., p. 49.
9. Although the struggle to democratize and to eliminate gender bias from science and technology is too immense a topic to be treated in this work, it is the subject of a growing literature. See, for example: Stanley Aronowitz's *Science as Power: Discourse and Ideology in Modern Society* (Minneapolis, MN: Univ. of Minnesota Press, 1988); Evelyn Fox Keller, *Reflections on Gender and Science* (New Haven, CT: Yale Univ. Press, 1985); Sandra Harding, *The Science Question and Feminism* (Ithaca, NY: Cornell Univ. Press, 1986); S. Harding and Jean F. O'Barr, eds., *Sex and Scientific Inquiry* (Chicago, IL: Univ. of Chicago Press, 1985); and the 1989 Massey Lecture by Canadian metallurgist Ursula Franklin (*The Real World of Technology*. Toronto: CBC Enterprises, 1990).
10 MOE, *The Public Review of the MISA White Paper*, p. 55.
11. Comments of R. Robinson, Assistant Deputy Minister, Environmental Protection Service, Environment Canada, House of Commons Special Committee on Regulatory Reform, *Minutes of Proceedings*, issue no. 6 (September 24, 1980), pp. 6-7, quoted by Schrecker in "Resisting Regulation," p. 10.
12. Winfield and Swaigen, "Water," *Environment on Trial*, p. 546.
13. Subsequent events, like the MOE's handling of the Kimberly-Clark case, have confirmed that such fears were not unfounded. Seven charges were laid against the company under the Ontario Water Resources Act, between April 1, 1981 and March 31, 1982. The government won convictions on all; Kimberly-Clark was fined $8,500. The Kimberly-Clark pulp mill in Terrace Bay, on Lake Superior, was given a ministerial order in 1982 to reduce its effluents to meet the "fish-kill standard" by October 1986. The company argued that it would have to close the mill, laying off 1,600 workers, and made no effort to implement the required changes. Kimberly-Clark claimed that a clean-up would require a $10 to $15 million expenditure on a settling lagoon and treatment system. Its 1985 reported profit from Canadian operations was $10.5 million; its reported U.S. profit was $267 million. Pollution Probe researched the company's financial situation in 1985, and found that the Canadian subsidiary had spent $14 million in 1983 to expand a Huntsville mill, $20 million in 1984 to expand a St. Hyacinthe mill, $10.9 million for a new boiler at Terrace Bay and $13 million for another expansion at St. Hyacinthe in 1985. Its 1985 sales revenues were $701.5 million. Thus the $10.5 million profit figure for 1985 probably reflected the amount set aside for shareholders after investment decisions were made. By 1986, increased public concern about dioxin contamination by pulp and paper mills, and, in Ontario, the Liberal Government's promise to defend the environment and its introduction of the MISA, made it difficult for the government to ignore Kimberly-Clark's noncompliance.

In January 1987 Environment Minister Bradley said he would issue a pollution control order requiring Kimberly-Clark to clean up its emissions immediately. The company then said that it could not meet these requirements so soon, and that it required government financial assistance. The alternative was a plant closure. Premier Peterson decided to take the decision out of the hands of the Environment Ministry and created a team of five provincial deputy ministers to come up with a plan acceptable to Kimberly-Clark. The government gave the company a three-year extension on the toxicity order. It did not demand any quid pro quo in the form of a guarantee that Kimberly-Clark would not simply continue to produce as usual, and then close the plant down after three years (the company was claiming that the plant was unprofitable). The environmental reporter for the *Toronto Star* had suggested that the government subsidize the clean-up in return for equity in the mill. Kimberly-Clark's president, Jack Lavallet, told the press: "What we're announcing is the continued survival of the mill." In May 1988 the company said it would build a $25 million secondary treatment lagoon and spend $6.7 million within the plant to reduce toxic discharges. In addition, the use of chlorine in the bleaching process would be reduced. See Pollution Probe news release, dated September 26, 1986; MOE, Legal Services Branch, *Prosecution Activity Reports*; Andrew Cohen, "The Politics of Pollution," *The Financial Post*, February 26, 1987, p. 17; reports in *The Globe and Mail*, January 26, 1987, p. B1, January 31, 1987, April 12, 1988, and May 13, 1988; reports in the *Toronto Star*, January 25, 1987, November 24, 1986.

The Ontario Municipal-Industrial Strategy for Abatement 85

A Guelph University biologist who conducted research on fish caught near the mill from 1989-91 reported that the company's pollution abatement did not appear to be working. (Martin Mittelstaedt, "Cleanup program fails in Lake Superior," *The Globe and Mail,* January 22, 1991, p. A4.)

In August of 1991, Kimberly-Clark pressured the NDP government of Ontario, Ontario Hydro, and the Canadian Paperworkers Union (CPU) to assist in financing a workers' buyout scheme of what one reporter called "a decrepit paper mill" in the one-company town of Kapuskasing, 800 kilometres north of Toronto. (Thomas Walkom, "Rae couldn't afford to let mill town fail," *Toronto Star*, August 14, 1991. See also: Bob Brent and Paula Todd, "Kapuskasing paper workers lose jobs or pay but mill saved," *Toronto Star*, August 15, 1991.) The same month, two native bands initiated a $1.3 billion lawsuit against the Kimberly-Clark Spruce Falls Power and Paper Co. and the Government of Ontario for sixty years of pollution in northern rivers.

14. St. Clair River International Citizens' Network, "Submission to the Ministry of the Environment on the MISA White Paper," September 1986. Copy in author's possession.
15. Windsor and District Clean Water Alliance, "Comment on the Municipal-Industrial Strategy for Abatement," September 12, 1986, p. 1. Copy in author's possession.
16. At a meeting of the SCRICN, September 22, 1986, one woman suggested that the Cancer Society be invited to participate in an upcoming public hearing on Great Lakes water quality. This would help make the important link between private industrial practices and health consequences for the general population.
17. Windsor and District Clean Water Alliance, "Comment on the Municipal-Industrial Strategy for Abatement," September 12, 1986, p.4.
18. Liaison Committee, "Comments on the Ontario Ministry of the Environment's Municipal-industrial Strategy for Abatement," August 28, 1986, p. 4. Copy in author's possession.
19. Interviews with union representatives in Sarnia, December 1986, May 1988.

[6]

The Great Lakes Water Quality Agreement Review

INTRODUCTION

The governments of Canada and the United States signed the Great Lakes Water Quality Agreement (GLWQA) in 1972, when public environmental consciousness was at a peak in North America. Water quality in the Great Lakes basin had visibly deteriorated due to eutrophication. (Phosphorus discharges stimulate algae growth, making the lakes incapable of supporting many fish species.) Lake Erie had been declared "dead." Considerable progress was made in reducing the nutrients discharged from municipal sewage treatment plants (STPs), but by the mid-1970s, concern was shifting toward the less visible problem of toxic chemical pollution. Thus, the 1978 GLWQA adopted an ecosystem approach to environmental protection and set a goal of zero discharge of persistent toxic substances.

The International Joint Commission (IJC) is responsible for monitoring progress under the Agreement. It is composed of six commissioners, three appointed by the United States and three by the Canadian government. A Water Quality Board (WQB), a Science Advisory Board, and a regional office (located in Windsor, Ontario) were created under the 1972 and 1978 Agreements. The 1978 Agreement required the United States and Canadian governments to review the Agreement after the IJC's third biennial report. This report was completed in March 1987. The agency responsible for overseeing implementation of the Agreement in Canada is the Review Board for the Canada-Ontario Agreement Respecting Great Lakes Water Quality, comprising representatives of the Canadian and Ontario governments. The Review Board was to advise the Canadian and Ontario governments on the 1987 process to amend or renegotiate the international agreement.

Environmental organisations saw the review period as an opportunity to mobilize public opinion on both sides of the border in support of the ecosystem and zero-discharge objectives of the Agreement. A 1985 report of the WQB had identified forty-two "areas of concern" (AOCs) in the Basin, and eight Great Lakes states, Ontario, and the two federal governments had committed themselves to "remedial action plans" (RAPs) to clean up these areas. Environmental groups wanted the review process to make public officials accountable to Basin communities regarding the implementation of the Agreement's objectives, including the RAP procedures and mandates. Moreover, they were concerned that there would be pressures to weaken the 1978 Agreement coming from the Reagan and Mulroney Governments. Given these goals, environmentalists were disappointed by the governments' and the IJC's apparent lack of interest in initiating a meaningful public consultation process. As late as February 1987, no such plans had been announced. (The Agreement was to be renewed by the end of 1987.) There had been only one opportunity for public input—at an IJC biennial meeting in Kingston in 1985. So the Great Lakes United (GLU) organisation (encompassing approximately 200 organisations from all over the Basin) decided to organise "Citizens' Hearings on Great Lakes Water

The Great Lakes Water Quality Agreement Review 87

Pollution," which were scheduled at nineteen locations around the Basin. Most of the locations were "areas of concern." These hearings were held between July 10 and October 30, 1986, and a report, called *Unfulfilled Promises: A Citizens' Review of the International Great Lakes Water Quality Agreement* was prepared and circulated by GLU's Water Quality Task Force in February 1987. The presentations made at these hearings provide valuable insights into the perceptions of citizens' groups regarding the causes of their areas' pollution problems, their own priorities, and the means to achieve these.

Perhaps as a result of the criticisms raised by the GLU hearings, the Review Board initiated its own—much more limited—public consultation process in June 1987. This involved: (i) an invitation to interested parties to submit written comments to the Board; (ii) a workshop with invited participants, held in Burlington, July 16-17, and; (iii) three public meetings, held in Kingston, Windsor, and Sault Ste. Marie from September 16-18. The Review Board then prepared its positions. The Protocol Amending the 1978 Great Lakes Water Quality Agreement was signed on November 18, 1987, by Canadian environment minister Tom McMillan, and the Administrator of the United States Environmental Protection Agency (EPA), Lee Thomas. Presentations made to the Review Board hearings were summarized in a document prepared by the Canadian Environmental Law Research Foundation (December 1987). A summary of the discussion at the Burlington workshop on the GLWQA was published by Environment Canada and the Ontario MOE. These documents and additional material are examined in order to distill from them the key themes presented by the citizens' groups and other participants.

THE GREAT LAKES UNITED CITIZENS' HEARINGS

The Task Force reported that over 1,200 people attended the hearings, and 382 of these made presentations. The most striking aspect of the representation—particularly in contrast to the government-sponsored workshop's participants—was the virtual absence of corporate management. (See table 5). The only large firm that sent a spokesperson to a GLU hearing was Dow Chemical Company of Canada. The hearing was in Sarnia, and Dow had been particularly concerned to defend and improve its public image since the August 1985 "blob" incident (discussed in detail in chapter 11). The Lambton Industrial Society also sent a spokesperson to the Sarnia hearing.

Even labour organisations were, for once, better represented (six United Auto Workers of America (UAW) locals, one Canadian Auto Workers (CAW) local, and the Windsor and District Labour Council). There were approximately 130 environmental and citizens' groups represented. Their concerns were shared and supported by various researchers associated with universities or institutes (twenty-six), by some elected officials, by other non-governmental organisations such as the League of Women Voters (whose members made twelve presentations), and by outdoor sports clubs (twelve). It was also evident that government departments at the state, provincial, and federal levels, felt compelled to defend and explain their progress in implementing the Agreement. About seventy-three United States officials and elected representatives from various levels of government testified before GLU's Task Force. From Canadian jurisdictions, there were thirteen federal and provincial officials, and eleven spokespersons from municipalities. Thirty-seven individuals also testified, most voicing concerns for environmental and human health in their areas.

It was evident at the Sarnia hearing that the Dow spokesperson, Steven Bolt, expected a hostile reception by the audience. (Dow managers had earlier experienced a rough ride when they spoke at a public meeting in Wallaceburg, following the media reporting of the Blob.) His speech provoked angry responses from a number of people—including two

TABLE 5
PARTICIPATION IN GLWQA PUBLIC CONSULTATION PROCESSES
(NUMBER OF PRESENTATIONS/PARTICIPANTS)

Category of Participant	GLU Hearings	Review Board Workshop	Review Board Hearings
U.S. environmental orgs. and citizens' groups	95	—	3+
US government and elected officials	73	1	—
Academics/Researchers	26	6	3
Citizens of U.S.	24	—	1
Canadian Citizens Groups	22	1	4
Canadian Environmental organizations	13	7	2+
Citizens of Canada	13	—	4
Canadian federal and provincial governments	7	17**	—
Canadian politicians or parties	12	—	3
League of Women Voters (U.S.)	12	—	1
Canadian municipal officials	11	3	—
U.S. Sports Clubs	11	—	1
Canadian Sports Clubs	1	1	—
Labour (US)	6	—	—
Labour (Canada)	2	2	1
Health authorities	7	3	—
Native Bands	6	—	—
Small firms	4*	—	—
Chambers of Commerce	2	—	1
Large Firms/Industry Assocs.	2	3	—
Others	23	—	2
TOTALS	382	44	25

* These appear to be small firms in the camping and sports supplies market.
** Includes the federal departement of health and welfare, which is also counted under "health authorities."
+ These figures include Great Lakes United, which is a binational organization.

SOURCE: GLU, *A Citizens' Review of the International Great Lakes Water Quality Agreement*; Review Board, *Summary of Discussion at the Workshop on the Great Lakes Water Quality Agreement*; MOE and DOE, *Public Meetings on the Review of the 1978 GLWQA*.

Dow employees, who repudiated both the assurances and the facts provided by their employer.[1] Perhaps because they did not anticipate a "fair hearing" at events organised by an influential environmental organisation, the companies stayed away. It was unlikely that their public relations managers would succeed in generating sympathy for the companies' position. Moreover, they might well be asked embarrassing questions—before public witnesses and the media—by the expert panels assembled by GLU. Clearly, this was not a milieu favoured by management for making their "responsible corporate citizen" case.

Corporate management prefer controlled tripartite situations where they can negotiate with government officials directly, and out of the public eye. Such an environment was provided, for example, by the Review Board's workshop for invited participants. The Canadian Chemical Producers' Association (CCPA), Canadian Manufacturers' Association (CMA), and the Canadian Pulp and Paper Association (CPPA) sent representatives to this event. Here, the conditions for influencing policy, without taking public relations risks, were far better: no media were present; about half the participants were representatives of various levels of government; and the environmental and labour representatives were relatively known entities. Moreover, the summary of the working sessions did not attribute any positions to particular participants. Industry representatives could feel free to state their concerns without fear of being publicly labelled self-interested. For example, "certain participants" repeatedly argued against the goal of "virtual elimination of toxic discharges," or "zero discharges," saying it is "impractical and unachievable." These participants, though not identified, very likely included the representatives of the CCPA, the CMA, and the CPPA.[2] By contrast, the citizens' groups which participated in the GLU hearings wanted to address as broad a public audience as possible, and they wanted all the media attention they could get.

The GLU Task Force report concluded that there is a widespread consensus among citizens' groups that "industry continues to fail to protect the environment." Many identify the profit motive as "the basic reason behind not being able to trust industry to protect the environment." This view was evident, for example, among the Wallaceburg and other groups downstream of Sarnia. They claimed that St. Clair County has the highest cancer rate in Michigan. They demanded zero discharge, and the compliance of companies regardless of the price. Janice Gunning of Mt. Clemens, Michigan, a spokesperson for the SCRICN, stated: "We want aggressive prosecution of polluters; we want polluting to become very unprofitable. Pollution must stop now."[3]

But the conclusion that capitalism is necessarily incompatible with environmental goals is not obvious to many of these citizen and environmental activists. Their proposals for dealing with private polluters can be surprisingly radical in the extent to which they challenge capital's traditional rights to make production and investment decisions. In addition, they often imply that firms will have to accept smaller profit margins, as a result of regulations to be enforced by governments. However, such demands may be accommodated within social democratic discourse; only in radical ecology or eco-socialist circles is transition towards non-capitalist modes of production and consumption being proposed. This does not diminish the importance of the perceptions of the mainstream of the citizens' movement, insofar as they form the basis for a more radical critique of capitalism. All the citizens' groups accept, to some extent, the existence of a conflict between their goals and those of the industrial polluters. Their members hold different views, however, about the changes necessary to resolve this conflict. The common ground is a widely generalized set of demands having to do with placing social priorities above those of capital accumulation and with the democratization of decision making. These are advocated both by those for whom they constitute steps in a more radical, long-term agenda, and by those who are merely seeking renegotiated terms for capitalist accumulation.

With this in mind, I summarize some of these perspectives under the following themes: environmental and health priorities versus profit; democratization of the State; a "people's State"; and natural resources as a collective trust.

ENVIRONMENTAL AND HEALTH PRIORITIES VERSUS PROFIT

Many of the speakers at the GLU hearings urged the Canadian government not to reopen the Agreement for negotiation. They were afraid that the Reagan and Mulroney administrations (being enamoured of the virtues of unrestrained private enterprise) would take the opportunity to weaken it. As a result, the GLU Task Force recommended that the Agreement not be renegotiated, but supported amendments which would broaden and reassert its mandate (e.g., to include the St. Lawrence River in the IJC's jurisdiction).

The GLU report concluded that: "The public also insists that industry accept the public's right to have input into corporate decisions affecting pollution." Numerous demands were made for restrictions of management's rights to produce environmentally harmful products, to use polluting technology, or to discharge their effluents at public cost. Among these were:

1. stricter requirements for pre-testing of new chemicals;
2. banning deep-well injection of wastes;
3. requiring industry to "change production processes to minimize the use of hazardous materials";
4. regulations to force companies to reduce, reuse, and eliminate hazardous wastes before the waste leaves the plants, before they will be licensed to operate (Cornwall hearing);[4]
5. timetables to force polluters to reduce their releases of persistent toxic substances to zero (Greenpeace, Chicago hearing).

Despite such proposals, environmentalists tended to fall back on public spending as a solution to pollution problems. For example, GLU recommended that the federal, provincial, and municipal levels of government get together to fund the revamping of municipal sewer systems around the Basin, and criticised the federal government for refusing to contribute. Alternatively, they could have demanded that the companies pay for pre-treatment plants for their effluents, that all industrial discharges to municipal sewers be capped after a certain date, and that companies help pay for sewer remediation, in repayment for the years of free dumping they have enjoyed at taxpayers' expense.

Another view of capitalist society offered by some citizens focused on consumption norms. The general proposal was that "consumers must demand products that result in less environmental degradation." A clergyman who spoke at the Sarnia citizens' hearing argued: "We as the consuming public need to stop using these chemicals in and around our homes. As long as we demand them, they will be produced and we are reaping the whirlwind of our greed."[5] A speaker at the Toronto citizens' hearing said:

> We must come to understand our personal and immediate responsibility for the state of our world and provide solutions. Our chosen lifestyle, our consumer practices all impact our environment and directly lead to polluted water, air and land. We must consciously accept our responsibility for such situations and consciously change our lives to protect our environment.[6]

In a discussion about the purposes and goals of citizens' groups, Kristina Lee of the Wallaceburg Clean Water Committee emphasized the responsibility of individuals to educate themselves about the consequences of their lifestyle choices.

> I think we are so busy throwing stones at industry, that in our own back yards we are not doing what we [should]. I know that a lot of [environmental activists] get upset with this [approach]... O.K., starting with household things, people will flush things down the toilet and think nothing of it; will put all those chemicals in the cupboard, and then the garbage... [It goes] to the dump. To me, I am just as guilty as the industries... Look at the saran wrap and styrofoam that I buy. I am the consumer...industry makes more of it. So how can I blame the industry, when I'm the one who buys the product? That's the philosophy that I look at.[7]

This type of argument has two possible directions. On one hand, it can begin with the assumption that capitalism's drives toward ever-increasing production, and the commodification of every sphere of social existence, are at the root of the consumer's dilemma. We do have, as individuals, some choice regarding what and how much we consume. However, capitalists—through their control over investment and production decisions, and their means of structuring mass consumption norms, are able to greatly mould and constrict our choices as individual consumers. The struggle to change the choices offered, therefore, must be a collective one, and one which addresses the nature of control over production decisions. Thus, for example, when the Greenpeace spokesperson at the Sarnia hearing denied the need for many of the chemicals produced, he was raising questions about why they are produced, and why consumers are led to believe they are "essential to a good quality of life." In other words, he located the problem at the point of production—of control over production.[8]

Kristina Lee's argument, however, began with different assumptions. As she was aware, her emphasis is challenged by other environmentalists, who take a more militant line with industrial polluters. Lee placed primary responsibility for the production of environmentally harmful goods in the realm of the consumer. She drew an analogy with food products:

> I don't know [enough] about the things in my cleaning cupboard. And I've been in this business for a while. I feel, that in order for our society to really understand, we have to have the same concept about chemicals that we do about nutrition. I don't feed my kids junk food...Why can't I do the same thing with the chemicals I use? That's the kind of philosophy that I think we have to have in terms of the environment...
>
> Now, just because I [don't] buy potato chips doesn't mean I'm going to put the potato chips people out of business, but I think, to use nutrition as an example, look at how—since the 1960s and 1970s—the companies...are looking at "no salt added," "no sugar added." I mean, they're really getting into the business of nutrition. Eventually, if the public becomes as educated about the chemicals as we are about nutrition...the companies are then going to have little [labels] saying: "This is not environmentally hazardous." They're going to start advertising that ... I think that's where the education comes in. It's a far-off thing, but that's what I'd like to achieve...[9]

But as her analysis in other respects showed, Lee knew that neither nutritional nor environmental labelling are sufficient solutions to health problems or resource exploitation. She agreed that the nutrition problem has not been resolved. The growth in the consumption of fast foods with high fat and sugar contents has been dramatic in North America. Obesity, anorexia, bulimia, dieting obsession, and various other eating disorders are rampant. Many people cannot afford to buy enough nutritious food, while others throw out mounds of food waste. These problems cannot be resolved without addressing the nature of agricultural production processes (chemical-intensive vs.

organic, scale, etc.), or the food processing industry, which are linked to the ownership of the means of food production, the nature of the distribution system, the nature of work, unemployment, and so on. Nor can governmental regulation be fully relied upon to protect public health from the profit-motivated objectives of the food and pharmaceutical industries.

DEMOCRATIZATION OF DECISION MAKING

Democratization is generally seen as the first step, or necessary precondition, to asserting environmental and health priorities over those of the private sector and bureaucrats. Thus, the GLU report observed that "public access to information and opportunities to be involved in decision-making are basic rights." The citizens' groups made innumerable criticisms of governments' commitments to public information and participation. These were described, for example, as "woefully inadequate and grossly under-funded." The GLU Task Force recommended that "all governments and the IJC provide full and timely disclosures of information."[10]

It was pointed out at the GLU hearings (and also the Review Board hearings) that the Water Quality Board (WQB) members have a conflict of interest when it comes to evaluating the progress of the Agreement. "There is a built-in bias and an incentive not to be openly critical of the shortcomings of the agencies they are employed by."[11] Many organisations recommended that representatives of non-governmental environmental and public interest groups be appointed to the WQB in order to balance the interests represented. The IJC was also advised to set up a "citizens' advisory board," made up entirely of non-government, citizen representatives, to "hold public hearings, issue reports, and make recommendations to the IJC."[12] In addition, the IJC was urged to open its board meetings to the public, and to release all reports to the public.

THE DEMAND FOR A "PEOPLE'S" STATE

Certain arguments of the citizens' groups imply not only that the State should be less biased towards the interests of the private sector, i.e., that the State should be more "fair," or "neutral," but that the State should be more popular in its orientation. The citizens' groups' conception of democracy is that the State should consistently act in the interests of the general welfare of "the people," and not primarily in defence of the interests of the private sector. The problem, obviously, is to what extent these groups view the two functions as being in conflict. Here again, there are contending perspectives within the environmental movement. In general, certain demands which seem to represent a broad consensus do imply a deepening *popular* role for the State. Resistance to such pressures by the private sector and by State agencies has the effect of radicalizing the citizens' interpretation of the conflict.

Citizens' and environmental groups have repeatedly demanded public funding for research that will, ultimately, benefit the "general welfare" priorities of health and environmental protection. They want such spending to be made a priority over other areas of spending, which are seen to benefit primarily the private sector. They also want the State to assume the role of guardian more effectively, either by doing its own research on the public's behalf, or by compelling the private sector to prove that new products are environmentally safe before permitting companies to produce and market such products. A member of the Grand Calumet River Task Force complained that, as things now stand, the EPA (US) places the burden on citizens to prove harmful effects.[13] A Michigan State Representative told the GLU hearings: "for every environmental lobbyist, there are about 15 lobbyists for private industry." These groups also want more accountability of government agencies to the public. One of the recommendations emerging from the

GLU hearings, for example, was that Congress and Parliament should hold annual hearings on the implementation of the GLWQA.

A strongly voiced demand is that the government should stop protecting private industry by suppressing information and not prosecuting offenders. At the Sarnia hearing, a DOW employee recounted a series of incidents in which he had reported pollution violations to the local MOE office, only to be stonewalled, and even reported to his employer. Members of the two Wallaceburg groups, interviewed in May 1988, expressed suspicion of the governments' "closeness" to private firms. Joseph Cummins, a plant scientist at the University of Western Ontario, and known for his environmental activism and work with Greenpeace, listed in a brief to the Review Board cases where critical reports had been withheld from the public for up to five years. Among these was a survey of point sources of chemical pollution in the St. Clair River, made by the MOE and Environment Canada in 1979 and 1980, but not released until September 1985. Although this survey had found toxic pollutants at levels high enough to warrant serious concern, no new abatement measures were ordered. Nor did the IJC reports of 1982, 1983, or 1985, refer to these data. Instead, they said that a joint study between the MOE and Environment Canada was ongoing. Cummins claims that: "In fact, the 1979-80 [study] was the only study of priority organics at point discharges that was undertaken. The failure of the IJC to demand publication of that study during the years that they published repeated reports of "improving" water quality may have seriously compromised Canadian representatives of that important commission."[14] Cummins gave other examples of government withholding of information which would have focused public attention on specific private polluters: a study of lead emissions from the Ethyl Corp. of Canada plant (Corunna), completed before 1985, but still not released as of 1987; an MOE study of hexachlorobenzene pollution near Algonac, Michigan, completed "recently," but not released; the concealment of discharges of a dangerous by-product of a fertilizer manufacturer in Corunna (beginning in 1985), until "public disclosure" in August 1987.[15]

A member of the Citizens Coalition for Clean Water, Wallaceburg, expressed the anger and frustration of citizens who are denied access to information which crucially concerns their welfare.

> Right now, if there's a big spill in Chemical Valley, it's bad enough for them to shut our water service down, as they have done, on three occasions. You know who quits drinking the water? The Mayor and the water commissioner. Nobody else knows about it... They don't tell nobody. If it wasn't for Greenpeace, we would never have known about the Blob.[16]

The citizens of Wallaceburg were livid when they found out that government officials responsible for the environment had known for years about the toxic chemicals in their waterways, but had decided not to act—not to enforce their own laws—and thereby had colluded with the polluters. The anger of the citizens toward the State was immense. This was a betrayal of the public interest, and meant that the State was out of control and could not be relied on in any sense to protect them.

Sarah Miller, a member of the citizens' group Stop Contaminating our Waterfront, Toronto, told the GLU Task Force that although the federal, provincial, and municipal governments had had a report documenting pollution violations at the Leslie Street Spit for three years, they had not released it to the public. The Environment Canada report showed that over 50 percent of the material dumped at the Spit in 1983 exceeded government regulations for acceptable contamination levels. The report was released to the public a month after the Toronto GLU hearing.[17]

The assumption that "government = elected representatives = accountability to citizens" has been eroded, and in some cases has crumbled altogether. The GLU report pointed out that people understand the motives behind private capital's behaviour (profit), but that they feel betrayed by the State which was supposed to be their guardian: "Indeed, the public is generally more hostile towards government than towards industry when they express their concerns about water quality. They feel let down because *the government's job is to protect the public.*"

Some activists have concluded that citizens have to construct their own, "dual power" structures for pressuring both polluters and the State. This path was suggested by Greenpeace's proposal of an Environmental Control Commission to oversee MISA. A "people's power" strategy is also implied in statements such as: "The environment has become too important to leave to governments."[18]

RESOURCES ARE SOCIAL PROPERTY

A very prevalent theme in the arguments of environmentalists is that we should, as a society, view natural resources and the environment as if we were their trustees; we have use of them in the present, but they belong also to future generations. Many citizen activists explain their involvement in terms of an obligation to their children, or to children in general. Moreover, they challenge the right of private companies to pollute an environment, and to plunder resources, which, in their view, belong to society as a whole. Firms may have temporary licences to exploit the environment, but these licences are conditional, and it is the broader society which is entitled to determine and to enforce these conditions. These—as we saw in the section dealing with the opposition between environmental and profit priorities—may extend to telling companies what they can produce, how, and in what quantities, and (in regard to exports) to whom they may sell.

Judith White, representing the Lake St. Clair Advisory Committee at the GLU citizens' hearing in Sarnia, described the river and lake as a "soup" from which the surrounding communities draw sustenance. Although the "soup" belongs to the citizens, it is being contaminated by polluters:

> Consider: poisons belched into the air, poisons sluicing overland and poisons gushing from pipes, much of this quite legal, and all of it landing in our water. Ironic because the very people who do it, or permit it, or tolerate it, or mutely accept it—and that is most of us—would be grievously repulsed at having to share a stranger's fork. And yet we drink. Suffer another of my poor analogies. Would you permit me to spit in your soup?... In truth we must learn to perceive all manner of toxic discharge as a personal violation and a personal threat.[19]

Kristina Lee, of the Wallaceburg Clean Water Committee, described the private sector's approach to environmental use as short-sighted, and contrasted it to the environmentalists' sense of long-term responsibility to preserve the planet.

> We shouldn't be looking only seven or ten years down the road. What about 500, 1,000 years from now? Let's hope the human species is going to be around in the next ten generations! I've never heard a company [talk about the long term] when they say "Oh, there's no environmental impact..."[20]

This view is expressed as well by the native peoples affected by industrial capitalist development. The Walpole Island First Nation representative argued at the GLU hearing in Sarnia:

> We are realizing that both non-native and native people have something to share and learn from each other. You are in a position to offer scientific and technical expertise to measure the changes to our Mother Earth that we cannot see. We are

offering to you a spiritual understanding of the wholeness, the oneness of our living earth. She takes good care of us, we want to take good care of her.[21]

LABOUR PARTICIPATION IN THE GLWQA REVIEW

Labour representation at the GLWQA hearings organised by GLU was more grass-roots than in the other processes we have examined so far. Although there were only eight union presentations made to the Task Force, seven of these were made by local environment committees, and one by the Windsor and District Labour Council. Nevertheless, union presentations amounted to only eight out of 382, and there were no labour representatives on the Task Force itself, although at least thirty-six of GLU's 200 member groups were union organisations.[22] It also seems apparent that labour was the "weak link" as the hearings moved from one toxic hot spot to another. First, union participation was concentrated in Michigan, and to a lesser degree in Buffalo, NY, and Ohio. Only three Canadian organisations made statements. Two of these were CAW locals. The third, the Windsor and District Labour Council, was represented by its president—the Vice President of CAW local 444 in Windsor. So only one industrial sector was represented. Yet the worst industrial polluters included coal-burning and petrochemical plants, pulp and paper mills, and others whose workers took no part in the hearings. The poor representation of union organisations raises the question: did GLU consistently inform union organisations about the hearings and invite them to testify?[23]

In many places, there were no labour representatives at all. For example, in Gary, Indiana, where the steel industry is a major polluter, the Steelworkers were absent. So when the GLU report claims that "the message...came through...that the perceived schism between industry and the environment must be replaced by the recognition that economic development and environmental quality go hand in hand," the questions arise: Who put this view forward? Is it coming from the unions? Is it getting to the unions? Is "the message" backed up by an environmentalist effort to involve labour in its agenda for reform?

A hearing was held in Grand Rapids, Michigan, not far from White Lake, where, in the late 1970s, labour organisations backed Hooker Chemical against citizens demanding a halt to the production of the highly toxic pesticide, C-56.[24] At Sarnia—heart of the petrochemical industry—there was no declaration of support for the objectives of the GLWQA from the ECWU, from the Labour Council, nor from any other labour organisation. In Windsor, no one from the UAW (Detroit) came to speak against the Detroit Incinerator's construction without state-of-the-art pollution technology (see chapter 13). Although the Task Force reported that "labour leaders from Milwaukee, Grand Rapids, Windsor, Cleveland, Toronto, and Buffalo stressed that this seeming contradiction [between jobs and the environment] is based on a short-term, narrow perspective," these assertions generally lacked any reference to concrete alternatives. Those I was able to obtain amounted to the usual rhetorical denunciation of "bad" capitalists or negligent governments. The trouble is, the contradiction is not "seeming" but real, given the logic of capitalism; the problem is whether or not environmentalists or unions are going to tackle it with specific economic analyses and proposals, and whether these will be articulated to one another by shared principles.

A second reason to question the superficial treatment of labour participation has to do with its assumptions about who these leaders represented. Interview work with union officials and attendance at various multipartite meetings indicate that the union representatives who appear at such events are generally detached from the rank-and-file, insofar as this base is uninformed and alienated from the activities sponsored by its executive leadership. As the GLU citizens' hearings were the process most likely to attract local-level union involvement (contrasted, for example, with more geographically centralized and more formal governmental or legislative hearings), the turn-out must be seen as disappointing, and evidence of the very great gap between labour and environmental organisations. The recommendations which emerged from the hearings also reflect the inadequacy of both union contributions, and environmentalists' and citizens' attention to the issue of building alliances with labour. The report contained virtually no economic analysis or specific proposals to bridge the labour-environmentalist divide.

At the Review Board-sponsored workshop, there were only two labour representatives out of a total forty-four participants. Again, the CAW was represented by the president of its Local 444 (Windsor-Chrysler) environmental committee, Rick Coronado. (Coronado would also later present the only labour brief to the Review Board when it held its public hearings on the GLWQA.) The Ontario Federation of Labour (OFL) representative, Duncan MacDonald, attended as a member of the OFL's Energy, Conservation and Pollution Control Committee—the same committee which is supposed to have played such an influential role in the Environmental Contaminants Act Amendments Consultative Committee, but disappeared during the CEPA debate. It is worth noting that the OFL did not participate in the citizens' hearings organised by GLU, but did send a representative to the government-sponsored "multi-partite" workshop. Such multipartite forums have been the preferred context of OFL and Canadian Labour Congress work, as CLC National Representative David Bennett stated with regard to the Environmental Contaminants Act and Canadian Environmental Protection Act review processes.

There is very little in the summaries of the workshop or the Review Board hearings to indicate that strong arguments were made for "sustainable development" planning for the different industrial sectors. Discussion focused on environmental quality goals and regulations, but not on costs and who would pay. The assumption of all parties seems to have been that governments will pay for whatever costs companies cannot be persuaded to pay (without adverse consequences for employment and investment). This social democratic perspective was also found to be characteristic of union officials interviewed in the 1986 to 1988 period (see parts 3 and 4).

NOTES

1. Bolt argued that the situation is actually getting better. The problem is one of perception: increasingly sophisticated testing methods are allowing scientists to detect ever lower traces of toxic substances in the environment. Thus, it is our improved technology that is "frightening us to death," rather than the presence of the chemicals. In response to this, a Dow employee and part-time biologist angrily told the audience that the St. Clair River is "a toilet bowl," and that the facts are good cause to be frightened to death (author's notes).
2. See Review Board of the Canada-Ontario Agreement respecting Great Lakes Water Quality, *Summary of Discussion at the Workshop on the Great Lakes Water Quality Agreement* (July 16-17, Burlington, Ont.), prepared by the Canadian Environmental Law Research Foundation, December 1987, pp. 10, 14.
3. Janice Gunning, quoted in Great Lakes United, *Unfulfilled Promises: A Citizens' Review of the International Great Lakes Water Quality Agreement* (Buffalo, NY: GLU Water Quality Task Force, February 1987).
4. Citizens of the Cornwall area, and members of the Akwesasne Mohawk Reserve bordering New York, Ontario, and Québec, have particularly urgent reasons for making these demands. In the 1980s Québec industries were discharging more than 100,000 metric tonnes of waste containing oils, greases, heavy metals, and carcinogenic chemicals into the St. Lawrence each year. Reynolds Aluminum poured 300 pounds of fluoride per hour out of its smokestacks until required to install filters. The fluoride weakened the bones of Mohawk cattle and killed vegetation and cattle. A 1991

report stated that children on the Akwesasne Reserve were suffering from flouride poisoning. (André Picard, "Mohawks forecast pollution disaster," *The Globe and Mail*, July 15, 1991, p. A4.) Five hazardous waste dumps on ALCOA's plant site, and two on Reynolds' property are the suspected sources of toxic chemicals in the fish, birds, and wildlife of the area. The fat of one snapping turtle contained 835 ppm of PCBs, 600 ppt of dioxins and 4,900 ppt of furans.

The General Motors foundry on the New York side is a dump for PCBs, at such high concentrations that they can be smelled from the river. Samples from a 200-pound Lake Sturgeon netted from the St. Lawrence by native fishers were found to contain 3.41 ppm of PCBs in its meat, 7.95 ppm of PCBs in its eggs, and 10.2 ppm of PCBs in its liver. It also had 167 ppt of 2,3,7,8-TCDF— the highest levels of dibenzofurans the Canadian Department of National Health and Welfare labs had ever seen. By the time the test results were sent to the fishers their families had eaten the sturgeon. This story is related in the GLU Task Force report, *Unfulfilled Promises*, pp. 19-20. The Akwesasne Mohawks were suing Reynolds, General Motors, a Domtar paper mill, and a C-I-L chemical factory in Cornwall for damages. See "St. Lawrence ranked among most polluted waterways," *The Globe and Mail*, August 1, 1988, p. A3. Alcan operations on the Saguenay River (which drains into the St. Lawrence) are believed to be responsible for the toxins that are poisoning the Beluga whale. The Belugas are dying of bladder cancer, hepatitis, pulmonary fibrosis and other diseases. At least a dozen of the remaining 500 are dying every year. See *The Detroit Metro Times*, June 8-14, 1988, pp. 10-12; and "St. Lawrence ranked among the most polluted waterways," *The Globe and Mail*, August 1, 1988.

By November 1991, some progress had been made on reducing the tonnes of toxic liquid waste poured daily into the St. Lawrence by some 3,900 industrial plants and by municipal sewers. However, the technical director of the St. Lawrence (federal-provincial) Action Team acknowledged that the 90-percent reduction target could take another decade, and "blamed delays in the regulation of pulp-and-paper mill effluent and the reluctance of some of the river's top polluters to co-operate." See André Picard, "Top polluters slow St. Lawrence cleanup," *The Globe and Mail*, November 22, 1991.

5. Reverend Thomas Schoenherr, quoted in *Unfulfilled Promises*, p. 44.
6. Annie Booth, quoted in *Unfulfilled Promises*, p. 44.
7. Kristina Lee, interviewed in Wallaceburg, May 5, 1988.
8. Scott Shibley of Greenpeace argued that the chemical and petrochemical products produced in the Valley are not essential to a good quality of life—that their very production is incompatible with an "ecosystem approach" to preserving the environment. (Author's notes.)
9, Interview with Kristina Lee, Wallaceburg, May 5, 1988.
10. The focal point of these criticisms was the remedial action programmes, which are examined in the next chapter.
11. *Unfulfilled Promises*, p. 7.
12. Ibid., p. 7. See also presentations from Adkin, Samis, and Sewell to the Review Board, in DOE and MOE, *Public Meetings on the Review of the 1978 Great Lakes Water Quality Agreement*. A Report submitted to the Review Board for the Canada-Ontario Agreement Respecting Great Lakes Water Quality. Prepared by the Canadian Environmental Law Research Foundation (Toronto: December 1987).
13. *Unfulfilled Promises*, p. 42.
14. "A submission for the International Joint Commission regarding improvements to the Great Lakes Water Quality Agreement of 1978," in DOE/MOE, *Public Meetings on the Review of the 1978 GLWQA*, Appendix 7. Cummins presented this brief at the Windsor meeting sponsored by the Review Board.
15. The last example refers to the MOE's permit to C-I-L to dump waste from its phosphate fertilizer operation into the St. Clair River. An October 1985 permit to C-I-L to dump effluent was based on an "emergency appeal" from C-I-L; no public review was held. Apparently C-I-L threatened immediate closure if required to spend money on an alternative to dumping. The plant was subsequently "decommissioned" (shut down); however, existing effluents were to be discharged at a rate of 8 million gallons per day for the next fifteen years. Its effluent contained ammonia, phosphates, radioactive by-products (uranium and radium), and dinitrotoluene (DNT) (a chemical by-product of explosives manufacture). Once citizens' groups became aware

of this discharging, C-I-L attempted to reassure them that the process was both environmentally acceptable and necessary (no alternative)—and that C-I-L was treating effluent before discharging. Apparently, C-I-L was invited to attend a public meeting in Wallaceburg in August 1987, but declined. According to Kristina Lee of the Wallaceburg Clean Water Committee, C-I-L executives were "scared out of their minds" by the reception they anticipated, following meetings between Dow Chemical and other chemical companies, and angry citizens in Wallaceburg and Sombra. (Kris Lee, interview by author,Wallaceburg, Ont., May 3, 1988.) SCRICN members went on a tour of C-I-L; the company wanted to "prepare" and "inform" concerned citizens about the dumping process. The SCRICN decided to write a letter to the MOE expressing its concerns: the Ontario Government has no legal guidelines for DNT emissions; and the government monitoring station is located upstream of C-I-L. In addition, the two environmental groups in Wallaceburg, City officials, the NDP candidate, and the Walpole Island First Nation sent letters to the MOE regarding C-I-L. (Author's notes from a SCRICN meeting, July 22, 1987, Windsor, Ont.) This incident also illustrates the differences between the two Wallaceburg groups, which is examined later. The Citizens' Coalition for Clean Water, which declines to participate in the SCRICN, did not go on the C-I-L tour; it will not accept any tours or other invitations from the chemical valley firms.

16. Don Laprise, interview by author, Wallaceburg, Ont., May 7, 1988.
17. *Unfulfilled Promises*, p. 34.
18. Annie Booth, North York resident, at the Toronto GLU hearing; quoted in *Unfulfilled Promises*, p. 35.
19. Judith White's written brief to the GLU Water Quality Task Force, October 1986, p. 2. Copy in possession of the author.
20. Lee, interview by author in Wallaceburg, May 3, 1988.
21. Laurie Montour, representing 1,800 members of the Walpole Island First Nation, Sarnia, October 9, 1986. Quoted in *Unfulfilled Promises*, p. 30. The Montour and White briefs, among others, also raise the issue of the relationship between the popular groups and scientists, or "experts." This question is returned to in chapter 7.
22. Ibid. These included 32 UAW, two CAW, one United Transportation Union, and the Windsor and District Labour Council.
23. I wrote to one of the key organisers of the GLU hearings for information about GLU's contacts with labour, but received no reply.
24. See John J. Berger, *Restoring the Earth* (New York: Alfred A. Knopf, 1985), pp. 139-140. C-56 (hexachloro-cyclopentadiene) was a component of Mirex and Kepone, pesticides now banned.

[7]

Brush-fires of Democratization: The Remedial Action Plans

INTRODUCTION

The 1985 report of the Water Quality Board (WQB) (established under the Great Lakes Water Quality Agreement) recommended the development of Remedial Action Plans (RAPs) for the geographic Areas of Concern (AOCs) identified by the International Joint Commission (IJC). Since six of the forty-two AOCs are shared by two jurisdictions (Canada and the United States), this meant that forty-eight RAPs would be submitted to the IJC for approval. Although the initial deadline for completion of the RAPs was set for December 1986, this soon proved to be unrealistic. Few had been drafted by 1989, and the time-table for implementation extends to the end of century. The purposes of the RAPs, as described by the IJC, are to "identify specific measures necessary to control existing sources of pollution, abate environmental contamination already present, and restore beneficial uses."[1]

The RAPs are perhaps the most potentially "grass-roots"-oriented of government initiatives so far. Given their geographic and ecosystem frameworks, they could be vehicles for local and regional citizen involvement in long-term planning—not only for ecological objectives, but for their socioeconomic implications. Not surprisingly, then, the structures for public participation in the RAPs have been the focus of citizen and environmental group lobbying of the various jurisdictions. Corporate management has also recognized the potential of the RAPs and their public advisory or decision-making bodies to affect the conditions of their operations, and have lobbied hard for strategic positions. Union involvement varies according to the specific characteristics of labour organisation and culture in each AOC.

The organisational framework of the RAPs is bureaucratically rather complex. Figure 1 attempts to illustrate the relationships (advisory and authoritative) linking the public participation processes to the State agencies.

FORMATION OF THE RAP TEAMS AND PUBLIC ADVISORY COMMITTEES: WAR OF POSITION

As figure 1 suggests, specific criteria for public participation processes were not set out in the initial schema. By the fall of 1986, it had become apparent that considerable confusion and inconsistency existed regarding the structures for such involvement. Great Lakes United (GLU) pointed out in a memorandum to the WQB that public involvement had been encouraged and accommodated in only a handful of AOCs.[2] These included the Green Bay (Wisconsin), Grand Calumet (Gary, Indiana), and Toronto harbour RAPs. In the Green Bay process, while a Citizens' Advisory Committee (CAC) had been established, there were, from the point of view of citizens' groups, serious problems with its composition and structure.[3] In the Grand Calumet area, citizens' groups were successful in pushing for a clean-up plan and its implementation, but the plan itself was produced by the Chicago Region V office of the Environmental Protection Agency (EPA). In

FIGURE 1
REMEDIAL ACTION PLAN PROCESS, CANADIAN JURISDICTIONS

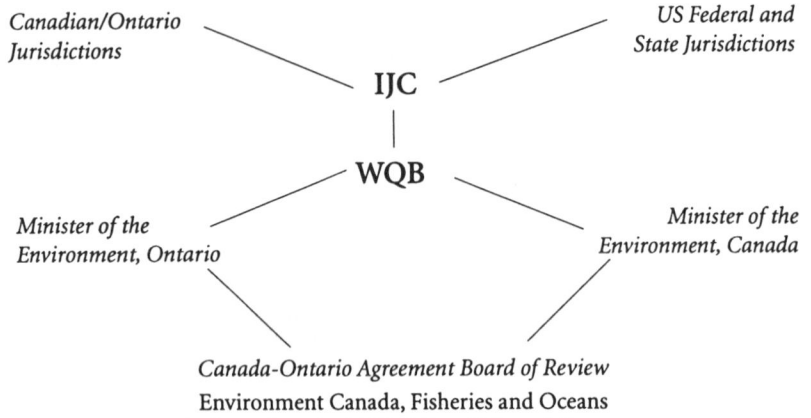

Canadian/Ontario Jurisdictions — IJC — US Federal and State Jurisdictions

IJC
|
WQB

Minister of the Environment, Ontario — WQB — Minister of the Environment, Canada

Canada-Ontario Agreement Board of Review
Environment Canada, Fisheries and Oceans
Agriculture Canada, MOE, Min. of Natural Resources,
Ontario Ministry of Agriculture and Food

Federal-Provincial RAP Steering Committee
To oversee and coordinate preparation of 17 RAPs, hire
consultants and manage budgets. Composed of: Water Resources
Branch, MOE; Operations Division, Intergovernmental and Strategic
Projects Division; Environment Canada and MOE communications
branches; other Environment Canada and MOE officials.

17 RAP Teams
Composed of government officials. To report to the Steering
Committee, develop RAPs, and oversee public participation.

Public Participation
Mode of public participation to be determined by each RAP team,
according to general criteria; may take the form of Public
Involvement Committees (subcommittees of the RAP officials),
hiring consultants, or Citizens or Public Advisory Committees
(having varying compositions), public hearings, newsletters, etc.

Toronto, where there already existed considerable municipal involvement in a waterfront clean-up, as well as environmental-citizens' expertise, various groups proposed to the Neighbourhoods Committee of City Council in October 1985 that "a special committee of concerned citizens groups and appropriate City staff be established to draft a RAP for the Toronto Waterfront." They wanted to be involved in the planning process directly, as decision makers. A working committee was created by the City Council to draw up a Waterfront Remediation Action Plan (WRAP) "through citizen input," working independently of the Ontario Ministry of the Environment (MOE) and Environment Canada (DOE), who were preparing their own plan.[4]

In these three cases, where significant public involvement had been achieved by the fall of 1986, it was evident that this involvement was still inadequate; indeed, its success was occurring despite, rather than because of, governmental policy. In other areas, complaints were being voiced by citizens and environmental groups about their exclusion from the crucial planning stage. Citizens' groups were not satisfied with the governments' framework for public participation, which was to let citizens review the plan once it was drafted. The Windsor and District Clean Water Alliance, for example, protested in October 1986 that:

> We are assured that the public will be informed, but only after the fact. Once the RAP programme has been drawn up the public will be invited to comment on its proposals. This is not good enough. What is at stake is our environment, our health, and that of future generations. And if the past is any indication, governments are not prepared to protect the public and exercise restraints on industrial and other polluters without significant public input and pressure to do so.[5]

The government officials in charge of the RAPs had made a clear separation of functions between the RAP teams, composed of MOE, DOE, and other government officials, and the public or citizens' advisory committees (PACs or CACs) or the "public involvement process." The RAP teams' mandate, according to these officials, was to first "inform the public" about environmental problems in the area, and then to draw up the remedial action plan, which would involve primarily technical expertise. The plan would then be submitted for approval or amendment to the public review process. In almost every case, as table 6 shows, the RAP teams hired private consultants to manage relations between themselves and the citizens' groups. The "public involvement process" was viewed as a separate aspect of the development of the plan—one appended in various fashions to the "core (technical) task" of the government experts for political reasons. The process initially envisaged, therefore, allowed no place for citizens to define the terms of reference or the scope of the RAPs, and certainly excluded any discussion of long-term local development goals relating to socioeconomic interests.[6]

For many of the citizens' groups, more meaningful participation would mean the dissolution of the barrier between the technical/bureaucratic authorities and the local population, allowing the citizens to contribute their knowledge and to influence the scope and priorities of the RAP. The exclusion of the citizens' representatives from seats on the RAP teams themselves (in all but one case) has been viewed as a decision by the MOE and other authorities to maintain ultimate control over the development of the RAPs.

When in addition to this exclusion on "technical" grounds, citizen activists saw the integration of corporate representatives and company scientists into the MISA technical committees, and their substantial representation in the PACs of the RAPs, they became increasingly critical of the "unpopular" or pro-private sector bias in the process.[7] The Ohio Environmental Council wrote to the Director of the Ohio EPA:

Table 6
Public Participation Process in 17 AOCs

Remedial Action Plan Area of Concern	1	1a	2	3	4	4a	5	6	7	8	9
Bay of Quinte[a]	X	X	X		X				X	X	
Collingwood Harbour[b]	X	X								X	X
Detroit River[a]	X		X								
Hamilton Harbour[c]	X				X		X			X	X
Jackfish Bay[b]	X	X								X	
Niagara River[d]		X			X	X			X	X	X
Nipigon Bay[b]	X	X								X	
Peninsula Harbour[b]	X	X								X	
Port Hope[b]	X	X						X		X*	
Spanish River[b]	X				X	X				X	
St. Clair River[a]		X	X	X						X	
St. Lawrence River[a]	X	X			X					X	X**
St. Marys River[b]	X	X				X				X	X***
Thunder Bay[b]	X	X								X	
Toronto Harbour			X				X				
Severn Sound[c]		X			X					X	X

[a] developments as of September 1988
[b] developments as of October 1988
[c] developments as of January 1989
[d] developments as of December 1988
[e] developments as of November 1988

Legend
1. stakeholders' groups contacted by newsletter, RAP team or government-hired consultant
1a. consultant hired to liaise with public
2. citizens' Advisory Committee
3. citizens' representatives on the RAP team
4. funding for citizens' representatives
4a. no funding for citizens' groups for education will be provided
5. autonomous citizens' / environmental RAP
6. citizens' group principal liaison with the public
7. union involvement
8. public meetings / open house (no regular consultation, no consultant)
9. citizens' public advisory committee will be formed.

SOURCE: RAP Newsletters; WQB, *1987 Report on Great Lakes Water Quality*, Appendix A; personal communications with RAP co-ordinators and citizens' groups.

* RAP dominated by the Atomic Energy Company of Canada Ltd. (AECL)
** Mohawks "very" involved
*** Unions were contacted, but with little response

Brush-fires of Democratization

During the past several months the Ohio EPA released draft Remedial Action Plans (RAPs) for the Cuyahoga and Black river areas of concern (AOCs). Both were prepared by USEPA [United States Environmental Protection Agency] contractors without meaningful public participation. In their current condition, these draft RAPs are of limited usefulness and reflect poorly on Ohio EPA which must develop final RAPs from them.[8]

Similar concerns were expressed by members of the Windsor and District Clean Water Alliance and the Great Lakes Institute regarding the Michigan Department of Natural Resources' reluctance to allow public involvement in the drafting of the Detroit River RAP.[9] Citizens' groups in Windsor would also find themselves struggling for access to decision-making bodies in the preparation of the Canadian jurisdictions' Detroit River RAP.

When the WQB held a forum for RAP co-ordinators (government officials) in Windsor, October 20-21, 1986, GLU took the opportunity to push for specific commitments regarding public participation. GLU's director made a presentation to the co-ordinators,[10] in which he proposed that:

1. Citizens' Advisory Committees (CACs) be developed for each RAP, to "assist the agency and agency consultants in the writing, finalization, and implementation" of the RAPs;
2. CACs should have representation from the general public, the private sector, and local government;
3. criteria for the creation of these committees should be drafted by the WQB in order to make the terms of public access to the RAP processes more consistent;
4. the CACs should be able to make recommendations for immediate clean-up activities for known contamination sources, while awaiting completion of various studies;
5. there be criteria for built-in review mechanisms, such as annual public hearings on RAP implementation;
6. the CACs be involved in the budgetary process.

These proposals were not generally adopted, however. Governmental authorities replied that the structures for public participation should remain "flexible," given the differences among the AOCs.[11] In a meeting between public representatives and the Michigan Department of Natural Resources (DNR) held in the fall of 1986, the DNR reiterated its intention not to involve the public until "after the RAP has been fully designed." Moreover, the public representatives concluded that "public participation seems to be regarded as a process of 'informing' rather than 'involving' the public."[12] The latter observation reflects the experience of citizens' groups throughout the Basin in dealing with government agencies unaccustomed to sharing their decision-making authority with popular organisations.

Because of public pressure to create Citizens' Advisory Committees, or at least some general criteria for citizen involvement in the drawing-up and implementation of the RAPs, the Ontario MOE did make an attempt to come up with "an overall approach to public consultation" in the Ontario jurisdiction.[13] In March 1987 the MOE produced a draft document proposing a "generic" public consultation approach and procedures to be followed for each RAP. It was to be discussed with Environment Canada officials before being finalized.[14] The stages it set out may be summarized as follows:

1. Inform/educate the public; identify "stakeholders" (brochures, media presentations, open houses/workshops, speaking engagements by government officials);
2. Identify public's priorities regarding water use goals (workshops with stakeholders: key industries, municipalities, local citizens' groups; a consultant could be hired to "facilitate dialogue"; public meetings, solicitation of written briefs, surveys, etc.);

3. RAP team drafts plans to attain goals identified in stage 2, then presents them to the public for review. Revisions to the plan will then be made (workshops, etc.);
4. Preparation of the RAP document by the RAP team and its circulation to stakeholders for review;
5. Preparation of final RAP;
6. Continuing consultation with the public during implementation (unspecified).

The problem with this carefully laid-out series of steps was that, in reality, the "inform the public"/"listen to the public" functions could not be so neatly controlled and separated. Clearly the Ministry wanted to retain its prerogative to actually author the RAP documents—taking into consideration, of course, public "input." But the public in many cases pressed for a more active role, and could not see why they should not be permitted to help draft the plans directly, working with the government scientists and officials.[15] Some groups were asking for positions on the RAP teams themselves—not merely on CACs.

One reason for the MOE's reluctance might be the government's anticipation of conflict among "stakeholders." "Public" included "industry," municipal governments, and citizens' groups, among others. How would the Ministry establish the relative weights of "stakeholder" representation in the RAPs? How could it avoid accusations of bias from the private sector, on one hand, and from citizens' groups, on the other? (This conflict indeed developed in the St. Clair River Binational Public Advisory Committee, as described below.) By permitting all "public" actors an advisory role only, the government could control the pace and direction of regulatory change and enforcement. The more radical environmental and citizens' groups could not point to industry representation on RAP teams as proof of bias towards the private sector's interests. (Industry would, nevertheless, be well-represented in the consultation process, through the MISA technical committees.)

The MOE had another concern as well: it saw the RAPs—like the MISA and other programmes—as dependent for their success on private sector co-operation—especially given the inadequacy of budget procurements for government implementation of the RAPs. The MOE and Environment Canada had no desire to alienate the private sector by radically shifting the balance of representation within decision-making processes in favour of the citizens' groups.

In a word, the MOE tried to maintain its role as ultimate arbiter of these "interests," while maintaining the appearance of commitment to enhanced public participation. Indeed, at the IJC's second forum for governmental RAP co-ordinators, participants said that one important function of public participation is to "establish government credibility—trust."[16] The attempt at a "generic" approach to public participation soon broke down, as a result of citizens' group pressures, on one hand, and the Ministry's attempts to preserve its credibility as an impartial arbiter of interests, on the other. Some of the RAP experiences are examined in greater detail in this section.[17]

By the fall of 1987, long after the date that the RAPs were to have been written and submitted to the WQB for review and approval, the "public participation" battle was, if anything, growing more intense and more bitter. GLU and many citizens' groups were advocating the creation of advisory committees, but they had been established in only four of the forty-two AOCs (Green Bay, Wisconsin; Rouge River, Michigan; Buffalo River, NY; Oswego River, NY).[18] Loud complaints were heard from citizens at the Review Board's hearings in Ontario in September, concerning the denial of funding, and exclusion from RAP planning.[19] GLU organised a workshop for citizens' groups on "Citizen Action in Developing Cleanup Plans for the forty-two Great Lakes Toxic Hot-spots" in September 1987. The timing of the GLU workshop may have been related to the IJC's scheduling of its second forum for RAP co-ordinators, to be held in Toledo, November 19-20. Citizens' groups were urged to lobby the governmental officials to adopt their proposals for public

Brush-fires of Democratization

participation. Seventy organisers attended the GLU-sponsored workshop. Sharing their experiences, they concluded that they were all having to "fight on a case-by-case basis for full inclusion in the RAP planning process,"[20] and that "despite governmental platitudes about public involvement in RAPs, most jurisdictions are still treating the public as an afterthought—a final hoop that the finished plan must be passed through."[21] Sarah Miller, of the Canadian Environmental Law Association (CELA) and GLU, and involved in the Toronto RAP, said: "With the exception of Hamilton Harbour, public involvement in RAP planning is not adequate. The Canadian and Ontario governments' efforts are perceived as fragmented, disorganised, slow and lacking continuity."

The citizens urged the IJC to adopt a set of principles regarding public participation which it would use to evaluate the RAPs. They also demanded adequate funding from governments to make effective citizens' participation possible. By fall 1987, in the State of New York, public participation funding had been allocated for only one of the State's six RAPs. In Ohio—with the exception of the Maumee River RAP—only one staff person had been assigned to work on the State's four RAPs. There had been no hearings and no public meetings. In Wisconsin, Governor Thompson vetoed funding for the Milwaukee and Sheboygan RAPs. No money had been appropriated to implement the new provisions of the US Clean Water Act (which would encompass the RAPs). No funding for public participation had been forthcoming in the Grand Calumet AOC, or in Oswego, NY. In Canada, this had been the experience of groups in the areas of Cornwall, Bay of Quinte, and Niagara River, among others.[22]

Since by September 1987, RAP teams in all forty-two AOCs had submitted status reports to the IJC, including an environmental assessment, a statement of progress, and a time-table for studies and completion,[23] it was obvious that the public participation aspects of the RAPs were lagging far behind the technical studies and decisions. Participants in the GLU workshop said that public advisory committees were being set up too late for their representatives to be involved in setting the goals and the timetables.[24] The "advisory" role of the public committees was also viewed as a problem. In some cases, the PAC's advice was being ignored. In addition, with timetables already set, there was a tendency for government agencies to try to rush through the public reviews of reports prepared for the RAP.

The GLU workshop drew up a number of recommendations regarding public participation for presentation to the IJC and to governmental authorities. They also decided to network more effectively. Initiating a newsletter to keep all the groups informed about developments in other areas, and requesting status reports on public participation in each RAP area, were two means proposed to improve communications among citizen activists.

Overview of Selected RAP Experiences

The MOE's preferred framework for public participation was the organisation of "stakeholders'" groups by a hired consultant. These groups would meet separately, and provide written input to the writers of the RAP (government officials).[25] In addition to this, the consultant might be required to organise public meetings where RAP team members provide information and hear various views about the plan. This was the set-up, for example for the Hamilton Harbour RAP.[26] The process outlined for many of the Ontario RAPs in the IJC's 1987 *Report on Great Lakes Water Quality*, "Appendix A" ("Progress in Developing Remedial Action Plans for Areas of Concern in the Great Lakes Basin"), typically included public meetings, perhaps the distribution of newsletters, and the hiring of a public involvement consultant (as described, for example, in the status reports for Collingwood Harbour, Penetang Bay to Sturgeon Bay, Spanish River, Wheatley Harbour,

Bay of Quinte, Peninsula Harbour, Jackfish Bay, Nipigon Bay, St. Lawrence River (near Cornwall), and Thunder Bay (Kaministikwia River)). In only a handful of AOCs were more intensive public participation processes initiated; these were the products of citizen groups' and environmentalists' pressures. Table 6 sketches the kinds of public participation programmes that had developed by the spring of 1988 in the seventeen Ontario/Canada areas of jurisdiction.[27]

The Detroit River RAP has been the site of a battle between citizens' groups and the two principal governmental authorities (MOE, Michigan DNR) over the nature and extent of public participation in the drafting and implementation of the plan. In December 1986, environmental activists on the Canadian side became concerned that the DNR was not going to allow or fund any citizens' participation in the RAP's writing, but would initiate a public review only when the plan had already been drafted.[28] In order to prevent the same thing happening on the Canadian side, they wrote to Minister Bradley, proposing that the Great Lakes Institute (GLI)—which had been at the hub of environmental issues locally for some time—be designated by the MOE to co-ordinate public participation.[29] In February 1987, Bradley replied that his ministry would be hiring a consultant to co-ordinate public participation, and that the GLI was welcome to tender an application. The GLI's proposal, submitted in May, emphasized the Institute's extensive interactions with government agencies, local businesses, other researchers, labour, and citizens' groups from Sarnia to Detroit.[30] Biologists at the Institute had carried out work on water quality in the St. Clair and Detroit river systems since 1982. In the procedures for consultants' reporting to government officials, the GLI proposed that its RAP organiser would participate in the RAP team meetings. An intensive programme of public participation was outlined, stretching from May 1987 to March 1988. The GLI submission had the backing of the Windsor and District Clean Water Alliance, the Windsor and Essex County Water Quality Liaison Committee (between the public and City Council), the Windsor and District Labour Council, and others.

However, before the end of the month, it was known that the MOE had awarded the public participation contract to a firm of consultants from Toronto, Michael Michalski Associates.[31] This decision was protested at a public meeting held May 27, by a representative of the Clean Water Alliance and the CAW 444 environmental committee:

> We do not understand how the MOE and the DOE can in effect bring in an outside group to start a process with the public that as we have stated already exists now. Clearly an outside consultant will have some difficulty in garnering public support for such an important project... We are very disturbed by the process that the MOE and the DOE have pursued in selecting a consulting group. Therefore, the Windsor and District Clean Water Alliance and affiliated groups such as the Canadian Auto Workers Environmental Committees and the Windsor and District Labour Council Environment Committee and the Environmental Health Committee will be seeking alternatives to the present situation and that will include a programme that is not inconsistent with the Toronto Waterfront Remedial Action Programme.
>
> We are shocked and disappointed at the chain of events that has cut off and stopped the very essence of community action and involvement.[32]

But of course the citizen and labour activists did have an understanding of why this decision had been made. It was the Great Lakes Institute's biologists who had first discovered evidence of the St. Clair River blob in 1984, and pressed for the release of test results from the MOE. The author of the GLI's proposal for the Detroit RAP, Catherine Alpaugh, had been the political analyst and public liaison for the Institute during the escalation of citizens' groups' activities in the Chemical Valley. She had been a high-profile media contact for the Institute during the blob story. In addition, she had worked with the Windsor and District Clean Water Alliance, had helped citizens' groups write critical responses to the draft MISA white paper, and had acted as the GLI representative in the St. Clair River International Citizens' Network. She was well known to public relations managers in the chemical companies, and to officials at the MOE, for her work as critic and organiser. Had the GLI been awarded the contract for the Detroit River RAP, Ms. Alpaugh would have been the co-ordinator, and liaison, between the MOE officials and the citizens' and other organisations. Both she and the Institute were identified by government officials as being "anti-industry."[33]

To this point, the various citizens', environmental, and other groups had been participating in "stakeholders'" meetings organised by the consultant for the Southeast Michigan Council of Governments (SEMCOG). As word spread that a consultant from Toronto had been given the job of organising public participation on the Canadian side, many people began to talk about doing what citizens had done in Toronto—that is, drawing up a plan independently of the MOE, working with municipal officials. (To add insult to injury, the Toronto consultants asked the GLI for its contact lists and other assistance, to initiate a public input programme.)

The new consultants organised a public meeting in Windsor on June 8, and took out some newspaper space to inform people about the RAP. At a meeting in Detroit in October, it was announced the RAP team would allow the formation of a binational public advisory committee (BPAC), composed of 20 representatives each from Canada and the US. Four members of the BPAC would liaise with the RAP team, beginning in January 1988.

The stakeholders' meetings held in May revealed some interesting differences between the expectations and objectives of "industry" and environmental groups. May 22 a meeting was held for "industry and shipping" representatives, including General Motors, General Chemical, Great Lakes Steel, Michigan Consolidated Gas Company, and the Windsor and District Chamber of Commerce. These representatives expressed "surprise that current problems exist," and questioned the credibility of the toxic hot spot label given to the AOCs.[34] They conceded that the waterfront land could be improved to make it more suitable for "redevelopment," but felt that the public did not appreciate how much money the companies had already spent on environmental concerns. They said that the press was misinformed and contributed to public misunderstanding about the seriousness of the problems. Moreover, they stressed that some environmental degradation was the necessary consequence of economic prosperity—the jobs and taxes the companies provide to local workers and governments.

> [P]eople are not aware of the amount that has been done by industries on both sides of the river (Example: Great Lakes Steel has spent 100 million to come into compliance; Windsor companies have spent millions also)…
>
> It is important that existing industries coexist with other uses. (Windsor, Detroit, Downriver areas). The region needs the jobs and the tax base that industries bring. 90-95% of the current industries use the river to their advantage and 70% of the industries on the river are dependent on it for transportation. Shoreline land uses are changing to office and residential. Public tax bases are largely from industry…
>
> The region can't ignore the benefits of commercial growth related to the river.[35]

A week later, a stakeholders' meeting was held with representatives of environmental and conservation organisations. These included the Grosse Isle Conservation Club, MI;

Grosse Isle Natural Resource Committee; UAW Conservation Department, Detroit; Sierra Club, MI; United Conservation Clubs; National Wildlife Federation, Mi.; East Michigan Environmental Action Council, Mi.; League of Women Voters; Great Lakes Institute; CAW Locals 1973 and 444; Windsor and District Clean Water Alliance; and Wayne County Bass Anglers Club. Interestingly, the labour representatives attended this meeting, and not the meeting for "industry" representatives, described above. They included: Rick Coronado, from CAW Local 444 (Chrysler); Gordon Taylor and Jack Ewart from CAW Local 1973 (GM); and Russ Gossman from the UAW's Conservation Department in Detroit. These participants' concerns about water quality were much more numerous and detailed. Points were made repeatedly concerning the need for more public participation in decision making. While the "industry" reps had talked about the need to *maintain* the "balance" of interests in the process, the environmental groups were arguing that balance had to be *established* by adding more citizens' weight.[36]

The public participation process also went somewhat awry for the MOE in the St. Clair River AOC. Although the government's status report on the RAP submitted to the IJC in April 1987 outlined the usual framework for public involvement (consultant, stakeholders, public meetings, public review of drafted RAP), by July the MOE had agreed to work with a bi-national Public Advisory Committee, and was considering a request from the SCRICN for representation on the RAP team itself.[37] The Ministry's response can probably be explained by two factors. First, the SCRICN had formed in response to an immediate health threat—chemical contamination of communities' water supply and of the food source for the native people at Walpole Island. The Network's members had been vocal lobbyists and were in a position to embarrass the Liberal Government if it did not show satisfactory progress in dealing with the chemical companies and utility corporations polluting the river. They had begun lobbying the MOE for a role in the RAP as early as October 1986.[38] The Chemical Valley had been the most important test of the Liberal Government's commitment to environmentalism from the outset. The stiffest opposition to the Spills Bill had come from the large chemical companies. The "blob" disaster of August 1985 had been one of the main impetuses behind the introduction of the MISA in 1986. The petrochemical sector was the first industrial sector targeted for regulation under the MISA. Moreover, because of past practice, the MOE's credibility as a defender of the public interest needed major restoration. Bradley acknowledged, not long after taking office, that officials in the ministry had been too close to industrial interests. In environmental circles it was common knowledge in 1986 that:

> Mr. Bradley faces serious internal problems in his ministry. It is no secret at Queen's Park that the Minister felt a number of long-time environment bureaucrats were giving polluters an easy ride. The Minister has clashed with his administrators, who say it is their job to run the personnel side of the department. The key post of communications director has been vacant for nearly a year and is not even listed in the latest government phone book.[39]

Second, the recent decision not to award the public participation contract for the Detroit River RAP to the Great Lakes Institute had seriously alienated citizens' groups and activists. If this situation worsened, or was reproduced in other areas, the government's credibility would be increasingly under attack. No doubt wishing to prevent a repetition of the Windsor fiasco, the MOE acceded rather readily to the proposals coming from the St. Clair River Network.

The SCRICN's requests were supported by Great Lakes United. In August 1987, GLU proposed that a CAC be created, with 25 to 35 members drawn from different constituencies. The CAC would specify goals for the RAP, recommend remedial actions, comment on who should pay for them, act as a liaison between the public and government agencies, and serve as a kind of watchdog, to hold governments and polluters accountable once the plan was implemented. In addition to the CAC, other public education activities would be planned.[40]

In September 1987 the governments announced the elements of their public participation programme for the RAP. It would include a binational public advisory committee (BPAC).[41] The governments also found a way to avoid the problem of private sector or citizen participation in the RAP team itself, and hence in the process of decision making rather than a merely advisory role. They decided that the BPAC members would choose from among themselves two members from each of Ontario and Michigan to sit on the RAP team. The nation cleavage neatly obscured the interest cleavage that such a selection would inevitably entail. So the struggle began for representation on the BPAC, for structures and procedures that would serve different interests, and for the plan's principles and specific measures.

The chemical industry's position was expressed by its representative, Ron Denning, of the Lambton Industrial Society:

> The last three years have seen, on both sides of the river, from Sarnia-Port Huron to Detroit, the formation of well over a dozen new groups involved in promoting both narrow and broad environmental issues. Umbrella organizations have formed as the process of citizen networking has been prompted using public funds. To be successful, the RAP process should provide an opportunity for genuinely concerned, nonaligned citizens to hear the facts, ask questions and create informed opinions on the St. Clair River. If we are to arrive at a proper consensus, no one sector of society, whether industrialists, environmental consultants, special interest groups, organized labour, local politicians, or even government officials can be allowed to dominate the process...
>
> When all is said and done, we that live here, too deserve a voice in the future of this area.[42]

When the BPAC was formed, it included forty-four members (see table 7). As the citizens' groups immediately noted, "industry" had eleven representatives on the Committee, compared to their six.

At the first meeting of the BPAC, April 13, 1988, conflicts emerged over the composition of the Council and its procedural rules—decisions which would affect the subsequent balance of power among interests represented. A labour-management split also became apparent. While the government and business representatives favoured the adoption of Roberts Rules of Order, members from the citizens groups were intimidated by the formality of these procedures and asked that "flexibility" be allowed, to encourage discussion. Roberts Rules were adopted, but a By-laws Committee was formed to make recommendations on procedures. Denning, of the Lambton Industrial Society, moved that the By-laws Committee consider a rule that a two-thirds majority be required to carry a motion. Denning's rule would make it impossible for the handful of environmentalists to push through a motion when industry representatives were absent. (The RAP team had proposed a formula for voting whereby action could be taken on an item by a majority of the number needed for a quorum [12], but without actually having a quorum of members present.) The two-thirds majority rule would also make it generally more difficult for motions to be passed, thus delaying action by the Council. Insofar as management representatives saw their role as primarily one of limiting public-relations damage to their firms, or successes for the environmentalists, i.e., a defensive position, they saw any rules

TABLE 7
ST. CLAIR RIVER RAP BPAC MEMBERSHIP, MAY 1988

Sector	U.S.	Canada	Total
Agriculture	1	1	2
Business & Industry	3	6	9
Citizens at large	3	2	5
Community groups	1[a]	—	1
Conservation & Environment	3	3	6
Health authorities	3	1[b]	4
labour[d]	—	1	1
Municipal	3	4	7
Native people	—	2[c]	2
State/Provincial	4	1	5
Tourism and Recreation	1	1	2
Totals	22	22	44

[a] Port Huron League of Women Voters
[b] Dr. Lucy Duncan, Lambton Medical Officer of Health
[c] Walpole Island Band and the Chippewa of Sarnia Band
[d] By September 1988, two more labour representatives had been added: Ron Tack, of the Chatham and District Labour Council, and Al Whitsitt of the UAW, Marysville, Michigan. (Information provided by J. A. Moore, co-ordinator, Detroit/St. Clair/St. Marys Rivers RAPs, September 23, 1988.)

which would slow down the work of the Council as advantageous.

Management representatives were obviously on guard for any development which might shift the balance of power in the Council in favour of the citizens' and environmental groups. When John Jackson of the SCRICN moved that one more item be added to the list of the BPAC's mandate—that it should advise the RAP team on the public involvement programme—industry representatives like Denning opposed. Although the suggestion was in keeping with the other tasks outlined in the mandate, and quite clearly an appropriate task for a public advisory council, Denning and others were primed to see anything emanating from Jackson as subversive of their interests. The ensuing debate was eye-opening for members of the citizens' groups. According to Kristina Lee of the Wallaceburg Clean Water Committee, the management reaction made her realize how worried the chemical companies were about the direction and influence of the new structures for "public participation."[43] Lee's motion that a representative from the Great Lakes Institute should be added to the Council was defeated. In what seems to have been a move to remove Jackson and to prevent CAW participation from Windsor, business representatives moved that no alternates should be accepted who come from anywhere but the Port Huron-Sarnia area. This motion was defeated.

The chemical company representatives also attempted to limit labour participation. Cal Douglas, a postal worker representing the Sarnia and District Labour Council, moved (seconded by Kristina Lee) that Rick Coronado be added to the BPAC as a labour representative. They argued that labour was under-represented. Coronado is well known in the region as an environmental activist, because of his leadership in the Windsor and District Clean Water Alliance, CAW Local 444 (Chrylser), and the Windsor and District Labour Council. This motion was opposed and defeated.[44]

Brush-fires of Democratization

According to Lee's description of the meeting, the tension between Cal Douglas (the sole labour representative) and the management representatives "could have been cut with a knife." The chemical company members became angry when Douglas referred to specific firms in the course of listing pollution problems in the Valley. This demonstration, once again, was enlightening to the citizens. Although still skeptical about the willingness of organised labour in Sarnia to side with the citizens' groups against chemical company employers, members like Lee were impressed by Douglas' aggressive stance at the meeting. At a subsequent meeting of the SCRICN (May 2, 1988) Douglas was described as a possible ally—a "brother of Rick."[45]

As we will see in chapter 11, while the SCRICN groups were trying to maintain a co-operative relationship with the chemical companies, and had attended meetings organised by industry associations (like the Lambton Industrial Society), the RAP experience presented them with their first encounter with the potential for labour support from Sarnia. They were cautious, but impressed by a strong pro-environment position from labour representatives. If this labour role continued, it might provide a counterforce to the strategy of co-optation of the companies. In any case, at the outset of the public consultation process, the citizens were already developing a clearer understanding of the dynamic they could expect within the Council. In particular, they were keenly aware of their representational disadvantage, and how important this imbalance was likely to be.

These lessons were also being learned in other areas. By the spring of 1989 the Citizens Advisory Committee for the Green Bay, Wisconsin, RAP had come to a number of conclusions about the process after two years of involvement. One participant argued for more clarity about real conflicts of interest between "community and industry interests." Providing a very apt description of the nature of the struggle, she advised citizens to obtain a voice in the selection of the committee that will *implement* the RAP:

> Insist on having input on committee selection. At least three outspoken, hard-headed environmental advocates should be appointed and should plan to work closely together; otherwise a strong potential exists for isolating and discrediting single environmental representatives. The industry, business and agency reps will "gang up" on them. Other interest groups should also be represented by strong RAP supporters, such as sportsmen and recreationists. But look out for hostile business leaders who also belong to the local duck or yacht club. They might be appointed to represent otherwise supportive groups but team up with industry representatives against RAP implementation. If this sounds like struggle, it's because *it is*. Sometimes it feels like guerrilla warfare.[46]

Guerrilla Citizens in the 1990s

In 1993 the Lake Michigan Federation conducted interviews with RAP participants to write a report on citizens' views of the process. The conclusions suggest that citizens' stamina and enthusiasm for the process were waning, largely because "in no RAP process has the public been fully integrated into the development of their cleanup plans." Moreover, the process had become too "technical," and "without adequate support, community members cannot effectively participate in necessary discussions... As a result, many lost interest in participating."[47]

With these conflicting agendas the RAPs for the AOCs were soon stalled in the trenches. Progress on the cleanups was proving extremely slow. John Jackson, then president of Great Lakes United, stated that "ten years after the Areas of Concern...were designated by the IJC in 1986, only one has been cleaned up."[48] Ambivalent commitments to the ecosystem and "zero discharge" goals on the part of the government agencies gave way to outright abandonment of the RAPs in the mid-1990s. Governments on all sides withdrew funding for the RAPs, cutting environmental budgets severely, and turning the programmes over to the citizens in the name of encouraging "local leadership" and "community control." The President of Great Lakes United had another view of the governments' intentions: "This shift has nothing to do with providing for local control. It is purely the product of trying to save money."[49] In 1995 the newly combined Ontario Ministry of the Environment and Energy (MOEE) announced that it would no longer financially support RAP public education activities. Surveying the state of the RAPs in the winter of 1995-96, Great Lakes United's field coordinator, Y-Lang Nguyen, reported:

> Most of the people who sit on the Public Advisory Committees are volunteers with limited time and resources who need government financial and technical support if their participation is to be effective. It is bitterly disappointing for many PAC members to see governments withdrawing support after all the work they have put into the process. Some are simply calling its quits, a terrible loss to community cleanup efforts.[50]

As for the goal of zero discharge, "governments on both sides of the border are increasingly relying on voluntary programs to reduce the emission of pollutants," despite evidence that "regulations are the overwhelming motivation of polluters in reducing their discharges."[51] The advances of anti-ecological, anti-egalitarian, neoliberalism in Canada have in the space of ten years rapidly driven back many of the gains made by the environmental, women's, and labour movements, among others. Citizen environmentalists were engaged by the mid-1990s in a "guerrilla warfare" whose lines were ever more sharply drawn in democratic/anti-democratic terms, and which more than ever demanded alliances with other social actors fighting for alternatives. In this conjuncture lies the potential for new coalitions, and these are indeed emerging in Ontario, in the form of green work and social justice alliances. These developments are discussed briefly in chapter 14.

NOTES

1. IJC, "Remedial Action Plans for Areas of Concern," (Windsor, Ont.: pamphlet, no date).
2. David Miller, Executive Director, GLU, memo to Great Lakes Administrators, Water Quality Board Members, and Remedial Action Plan Co-ordinator, October 14, 1988.
3. Rebecca Leighton, "Developing a Remedial Action Plan: The Green Bay Experience," *Great Lakes United*, Fall 1986.
4. Theresa Zanatta, "Toronto plans own clean-up," *Great Lakes United* (July 1986).
5. Rick Coronado, chairperson, "Public Participation: An Address to the Great Lakes United Citizens' Hearings on the GLWQA," University of Windsor, October 7, 1986, p. 3. Unpublished speech, in author's possession.
6. Most of the RAPs I have reviewed have more or less conformed to this process, at least initially. In some cases, citizens have been able to subject the RAP team's technical role to varying degrees of direction from the public advisory structures.
7. Sally Lerner observed in her study of "volunteer stewardship" around the Great Lakes Basin that what unites citizen initiatives is a perception that "there appears to be an increasingly explicit failure of political will in the State and corporate sectors to address the urgent protection and rehabilitation needs of the Basin" ("Environmental Constituency-Building: Local Initiatives and Volunteer Stewardship," in *Alternatives* vol. 13, no. 3 (September/October 1986), p. 55).

With regard to citizens' views of science, Donna Smyth prepared an excellent documentary for CBC Radio in 1985 based on interviews with citizen activists across the country. See "Finding Out—the Rise of Citizen Science," broadcast on "Ideas," January 8-22, 1985. An

Brush-fires of Democratization 113

alliance between scientific and professional experts and capitalist interests was identified by citizens involved in campaigns against spruce budworm spraying in Nova Scotia, toxic chemical pollution of the Niagara River, uranium development in Nova Scotia and Saskatchewan, nuclear power development in Ontario and New Brunswick, and by citizens fighting for compensation as a result of exposure to urea formaldehyde foam and phenoxy herbicide (containing 2-4-D and 2-4-5-D dioxins—also known as Agent Orange when it was used against the Vietnamese).

8. Letter from Stephen Sedam, Executive Director, Ohio Environmental Council, to Warren Tyler, Director, Ohio EPA, dated December 23, 1986. In possession of author.
9. See letter from Coronado (Windsor and District Clean Water Alliance), Haffner (Great Lakes Institute), and Alpaugh (GLI), to James Bradley, December 6, 1986. In possession of author.
10. IJC, WQB, "*Summary of the Forum for Remedial Action Plan Co-ordinators,*" Windsor, Ont., October 20-21, 1986, Appendix 3 (Windsor, Ont.: IJC, 1986).
11. See, for example, letter from the Director of Michigan's DNR to David Miller, of GLU, November 6, 1986. In possession of author.
12. See letter from Coronado, Haffner, and Alpaugh, to James Bradley, December 6, 1986.
13. Letter from James Bradley to Coronado, Haffner, and Alpaugh, February 5, 1987.
14. MOE, Intergovernmental Relations Office, "Public Consultation Process for Remedial Action Plans,"(Toronto: MOE, March 1987).
15. For example, the GLI staff person responsible for drawing up the Institute's proposal to act as a public participation co-ordinator for the Detroit River RAP (Canadian side) viewed the "stages" outlined by the MOE as essentially collapsible—not mutually exclusive or discrete. Written comments on the MOE document by M. C. Alpaugh, in author's possession.
16. IJC, Great Lakes Water Quality Board, *Summary of the Second Remedial Action Plan Forum*, Toledo, Ohio, November 19-20, 1987 (Windsor, Ont.: IJC, 1987), p. 8.
17. The RAP stories provide important insights into the ongoing struggles to democratize State structures, the relationships between private industry and the State, and the changes occurring within the citizens' movement. These ongoing struggles deserve a more thorough study than can be undertaken here.
18. GLU, "RAP Update"(Windsor, Ont.: GLU, September 1987).
19. The author attended the Kingston hearing, September 16, 1987. Citizens from the Bay of Quinte area protested that they had been denied funding necessary to enable them to participate in the RAP, and that their expertise and commitment to environmental clean-up of the Bay had been disregarded by government officials.
20. GLU, *Citizen Action in Developing Clean-up Plans for the 42 Great Lakes Toxic Hot-Spots*, Report from a Remedial Action Plan workshop for citizens and community leaders, Buffalo, NY, September 11-13, 1987 (Windsor, Ont.: GLU, 1987), p. 6.
21. Tim Eder, "Back up promises with funding workshop concludes," *Great Lakes United* (Fall 1987).
22. John P. Laue, "The Grand Cal," *Great Lakes United* (Fall 1986); GLU, *Citizen Action*, pp. 10-11, 15; and GLU, "Citizens RAP governments on clean-up plans," news release (Windsor, Ont.: GLU, November 10, 1987).
23. GLU, "RAP Update," September 1987.
24. GLU, *Citizen Action*, p. 7.
25. Managing the stakeholder groups separately has some important implications. Not bringing citizens' groups and private management representatives together in the same forum minimizes the exposure of the citizens to views which might radicalize their perceptions of private sector interests. It also reduces the opportunities for alliances among labour, citizens, and other "stakeholder" groups to form.
26. The Center for the Great Lakes, Chicago/The Centre for the Great Lakes Foundation, Toronto, "Fact Sheet: Hamilton Harbour, Ontario," September 9, 1987. In author's possession.
27. I wrote to each RAP co-ordinator requesting information about citizen and labour participation, composition of public advisory committees, and so on, and received responses from fourteen areas of concern.
28. Letter from Alpaugh, Coronado, and Haffner, to James Bradley, December 6, 1986.
29. Ibid.
30. Great Lakes Institute, "Co-ordination of the Public Participation Program for the Detroit River

Remedial Action Plan," Proposal to the Ontario MOE, submitted May 8, 1987. Obtained from the GLI in 1987; in author's possession.
31. Detroit RAP Newsletter, *Issue One*, published by the MOE and the DOE (Fall 1987), p. 2.
32. "Statement from the Windsor and District Clean Water Alliance to the Southeast Michigan Council of Governments and the Michigan Department of Natural Resources, MOE, and DOE," read by Rick Coronado at the Detroit River Water Quality Workshop, May 27, 1987. Copy in author's possession.
33. This was said to a member of the CWA who reported it to the GLI liaison.
34. Minutes of the May 22, 1987 meeting obtained from Dean Edwardson, Canadian co-ordinator, Detroit River RAP.
35. Ibid.
36. Minutes of May 27, 1987 meeting, provided by Dean Edwardson, Canadian co-ordinator, Detroit River RAP. In author's possession.
37. At a SCRICN meeting held July 22, 1987, and attended by the author, it was reported that the Network had sent a letter to McMillan and Bradley requesting: (*a*) membership on the RAP team; (*b*) formation of a CAC. The Ministry had responded favourably. At that meeting, members discussed how they would contribute to the RAP team, whom they would choose as their representatives, and how these individuals could be supported (child care) and funded for the trips to Toronto. The group chose two representatives for the RAP team, and two alternates. As three were women, and two of these had small children, child care was a necessary condition for their participation. An older woman in the group offered to look after the children when the mothers had to attend meetings.
38. At a meeting October 27, 1986 the SCRICN members agreed to send a letter to the governments urging them to get moving on the RAP for the St. Clair River. They also planned to hold a meeting with representatives of the Ontario and Michigan environmental ministries to make proposals in the presence of the media (author's notes).
39. Michael Keating, "Where there's smoke, polluters beware: cleaning up the environment is an Ontario priority," *The Globe and Mail*, August 9, 1986, p. A4.
40. Tim Eder, field co-ordinator for GLU, "A proposal for a citizens' advisory committee for the development of the St. Clair River Remedial Action Plan," August 17, 1987.
41. MOE/DOE, *St. Clair River RAP Newsletter* (September 1987).
42. Ron Denning, "Remedial Action Plan—it's up to all of us," *St. Clair River RAP Newsletter*, p. 2. (The slogan of the Lambton Industrial Society is "We Live Here Too!")
43. Kristina Lee, interview by author, Wallaceburg, Ont., May 3, 1988.
44. Unfortunately, members' votes are not recorded in the minutes. It would be interesting to know which way the government members voted on these motions.
45. Relations between the citizens' groups in the valley and unions are discussed in more detail in part 3. Douglas was replaced in the summer of 1989 by Paul Carter, a chemical worker, representing the Sarnia and District Labour Council.
46. Rebecca Leighton, "Lessons from Green Bay: How to Make a RAP Work," *Great Lakes United* (Spring 1989), p. 1.
47. Kathy Bero, "RAP Study: Tell Us What's Going On!," *Great Lakes United* (Winter 1993/94), p. 7.
48. John Jackson, "If Not RAPs, What?" in *Great Lakes United* (Winter 1995-96), p. 30.
49. Jackson outlined the government funding cuts to the RAPs in *Great Lakes United* (Summer 1995), p. 16. They included a 70-percent reduction by the end of fiscal year 1995-96 from the U.S. Environmental Protection Agency (below its 1994-95 year contribution); the elimination of funding from the State of Michigan; the concentration of all funding from the State of Wisconsin on only two AOCs; the reduction of the Minnesota staff for the St. Louis River RAP by half; and Environment Canada's nearly 30-percent budget cut over the next three years. In the spring of 1996, citizen environmentalists were further disheartened by the new Harris Conservative Government of Ontario's announcement of a 30-percent reduction in the budget of the Ministry of Environment and Energy (now merged). Staff numbers are expected to be cut by 40 percent. The executive director of Great Lakes United, Burkhard Mausberg, pointed out that the Harris government budget cut "comes on top of already devastating reductions in the Ministry's budget. The 1996-97 funding will be down a stunning 59 percent from the 1992-93

budget of $434 million." The budgets of the Ministry of Natural Resources and local conservation authorities were also to be cut by 29 and 70 percent respectively. Simultaneously, the Conservative Government of Ontario had moved rapidly to repeal various environmental acts, and had chosen not to renew the Intervenor Funding Project Act which allowed citizens to obtain funds to participate in public hearings. See "Ontario and environment: galloping backwards," *Great Lakes United*, vol. 10, no. 3 (Spring 1996), p. 2.

50. "Governments abandoning hot-spot cleanup plans," *Great Lakes United*, vol. 10, no. 2 (Winter 1995-96), p. 12.
51. Jackson, "RAPs: Will there be money for actual cleanup?" in *Great Lakes United*, vol. 9, no. 4 (Summer 1995), p. 16. In the same article Jackson cited figures from a report by KPMG Consulting, a Toronto consulting firm, which found that only 14 percent of firms surveyed said their motivation for reducing discharges was voluntary. A more detailed analysis is provided in Jackson's "The spread of 'regulatory voluntarism': Abandonment of the goal of zero discharge," in *Great Lakes United*, vol. 9, no. 2 (Fall 1994), p. 16.

PART III

CORPORATE UNIONISM AND SOCIAL MOVEMENTS:
THE ENERGY AND CHEMICAL WORKERS

[8]

The Political Economy and Culture of a Union: The Energy and Chemical Workers Union in the 1980s

INTRODUCTION

Political and economic conditions both determine, and are shaped by, the strategic perceptions and choices of social actors. In this chapter we examine the interactions between developments in the energy and petrochemical industry globally and in Canada, and the strategies adopted by employers, governments, and union leaders in their efforts to direct or respond to these changes. The origins of the ECWU within the North American labour movement, as well as within a sector of the economy dominated by large multinational firms and characterised by a capital-intensive production process, are among the factors which help to explain the particular orientations of chemical workers and their union representatives regarding management-labour relations, the appropriate social and political roles of unions, and alliances with other groups of workers or with non-union social actors.

The 1980s were a period of global restructuring within the energy and petrochemical industry, coinciding with a peak of public consciousness about toxic chemical pollution and demands for expanded environmental regulation of the industry. Union strategy is calculated in the context of such changing conditions: priorities are challenged and redefined or reasserted. Strategic choices are the products not only of interpretations of what is "possible" to achieve, but also of political-ideological struggles about the social objectives of unionism. How are the interests of defending wages and job security related to such concerns as egalitarianism (e.g., addressing wage differentials within the membership, including those based on gender or race), solidarity (with other groups of workers, with the unemployed, with other social struggles), improving the quality of life, defending nature and the rights of other species, and so on? The answers to these questions provide the outlines of what might broadly be called the prevailing "culture" of the union as compared to other unions. No culture is homogeneous, however, and there are significant differences of experience between men and women, whites and other racial groups, categories of workers, and between union leaders and rank-and-file workers. In the analysis of union responses to energy policy and to pollution issues in southern Ontario, an effort is made to identify the internal conflicts as well as the predominant tendencies in ECWU strategy.

Now that the ECWU has merged with the Communications Workers and the Paperworkers unions to become the Communications, Energy, and Paperworkers Union (CEP, 1992), the "culture" of the new amalgamated organisation will be the product of complex interdynamics which remain to be investigated. However, it may be expected that in the short term the particular cultures of each of the founding member organisations will remain relatively intact, given their rootedness in sectorally distinct memberships and industries. This study of the ECWU's positions may indeed provide important insights into the internal dynamics and strategic positions of the newly formed CEP.

Chemical and energy industry workers are at the heart of key sectors of the advanced capitalist economy. The ecological critique of consumerism, wasteful lifestyles, socially unnecessary and environmentally harmful production, and the effects of the multitude of chemicals which permeate our daily lives, has profound implications for these sectors. The industrial capitalism criticised by ecologists is virtually epitomized by the energy and chemical sectors. Even a partial list of environmental campaigns in Canada indicates how centrally the chemical industry concerns the movement (table 8). The positions taken by energy and chemical workers influence the outcomes of struggles between citizen-environmentalists and the owners of capital in these sectors. As the following chapters show, unions have played significant roles in regulatory processes—roles which have been largely overlooked in analyses of energy and environmental policy formation.

TABLE 8
CAMPAIGNS AFFECTING THE ENERGY AND PETROCHEMICAL INDUSTRY

- Conservation of non-renewable energy resources.
- Reduction of the production/consumption of plastics and foam products.
- Recycling, reuse of chemical products and of other products (which will reduce overall demand for chemical products).
- "Make the polluter pay" for the costs of environmental abatement technology, pollution clean-up, etc.
- Ban on the production of CFCs, many pesticides and fertilizers.
- Organic farming as an alternative to chemical-intensive (and capital intensive) agriculture.
- Changing the production processes of various industrial sectors to eliminate or reduce environmentally-harmful by-products, e.g., the campaign to make pulp and paper mills.
- Replace chlorine-bleaching of pulp with an oxygen process used in Sweden, to reduce dioxin effluent and residues in white paper products.
- Moratoria on nuclear power, uranium mining, and tritium and plutonium processing.
- Removal of lead from fuel.
- Reduction or elimination of automobile emissions.
- Ban on production of asbestos.
- Increased fines for companies which violate pollution laws.
- Legislation requiring testing of all new chemical products before they will be approved for marketing.
- Compensation for workers whose health has been harmed by exposure to chemicals.
- Elimination of chlorine from industrial production.

THE ECWU: ORIGINS, STRUCTURE AND MEMBERSHIP

The ECWU, formed as an autonomous Canadian union only in 1980, was—until its merger with the Communications Workers and Paperworkers unions in 1992—the largest Canadian union representing workers in the energy and chemical sectors. By the end of 1988, its membership was approximately 39,000, encompassing more than 400 workplaces and about 202 locals. It was ranked by Labour Canada as the 25th largest union in Canada.[1] However, of an estimated workforce in the industry of 200,000, the ECWU represented only about 19 percent—or one-fifth—of the workers in the industry.[2] As the figures in table 9 suggest, ECWU (now CEP) bargaining units are generally small,

TABLE 9
STRUCTURE AND MEMBERSHIP OF THE ECWU, 1985

Province	Metropolitan Area	Total Members	Women Members	No. of Locals	No. of Employers
Newfoundland	—	54	0	3	3
	St. John's	14	0	1	1
Prince Edward Island		0	0	0	0
Nova Scotia	—	624	177	10	11
	Halifax	25	9	1	1
New Brunswick		379	9	4	6
	Saint John	267	1	—	3
Quebec	—	5,636	935	52	76
	Quebec City	487	41	5	15
	Trois-Rivieres	280	235	1	1
	Montreal	3,515	547	29	40
Ontario	—	15,524	1,949	79	112
	Ottawa-Hull	455	48	2	3
	Toronto	5,732	1,093	21	40
	Hamilton	276	5	4	4
	St.Catharines-Niagara	449	0	2	2
	Kitchener	58	3	1	1
	London	598	127	6	6
	Windsor	365	127	3	3
	Thunder Bay	46	15	1	1
Manitoba	—	433	49	3	5
	Winnipeg	419	49	2	4
Saskatchewan	—	3,504	664	—	24
	Regina	1,660	596	3	4
	Saskatoon	115	5	1	5
Alberta	—	3,310	173	18	32
	Calgary	375	3	3	3
	Edmonton	2,319	122	7	19
British Columbia	—	1,032	58	7	21
	Vancouver	673	47	3	17
Yukon & NWT	—	0	0	0	0
TOTALS	National	30,496	4,014	190	290
	Metropolitan Areas	18,128	3,073	97	173
	Other areas	12,368	941	93	117

SOURCE: Statistics Canada, Corporations and Labour Unions Returns Act, Report for 1985. Part II - Labour Unions. Table 2, pp. 96-271.

widely distributed, and many are in smaller centres or in remote areas. By sector, the largest component of the union membership is drawn from industrial chemicals, followed (in approximate order) by: natural gas; petroleum refining, distributing, and marketing; pharmaceuticals; mining (uranium, potash, salt); chemical-based finished products, food and beverages; and related products and services.[3]

The nature of the membership also varies quite significantly by region. In Québec, most of the locals represent workers in small factories producing textiles, food, or chemical products. Alberta membership is drawn mainly from oil field, petroleum refining, and natural gas workers. In Saskatchewan, the ECWU represents uranium and potash miners. Three of the most significant locals in Cape Breton (at heavy water plants) bargain with Atomic Energy of Canada Ltd. In heavily-industrialized southwestern Ontario, the ECWU represents mainly chemical industry workers, with a concentrated industrial chemicals workforce in the Sarnia area. The national headquarters of the union was located in Edmonton, Alberta.

At a biennial convention, delegates elected a National Director (after 1986, the President), a Secretary-Treasurer, three Executive Board members "at large," and five Executive Board members representing geographic regions. The Executive Board was called "rank and file" because its members could not be employees of the national union, but must be "rank-and-file" members. In fact, they were usually members of local executives—fairly highly placed in the union hierarchy—and eventually candidates for staff positions. The National Director and Secretary Treasurer reported quarterly to the Executive Board, which was supposed to monitor their work and oversee implementation of policies adopted by the conventions. There were also four regional co-ordinators and seven area councils. The latter were responsible for "voluntary programs"—in particular, educational seminars.

The petrochemical sector is highly capital-intensive. The Canadian Chemical Producers Association's (CCPA) brief to the MacDonald Royal Commission on the Economy in June 1983 stated that, in 1982—before the full effects of the recession and rationalization—the fixed assets per employee in the chemical manufacturing sector (synthetic rubber, synthetic resins, inorganic chemicals, organic and specialty chemicals, fertilizer chemicals) averaged $287,000. Value-added per employee in the chemical and chemical products sectors averaged $68,000 in 1981. This was higher than for any other manufacturing group, with the exception of petroleum and coal products, and tobacco products, and was 60 percent above the level for manufacturing as a whole. For the manufacturing firms represented by the CCPA, value-added per employee that year was over $100,000.[4] The unionized workforce in the industrial chemical sector comprises mainly skilled trades and process workers, and these are almost exclusively male.

The roots of the ECWU lie in attempts to unionize oil field and gas workers in Texas, California, and Colorado in the early part of the century. Labour organisers struggled until the Second World War to establish national unions in the oil and petrochemical industries, against the opposition of powerful, increasingly oligopolistic employers, and despite the devastating effects of the Depression. The International Association of Oil Field, Gas Well, and Refinery Workers of America (IAOFGWRWA), which held its first convention in 1918, was reduced to 300 members (from 30,000) by 1933. In 1937 the IAOFGWRWA changed its name to the Oil Workers International Union (OWIU), and in 1948 the OWIU extended its jurisdiction into Canada. In 1955, the OWIU and the United Gas, Coke, and Chemical Workers' Union merged to form the Oil, Chemical, and Atomic Workers' Union (OCAW). Developments in the mid-late 1970s led to the separation of the Canadian districts of the International Chemical Workers (ICW) and the OCAW from their international (U.S.-based) bodies, and their eventual merger in 1980.

Since the end of the Second World War, unionization of petrochemical workers has been impeded by divisions within the workforce, inter-union competition, and the opposition strategies of employers. The structures of the oil and chemical industries partially explain the difficulties of workplace organising, and the jurisdictional competition among unions. Another factor shaping union strategy is the ability of employers, given the rapid advances in technology and labour productivity, to create the conditions for company unionism.[5] In addition, oil field workers, and those involved in natural gas extraction, are typically scattered around drilling rigs and pumping stations which are located in remote areas, and are highly mobile. Workers in the distribution sector have also proven difficult to organise, as they work in small, relatively isolated units (pipelines, tank cars, motor transport). A smaller workforce overall, but more concentrated and stable, are the refinery workers.

Since the first quarter of the century, ownership of refinery capacity has been highly concentrated, and these owners—notably the Rockefellers—pioneered the "employee association." The petroleum industry was colonized early by company unions, which defended "open shop" and resisted alliances with other workers. Rapidly increasing labour productivity in a capital-intensive industry had several consequences. First, the "productive" workforce began to shrink after the Second World War, while the (non-union) scientific and supervisory employees grew in number. Second, employers have been able to maintain wages at levels well above those for other industrial workers. Workers in the oil company unions, as Ann Forrest points out, were "the recipients of benefit packages which included sick pay, paid vacations, and pensions well before unions managed to wrest these concessions from employers in the manufacturing sector generally."[6] This trend has been maintained to the present, as table 10 indicates. While industrial chemical workers have narrowed the wage differential with petroleum sector workers significantly, there remain wide gaps between the wages of these workers and other categories of chemical industry workers, let alone other manufacturing sector workers.[7]

Although the figures given in table 10 represent only monthly (or "snapshot") reportings, rather than annual averages, which would give a more accurate depiction of trends, they do provide a general picture of the wage differentials for different sectors over the seven-year period 1980–1987. The percentage differences in wage rates between petroleum products and industrial chemicals, and between industrial chemicals and (a) textiles, (b) fertilizers are given in table 11. From these data it appears that while wage differentials between petroleum products workers and industrial chemicals workers had narrowed to approximate parity by 1987, the wide differential between these two categories and other chemical industry workers (in textiles and fertilizers) remained.[8]

Wage inequalities have regional and gender characteristics as well as occupational ones. According to December 1987 reported wage rates (table 10), petroleum and coal products, refinery, crude oil and gas, uranium, chemicals, and plastics industry workers all earned wages well above the manufacturing average. However, other sectors, also represented by the ECWU, fell *below* the average manufacturing wage in the same month. These included: food and beverages, textiles, rubber and plastics, synthetic fibres, pharmaceuticals, and paints and varnishes.

Notably, the most poorly paid sectors (textiles and rubber and plastic products) are those with some of the highest percentages of females in the workforce. For some of these categories, female participation in the workforce in the early 1980s was estimated by Statistics Canada as follows: food and beverages (24 to 27 percent); rubber footwear (50 percent); leather products (48 to 60 percent); textile products (27 to 37 percent); pharmaceuticals (37 to 43 percent). Women comprise a relatively small proportion of the highly paid workforces, such as refineries (6 to 8 percent); and industrial chemicals

TABLE 10
AVERAGE WEEKLY EARNINGS (HOURLY WAGE EARNERS ONLY)
ECWU-RELATED INDUSTRIES (WITH OVERTIME)

Sector	1980[a]	1987[b]
All manufacturing	323.27	471.98
Petroleum and coal products	470.11	701.25
Petroleum refineries	478.56	719.06
Crude petroleum and natural gas	—	741.70
Uranium mines	—	802.71
Food and beverage	296.48	431.44
Textile products (industries)	261.12	390.31
Rubber and plastics	—	407.77
Synthetic fibre, yarn, cloth	286.03	449.73
Chemicals and chemical products	356.54	527.25
Pharmaceutics and medicines	278.01	442.17
Paints and varnishes	317.71	415.14
Soap and cleaning compounds	376.49	504.88
Industrial chemicals	441.89	700.94
Fertilizers (mixed)	—	514.20
Plastics and synthetic resins	—	594.77

[a] Based on Dec. 1980 data
[b] Based on Dec. 1987 data, including overtime, firms of all size.

SOURCE: Statistics Canada. *Employment Earnings and Hours*, Vol. 59 (Jan. 1981), pp. 8-15; Vol. 66 (Jan. 1988), pp. 40-45.

TABLE 11
WAGE DIFFERENTIALS FOR SELECTED SECTORS, 1980-87
(PERCENTAGE DIFFERENCES)

Year	Petroleum:	Industrial chemicals:	(a) Textiles	(b) Fertilizers
1980	6.0	40.9	N/A	
1981	7.3	44.5	N/A	
1982	12.7	41.9	N/A	
1983	12.0	44.9	42.3	
1984	10.4	43.4	44.8	
1985	4.4	48.2	49.1	
1986	-2.9	44.5	33.7	
1987	0.04	44.3	26.6	

SOURCES: Statistics Canada. *Employment Earnings and Hours*: vol. 59 (Jan. 1981), pp. 8-15; vol. 60 (Jan. 1982), pp. 8-15; vol. 60 (Dec. 1982), pp. 8-15; vol. 61 (Sept. 1983), pp. 62-71; vol. 62 (Dec. 1984), pp. 62-69; vol. 63 (Dec. 1985), pp. 40-49; vol. 65 (Jan. 1987), pp. 40-45; vol. 66 (Jan. 1988), 40-45.

The Political Economy and Culture of a Union 123

(9 to 11 percent).[9] According to these data on wage differentials and gender, it is evident that the predominantly male chemical workers in Sarnia comprise a relatively privileged workforce, vis-à-vis both other sectors of the ECWU membership, as well as other industrial sector workers. The fact that women tended to occupy low-wage ghettos within ECWU locals, and within the membership overall, was recognized in resolutions passed at the union national convention in 1984. Resolution 10 called on the union to "support through legislative lobbying, effective negotiations, and any other means available, the elimination of lower-scale wage pockets, and strive for recognition of equal-pay-for-work-of-equal-value principles."[10]

Male members and male-dominated local union executives were viewed by women delegates as part of the problem. A delegate at the 1984 convention described the situation at her textile factory in Trois-Rivières:

> We [women] work on the bonus plan—of course we have a basic salary, but to have the same wages as men who are on an hourly basis, we have to work 25 to 30 percent more, which means that we do piece work, and it is discriminatory... [O]ur members have to be made aware because we have a problem in our mill, for instance, they post jobs. It's all nice, but men do not apply because women used to have those jobs. Women do not apply to other jobs because they used to be held by men and if they do they are not going to be accepted or they will be treated disgustingly... [T]here remain some men who have some way to go.[11]

It is difficult to explain the situation of the women workers, especially in cases where they form the majority of the workforce, in any way other than that the male membership has actively collaborated with employers in perpetuating the inequalities, e.g., by controlling local bargaining and refusing to stand on the issue of the gendered wage disparity. The female delegates at the 1984 convention stressed that what was required, for the resolutions to be implemented, was a concerted effort by the union to challenge its male members' sexist attitudes and privileges. One way to do this would be to put equal-pay-for-work-of-equal-value at the forefront of the union's national bargaining programme. However, this had never been proposed. Instead, the official union view has tended to attribute blame for the women's situation solely to exploitative employers.

Another factor which contributes to the character of unionism in the petrochemicals industry is the legacy of company or "independent" unions. These have proven to be very entrenched in the oil sector, particularly, but also in certain of the chemical companies (e.g., DuPont). This is the case in both the US and Canada. In the 1950s, "independent" unions dominated the unionized workforce, with OCAW, the International Chemical Workers, and District 50 (CIO) dividing the rest.[12] An attempt to form a National Coalition of Oil Unions between 1951 and 1954, leading to merger, was prevented by the opposition of the "independent" unions.[13] Forrest reported in 1976 that the OCAW's main rivals for jurisdiction in oil were the independent unions.[14] In Canada, where the oil industry is dominated by subsidiaries of US multinational corporations, similar developments have occurred. Imperial Oil still had an "independent" union at the end of the 1980s. Significantly, Imperial Oil was the first company to locate in the Chemical Valley where it dominated the economy of the area for decades. ECWU workers interviewed in Sarnia in 1988 described Imperial Oil workers as "un-unionized" and as an historically conservative—even "backward"—force in local labour struggles.

The chemical industry's structure has also presented unions with unique obstacles to organising. Extensive horizontal and vertical integration within firms, mergers, joint ventures, and rapid product diversification have contributed to conflict among unions over jurisdictions. Merger talks between OCAW and the ICW, held in 1958, 1964, and

1971, were unsuccessful, as were merger discussions with the United Rubber Workers in 1975. When, in 1976, the Canadian District of the ICW broke away to form the Canadian Chemical Workers' Union (CCW), battles developed between the ICW, the CCW, the Canadian Paperworkers, the United Steelworkers of America (USWA), OCAW, the Tobacco Workers, and Confédération des Syndicats Nationaux (CSN) and Confédération des Syndicats Démocratiques (CSD) affiliates for the former members of ICW in Canada. When the Canadian District of OCAW separated in 1979 to form the Energy and Chemical Workers' Union (ECWU), the new union's affiliation to the CLC was opposed by the USWA on the grounds of competing jurisdiction in coke and other areas. Union organising efforts in Canada have therefore been seriously undermined by union competition for a relatively small, and widely scattered workforce. Following its independence in 1980, the ECWU pursued mergers with other unions. Mergers and transferred affiliations were the main sources of new members over the decade.[15]

Jurisdictional problems for the unions are created by the widely diversified nature of the petrochemical industry. At the same time, the dominance of a small number of large firms (listed in tables 12, 13, 14), has helped employers deal with the unions from a position of strength. The oil and chemical companies have co-operated to establish uniform wage standards and to supply one another during strikes. They collaborate (mainly through their industrial associations) to lobby governments on various policy issues (e.g., energy and environmental policies). Moreover, the petrochemical companies have resisted negotiation with unions on other than a *local* basis, thereby attempting to lessen the attraction of national unions to their workforces, and to isolate bargaining units.[16]

TABLE 12
THE "TOP TEN" US CHEMICAL COS., 1984-86

Company	1984	1985	1986
Du Pont	1	1	1
Dow Chemical	2	2	2
Exxon	3	3	3
Monsanto	4	4	6
Union Carbide	5	5	4
Atlantic Richfield	8	6	5
Shell Oil	6	7	8
Celanese	7	8	10
Amoco	9	9	9
W.R. Grace	10	10	12
BASF	—	12	7

SOURCE: *Chemical and Engineering News* (May 5, 1986; May 4, 1987).

Finally, chemical workers are also divided by the internal hierarchies of the labour process itself, by shift work, by race, and (as mentioned with regard to wage ghettoes) by gender. While a handful of excellent studies of these factors exist for British and United States chemical workers, this is a neglected area of sociological research in Canada.[17] In general, at least for the large petrochemical complexes in the Chemical Valley, one can say that the non-clerical and non-managerial workforce falls into two main categories: skilled

TABLE 13
LEADING CHEMICAL COMPANIES IN CANADA, 1988

Company and Year End	Profit[a] ($000)	% Change	Revenue Ranking (out of top 1000)	Assets ($000)	Capital Spending	No. of Employees	Major Shareholder	Private/ Public
Dow Chem. Can. (Dec. 88)	363,061	180	19	2,024,737	76,000		Dow Chem. US	pr.
DuPont Chem. Can. (Dec. 88)	99,910	10	84	762,938	106,621	4,052	DuPont US	pu.
PPG (Dec. 88)	57,909	12	89	453,001	48,500		PPG Industries Inc. US	pr.
Celanese (Dec. 88)	48,904	72	178	305,233	24,490	2,102	Celanese US	pu.
C-I-L (Dec.'88)	48,000	20	26	1,227,000	n/a		Imperial Chem. Ind.(UK)	pr.
Union Carbide (Dec 88)	42,266	65	145	802,076	72,138	2,800	Union Carbide US	pu.
Monsanto (Dec. 88)	27,810	16	109	181,860	7,100		Monsanto Co.US	pr.
Canadian Oxygen (Sept. 88)	11,740	11	294	147,341	46,643		BOC Group PLC (UK)	pr.
BASF	7,124		159	126,734			BASF AG Corp. W.Germ.	pr.
Allied Signal (Dec. 88)	(US) 22,733		98	(US) 337,982			Allied Signal Inc.US	pr.
Eli-Lilly (Dec 88)	n.a.		259	63,615			Eli Lilly & Co., US	pr.
Hoechst (Dec. 88)	16,489		201				Hoechst AG, W. Germany	pr.

[a] Net income after taxes, excluding extraordinary gains or losses.

SOURCE: *Globe and Mail Report on Business* (July 1989).

TABLE 14
LEADING INTEGRATED OIL COMPANIES, 1988

Company and Year End	Profit[a] ($000)	% Change	Revenue Ranking	Assets ($000)	Downstream as % of Total Assets	No. of Employees	Major Shareholder	Private/ Public
Polysar (Dec. 88)	319,000		12	2,425,000			Nova Corp. (Alta)	pr.
Imperial Oil (Dec. 88)	501,000	-33	13	9,676,000	27	12,161		pu.
Shell Canada (Dec. 88)	427,000	22			37	7,186		pu.
Texaco Canada (Dec. 88)	333,000	4	11	4,097,000	37		Imperial Oil (Ont.)	pr.
Petro-Canada (Dec. 88)	126,000	-41		8,611,000	36	7,307	Govt. of Canada	Crown
Total Petroleum (Dec. 88)	72,749	352	55		59			pu.
Suncor (Dec. 88)	-49,000	-202	86	2,023,000	26	4,080		pu.
Nova Corp.	424,000	137	31	8,242,000		13,000	Nova Corp. (Alta)	pu.
Gulf Canada	67,000	-61	114	3,717,000		3,000		pu.
Amoco Cdn. Petroleum (Dec. 88)	-52,250	-136	17	7,242,499			Amoco Corp. US	pr.

[a] Net income after taxes, excluding extraordinary gains or losses.

Source: *Globe and Mail Report on Business* (July 1989).

trades (maintenance) workers, and "process" workers and operators (in which I include lab technicians). The maintenance and process workers are typically scattered over a large plant site, and are divided by shift work.[18] Technical and supervisory personnel (engineers, chemists, supervisors) are generally excluded from the bargaining unit, and present a problem for unionized workers in that they are capable (in some circumstances) of running the plants during strikes.[19]

At Polysar, the "productive" workforce breakdown is shown in table 15. Four different working arrangements were common in the 1980s:
- day employees
- 8-hour shift employees (rotated weekly)
- 12-hour shift employees
- 4 P.M. to midnight shift (janitorial staff)

Seniority, contracting out, and attempts to change job categories (to "deskill," make workers more "flexible") have been key issues of concern, especially to the skilled trades employees.

TABLE 15
WORK FORCE CATEGORIES, POLYSAR, 1986-88

Category	Percentage of productive or "blue-collar" work force
Skilled trades	27.3
Process workers	45.5
Truck drivers, warehouse workers, fire-fighters	16.4
Janitorial and grounds	10.9
Total	100.0

SOURCE: Estimates based on the numbers of stewards recognized for each group in the 1986-88 collective bargaining agreement.

From this overview of the origins of union organisation in the sector and of its membership, we may make some general observations. The workforce in the oil, petrochemical, and industrial chemical sectors is not highly unionized compared to other sectors, (e.g., automobile assembly and parts production in Canada). It is also relatively highly paid, compared to other manufacturing sector workers (including other groups within the same union), and—apart from the initial fight for the right to organise—does not have a particularly militant history in its dealings with employers. The energy and petrochemical industry is dominated by large firms which have succeeded to a considerable degree in maintaining "independent" unions (in the oil industry), and in warding off sector-wide bargaining. The characterisation of the chemical industry unions as "business unions," however, requires further explanation, since it has to do with the formation of chemical workers' identity as professional, technical (or in any case, *not* "blue collar") workers, and with the nature of the relationship between union leaders and corporate managers. These aspects of ECWU culture are crucially important to chemical workers' perceptions of their interests and of alliances vis-à-vis other groups of workers as well as social actors such as environmentalists.

RECESSION AND RESTRUCTURING IN THE PETROCHEMICAL INDUSTRY

An Era of Crisis

In the early 1980s the petrochemical industry worldwide entered a serious recession. In Canada, the crisis of profitability was exacerbated by federal government regulation of the energy sector. The petrochemical companies organised to lobby the federal government to change energy policy; in the post-Trudeau era, they found a sympathetic reception. The ECWU participated in two task forces formed to advise the federal government on energy sector policy. These task forces reported in June 1978 and February 1984. This section examines the international and national political economy of the petrochemical industry, focusing on the late 1970s to 1980s period, the nature of the crisis, and the strategy of the integrated multinationals to restore profitability. The bargaining and political strategies adopted by the OCAW Canadian District (later the ECWU) in this transitional period are important to understanding the union's positioning within the Canadian labour movement, as well as in relation to other social actors.

From the 1950s to the early 1970s, the petrochemical industry had a substantially faster rate of growth than most other industrial sectors. The highest rates of growth were experienced from 1960 to 1973: "In the whole of the OECD area, while total industrial production rose during the period by 5.6 percent at an annual rate and chemical production by about 9 percent, petrochemical production showed a rate of growth varying between 10 and 17 percent according to the product (butadiene: 10 percent; benzene: 13 percent; propylene: 16.5 percent; ethylene: 17 percent)."[20] The reasons for this were, first, rapid general economic growth (increased demand for products—industrial and consumer goods—incorporating basic chemicals), and second, the development of new products. Many of these were substitutes for "natural" products; the chemically-based substitutes were relatively cheap, due to—among other factors—the abundance of the hydrocarbon raw materials (oil and natural gas). Between 1960 and 1980, the "apparent annual chemical consumption per capita in Western Europe increased from approximately $70 (US) to $600 (US).[21] The rate of growth hit its peak in the second half of the 1960s, and slowed down from 1970 to 1973, corresponding to the general trends in industrial growth. There was also a saturation of markets for which basic organic chemicals are produced. In some cases there was even a return to natural products, due to a change in consumer attitudes, or to increasing costs of the raw materials for synthetic products (which made the "natural substitutes" more cost competitive). In the late 1970s and early 1980s the environmental goal of a "chemical-free society" challenged the chemical companies' slogan: "chemicals for a better society." The OECD lists "increasing concern for environmental protection and waste prevention through increased recycling and longer product life," as well as concern for energy conservation, as factors contributing to the decline in chemical products demand at this time.[22]

Market saturation is illustrated by worldwide trends in ethylene demand. From 1965 to 1974, ethylene demand grew at a rate of 16 percent per annum (p.a.). From 1975 to 1979 this rate was 4.2 percent p.a., and from 1980 to 1987, 4.0 percent.[23] Between 1980 and 1987, growth rates for ethylene and propylene in the OECD countries were only 2 to 4 percent, compared with 11 to 14 percent in Latin America and 15 to 18 percent in Asia. While the developing countries were striving for greater self-sufficiency in basic chemicals, rapidly expanding these capacities, growth in the developed countries in the 1980s occurred mainly in the new specialty chemical and commodity plastics areas. Between 1982 and 1987, not a single new ethylene plant was planned in the United States. Growth in demand for ethylene, on the scale experienced from the 1960s to 1970s, is not expected to recur, so long as the United States and Western Europe account for about two-thirds of total ethylene consumption, and their markets are relatively saturated. A second factor explaining the slow-down in growth is the stagnation in productivity gains which had set in by the early 1970s. As in other industrial sectors, the additional benefits from increasing plant size and from energy saving measures had begun to diminish; many basic petrochemical technologies had matured.[24]

By 1974, growth in petrochemical production within OECD countries had begun to decline, and in 1975 there was a substantial decline in *output*, especially for benzene and butadiene (used in the production of plastics and foams, and synthetic rubbers, respectively). By 1985, the OECD was predicting that "market saturation" conditions would continue and even intensify: "from now on, growth in total demand for bulk petrochemicals (i.e., the main thermoplastics and their precursors) is likely to keep in step with general economic growth."[25] The productivity trends were not, however, evident to most investors in the late 1960s and early 1970s, when growth rates encouraged new investment in petrochemicals. In the 1970s, oil companies entered the primary petrochemical and thermoplastics markets, believing that their control of feedstock sources would give them a cost advantage. Investment in new capacity matured after the first oil shock and coincided with the onset of the recession. Overcapacity was also caused by the wave of investment in developing countries at the end of the 1960s and early 1970s, and relocation of petrochemical production to oil and gas producing countries was accelerated by the oil shocks.

Stagnation in productivity, market saturation, and growing competition had begun to affect rates of growth and profitability in the petrochemical and chemical industries before the impacts were felt of the oil shocks of 1973 and 1979. The steep increases in feedstock prices had complex consequences for firms, depending on their access to oil or natural gas feedstocks, government policies, the degree of intra-firm integration, and other factors.[26]

RESTRUCTURING TRENDS

Restructuring in petrochemicals, as in other sectors, has followed a now familiar pattern, including: innovation in production technology and labour processes, product specialization and differentiation; mergers and takeovers (leading to greater vertical integration and diversification within firms); and reduction of capacity in traditional product lines (growth in production of which is now occurring in developing countries), effected by plant closures and cut-backs.

In Canada, the most ruthless stage of petrochemical industry restructuring was more or less completed by the end of 1985. The combined profits of Canadian chemical manufacturers (excluding fertilizer materials) fell from $559 million in 1981 to $285 million in 1984. Petrochemicals dived deepest; producers reported losing $132 million in this sector in 1984, compared to combined profits of $200 million in 1981. Canadian chemical companies reported a combined loss of $17 billion for the 1982-86 period.[27] The workforce in the chemical industry declined from about 30,000 in 1981 to 25,000 in 1985.[28] According to the ECWU, 60 percent of its bargaining units reported lay-offs in 1982. In July of that year, 20 percent of its entire membership was on lay-off.[29] Between 1983 and 1986, employment at major chemical companies declined as shown in table 16.

There was an increasing emphasis on export products and markets, given the relative saturation of the Canadian market (hence support from this sector for a free trade agreement with the United States). Petrochemical plants in eastern Canada were converted so that they could use natural gas as a feedstock, to take advantage of its availability in Canada and its comparatively lower price.

There has been a continuing slump in demand for chemicals used in mining, oil and gas industries, and agriculture, despite general economic recovery. Production of chemicals

TABLE 16
CHEMICAL COMPANY EMPLOYMENT IN CANADA, 1983-1986

Company	Work Force	
	1983	1986
C-I-L Inc.	6,700	5,600
Celanese Canada	3,400	2,100
Du Pont Canada	5,000	4,600
Union Carbide	4,200	3,300

SOURCE: *Chemical and Engineering News* (June 8, 1987, p. 70)

used in fertilizers decreased by 12 to 13 percent during the 1980s.[30] Carbon black production decreased 11 percent from 1985 to 1986. Other significant decreases have occurred for hydrochloric acid, nitric acid, and sulfuric acid. Some organic chemicals have also been cut back since 1985: benzene by 8 percent, toluene by 17, and xylenes by 14 percent. Inorganic chemicals production has also decreased for some commodities. Plastics, on the other hand, all experienced growth in production—low density polyethylene by 21 percent. Prices from 1984 to 1985 declined overall for basic chemicals (organic and inorganic) but increased for specialty chemical products. The average profits of C-I-L, Celanese, DuPont, and Union Carbide (all publicly-traded companies whose profit figures are made public) increased by 35 percent from 1985 to 1986, although their combined sales increased by only 2.8 percent, reflecting the shift to production of higher value-added products and other factors.[31]

Canadian-based chemical companies did very well, over all, in 1987. The combined profits of the big four publicly traded companies (C-I-L, Celanese Canada, DuPont Canada, and Union Carbide Canada) rose by 50 percent in the first nine months of 1987. During the same period, sales rose by only 2 percent.[32] A large portion of these profits came from exports.[33] In 1988, before-tax profits for forty of the CCPA's seventy-three members increased by an average 111 percent. These firms estimated their aggregate pretax profit at $2.6 billion (Canadian), up from $1.2 billion in 1987. The association attributed the dramatic 111 percent rise in profits in 1988 to "stable energy costs, strong gains in productivity, and the redirection of product mixes to more sophisticated but more expensive items."[34] Consistent with the trend in the United States, 1988 sales for the same 73 companies rose by 22 percent over 1987—a figure significantly *less than* the rate of growth in profit margin. In the case of Shell Canada, profits increased from $154 million (Canadian) in 1986 to $350 million in 1987—an increase of 127 percent. Sales revenues, however, increased by only 0.83 percent (from $4.82 billion to 4.86 billion).[35] In addition to the shift to higher value-added product lines, high profits reflected higher productivity; the chemical industry was operating at about 93 percent of capacity in 1988, and some closed facilities were being reactivated. However, employment at the end of the 1980s expanded by only about 2 percent.

Because overall growth in GNP in the industrialized countries remained slow (relative to rates preceding the late 1970s), chemical industry analysts did not expect such high profit increases to continue in the long term. The CCPA was predicting at the end of 1988 that sales growth would slow to about 8.5 percent, and the increase in pretax profits would decline to an average 5.6 percent in 1989. The association claimed that increasing costs of compliance with health, safety, and environmental regulations would offset future productivity gains. The average wage increase in the industry for 1988 was 5.4 percent, somewhat better than the overall (Canadian) average.[36]

CORPORATE AND UNION STRATEGIES IN THE CANADIAN ENERGY SECTOR

CORPORATE STRATEGY

The second oil shock made ethane more attractive than oil as a feedstock, and this meant that areas with large reserves of natural gas, like Alberta, were seen as potentially competitive regions of production.[37] Moreover, because of federal government energy policy, feedstock prices were held below world levels following the 1973 oil shock. This gave the petrochemical companies a great advantage, and created an incentive for investment in new capacity in Canada. World-scale plants were built to export to the USA. A 450,000 tonne naphtha cracker came on stream in Ontario in 1978. In 1977 Dow undertook the "largest single commitment the Dow Chemical Co. has ever made for a petrochemical project anywhere in the world": a huge ethane-cracking plant at Joffre, Alberta, which Dow designed, constructed, and trained operating personnel for, on behalf of Alberta Gas Ethylene, a subsidiary of Alberta Gas Trunk Line. (Six other companies built four new plants in Alberta to extract ethane from natural gas.) The entire ethylene capacity of 1.2 billion pounds per year was purchased by Dow. Seven hundred million pounds per year were consumed at Dow's new world-scale ethylene dichloride, vinyl chloride, and ethylene oxide/ethylene glycol plants at Fort Saskatchewan. A world-scale caustic and chlorine plant, and a facility to manufacture styrofoam—the largest of its kind in the world—have also been built at Fort Saskatchewan since 1977. Five hundred million pounds of ethylene per year are transported via the 1900 mile pipeline constructed in 1979, connecting Fort Saskatchewan with Sarnia. The Cochin pipeline cost $350 million. Dow, having a one-third share (with Dome Petroleum and two other partners), spent over $100 million for the pipeline. Dow claims that its investment in Alberta between 1977 and 1980 amounted to $600 million of new capital.[38]

Just as the "boom" projects, initiated in the 1970s, were being completed, market conditions changed. Combined with a slump in domestic demand and world export markets, was a growing price disadvantage with regard to feedstocks.[39] 1982 was the worst year of the recession for this industry. Alberta Gas Ethylene shut down operations for several months. Petrochemical producers in eastern Canada were particularly hard-hit. The Canadian government responded with an offer of "short-term assistance" (repayable contributions and loan guarantees) to eastern petrochemical producers, conditional upon equivalent provincial government assistance. The government also appointed an "industry-labour" task force to assess the long-term outlook, including regional aspects, and to make recommendations for a "national policy framework."

The federal government's National Energy Programme (NEP) (October 1980) was intended to give Canadian producers a feedstock price advantage, but the five-year Canada-Alberta Agreement (1981) was based on the assumption that world prices would continue to rise.[40] When this did not happen, and when the pricing schedule negotiated in Canada actually surpassed world market prices, the petrochemical industry began to call for "deregulation" of energy pricing.[41] In their February 1984 report to the federal government, the members of the Petrochemical Industry Task Force tried to demand a reversal in policy without appearing to have ever supported government regulation of energy prices.[42]

> Canada has abundant hydrocarbon resources that are the basis of the raw materials for the petrochemical industry. Despite this, the Canadian petrochemical

industry lost its competitiveness in 1982 when *the market responsive systems* in the US and elsewhere resulted in substantially falling feedstock prices at the same time as the feedstock costs in Canada were rising due to regulated oil and gas prices... Therefore, the Canadian petrochemical industry requires government policies that allow for *flexible* feedstock prices that can move with those of our *market responsive* competitors (emphasis added).[43]

However, because many of the largest companies are integrated (have upstream operations in oil and natural gas extraction and refining), they also asked for changes in the NEP's taxation policies, to ensure that the oil and natural gas producing sectors would not suffer a decline in profitability as a result of lower prices. The task force argued that

the upfront fiscal burden on oil and gas resources in Canada should be reduced to the maximum extent possible and that government should rely on existing forms of corporate taxation for revenue generation... The Task Force also wishes to highlight the *interdependence* of the oil and gas industry and the petrochemical industry in Canada... Because of this *interdependence*, the Task Force urges that the feedstock recommendations be implemented in a way that will not impair the oil and gas industry (emphasis added).[44]

Notably, in making these arguments, the petrochemical industry kept referring to the "surplus," or "excess," in Canadian natural gas supplies.[45]

The chemical companies indeed took advantage of the recession to press for a dismantling of the Liberal Government's entire energy sector programme. They blamed government regulation and "monopoly" (PetroCanada) for their inability to compete with US-based producers; they called for the abolition of restrictions on foreign investment, arguing that MNCs provide Canada with "ready access to the global pool of the latest technology";[46] and they urged domestic policies to "improve the environment for business." These included less taxation, and less environmental and other regulation.[47] To drive home their point, the petrochemical companies warned the government that failure to act on the recommendations of the Petrochemical Industry Task Force would result in a virtual freeze on further investment. In his presentation to the Senate Standing Committee on Energy and Natural Resources (review of the National Energy Programme), Dow Chemical Canada's president stated that the "inflexibility of the NEP also led to the cancellation of about three billion dollars of new petrochemical investment in Western Canada over the last three years."[48]

THE ECWU AND CANADIAN ENERGY POLICY

The Nationalist Phase

The 1978 Consultative Task Force on Petrochemicals was one of twenty-three such groups appointed by the federal government to examine the prospects of various industrial sectors. Its chairperson was Norman Kissick, CEO of Union Carbide Canada. Of seventeen members, there were only two union representatives, from the OCAW and the United Rubber Workers of America (Canadian districts). Eleven were high-ranking executives of multinational petrochemical companies (Monsanto Canada, Polysar, C-I-L, Dow Chemical Canada, Alberta Gas Ethylene Co., Gulf Oil Canada, Celanese Canada, DuPont Canada, Esso Chemical Canada, and Petrosar). There were also three provincial government representatives, and a professor of business administration. Its primary goal was "to formulate recommendations leading...to an industry with an adequate level of profitability at international costs."[49] The second goal was to improve the industry's "position to utilize Canada's strong hydrocarbon resource base" to increase petrochemical exports. The task force majority made a list of recommendations to the government, some of which are outlined briefly here. The sole dissenting voice on a number of points belonged to the OCAW representative, Henri Gauthier. In his registered disagreements or counter proposals are the outlines of the energy policy statement which the ECWU would adopt two years later, upon becoming an independent Canadian union.

The first recommendation of the Report of the Consultative Task Force on Petrochemicals (June 1978), stemmed from the companies' complaint that construction labour costs in Canada were higher than in the United States (Gulf Coast).

[L]arge, skilled labour forces must usually be assembled in Canada for each major construction project. The local labour pool is normally not large enough and tradesmen must be brought in from other parts of the province, other provinces and other countries. Because of the reluctance of construction workers to move to a new location, *in part due to the availability of unemployment insurance*, it has been necessary to provide a considerably greater package of wages and fringe benefits than is necessary on the Gulf Coast.

This lack of competition within the skilled construction labour community has also led to *work practices which reduce productivity* at the construction site. Again, this is in contrast with the situation on the US Gulf Coast where considerable competition exists and where a high proportion of petrochemical construction is done by non-union tradesmen (p. 3) (emphasis added).

The task force recommended measures, therefore, to increase "labour mobility," to make collective bargaining more "competitive" (thereby lowering wage rates in Canada), and to limit the right to strike. The OCAW representative, while not defending, in principle, the right of Canadian workers to the higher standard of living achieved through collective bargaining, drew the line at limiting the right of construction workers to strike.

A second proposal, mentioned in the preceding section, was to use energy policy to promote the development of high value-added manufacturing industry in Canada, via lower domestic energy prices. This nationalistic-sounding goal coincided with the interests of the large integrated petrochemical companies at the time, since the world price was still higher than the domestic price negotiated by the Alberta and federal governments. The OCAW was in agreement with this goal.

A third recommendation was that the Canadian government should negotiate domestic status for Canadian refineries, to facilitate the export of Canadian oil and gas to the United States. The OCAW representative opposed "any export of Canada's indigenous resources." The goals of national self-sufficiency and conservation for future generations' use were popular among the left-nationalists who were key figures in the Canadian District of the OCAW at the time. Growing conflict with the international (US) leadership of the OCAW over energy policy—according to Canadians active in the union at the time—was one of the factors leading to the separation move in the late 1970s.[50]

When the chemical company executives recommended that the government reduce corporate taxation, and grant higher investment tax credits, the OCAW member countered that the government "should secure equity participation in return for increased tax advantages provided to the companies." (This proposal was rejected explicitly by the Canadian government in its response to the task force Report, in favour of a free-market approach to economic growth.)

The next two recommendations were contradictory in principle, if not in terms of the interests of the petrochemical companies. The company executives asked the Canadian government to negotiate "a bilateral free trade agreement with the US for a limited group of petrochemicals [primary and intermediate industrial chemicals] using…the export of additional quantities of natural gas as bargaining leverage." In the next paragraph, they asked for greater Canadian tariffs on the importation of higher value-added products, again, to promote downstream industrial development. The OCAW representative opposed a bilateral free trade deal, apparently on the grounds that such a deal might "undermine" Canada's position at GATT negotiations. His silence on the second point may be explained by the nationalist economic views referred to above.

Interestingly, when the task force majority called for less government regulation in the areas of "Health, Safety, and Fairness," and proposed that such regulations be subjected to socioeconomic impact analysis, there was no response from either of the union representatives. Additionally, the companies asked that chemicals regulation be based on proven harm, rather than on unproven safety criteria, and that they be legislated only "after consultation with industry and labour." Again, no union objection was recorded.

Finally, the executives recommended limiting or eliminating "further nationalization or direct government participation" in the petrochemical sector. OCAW's representative disagreed with this approach, instead advocating *more* government involvement in planning the development of the sector. Although his statement was rather obliquely worded, it implied that, because the sector is dominated by multinational companies, Canadian government intervention (through Crown corporations) is necessary to protect national interests. The ECWU would later support such a policy.

In its response to the task force report, the federal government emphasized its desire to create a corporatist framework for the development of a consensus on economic policy. Its primary concerns were described as: (i) to increase industrial "competitiveness"; (ii) to support regional development goals; and (iii) to "enhance government, business, and labour co-operation."

> [The government] has reaffirmed its belief that the principal actors in the Canadian economy must be the individual firm and its labour force and that the route to economic prosperity is via the market system. It has also endorsed the principle that the stimulation of economic growth and job creation are among Canada's first priorities, and to achieve these it is important to foster an environment of understanding in which more effective consultation can take place among labour, business, and government.[51]

To further these corporatist objectives, the government had also appointed an "Overview Committee" to review the twenty-three industry task force reports and to make a consensus report to the government. This Overview Committee consisted of five Canadian Labour Congress (CLC) representatives, five business representatives, and one academic, with the chairperson appointed from the private sector. At the end of this 1978-79 consultation period, the Conservative government did not seem to have moved significantly from the status quo ante position of the Liberals: the private sector was to continue to determine, fundamentally, the direction of the economy, while the government would ameliorate the undesirable social effects of this model of growth with various regulatory policies. In the petrochemical sector, this meant that multinational corporations would continue to control the oil, gas, and feedstock resources of the country, and their interests would predominate in the making of Canadian energy policy. The one exception to this rule would be PetroCanada—the federal government's attempt to affect investment decisions and to secure domestic interests in the petrochemical sector.

Following its not very successful attempt to influence energy policy through the corporatist consultation process, the ECWU took advantage of its new independence from the international union to adopt an energy policy statement at its founding convention in 1980. The statement included the following principles and proposals.

General Principles
1. essential domestic energy needs must be met;
2. energy self-sufficiency should be achieved as soon as possible;
3. energy development should take into account the needs of future generations, and of the regions;
4. energy policy should be related to industrial strategy and to fiscal and social polici
5. energy development must be made compatible with environmental and health goals and the rights of native peoples;
6. energy development should promote transition from non-renewable to renewable sources;
7. Canadian ownership and control of the sector should be maximized, beginning with the creation of a national energy corporation; the ECWU proposed the formation of a vertically integrated firm, from an expanded PetroCanada and the nationalization of Imperial Oil (Canada);
8. a low cost transportation policy to encourage industrial development.

The document proposed:
1. conservation programs instead of market (price) mechanisms to lower energy consumption, on the grounds that the latter hurt low-income consumers most;
2. adjustment measures to support workers in energy supply industries;
3. more money for research into renewable resources, such as passive and active solar systems, photovoltaic conversion of sunlight to electricity, wind-generated electricity, and biomass conversion to gaseous and liquid fuels, all of which are more environmentally safe as well as more labour-intensive sources of energy supply;
4. energy prices set in Canada on the basis of domestic costs of production and the investment required to achieve self-sufficiency, not on OPEC or world prices;
5. maintenance of a two-price system for oil and gas;
6. compensation for western oil-producing provinces for lost revenues (due to lower domestic prices), in the form of an industrial strategy which lays the bases for their long-term economic growth;
7. limitation or ban on exports of Canadian oil and gas (recommended by the OCAW and the CLC to the National Energy Board in September 1978).

This document remained the official ECWU position on energy policy well into the 1980s. The 1982 National Convention of the union reaffirmed support for "Canadianization of the petroleum industry."[52] Then came the recession, and the beginning of a concerted industry campaign to redesign Canadian energy policy. With the petrochemical companies predicting the "disappearance" of the industry, the union sided with employers in an effort to persuade the Canadian government to deregulate energy prices, abandon the two-price system, reduce corporate taxation, and remove the obstacles to foreign investment. The left-nationalist tone of the late seventies became a decidedly corporatist one, although in some ways still cloaked by nationalist-sounding rhetoric.

The 1983-84 Petrochemical Industry Task Force

> Brothers and Sisters, we more than any other trade unionists in this country have an obligation to try to ease that stranglehold that the government has placed on our employers, on our source of income, on our livelihood.[53]

The ECWU's participation in the 1983-84 Petrochemical Industry Task Force, the union's subsequent support for the task force's recommendations, and the executives' rationalization of its positions to members at the 1984 national convention, all support the view that the ECWU leadership had embarked on an essentially corporatist path as a strategy to steer the union through the recession. The task force participation coincided, moreover, with the adoption (in the early 1980s) of the "continuing dialogue" programme, which members of the national staff and executive promoted as an alternative to confrontational labour-management relations.

The composition of the 1984 task force was much the same as that of the 1978 task force, with an important exception. With the industry in crisis, creating an "urgent need" for labour-management "co-operation," the national director of the ECWU, Neil Reimer, was appointed co-chairperson of the task force. Reimer was the only labour representative on the task force; other unions in the sector were excluded. The other chairperson was the president of Shell Chemical Canada, interestingly, the company which had implemented a "new management philosophy" at its Sarnia plant in the late 1970s, and with whom the ECWU was conducting a "continuing dialogue." The task force secretary was the president of the CCPA, and all the members were corporate executives, representing: Esso Chemical, Celanese, Polysar/Petrosar, C-I-L, Dow Chemical, Union Carbide, Hercules Canada, DuPont, Petromont, Ocelot Industries, and Novacor Chemicals. The Alberta Federation of Labour, the CLC, and the ECWU were the only labour organisations which made presentations to the task force.

According to Reimer, the ECWU's brief to the task force was "well received and incorporated to a large degree in the final report which the task force issued."[54] Among the union's recommendations were:

1. that government royalties on oil and gas producers should be reduced, to lower the cost of feedstocks for the petrochemical industry ("Governments must back away from their excess reliance on revenues from oil and gas.");
2. that "joint labour-management efficiency studies should be a prerequisite for federal assistance to industry";
3. that government should take measures to increase export markets for petrochemicals;
4. that governments should help finance plant conversion to allow producers to use alternative feedstocks more flexibly.

In addition to these recommendations, the ECWU leadership endorsed the entire task force report, which they viewed as "*the necessary strategy to... strengthen the petrochemical industry and its related employment opportunities in Canada*" (emphasis added).[55] This time there was no dissenting labour voice; the ECWU energy policy statement was nowhere to be found; and no distinction was made—either in the report or in the executive's reporting to members—between the interests of the multinational petrochemical firms and those of their workers.

The federal government response to the task force report, released in July 1984, was considered inadequate by the ECWU leadership. In a position paper on the response, presented for approval to the delegates at the 1984 national convention, the government was condemned for not immediately implementing the task force recommendations.

> No new initiatives were tabled to increase flexibility of natural gas pricing for industry... One area where the federal government could do more, is to reduce front-end taxes on feed stocks... *The ECWU supports market response Energy Pricing System*—we support the transition assistance programme for plants to provide feed stock flexibility (emphasis added).[56]

Stuart Sullivan, the Ontario Co-ordinator of the ECWU, gave a glowing defence of the petrochemical companies' efforts to survive and compete, despite perverse government policies.

> [The Petro-Chemical Industry] is the only industry in Canada that meets the full criteria of the policies of the labour movement...that our natural resources should be developed within our national boundaries to the fullest extent possible, and name me an industry that does that other than the Petro-Chemical Industry... The only industry in Canada, and they are not asking for assistance in terms of a hand-out, all they are saying to the government is "could you slow down the bleeding, just a little bit, please, because you are bleeding us to the tune of 75% to 94% of our operating cost or feed [stock] cost." They said "could you just lower that a little bit so that we can continue to compete on the world markets." And, the response of the government has been very negative to [the] point "O.K. we will study it, we will look into it—if the provinces agree to do something."[57]

After citing an example of what amounted to an investment boycott threat, Sullivan blamed not the profit goals of the company, but the government for the potential loss of investment in the industry.

> [At] Polysar where we have a fine new butyl plant...the company officials said that if we had known what the federal government were going to do...we would have had to build that plant in Orange, Texas. And, in all probability on their books it is the last major expansion for Canada. All future major capital investments will have to be outside of Canada *because they cannot trust the government*... They are a Canadian corporation, but they are being driven out by this policy (emphasis added).[58]

In these statements, nationalist rhetoric (including the industry's claim that the short-term plunder of energy resources amounts to an "upgrading" of Canadian supplies and a desirable form of industrial development) was used to sell the task force recommendations to the membership. Reimer stated at the 1984 convention that the petrochemical industry task force used "models" that showed: (i) Canada has the "largest amount of reserve per capita of natural gas in any industrialized nation"; (ii) "if the government implemented the recommendations of the petrochemical task force not only would the jobs that you have be protected—it would create 170,000 to 230,000 man years of work in the next ten years. I am told that equates to 10,000 new jobs for ten years."[59]

Thus, concerns about resource depletion could be dismissed, and the employment crisis averted, if only the government would co-operate. When one delegate dared to question the anti-conservation logic of the position paper, he was promptly put in his place.[60] The delegate said:

> I thought there was a big hullabaloo a few years ago about conserving all this stuff [energy resources] for our own, all [that] oil and stuff for our own use... If we were not going to save it we are going to lose it and be paying higher and higher prices later on and we won't have it for ourselves because we have been exporting it and I don't see why we should be trying to increase export markets, in that case.[61]

Presumably this man was referring to the ECWU's energy policy statement of 1980, which emphasized self-sufficiency as a goal for downstream manufacturing (not maximization of exports to sustain the short-term profitability of multinational corporations), conservation, and Canadianization (necessary to achieve these priorities). He was, in effect, told by Reimer that he was ignorant, and that the path advocated by the task force was the only one possible. After another long speech by a national staff representative, in support of the executive's position paper, it was unanimously adopted. Delegates were told that the new policy was excellent, well-researched, and that the national director had brought prestige to the union by co-chairing the task force.

This is not to say that membership support for this response to the industry's crisis was merely passive. The Sarnia area locals had formed their own "task force" in 1983, to prepare a brief for the government-appointed body. They hired a consultant and formed a committee, and their report apparently agreed with the recommendations adopted by the union's national executive.[62] This is not surprising, since their employers and their union representatives were telling them the same story of desperate struggle for survival and the jobs waiting to be created once the federal government could be persuaded to see the light. The outline of this story was provided by Sullivan and Reimer, the two main supporters of the task force (and, not surprisingly, of the "ongoing dialogue" programme). According to Sullivan:

> Your jobs are at this moment in the greatest jeopardy they have ever been since I have been a member of this union and I have been a member of this union for close to thirty years. And, it is because of government inaction, and when you are out there talking to your friends and relatives...maybe you should be pointing out to them what this industry means to you, to the neighbourhood, to the country in which we live... [Try] to envision what would happen...if we did not have the Petro-Chemical Industry.[63]

Of course there was ample reason for insecurity about job loss. An estimated 1,000 ECWU jobs were lost in the oil industry between 1981 and 1985.[64] As table 17 shows, plant closings hit the oil refineries particularly hard. According to the ECWU, over 30 percent of their units in Ontario were experiencing either lay-offs or work-sharing by the fall of 1982.[65] In the Sarnia area, over 2,000 jobs were lost through attrition and early retirement schemes, as a result of technological change, between 1982 and 1984.[66] In 1984 there were all kinds of rumours and threats of more plant closures. In this context, the national director and his staff willingly accepted a corporate strategy of recovery which promised to save, and to create more jobs in the industry.

There are important implications of this change in energy policy for the union's relationship with environmentalists concerned with resource conservation. Clearly, the 1980 statement contained many points of agreement with the environmentalist agenda for the energy sector, whereas the 1984 position, which contains some of the seeds of the energy section of the 1988 Free Trade Agreement, conflicts with environmentalist conceptions of "sustainable development."

Post-1984 ECWU Energy Policy

After many of the Petrochemical Industry Task Force recommendations had been implemented, and when industry restructuring was more or less established, the ECWU leadership revived some of its earlier nationalist views on energy policy. Union executives argued against the Conservative government's deregulation thrust, using oil pricing as an example of the adverse effects of deregulation on workers. The Secretary-Treasurer, Bob Stewart, claimed that deregulation of oil pricing and the "Western Accord" had resulted not in lower petrol prices but in higher federal tax on gasoline sold to consumers (as the government tried to recoup its revenue losses).[67] The elimination of a "made in Canada" oil price system, said Stewart, had reduced the ability of the National Energy Board to control imports and exports.[68] The ECWU opposed the Conservative government's intention to privatize PetroCanada, as well as the energy provisions of the Free Trade Agreement, criticising governments and corporations because "their short-term profit oriented market system has blinded the officials to the very serious concerns on sovereignty, and long-term energy supply."[69]

TABLE 17
PLANT CLOSINGS AFFECTING ECWU MEMBERS, 1982-1988 (PARTIAL LIST)

1982	Provincial Refinery, Come-by-Chance, NF
	Gulf Refinery, Port Hawkesbury, NS
	B. P. Refinery, Montreal, QC
	Texaco Refinery, Port Credit, ON
	Shell Oil Refinery, Oakville, ON
	Gulf Refinery, Kamloops, BC
	Five Gulf refineries in Western provinces
	Five Imperial Oil refineries in Western provinces
	Two Maple Leaf Mills plants, ON
	Chipman Chemicals, Moose Jaw, SK
	Toyotex Ltd., Trois-Rivières, QC
1983	Gulf gasoline and distillation units, Clarkson, ON
	McMillan Bloedel plant, London, ON
1984	Texaco Refinery, Edmonton, AB
	Melcher's Distillery, Berthierville, QC
1985	AECL heavy water plants, Hawkesbury and Glace Bay, NS
	Texaco Refinery, Port Credit, ON
	Gulf Oil Refinery, Montreal
1987	Pall Canada filters plant, Brockville, ON
	American Cyanamid, Welland, ON
	Canada Cup, Toronto, ON
	Western Co-op Fertilizer, Calgary, AB
	Cominco Fertilizer, Calgary, AB
1988	Pfizer Canada citric acid plant, Cornwall, ON

SOURCE: *ECWU Journal*, 1982-1988 issues.

Reg Basken, the national director who succeeded Neil Reimer in 1984, participated in an "Energy Options" study group appointed by the federal government. Basken said he would use the information obtained from this group to "redraft the Energy Policy for our Union," and that the Energy Committee of the CLC would have a new energy policy prepared for the CLC convention in Vancouver in May 1988. (Reg Basken chaired the CLC Energy Committee.) The CLC policy statement that emerged essentially reaffirmed the general principles of the ECWU's 1980 energy policy. In addition, it discussed the Tories' Free Trade Agreement (energy provisions) and how privatization and spending cuts affect national energy conservation and other goals. There was more focus on the issue of nuclear energy, in regard to which the Congress postponed taking positions which would antagonize certain groups of workers, by creating a task force to report to the 1990 Convention. The privatization of PetroCanada, Eldorado Nuclear, and Atomic Energy of Canada was opposed in the 1988 document, as in previous CLC statements.

The objective of keeping the costs of oil and gas feedstocks for the petrochemical industry relatively low is supported in the name of a diversified domestic industrial base.[70] However, given that a large portion of most petrochemical producers' sales are made to US markets, and that no specific measures to encourage "diversification" were proposed, this objective seemed more likely to secure the short-term "export-competitiveness" of the multinational petrochemical companies, than to reorient Canadian oil and gas production according to domestic consumption and conservation criteria. Taken alone, the use of "indigenous oil and gas supplies" to promote petrochemical industry production does not conflict with the interests of the companies—far from it. In other words, there does not appear to be a real contradiction between the CLC and ECWU's support for low energy prices to promote domestic industrial development, and the interests of the petrochemical companies in securing "competitively priced" feedstocks.

There would be, on the other hand, a conflict if restrictions on the production of oil and natural gas and on petrochemical exports were to be imposed—if domestic demand and conservation were to determine production levels and prices—thereby blocking the maximization of (export) sales. The CLC does call for a "self-reliant energy policy," but it is unlikely that the big, integrated petrochemical companies would consider limitations on exports an acceptable condition of corporate citizenship. Indeed, they were key supporters of the Free Trade Agreement precisely because they wanted to increase exports.[71] However, this apparent contradiction is not discussed, or even acknowledged, in the CLC document. Instead, a distinction is made between the petrochemical industry which must be encouraged to "create processing and manufacturing opportunities," and "the transnational energy corporations." The document views the energy provisions of the Mulroney Trade Deal as "the capitulation of Canadian interests to those of the US and the transnational energy corporations." Since many of these companies are oil and gas producers with downstream petrochemical operations, it is not evident that such a separation of interests is valid. Certainly this would seem to be a problem for the ECWU, whose members are drawn from all energy sectors and downstream industries.

The thrust of the ECWU-CLC positions was to limit exports (not extraction) of oil and gas, but not exports of petrochemicals or downstream products. The thinking appeared to be that this arrangement would create more processing jobs in Canada (assuming access to the United States market) and no loss of energy sector jobs. The strategy had nothing to do, therefore, with the conservation of non-renewable resources or environmental protection; the main concern was the protection of oil and chemical workers' jobs.

Yet even in this respect the strategy was short-sighted. Changes in demand for petrochemical products, and demands from environmentalists for the phasing-out of certain chemical industry commodities (e.g., polymers, plastics, chlorine), combined with technological change (increasing the capital/labour ratio), were also affecting chemical workers by the late 1980s.[72] Cheap feedstock policies were insufficient to bring about the creation of more jobs in the absence of a more radical subversion of the free market mechanisms underpinning the energy industry (e.g., in the form of nationalization of the industry, a programme of public investment in labour-intensive areas of energy conservation, alternative energy source development, recycling technology, etc.). This kind of nationalist, conservationist energy policy would no doubt have triggered an investment boycott, plant closings, and a campaign against government policy not unlike that waged against the National Energy Programme. The ECWU's choice in 1988 was to either join environmentalists and others in arguing for a national energy strategy not unlike its 1980 stance, and defending it against predictable reaction, or to support the interests of the multinational petrochemical firms in the hopes that cheap feedstock prices (low royalty rates) would create jobs for energy and chemical workers. One might say that the union tried, unsuccessfully, to do both.

CONCLUSIONS

When the petrochemical companies waved the banners of industry "disappearance" from Canada and massive job loss in the early-to-mid 1980s, the ECWU leadership accepted the logic that reducing government royalties on oil and gas extraction, deregulating prices, and increasing exports were the only ways to preserve and to create jobs. By the end of the 1980s, the factors that had led the ECWU leadership to ally with employers against government regulation of the industry had changed little, making their commitment to a self-reliant, domestic-needs oriented, and conservationist energy policy less than credible. The leadership remained committed to elite-corporatist and institutional forms of negotiation with employers and government. The focus of ECWU bargaining was the preservation of the privileged wage position (relative to other sectors) and the job security of an ever-shrinking minority of skilled workers. The conditions which would be necessary to successfully implement the energy policy outlined in 1980—including a radical education and mobilization of rank-and-file members behind the strategy, grass-roots alliances, public education work, collaboration with radical economists, etc.— were no more present than they had been in 1984. Although the worst of the restructuring and consequent job loss in the sector seemed to be over, the workforce was being reduced by technological change, while at the same time ownership was becoming increasingly concentrated.

NOTES

1. See the ECWU's *5th Constitutional Convention Proceedings* (Edmonton: ECWU, 1988), p. 11.
2. In 1978 the Petrochemical Industry Consultative Task Force put direct employment in the industry at 11,000, and employment in downstream industries at around 220,000. Petrochemical Industry Consultative Task Force, 1979, *Report of the Consultative Task Force on Petrochemicals* (June 1978), p. 2. The 1984 task force (see note 43) estimated that petrochemical companies employed 18,000 directly, 50,000 in "upstream industries and services," and 125,000 in downstream industries.
3. ECWU, "The Energy and Chemical Workers' Union: A United Voice for 35,000 Employees in Canada's Resource Sector," no date, p. 2.
4. See the CPPA, "The Key Role of the Chemical Industry in Canada's Economy," (submission to the MacDonald Royal Commission on the Economy), June 1983, p.4.
5. Mario Creet has argued that the "quiescence" of workers in the chemical industry may be traced to the late nineteenth century, and to the characteristics of the industry itself: rapid technological change which was deskilling, concentration of ownership, high capital investment, and rapid growth, which carried through to the 1960s, and allowed employers to pay relatively high wages. See "The Quiescence of the Chemical Worker" (unpublished paper, Queen's University, April 1985).
6. In the mid 1950s, the oil industry in the United States employed about 135,000 refinery workers. By 1976, this number had declined to 90,000 workers producing "twice the amount of petroleum products as their counterparts in the 1950s." See Ann Forrest, "History of Unionism in the Petro-Chemicals Industry" (unpublished paper, September 1979), pp. 23-24.
7. M. Rothbaum observed that wage differentials were a source of conflict within the OCAW after its merger with the oil workers in 1955. Melvin Rothbaum, *The Government of the Oil and Chemical Workers of America* (New York and London: Institute of Labor and Industrial Relations/Univ. of Illinois/John Wiley and Sons, 1962).
8. Figures showing similar differentials for US chemical workers are given in *Chemical and Engineering News*, June 9, 1986, p. 62. The fertilizer industry had been in a slump for some time because of the relative saturation of the market, and the depressed agricultural economy. A number of fertilizer plants closed during the recession. (See table 17 on plant closures.) Significant wage increases for workers in this sector in 1986-87 indicated a general upturn in profits, following restructuring.

9. These estimates are taken from Statistics Canada, *Employment Earnings and Hours* vol. 60 (December 1982), pp. 8-15. The ranges indicate the differences in employment between November 1981 and 1982. Generally, women's share of jobs in these sectors declined, probably because of the recession. Statistics on female workforce participation are not given in this source after 1982.

    This distribution of women workers by industry corresponds with the higher percentages of women found in ECWU locals in the metropolitan areas of Québec and Ontario. In Ontario, women comprised 12.6 percent of the ECWU's members in 1985; in Québec this figure was 19.2 percent. In Trois-Rivières, 83 percent of the members in one local were women. This compares to the 7.8 percent of members in "non-metropolitan" (resource extraction and refining) areas, and to the 13.2 percent of all union members who were women.

    Although the numbers of women in Alberta and B.C. locals were very few, Saskatchewan was something of an exception. In this province, about 19 percent of ECWU members were women, and the president of the Saskatchewan Area Council was a woman. The figures cited are based on table 9, and on Statistics Canada, *Corporations and Labour Unions* (1985), op. cit. According to Statistics Canada, women comprised 14.1 percent of the ECWU's national membership in 1983, and 13.4 percent in 1984.
10. See ECWU, *Proceedings of the Third Constitutional Convention*, July 16-19, 1984 (Edmonton: ECWU, 1984), p. 62.
11. Louise Sampson, delegate from Local 119, in ibid., p. 64. This delegate could probably have added that men were not likely to apply for lower-paying (women's) jobs, and were likely to see women as a threat to their monopoly of the better-paying ones. A good description of such a conflict is given by Stan Gray, in his account of sexism in the workplace, "Sharing the Shop Floor," in G. Hofmann Nemiroff, ed. *Women and Men* (Montréal: Fitzhenry and Whiteside, 1987).
12. See Arnold R. Weber, "Competitive Unionism in the Chemical Industry," *Industrial and Labor Research Review* (October 1959).
13. Rothbaum, *The Government of the Oil and Chemical Workers of America*, p. 34.
14. Forrest, "History of Unionism," p. 24. According to the (US) National Petroleum Refiners Association, of 37,052 oil refinery workers in the United States, 25,251 were covered by OCAW contracts in 1987. The remaining 11,801 were either non-union or non-OCAW represented. (Bob Williams, "Toting familiar demands, OCAW faces uphill fight in negotiations," *Oil and Gas Journal* vol. 85, no. 51 (December 21, 1987), pp. 14-16.)
15. This statement is based on data from the *ECWU Journal* (1981-1988 issues), and *Proceedings* of the 1986 ECWU Convention.
16. By the 1970s, OCAW was trying to implement national bargaining programs, and the ECWU followed this path in the 1980s. The ECWU also formed national bargaining councils (by sector and by firm) to co-ordinate bargaining strategies among locals. This parallels the development of national bargaining councils by the Canadian Autoworkers—a union which also has to negotiate with multinational corporations—as well as the creation of "world councils" by the International Chemical and Energy Workers' Federation (ICEF), to which the ECWU was affiliated.
17. See Huw Beynon and Theo Nichols, *Living with Capitalism: Class Relations and the Modern Factory* (London, Henley, and Boston: Routledge and Kegan Paul, 1977); Theo Nichols et al., *Workers Divided* (Glasgow: William Collins Sons & Co., 1976); David Halle, *America's Working Man* (Chicago and London: The Univ. of Chicago Press, 1984).
18. Union organisers at Fort McMurray (Syncrude, Suncor plants) complained in 1983 that: "Companies there arrange the working schedules to prevent workers from communicating among themselves." (Unnamed ECWU organisers, quoted in the *ECWU Journal* no. 7 (Fall 1983), p. 4.)
19. Just before the strike deadline in May 1988, Dow Chemical (Sarnia) management locked out their workers and brought in workers from (non-union) plants in Fort McMurray, Alberta, as well as their sales and marketing employees, to keep the plants running.
20. OECD, *The Petrochemical Industry: Trends in Production and Investment to 1985* (Paris: OECD, 1979), p. 7.
21. This represents a more than threefold real increase after adjusting for chemical prices. These

figures are given by the OECD, Environmental Directorate, in *Economic Aspects of International Chemical Control* (Paris: OECD, 1983), p. 15.
22. OECD, *Petrochemical Industry: Energy Aspects of Structural Change* (Paris: OECD, 1985), p. 78. Graham D. Taylor and Patricia E. Sudnik, in their history of DuPont, refer to environmental regulation in the US (e.g., the 1976 Toxic Substances Control Act), and the consumers' movement, as factors contributing to the industry's problems in the 1970s. They also include increasingly strong unions and rising labour costs in their explanation of profit squeeze in the chemical industry. See *DuPont and the International Chemical Industry* (Boston: Twayne, 1984).
23. Walter Vergara and Donald Brown, "The New Face of the World Petrochemical Sector: Implications for Developing Countries," *World Bank Technical Paper*, number 84: Industry and Energy Series (Washington DC, The World Bank, 1988), p. 20.
24. Petrochemical commodities are also relatively standardized; until recently, there was little product differentiation to affect market shares or prices. In 1986 *Chemical and Engineering News* reported that: "the ratio of added value to fixed cost [in the petrochemical industry was] at about unity. In terms of value added, the industry has been virtually flat for the past 10 years... Since the industry has added capital assets of about 50% during this period [1975-1985], capital productivity growth has been negative" (April 28, 1986, p. 10).
25. *Petrochemical Industry: Energy Aspects*, p. 11. Thermoplastics include polyethylenes, polypropylene, polyvinyl chloride, and polystyrene. "Precursors" refers to the primary and intermediary products. These are, respectively: ethylene, propylene, butadiene, benzene, and ammonia, and; ethylene oxide, ethylene glycol, dichloroethane, vinyl chloride, ethylbenzene, and styrene.
26. European and Japanese producers, who are primarily dependent on naphtha (a derivative of oil), were hurt much more by the sudden rise in oil prices than were their counterparts in the US. In Europe, the share of energy production costs in total ethylene production rose from 46 percent in 1973 to 85 percent in 1980 (OECD, *Petrochemical Industry: Energy Aspects*, p. 13). In the US, where petrochemical producers rely more heavily on ethane (a derivative of natural gas), the price increase was more gradual, and remained lower than naphtha prices. The US producers' advantage was mainly due to government regulation of oil and natural gas prices. Ethane prices in the US went up eight times between 1972 and 1981, compared to fourteen times in Europe (ibid.). After 1981 the US firms began to lose their advantage over European producers because of: (i) deregulation of oil prices; (ii) gradual deregulation of natural gas prices; (iii) a cyclical downturn in naphtha and petroleum prices in Europe; and (iv) the rise in the value of the dollar.
27. Dennis Slocum, "Chemical companies ponder past mistakes," *The Globe and Mail*, May 23, 1988.
28. N. Hunter, "Chemical sector's profit recovery is still far off," *The Globe and Mail*, November 23, 1985.
29. *ECWU Journal* no. 6 (Spring 1983), p. 6; and no. 3 (July 1982), p. 8.
30. *Chemical and Engineering News*, June 8, 1987, pp. 70-71.
31. Dermot O'Sullivan, "Earnings of Canadian chemical firms improved last year," *Chemical and Engineering News*, February 23, 1987, p. 19.
32. Earl Anderson, "Profits make a strong recovery for the [Canadian] chemical industry," *Chemical and Engineering News*, December 14, 1987, p. 43.
33. DuPont Canada found strong demand for its industrial yarns, polyethylenes, and specialty polymers. Celanese Canada had "exceptionally brisk" chemical sales to Europe. Over all, Canadian chemical exports increased by around 9 percent in 1987. Plastics exports were up by around 25 percent. Fertilizer sales in foreign markets, however, remained depressed, with declines from 15 to 40 percent (Earl Anderson, "Profits make a strong recovery," *Chemical Engineering News*, December 14, 1987, p. 44). The demand for plastics (polystyrene, polyvinyl chloride, polyethylenes) has created strong demand for ethylene. Canadian producers increased ethylene output by 14 percent from 1986 to 1987 and plants were running at full capacity.
34. Patricia Lush, "Chemical sales forecast to slow," *The Globe and Mail*, December 28, 1988, p. B1.
35. *The Globe and Mail* (business briefs), n.d., December 1987.
36. Ibid.
37. Dow Chemical of Canada and other companies made this point in their briefs to the MacDonald Royal Commission on the Economy, in 1983 and 1984. Lower feedstock costs translate into a

substantial advantage in production costs of ethylene and significant savings in the production costs of downstream petrochemicals.
38. Dow Chemical Canada brief to the MacDonald Commission, November 1983, p. 2.
39. In late 1978, Canadian oil prices—regulated since 1973 under federal-provincial agreement—were approaching world levels. Then, between October 1978 and mid-1980, the world price more than doubled. In June 1979, Prime Minister Clark agreed to raise Canadian oil prices to international levels "as quickly as possible." See Larry Pratt, "Energy: The Roots of National Policy," *Studies in Political Economy* 7 (Winter 1982), pp. 27-59.
40. The feedstock price advantage was at the expense of the oil and gas producers, and was based on a "blended" oil price (domestic and imported average) and on keeping natural gas prices lower than oil. The 1981 agreement provided that oil and natural gas prices would rise much more quickly than under the NEP, and eliminated the export tax on gas.
41. At one point in 1982, the price of ethane was 25 percent higher in Alberta than that paid by US producers in the Gulf of Mexico.
42. In their 1978 task force recommendations to the Canadian government, the petrochemical companies argued that Canada's "strong energy resource position" should be used to keep energy prices for domestic industry lower than the export, or world market price. See the *Report of the Consultative Task Force on Petrochemicals* (June 1978), p. 6. (Cited in note 2.)
43. Petrochemical Industry Task Force (1983-84), *Petrochemical Industry Task Force Report* (February 1984), p. 15.
44. Ibid., pp. 16-17. These recommendations were made also in the CCPA, Dow Chemical, and other chemical company briefs to the MacDonald Royal Commission on the Economy in 1983-84.
45. The petrochemical companies used this claim to argue for increasing energy exports to the US under the Canada-US Trade Agreement. The OECD, however, predicted in 1985 that oil and gas reserves would begin to run out in the 1990s, and that the discoveries-production ratio would fall permanently below unity. The OECD advised the industry to accelerate research into processes for using coal and biomass products as feedstocks (e.g., synthesis gas chemistry). See OECD, *Petrochemical Industry: Energy Aspects*.
46. Dow Chemical Canada brief to the MacDonald Commission, November 1983, p. 1.
47. Ibid., p. 10.
48. Dow Chemical Canada, "Remarks to the Standing Senate Committee on Energy and Natural Resources Review of the National Energy Programme," May 8, 1984. In author's possession.
49. *Report of the Consultative Task Force on Petrochemicals* (June 1978), p. 2.
50. This view was expressed by Ivan Hillier, former president of the Dow Sarnia chemical workers' local, and long-time activist in the OCAW and ECWU, in an interview with the author in May 1988 in Sarnia, Ont.
51. Government of Canada, "Response of the Federal Government to the Recommendations of the Consultative Task Force on the Canadian Petrochemical Industry" (May 1979), p. 4.
52. *ECWU Journal* no. 3 (July 1982), p. 7.
53. C. Stuart Sullivan, Ontario Co-ordinator, ECWU, speaking at the 1984 national convention of the ECWU (Ottawa, July 16-19), in *Proceedings of the Third Constitutional Convention*, p. 163.
54. Ibid., p. 159.
55. Ibid., p. 159.
56. Ibid., p. 161. Note that the ECWU had opposed "deregulation" of energy prices in 1978; in 1984 they referred to this—now desirable policy—as "the more flexible approach." See, for example, the *ECWU Journal* no. 8 (Spring 1984), p. 12.
57. ECWU, *Proceedings*, 1984, pp. 126-127.
58. Ibid., p. 163. Sullivan also confirmed in a statement made at the 1988 Convention of the ECWU, that in his view the alternatives at the time were either to support employers' demands for lower energy prices, or to accept more plant closings. See ECWU, *Proceedings* (1988), p. 202.
59. Reimer, in ECWU, *Proceedings* (1984), p. 16.
60. Judging by the 1984 convention proceedings, the national executive and the executive board controlled both the agenda (submitting the resolutions, presenting faits accomplis) and the process. Key staff representatives or executive members dominated the floor, promoting their

various resolutions. The "top's" privileged expertise, and prestigious associations were used to denigrate members, e.g., comments such as: "let me take you to school" (Reimer to a delegate); "I would consider most of the people in this room somewhat short of facts" (national rep. responding to questions about the Petrochemical Industry Task Force positions). Troublesome delegates were dismissed or cut off by the chairperson, Reimer; their points were sometimes ignored. Meanwhile, a great deal of self-congratulation went on among executive and staff officials.

61. ECWU, *Proceedings of the Third Constitutional Convention*, 1984, p. 164.
62. The Sarnia locals' brief is referred to by Stuart Sullivan and R. Pratt (national rep) at the 1984 convention (Ibid., pp. 162, 165).
63. Sullivan, Ibid., p. 126.
64. *ECWU Journal* no. 13 (Spring 1986), p. 6. The same source claims that, in the United States, there were 135 refinery closures in this period, resulting in the loss of over 20,000 jobs.
65. *ECWU Journal* no. 5, p. 4. Structural unemployment in 1983 was averaging 10 percent (*ECWU Journal* (Fall 1983), p. 3).
66. Figure given by Stuart Sullivan, ECWU, *Proceedings* (1984), p. 162.
67. The Western Accord of March 1985 lifted most controls on oil and deregulated pricing. Market laws were restored to natural gas policy in October 1985, with the Agreement on Natural Gas Markets and Prices. Conservation and alternative energy programmes were replaced by the National Conservation and Alternative Energy Initiative, which—despite its name—"resulted in significantly less spending on those technologies." See the CLC Energy Committee's "Energy Policy Statement" (Doc. No. 19) presented to the 17th Constitutional Convention (May 9-13, 1988), p. 1.
68. *ECWU Journal* no. 12, p. 4.
69. Reg Basken, in the *ECWU Journal* no. 18, p. 3. On PetroCanada, see *ECWU Journal* no. 17 (August 1987), p. 16. The ECWU always supported the formation and continued operation of PetroCanada, and indeed takes credit for pushing the Canadian government to create the crown corporation. However, in the Petrochemical Industry Task Force report the union remained silent on the issue of "government monopolies."
70. See the CLC's "Energy Policy Statement" (May 1988), p. 2.
71. The FTA stipulates that Canadian exports of oil and natural gas to the United States may not be reduced for reasons of domestic conservation of supply. Exports may be cut only if the production for domestic consumption is cut proportionately.
72. For a detailed study of the effects of environmental regulation on technological innovation and industrial strategy in the cases of paints, polymers, plastics, and pesticides, see Arthur P. J. Mol, *The Refinement of Production: Ecological Modernization Theory and the Chemical Industry* (Utrecht: Van Arkel, 1995).

[9]

Collective Bargaining and Union-Employer Relations

NATIONAL BARGAINING PROGRAMMES, 1981-88

The priorities and achievements of OCAW/ECWU collective bargaining are examined here with a view to identifying the importance attached by leaders and rank-and-file members to "social unionism" concerns such as reduction of work time (solidarity with the unemployed; quality of life of union members); reduction of wage differentials and gender and racial equality (internal egalitarianism); occupational health and safety; and industrial pollution.

REDUCTION OF WORK TIME

By the early 1970s the stresses of shift work and the forty-hour work week were producing higher rates of absenteeism and turnover. A survey of ninety-four bargaining units in 1972, encompassing 1,799 members, showed that there were conflicting views within OCAW's membership about the importance of reducing work time. Summarizing the survey results, Wayne Roberts says: "Younger workers wanted longer days and a shorter work week. Older workers didn't think they could handle the longer shifts. Although 72 percent of the members wanted shorter hours, only 42 percent said they'd strike over the issue."[1] In the absence of membership consensus on the form work reduction should take, or the priority this should warrant in bargaining with employers, the Canadian leadership of the OCAW decided to negotiate a deal with the company whose management seemed most open to the idea—Gulf Oil. The oil workers' bargaining unit approved work time reduction as a priority at their meeting in February 1973. Subsequently (in July 1973):

> Gulf agreed to the 37.3-hour week and wage increases of 22 percent over a three-year contract. The wage increase, most of which came due immediately, offset the loss of hours and provided a small raise. A new work schedule bundled the shorter hours into 17 extra days off per year, timed to coincide with other holidays. Oil workers call them "Golden Fridays." It was a "historic breakthrough," Reimer [Canadian director of the OCAW] told *Union News*, "the first time a company and a union have negotiated a shorter work week with the retention of the eight-hour day on a national and industry basis."[2]

Notably, this wage increase more than made up for the loss of earning hours—a deal much more difficult to extract from employers in less profitable, less capital-intensive sectors of the economy. The wage increase agreed with Gulf Oil made up for 2.7 hours of lost overtime wages. But at other companies, overtime hours averaged four to six hours. Nevertheless, workers at other oil refineries supported the national agreement, which was eventually accepted by Shell and Texaco. In 1973-74, shorter work week contracts were negotiated in the Chemical Valley with Fiberglass, Polysar, and Cabot in Welland. This was also one of the demands at issue in the 1973 strike at Dow Chemical in Sarnia, which lasted thirteen weeks and ended in Dow's acceptance of OCAW's demands. However, as the era of Fordist crisis set in, companies would become less willing to agree to such reforms. Roberts remarks in his 1990 history of the ECWU:

> There was a time to grab for shorter hours, and that was in the late 1960s and early 1970s. After that the shorter work week became a "frill" compared to the problems of inflation in the mid-1970s and concessions and international competition in the 1980s.

Far from being a "frill" for workers, the shorter work week became an essential solution to structural unemployment in the 1980s. Yet the 37.3-hour work week was often not observed in practice, and calls for a 36-hour work week did not translate into collective bargaining.

In early 1981 the ECWU was able to negotiate a uniform wage settlement with the oil and petrochemical industry at the national level. At the time, it was the highest wage increase obtained in any major industry (subsequently exceeded by the Canadian Paperworkers Union and the International Woodworkers of America in BC.). The agreement was for two years. In the second year, the oil companies agreed to an additional 1.5 percent wage increase, which brought the second year increase to 13.5 percent. The petrochemical companies, however, refused to grant this additional increase because of the recession, which worsened in 1982. By 1983, as bargaining approached again, the uniform rate structure was beginning to crumble; many of the petrochemical companies had already demanded concessions.

The October 1982 National Bargaining Conference of the ECWU established three priority categories of concern: wages and benefits; job security; and union recognition. Nothing was proposed regarding health and safety, environmental protection, or job creation (e.g., reduced work time). Similarly, the National Bargaining Format in 1983 included: a one year agreement; a general wage increase of 6 percent; a union orientation programme for new members; extended leave of absence for union business; job security clauses; and improved notice of lay-offs and terminations.[3]

The National Bargaining Programme discussed in 1984 did include a call for a shorter work week. The national director of the union proposed that a thirty-six hour work week should be phased in by 1986.[4] A resolution passed at the 1984 convention urged *governments* to phase in a thirty-two hour work week over the next three years, with no loss in take-home pay. It also proposed a ban on compulsory overtime.[5] However, some delegates pointed out that membership support for such measures was lacking, that members were more concerned about making as much money as possible (especially in cases where lay-offs were threatened) than with measures to create new jobs for others. According to one delegate:

> The fact is that we all…pay lip service to [shorter work weeks]…but, somewhere along the line, the trade union movement has to deal with a few realities… In the Local union that I represent…in the month of July, 1984, some of my members have worked 500 hours of overtime, already; that is 20 hours a week—that means they are taking somebody's job away every week… [T]his amount of overtime is being put upon a salary or an income of close to $34,000 a year flat rate. I mean we have members of our union this year that are going to make $50,000 a year… but where do we go to when we look at it from a social justice point of view? It is not there.[6]

A delegate from a textile factory in Trois-Rivières, employing mostly women, said that union officials there were "unable to get the employees to understand that overtime is cutting jobs." She proposed that if the union's long-term objective were to reduce the work week, it should begin with an educational campaign among rank-and-file members, leading up to their agreement to a ban on overtime work (including voluntary overtime). In this case, it was not a question of a relatively well-paid, permanent workforce trying to make $13,000 on top of their regular pay, but of a highly insecure workforce, earning lower wages, and frequently on and off unemployment-insurance contributions (UIC), trying to save up enough money to live during periods of lay-off. The sacrifice required, therefore, in the name of solidarity with other workers, was considerably greater. As this delegate pointed out:

> The Resolution before us is rather nice, but I believe that it is a dream; we must first sensitize our membership and make them fully understand the objective of our Union—why we are asking them to renounce overtime. To renounce overtime is to refuse money and therefore, we must make them understand why they are asked that sacrifice. It is for the progress of the labour movement and all the workers, organized or not.[7]

No such educational campaign was proposed, however, in the form of a resolution, and there was no response from members of the executive to the concern expressed by delegates that the 32-hour resolution be supported by concrete actions by the union.

A second problem with this bargaining goal was the reality of employers' refusal to negotiate it. The resolution took the form of an appeal to *government* to implement the shorter work week through legislation. This led to an appeal by a member of the national staff close to the New Democratic party (NDP), for everybody to vote for that party in the September 1984 election. It was explicitly admitted by staff that the union had no intention of negotiating for shorter hours with employers through collective bargaining. Dave Pretty, National Rep. for the Sarnia District, summed up what amounts to the union's retreat from all fronts except parliamentary support for the NDP.

> We don't even have a 40-hour work week. I service a number of collective agreements that say: the basic work week shall be 40 hours per week. Well,...the actual work week is an average of 42 hours a week... We have Local 21—Cyanamide and the Welland Plant, Garner Road near Niagara Falls, where there is 25% of a 400-man workforce that is slated for or now on unemployment... What did the Company say when we said let's talk about reducing those hours? "Well, we can't afford that—that's too costly." What does Domtar say? Domtar says 5 and 4—there ain't no more. And they got the 42-hour work week, then paying time and a half on average for the last 25 years for that extra 8 hours every four weeks but there ain't no way that those folks are prepared to come down to the basic reality of a 40-hour week... So, Brother Chairman, sisters and brothers, delegates, let's don't plan on having a lot of strikes in order to accomplish this, let's recognize the fact that in order to support R [Resolution]-7, we are going to have to convince two million Canadians [to vote NDP].[8]

As the convention continued to adopt various bargaining objectives, such as job security clauses, some delegates became aware of a contradiction between the radical rhetoric of the convention, and the realities facing them in their workplaces. A delegate from local 593, Oakville, questioned:

> How come we in fact propose to state to the world and to the labour movement in Canada that we believe in strengthening job security clauses in collective agreements, that we believe in reduction of the work week to provide increased

Collective Bargaining and Union-Employer Relations 149

employment... How come we stress these things and yet be told by our leaders that we should try and go back to the individual bargaining units, and convince our members that yet again in 1985 we propose that the contract not be opened but merely extended. There will be no negotiations nationally on these issues because we have already been told by several of the senior National Reps. that it is not there... I am confused, Mr. Chairman.[9]

The delegate received no reply.

Work hours were considered unnegotiable in this period; the union staff and executive members attempted neither to implement campaigns to raise the consciousness of rank-and-file members regarding the long term objectives of the movement, nor to organise a strong nation-wide collective bargaining campaign targeting key objectives.[10] This reflects, probably, both the reality of high unemployment and a shrinking membership, and the leadership's predisposition to avoid confrontation with employers, instead pursuing consultative and electoral paths of action.

Petrochemical industry profits began to recover by 1986, and the worst of the lay-offs seemed to be over. However, falling oil prices led the oil companies to pressure the unions for wage "roll-backs." In this context, the bargaining programme for 1986-88 remained relatively cautious. Its main elements were:
1. a seven percent wage increase (over two years);[11]
2. job security clauses;
3. more vacations;
4. "dialogue" between the National Bargaining Committee[12] and employers, regarding:
   a. early resolution of local demands
   b. reducing overtime
   c. ensuring adequate leave of absence for union business
   d. strengthening "continuing dialogue"
   e. dialogue with local union committees about pension improvements[13]

The National Bargaining Programme for 1988-90 included:[14]
1. a two-year contract;
2. wage increases of about 4.5 percent a year;
3. six months notice of permanent workforce reduction;
4. a union Safety, Health, and Industrial Relations Training Fund.

OCCUPATIONAL HEALTH AND SAFETY

Since its separation from OCAW in 1979-80, the ECWU had not been particularly active in health and safety education, research, and bargaining. The national co-ordinator for health and safety, Dan Ublansky, interviewed in 1988, suggested that this was because the union lacked the resources for research which had been available through the OCAW.[15] Most of the union's activities in this regard had been directed toward government lobbying, to improve occupational health and safety legislation, rather than contract negotiations or strike actions.[16]

In the fall of 1987, the ECWU decided to create a National Health and Safety Committee, initiating a renewed role for the union in this area. The union was successful in negotiating with major employers in 1988 (including PetroCanada) the creation of a Safety, Health, and Industrial Relations Training Fund. Employers would pay three cents per hour to the National Union for each full-time employee's regular hours of work. This was presented to workers as a concession exacted from employers. "Off the record," one union official explained that the three cents was actually to be deducted from the negotiated wage increase. Union officials doubted that members would support a deduction from their wages, even for a health and safety training fund. So it was presented to them, "in disguise," as an additional three cents per hour (employer contribution) on top of their wage increase.

This episode says something about the nature of the relationship between the union leadership and its membership. While the goal of improving health and safety education and training is certainly one to be supported, and a number of rank-and-file activists have dedicated themselves wholeheartedly to efforts to improve working conditions, union officials admit that they have failed to involve the rank-and-file membership in an effective, ongoing, campaign. As the delegate from Trois Rivières observed with regard to the reduced work hours issue, membership support for such policies needs to be created through educational work undertaken by the union, and by a demonstrated commitment from the leadership. This implies a dynamic, interactive relationship between union representatives and the rank-and-file, a priority of funding for educational programmes, and so on. This kind of internal culture did not appear to be present in the ECWU of the 1980s.

GENDER EQUALITY

One "non-traditional" area of concern which was making some progress within the union was "women's issues." This was due to the persistent efforts of women activists in the union to have equal pay, parental leave, and other such concerns placed on the bargaining agenda. Before 1984, very few women were to be found in any official union positions.[17] (The union estimated that, by 1989, women comprised between 12 and 15 percent of total membership.) At the 1984 Constitutional Convention, delegates voted—after an unusually long debate (most resolutions recommended for concurrence by the Resolution Committee were passed without much discussion)—to make one out of three executive board members at large a woman. This was a temporary affirmative action measure, to be reevaluated at subsequent conventions. A Women's Committee was also formed; it was to report to the next convention on problems and policies related to women. Policies on wage discrimination and maternity leave were adopted in principle, although they were not placed on the agenda of the national bargaining programme.

The Women's Committee report to the 1986 Convention revealed that only 50 percent of ECWU contracts contained maternity leave provisions, and that "contractual language on harassment, parental leave, and affirmative action are virtually nonexistent, as is company or union provided child care." Moreover, the Committee was "not surprised to find that educational programmes that have some focus on women's issues were not taking place."[18] At this convention, resolutions were passed to create a Women's Standing Committee, and to adopt a policy paper on "personal/sexual harassment."[19] The principle of pay equity was endorsed by the delegates once again, and included in the union's educational programme. However, local bargaining units were not obligated to negotiate pay equity.

By 1988, the women seemed to have concluded that convention policies and efforts at persuasion alone were not going to bring about real changes in union practice. At the Convention held that year, they moved that the women's position on the executive board be made permanent, through an amendment to the constitution. This engendered considerable debate, leading members of the executive and national staff to express "surprise" and "dismay." Sullivan urged delegates to support the resolution, if not because of agreement with the principle of affirmative action, then to protect the "credibility" of the union in the labour movement. Eventually the motion was passed. The second significant development at this convention was a resolution calling on local unions to "negotiate clauses to close the wage gap, including across the board wage settlements instead of percentages to assist those in the low end of the pay scale."[20] Another resolution called

Collective Bargaining and Union-Employer Relations 151

on local unions to bargain for parental leave. These were passed without debate, but it was left up to local unions to implement these policies, and women's issues had no place in the national bargaining programme.

CONTINUING DIALOGUE

Very little written information is available about the changing nature of labour-management relations in the Canadian energy and chemical industry. General statements are made additionally difficult by the fact that conditions in the oil fields, refineries, industrial chemical plants, smaller chemical products manufacturing plants, nuclear facilities, and so on, vary greatly. Some work does exist on labour-management relations, and the union's mediating role, in the cases of some of the large chemical companies in Britain. Nichols and Beynon examined the "New Working Arrangement" introduced at "Chem Co" in southern England in the 1970s. Shell U.K.'s "New Philosophy" programme, implemented in the 1960s, is the subject of a book by Blackler and Brown.[21] In 1979, Shell Chemical Co. of Canada introduced a similar programme at its Sarnia site, with the participation of the ECWU.[22]

In the early 1980s the ECWU leadership introduced the "continuing dialogue" programme. Its co-ordinator, "Buck" Philp, described its purpose as: "to improve relationships, correct sloppy operations and increase the viability of the plants through a cooperative approach."[23] According to Stuart Sullivan, Ontario Region Co-ordinator for the ECWU and one of the programme's key supporters, the dialogue was supposed to let the union participate in developing the "social and technical environment" in the firm.

> Ongoing dialogue is what we call it, where we have committees established. For instance, at Domtar, we have a committee at the top of the house, which consists of Reg Basken [National Director, ECWU] and the corporate vice president of Domtar. They meet about once a year, and have a working/steering committee.[24]

The steering committee comprised three ECWU officials and three management persons. Its job was to review "the whole work relationship and to promote a better working relationship, understanding, opening up the lines of communication so they get right up to the people who are the decision makers, like the President [of the company]." The committee made recommendations, and suggested processes for particular plants to implement. It advised on whether particular changes violated corporate or union policy, and "encourage[d] them to get together." According to Sullivan, the committee also reviewed the minutes of plant committee meetings and kept up pressure for changes to be implemented. He gave the example of a "success" with the programme: labour relations at Domtar. ECWU held the bargaining rights for twelve groups of Domtar workers (including a salt mine), totalling just over 900 workers (or 10.5 percent of the company's unionized workforce). Between 1971 and 1982, there were twenty-two legal and nineteen wildcat strikes in ECWU-represented Domtar plants; management was openly anti-union. ECWU officials claim that in March 1982 they invited Domtar managers to meet with union staff to form a joint Domtar Task Force to improve labour relations.[25] The company agreed. The Task Force subsequently achieved mutually acceptable guidelines for bargaining and bargaining dates, thereby avoiding strikes.[26]

Union officials say that the programme began with the oil industry, and specifically with the Gulf Canada Task Force, created in 1983. The idea, it seems, was for the union and the employers to collaborate to pull the companies through the recession.[27] By the late 1980s, according to Sullivan, some kind of "continuing dialogue" programme existed in about 20 percent of ECWU-represented plants across the country, among them: Canadian Cyanamid, Upper Canada Marketing, PetroCanada, and Shell Chemical

Canada (Sarnia). Shell Chemical Canada was, in the view of one union official, the "most prominent," "formal," and "stable" QWL programme in existence at any (ECWU) plant, having been in place since the plant was built. Union lawyer Dan Ublansky described the Shell programme as "a team approach to the operation of the plant." In lieu of a collective agreement, there is a short statement of principles and objectives. "It does not deal with the nitty-gritty of working conditions; all these things are to be dealt with on a co-operative basis, from day to day."[28] According to union officials, conflicts are usually settled by referral to a "good practices handbook."

> The entire operation still runs [in 1990] 24 hours a day, seven days a week, with a bare minimum of supervision. Workers and co-ordinators have divided themselves into six operating, or "process," teams and one maintenance, or "craft," team. Each team manages its own affairs... Unions and managers work as equals in the design plans, training programmes, and hiring decisions.[29]

When in-plant co-operation fails, a "special co-ordinator" from the national union executive "will go in and work with the [local] union and the company, trying to get them to start working out mutual ways, developing trust..."[30] Thus the national union officials act, in effect, as mediators between the local workforce and local management.

While the recession no doubt created greater incentives for employers and union leaders to implement such agreements, the ECWU's interest in a "co-operative" or "consultative" relationship with employers goes back to the mid-1970s. The National Director at the time sought to participate in consultative bodies involving government, private employers, and the unions, such as the Major Projects Task Force of the federal department of Industry, Trade, and Commerce, and the PetroChemical Industry task forces. Shell approached the ECWU leadership in 1977 with an invitation to participate in a joint union-management organisation design task force "responsible for designing a new chemical plant in keeping with the principles of socio-technical systems thinking."[31] Union officials (Reimer, Sullivan, Basken) took the lead in persuading the Sarnia area ECWU council and other national union officials that Shell's "new paradigm" was compatible with the union's objectives of "enhancing the quality of life of our members."[32] The ECWU participated in the Canadian Labour Congress's (CLC's) committee on quality of work life (QWL) programmes, and in 1981, Reimer described QWL as "a major programme of our union."[33] At the 1982 Convention, the Executive Board introduced a "Programme on Improvements in Working Conditions." This was intended—without undermining the collective agreement—to create a process (like the steering committee) to "continually review and monitor" issues related to working conditions. The idea was not, primarily, to improve productivity, but to give employees (through the union) "greater decision making authority." A five-day seminar on QWL, held in October the same year, organised by the Management School of the University of Montréal, was attended by ECWU representatives and petrochemical employers.[34]

In the Shell U.K. case, the Tavistock Institute of Human Relations helped a special management group to write a new corporate philosophy statement, and its social scientists acted as consultants on its implementation.[35] Blackler and Brown observe that the impetus behind the initiative was declining profitability, attributed to diminishing labour productivity and increasing world competition. Also mentioned is the "problem" of "an emerging ecological lobby whose activities promised to limit oil usage and to lead to pressures on companies to pollute less." Management's project was to reassert control over its employees, to overcome union resistance to lay-offs, contracting out, the introduction of labour-saving technology, and the elimination of "restrictive work practices." The solution, incorporated in the "new management philosophy," was to make it our long term policy to secure a fundamental change in attitude *on the part of employees* where, in a climate of mutual trust and confidence between man [sic] and management, it becomes possible for them to commit themselves fully *to the company objective* of having its work carried out with maximum efficiency and productivity (emphasis added).[36]

A similar conjuncture existed within the Canadian petrochemical industry in the early 1980s. Indeed, the Tavistock Institute also played a role in developing the QWL plan for Shell Canada.[37]

For the ECWU leadership, the initial conception of the continuing dialogue programme (CDP) seems to have emphasized the goal of advancing workplace democracy, albeit not as part of any explicitly radical agenda.[38] The CDP was associated with the goal of putting union representatives on the boards of directors of firms—especially the crown corporations.[39] This conception predominated in official statements about the CDP until 1982, and recurred subsequently. However, with the deepening of the recession, it was supplanted by a greater emphasis on the "mutual" concern of employers and employees to improve productivity and to help the industry compete internationally. The union was struggling to defend jobs and wages; "quality of work life" issues were not considered negotiable. In this context, it is interesting that the CDP was described as a "key focus" of the 1982-84 National Bargaining Programme.[40] In addition, after 1982 the "dialogue" was increasingly viewed as being most appropriately one between top levels of management, and national-level representatives of the union. Some local unions were confused about how to respond to employer initiatives. They were being told to engage in "continuing dialogue" programmes which seemed linked to management schemes to improve productivity at workers' expense. The "dialogue" seemed to be taking place in board rooms, while the "bargaining" was being fought out on the shop floor. In 1985 the ECWU's National Director, Reg Basken, admitted that employers were more interested in increasing productivity than in increasing workers' participation in decision-making.[41] However, what emerges most strikingly from recorded discussions of the CDP is a large gap between the perceptions of rank-and-file members and those of the highest levels of the union hierarchy regarding the goals and achievements of the programme. Basken's admission, for example, was followed by a re-endorsement of the programme, and of its goals to improve the quality of work and "ease confrontation between employers and workers."

Meanwhile, on the shop floor, management-inspired schemes to improve productivity and to "dialogue" directly with employees were making local union officials question the direction of the CDP. At the 1984 convention a Québec delegate related his membership's experience with their employer, Cyanamid Canada (one of the firms mentioned by Sullivan as having a CDP in place with the union). As was the case at Domtar, after a period of conflict during which "the members were militant," the company "streamlined its style of management." "It promoted participation programs," and introduced "The Key to Innovation." Employees who would give management some idea for improving productivity, would receive a reward—a weekend trip or $1,000. One employee, getting into the spirit, submitted an idea to eliminate eight jobs. Management was, of course, delighted. Cyanamid also introduced a "Quality of Work Life Programme." They surveyed employees about their attitudes, and then used some of the results to challenge the representativeness of the union's bargaining positions. The company also hired a consulting firm to "set up a strategy of direct communications with employees," thereby by-passing the union, and challenging its legitimacy as a bargaining agent. Delegates at the 1986 convention also described a workplace reality which contradicted the national executive's ideal picture of continuing dialogue. One delegate pointed out that "we discuss things [with management] all the time anyway," and that whatever they got they had to bargain for. Another delegate, employed by Husky Oil, Lloydminster, described an intransigent management which could be forced to make concessions only through hard bargaining. These delegates seemed to be saying that real gains for workers would inevitably entail "adversarial" or "confrontational" relations with employers.

Other employers, however, like Cyanamid, had attempted to convert QWL programmes into vehicles to attain their own objectives. Even Dow Chemical Canada (Sarnia Division), known for its paternal and authoritarian management style, decided in 1987 to implement a programme called "Continuous Improvement Process," and "Management Philosophy Core Values." The key elements were "teamwork," "reward and recognition programmes," and "using employee input within the overall company point of view."[42] Suddenly the management was encouraging employees' "personal freedom," "creativity," "self-motivation," and "innovation." Nevertheless, this new philosophy did not soften management's treatment of rank-and-file activists in the much-emphasized priority concern areas of health and safety and environmental stewardship. Workers active in both these areas confirmed in interviews that encouragement of "self-motivation" was intended to apply quite specifically to the company's profit and public image objectives (see chapter 11).

Continuing dialogue also seemed to be having questionable results at the Shell Chemical Plant near Sarnia, where workers were on the verge of a strike in 1988. Union officials implied that the main issue was management's refusal to fulfil its part of the "co-operative" bargain (embodied in the statement of principles).[43] A member of the local executive, quoted by Roberts, explained that by 1988, "the union felt it was on shaky ground, with no way to protect people, so we insisted on a clause that recognized [that] the good practices handbook and philosophy statement could be taken to an arbitrator."[44]

Despite these indications that the companies were obtaining more from continuing dialogue and QWL programmes than their workforces, national officials of the ECWU continued to be quite committed to a "consultative" relationship, conducted mainly between themselves and corporate executives. At the 1986 convention, the Executive Board introduced a resolution which re-endorsed the CDP, and committed the union to "proceed with its efforts to establish a continuing dialogue programme wherever and whenever we can get the employers involved in meaningful discussion." Speaking in support of the resolution, national representative Buck Philp, argued along two lines. The first—which subsequently became a pervasive conception of the CDP among lower levels of the union hierarchy—was that CD was simply *a continuation of collective bargaining*. Talking to employers frequently (during the life of the agreement) would make contract negotiations easier. This was also the interpretation of CDP given by the National Director, Reg Basken, in his address to the convention. He explained CDP as meaning: "if you can't get it at the bargaining table, we'd better talk about it and see if we can get it some other way," leaving open the question of what the bargaining power of the union is supposed to be, once the threat of strike is removed. At the 1988 Convention, Basken said: "There is no magic in continuing dialogue, it's just a better way for some. If it works, we use it. If we're used in it, we throw it out." He argued that employers were going to have to see unions, not as a "third party," but as "an equal partner in the plant, in the offices." This line suggests that members can only *gain* through such a relationship with management. There is no mention made, in this version, of a *quid pro quo*.

The second argument made by Philp in his 1986 statement revived the corporatist "recession" theme:

Collective Bargaining and Union-Employer Relations 155

> Over the last several years we have had to look at it from a somewhat different light as well. We have had a great many plant closures in this country. We have had to deal with those. We have had to look at the industry's position as a result of the crunch [oil crisis] and it's been difficult...
>
> There is a serious short term problem for the industry and we have to address those things. It's a simple matter, as I said during the National Bargaining Programme [report], those companies have to be healthy for our membership to be healthy, and I mean financially healthy. So [continuing dialogue] is an important programme for this union. It is the kind of programme that can produce a lot of good things for our members, good results and can produce them without having to pound the bricks.

Here we find that Continuing Dialogue is a *substitute* for collective bargaining in a context of generally weakened union bargaining power. In other words, the CD programme was viewed as part of a *defensive* strategy to prevent job loss and keep the companies "healthy."

Moreover, collective bargaining, entailing the possibility of strikes, was seen as an "adversarial" approach to management-labour relations. The union leadership's view of the latter as "out-dated," was the counterpart of its desire to create a "professional" image for the ECWU (and themselves). National officials of the union tended to identify themselves more closely with the educational and occupational standings of their management counterparts than with those of industrial workers. Their statements emphasized the "professional," "highly skilled" nature of the membership and the union, and the "high-tech," and "cutting-edge" nature of the industry. They stressed the business-like relations between union and employers and government, union leaders' roles in consultative bodies, union sponsorship of medical research (e.g., into osteoporosis), and other factors which, in their view, set them apart from other industrial workforces and their unions.[45] One former ECWU official summed up this distinction by saying that ECWU leaders and members "are more sophisticated in their approach to union problems" than other industrial unions. He attributed this to a higher level of education. (He claimed that the average chemical worker has completed high school and often some courses at community college.) This official contrasted the "higher" level of bargaining skills, and the more "business-like" approach of ECWU officials, to the bargaining behaviour of the "dirty fingernail group."

Indeed, Rankin makes important points with regard to the particular conditions for the success of the "team approach" to plant operation in the chemical industry, in his analysis of the Shell Chemical Co. (Sarnia) case (Local 800).

> A bargaining unit of 160 is significantly different in structure, process, and culture from one of several thousand. In the latter, for example, the opportunity for face-to-face contact among the membership is severely limited. It will be important, therefore, to monitor the experience of the UAW in General Motor's new Saturn plant ...
>
> The relative homogeneity of local 800 members in terms of age, sex, education, language, and ethnic origin makes integration less problematic than in many work settings...
>
> These members were selected from over 2,500 candidates. It is possible, therefore, that local 800 is composed of an élite group of workers who are not representative of the general population...[46]

The workforces in most chemical plants are relatively small, given the highly capital-intensive nature of the industry, which has already been noted. The gender and racial "homogeneity" referred to also seems typical of chemical workers in the Chemical Valley. As for the "elite" status of chemical workers, success in the competition for the relatively small number of available positions would certainly lend itself to this self-perception, although Rankin seems to be referring to factors such as level of education (minimum 12 years, or high school, were required). The active cultivation of an "elite" identity among chemical workers by employers and union officials is not, unfortunately, considered in Rankin's analysis of Local 800.

Rankin notes that some analysts view arrangements like that at Shell Chemical as examples of "associational unionism," in which "social skills (e.g., communication, negotiation) are critical."[47] Implied by this term, also, is close co-operation between union and management aimed at achieving jointly-agreed goals (regarding productivity, output, quality, etc.). It is not difficult to see that such close co-operation ("team work") with management, involving a small workforce, and on a day-to-day basis, both requires and creates a culture which is very different from the kind of militant industrial unionism (informed by Marxist-inspired educational programmes) which characterises the Canadian Auto Workers (CAW).

Conclusions

The "business-like" self-image of the chemical workers is important not only because it helps to explain the union elite's predilection for rubbing shoulders with corporate executives and government officials, but because it is part of a union "culture" which meshes rather well with corporate ideology. Chemical workers' image of themselves as highly-skilled and knowledgeable employees, in possession of privileged knowledge about the operations of complex plants, has important implications for their attitudes towards alliances. In the Chemical Valley case study developed in chapters 10 and 11, two possibilities emerge. First, in a confrontation between employers and environmentalists where jobs are threatened (or even where they are not), workers may have a strong identification with the companies' view of the corporation as a highly-skilled and competent *team*. Their special knowledge may unite them against the "ill-informed," "alarmist," or "sensationalist" claims and fears of the environmentalists, who are, after all, only lay persons. What do they know about how safe the plants or the chemicals are? What do they know about the importance of chemicals in every aspect of modern, industrial life? (The companies promote a view of their products as essential to other industrial sectors, and to a plethora of consumer goods, eagerly demanded by the public.) Sexist ideology comes into play here, as well. The concerns of the citizens' groups are sometimes discredited by their feminization. Masculine gender roles prevent largely male workforces from identifying with such groups.[48]

A second possible development of this self-image is a sense of "charity" or "generosity" towards the citizens' groups who are struggling to make sense of chemical complexities, and who could benefit from the advice and knowledge of the chemical workers and/or their union. However, until now, the first theme appears to have predominated in chemical workers' attitudes towards the environmental and citizens' groups. This elite union-company culture provides a rationale for remaining aloof from the environmental groups, and it is this relationship which is examined more closely in chapters 10 and 11. As the picture developed in this chapter of the ECWU leadership's strategic orientations suggests, however, the "elite" culture is much more in evidence at the executive levels of the union than among the rank-and-file. The identity of chemical workers must be actively cultivated and reinforced both by the employers' ideological campaigns, and by the discourse of union leaders. Sites of resistance to the elite-corporatist or "business"

Collective Bargaining and Union-Employer Relations

unionism approach do inevitably emerge, often in the areas of workers' health and safety, and—more rarely—with regard to environmental responsibility.

NOTES

1. Wayne Roberts, *Cracking the Canadian Formula* (Toronto: Between the Lines, 1990), p. 119.
2. Ibid., p. 121.
3. Companies which first agreed to the above include: Texaco, Shell, PetroCanada, BP (now PetroCanada), Husky, and Irving Oil. Companies more determined to win concessions included: Gulf Oil, Chevron, and Imperial Oil. (*ECWU Journal* (Spring 1983), p. 10.)
4. Neil Reimer, in ECWU, *Proceedings of the 1984 National Convention*, p. 17.
5. Ibid., Resolution R-7, p. 34.
6. T. Appleton, delegate, Local 691, quoted in ibid., pp. 35-36.
7. Louise Samson, delegate, Local 119, quoted in ibid., pp. 38-39.
8. Dave Pretty, quoted in ibid., p. 37.
9. B. Clarke, delegate, Local 593, quoted in ibid., p. 121.
10. Tom Rankin, in his study of the Shell Chemical Plant in Sarnia, states that among the ECWU's achievements is the negotiation of a 35-hour work week. (See Rankin, *New Forms of Work Organization: the Challenge for North American Unions* (Toronto: University of Toronto Press, 1990), p. 65. He does not, however, say where this occurred. The Shell plant was on a 37.33-hours per week, 12-hour rotating shift or 8-hour day system (Ibid., p. 72).
11. The wage increases proposed were 4 percent, February 1, 1986, and 3 percent February 1, 1987, plus an additional $500 lump sum payment for groups in refining and package operations. For marketing, proposed increases were 4 percent on February 1, 1986, and effective February 1, 1987 a lump sum payment of $700, and a further lump sum payment on August 1, 1987. Shift differentials were to be raised in accordance with that percentage increase. This "model" agreement was signed with PetroCanada, February 14, 1986. See "National Bargaining Programme Report," *ECWU National Convention Proceedings* (1986), p. 101.
12. The 1986-1987 National Bargaining Committee included: Reg Basken, ECWU President (title changed from National Director in 1986); Stuart Sullivan, Ontario Co-ordinator; R. T. (Buck) Philp, National Programmes Co-ordinator. It was assisted by Neil Reimer, National Director Emeritus. According to Philp, this committee met with "all of the major companies in the industry and it became apparent very early that the only company that was prepared to take a lead ... was PetroCanada" (Ibid., p. 101).
13. *ECWU Journal* no. 13, p. 6. It is notable that the main issue leading to the strike at Dow Chemical's Sarnia Division, which lasted from May to the end of November, 1988, was the union members' pension plan.
14. *ECWU Journal* no. 18, p. 13.
15. According to the terms of their separation, however, Canadian locals were granted continuing access to OCAW's technical expertise and vice versa, with charges only for staff time. (*ECWU Journal* vol. 1, no. 1, p. 5.)
16. For example, National Rep., John More (Ontario region) is credited with playing "a very important role in assuring proper safety and health standards are [adopted] in the province and that adequate funding from government sources continues to provide the financing for the Ontario Federation of Labour's Occupational Health and Safety Centre" (*ECWU Journal* no. 3, pp. 10-11). Basken and other union leaders (national and Ontario levels) met with Ontario Minister of Labour, Greg Sorbara, to discuss changes to the Occupational Health and Safety Act in February 1988. (*ECWU Journal* no. 18 (Jan/Feb. 1988), p. 13.) Dan Ublansky drafted a brief to the Canadian government on reforms to the Workers' Compensation system. An exception to this "parliamentarist" strategy occurred when potash miners at the Lanigan mine in Saskatchewan went on strike, mainly to protest deteriorating safety conditions. The strike lasted ten and a half months. See ECWU, *Proceedings of the Fourth Constitutionl Convention* (1986), pp. 61-62, 283-84; and ECWU, *Proceedings of the Fifth Constitutional Convention* (1988) p. 130.

17. Barb Risling, President of Local 677 (Domtar, Saskatchewan) was the "women's representation" on seemingly every union committee.
18. ECWU, *Proceedings* (1986), p. 50.
19. The women's (standing) committee began to publish a newsletter, as well as articles (a women's page) in the *ECWU Journal*. Their key concerns were pay equity and health and safety problems.
20. ECWU, *Proceedings* (1988), p. 206.
21. The works referred to are Huw Bey   n and Theo Nichols, *Living with Capitalism: Class relations in the modern factory* (London: Routledge & Kegan Paul, 1977), and; F. H. M. Blackler and C. A. Brown, *Whatever Happened to Shell's New Philosophy of Management?* (Farnborough, Hants., England: Teakfield, 1980).
22. This experiment is described by Wayne Roberts in *Cracking the Canadian Formula*. The Shell chemical plant's QWL design is the subject of a doctoral dissertation by a former senior manager at Shell (Norman Halpern, "Strategies for dealing with forces acting on the process of organization change in a unionized setting: A case study" (Education, Adult and Continuing Ed. Dept., University of Toronto, 1983)), and a dissertation by Tom Rankin, "Unions and the emerging paradigm of organization: The case of ECWU Local 800" (Collective Bargaining, Shell, Sarnia) (Sociology, Industrial and Labor Relations:University of Pennsylvania, 1986), later published as *New Forms of Work Organization*, see note 10.
23. Quoted in *ECWU Journal* no. 12, p. 4.
24. Stuart Sullivan, interview by author, Sarnia, Ont., May 1988.
25. *ECWU Journal* no. 5 (Fall 1982), p. 9.
26. This case would make an interesting study in itself. What were the issues which caused repeated strikes—many unauthorized—by rank-and-file workers at Domtar? Has "continuing dialogue" addressed these problems, or was it a vehicle to pull rank on the local executive and activists? Did the recession, hitting its depth in 1982, have anything to do with the new quiescence of this workforce?
27. I have been able to find only a few references to this Task Force. An analysis of it would require further interview work with union and company officials.
28. Dan Ublansky, interviewed in London, May 3, 1988.
29. Roberts, *Cracking the Canadian Formula*, p. 241.
30. Sullivan, interview, May 1988.
31. Rankin, *New Forms of Work Organization*, p. 66.
32. Ibid., pp. 123-124.
33. *ECWU Journal*, vol 1, no. 1 (June 1981), p. 9. See also, "Quality of Worklife benefits everyone," Ibid., p. 15. Rankin's study confirms that the national executive of the ECWU adopted a policy "strongly supportive of QWL initiatives" in 1981 (Rankin, *New Forms of Work Organization*, p. 124).
34. Interestingly, the opinion of an unidentified union participant about the seminar was that it was "an attempt to use 'Quality of Work Life' as a marketing device to promote the interests of employers." Quoted in the *ECWU Journal* no. 6 (Spring 1983), p. 5.
35. See Blackler and Brown, *Whatever Happened to Shell's New Philosophy of Management?*, pp. 3-19.
36. Excerpt cited by Blackler and Brown, ibid., p. 22.
37. Roberts, *Cracking the Canadian Formula*, p. 242.
38. A teacher who worked with the ECWU in Alberta, developing labour relations simulation games (in 1986), described the union participants "not [as] wild-eyed radicals bent on destroying the capitalist system, [but as] a caring, professional group, who [sic] was concerned with education and protecting workers within the market system." This comment was quoted approvingly in the *ECWU Journal* no. 18, p. 15.
39. Upon Reimer's retirement as national director in 1984, the Officers' Report Committee of the ECWU recommended that:

> [I]n the interests of working people and the union movement, that the Union promote Brother Reimer and secure a position on Boards and Agencies as well as on the Directorates of Corporations, such as Polysar, Atomic Energy of Canada, PetroCan, and other such International, Federal, or Provincial agencies related to the interest and jurisdiction of the Union. (*Proceedings* (1984), pp. 115-116).

Collective Bargaining and Union-Employer Relations 159

40. Resolution 5, in ECWU, *Proceedings* (1984), p. 54.
41. *ECWU Journal* no. 12, p. 3.
42. Dow Chemical Canada, *Dimensions* (October/November 1987).
43. Interviews with Stuart Sullivan and Dan Ublansky. See also ECWU, *Proceedings* (1988), p. 106.
44. Judy McKibbon, quoted by Roberts, *Cracking the Canadian Formula*, p. 245.
45. Interestingly, the osteoporosis campaign mirrors Dow Chemical's charitable campaign to support organ transplants.
46. Rankin, *New Forms of Work Organization*, pp. 152-153.
47. Ibid., p. 155. Rankin refers particularly to the work of C. Heckscher, author of *The New Unionism* (New York: Basic Books, 1988).
48. "Feminizing" the enemy is also used to ridicule employers in other contexts. On the Dow Chemical workers' picket line during the 1988 strike, I observed strikers making homophobic gestures implying that management was homosexual.

[10]

Chemical Workers and Toxic Pollution Issues

INTRODUCTION

The next two chapters examine the relations among chemical workers, their union, citizens' groups, environmental organisations, corporations, and the Ontario and federal government ministries responsible for environmental quality, in the highly industrialized southwest of Ontario from the 1950s to the 1980s. The earliest concerns of "Chemical Valley" residents were air pollution and phenol- and oil-tainted water. From the mid-1960s to the 1970s, mercury contamination of the St. Clair River and downstream water bodies, caused by Dow Chemical Canada and the Wyandotte Chemical Corporation of Michigan, led to a banning of commercial fishing. Chemical workers were later affected by environmental lobbying to ban leaded gasoline, and by the 1980s campaign to stop the contamination by the chemical industry and public utilities of the St. Clair River and downstream water bodies.

DEVELOPMENT OF THE CHEMICAL VALLEY AND THE PETROCHEMICAL WORKFORCE

For the first half of the nineteenth century, the main economic activities in the area now known as Lambton County were lumbering, fishing, agriculture, and iron foundries. Anglo-Saxon settlers predominated. The growth of a petrochemical industry in the Sarnia area was based on the presence of oil, discovered in the 1850s, and of the huge salt beds which underlie most of southwestern Ontario. (Around Sarnia, the salt bed lies about 1,500 to 2,000 feet below the surface.) Sarnia was also close to markets for chemical products. Other factors included the proximity of water for the processing plants and for transportation, and the availability of land for the large production sites, which was expropriated from the Chippewa Indian Reservation.

The development of oil refining and shipping, and industrialization in the second half of the century attracted eastern and southern European immigrants. During at least the first four decades of the twentieth century, racism divided the workforce and allowed employers crucial victories. In 1906, Anglo-Saxon workers persuaded the town council to forbid building contractors to employ "foreign" (mainly Italian-born) workers.[1] Longshoremen at the Northern Navigation Company docks in Point Edward went on strike in 1910 because Italians were hired. Another strike at the docks, in 1915, also manifested racism. The worst incident occurred in 1937, at the Holmes Foundry. A group of strikers, mainly Italian- and Polish-born immigrants, who had occupied the Foundry, were beaten and driven from the plant by a "mob of Anglo-Saxon citizens, encouraged by the plant management and assisted by the law enforcement bodies."[2]

The chemical industry became established in Sarnia during and immediately following the Second World War, launched by public investment.[3] Shortly after the war, Dow began to produce and export "Styron," a polystyrene plastic, using styrene monomer from another Dow plant. The Leduc, Alberta, oil discovery of 1947 led to the construction of

Chemical Workers and Toxic Pollution Issues 161

an oil pipeline from Alberta to Wisconsin. Tankers then carried the oil to Sarnia, where Imperial Oil undertook a major expansion of its refining operations. Around this time, Fiberglas also started construction of its plant at Sarnia. In 1949, Dow began to produce ethylene glycol, chlorine, ethylene, vinyl chloride monomer, chlorinated solvents, and styrene. Imperial Oil began to produce detergent alkylate, and, by the late 1950s, the petrochemicals ethylene, propylene, and butadiene. The last three were sold to Dow and to DuPont, for production of polyethylene and other chemicals, and to Polymer Corporation for production of rubber. In the early 1950s, Sun Oil, a US-based firm, decided to build a refinery in Sarnia. The oil pipeline was extended from the Lakehead to Sarnia at this time. Cabot Carbon started production of carbon blacks (used primarily in rubber-tire production), and Ethyl Corporation began producing tetraethyl lead (an anti-knock additive for gasoline). In 1959, DuPont Canada constructed a plant for the manufacture of polyethylene resin.

The establishment of new plants and expansion of existing sites continued well into the 1970s, with a major boom in the late 1960s.[4] By the 1970s Sarnia was the location of petrochemical operations for Dow Chemical, DuPont, Polymer Corp. (which later became Polysar), Fiberglas, Cabot Carbon, Ethyl Corp., Allied Chemical, C-I-L, Shell Canada, and Union Carbide. Figure 2 shows the location of chemical and other plants along the St. Clair River, from Sarnia in the North, to Walpole Island and Lake St. Clair.

The Oil Workers, the United Gas, Coke and Chemical Workers, and Mine Workers unions moved into Sarnia in the 1940s. There was intense rivalry between the unions for members until 1955, when they merged to form the Oil, Chemical, and Atomic Workers International Union (OCAWIU or OCAW). OCAW negotiated a landmark contract with Polymer in 1957, which gave workers a 20-percent wage increase, double time for Saturday and Sunday, three weeks of paid vacation with fifteen or more years employment, and benefits associated with compensation for injury, sick pay, and retirement. There were also "sweeping changes in hours of work, grievance procedure, seniority rights, promotions, leaves of absence, safety and health [and] recognition of the function of union committees and stewards."[5] This contract attracted technicians, who sought to join the bargaining unit and were certified the same year. In 1959 there was a strike at Polymer, mainly over the issue of trades recognition, which lasted from March 18 to June 27.[6] At that time, it was the longest strike in the history of the Canadian chemical industry, and it served to politicize a number of the union members who became leaders in the 1960s.[7]

The late 1960s were, for the chemical workers as for other workers, good times. Sarnia had the highest average industrial weekly earnings in the country ($133) in 1967, followed by Oshawa, Sudbury, and Windsor. (The Canadian average weekly wage was $104.73.[8]) As late as 1972, there had been only two strikes affecting the chemical plants. These were a 1956 strike at Fiberglas, which lasted a month and a half, and the 1959 strike at Polymer Corporation. In October 1973, workers at Dow Chemical Canada in Sarnia went on strike for a precedent-setting demand: reduction of the work week from 40 to 37.3 hours. The strike lasted until late December, ending in a victory for the union. In that year, six companies negotiated with OCAW regarding the 37.3-hour work week. The three key goals in bargaining were hours of work, wages, and vacations.[9] Employment in the petrochemical plants in 1972 was estimated at 9,200, out of a total population of 60,000 for Sarnia. Between 1967 and 1972, five new plants opened in the area, but in 1971 the unemployment rate was about 9 percent. This was attributed to automation of the oil refineries and company streamlining.[10]

By 1978, OCAW had organised nine plants in Sarnia and Lambton County. Its membership was about 3,400, with the largest group at Polysar.[11] Non-union plants included

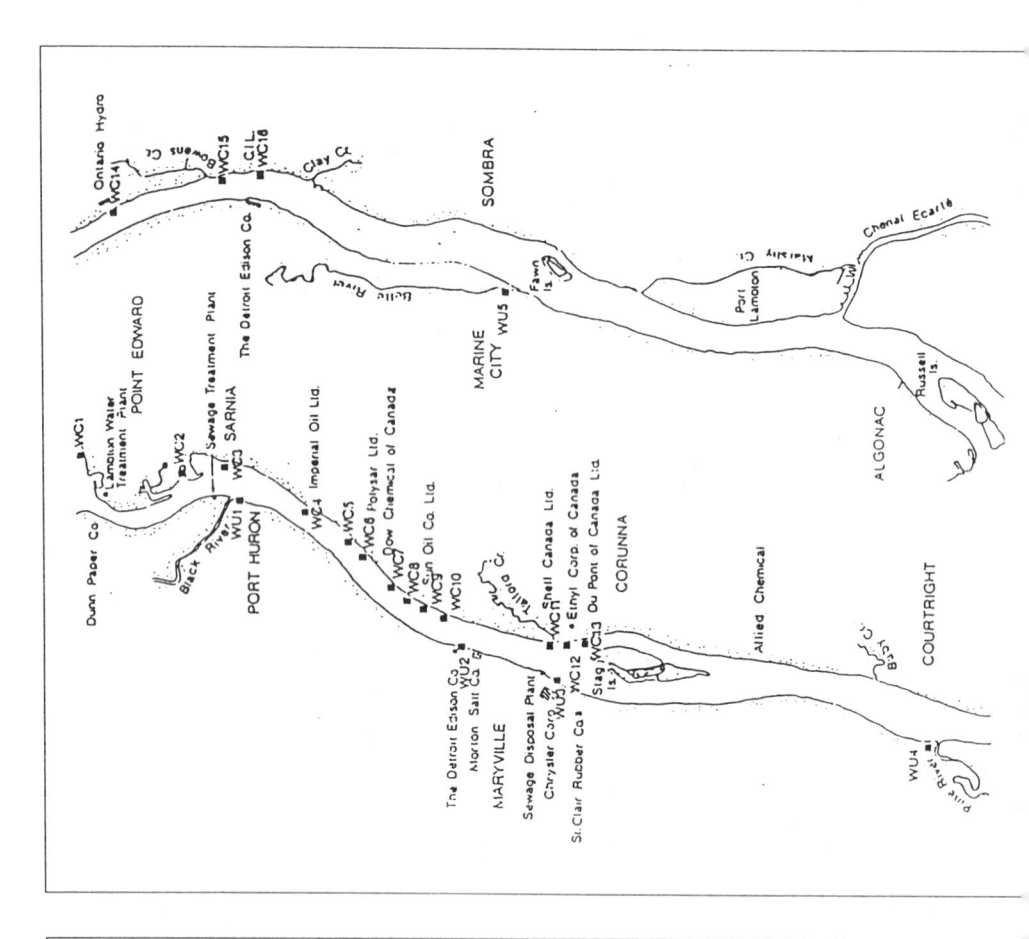

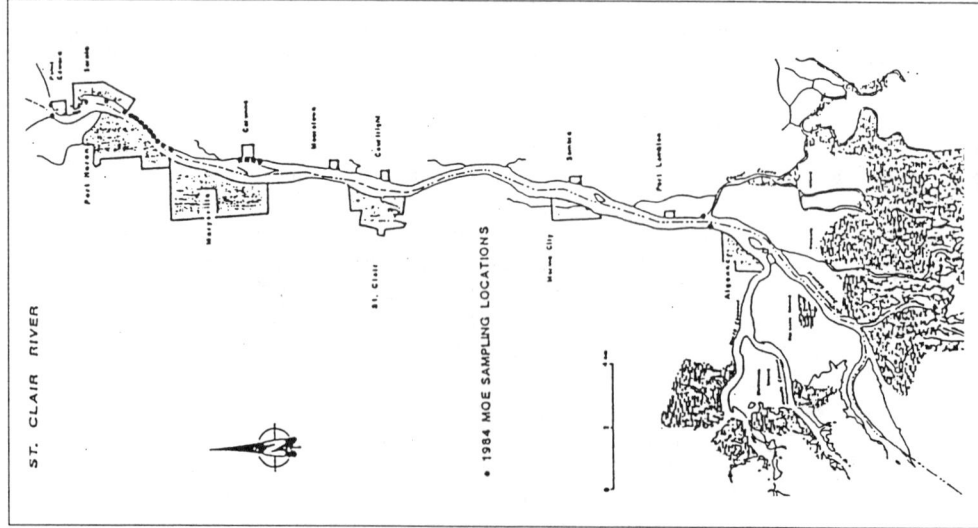

SOURCE: Environment Canada and the Ontario Ministry of the Environment, *Pollution of the St. Clair River (Sarnia area): A Situation Report.* December 1985. Includes sampling stations.

Chemical Workers and Toxic Pollution Issues

DuPont, Union Carbide, and Petrosar. The latter was owned by shareholder companies: DuPont of Canada (20%), Polysar (40%), Union Carbide Canada (20%), and the Canada Development Corporation (20%). There was an independent union at Sun Oil, recognized under the Ontario Labour Relations Act. Imperial Oil had an employee council. A local of OCAW was certified at Ethyl Canada in November 1979, shortly before major lay-offs were to affect the workforce. New organising efforts seemed to stagnate in the Sarnia area, as unemployment levels climbed throughout the 1970s. Among construction workers, unemployment had reached about 30 percent by 1980, according to the *Sarnia Observer*. This meant that, outside of permanent jobs in the plants, there were few employment options for skilled trades workers.[12] In January 1981 the Sarnia and District Labour Council started a Labour Assistance Information Centre. The recession, which reached its depths in the petrochemical industry in 1982, put further pressure on workers to lower their bargaining expectations. Dow Chemical (Sarnia) asked its workers to accept a smaller pay increase that year—4 percent instead of the 12 percent already negotiated. The 800 members of Energy and Chemical Workers Union (ECWU) Local 672 voted against this concession, by 96 percent. Instead, the company cut back the salaries of its non-union, salaried employees.[13] Petrosar reduced its workforce from 1,090 in January 1982 to under 680 in January 1983.[14]

By the time 1983-84 bargaining began, employers' campaigns to create a crisis consciousness among the industry's workforce had taken effect. ECWU leadership had already more or less accepted the companies' explanation for the recession, as well as their prescriptions for recovery. In February 1983, workers at the chemical plants in Sarnia were collecting signatures to petition the government to deregulate oil prices, "in an attempt to save their jobs."[15] A petition signed by 11,000 people (about 18 percent of the population of Sarnia) was presented to area members of Parliament. In January 1983, 92 percent of the 1,650 workers at Polysar (Sarnia) ratified a one-year contract that held them at the current rates of pay until March 1984, when a 6 percent wage increase would come into effect. The President of the Polysar local (of the ECWU), Bob Healey, was quoted as saying that the union "'fully understands the economic hardships facing the company.'"[16] The *Sarnia Observer*, historically very pro-employers, praised the new docility of the chemical workers:

> Unions have often been criticized for failing to consider the future while trying to obtain as much as they can now. But this community has some good news on the labour front... Terms of the [new Polysar] contract provide for no increase in wages this year and a six-per-cent increase in 1984...
>
> The fact the union was willing to approve a contract which called for such a small increase in wages is good news for this area, and will hopefully lead to further concessions to help industry...
>
> [T]he time has arrived when the companies can no longer afford such luxurious wages.[17]

The Polysar concessions were followed by Dow workers. On March 9th of the same year, the *Sarnia Observer* editorialized on the ECWU's request to participate in the Petrochemical Industry Task Force:

> The inclusion is welcome provided the union remains objective and helps to find solutions to the economic problems facing the whole industry, not just union members...
>
> The union should be prepared to agree to concessions and lower expectations, to ensure the economic survival of the industry...

> The task force may provide an opportunity to show how the union accepts this responsibility by working hand in hand with government and industry.

As the analysis of ECWU strategy in chapter 8 shows, the union leadership did not disappoint the editorial writers at the *Sarnia Observer*.[18]

However, a strike at Ethyl Canada, which began in June 1983 and lasted until late November, was sharply criticised by the local newspaper. The major concern of the workers was job security.

> Militancy among union leadership has eased in light of high unemployment and concern about job security... [However], Ethyl Canada workers have been on strike for several months, with the major issue...job security. But where's their job security on the picket line? It's time for Ethyl employees to review their situations and realize their futures rest working in the plant, not pounding the pavement on the picket line. With the current controversy over leaded gasoline, the plant faces other problems in the months ahead.[19]

In this case the newspaper and the employer were able to use the threat of environmental regulation as well as economic conditions to blackmail the workforce. The terms of the settlement included a 6 percent wage increase effective April 1, 1983, and a 5-percent increase effective June 1, 1984. The workforce was reduced to 87 from 145; the union managed to save twelve jobs which had been scheduled for elimination. Four workers were fired and four more were disciplined with suspensions because of "strike-related incidents."[20] (It is interesting that, when the strike was in its fifth month, area police forces decided to rehearse responses to a mock hostage-taking of a "senior executive of a Sarnia Chemical Company" at the Sarnia airport.) By March 1985, there were more than 8,000 people in the Sarnia-Lambton area collecting unemployment insurance, and more than 760 on welfare payments.[21] The chemical companies were using early retirements to reduce their workforces; many workers were on temporary lay-offs due to production cutbacks in the plants.

This was the changing local context of the union's responses to environmental problems from the 1950s onward. Despite the concentration of unionized workers in the Sarnia area (almost one in six Sarnia residents worked in the petrochemical plants by the mid-1970s), Lambton County remained Conservative Party turf, with an anti-labour local press. The community culture in relation to the union was therefore very far from the "blue-collar town" milieu of Windsor, just downstream.[22] Sarnia, indeed, was much closer to being a "company town," not unlike Midland, Michigan, corporate headquarters of Dow Chemical Company. There were, however—as the following cases reveal—dissenting and oppositional voices to the practices of the companies, and to the quiescence of the union.

1950S-1960S: AIR AND WATER POLLUTION IN THE CHEMICAL VALLEY

Although Sarnia residents' protests about air pollution, and concerns voiced by downstream communities about pollution of the St. Clair River, were occasionally heard during these decades, chemical companies succeeded in avoiding stricter regulation. This was due to a combination of factors: the cozy relationship between employers, local politicians, and the Conservative government of Ontario (which, along with municipalities, was primarily responsible for industrial pollution control); the propaganda efforts of the chemical firms, the *Sarnia Observer*, and local ("pro-development") city officials; the absence of scientific or organised environmentalist support for the attempts of local groups to draw attention to pollution problems; and the willingness of chemical industry workers (and other workers whose livelihoods were dependent upon the presence of the industry) to turn a blind eye to the environmental costs of their relative affluence.

The development of petrochemical complexes in the 1940s and 1950s was accompanied by emissions of sulphur dioxide, hydrocarbons, oxidants, suspended particulate matter, dust fall, aerosol, and hydrogen sulphide (rotten-egg smell). The combined effect was a noxious smog, which, in addition to causing short-term nasal, skin, and respiratory problems, exacerbated allergic conditions, and had long-term health effects. Samples of surface water from the St. Clair River were tested for oil, total organic carbon, turbidity, phenol, and chlorides. (Phenol and oil affected the smell and taste of fish, and were a concern for commercial fishers and tourist-industry businesses.)[23]

In the early 1950s, the Ontario Research Foundation (ORF), a research organisation closely associated with the petrochemical companies, was the main source of data on pollution in the Chemical Valley. The International Joint Commission (IJC) used ORF data to monitor pollution in the area. The St. Clair River Research Committee (SCRRC) was established in 1952 to study the smog problem in Sarnia. It was funded by ten petrochemical companies and the Ontario Government, and worked closely with the Ontario Research Foundation (ORF).[24] In June 1955, members of the SCRRC included executives from DuPont Canada, Shell Canada, Ethyl Corporation, and Imperial Oil. Its key figure for some years was Dr. R. K. Stratford, Imperial Oil's "scientific advisor." The SCRRC arranged tours and hosted meetings with chemical company officials for IJC and Ontario government delegations in 1954 and 1955, and generally acted as a "scientific" liaison between governments and the firms. The industries' efforts to convince these authorities of their achievements in ameliorating the pollution problems seem to have been successful. According to a *Sarnia Observer* story in February 1957, the Select Committee of the Ontario Legislature "commended [the SCRRC] for its trail blazing in the study of pollution and its control."[25]

And in fact, the chemical companies had begun to install some pollution-abatement equipment. The *Sarnia Observer* gave high-profile coverage to Dow and Cabot Carbon's installation of $900,000 worth of such equipment in 1956, and Imperial Oil's reduction of air emissions (gaseous hydrocarbons, dust fall, fumes, odour) and emissions of phenol and oil into the river.[26] In 1957 the SCRRC hired a biologist to study the effects of water pollutants on aquatic animal life. Late in 1958 he reported that the problems were not serious, emphasizing the capacity of the river to absorb pollutants and render them "harmless." These findings were reported by the *Sarnia Observer* under the headline: "[Biologist] Reports River 'Cures' itself of Pollution."[27] During this period, the companies were testing only surface water. This was the first reported study of aquatic life (insect larvae, underwater snails, clams, and worms). Testing of species higher in the food chain, which bioaccumulate toxins (such as mercury, detected by a Ph.D. student in 1967-70), and of river *sediment* (where a mess of toxic chemicals was discovered in the 1980s), was not carried out. The government of Ontario established its own testing station only in 1958, when the Ontario Water Resources Commission (forerunner of the Ministry of the Environment) located a lab at Point Edward.

By 1960 the chemical companies, their research organisations, and the local media were proclaiming the end of the pollution problem. The credit for this achievement was attributed glowingly to the companies' self-motivated commitment to a clean environment. The director of chemistry of the ORF said that Sarnia's "relatively clean" slate was due "almost entirely to the originators and members of the SCRR Committee, who have acted as voluntary guardians of the air and water resources of the city."[28] The *Sarnia Observer* highlighted the chemical industry's sacrifices toward this cause, noting that between 1952 and 1960 Sarnia firms had invested $14,400,000 in anti-pollution controls and procedures.[29] In 1964 the newspaper concluded that: "The fact that the effect of pollution while not entirely eliminated has seemingly been arrested should be satisfying to people downstream."[30] The paper maintained this theme throughout the 1960s. A 1965 story emphasized that:

> While pollution of the country's lakes and streams...has caused Ottawa to jump into the fray, pollution in the St. Clair River is less than it was six years ago. Much of the credit for this improvement can be credited to a voluntary committee composed of representatives of major industries of the Chemical Valley which in 1952 teamed up with the Ontario Research Foundation to form the St. Clair River Research Committee.[31]

In May of that year, the *Sarnia Observer* ran a front-page headline: "Local Waters Given Clean Bill: Pollution Said No Problem in Sarnia Area." The source for this pronouncement was the Chairperson of the SCRRC, who was also the plant chemist at Ethyl Corporation. Another headline in August read: "Industrial air pollution is not a cause for alarm in the Sarnia area." Again, the source was the chairperson of the SCRRC. The editorial which accompanied this story lent credibility to the "careful research" of this organisation, while questioning the motives of pollution critics.

> The report of the St. Clair research committee, well documented as it is, will not remove the idea, however, that Sarnia air is over-polluted. This is something akin of floridation and the theory that cigarette smoking causes cancer. Views on these matters can be quite strong, yet they are not convincing to all.
> What must be remembered in the matter of air and water pollution is that local industries are well aware of the potential problem and generally are doing all in their power to make whatever adjustments are necessary because they are all good corporate citizens for which Sarnia is fortunate. They have expended many tens of millions of dollars and they employ most of our people... The housekeeping in virtually all plants is such that industrial accident rates here are low because employees co-operate with management's desire to remove hazards.
> Let us, therefore, proclaim our astonishingly good record for clean air despite the nature of our industries. The committee's report should make most Sarnians proud.[32]

By 1966, however, some dissident voices were being heard. A Sarnia allergist said he was "concerned about complex organic chemicals in the air which are not being measured. Among these benzpyrene, a cancer inducing chemical."[33] While his concerns did not get front-page coverage, they were taken up by a Liberal MPP in the Ontario legislature, Andrew Thompson. In response to Thompson's charge that Sarnia air pollution was reaching dangerous levels, the Conservative MPP for Lambton West, J. Ralph Knox, said: "I would like to stress the fact that industry is making a great deal of progress in its endeavours to bring under control any pollution that might emanate from their plants." Referring to concerns about lachrymators (oxides, dust, etc., which cause eye and sinus irritation), Knox assured his colleagues that "he had lived in Sarnia for more than 38 years and had yet to cry."[34]

In the summer of 1966 Sombra residents formed "an association to fight present pollution and organise a voice of the people to deal with future matters." The "officers" included a "developer of a million dollar resort on nearby Fawn Island," who was named president, three male directors (including a doctor), and a Mrs. Randy Purser, secretary. They called themselves the St. Clair District Association. The focus of their concern was

Chemical Workers and Toxic Pollution Issues 167

the Chinook Chemical plant, which produced methylamines. Its emissions polluted the air with a nauseous odour, settling on vegetation, clothing, buildings, and the river water. Aside from damaging tourism and property values, it was causing respiratory problems. Residents of Marine City, Michigan had also formed an anti-pollution group.[35] In their continuing attempts to counter such concerns, the SCRRC held a symposium in Sarnia in April 1967. Its chairperson, Dr. E. R. Morton, reassured the public that "pollution in the Sarnia area is essentially under control and levels compare favorably with or better than other major industrial communities in North America." (Sarnia was actually compared with Hamilton, Toronto, and other much larger industrial centres.) A city alderperson congratulated the SCRRC for its "honesty."[36]

Also in 1967, the SCRRC became the Lambton Industrial Society (LIS), "an environmental co-operative," funded entirely by the area's petrochemical companies, and composed of their representatives. The LIS would continue to commission research by the Ontario Research Foundation, and to depict itself as an impartial, scientific liaison between the industry and the public. The formation of the LIS may have been in part a response both to growing citizen protests against area pollution, and the introduction by the Ontario Government of the Air Pollution Control Act, which entered second reading in April 1967. Also, in July 1967 the IJC initiated an air pollution study, to be completed by September 1969. In addition to these factors, information emerging about mercury contamination of the St. Clair River was pointing toward a credibility crisis for the chemical companies.

In July 1968 the LIS released a one-year study of air pollution. Not surprisingly, the report said that Sarnia's air was pretty good—better than Los Angeles'. The *Sarnia Observer* editorial on the report complained that, despite all the evidence presented by the companies, people continued to have a false idea that Sarnia had an air pollution problem. Despite this injustice, however, the LIS would "continue its extensive research into the problem. That, of course, strongly supports the concept of good corporate citizenship which our industries demonstrate."[37] However, in 1968 and 1969 other reports documented heavy pollution of Sarnia Bay, and the IJC officials began to be more critical of industry for polluting the St. Clair River.[38]

Throughout these decades, the residents of Sarnia itself, including the thousands of workers employed in the refineries and chemical plants, seem more or less to have agreed with the view of the *Sarnia Observer* that the pollution was more than compensated for by the benefits of having the industry's investment and jobs (i.e. that this was the choice). The theme was that a certain amount of pollution was necessary and reasonable in order for the industry to continue to provide these benefits.[39] The industry, meanwhile, vested itself with the scientific authority to judge what was reasonable and necessary. In the absence of strongly contradicting evidence, collected by governmental or other publicly funded scientific bodies, it was no doubt easier to believe the claims of the SCRRC, the ORF or the LIS than to give much credence to the complaints of housewives about laundry being dirtied on the clothesline, or of cottage owners about tainted water. Indeed, concerns about air pollution could be denigrated as "sissy," as the comment of the Conservative MPP, Ralph Knox, implied.

Sarnia workers were not alone in this refusal to take pollution problems seriously. Unions during this era were primarily concerned with achieving material gains through collective bargaining. Much less was known about the links between pollution and health. Even health and safety conditions in the plants—an area where employers' willingness to sacrifice human health for profit would have been evident to most employees—did not rank highly on the agendas of unions. When Ivan Hillier began his agitation about mercury vapour in the Dow Chemical Chlor Alkali plant, he had to convince not only the Ministry of Labour inspectors and his employer of the dangers posed, but also his co-workers. Even in the mid- to late-1980s, health and safety activists in the chemical plants were having a difficult time convincing their co-workers to observe regulations and to support struggles against such hazards as asbestos exposure.[40] Despite years of health and safety committee campaigns and union courses, a macho attitude toward such concerns persists among male industrial workers. Concern for one's physical security and well being is seen as unmanly. Chemical workers take a certain masculine pride in the dangerousness of their work. At the same time, they feel that if they are prepared to handle hazardous chemicals, the public should accept the same risks; anything else implies that the lives of chemical workers are more expendable than those of the public "outside." This logic explains why workers become angry about the complaints of people not exposed to the same daily health risks at work, for example, cottage owners protesting acid rain, or parents worried about asbestos insulation in school buildings.[41] If such attitudes are common in the 1980s, they were even more pervasive in the 1950s and 1960s. In addition to these factors, one should consider that there was no "environmental movement" to mobilize public opinion and lobby government during this period. Pollution Probe did not become active in Sarnia until 1970. Governments were only beginning, at the end of the 1960s, to consider the necessity of stricter environmental legislation.

THE MERCURY STORY

In 1962, Ivan Hillier, a Dow Chemical Canada process operator, and at that time the president of the Sarnia and District Labour Council, began to agitate about the health hazards posed to Dow employees by mercury vapours in the Chlor Alkali plant where he worked.[42] He also criticised the company's polluting activities, and did some research into the scientific evidence about mercury contamination and its effects. In September he presented a brief to the Ontario Federation of Labour (OFL) Executive Council about the health effects of mercury exposure in the workplace. Hillier and an OFL official asked the Chief Inspector of Industrial Hygiene at the Department of Health (Toronto) to make Dow clean up mercury puddles and residues. Dow was notified in advance by the Department that an inspection would take place September 26. Management met to plan a defence; with the help of the company doctor they prepared "scientific" explanations for earlier findings of mercury contamination of employees. They also ordered a thorough clean-up of the area to be inspected. The inspector's report more or less accepted the company's arguments, and concluded that health risks were not significant. The union countered with a report claiming that the Department had failed to test during normal conditions, as a result of giving advance warning to the employer, and had failed to perform critical tests which would have revealed greater levels of mercury contamination. The union demanded a more thorough and objective investigation, and threatened to send its own report to the leader of the Ontario New Democratic Party (NDP) if actions were not taken. Another clean-up and further tests were done, but not to the union's satisfaction.[43] In February 1964, the OCAW local sent its brief to the leader of the NDP, Donald MacDonald, who called on the Minister of Health, Mr. Dymond, to instigate a thorough investigation of working conditions at Dow Chemical. The Minister responded that this had already been done. A few days later, the Conservative MPP for Lambton West, Ralph Knox, wrote to the Assistant Vice President in charge of Public Relations at Dow, asking for direction on the issue.

> I have to decide for myself whether I want to make a speech at all. Whether if I do, I want to bring this matter up again, and whether I might embarrass you or

the Department of Health any further by what publicity it might get or by whatever further remarks might be made by Donald MacDonald and his ilk. Please let me know whether your company feels it wants to carry this matter any further.[44]

Meanwhile, the situation of workers at Dow Chemical received little coverage by the *Sarnia Observer*, which agreed with the claim of chemical companies in 1970 that no one in North America had known anything about the environmental or health effects associated with mercury before that date. Yet by the mid-1960s, some Canadian scientists had begun to assimilate data on mercury contamination from other parts of the world. In 1965-66, the head of the Canadian Wildlife Service Pesticides Branch, J. A. Keith, tried to find a biologist to do a study of mercury in the Canadian environment, but without success. Swedish biologists were worried about mercury contamination of the environment in the mid-1960s. The mass mercury poisoning at Minimata, Japan, had occurred in 1953, and had been conclusively linked to mercury by the 1960s. Indeed, mercury poisoning cases had occurred in many parts of the world by 1970. In May 1969 the Ontario Water Resources Commission (OWRC) found concentrations of mercury in the river sediments near Dow's effluent outfalls, and initiated a study of fish. Although the results of fish testing revealed high mercury levels, the OWRC "did not feel that the reliability of the testing method had been conclusively established."[45] The mercury story broke only in March 1970, when a Norwegian Ph.D. student, Norvald Fimreite, reported his findings of high levels of mercury in St. Clair pickerel, pheasants, and partridges. When the results of this three-year study received considerable press coverage, the government of Ontario was obliged to impose a ban on fishing and hunting in the area.[46] Commercial fishing was banned in the St. Clair River, Lake St. Clair, the Detroit River, and the western end of Lake Erie. Michigan also banned commercial fishing in its jurisdiction. Dow Chemical was ordered to eliminate mercury emissions to the river. Within three days, the company had installed temporary seals. These were later replaced by permanent measures.[47] The Ontario and federal governments agreed in April 1970 to share the costs of interest-free loans to commercial fishers, and to seek compensation from the polluters.

Attention turned to Dow Chemical's dumping of mercury-contaminated effluents into the St. Clair River. While the company claimed that mercury "losses" were rare and accidental, workers at Dow told NDP politicians that they had been told not to dump mercury effluent *while the river was being monitored*, and that Dow knowingly dumped mercury into the sewers. Hillier asserted, once again, that the company "permitted pools of mercury to lie around the plant areas and took inadequate measures to protect employees from it." The leader of the NDP demanded that a committee of the legislature be struck to investigate these allegations. In May of 1970, officials of Dow Chemical met with the OWRC to present their case.

The years 1970-72 were a high point of political activity by members of the OCAW in the Sarnia area, coinciding with the period of union bargaining strength described above. Politically, their employers were on the defensive, subject to intense public scrutiny for their corporate behaviour; NDP victories in British Columbia, Saskatchewan, and Manitoba provided impetus for union identification and alliance with the NDP in Ontario and federally; and the arrival of environmental activists in the area provided expertise for public campaigns. Key officials of the OCAW became candidates for the NDP, and published items in a tabloid called *The Sarnia Democrat* (issued monthly from 1970 to 1972). This paper became a forum for attacking the polluting activities of area industries, as well as the credibility of the Lambton Industrial Society.

At the beginning of March, just before Fimreite's findings were made public, a committee of the Sarnia and District Labour Council, composed almost entirely of OCAW officials, met to plan an Environmental Health and Pollution Seminar. It was to take place over two days, and to include a public forum and a workshop, with invited experts. The objectives were: "to alert the public to...pollution and its health environmental [sic] damage, setting up a possible citizens' committee for action against pollution, to request that the two governments concerned give sufficient power to the IJC to enact laws for punishing offenders." The scope of envisaged alliances was impressive: scientists/academics, MPs, the University Women's League Industrial Pollution Abatement Committee, Port Huron Pollution Probe, London Pollution Probe, National Indian Brotherhood, Cancer Society, local elected officials, unions, students, and others.[48] Following the announcement to the media of Fimreite's mercury findings, the Sarnia and District Labour Council used the opportunity to publicize its workshop (planned for April 11-12), as well as its pollution concerns.[49] About 150 to 200 persons attended the environment workshop. However, Bob Sage, president of the Labour Council, was very disappointed with the turnout from the unions. Only twenty-five of the Council's 6,000 members attended. He explained this as the consequence of fear and apathy: "Union members are afraid they'll lose their jobs if they discuss in public that there may be pollution at their plants... They have always been scared and they still are... They seem to feel that they pay their dues and that's it."[50]

Also in April 1970, a Pollution Probe group formed in Sarnia. Its chairperson was Dr. James Higgins, a research chemist at Imperial Oil. Twenty-six citizens turned out for its founding meeting. Ivan Hillier became a "co-ordinator"—one of a nine-member executive. Duncan Longwell, a lab technician at Polysar, became vice-president.[51] The targeted issues were sewage treatment, air pollution, water pollution, and mercury. Jim Charrington, the secretary of the Sarnia and District Labour Council, was at this meeting. His views were described by the *Sarnia Observer* reporter as "controversial." The views of Dow Chemical on local pollution problems, however, were given one third of the article's space, and were treated very seriously.[52] Dow took out space in the same issue of the *Sarnia Observer* (i.e., the issue announcing the formation of the Pollution Probe group) to assert that the mercury had not been dumped, but had leaked, in amounts undetectable by available technology. (Interestingly, the technology suddenly became available once the mercury in the river was discovered and attributed to Dow.) A few days later, an editorial in the local newspaper emphasized the "lack of information" about the pollution situation, and advised against "witch hunts" against the chemical companies. "We should not substitute Pollution for Communism in the McCarthy context," the editors cautioned.[53] On April 28 Pollution Probe Sarnia had its first public meeting, which drew almost 200 persons. The theme was consumer action, and Norvald Fimreite was a speaker. Thirty-five new memberships were sold, bringing total membership to at least sixty-one.[54]

In May the Queen's Park hearing began into mercury contamination of the St. Clair River system. The committee was chaired by Conservative MPP William Newman, and its members included Donald MacDonald of the NDP, Lorne Henderson, MPP for Lambton County, and James Bullbrook, MPP for Sarnia. Witnesses called included a Dow chemical engineer and management executives, representatives of the OWRC, and Ivan Hillier. The investigation provided some interesting insights into the relationships between the government agencies responsible for monitoring workplace conditions and environmental practices (i.e., the departments of Health and Labour, and the OWRC) and Dow Chemical. Hillier accused government environment and labour officials of collusion with the company—of refusing or neglecting to carry out necessary inspections and testing, and of withholding results from the public. He said that the government was as much to blame for the mercury situation as the company, and that the law suits announced by the

Chemical Workers and Toxic Pollution Issues

government of Ontario against Dow Chemical Canada and its parent company in Midland, Michigan, were ludicrous.[55]

The director of OWRC's industrial wastes division was asked why his agency had not conducted more rigorous inspections of the Dow site. His response covered a number of points. First, Dow controlled entry to the site and inspectors, instead of insisting on an automatic right of entry, were notifying management and arranging visits in advance. Second, government inspectors did not have the technical staff to do the necessary tests, and had to rely on help from Dow engineers. Third, the agency assumed that Dow was reporting honestly and not cheating. Fourth, the OWRC needed "a good working relationship" with management so they would co-operate and notify the Commission if there were spills. The OWRC did not have the resources to do adequate monitoring itself. Finally, the fines levied against polluters (in the rare instance of prosecution) were so small that they did not cover the government's costs of investigation of violations. The maximum fine for each instance of water pollution in 1970 was only $1,000.[56]

All of this, needless to say, created a major crisis for Dow Chemical. Not only was the corporate image severely damaged—at a time when the napalm-Vietnam campaign against Dow Co. (Midland) was escalating—but law suits and new government legislation were threatening to carve out portions of company profits. During May and July 1970, the State of Michigan threatened to sue the chemical companies (Dow and Wyandotte) for mercury pollution of the St. Clair River. The State of Ohio filed a suit with the US Supreme Court, attributing total liability for mercury pollution clean-up to the chemical companies. The government of Michigan stated its concern that "the Ohio action doesn't go far enough." The Canadian deputy minister for water resources told a meeting of anti-pollution groups in July that the government was studying the question of liability in cases of industrial water pollution.[57] When the mercury story had first received wide media coverage, in late March, the Ontario NDP had gone so far as to demand the closure of the Dow Chemical Company "until it is established beyond any doubt that their processes will cause no further pollution of the river."[58] Locally, the chemical companies found themselves confronted with opposition, however small and vulnerable it was in reality: several area anti-pollution groups and an environmental campaign by an NDP slate in the municipal elections of November 1970.

Hillier—who seemed to be everywhere at once during this period, including the executive of his OCAW local, the Ontario Council of the OCAW, the Sarnia and District Labour Council, Pollution Probe, and the Sarnia NDP—ran as a candidate for the NDP in the 1970 municipal elections. He and the other candidates, including Polysar worker Duncan Longwell, were strongly critical of the industry's pollution record, and were calling for nationalization of industries "having a poor pollution record."[59] Longwell recalls that during the campaign an incumbent on City Council exclaimed: "When I smell the stuff coming from Chemical Valley, all I smell is money!"[60]

During the summer a split had developed within the Sarnia Pollution Probe chapter between the NDP/union members and the chairperson, Dr. Higgins. The former wanted the group to endorse the NDP slate for the municipal elections; Higgins wanted to keep pollution issues "above" politics. Rather than focus on legislative/political change, he wanted to direct the group's activities toward individual/consumer-oriented educational work with the general public and in high schools.[61] From this point onward, it appears that Hillier and a handful of other union activists focused their energies on the NDP and on events organised by environmental activists from the Toronto and Peterborough Pollution Probes (e.g., two conferences on labour and the environment, involving union representatives, academics, and NDP members).

In 1971 the mercury issue trailed off into legal battles over compensation for fishers and others affected by water contamination, hearings, and studies of pollution in the area. In March the IJC held a hearing in Sarnia on air pollution, which had worsened due to the start-up of an Ontario Hydro plant and increased emissions of sulphur and nitrogen oxides from the Detroit Edison plant at St. Clair, Michigan. The Mayor of Sarnia, Paul Blundy, acknowledged at the hearing that air pollution was bad and that more control was needed, although he congratulated local firms for their efforts.[62] Meanwhile, public opinion in Sarnia was divided on the issue of corporate liability for pollution. According to Barbara Thompson, author of the Sarnia Pollution Probe *Mercury Report*, made public in November 1971:

> The question of the probable effects on the City of Sarnia by a successful damage suit against Dow Chemical is a matter of some great concern to the residents of this area...
>
> There appear to be, however, two major opinions regarding this issue. Some residents have expressed the concern that a large settlement from Dow might force the company to close down the Sarnia plant and therefore cause a great deal of unemployment and economic distress. Others, including the Ontario government, feel that the company could well afford to pay the multi-million dollar suit and still maintain its operation (p. 44).

One person Ms. Thompson named as expressing the latter view was Ivan Hillier. Given his relative isolation in the campaign to bring Dow Chemical to account, it is questionable how "major" the second opinion was in Sarnia at the time.

In 1972 Hillier and the local NDP contingent continued to use the pages of the *Sarnia Democrat* to raise pollution issues. They also attacked the Vietnam war, and took left nationalist positions, including a call for the nationalization of oil companies—especially Imperial Oil (June 1972 issue). They criticised the sale of the Crown corporation, Polymer, to the Canada Development Corporation, and accused Shell Oil and Imperial Oil of being corporate welfare bums. Not surprisingly, all this activity did not endear Hillier to his employer nor to the conservative elite which had traditionally shaped public opinion in Sarnia. When he became involved with Pollution Probe, he and his wife received threatening phone calls. He had his number changed twice. He received hate mail at home and at work. According to Hillier, "communist" literature was delivered to his union office to discredit him. After he complained to the RCMP, they and the city police raided his house when he was out of town, on the pretext of a drug search. They produced a clay pipe and accused his fourteen-year-old daughter of smoking marijuana, although they did not lay charges. The editor of the *Sarnia Gazette* wrote a defamatory editorial about Hillier and other activists, which led to a law suit.[63]

Throughout a decade of involvement with the mercury and other local pollution issues, Hillier's campaign was more or less a one-man show. Although during this time he was almost continuously either president of his local (OCAWIU 672, Dow) or president of the Labour Council, there was no official union endorsement of his struggle. Hillier did not act as a representative of the OCAW or of his local. This fact was acknowledged by other ECWU officials interviewed in 1988.[64] Moreover, the labour relationship with Pollution Probe was not an official or organisational one, but primarily one with Hillier and a few others acting independently. The area unions remained passive during this period of heightened environmental-corporate antagonism. Apart from the environment workshop sponsored by the Labour Council in March 1970, which was poorly attended by unionized workers in the area, there is little evidence of union involvement in the issue. When asked why he chose to fight this battle as an individual citizen, rather than as the head of a union, Hillier replied:. "I had the strong feeling that if I had raised it as an issue with the Labour Council, and sought [their] endorsement, maybe I wouldn't get it, because of the...right wing element."[65]

While chemical workers had achieved relative affluence and security by the early 1970s, the economic conditions underpinning these gains had begun to change. Rising unemployment had led in 1972 to the creation of a local coalition called "People Under Social Hardship." There was considerable fear that Hillier's activities were going to cost chemical workers their jobs. He was not only harassed at work by his employer (and he received little protection from the union), but was also criticised by co-workers. For these reasons, he chose to work through the NDP and Pollution Probe. It was these organisations—not the OCAW—which took up the cause of industrial pollution in Sarnia. With the changing economic and political climate of the mid-1970s, these organisations slipped back into a marginal existence or left the scene altogether.[66] Pollution Probe in Sarnia seems to have declined after the mercury scare of 1970. One of the reasons for this may be the absence of a larger community of radical intellectuals and activists in Sarnia, who might have sustained a more long-term and political *raison d'être* for the group.

The Lead Issue

The Energy and Chemical Workers' Union was faced in the 1980s with growing concern about the effects of lead in the environment. One aspect of this concern was the campaign to remove lead from gasoline. Another was the mobilization of citizens in neighbourhoods of Toronto to stop lead emissions from industrial plants.

The Campaign to Ban Leaded Gasoline

National environmental and health organisations as well as neighbourhood and parents' groups in Toronto led the campaign to make the federal government legislate a ban on lead in gasoline, following growing evidence in the late 1970s and early 1980s that exposure to lead emissions (from car exhaust and smokestacks) was affecting the neurobehavioural development of children in North American cities.[67] A study by the Department of National Health and Welfare, completed in 1982, determined that the blood lead level considered dangerous needed to be lowered.[68] The environment minister at the time, John Roberts, promised that lead in gasoline would be reduced.[69] The oil refineries responded by lobbying against a total lead ban, arguing that the costs of renovating their facilities would be passed on to consumers. They pointed out that some plants producing tetraethyl lead would close, laying off between 160 and 330 workers. The jobs of ECWU members at Ethyl Canada Corporation (Corunna) and DuPont Canada (Maitland) were threatened. There was a notable convergence of views among the management of Eythl Canada Corporation, the *Sarnia Observer*, and the ECWU representatives on the lead ban issue. All of them tried to oppose the new regulation without appearing to dismiss the public's health concerns.

The President of Ethyl Canada "denied that the [existing] 0.77 [gms/litre] standard poses any danger to human health," and pointed out that consumers would have to pay two cents a litre more for gasoline as a result of the new regulation.[70] Ethyl Canada and DuPont claimed that "there are no studies that *prove* that lead from tailpipes is causing harm to humans, particularly in Canada."[71] In a March 1983 editorial, the *Sarnia Observer* tried to support Ethyl Canada's position without saying that lead emissions were a good thing. The writers made an argument—repeated by the ECWU—that other pollution problems were more pressing, and that the evidence regarding lead was not entirely convincing. They suggested that the ban be postponed pending "*more research* on [lead's] effects."[72]

In a May 1983 brief submitted to the Minister for National Health and Welfare, the ECWU tried unsuccessfully to reconcile a stated commitment to occupational health and safety and public health with opposition to a reduction of lead in gasoline.[73] The ECWU brief began by pointing out, quite rightly, the hypocrisy and inconsistency of the government in applying stricter health standards in the public health than in the occupational health spheres. Although workers had been exposed to lead for many decades, occupational exposure was not the impetus behind, nor the subject of, the new regulatory concern. The blood lead level considered dangerous in the Department of National Health and Welfare report was 30 micrograms/decilitre (ug/dl). The threshold level in the Ontario Occupational Health and Safety Act was 60 ug/dl, and no proposals had been made to lower it.[74]

However, the brief then went on to question the legitimacy of the concern about environmental lead exposure. It used the very argument which, historically, has been used by employers and the scientific establishment to delay or avoid altogether measures to protect workers' health. The ECWU argued that there was *insufficient evidence to establish a cause and effect relationship* between lead exposure and health effects such as neurobehavioural problems in children.[75] They referred to various scientific studies whose conclusions were not considered decisive, including data from the blood screening of children in the South Riverdale neighbourhood of Toronto in 1982 and 1983. (Canada Metals, one of the plants whose lead emissions had caused the high lead levels in the area, was the site of an ECWU local.) The ECWU emphasized that lead levels in these children were not considered significant, while downplaying the fact that lead abatement programmes had been instituted in the area after 1973, when lead blood levels were significant. In a rhetorical question with depressing implications, the brief's authors asked whether preventative measures were called for, "in order to avoid the potential loss of four or five I.Q. points among those few children [whose lead levels] may be high enough to produce such effects?" Such dubious benefits, they argued, should be weighed against the loss of up to 300 chemical workers' jobs. The "absence of proof" argument was repeated by ECWU officials interviewed in 1988, even though studies since the early 1980s had strengthened the case against lead.

The second line of argument was that other sources of lead contamination had not been subjected to the same scrutiny as leaded gasoline, and that unless this was done, it was unfair to impose restrictions on the latter.[76] They did not call, however, for the reduction or elimination of lead emissions from factories, from paint and other products, *and* gasoline. Instead, they argued: If you are going to ban lead, then ban everything else which is potentially harmful to children or foetuses. Otherwise, don't pick on us.

The self-serving and ethically unconscionable nature of these arguments is particularly sad given the exposure of many chemical workers to lead and other toxic substances in their workplaces and communities. The devil's choice of short-term job security at the cost of the long-term consequences of ignoring such working conditions is reflected in the tortuous logic of the ECWU brief on lead regulation. The union could not simply deny that there are links between lead exposure and health problems. In addition, it had a good case that its own occupational health concerns had in the past been ignored by governmental authorities and employers, and that environmental groups were also neglecting workers' concerns. Yet it seized on any means to *minimize* the credibility of health risks in this case. In doing this, the union reinforced an opposition between its members and those people "outside" whose interests as parents, environmentalists, or residents of neighbourhoods were separated from the interests of all of the above as workers. Ultimately the reference to the occupational exposure of workers to lead expressed not a solidarity with those "outside" the workplace, but the same kind of resentment that was described above: "If we are prepared to suffer these things, the public—which is less affected—has less right to complain, and should not jeopardize what we have attained at such cost."

The ECWU's director of health and safety, Dan Ublansky, expressed similar feelings in a 1988 interview:

> [Ublansky]: ...[T]here is a difference in attitude between our people and the citizens' groups. Our people deal with this crud every day, so they're familiar with it. It's not the fear of the unknown there. They have a pretty good idea of what the risks are. I think the community groups...tend to be more alarmist... I think part of the reason why [environmental and labour] groups can't get that close is that there is some element of hypocrisy between the way workers' health problems are dealt with versus the citizens' complaints. That's one of the reasons we were so pissed off about the lead thing. We felt...the degree of the hazard posed by lead in gas, compared to the risks that a lot of our members were facing, was far out of proportion. To prioritize leaded gas as being number one on the legislative hit list, compared to some of the other problems, we thought was unfair.
>
> [A]: Do you mean, [compared to] the conditions of workers who were producing leaded gasoline?
>
> [U]: Not only the people who were producing it, but what I'm saying is that as a substance, [it was wrong] to say that lead was the number one priority, that there had to be legislation.
>
> [A]: But why not [regulate leaded gasoline]?... It was something [environmentalists] thought they could achieve.
>
> [U]: Exactly. And that's where we run into problems, because...you blew away two or three hundred of my members by taking the easy victory... It was something they thought they could get, so they went for it.

In the end, the victory on leaded gas was not so "easy," due to the lobbying efforts of employers and the union. Federal Environment Minister Charles Caccia announced in December 1983 that lead in gasoline would be cut by about 60 percent by 1987 (by lowering the maximum level to .29 grams per litre), and a committee would be established to study the effects of lead on Canadians' health.[77] Federal officials estimated the cost of refinery modifications needed to get more octane from raw fuel to be $120 million to $240 million. This would add 0.1 to 0.2 cents a week to an average gasoline bill for a leaded-gas car. Caccia said his decision to implement a reduction, rather than a total ban, represented "a prudent approach between the health implications of continuing automobile lead emissions and recognition of the economic implications." He promised that displaced workers would get "highest priority" in retraining programmes.

Environmental groups had wanted the new lead standards to take effect by 1985; the four-year period of grace granted to the refineries represented a partial victory for Ethyl, as did the government's decision not to implement a total ban. Ethyl said the new standards would not be difficult to achieve.[78] It announced in December that it would lay off or grant early retirement to about fifty employees of the tetraethyl plant in Corunna.[79] However, one of the reasons for the decision to close down the Corunna plant, according to Dave Pretty, the Sarnia and District representative for the ECWU, was anticipation of the free trade agreement between Canada and the United States. Ethyl's main market for leaded gas was in the United States. Ethyl made an agreement to market (in Canada), through DuPont, tetraethyl lead produced in the United States. In this way, the company could consolidate its production while retaining access to a secondary (Canadian) market.[80] Overall, the lead regulation did not appear to be the main cause of the company's decision to close down its Corunna plant. Moreover, similar regulation in the United States was shrinking the market for tetraethyl lead, and petrochemical firms were looking for new substitutes.[81] By September 1985, Ethyl Canada had begun production of a new product, diesel ignition improver. The company planned to produce four million lbs./year, at $1 million in sales, in a plant employing six persons. Nor did lead regulation seem to affect company profits too adversely. The parent company, Ethyl Corporation of Richmond, Virginia, reported 1985 and 1986 profits of $117.1 million and $177.7 million respectively, and profits and sales were still climbing in 1987.[82]

In 1985, the Royal Society of Canada published a report which supported findings that had already been established in the United States several years earlier. The level at which lead was said to have harmful effects was 25 ug/dl of blood. The Royal Society report also recommended a seven year time-line for the gradual phasing-in of lower lead levels in gasoline. The Canadian government, on the basis of these recommendations, set a 1993 deadline for the reduction of lead in gasoline to .026 grams/litre (the standard adopted by the United States in 1986). In response to these recommendations, a coalition of groups formed demanding a 17-month time-line for the implementation of new regulations, which they argued was technically feasible. (Pollution Probe, Friends of the Earth, and the Canadian Environmental Law Association participated in the coalition.)[83] They viewed the Royal Society report as a delaying tactic, and its recommendations as far too lenient. In his account of the lead-ban campaign, David Lees claims that successive federal cabinets had caved in to pressure from the Petroleum Association for Conservation of the Canadian Environment (PACE) (which, despite its name, "lobbies on behalf of the petroleum industry"), the International Lead and Zinc Research Organization, along with Esso and the companies mining lead.

> "McMillan [the new federal environment minister] told us privately that he had been under terrific pressure from the industry not to cut back on the lead in gasoline," said McElgunn [a researcher with the Learning Disabilities Association of Canada]. "He told us that personally he wanted to go to virtually no lead by 1989, but that his fall-back position with the industry was that he would settle for 1990.
>
> "McMillan is the third environmental minister I've dealt with on this issue. and they all wanted to get lead out of gasoline. When I met Charles Caccia after he took the standard from 0.77 to 0.29 he was furious... He said, 'Barbara, give us hell. We should have gone to zero.' They always mean well but something always happens."[84]

By 1988, the coalition was supported by new medical evidence showing that "children can be harmed at blood lead levels as low as six micrograms a decilitre."[85] Under pressure, Federal Environment Minister Tom McMillan said he would study the new data and consult with the refineries. In September 1988 the government announced that it would move up the deadline for reduction to December 1, 1990.[86]

CANADA METALS AND TORONTO REFINERS AND SMELTERS: TWO CASES OF INDUSTRIAL LEAD EMISSIONS

Canada Metals was one of at least two plants targeted by area residents for lead emissions in the 1980s. This was also a plant where ECWU members were exposed to lead fumes, and the lesson drawn by the union lawyer, Dan Ublansky, seemed to be that workers can take care of these problems when they are left to themselves, and citizens do not interfere.

> We were having problems in the plant... the Ministry of Labour was involved as well as the Minister of the Environment. There was an intensive four-way

co-operation to try to control [lead emissions] both in the plant and outside. And a lot of money has been spent. Canada Metal has been working to control their emissions over the last four-five years.

Interestingly, Ublansky omitted to mention another factor explaining these efforts, namely the involvement of citizens from the surrounding neighbourhood. According to Kathy Cooper, an activist in the lead issue in Toronto, management at Canada Metals had shown some willingness to accept responsibility for the lead problem and to initiate a clean-up, *but this was largely due to the presence of a very vocal citizens' group*—in this case the South Riverdale Community Health Centre (SRCHC).[87] Moreover, following the closure of the Toronto Refiners and Smelters (TRS) plant (discussed below), Canada Metals purchased the plant's equipment, planning to expand its operations in South Riverdale. This greatly concerned the area residents, whose ultimate goal was closure of the plant. They felt that the operation of a lead-recycling facility (the plant recovered lead from batteries) across the street from a school, and in an area already heavily polluted, was a health threat to children and to long-term residents.[88]

Tests conducted by the Toronto Public Health Department around Toronto Refiners and Smelters (a Steelworkers' plant) in the summer of 1985 had found that some of the children in the area of these plants had nearly 60 percent more lead in their blood than the average Ontario child.[89] Ministry of the Environment data showed that, in 1985, lead concentrations around Toronto Refiners and Smelters exceeded the limit allowed under the Ontario Environmental Protection Act.[90] In 1975 the company had been issued a government order to clean up, but over ten years the MOE's regional office in Toronto had "preferred to negotiate pollution agreements with the companies rather than force them to clean up."[91] For years, local residents—mainly parents concerned for their children's health—had been trying to get the government to enforce controls on these polluters. In 1986, a Canadian Environmental Law Association lawyer filed charges against Toronto Refiners and Smelters on behalf of the Niagara Neighbourhood Association Lead Pollution Committee, citing the failure of the Ministry of the Environment to prosecute despite continuing violations of the Environmental Protection Act. The Ontario Environment Ministry under James Bradley negotiated an agreement with the company to meet government requirements by January 5, 1987, or face prosecution.

Meanwhile, one wonders what working conditions *inside* these plants must have been like. The clean-up order for Toronto Refiners and Smelters called on the company to "improve its ventilation and filtration system to the outside."[92] In May 1988 the Ontario New Democratic Party leader, Bob Rae, took up the case in the legislature of a Toronto Refiners and Smelters worker, who had been employed at the company for thirty years, and who was suffering from serious lead poisoning. He had been denied a permanent disability pension by the Workers Compensation Board.

According to a South Riverdale community organiser and member of the SRCHC, community relations with the unions at Canada Metals were sporadic and conflictual.[93] The workforce at Canada Metals in 1989 was about 104, the majority of whom were members of the ECWU. A small group, and that most exposed to lead in the plant, consisted of pipefitters who belonged to a different union. The SRCHC organiser claimed that the neighbourhood group had tried many times to establish relations with the unions over a period of fifteen years. During this time, union representatives very rarely attended neighbourhood meetings; the group's contacts were with ex-employees. Indeed, the citizens perceived that the workers at Canada Metals "have always seen us as a threat."[94] The South Riverdale citizens met every six weeks with representatives of the Departments of Public Health and the Environment, and the owner of the plant. At one of these meetings the plant owner agreed to ensure that union representatives would attend a meeting with community representatives. This meeting took place in June 1989. According to the SRCHC organiser, local and national representatives of the ECWU, as well as a local representative of the pipefitters, were present. They expressed anger at the neighbourhood residents for threatening their jobs; one man said that, although he had worked at Canada Metals for thirty-five years, he was "still alive." When asked if they would continue to meet with the citizens, the response was that they might do so, if the owner approved. As of mid-August, the citizens had not heard from the unions, and were not expecting to.

In response to questions about how the citizens had attempted to address the concerns of the workers for job security (e.g., whether they had prepared any briefs for the Minister of Labour), or to involve themselves in occupational health and safety issues, the SRCHC member indicated that the citizens had been cognizant of these issues. While they had not met directly with the Ministry of Labour, they had endorsed OFL criteria for retraining and interim support of displaced workers, and had made this clear to the union representatives. The SRCHC member also noted that Canada Metals had successfully contested Ministry of Labour work orders for improvements to working conditions in the plant, which would indicate either that the unions were not concerned with these conditions, or had been unsuccessful in documenting them and in demanding enforcement of MOL regulations.[95]

The overall picture provided by the available evidence, then, is one of a workforce closely attached to the interests and perspectives of its employer, and unwilling to risk plant closure by allying in any way with the interests of the neighbourhood, or indeed, to defend its own health. The owner of Canada Metal was managing the environment-and-health-versus-profits conflict by "co-operating" with organised citizens and government officials to ameliorate external pollution problems. At the same time, the company was acting to weaken its opposition by targeting vulnerable elements for aggressive actions. For example, Canada Metals sued a CBC Radio documentary-maker in the 1970s for a programme prepared for broadcast on the lead pollution problem in Toronto.[96] In the 1980s, the company threatened to sue an individual who was producing a neighbourhood newspaper in South Riverdale critical of pollution from the plant. Clearly, the company had also counted on at least the passive support of its workforce. One can only speculate on the outcome of this conflict had the union and the citizens adopted a joint strategy.

The Toronto lead pollution cases raise a number of questions. Did the unions try to improve the conditions of workers exposed to lead by linking the issue to the concerns of other citizens? Did environmental and citizens' groups demand transitional measures to assist workers who would lose their jobs due to lead regulation and environmental law enforcement? Regarding the unions, the answer seems to be a pretty clear "no." As for the citizens, it seems that their lobbying on the employment issue could have been more direct, and a greater priority, although they did try to work with the unions. These questions are examined further in the following section.

The Junction Triangle

Pollution problems in the Junction Triangle (JT) area of Toronto also involved the ECWU. The JT is a mixed industrial and working-class residential neighbourhood in west end Toronto. In the 1980s, about 6,000 people lived there—over half of them of Italian, Portuguese, Ukranian or Greek origin. It was the location of about twenty manufacturing plants using or producing chemical products. Amongst the worst polluters in the late

Chemical Workers and Toxic Pollution Issues 179

1970s were Anchor Cap and Closure (odours caused by emissions from the lacquer lithograph and plastisol ovens, noise); American Standards (odours, noise); Glidden Paint Company (odours and fumes from manufacture of resin, adhesives, and varnish); Canadian General Electric; Seiberling Rubber; and others.[97] Glidden Paints was one of the ECWU plants in the area. During the 1970s it had successfully evaded the requirement to install pollution control towers.[98]

Since the mid-1970s, JT residents, suffering from a variety of pollution-related ailments and stress, had been pressuring Toronto City Council to take some actions against the polluters. In 1982 a group of residents formed The Watchdog Committee Against Pollution. The City's Department of Public Health undertook a health study of residents which was released in 1984.[99] The authors of the study concluded that the health problems of JT residents were no worse, on average, than those of residents of other neighbourhoods in Toronto.[100] However, the more detailed observations of the study gave reason for concern. The number of persons reporting occupational exposure to risk factors "potentially hazardous to health" over a period of at least a year could hardly be considered acceptable, even if all three areas reported similar data. The numbers reporting residential exposure to hazardous risk factors was also high. The significant difference in the data reported for workplace and residential exposure to pollutants may have been the result of perceptions or fears about reporting workplace pollution, although this possibility was not considered by the authors: "It is an *important negative finding* that the adults of JT report no difference in exposure to risk factors potentially hazardous to health *at the work site, i.e., occupational exposure.*" (See tables 18 and 19.)

TABLE 18
% OF ADULTS REPORTING OCCUPATIONAL EXPOSURE TO RISK FACTORS
POTENTIALLY HAZARDOUS TO HEALTH
(FOR MORE THAN ONE YEAR)

Category	Comparison Area (TR)	Junction Triangle (JT)	Neighbouring Area (NA)
Noise	40.2	44.7	45.0
Dusty particles	39.8	37.3	41.9
Chemicals or Solvents	18.9	18.8	21.8
Gas, chemical fumes or smells	22.4	17.7	24.0
All factors above except dust	27.9	25.0	31.2

SOURCE: W.O. Spitzer, "A Study of the Health Status of Residents of the Junction Triangle, Toronto," (City of Toronto, Dept. of Public Health, April 1984), Table 13.1, p. 64.

The authors stated: "With respect to *residential* exposure to risk factors potentially hazardous to health, however, a marked excess was reported in the Junction Triangle compared to the comparison area (TR). The difference was statistically significant and a gradient was evident."[101] Moreover, the study found reason to worry about the health of children in the area.

TABLE 19
% OF ADULTS REPORTING RESIDENTIAL EXPOSURE TO RISK FACTORS POTENTIALLY HAZARDOUS TO HEALTH (FOR MORE THAN ONE YEAR)

Category	TR	JT	NA
Dusty particles	14.3	34.5	32.1
Heavy traffic	29.2	45.5	44.9
Gas, chemical fumes or smells	11.9	66.2	45.2
All exposures except dusty particles	32.7	76.3	62.6

SOURCE: W.O. Spitzer, "A Study of the Health Status of Residents of the Junction Triangle, Toronto," (City of Toronto, Dept. of Public Health, April 1984), Table 13.2, p. 64.

[T]he two-week prevalence of cardinal symptoms[102] was a priority variable, and the cardinal symptoms chosen were among the most probably associated with the chemical substances detected in the environment of the Junction Triangle. The differences in the two-week prevalence rates of such symptoms among children in the JT and TR areas were clinically and statistically significant and there was a clear gradient from the JT to the NA to the TR... Moreover, a trend that did not favour the children of the JT was observed when a more comprehensive set of 12 symptoms was examined at two-week and one-year prevalence rates.[103] In both cases, the gradient persisted and the differences in the one-year prevalence rates were statistically significant...

We conclude that there is enough evidence of unfavourable health experience among children in the JT area to warrant more in-depth and more clinical evaluation of their health problems.[104]

The authors recommended a health study of children, pollution controls on industry, and a cancer study.[105]

Despite these findings, an official of the ECWU focused only on the conclusion that overall the health status of residents of the Junction Triangle seemed no worse than that of residents of other Toronto neighbourhoods. Moreover, the "problem" was identified as affecting *residents* primarily, rather than workers. The ECWU had taken no part in demanding that the health study be carried out; nor had it sought to have occupational exposure included.

Some of our locals in the Junction Triangle in Toronto have been under fire a couple of years ago—at least the companies they worked for—Glidden Paint, a number of the paint plants in the west end. There's a lot of industry located right in the middle of a residential area. The neighbours were complaining about smells and health problems. They put a lot of pressure on the City of Toronto and a health study was done...which said everything was O.K. I guess that ended the pressure out of that area...

The extent of the danger wasn't documented. There were some stories and some complaints. As far as the health and safety within the plants were concerned, it wasn't a particularly strong issue. We weren't getting complaints from our members in the plant about health problems. Not necessarily to say that there weren't any. Normally, if there are serious problems, we hear about it. Because there was publicity going on around them, I would have thought that if any of the people inside the plant were also... Some of them were also residents of the area... Anyway, that's one area where the companies were under fire, but they managed to stonewall their way out of it (emphasis added).[106]

What is striking about this response is the willingness of the union to turn a blind eye to conditions both within and without the plants—i.e., not to investigate, lest a problem be confirmed. Despite the attention being focused on the health effects of the very chemicals to which they were daily and directly exposed, workers appear to have chosen not to get involved in the anti-pollution struggle. They remained "neutral" rather than ally with—in this case—their neighbours.

It is also interesting that a union official again deployed a defence often used by employers, implying that there was insufficient scientific evidence to legitimate concerns about either residents' or workers' exposure to pollutants. Given that the union was not demanding that testing of the workplaces be done, or carrying out any data collection of its own, or participating in the citizens' efforts to get information, one wonders where the documentation was supposed to come from. Ublansky also referred again to the idea that workers are less concerned about the risks because they have more knowledge about what is going on inside the plants; this superior knowledge sets them apart from the alarmist laypersons outside.

[Regarding the] Junction Triangle, the early stories that came out in the newspaper—you know, people questioning what they were being exposed to—well, that sort of information was readily available if they had gone to the union. In fact, I recall going to an NDP-sponsored environmental workshop about four or five years ago, when this Junction Triangle thing started, and the community people were there, and they said to us: "We want this information." I said to them, "if you want it, it's easily obtained. We can get that for you." But there had never been that kind of attempt coming from the environmental people. They seemed reluctant to jump in with the labour groups. I think they see us as being more aligned with the company than with the community.

In this quotation one also finds the expectation that it is the environmental or citizens' groups which must overcome the barriers to alliance with the union; it is their responsibility to demonstrate to union members the legitimacy of their concerns. The rather demanding scientific criteria which this union, at least, seemed to require before it would question the actions of an employer, posed an obstacle to such alliance. More importantly, the condition implicit in these cases—that the parties courting alliance must produce guarantees of job security—is really an impossible one for any actor but the State, or a regional planning body to meet. In a local struggle, it is highly unlikely that a citizen's group could meet the security concerns of the union.

NOTES

1. Patricia Drimmie, *A History of Labour in Sarnia and Lambton County* (Sarnia and District Labour Council, 1978), p. 6.
2. Duart Snow, "The Holmes Foundry Strike of March 1937: 'We'll give their jobs to white men!,'" *Ontario History* (Ontario Historical Society, 1977), p. 3.
3. In 1942 the Canadian government created the Polymer Corporation to produce rubber; Sarnia was the chosen site. The government made agreements with three companies which would operate the

plants and be paid management fees. These were St. Clair Processing, a wholly-owned subsidiary of Imperial Oil; Dow Chemical of Canada; and Canadian Synthetic Rubber (formed by Dominion, Firestone, Goodrich, and Goodyear). By 1951, all of the agreements had been terminated.
4. At the beginning of the decade, St. Clair Chemical (now Welland Chemical) began production of anhydrous aluminum chloride (used as a catalyst in the petrochemical industry). Allied Chemical built its plant south of Corunna for the production of TDI, one of the raw materials for polyurethane foam (and a very toxic chemical). In the mid-1960s, C-I-L built a fertilizer complex south of Courtright. The Lambton coal-fuelled generating station started up in 1969. Dome Petroleum built a gas separation plant. Liquid Carbonic built a CO_2 plant at C-I-L in 1969 (H_2 was added in 1975). In 1967-68, area plants invested about $343.6 million in new capacity. In the late 1970s Union Carbide built a polyethylene plant in the Sarnia area. DuPont expanded its capacity at Corunna, and Shell added isopropanol and polypropylene units.
5. Drimmie, *A History of Labour in Sarnia and Lambton County*, p. 26. See also, *Sarnia Observer*, February 9, 1957, p. 13; March 2, 1957, p. 9. Polymer joined Polysar in 1973, and was acquired by the Canada Development Corporation. It produces synthetic rubbers and latexes.
6. *Sarnia Observer*, May 13, 1959, p. 21; June 22, 1959, p. 1.
7. Among these were Duncan Longwell, still a Polysar worker in 1986, and David Pretty, who became a union staff member in 1968. Both were interviewed by the author in December 1986.
8. *Sarnia Observer*, January 4, 1968, p. 13.
9. *Sarnia Observer*, January 17, 1974, p. 15.
10. *The Financial Post*, (Report on Ontario), October 21, 1972.
11. Drimmie, *A History of Labour*.
12. *Sarnia Observer*, July 29, 1980, p. 4.
13. *Sarnia Observer*, March 9, 1982, p. 1.
14. *Sarnia Observer*, January 20, 1983, p. 1.
15. *Sarnia Observer*, February 3, 1983.
16. *The Globe and Mail*, February 1, 1983, p. B11.
17. *Sarnia Observer*, February 3, 1983, p. 1.
18. When the Petrochemical Industry Task Force Report was released in February 1984, it received the approval of the *Sarnia Observer*. The newspaper was also pleased by the Conservative electoral victory in September 1984, and urged the new government to deregulate feedstock prices. Moreover, it opposed any public ownership or regulation of the industry. See the *Sarnia Observer*, Feb. 7, 1984 (editorial); Nov. 5, 1984 and Feb. 8, 1986.
19. *Sarnia Observer*, October 27, 1983, p. 1. Note how the tone—and even the language—of this editorial was echoed by the ECWU's Secretary-Treasurer, Buck Philp, at the 1986 Convention (chapter 8).
20. *Sarnia Observer*, November 21, 1983, p. 1.
21. *Sarnia Observer*, March 23, 1985.
22. In the 1980s it was joked that "in Windsor, Bob White walks on water." (Bob White was the President of the CAW at that time.)
23. Marcella Brown, "Air Pollution Down Here, Society Reports," *Sarnia Observer*, June 25, 1970, pp. 25, 26; Lambton Industrial Society, "Environmental Quality in Sarnia, Ontario, 1969" (June 17, 1970).
24. Supporting members included: Imperial Oil, Polymer Corporation, Dow Chemical, Fiberglas Canada, Mueller, Holmes Foundry, Cabot Carbon, Canadian Oil, Sun Oil, and Ethyl Corporation.
25. *Sarnia Observer*, February 7, 1957, p. 13.
26. *Sarnia Observer*, January 19, 1957.
27. *Sarnia Observer*, October 23, 1958, p. 17.
28. *Sarnia Observer*, November 24, 1960, p. 17.
29. *Sarnia Observer*, November 26, 1960, p. 9.
30. *Sarnia Observer*, (editorial) July 3, 1964, p. 4.
31. *Sarnia Observer*, May 1, 1965, p. 11.
32. "Sarnia Air is Cleaner Than Many Thought," *Sarnia Observer*, (editorial) Aug. 13, 1965, p. 1.
33. *Sarnia Observer*, May 3, 1966, p. 9. There was also a CBC documentary on the pollution in Sarnia, aired around this time, called "Air of Death" (cited in R. W. Ford, *A History of the*

Chemical Workers and Toxic Pollution Issues 183

     Chemical Industry in Lambton County (Canadian Society for Chemical Engineering, 1976), p. 17).
34. *Sarnia Observer*, May 3, 1966, p. 9.
35. *Sarnia Observer*, July 5, 1966, p. 9.
36. *Sarnia Observer*, April 17, 1967, p. 13.
37. *Sarnia Observer*, July 11, 1968, p. 4.
38. *Sarnia Observer*, July 16, 1968, p. 4; November 12, 1968, p. 11; January 23, 1969, p. 13; February 26, 1969, p. 19.
39. This idea was expressed by the President of the Ontario Area Council of the ECWU in a 1988 interview: "I think our problem is that we have to weigh both sides... You can have fresh, clean air, or a country that's not productive" (Charlie Stevens, interview by author, Sarnia, Ont., May 5, 1988).
40. Interview with "Peter," health and safety activist at Dow Chemical (Sarnia), May 5, 1988. At that time Dow was using the most dangerous form of asbestos (blue, or crocidolite). They had replaced the mercury cells in the chlorine unit with asbestos diaphragm cells.
41. These views emerged in interviews with chemical workers and union officials in Sarnia, steel and coke oven workers in Sydney, and at the 1986 Jobs and the Environment Conference in Hamilton.
42. Documents used in preparing this section include copies of briefs and correspondence obtained from Ivan Hillier, newspaper coverage in the *Sarnia Observer* and the *London Free Press*, and the report *Mercury in our Environment (with special reference to the St. Clair River System)* by Barbara Thompson (Sarnia: Pollution Probe, 1971), whose appendices include correspondence with Dow, and the OCAW brief to Donald MacDonald (1964).
43. Just after the second testing was done, there was a release of chlorine gas from the chlorine plant where Ivan Hillier was an operator. The company immediately blamed Hillier for this occurrence. He protested that such leaks were common, and that the company was acknowledging this one, and was blaming him, in order to discredit him. See the OCAW brief in Thompson, *Mercury in our Environment*.
44. Letter from Ralph Knox, dated February 28, quoted in Appendix IV, Ibid.
45. Ibid., p. 40.
46. The same pattern of government protection of the companies and of the rupture of this arrangement by an independent actor occurred in the mid-1980s, with the "discovery" of the St. Clair River "blob" by divers of the Great Lakes Institute (chapter 11).
47. A ministerial order was served on Dow Chemical by the Ontario Department of Energy and Resources Management under the terms of the Ontario Water Resources Commission Act. See Thompson, *Mercury in our Environment*, Appendix VII. In addition, pulp and paper mills were ordered to stop using mercury slimicides by April 15, and a study of the mercury problem was undertaken by Michigan agencies, the OWRC, the Department of Lands and Forests, the American Bureau of Commercial Fisheries, and the US Food and Drug Administration.
48. Minutes of this meeting were obtained from Ivan Hillier.
49. March 28, 1970 statement by Jim Charrington, public relations officer for the Sarnia and District Labour Council.
50. Sage, quoted in "Claims all Lakes area poisoned by mercury," *London Free Press*, April 13, 1970. In relation to Sage's comment about workers' fear of employer retaliation, it should be pointed out that in 1970 Ontario did not even have the Occupational Health and Safety Act to protect employees, let alone "whistle-blower" protection for reporting pollution offences.
51. Duncan Longwell, interview by author, Sarnia, Ont., December 5, 1986.
52. *Sarnia Observer*, April 10, 1970, p. 13.
53. *Sarnia Observer*, April 14, 1970, p. 4. A *Sarnia Observer* April 25 editorial on amendments to the Canada Water Act, which would impose fines on industrial polluters, defended the "good citizenship" of local firms.
54. *Sarnia Observer*, April 28, 1970, p. 2.
55. The government announced at the end of March 1970 that it would sue Dow Chemical for $35 million for damages and the cost of clean-up. The suit was dropped in June 1978. The government accepted an out-of-court settlement which awarded $250,000 to fishers who had lost their livelihoods in 1971. The fishers' lawyer said this amount was "a paltry sum, a puny settlement." It prohibited claimants from taking any future action against Dow. The ban on fishing was still in effect.

The Canadian Environmental Law Association said the outcome would be "an open invitation to more industrial environmental abuses in the future" (*Sarnia Observer,* June 7, 1978, p. 1; June 8, 1978, p. 1).
56. The director's testimony was reported in the *Sarnia Observer,* May 21, 1970.
57. *Sarnia Observer,* July 22, 1970, p. 1.
58. *Sarnia Observer,* April 1, 1970, p. 19.
59. See the November 1970 issue of the *Sarnia Democrat.*
60. Longwell, interview, December 5, 1986.
61. See the *Sarnia Observer* reports of August 5, 1970, p. 19; August 7, 1970, p. 11. It is interesting that this split also characterised the St. Clair River International Citizens' Network in the 1980s. In the latter case, the more radical positions and pressure to ally with the NDP stemmed from the union representatives in the coalition, while the "professional" members (teachers, dentists, those in management occupations) preferred an individual "consciousness raising" approach, emphasizing individual choices as consumers. A similar division developed in the Fermi II citizens' group in Amherstburg, between CAW members who were involved with the NDP, and other members (retired people, teachers, students).
62. *Sarnia Observer,* March 10, 1971, p. 1. Ivan Hillier had run against Blundy for the Mayor's seat in 1970.
63. Interview with Hillier, May 6, 1988. See also, "Is There Really a Movement to 'Get Ivan Hillier' In Sarnia?" (editorial), *Sarnia Observer,* 1972 (no date).
64. Interviews with Dan Ublansky (May 3, 1988, London, Ont.), Stuart Sullivan, Charlie Stevens.
65. Interview with Ivan Hillier in Sarnia, May 1988.
66. Nevertheless, the commitment of Ivan Hillier, Duncan Longwell, and other chemical workers to this struggle against industrial pollution provides some important insights into the possibilities that can occur when industrial workers become militants and make great personal sacrifices in defence of principles. For these men, the existence of support from activists in the NDP and Pollution Probe was important in sustaining and giving political direction to their efforts. Also, it is worth noting that their struggle began with a health and safety conflict: their employer's willingness to ignore the effects on workers of mercury exposure informed their approach to the profit-versus-health/environment conflict outside the plant.
67. The National Research Council of Canada, Associate Committee on Scientific Criteria for Environmental Quality, conducted studies on lead in the environment in 1973 and 1979. See *Effects of lead in the environment, 1978—quantitative aspects* (Ottawa: NRC, 1979). The Ontario Ministry of the Environment, Air Resources Branch, produced an "Update Report on Lead Levels near Toronto Lead Plants during July, August, and September 1978"(Toronto: MOE, 1978) in response to public concern.

    Calvin Sandborn, staff counsel for the West Coast Environmental Law Association, notes in a 1988 article that since at least the eighteenth century, symptoms of lead poisoning were known to include mental impairment, gout, and sterility. In 1923, oil companies began to add lead to gasoline as an "anti-knock" agent. Before 1925, thirteen production workers had died and "scores of others" had become insane after exposure to lead fumes. The American Medical Association and various medical experts urged the Surgeon General to ban lead use. One researcher warned: "Tetra ethyl lead is 200 times more deadly than strychnine... there is a danger of universal lead poisoning." However, "industry pressure led to the reinstatement of leaded gasoline" in 1926. See "We're taking too long to get the lead out," *The Globe and Mail,* October 18, 1988.
68. Department of National Health and Welfare, *Human Exposure to Environmental Lead* (Ottawa: DNHW, November 1982).
69. Michael Keating, "Ottawa predicts 60% cut in gasoline lead by 1987," *The Globe and Mail,* December 22, 1983, p. 4.
70. "Company disputes Caccia's estimate for reducing lead," *The Globe and Mail,* December 24, 1983, p. 12.
71. "Ottawa predicts 60% cut in gasoline lead by 1987," *The Globe and Mail,* December 22, 1983, p. 4 (emphasis added).
72. *Sarnia Observer,* editorial, March 15, 1983 (emphasis added).
73. ECWU, "Human Lead Exposure to Environmental Lead" (Comments Submitted by the Energy

and Chemical Workers Union on the Report Prepared by the Department of National Health and Welfare for the Department of the Environment), May 1983. Copy in possession of author.
74. At the Ethyl Canada plant in Corunna, high lead levels in the blood of employees had resulted in people leaving their jobs. According to an ECWU official, an unusually active occupational health and safety committee at Ethyl had lobbied, in the early 1980s, for Ministry of Labour intervention to have the workplace cleaned up. (David Pretty, ECWU Sarnia District representative, interview by author, Sarnia, Ont., December 4, 1986.)
75. The lead story has some striking similarities to the union's handling of the asbestos issue in Canada, in which the "insufficient evidence" argument was also used to downplay evidence of occupational diseases. The asbestos case, which there is not space to review here, is one of the most terrible stories in the history of Canadian workers' health. The regulatory aspects are summarized by Kathryn Harrison, George Hoberg, and Gregory Hein, in *Risk, Science, and Politics* (Montréal: McGill-Queen's University Press, 1994), chapter 7. Unfortunately, these authors' discussion of "interest representation" omits any analysis of the positions taken by unions in Québec and Ontario.

Despite overwhelming medical evidence, collected since at least the 1930s, of a relationship between exposure to asbestos fibres and the diseases of asbestos, lung cancer, mesothelioma, and other kinds of cancers, the governments of Canada and Québec, mining companies, the Québec Federation of Labour, asbestos miners themselves, and the Steelworkers' union, have opposed the banning of the substance. Other sectors of the labour movement (the public sector unions, the OFL, the BCFL, and the construction and other asbestos-using unions) have supported the call for a ban, with transitional planning for affected workers. See Ray Sentes, "Asbestos, Jobs and Health," *The Facts* (CUPE) vol. 8, no. 6 (November/December 1986).

At the Johns-Manville Transit Pipe Company in Westhill, Ontario—an ECWU plant inherited from the International Chemical Workers—by 1986 more than 110 workers had contracted asbestos-related diseases, and sixty-eight more had died from them, out of a total workforce of 714. These were only the cases that had been reported for compensation claims. See Linda Jolley, "Regulating a Toxic Substance: The Impact on Workers," paper presented to the Conference on Jobs and the Environment, November 21-23, 1986, Hamilton, Ontario. In *Cracking the Canadian Formula*, Roberts quotes union reps who admit that many of the workers at Johns-Manville "wanted to avoid the truth, and we [the ICW] helped them avoid it" (Toronto: Between the Lines, 1990, p. 228). Another tragedy may be in the making, this time under new corporate and union management. According to Robert's account:

> Manville's Scarborough plant also dropped out of the news. The building's new owners, Manson Insulations, kept on some 70 ex-Manville workers, who have stayed on with the Energy and Chemical Workers Union. "Manson is a hell of a lot more ruthless than Manville," local union president Ken Montgomery told *Our Times* magazine in November 1987. In this plant, silica is widespread, and it's as harmful to the chest as asbestos. Montgomery says, "Working conditions have worsened. As far as dust is concerned, the working conditions never improved. They are still hazardous" (ibid., p. 233).

76. Charlie Stevens, a Cabot Carbon employee, said: "They claim leaded gas is poisoning everybody, but the government has never really proved to us that the leaded gas is what they were getting the readings from. Areas where they took readings were...where lead was produced other than through leaded gas." In fact, studies in the United States had already shown that "anywhere from 40 percent to 70 percent of the lead in the blood of urban children comes from gasoline." See David Lees, "Club Lead," *Toronto Life Magazine*, December 1986, p. 43.
77. The Canadian Council on Children and Youth and the Canadian Association for Children and Adults with Learning Disabilities had urged Caccia to eliminate lead altogether.
78. A December 23, 1983 editorial in the *Sarnia Observer* praised the dilution of the regulation.
79. *Sarnia Observer*, September 25, 1985; December 9, 1985.
80. As of 1988, however, the workers at Ethyl Canada were still benefiting from an unexpected reprieve from Ethyl's restructuring plans. An explosion at one of Ethyl's United States plants meant that production of tetraethyl lead would temporarily have to be continued in Canada. Workers were hired back, and the plant was running seven days a week.

81. For example, a chemical engineer at Queen's University in Kingston invented an alcohol separation process to "speed up production of ethanol—a form of alcohol used widely as a lead substitute in unleaded gasolines" (*Kingston Whig-Standard*, January 29, 1987, p. 23). However, ethanol, when burned in combination with gasoline, may produce greater emissions of nitrogen oxides and aldehydes, producing more smog. When ethanol is produced from the fermentation of sugar cane waste, the resulting emissions are slightly better than gasoline. Another substitute, methylcyclopentadienyl manganese tricarbonyl, or MMT, has been discovered to cause brain and nerve damage, and has been banned in some US states for over seventeen years. (CAW Local 1520 "Environment Committee Report" in *Local 1520 Newsletter*, St. Thomas, Ont., 1996 [no date]). The Canadian Government has introduced Bill C-29, which would ban the importation of MMT, which is produced by Ethyl Corp. of Richmond, VA. See Norm Ovenden, "Final Assault on anti-MMT bill," *The Edmonton Journal*, October 30, 1996, p. B1.
82. *The Globe and Mail*, January 26, 1987.
83. Other members of the Canadian Coalition for Lead-Free Gasoline included: the Canadian Council on Children and Youth, the Canadian Institute of Child Health, the Canadian Teachers' Federation, Greenpeace Foundation, Learning Disabilities Association of Canada, Niagara Neighborhood Association Lead Pollution Committee, South Riverdale Community Health Centre, STOP (Montréal), and Toxics Watch Project (Edmonton).
84. Quoted in Lees, "Club Lead," p. 44.
85. Craig McInnes, "Ottawa urged to speed reduction in lead levels," *The Globe and Mail*, June 16, 1988, p. A8.
86. The additional cost to the petroleum industry was estimated at $250 million. (Ross Howard, "Ottawa advances deadline for elimination of leaded gas," *The Globe and Mail*, September 14, 1988.) See also: "Leading refiners support quicker removal of lead," *The Globe and Mail*, September 15, 1988.
87. Kathy Cooper is also the co-author of *The Citizen's Guide to Lead* (Toronto: New Canada Press, 1986), and a researcher at the Canadian Environmental Law Association. I spoke with her in Toronto, July 31, 1989.
88. According to figures provided by a member of the SRCHC on the health of people in the postal code group closest to Canada Metals and several other industrial plants, the death rate among men from respiratory cancer is 63 percent higher than in any other postal code group in Toronto. The heart disease rate among women is 33 percent higher. The hospital admissions rate is double that of other postal code areas in the city. In a documentary program on the lead issue prepared for the CJRT Open College program, the Metro councillor for Ward 7 in Toronto, Roger Hollander, reported that citizens had succeeded in lobbying the Ontario government to implement a soil removal and replacement program in 1987, as well as to order the use of pollution filters by companies emitting lead. However, monitoring of Canada Metals in 1990 showed that it had exceeded maximum levels for lead emissions eleven times in that year. Also, the blood of children in the neighbourhood still contained higher blood levels than that of children from other areas of the city. See "The Environment (COCR 925)," a CJRT Open College Course, written by Jay Ingram and Beth Savan, executive producer Shirley Gibson (CJRT Open College, Ontario, 1991, 1994). This course was purchased by Athabasca University and is available as "Environmental Studies 252: The Environment: Issues and Options for Action," Program 19 (Athabasca, Alta.: Athabasca University, 1994).
89. Lees cites research in the United States that "has linked levels as low as eight to ten ug/dl with behavioral changes and abnormal brain activities in babies. In children, disruption of the body's ability to produce hemoglobin becomes apparent at twelve ug/dl, and at fifteen ug/dl, hyperactive behavior, a decrease in IQ, slower reaction times and shortened attention spans are evident" ("Club Lead," p. 43). More recent research has confirmed these links, and also correlated high lead levels in the bone to violent, aggressive behaviour. Researchers argue that bone lead levels may be more significant than blood lead because they are a measure of lead accumulation over a long period of time. "A child could have high bone lead while his blood levels are not high at the time they are measured." (Dr. David Bellinger, quoted in Jane E. Brody, "Lead linked to delinquency," *The Globe and Mail*, February 8, 1996, p. A6.) For a comprehensive review of US research on lead, which focuses on the widespread problem of lead poisoning in children, see

Karen L. Florini, George D. Krumbhaaar, Jr., and Ellen K. Silbergeld, "Legacy of Lead: America's Continuing Epidemic of Childhood Lead Poisoning: A Report and Proposal for Legislative Action". (Washington, D.C.: Environmental Defense Fund, 1991).
90. See MOE, "Environmental Review, Toronto Refiners and Smelters" (Toronto: MOE, September 1987), and MOE, "Lead Concentrations in Soil on Residential, Public, and Publicly Accessible Commercial Properties in the Vicinity of Toronto Refiners and Smelters, Toronto, 1985-1987" (Toronto: MOE, June 1988).
91. Christie McLaren, "Group pushes for action against refinery," *The Globe and Mail*, August 1, 1986, p. A12.
92. See "The Case of Giuseppe Ianuzzi," *New Democrats Communique*, May 24, 1988. Rae raised Mr. Ianuzzi's case in the Ontario Legislature the same day.
93. This individual, interviewed August 18, 1989, preferred not to be identified by name.
94. SRCHC organiser, interviewed August 18, 1989.
95. In 1986 the Ontario Co-ordinator of the ECWU said: "We know that our metal workers [at] Canada Metals [are] being exposed to lead poisoning and have constantly balanced their economic security against their health" (ECWU, *Proceedings of the 4th Constitutional Convention* July 14-17, 1986 (ECWU, 1986), p. 38).
96. In 1975 Max Allen produced a program for CBC's *As It Happens* called "Dying of Lead." A court granted the companies named an injunction to prevent certain parts of the documentary from being aired. This action was followed by a libel suit against Allen and the show's producer.
97. See the Ontario MOE list of companies in the Junction Triangle with pollution problems, updated fall 1978, in City of Toronto Planning Board, *Neighbourhood Plan Proposals: Junction Triangle* (May 1979), pp. 32-33.
98. Ublansky referred to a number of "paint plants" unionized by the ECWU in the west end, but did not specify which ones. Inmont (resins and paints), Viceroy (paints and solvents), and Nacan (adhesives) were all cited for pollution problems in: Mayor of Toronto, "Action Task Force on Chemical Spills and Air Emissions in the Junction Triangle" (1982). An explosion at Nacan Products in July 1988 put thirteen persons in hospital suffering from exposure to fumes. Nacan, under intense criticism from residents, subsequently moved the part of its manufacturing process that uses flammable raw materials to other plants in North America. See Craig McInnes, "Explosion prompts call to relocate industries," *The Globe and Mail*, July 14, 1988, p. A9; Lila Sarick, "Part of Toronto factory stays shut after blast," *The Globe and Mail*, July 28, 1988, p. A5.
99. Walter O. Spitzer, principal investigator, "A Study of the Health Status of Residents of the Junction Triangle, Toronto, Final Report"(Dept. of Epidemiology and Biostatistics, McGill University, April 1984). Available from the City of Toronto, Dept. of Public Health, 1984.
100. The comparison area, TR, was chosen for its demographic similarity to the JT and the absence of heavy industry within its boundaries. Where its residents worked, their occupations, etc., were not, however, taken into account in comparing results to those of the JT.
101. Spitzer, "A Study of the Health Status of Residents," p. 68.
102. Cardinal symptoms include: itching, burning, or running nose; itching or burning skin; throat irritation; tiredness or fatigue; itching, burning or watery eyes.
103. These symptoms included the cardinal symptoms, plus: trembling of the hands; tingling in the hands, feet, fingers, or toes; loss of feeling or weakness in the above; feeling of suffocation, nausea, shortness of breath with very mild exertion.
104. Spitzer, "A Study of the Health Status of Residents," p. 69-70.
105. A cancer study was carried out by the Ontario Cancer Treatment and Research Foundation and the City of Toronto, Public Health Dept. in 1986. See "Junction Triangle historical cohort cancer study: a study of cancer incidence in an urban neighbourhood" (City of Toronto, Dept. of Public Health, 1986).
106. Dan Ublansky, interviewed May 3,1988, London, Ont.

[11]

Toxic Chemical Pollution of the Chemical Valley in the 1980s

INTRODUCTION

Not until the mid-1980s did pollution problems in the Chemical Valley again pose serious problems for the chemical companies. By this time, the health hazards of toxic wastes and emissions had become a primary focus of environmental organisations. Groups formed in the Chemical Valley to protest pollution from Allied Chemical and Tricil, but these battles never drew the attention that the discovery of the "toxic blob" in 1985 would attract.

Allied Chemical's plant in Moore Township had produced toluene di-isocyanate (TDI), used in the production of foam rubber.[1] Gas leaks from the plant (which the residents called "gas attacks"), and the fear of a major gas "spill" created opposition to the plant's operation in the area. Allied Chemical closed the plant in December 1978 and was looking for a buyer. In May 1979, residents of Moore Township petitioned their township council to rezone Allied Chemical's property from "special heavy industry" to "agricultural holding," so that no other chemical producer could resume operations there. The councillors, however, replied that they had no right to saddle Allied Chemical with an unsellable plant.[2]

Around the same time, opposition began to emissions from Tricil's incinerator. In the summer of 1978, emissions from the 225-foot stack of the incinerator were causing "considerable smoke and smells" for residents of the Lambton area. Farmers whose land bordered the facility complained about escaping liquid chemical waste stored in open pits. Overflow ruined one farmer's crop; a municipal ditch was contaminated. Local residents pressured the Ministry of the Environment (MOE) to act. After private negotiations with Tricil, the MOE issued a control order requiring better venting on tanks, monitoring of the incinerator stack, and maintenance of a minimum temperature for burning wastes. Meanwhile, its incinerator had been shut down.[3] Tricil had begun trucking waste from Mississauga to a Sarnia landfill and incinerator site. Residents' concerns were increased when the MOE announced plans to drill an injection well for liquid wastes, which they feared might contaminate ground water.[4] These events were the impetus for the formation of the Lambton Anti-Pollution Association (LAPA) in the summer of 1978; it initially had 150 members.

Mainly because of LAPA's lobbying, the MOE eventually ordered Tricil to build a taller incinerator stack, thereby reducing the smoke fall on surrounding farm lands. Once the air pollution problem was ameliorated, some members of the LAPA demobilized. However, others were not satisfied by this "solution" to the waste problem. Their campaign against Tricil's pollution, impelled initially by its direct effects on their health and environment, had led them to ask more far-reaching questions about the generation and disposal of waste in their society. The experience had also made them more critical of government agencies and politicians who had acted slowly and ambivalently to protect citizens' interests, and about the decision-making process itself (suppression of information, relationship between government and private owners, disadvantages of citizens in obtaining scientific and legal expertise). By February 1981, the LAPA claimed only about fifty members, with a ten-member executive, but these people were now committed in a long-term way to environmental vigilance. The co-president of the Association, Bob Marsh, was quoted in the *Sarnia Observer* as saying, "I don't think the Ministry controls the kind of waste that's incinerated well enough... By the time a group of citizens can get the scientific evidence...the data on air quality ... the pollution has gone on for years." The group was asking the government to spend more money on "research and development of new waste management techniques."[5] In 1985, the Lambton Anti-Pollution Association, now eight years old, was fighting an application by Tricil for a $1.5 million expansion of its Telfer Sideroad chemical landfill site. According to the local newspaper, they had "charged [that] the ministry has already approved the expansion in principle and is only going through with a...hearing on the matter as a formality."[6] The Energy and Chemical Workers Union (ECWU) played no discernible role in the activities of the Moore Township or Lambton anti-pollution groups. Neither Allied Chemical nor Tricil were ECWU plants.

The area experienced its first national environmental exposure since the mercury crisis following the discovery in August 1985 of the St. Clair River toxic "blob." The river system (connecting lakes Huron and Erie) and the chemical industry became the focus of attention of environmental organisations (especially Greenpeace and Great Lakes United), the media, and legislators. The responses to the events described below by citizens' groups, chemical company management, and the ECWU, are the subject of this chapter.

THE ST. CLAIR RIVER BLOB

In August 1985 Dow Chemical spilt 40,000 litres of the dry-cleaning solvent perchloroethylene (PCE), a known animal carcinogen and suspected human carcinogen. About 11,000 litres reached the St. Clair River. The PCE dissolved other contaminants in the river sediment, forming blobs of a black chemical mix containing a variety of polychlorinated organic compounds at significant levels in addition to perchloroethylene. Similar materials had been found in that area a year earlier. Between August and December, Dow spent about $1 million vacuuming up the blob. Blobs are still forming in the area, and other sources of chemical seepage are being investigated. It is now feared that the sources of the chemicals seeping into the river are the caverns and deep wells under the river bed itself, or migration routes from the wells to the river bed through rock formations. Chemicals continue to accumulate in the railway tunnel that runs under the river, connecting Sarnia and Port Huron.[7]

Immediately following the August 1985 discovery of the blob, Ontario Environment Minister James Bradley and federal Environment Minister Tom McMillan ordered an investigation into St. Clair River pollution. Testing was carried out from September 1 to December 31, 1985, and the report was released in January 1986. Five toxic organic compounds were detected in *treated* drinking water during this period (1,2,4,5-tetrachlorobenzene, 1,2,3,5-tetrachlorobenzene, pentachlorobenzene, benzene, and carbon tetrachloride). Although the report pointed out that these compounds were detected at levels below existing "water objectives," it recommended continued monitoring of water treatment plants, the development of "drinking water criteria" for these chemicals, and "contingency treatment technology" for use after chemical spills.[8]

The story of the blob uncovered not only the extent of long-term chemical dumping in the river, but also the degree of collusion between officials of the MOE and the chemical industry. Evidence of the blob had been discovered by biologists from the Great Lakes Institute in Windsor, in August 1984, who sent samples for testing to the MOE. But the MOE withheld the test results until September 1985. Moreover, it came to light that officials of the MOE had known about the toxic contamination of the river since at least 1976. A major study by the federal and provincial ministries of the environment of point-source discharges, completed in 1980, h. ' been suppressed. It was finally released in the fall of 1985, after public concern about water quality had been aroused by the discovery of the blob. This study stated that both levels of government had known that the contamination was widespread, but that no adequate clean-up measures had been implemented.[9] In the wake of the blob discovery, it was revealed that the Sarnia District Office of the MOE had also withheld information from the government. The District Officer of the MOE in Sarnia was charged with issuing forged documents (relating to treatment of toxic waste by Canflow Services). After an investigation, the head of the District Office was dismissed. Dow Chemical was charged with four counts of spilling a hazardous substance and fined $16,000.[10]

The blob episode set in motion a number of reactions. First, a number of citizens' organisations were formed to monitor environmental conditions and sustain pressure on government authorities for stricter regulation of the industries. Second, public concern provoked the Liberal government of Ontario to initiate steps to ameliorate the pollution problems in the area, particularly with regard to drinking-water quality.[11] The Ministry of the Environment of the new provincial Liberal government introduced the Municipal Industrial Strategy of Abatement (MISA) (discussed in chapter 5), under which the petrochemical industry would be the first industrial sector to be subject to new environmental regulation. The following section focuses on the relationship between the citizens' groups and the union in the "post-blob" period.

THE CITIZENS AND THE UNION

In April 1988 the workers at Dow Chemical Company (ECWU Local 672) in Sarnia decided to strike for a better pension agreement, and for job security for their "revamp" construction workers' unit. The company brought in 600 strike-breakers just before the strike deadline, and both sides prepared for a long siege. As part of its efforts to mobilize public support, the union pointed to the potential environmental dangers of this situation. The president of Local 672, John Haley, said his members were "worried about the safety and environmental threats posed by operating with employees who are inexperienced and unfamiliar with the volatile, highly complex processes."[12] Greenpeace (Toronto), demonstrating a keen tactical sense of timing, sent a group of volunteers to Sarnia to monitor the St. Clair River at Dow's sewer discharge points, and informed the media that they feared for public health and the environment.[13] Dow management hastened to assure the public that "the operation will run safely, as it did in the 1973 strike. If there is any mishap, [the spokesperson] said, the company 'absolutely' will obey provincial law and report it immediately to the Environment Ministry." The local office of the MOE said it would place Dow Chemical under "increased scrutiny" during the strike.[14]

Meanwhile, a member of the union strike committee had begun to piece together bits of information about Dow's "clean-up" of the blob. From conversations with lab technicians and truck drivers who had been involved with testing and disposing of the sediment, he had constructed the following version of events.[15] The drivers of the vacuum trucks took the sediment to a settling pond on Dow's site, where it was stored until about December 1987. It was then loaded into a cement truck and moved to the plant where perchlorethylene is made, to be treated. The water drawn out of the sediment was taken to an area which removes chlorinated solvents from liquids. Before being finally transported to the LaSalle Road landfill (on Dow property), the sediment was tested for levels of perchloroethylene and carbon-tetrachloride. It was not, however, tested for anything else, notwithstanding evidence that the sediment had been contaminated with a number of dangerous compounds (biphenols, hexes) documented in the earlier ministry and Dow tests.[16] (The Ministry of the Environment later admitted, after the NDP raised the issue in the legislature, that it had not tested the dump site for these chemicals; the reason given was that Dow was not licensed to dump them there.[17])

Union members repeatedly asked management about the presence of hexes because they could smell them, and were told not to worry about it. A lab employee, however, eventually informed the drivers of his suspicions that they were handling hazardous waste. Not until March 1988, when the knowledge that inadequately treated waste was being dumped in the LaSalle Road landfill was spreading among the workers, did Dow begin testing samples for Dowtherm (containing biphenol oxide, methyl biphenol) and hexes. A few weeks after testing for hexes had begun, Dow management stopped the trucking of sediment to the landfill. Workers reported in May that equipment used on Dow's site to transport and store the sediment was contaminated. Interestingly, the cement truck "disappeared" on a trip to London, and Dow later claimed that it had been "lost."[18]

This information, if made public, could have damaged the credibility both of Dow's stated environmental vigilance, and the monitoring and enforcement effectiveness of the MOE. It also could have undone some of Dow's efforts to establish good relations with citizen activists in the downstream communities. The company had recently sent letters to members of the St. Clair River International Citizens' Network (SCRICN), informing them that the company had proposed to construct on its site a rotary kiln for the destruction of toxic chemical waste. In the light of the information about the hexes at Dow's dump site, it is likely that the impetus for this proposal was the need to dispose of the hexes. A kiln would also be profitable, if used to destroy waste from other area plants. In the letter, Dow claimed that it had turned a new leaf, and wanted to involve the public in the approval process. The letter did not, however, mention the hexes.[19]

Shortly before the illegal landfill dumping became public, members of SCRICN held a meeting in Wallaceburg.[20] The major item on the agenda was strategy for their participation in the Bi-national Public Advisory Committee which had just been appointed for the St. Clair River Remedial Action Plan (see chapter 7). However, the members present also discussed the implications of the Dow strike. It was pointed out by the author (an observer at the meeting) that the strike could provide an opportunity for the SCRICN to make a link with the chemical workers. The strike-breakers were unfamiliar with the operations of the plants on the Dow Sarnia site, and there was concern about the risk of a serious accident. Already, there had been a report of a chlorine gas leak. It was suggested that the SCRICN lobby the Ontario Ministers of Labour and the Environment to have the strike-breakers removed and the plants closed for the duration of the strike. This would increase the pressure on Dow management to negotiate and to end the strike quickly. (The 1973 strike went on for three months because the company was able to run the plants using non-union employees.) For getting involved in the strike in this way, they could ask for a *quid pro quo* from the union, e.g., that the union agree to participate in the SCRICN. (The union had, after all, raised an environmental concern at the outset of the strike.)

The responses to this proposal provide some important insights into the problems of building labour-environment alliances. First, some members argued for "non-alignment" during the strike. These individuals referred to Dow management's efforts to improve its environmental image and relations with the citizens' groups; they were worried that appearing to side with workers during the strike would jeopardize their new relationship and "influence" with Dow. The wife of a local dentist feared that the SCRICN would lose its political "neutrality" and thereby its credibility with the public: "I'm concerned about the environment," she said, "I don't want to get involved in a strike." The same position was voiced by her husband (also the chairperson of the Wallaceburg Clean Water Committee) on another occasion. (He was not present at this meeting.) At the Great Lakes United public hearing on the Great Lakes Water Quality Agreement, held in Sarnia in October 1986, he had advocated "dialogue" among government, industry and citizens, rather than "an adversarial approach," and argued that "fines [assessed against polluters] are not the answer."[21] These views should be seen in the context of an active campaign by Dow and the other chemical companies to win over the trust of the citizens' groups, discussed below.

The second response was that, even if SCRICN were to make such an initiative, a positive or serious response was unlikely. Even if the union agreed to send a representative to their meetings, it was predicted, it would soon return to business as usual after the strike. All the Network would have gained was an "anti-industry" image. A member of the Wallaceburg Clean Water Committee (WCWC), herself a member of the negotiating committee of the local teachers' union, explained this conclusion:

> Sarnia unions are...not very political. These people don't have very much "get up and go," as a rule; they have never been very activist. They have good jobs in an area where jobs are scarce. So I do not see these people as ever joining us... I have a feeling, and I think people in the group do, too, that once this [strike at Dow] is all over, the union people in Sarnia will go back to their swimming pools and their baseball games. They're not going to help us.[22]

It is important to add that this member was one of several with a much more critical view of the companies' strategy than that held by the dentist and his wife.

The history of the chemical workers in Sarnia, of the ECWU's relations with employers, and of the union's positions on environmental problems affecting the area, provide part of the context for the views expressed by members of the citizens' groups. They do not have a picture of chemical workers as a militant group prepared to take on employers for any social cause. Indeed, the same woman quoted above contrasted the ECWU to the CAW in Windsor.

> Windsor is a strike town, and very militant, and I think it's because of the auto workers. Auto workers are different from chemical workers... [With the CAW] I know it will be: "We'll rub your back, you rub ours" ... I don't think the [workers] in Sarnia will.

These perceptions had prevented those members of the SCRICN who were open to an alliance with the unions from approaching the ECWU in Sarnia. They had not actually tested their predictions by making any overtures.

Members of the citizens' groups were also conscious of the fact that the few chemical workers who had attended their meetings or public hearings on the environment were neither representatives nor representative of ECWU members. Kristina Lee of the WCWC put it this way:

> I don't know what their relationship is with the other labour people. Are they the black sheep? Nobody wants to sit with them at lunch time? I don't know who they are... I know they're not representative. But are they respected or listened to by the other people? If not, then we're not going to get anywhere. I think we have to have certain key individuals in Sarnia Labour Council who are respected by the other members... "Michael" [a Dow Chemical worker who attended

SCRICN meetings] has been around a long time, and yet he hasn't brought anybody else with him. I don't know whether he has any influence.

The concern for official recognition is about more than obtaining a formal endorsement; the citizens' groups need evidence that environmental concerns are of real interest to the union. From their perspective, it is the credibility not only of the "Michaels," but of the issue itself—that is, in the eyes of the union and the workforce—which is at stake. Their suspicion that most chemical workers did not share their environmental concerns is supported by the evidence on the chemical workers' views discussed below.

The groups comprising SCRICN had been lobbying provincial and federal levels of government for stricter regulation and enforcement since 1985. A triangular set of relations had developed involving this active segment of "the public," the companies/polluters, and government officials and agencies responsible for the environment. Labour organisations in the Chemical Valley had been notably absent from this struggle. The only evidence of labour involvement is some correspondence between the president of the Sarnia and District Labour Council, Don Heath, and area MPs concerning the information emerging in late 1985 about toxins in the St. Clair River.

Heath, a young shift worker in one of the chemical plants, attempted to set a more activist tone for the Labour Council during his term of office, which ended in 1986. He wanted to get the labour community involved with municipal and provincial elections, the rights of the unemployed and employment policies, the women's coalition, the race relations committee, and increasing its own membership (6,000 in 1985).[23] In a letter sent to Environment Minister James Bradley, Heath called on the government to create a legislative committee to investigate the St. Clair River situation, to finance an "independent" study by "a group such as Pollution Probe,"[24] and to initiate a health study for the people of Lambton and Kent counties.[25] In addition, the Labour Council was approached by the Citizens' Coalition for Clean Water (CCCW) (Wallaceburg) with a request for endorsement. Heath replied: "Your fight is our fight and anything we can do to facilitate the procurement of a continuously safe drinking water supply for the people of your area will be done." But the CCCW's primary goal was a pipeline from Lake Huron, so that they would no longer be dependent on the St. Clair River as a source of drinking water. (Citizens of Sarnia already drew their water from Lake Huron.) There seemed little the Labour Council could do to help Wallaceburg residents obtain provincial and federal funding for a pipeline, apart from the offer of moral support. The CCCW did not ask for participation in any joint actions; only for official endorsement and money.

There was no revival of the activities of the early 1970s, when the Labour Council had sponsored a public workshop on area pollution problems, and leading labour figures had linked pollution to profit and Conservative politics. Nor was there any public endorsement of the demands of the downstream citizens' groups by officials of the ECWU. Indeed, while the chemical companies had launched a vigorous campaign to assert leadership over the direction and tactics of the citizens' groups, and to restore their corporate citizenship credibility, the ECWU had no relationship with the people calling for stricter regulation of their industry.

Union officials interviewed in December 1986 and May 1988 did not perceive the new regulations as a serious potential threat to chemical company profits, and therefore to investment and jobs. They were not particularly informed about the legislative initiatives at the provincial and federal levels, and none were even aware of the activities of the SCRICN. When asked about the possibility of a future alliance with groups like the St. Clair Network, officials were cautious, in some cases suspicious, and argued that it was up to the citizens' groups to make the first move. How do we explain this absence? In addition to the factors examined in the previous episodes affecting the Chemical Valley, the strategy of the companies and the attitudes of union members towards environmental politics provide important insights into the problem of the chemical workers' quiescence.

THE COMPANY CAMPAIGN

The Bhopal disaster of December 1984 had the same effect on the public image of the chemical industry that Chernobyl had on the popularity of nuclear power. The multinational chemical companies based in the United States began a campaign to counteract the fears raised by Bhopal, including the "Community Awareness" and "Emergency Response" programmes initiated by the United States Chemical Manufacturers' Association. They were intended to reassure the public by informing communities near the plants of safety and emergency evacuation procedures. Not accidentally, the acronym for this initiative was CAER. The Canadian-based chemical companies adopted the United States CAER programme in 1985, and in September—immediately after the blob story had reached the media—CAER was adopted by the members of the Lambton Industrial Society (LIS).[26] Fourteen local companies formed the Community Awareness Committee (CAC). The CAC offered to provide speakers on the subject of "chemical emergency preparedness." The January 1988 newsletter of the CAC stated:

> A team of presenters from member companies is taking the CAER message to schools and other interested organizations in the Sarnia area. Last year they visited all elementary and some secondary schools. This year they are working their way through the rest of the secondary schools. They are finding a high level of interest among our young people in matters of environmental protection and public safety.[27]

The CAER programme became a useful means for the industry to defend its environmental record, following the fall 1985 revelation of the blob.

Individual firms began to offer plant tours, and to produce newsletters or brochures for the public. Dow—previously very secretive and security-conscious—began to offer plant tours to public groups in 1986. In May 1987, C-I-L held a four-day "open house" to "provide the public with information on the decommissioning of their phosphates operation."[28] Shell hosted a party for Lambton College students. Polysar held "Family Days" at its Corunna plant in June, this year allowing local residents to tour the plant as well. In October Esso invited families of employees to an "open house." The theme of this event was "home safety."

The Lambton Industrial Society (LIS) continued its efforts to safeguard the good corporate citizenship image of the chemical companies. In 1985 it added "An Environmental Co-operative" to its name and logo, and hired a public relations consultant to help write its annual report. It was active in area schools and among educators. Money was given to the local elementary school system for "the development of a future program involving a better understanding of the impact of industry in our area."[29] The LIS presented a display at the secondary school teachers' Professional Development Day at a local collegiate, and sponsored prizes for environmental projects at the Lambton County Science Fair. A presentation was made "in support of the Lambton Secondary School gifted students program," and during the year, "the LIS explained the function of the Society to nineteen principals from the Lambton separate school system."

Meanwhile, government lobbying was not neglected. One of the key speakers at the LIS annual meeting in May was the Director General of the Ontario Region of Environment Canada. In June the LIS made a presentation to a group of Canadian and United States legislators on Great Lakes water quality. It arranged a "social" meeting with

Ontario Environment Minister, James Bradley, and industry representatives in August. In December the LIS sent a delegation, accompanied by municipal officials, to see Bradley, "to express concern at the apparent lack of objectivity in dealings with Sarnia-Lambton environmental affairs."[30]

The displeasure of the LIS members with public and government reaction to the blob was expressed in the statement of the Society's president, Bob Sones of DuPont:

> The publicity this incident received was out of proportion to its environmental impact. The solid historical evidence of continual improvement in the quality of the river water over the past 30 years was lost in the rhetoric of the day... [T]he handling of these complex topics by certain media and some academics tends to reflect self-interest and the public is led to rely on these 'experts' for information on environmental matters... We must ensure that those who influence public opinion are in possession of the facts so they can present a balanced view on the quality of the environment.[31]

Among the LIS' efforts to instill this "balanced view" in the minds of "those who influence public opinion" were the organisation of a tour of Tricil, Suncor and Polysar by fourth-year science students from the University of Windsor (in October), and a visit by alumni of the University of Western Ontario (in September).

The company at the centre of the environmental crisis was Dow Chemical. Dow's response paralleled that of the LIS, and was based on a corporate image campaign initiated by the parent company in 1984. Dow Chemical (US) had become known as the company that supplied napalm for the Vietnam War, and subsequently fought the efforts of veterans to claim compensation for exposure to Agent Orange. In the early 1980s, Dow was called to account for its dioxin-containing emissions into Michigan waters, and its influential relationship with EPA administrators was exposed during hearings of the House Committee on Science and Technology. These experiences led Dow management to undertake the "Initiatives Program," described as "a multifaceted campaign aimed at employees, potential employees, journalists, customers, legislators, regulators, and the general public."[32] The (parent) company decided to spend $70 million over five years to improve its image.

> Dow's top management appointed a 12-member internal task force, comprised of public relations, marketing, research, and government affairs people to rebuild Dow's public policy...
>
> Developing a softer profile with the media was a key element. Dow set up a 24-hour, toll-free number for journalists. It also provided a $325,000 grant to the University of Missouri to help establish the country's first science journalism centre.
>
> Other elements include: putting Dow researchers on the media-tour circuit to talk about "positive topics" like advances in toxic waste disposal; multi-million-dollar support for an organ donation campaign; an annual slick booklet, "Public Interest Reports," which highlights Dow's good deeds; a comprehensive resource manual for plant managers, who are now responsible for community relations; and a national corporate advertising program.[33]

The "Dow lets you do great things" (humanitarian) television commercials were one element of this advertising programme. (Dow employees on strike in Sarnia in 1988 used this slogan sarcastically on their placards.)

One of the reasons Dow management felt compelled to initiate this campaign was that the restructuring of the corporation since the early 1980s had involved a downscaling of production in primary commodities and a shift towards high-value-added, finished consumer products. The company had, therefore, become more vulnerable to consumer attitudes, and to the threat of consumer boycotts. These efforts had produced some results within a few years. According to T. K. Smith, director of government and public affairs, Dow began an annual telephone survey in 1984 of more than 2,000 people "from all audience groups." The 1986 survey showed that "25 percent of journalists reported more favorable attitudes towards Dow than in the past. Dow's image among its own communities [employees and families] also improved, though regulators and legislators registered little change."[34]

In Canada, Dow also took up the organ donation campaign. The entire issue of *Dow Canadian Dimensions* (May 1986) was devoted to the company's participation. The timing and nature of the campaign are important and deserve some detailed examination. In 1985, Dow Chemical Canada became "a major corporate sponsor of Transplant International" and committed itself to "an ongoing employee information program and an aggressive community awareness campaign."[35] Dow made a video on organ donation which was broadcast on the "in-house" video system to employees, and on local television shows, including a one-hour television special on the Sarnia community TV channel. The show was hosted by Dow's Public Relations Manager, Sarah Thorne, and featured a representative of Transplant International, a local pediatrician, and a Sarnia resident who had received a kidney transplant. The show was broadcast several times. In addition, the family members of Dow employees were encouraged to show the video in their schools and workplaces. The public relations manager was addressing employee groups across the country on the subject of the company's humanitarian work. At the same time, Dow's general sales manager was working to tell "some of our larger customers" about Dow's commitment to Transplant International.[36] The Transplant International co-ordinator for Dow's Ontario District was organising a steering committee to "plan and implement seminars for the families of company employees." In the Sarnia area, Dow sponsored an employee-community night; the president of Dow's Sarnia division appeared on a live radio hotline show to talk about Transplant International. The company also co-sponsored a "Transplant International Community Night" with Sarnia's St. Joseph's Hospital. According to a report in the newsletter of Transplant International:

> Community events like these have generated a number of invitations for Dow employees to address local community groups. Presentations have been made to the local Optimists Club, The Airforce Club, Rotary, the local chapter of the Heart and Stroke Foundation, and the Pilot Club.[37]

Dow also held a press conference and breakfast for members of government and the media on Parliament Hill in April, 1986, at which the company announced a three-year financial commitment of $75,000 a year and a "resource support program." According to the president of Dow, Dave Buzzelli, "Dow chose to support this important social issue because of its potential impact on the quality of life in Canada. Our involvement reflects the company's long-standing commitment to corporate social responsibility."[38]

Organ donation was not the only good cause being supported by Dow, although the scope of the campaign illustrates the company's targeted audiences and approach. It is interesting that, between 1985 and 1987, the portion of Dow's total budget allocated to philanthropic donations almost doubled, levelling off in 1988. The amounts donated were: 1985, $362,000; 1986, $482,000; and 1987, $702,000.[39] Although the official explanation for the increase was "a desire to do more," there were more specific guidelines for the allocation of donations.

Dow is not in the business of giving away money. According to the guidelines, donations should be visible, have an impact and be justifiable to the company's shareholders.

The Sarnia District Contributions Committee covers all donations for the Sarnia-Lambton area. It receives the largest dollar chunk of the eleven sites because it represents company headquarters and the largest concentration of Dow Canada employees.[40]

In 1986 the Sarnia committee received over 120 requests for donations, suggesting the dependence of local charities or community groups on this potential benefactor. That year, Dow donated the insulation for a local arena, as well as building materials for the United Way building. Money also went to St. Joseph's Hospital, the United Way, the Salvation Army, Easter Seals, Crime Stoppers, Heart and Stroke Foundation, and the Sarnia Little Theatre. In December 1986, following the advice of Delbridge consultants, Dow announced a joint venture with the City of Sarnia to build an outdoor summer entertainment centre at the Dow People Place rink. The $125,000 price would be split between the city and Dow. Buzzelli said: "The waterfront is the greatest natural asset we have." Mayor Marcell Saddy "thanked Dow for its leadership role in the community and said 'it really goes to show this company has a concept of the quality of life in this region.'"[41] In 1987 Dow contributed $375,000 to the building fund of Sarnia General Hospital.

Indeed, Dow's benefactor role in Sarnia parallels its corporate strategy in Midland, Michigan, where the parent company has its headquarters. In Midland, nearly a third of the residents are Dow employees. An American business journalist wrote:

> Dow has been good to Midland, and everyone there knows it. But everyone also knows that what is given with one hand can be taken away by the other, and the combination of gratitude and fear inevitably keeps a constant low hum of tension in the background. Dow and Midland have been able to achieve their remarkable harmony only by enclosing themselves in a protective bubble of white suburban affluence... [42]

The "protective bubble" captures rather nicely the clannish solidarity of townspeople and employers in Sarnia, which is described below in relation to the blob crisis.

Dow was also developing its involvement in the educational system. An article in *Dow Canadian Dimensions* (October/November 1987) stated:

> By actively participating with educators and the educational system, Dow Canada is increasing the level of awareness and understanding of the chemical industry, helping students better grasp what Dow is all about. In addition, Dow has the opportunity to listen and learn of the concerns held by educators and students. The result, company officials hope, is an opportunity for Dow's views to be taken into consideration as policies, strategies and programs are developed.
>
> Dow Canada's involvement ranges from a partnership between Dow and a Sarnia high school, to the sponsorship of a high school student to work at Sarnia Division for part of the summer. And while most of the programs differ in various ways, they all have the one goal in mind—developing dialogue between industry and education.[43]

In the summer of 1987, Dow executives participated in a week-long conference with primary and secondary school science teachers, sponsored by the Canadian Chemical Producers' Association (CCPA). The Society, Environment and Energy Development Studies (SEEDS) Foundation (funded by the CCPA) was set up to influence the process of curriculum development in a way that "will reflect a change in attitude about the chemical industry."[47] According to the report, the teachers attended more than forty presentations, made tours of area plants, and "quickly realized the variety of complex issues surrounding the chemical industry." The president of the SEEDS Foundation said: "The purpose of the program is to come up with fresh material that examines all the issues from a balanced perspective..." The main objective of the conference was "to identify the teachers that will form a core of writers responsible for developing the new materials for both primary and secondary school audiences."

Dow was also involved in the "Partners Active in Resource Sharing" programme, "designed to join industry and the educational system in a mutually beneficial relationship." Buzzelli told teachers at Sarnia's Northern Collegiate and Vocational Institute: "We want to expose you to our business and operations so you can see our world from our perspective." In January 1986, ninety teachers from the Collegiate participated in an "orientation program" at Dow. As the director of the SEEDS Foundation stated, Dow was looking for "thought leaders." Dow also participated in a panel on Responsible Care at the Chem Ed Conference for North American science teachers held in Kingston in 1987. Dow's director of Environmental Sciences said that teachers "must take a significant part in shaping children's attitudes about chemicals and the role they play in the environment."[45] These activities in the educational sphere indicate that Dow shared the conviction of members of the citizens' groups that this is a crucial battleground of ideas.

Dow was, in addition, very busy during these years lobbying the Canadian and Ontario governments on environmental policy. The amendment of the Ontario Environmental Protection Act (Spills Bill), the review of the federal Environmental Contaminants Act, the subsequent Canadian Environmental Protection Act review, the perchloroethylene spill, and the ensuing MISA white paper of the Ontario government, necessitated continual company responses. In the 1960s there had been one "environmental control" employee at Dow; in 1986 there were forty.[46] In addition, Dow had established a Government Affairs office in Ottawa, and had hired former Liberal MP, Claude-André Lachance, to represent the company's interests. Lachance claimed in 1987 that the company's "persistent and systematic" work with government officials had achieved a degree of mutual trust and "a number of revisions" of the Canadian Environmental Protection Act.[47]

Meanwhile, Dow had undertaken a campaign to woo over to its point of view the citizen "thought leaders" in the communities downstream of the Chemical Valley. Shortly after the blob incident had broken in the media, and had resulted in the shutdown of the water purification plants in downstream communities like Wallaceburg, Dow scientists and managers went to Wallaceburg to reassure the citizens that everything was under control. They found that their audience was not prepared, this time, to accept either their assurances or their authority. A member of the Wallaceburg Clean Water Committee describes the meeting this way:

> After the perchloroethylene spill, there was an uproar, and Dow was invited to come down to Wallaceburg to explain what happened... These three guys came down in three-piece suits, you know, real businesslike. They did a presentation, and the town hall was packed. We're talking 25 people, but [that's big] for Wallaceburg. It was being taped on Cable T.V. Basically what they did was talk down to everybody. You don't come in a briefcase and three-piece suit to Wallaceburg and start telling people why they don't understand what's happening. That's what they did. I think their presentation was very slick... Poor Dr. Ford [Dow scientist] could not understand why he was being lynched in front of everybody.[48]

A member of the Citizens' Coalition for Clean Water (Wallaceburg) recounted:

> [T]hey come to a public meeting, stood up with graphs and maps, distorted out of this world, and lied to us, right on TV. The night they were there, we pretty nearly ended up in a brawl. The clerk got his neck shook that night. Cause we're tired of this crap.[49]

There are only about 11,000 people in Wallaceburg, but their anger made itself felt at Queen's Park. Moreover, it became the focus of national media attention. Dow management realized, after this "close encounter" with the public, that a major effort was necessary to restore its credibility, not only with opinion leaders in the communities affected by Chemical Valley pollution, but with politicians. The chemical companies were perceiving a rapid erosion of their old relationship with government agencies and departments, as the citizens' groups increasingly were demanding an equal (or greater) representation at the policy-making tables, and environmental issues were becoming politically prominent.

In the summer of 1986, the CCPA hired Decima Research to do a public opinion poll on attitudes toward the chemical industry. When the results revealed profound public mistrust of the chemical companies and fear about the health and environmental risks of toxic chemicals, the CCPA hired the consulting firm Pat Delbridge Associates to help the industry improve its public relations. Delbridge proposed that the CCPA set up its own "Community Advisory Panel," comprising "twelve to fourteen individuals who have the background and experience to enable them to assist the CCPA to obtain a broader understanding of community needs. The experience of panel members will likely include involvement with community, business, consumer and special interest organizations."[50] Various individuals from the citizens' groups, among others, were contacted by Delbridge (acting as the "neutral facilitator of dialogue") and invited to participate in the CCPA's Community Advisory Panel.

Two aspects of this initiative are very interesting from the point of view of the companies' strategy. First, the CCPA established the terms of reference and of membership of the Panel. It would pay the expenses of invited participants, but it would also set the agenda by means of an initial definition of the objectives, and by veto power over items tabled by the panel members. Second, discussions in the meetings were to be confidential; it was stressed that members were not to act as *representatives* of their groups or constituencies. However, the CCPA representatives would report back on the panel discussions to that body.[51] Moreover, the Panel was to be a "pilot project" from 1986 to 1987; if the CCPA determined that it was not suiting its interests, it would be discontinued.

Clearly, the CCPA wanted to sound out its arguments on a group of its critics in a "contained" forum. According to a report on the Panel's activities as of April 1988, the group's "main task" had been "to help the CCPA fashion a series of individual codes of practice which together will determine the standards of conduct which are expected of the CCPA membership."[52] In response to federal and Ontario environmental legislation, the CCPA had been arguing that the industry, if left uncoerced, would develop its own codes of monitoring, testing, regulatory, and safety practices. However, if governments persisted in regulating, the CCPA would attempt to make these codes the bases for the new regulations. In the lobbying around new environmental initiatives, the governments had been more or less seeking a middle road between the stringent and compulsory standards demanded by the environmental organisations and the more minimal and "honour system" proposals of the corporations. The CCPA appears to have concluded from this experience that it might be possible to neutralize or moderate the positions of the environmentalists by trying to work out a compromise, consensus set of proposals which could then be presented to the legislators. At the very least, the companies would have a good idea of the likely responses and proposals of the environmental critics, and could prepare their own positions accordingly. It is important to note that, because the CCPA was setting the rules of its relationship with the Advisory Panel, it was not obliged to accept any of the group's proposals. As stated by the Delbridge consultants:

> It would be wrong to suggest that this is a process without difficulties. The individual codes go through a series of a dozen or more drafts before they are advanced to the CCPA Board of Directors for ratification. Industry committees and subcommittees working on the development of the codes do not always agree with panel comments and vice versa. There are seven codes (this may be expanded) dealing with all facets of a chemical's "life" from research to disposal. Some are now finalized and approved by the CCPA Board, one is at a preliminary stage. The others are at various stages in the development process.

In effect, the CCPA was getting the benefit of strategic advice from some of its most articulate opponents, at the cost of about five (order in) dinners for fourteen per year (plus travel expenses). Moreover, it was benefitting from improved relations with targeted citizens' groups, and the publicizing of this new dialogue. What were the citizen and environmental participants getting? The answer to that depends on the resulting codes of practice, and the objectives with which the participants entered into the agreement (the dilemma posed by Kristina Lee, below).

The Downstream Communities

In May 1986 Dow Chemical also hired Pat Delbridge Associates to survey "community leaders in Michigan and Ontario communities for their opinions on global and local environmental problems."[53] Delbridge employees held meetings with targeted individuals in Detroit, St. Clair, Port Huron, Wallaceburg, Windsor, Chatham, and Walpole Island. However, the fact that they were employed by Dow Chemical Co. was initially kept secret from the interviewees. According to Kristina Lee of the Wallaceburg Clean Water Committee, shortly after the town hall debacle in Wallaceburg: "certain people in town, including [from] some of the environmental groups, got invited for dinner at The Oaks [a well-regarded hotel dining-room]." Delbridge had invited certain influential people in town, like the minister's wife, Lee's husband (a high school teacher), and the chairperson of the WCWC, for a discussion about "what do you see wrong with the industry?" When it was eventually revealed (after this event) that it was Dow who had hired the consultants, the citizens were told: "if we had told you it was us, you probably would not have said the things you said, and we didn't think you'd come."[54] (Dow had also made a video of the first Wallaceburg meeting, used subsequently as an educational tool for its public relations people. The theme was, what *not* to do when dealing with citizens.)

After the Delbridge survey, Dow began actively courting the members of the newly formed citizens' groups in the downstream communities. Members of the St. Clair River International Citizens' Network were invited to tour Dow's facilities and to meet with Dow management to discuss their concerns and be informed about progress in pollution abatement. From the outset, certain individuals were targeted; the more oppositional "community leaders" were excluded. In Wallaceburg, the question of the appropriate relationship with the chemical companies led to a split among concerned citizens into two groups: the Wallaceburg Clean Water Committee (WCWC) and the Citizens' Coalition for Clean Water (CCCW). The former encompasses a more professional, "middle class" group— many of them teachers—although the membership of both groups is mixed. The differences among the two groups are interesting from the point of view of the strategic tendencies developing within this grassroots base of the environmental movement. In many ways, the two groups appear to have much more in common than they have dividing them, and their approaches cannot easily be categorized in terms of degrees of political consciousness or militancy. There were also differences of view within each group.

In general, the WCWC members were open to a "dialogue" with company officials; they toured Dow, Polysar, and C-I-L, and attended meetings with management. They believed that pollution abatement can be achieved only by either persuading the companies that it is in their interests, or through coercion exercised by the State. They were pursuing both strategies simultaneously. Within the group, there were varying degrees of faith in the good will of the companies to change their behaviour. Every new incident of a pollution violation tested this faith. At the same time, the citizens were skeptical about the Ontario and federal governments' determination to enforce stringent environmental standards: government officials were viewed as untrustworthy but necessary allies. The citizens had learned how to use the media and to do educational work with increasing sophistication in order to prod elected politicians and bureaucrats in the direction of environmental regulation.

Some of these positions were expressed by Kristina Lee, a spokesperson for the WCWC. On the question of the group's relationship with Dow, she said:

> There's two philosophies. One philosophy says, "They're just one bit smarter than you; one step ahead of you. It's just a big con game... They are simply changing their strategy." The other philosophy says, "These people have to change. They have realized it isn't worth it." Look at what the perchloroethylene spill did to Dow. It made their corporate image look terrible... In those terms I think we have succeeded, because I think they have learned that it does not pay to try to cover up, which is what I think they did when they had the perchloroethylene spill. They tried to downplay it; they were not open with the public...
>
> Instead of [being] confrontational, we have decided to tour the companies, let them know who we are. We talk to them. How can you criticize a company when you've never been in [their site]?... [But] just because you're on their grounds, just because you're talking to them, does not mean that they've got you in their back pocket. That's the number one philosophy. A lot of environmental groups say, be careful, don't get too friendly with them, and they're right. I don't think you should ever become friends with them. It's like a business: an employer shouldn't become friends with an employee. We're in business...but that doesn't mean we can't talk. I think that's the philosophy we take. We don't want to be too friendly, and yet we want to be able to communicate. We will attend any functions. That could be seen as a weakness. [I know] the other group [CCCW] sees it that way.[55]

Lee was aware that the company wanted her co-operation and was going out of its way to disarm her. For example, Dow sent her letters by courier, delivered to her home, and invited her and her husband to industry functions. She insisted that she had not, and would not, let down her guard, but she had begun to assume that the success of her group's goals depended more on maintaining a co-operative relationship with Dow than on exercising the kind of political pressure which initially impelled Dow to seek the relationship. This is the assumption that the CCCW did not make. Lee believed that her group had more influence with Dow than the CCCW had, since the latter group had rejected any dialogue with the companies.

> I don't think that I...trust the industry any more than the other group [does]. Everything [the companies] do is planned—all of the letters we're getting—I would never underestimate the industry. [But] who does [the industry] take

more seriously? My perception [is] the industries have stopped talking to the other group—they're not invited to any functions... For example, we were invited to the Lambton Industrial Society Annual meeting, this year and last year. The other group was not invited. Maybe they're using me—I know they're using me—to make a point, to show that "it pays to talk to us; it pays to be civil to us, if you want to associate with us." John [Jackson's] been invited to Dow; he's actually speaking at one of the workshops as a member of a citizens' group. Now that's an honour. I don't care what you say. It doesn't matter what their reasons are.

But of course, it does matter what their reasons are. This point is supported by Lee's perceptions of what her group had accomplished vis-à-vis Dow: "I think we've been successful in showing companies like Dow that [they] can communicate with a town... I think we've changed their way of communicating." Interestingly, she did not connect this observation with her earlier sarcastic comment that Delbridge had recently held an expensive seminar for chemical company public relations people, to teach them "how to communicate" with environmental groups: "They've got it down to a science now," she said. Lee was caught between viewing her group as a guinea pig in this science project, and persuading herself that the citizens could stay "one step ahead" of the chemical industry strategists.

It was not evident, moreover, that other members of the WCWC felt this tension as keenly as Lee. The president of the WCWC, Doug Steen, supported Dow's desire to have the post-blob meeting closed to the media. According to Lee, Dow wanted "to talk to us in private; they didn't want the papers there." Nor did Steen want to alienate politicians by openly criticising their role in the area's pollution crisis. Other citizens, who later formed the CCCW, insisted that the meeting be as widely publicized as possible, so that the chemical company representatives and politicians would be held to account on the citizens' turf. A fight ensued which led to the separation of the citizens into two factions. According to Don Laprise, president of the CCCW:

> We lined up our first meeting, and "The Journal," channel 9 got a hold of us and wanted to come down and cover it; about four television stations [were going to cover it], and Doug Steen called me up, wanted me to go over. Number one mistake, I went... and he wanted this, and he wanted that—he was going to set up a committee—and I said, "fine," but knowing Doug, I didn't want to get involved. If I'm going to step on a politician's face I don't care what party he's from. Doug's not like that. Neither is anybody in his committee. I said: "We got too much time and money tied up in this, Doug." [The meeting] was for the next Thursday...
>
> He said, "if I pay your expenses, will you call that meeting off?"
>
> I said, "I'll see you, Doug," and I walked out of his house. The night of the meeting... he was hollering and screaming at us in the back room, with all the television cameras out there, 'cause he wanted this done, and that done. And I says, "No, Doug, it's not your meeting."
>
> [Doug said] "you don't give a politician hell."
>
> I don't like politicians... And that's why there's two groups.

The CCCW, in addition to taking a more populist ("all politicians are corrupt") stance towards both government authorities and the companies, uses tactics which are modelled after those of Greenpeace, and were viewed as being outside the bounds of acceptable political lobbying by members of the WCWC. Lee said: "They have adopted what I call the Greenpeace philosophy... I just do not feel comfortable being in that group." Laprise, indeed, stated his admiration for and trust of Greenpeace: "Greenpeace is one of our best allies... If it wasn't for Greenpeace, we would never [have] known about the blob." After trying unsuccessfully to get the City Council to do something to secure a water pipeline from Lake Huron, the CCCW decided to attract the attention of the provincial and federal governments. To this end, they put up signs along the St. Clair River, saying the water was dangerous. This created an angry reaction from councillors as well as local tourism businesses. The coalition members were called "rambos," and "mental terrorists," and were censured in the town council.[56] They set up a meeting with the federal Minister of the Environment, Tom McMillan, and offered him a glass of water containing about twenty drops of St. Clair River water (to symbolize the dilution of pollutants in Wallaceburg drinking water). McMillan declined to drink it.

For all the confrontational rhetoric of the CCCW president, the group's activities, like the WCWC's, focused on government lobbying. The CCCW presented a 2,500-name petition to area MPs, corresponded with Bradley and other politicians, and participated in the CEPA review (see chapter 4). Unlike the WCWC, however, it did not appear to have made any concrete proposals for the democratization of the political decision-making process, e.g., along the lines outlined in the SCRICN brief on the MISA white paper. In some respects, the CCCW's strategy was less far-sighted than that of the WCWC. While the CCCW worked to sustain a high profile for the pollution issue in the media, it did not engage in the kind of educational activities that the WCWC viewed as a priority (displays in shopping malls, presentations in schools, etc.). Also, while the CCCW claimed the larger membership (about 150), its actions seemed to be directed in an executive fashion. The WCWC, on the other hand, planned its course in a more participatory and consensual way, which was no doubt easier because of its smaller size. The WCWC also participated in the SCRICN, which the CCCW boycotted because the group wanted to focus on getting a pipeline, and because Laprise mistrusted the "Steen gang" and the SCRICN's coordinator, John Jackson.

Both groups were, however, fundamentally skeptical of industry's motives; both blamed the chemical companies' negligence and government complicity for the history of pollution of the St. Clair; both accepted the need to bring pressure to bear on government agencies to defend their interests; and both understood the importance of mobilizing public opinion. The key difference was in their relationships toward the polluters: while the WCWC had to some extent (not unambivalently) exchanged a critical, *agitant* role for a strategy of "dialogue," the CCCW remained intransigent. The division of the citizens into two groups, however, must be seen as a success for the strategy of the chemical companies and their consultants.

Sarnia: "I'm a blob-maker"
The companies had an even more notable success in defusing any potential environmental opposition on their own turf—Sarnia. Delbridge's survey of "community leaders" in that city revealed a pretty loyal group of local politicians and business persons (not to mention the ever-faithful *Sarnia Observer*, which published the pro-industry results of the Sarnia survey, while stating that the rest of the results were secret!). Delbridge reported the following views among this group:
1. a "lack of public understanding" and "inappropriate" government actions have resulted from biased media reporting which stirs up "hysteria";
2. people in Sarnia are being made to appear as if they are ignorant or unconcerned about their own health;
3. the largest chemical plants have the best pollution safeguards, yet they are the most criticized [unfairness];
4. it is the government's responsibility to pay for an improved sewer system for Sarnia [related to costs of industrial pollution abatement].

However, even this sympathetic group suggested that the chemical companies should be more open with the media and the public, presumably to put forward their strong case more effectively. Delbridge's key recommendation to Dow regarding Sarnia was to work on community and public relations.[57] As we saw above, Dow's first approach was to try to buy off community groups and social "leaders," reinforcing its position as local benefactor.

In reinterpreting the pollution crisis, Dow received considerable assistance from the *Sarnia Observer*, which consistently defended the chemical firms' environmental record and lauded their abatement programs. The *Observer* took a hostile line toward Greenpeace and NDP critics, and juxtaposed stories about the economic hardships of the chemical companies and job insecurity with stories about the financial pressures stemming from environmental regulation. Following the public exposure of the existence of the St. Clair River blob in August 1985, Greenpeace announced that its ship "Fri" would be stopping off in Sarnia Harbour. The *Sarnia Observer* responded with a "warning":

[L]et it be known now that Sarnia's Chemical Valley does not welcome any of the frivolous publicity stunts this group is known for...

Sarnia's Chemical Valley has been held out as an illustration on a world scale level of how industry and the community can live together safely and in harmony.

One often wonders whether Greenpeacers have become so caught up in an idealistic campaign that they have lost sight of the fact that industry is something many of us rely on for our very livelihood. Were it not for the Chemical Valley, Sarnia would not exist as the thriving community it is...

In Sarnia we are well aware of the hazards of the workplace and the potential dangers of working with volatile and lethal products. We do not need a bunch of fanatical environmentalists scaling one of our smoke stacks to unfurl a Greenpeace flag, to remind us that we are living with a potentially lethal giant...

But the group's actions are frequently misguided and have earned them enemies both at the corporate level and among average citizens who are equally concerned about the environment and the desire to leave a safe, healthy world for our children.[58]

On August 24th, Greenpeace members climbed the Bluewater Bridge (connecting Sarnia to Port Huron, Michigan), and hung a banner reading "Toxins Today, Tumours Tomorrow." (This action was still referred to three years later by members of the ECWU.) The group called on industry and governments to move towards a "zero discharge" goal quickly. By coincidence, the Ontario Minister for the Environment, James Bradley, and other politicians were in Sarnia the same day for a tour of Tricil facilities and of the river.[59] Naturally, the Greenpeace action was condemned by the newspaper as a "scare tactic."[60] The editorial repeated the theme that Sarnia residents and chemical workers are too well-informed about the real risks and benefits of the chemical industry's operations to be conned by a group of fanatics.

When the results of laboratory tests on samples from the sludge became public November 5, there was a striking difference in reaction between Sarnia and the downstream populations (as expressed by their newspapers). The *Windsor Star* ran a large headline "The St. Clair River Mess," over two stories on the toxins discovered and the investigation of collusion between the Sarnia MOE and the chemical companies.[61] An editorial demanded strong measures to stop pollution, even at the cost of chemical industry jobs.

Sarnia's Chemical Valley is quickly becoming a dreaded upstream neighbor with a shameful concern for our environment. Both the Ontario and federal governments should be put on notice that those of us who drink the water that carries its toxic effluent have had enough...

We ask this question—when will examples of extreme environmental abuse end? Before, we hope, thousands of people in Windsor, and other communities along the St. Clair and Detroit Rivers, become seriously ill from unconscionable neglect...

We urge Environment Minister Bradley to also consider the following concrete steps:

1. Adopt water quality standards that will give legal teeth to environmental prosecutions and replace weak and meaningless pollution guidelines now in effect.
2. Hold mandatory public hearings when companies seek certificates to dump waste into rivers and impose significant fines when abuses are recorded.
3. Consider jailing company executives who flaunt environmental laws and threaten the lives and health of Ontarians.
4. Install, immediately, carbon filtration systems—which can screen toxins—in all communities that rely on water supplies susceptible to industries in the Chemical Valley.
5. Stop all waste discharges into the St. Clair and other rivers as part of a long-term goal. The technology already exists to safely store or recycle dangerous chemicals.

Clearly, today's practice of negotiating with industry to clean up its potentially lethal activities doesn't work... Threats backed up with tough action seem the only recourse. If all else fails, then there is one remaining option. Shutdown serious offenders. Jobs be damned. Our rivers, our drinking water, our health—the future of our children—must not be endangered.[62]

By contrast, the *Sarnia Observer* editorial of November 6 called for caution, faith, and more facts. It argued that little was actually known about the toxins in the river, implying that the problem had likely been exaggerated. As for the accusations of collusion, the paper said: "Those making any charges about the activities of the LIS or the Ministry should be prepared to back them up." Moreover, the editors asserted that the government should not focus on the question of who was responsible for the "possible" pollution problem, but simply on methods of cleaning it up. Loyal area politicians were assigned their tasks: "MP Ken James and MPP Andy Brandt should ensure that the governments stick to the facts and the problems at hand rather than seeking scapegoats."[63] The two papers' positions represent a polarization of the options in such a way that neither could be acceptable to both citizens and chemical workers. While the *Star*'s "Jobs be damned!" could hardly be a grounds for attracting the support of Sarnia chemical workers, the *Observer*'s persistent refusal to admit the seriousness of the health and environmental problem reinforced the citizens' and environmental groups' frustrated determination to deal directly with the government.

The day after the *Sarnia Observer* editorial was published, Bob Rae arrived in Sarnia to tour the Chemical Valley stretch of the St. Clair River. He had been briefed by staff at the Great Lakes Institute in Windsor on the chronology of the blob. (It was GLI divers who originally discovered the blob in 1984, and who tried for a year to get the test results from the MOE.) According to the *Sarnia Observer*, Rae was "critical of the fact that it took 15 months after tests were done last year, before the presence of dioxins was revealed."[64] This was precisely the point to which the chemical industry least wanted to draw attention, i.e., its cover-up of a dangerous health and environmental situation, which amounted to flagrant disregard for the welfare of the downstream population. The *Sarnia*

Observer editorial on Rae's visit, interestingly, did not attempt to deny or disprove Rae's statement. Instead, it attempted to destroy his credibility by claiming that his motive was political opportunism. The *Observer* tried hard to re-mystify what had momentarily been made clear:

> Politicians of all colors are quick to respond to any incident in an attempt to score points for themselves and their parties. Many times, the response only further clouds an issue causing *undue concern on behalf of the public* the politicians are sworn to represent. Such a case occurred in Sarnia Thursday as New Democratic Party leader Bob Rae visited the area...
>
> Mr. Rae jumped on the bandwagon and said there must be attention to cleaning up the pollution... But having an opposition politician... making all kinds of inflammatory statements is not going to ease the fears of residents... Unlike other responsible people involved in the affair, Mr. Rae has spouted off without bothering to find out what is really sitting on the bottom of the river.
>
> His visit to the area will only serve himself and his party. He will be seen by some people as the protector of the environment, but he is not. There are many people concerned with what dangers the substance poses, but they are not running around creating a media circus over the whole affair. The only things missing from Mr. Rae's entourage on Thursday was a brass band and Ferris wheel... Enough *confusion* exists about the St. Clair River without tossing in Mr. Rae's unsolicited comments. Let's have more investigation and less drama as the truth is sought (emphasis added).[65]

Meanwhile, two reporters from the *Windsor Star* attempted to find out what Sarnia residents were thinking about this latest crisis.[66] The residents' views strikingly resembled those of the *Observer* editorialists, even echoing the same words. City officials, like the city manager and the head of the Sarnia-Lambton County Economic Development Commission, dismissed the concerns about water quality (not a problem for Sarnia, of course), and complained of the "bad mouthing" of Sarnia by "outsiders." The Mayor, Marcell Saddy, was dismayed at the criticisms of the chemical companies, "where we all make our livings." Repeating the favourite theme of the LIS, Saddy said: "The public gets *a clouded impression* of all this. The actual quality of water now is better than when the first records were ever made." Most of the people interviewed attributed the crisis to political posturings by the parties. Even a secretary at the Sarnia office of the MOE said: "The new guys [Liberals] want to make the old guys [Conservatives] look bad."

The views of chemical workers and their families were also canvassed. A security guard at Dow said: "It's all blown out of proportion." As for others:

> "I think they're making too big a thing out of it," said Sophie Finney, who has lived in Sarnia 15 years. "It's been this way for years."
>
> "The blob doesn't upset me a bit," said a 57-year-old woman who would not give her name but said her husband and son are employed by one of the chemical plants.
>
> "I think the companies are doing their best. I guess when you're born and raised on the river, it doesn't frighten you as much," she said, noting she has lived in the area all her life. "The media is just scaring people; my parents died of old age."
>
> "There were lots of things in the river years ago," said Joan Reid, who has lived in Sarnia 34 years. "I'm not worried."
>
> "I think it's been blown way out of proportion," Rick Maggs, an operator at

Dow, said. "*I'm a blob-maker*," he added, explaining that an operator makes the raw chemicals, turns the valves and does procedural checks to make sure there are no leaks. "It's not the people who work in the plants that are concerned," he said, "*it's the people who are uneducated*."

Mr. Maggs also said he has worked for Polysar, which makes synthetic rubber, and Esso Chemical Canada. All three companies are very conscientious about their responsibility to the environment, he said (emphasis added).

The journalists pointed out that the facts contradicted such complacency. A recently released Environment Canada report had stated that "more than 1,355.5 tonnes of oil, acid, paint, phenol, styrene, sodium hydroxide, vinyl chloride, xylene, and benzene...were dumped into the river between 1972 and 1984." Polysar had thirty-eight (reported) spills during the eleven years ending in 1984, Esso had thirty-seven, and Dow had twenty-nine (plus eleven in 1985 alone). Nevertheless, another Dow employee and member of his local's health and safety committee, Tony Isber, refused to consider these facts and defended his employer.

> Dow bashing is a favorite of the media and Greenpeace and the rest of them... [The blob] is probably just fuel oil from lake freighters. Look, Dow is probably not lily-white in this whole thing. There used to be some terrible sins take place here, but that was 20 and 30 years ago.

The ideas about necessary trade-offs and reasonable risks which underpin workers' acceptance of both dangerous occupational health situations and environmental degradation were expressed by the wife of a Dow worker. The gender ideology which approves the male "provider" role also comes into play here, as a factor legitimating the cruel sacrifice demanded of the insulator and his family.

Ethel Wright, whose husband worked as an insulator for Dow for 37 years until he contracted asbestosis, said she is confident the company will clean up the river.

"The way we look at it, sure he's going to die...but Dow has provided for our family very well. He always had a steady job, the money was always coming in, nobody ever went hungry," she said. "Dow's been good to us."

"I think Sarnia's a pretty nice place. Mind you, we've got the pollution. But we know we've got it. And anyone who doesn't like it has got to move away."

This woman was not arguing that the pollution problem (like her husband's asbestosis) was *unreal*, rather, that it was *necessary*.

Things seemed to get worse for the chemical companies. Vacuuming of the blob failed to eliminate it, leading to the realization that the sources must be seepage from underground caverns or elsewhere; the head of the Sarnia MOE office was dismissed; the Ontario Spills Bill was passed on November 29. The *Observer* appealed for the chemical industry to be given a fair hearing.[67] When MOE testing of downstream drinking water (at Windsor, Walpole Island, Wallaceburg, Amherstburg, Stoney Point, Mitchell's Bay and Stag Island) failed to detect traces of dioxins or other toxic chemicals, the *Observer* gave this news front-page billing (which they failed to do when the testing on the blob's contents was revealed). The Conservative MPP for the area, Andy Brandt, was quoted at length, praising the good record of the industry.

"I think the Sarnia area has been completely vindicated... We have to continue to strive for the highest standards and I believe these results confirm that we have been," the MPP said.

Mr. Brandt said the results suggest Ontario Environment Minister Bradley was "wrong" in all the "hyperbole he indulged in" surrounding the river's pollution problems.

Mr. Brandt said that while industry here is "by no means claiming perfection," the Chemical Valley has made "absolutely staggering improvements" in its emission levels to the river.[68]

However, citizens downstream did not feel particularly reassured. Members of the Walpole Island First Nation, as well as residents of Wallaceburg, had been using bottled water purchased in Michigan for drinking, cooking, and bathing infants. By November it had cost the Walpole Band $7,000 to transport this water to the reserve, and they were threatening to bill Dow Chemical. Residents of Wallaceburg were considering a charcoal filtration system for the town water purification plant, as well as the pipeline alternative. A pipeline to Lake Huron, it was estimated, would cost between $8 and $9 million. This would not, of course, resolve the crisis for the native people dependent on fishing and hunting for food and income, or for the local tourism industry. These concerns were compounded by the news in November that new blobs were appearing and the sources now seemed far more extensive than initially thought (including Dow's Scott Road landfill).

In mid-December 1985 a citizens' group was established in Windsor, focusing on the drinking water quality issue. This group would become the Windsor and District Clean Water Alliance. Its initial composition reflected the history of labour-oriented activism and NDP strength in the Windsor area. Among the founding members were Jim Brophy, a director of the Windsor Occupational Health and Safety Council, and Steven Langdon of the NDP. Brophy made an important connection between workers' occupational health and safety experiences and the environmental problem. He also tried to shift the strategic orientation of the group from government lobbying toward grassroots coalition building. According to a report of the organisation's founding meeting:

> Brophy said the record of both industry and government in protecting citizens has not been good. Workers serve as the "early warning system" for employers about dangerous chemicals.
>
> "If you're waiting for government representatives or scientists to come out and (do something)…then you're going to have a long wait. We cannot rely on a benevolent employer or government to protect us."
>
> Brophy said the key to a successful government lobby will be a "coalition of unions and citizens." "Without (public) activity, this problem isn't going to get any better. It's going to get worse," Brophy said.[69]

Langdon spelled out a wide-ranging agenda for the new group, including a public forum on the pollution problem in Windsor (at which government officials and industry representatives would be asked to account for their actions), legislative reforms (including an environmental "super fund" along the lines of that implemented in the United States), a judicial inquiry into the St. Clair River situation (a demand of the NDP during the mercury crisis as well), presentations at schools, and contacts with unions and local municipalities (to obtain support). It is significant that the Windsor activists were conscious of the absence of any similar concern from Sarnia citizens. Langdon commented: "We have seen in the past months that people in the Sarnia area have a vested interest in reducing the significance of the problem… So it has to be us who keep the pressure up and see to it that (the government and industry) solve the problem completely."[70]

The attitude of Sarnia residents to the pollution problem had not changed much by February 1986, when a *Globe and Mail* reporter interviewed some "community leaders."

The first, Ms. Nan Macnair, belonged to "a local wildlife group" which she described as "in the Sarnia vanguard when it comes to concern about pollution."[71] Ms. Macnair claimed that the blob "is not really a problem," and complained that publicity about it was ruining Sarnia's tourism appeal. At Christmas, Ms. Macnair and others tried to make the chemical plants a winter tourist attraction by "dressing them with special lights" and arranging bus tours from Chatham and Detroit. The executive director of the Sarnia General Hospital, Mr. Ernie Redden, said: "We think (the blob) is a non-issue. We're not that concerned about it."

These views are even more interesting in light of the fact that both spokespersons' organisations were the real or potential beneficiaries of Dow Chemical largesse, although these connections were not mentioned in the newspaper story. Ms. Macnair's organisation was not named, but it may well have been the St. Clair Region Conservation Authority, or a group seeking similar favour with Dow. Around 1985, Dow Chemical gave $10,000 to the St. Clair Region Conservation Authority to establish a conservation education centre at the Wawanosh Wetlands. The chairperson of the Sarnia District Contributions Committee of Dow Chemical Canada, Dick Ford, explained this generosity: "We thought it was worthwhile to the community and *the project had an environmental flavour that suited us*. In fact the building has been named the Fred Bremner Conservation Education Centre in honour of a pioneer Dow employee" (emphasis added).[72] The Sarnia General Hospital had submitted a request for funding to Dow Chemical Company "to help construct two new additions that will house the pharmacy, rehabilitation, ophthalmology, psychology, and pediatrics departments as well as a major Trauma and Advanced Life-Support Emergency Department and a burn unit." In 1987 the hospital received a gift of $375,000 to be donated over five years.[73]

The *Globe and Mail* reporter did note, however, that local media and Conservative politicians had succeeded in channelling local resentment about Sarnia's new image as "home of the blob" against Liberal and NDP politicians and the "Toronto media." She was surprised that no one seemed to be blaming the Conservative Party, "which was in power for the past four decades while some of the chemicals...were being discharged." Instead, Conservative politicians were contributing to an "us against them" mentality in Sarnia. Larry Grossman, leader of the Ontario Conservative Party, told a press conference in Sarnia: "the cheap and easy politics of *beating up on a community* [makes one, i.e., Bradley] feel pretty good at the start, feel like a pretty tough fellow, particularly when some of the Toronto media receive that stuff pretty well, but that sort of stuff catches up over time" (emphasis added).[74] Grossman accused the Liberal government of "suggesting to the continent that Sarnia is a dangerous place," and spreading "horror stories." Andy Brandt had also been busy in Sarnia, making the arguments that Bradley had no business prosecuting the chemical companies in the Chemical Valley because there were worse places in Ontario, and because Bradley had pollution problems in his own riding. Although these were hardly arguments for doing nothing in Sarnia, they were given prominence by Sarnia media. The weekly *Sarnia Gazette* ran Brandt's comments in a front-page article under the heading "The Truth Comes Out."

Implicit in the public statements of the companies, their political representatives, and the "loyal" press, was the threat of job blackmail. The fact that the chemical companies are the major employers in Sarnia was mentioned in almost every item on the pollution crisis. In February 1986, a story on the restructuring and workforce reductions at the chemical plants, and on area unemployment, was placed directly above another piece which warned that environmental pressures were adding to the companies' woes. The *Observer* praised the companies' valiant efforts to restore their economic competitiveness (the wage concessions of workers were mentioned not at all), and quoted the retiring president of Dow

Chemical Canada, who said: "There is potential for trouble as the government tries to cut back on pollution while industry attempts to produce more efficiently."[75] There was no attempt to examine the costs of environmental improvements, the long-term social costs of failing to implement such improvements, or the ability of the companies to pay. This was notwithstanding the fact that it was unthinkable that a major, integrated chemical complex could easily or profitably be transferred from Sarnia to another location. Moreover, one of the benefits of the measures subsequently announced by Dow was the creation of jobs for local workers, especially in construction.[76]

In May a cancer study was announced for Kent and Lambton counties, to determine whether this population had a higher incidence of cancer than populations in other parts of the province. There was another scandal that month when vinyl chloride gas and hydrogen chloride gas were released from Dow's plant, but downwind communities in Michigan were not alerted.[77] In June Bradley announced the Municipal-Industrial Strategy of Abatement (MISA), to be followed by new penalties for polluters in July. Greenpeace returned to Sarnia to hold a press conference on the MISA. The location they chose was the Suncor site, near the river.[78] This time the group was joined by representatives of several other environmental groups from the area. Their demands (to the government) had to do with broadening public participation in the regulatory process. The zero-discharge goal of Greenpeace (and the St. Clair River International Citizens' Network groups) was endorsed by Don Heath, president of the Sarnia and District Labour Council, in August.[79]

The chemical companies, like their counterparts in the United States, adopted the stance of victims of unfair persecution and public ignorance. Confirming the observation of the citizens that the companies were increasingly nervous about the decline of Conservative Party hegemony provincially, and the erosion of their cozy relationship with the MOE, the general manager of the Lambton Industrial Society (LIS) warned that:

> Proposed harsher penalties for corporate polluters threaten to explode the stable relationship between Ontario's environment ministry and Sarnia's petrochemical giants that has kept both out of the courts... [N]ew penalties could result in costly legal battles as firms and government lock horns over technical points of law. The result could be stalled environmental improvements and cleanups as higher courts are faced with interpreting legislation... While industry does not object to flagrant offenders being severely punished, it does not want companies with good track records being made victims.[80]

According to the *Observer*, environment minister Bradley's "hard-line approach to polluters [had] sent shock waves through the Chemical Valley." An unnamed "highly-placed industry source" complained that "there is a real Rambo, macho movement going on in the Ministry now...and it's hard to say anything without incurring the wrath of God."[81] (It was Andy Brandt who first described Bradley as using "Rambo-like tactics" against the chemical companies. Ironically, this "macho" label applied to a group around Bradley which included Julia Langer [now federal director of Friends of the Earth].) A "veteran" communications officer at the Ministry of the Environment was quoted as saying:

> [T]here has been a significant shift in the government to a tougher outlook on environmental issues... With the previous (Progressive Conservative) administration, if you put 10 gallons of something in the river... no one said to ignore it, but there wasn't the same emphasis on spills.

You are seeing people getting into key positions who were interested in the environment in school. And public meetings on the environment are attracting a lot of people.

Certainly, the "industry" had reasons for concern. The reference to education as a formative factor in the new orientation of these government officials has not, as we have seen in previous sections, been lost on either the chemical companies or the citizens' groups.

By late 1986 the citizens' groups in the St. Clair River Network and their national and provincial environmental allies (CELA, Friends of the Earth, Pollution Probe, Greenpeace) were waging a concerted campaign to restructure the relationships among themselves, government agencies, and the private companies. They were demanding an uncompromising commitment from the government to put health and environmental interests before private profit (although the extent to which these were viewed as incompatible varied considerably among and within these groups), and they were pushing for direct representation of citizens' interests within government decision-making structures. The companies were on the defensive, having suffered a major loss of credibility in the eyes of the public, along with the "stable" political relationship they had enjoyed with the Conservative regime. Both the companies and the Liberal government were trying to establish a new relationship which would have to accommodate at least some of the demands of the citizens' movement.

The element which continued to be missing from this array of interests was the chemical workers. The attitudes they had expressed in the immediate aftermath of the blob were repeated in late 1986 and early 1988, when a number of ECWU officials were interviewed in Sarnia. The opinions and observations of these union members illustrate some of the contradictory elements of the chemical workers' views of environmentalists, their relationships with their employers, and the role of the union.

UNION RESPONSE TO THE BLOB

Representatives of the ECWU explain their union's non-involvement in grassroots social movements, like environmentalism, in various ways. Among the explanations one finds: the apathy of the rank and file; guilt, or the knowledge of complicity in the polluting activities of employers; job insecurity; and an identification with employers' attitudes towards environmentalists and citizens' groups (i.e., the "outsiders"). There are, of course, many contradictions of these explanations in their statements. For example, when it was suggested that workers might hesitate to report pollution violations or to support environmental groups because of the threat of job blackmail, Charlie Stevens, a union official at Cabot Carbon, insisted that his employer was conscientious about avoiding and reporting environmental degradation. He suggested that, if there were a "definite" problem, the company would willingly co-operate with concerned citizens, the government, or the union in cleaning it up. In other words, in order to exonerate his members from any responsibility for the problem, or suggestion of self-interest, he denied the existence of any "real" problem. However, in the same interview, in the course of questioning the credibility of the citizens' groups' information, Stevens said that they should ask the union for help, because "companies aren't going to tell them what they want to know." "I've had a lot of experience with companies," he said. "They're not that nice." The question is therefore raised: what would the workers tell the citizens' groups, that the company does not want them to know, about the non-existent problem? The following excerpts from interviews with ECWU officials and rank-and-file activists express some of the themes of union relations with environmentalists.

"We Know Better"

Dow Chemical has spent in 1986...at least a million dollars, probably more, revising their operations so they can contain [pollution]. Some people spend a lot of time talking about the blob, and it has a negative impact on the community. But what I look at is...the things [that] are done to upgrade the facilities to make them more environmentally safe. In fact, in the...last *Labour Day Review* [1986] I [wrote] an article that touched on that. [Dave Pretty, National Staff Representative, Sarnia District, December 4, 1986]

****

Our union has never been one...to get into that war of the newspapers, or whatever. You know, Dow and their employees get into condemning each other but this time with the blob, you didn't hear labour coming out and screaming and hollering. Yeah, there were statements by [Labour Council President, Don] Heath, and those kinds of things. When Greenpeace was on its way we were informed by management, because they [had] their watchdogs out, watching for her [Joyce Maclean]... [Management] asked if we'd be having any input. I said, "Well, not unless we're asked. I don't know what I would tell her. It depends on what she wants to know, I guess." [Management said it was concerned that Greenpeace would do] something silly, or harmful, to the plant... [Ken Glassco, Chief Steward at Polysar, December 4, 1986]

****

[Question]: Do you think there is a feeling among the workforce in Sarnia that they are vulnerable to economic blackmail by the companies if they start to become more activist on environmental issues?

[Answer]: No, I don't think so, because we've been pretty out front if any companies do pollute. I don't say we [workers] call in the government every time they have a leak, or something like that, but I think the companies—at least the company I work for—if they have a leak they waste no time calling the Ministry. If the Ministry catches them, and they haven't reported it, they're in trouble...

Let's say I went and stood on top of a bridge [to publicize a pollution violation]; they [the employer] wouldn't think too much of it. But if there's *definite* problems... I'm sure the company would help you... [A]s far as protecting the environment, the union in Sarnia is fully prepared to go ahead and do something, *if there is something more they can do than they are now*...

Before, [the companies] used to [pollute] on purpose; they used to drain it. Now, the only time they get spills is when there's an accident. Some of our own people cause the accidents... That's the difference between [the SCRICN] and [our union]: we don't go to the newspapers and say all this—that they did it on purpose. But that's not protecting any company [that is] polluting... [Charlie Stevens, President of the Sarnia Area Council of the ECWU, and member of the union executive at Cabot Carbon, May 5, 1988. Emphasis added].

These officials find various ways to defend the environmental record of their employers, thereby marginalizing the existence of a problem which requires action on their part. Pretty and others refer to the money being spent by the companies on pollution abatement, thus repeating the assertions of the local media and the companies themselves. The actual history of virtually unregulated environmental degradation and citizen protest behind the implementation of these measures is ignored or downplayed.

The seriousness of the problem is not acknowledged. No opinion is offered on the relationship between pollution and profit.

Yet in other contexts union officials do admit that the companies deliberately pollute. Stevens, for example, (like other citizens of the Sarnia area), admits that this was a problem *in the past*. During the 1988 strike at Dow Chemical, workers used the company's environmental record (especially the emerging evidence that Dow had been illegally dumping toxic wastes in the LaSalle Road landfill) to depict their opponent as unethical and untrustworthy. Workers at Polysar tend to defend their own employer's environmental record, while freely admitting Dow Chemical's history of pollution and attempted cover-ups.

Ken Glassco's account of his predicament while awaiting the arrival of the Greenpeace ship also reveals the contradictory interests of chemical workers. On one hand, he knows that management's "watchdogs" are usually deployed against workers, particularly during strikes; he has some sympathy for the company's environmental opponents, as they approach the fortress. On the other hand, he is within the walls, and to some extent a beneficiary of the polluting activities directed by management. Management, at this pivotal moment, deploys a tactic calculated to provide workers with a socially responsible excuse to remain at least neutral in the conflict: it suggests that these environmentalists are unpredictable fanatics—that they would go so far as triggering a major environmental disaster in pursuit of their "extreme" goals. This completely unfounded suggestion is repeatedly used to divide workers and environmentalists. Greenpeace's media-oriented tactics are used by employers to discredit environmental concerns; they are also threatening and alien to the normal practice of the unions (legalistic, corporatist, parliamentarist).

At the same time, these tactics strike a chord of response among rank-and-file workers who have experienced collective and militant mobilization during strikes—moments when acts of sabotage or vandalism are not uncommon. They also know how unequally the "transgressions" of workers and employers are treated by authorities and media. Indeed, there is a mixture of admiration and resentment in workers' views of Greenpeace. These people who climb bridges and smokestacks, who repeatedly get arrested for defying the companies' "keep out" signs, are not so different from strikers who defy picketing injunctions and deal with police who are always enforcing laws which protect their employers' interests. But workers do not like being criticised, even implicitly, for their complicity and inaction. Put simply, the people on the bridge make them look bad. There is an element of injured machismo in the repeated assertions that workers are not "scared" by employers' threats, are not hesitant to take stances against pollution, are not "impressed" by the Greenpeacers. (Similar views were expressed by the autoworkers—see part 4.)

Guilt/Complicity

Management's ability to build a wall around the plant site and, at moments of crisis, effectively ensure the loyalty of their subordinates against the "outsiders," rests upon a certain degree of complicity of workers in pollution. This was admitted by various union representatives (and is reported in the case examined in the next section).[82] According to Ken Glassco, chief steward at Polysar:

> I think a lot of [chemical workers] felt hurt that it was Sarnia [where the blob happened]. If you read our newspapers during that time, the Chamber of Commerce was saying "There's nothing the matter with the blob," and running ads. I didn't hear anybody coming out [against the pollution]. You don't hear that kind of thing around here. I don't think it's a company town, but I guess a lot of

[workers] feel that if something's the matter, they may have been a part of it, and maybe they don't want to admit it. You didn't see people writing the editor, or if they did it wasn't [published] in the [Sarnia] *Observer*. They would write an article condemning the people that were [drawing attention to] the blob.

Charlie Stevens [Sarnia Area Council President of the ECWU] said that workers do not call the Ministry of the Environment "every time [the plant has] a leak." It was assumed that "leaks" are part of normal operations. Most of the plants are designed so that gases are automatically released into the atmosphere whenever the capacity of a unit is exceeded. This happens frequently. The rationale is that "safeties" are preferable to explosions, assuming that the company chooses not to upgrade the plants or install pollution technology.

Dave Pretty [National Rep., Sarnia District] gave the example of the chlorine solvents unit at Dow Chemical, which frequently releases chlorine gas into the atmosphere:

> They have to have "safeties" to avoid perhaps an explosion...which would be even worse. But they have a scrubbing system in the solvents unit [which] was never designed to handle these things to the degree that they are [being produced], so, the over-capacity goes into the atmosphere. In the [solvents] unit, they are putting up a $60,000 expansion of the scrubbing system. The unit was designed 15 to 20 years ago for a certain capacity. They keep increasing it and running at 120 to 130 percent of the nameplate of the original design.

"Steven," a Dow employee, described another example of pollution as "normal practice."

> Overheads and bottoms are two terms you run into in the plants. Whenever you heat something, you drive something off the top, chemically, which we call overheads. There's always a stream of stuff that doesn't get evaporated and blown off, and that's called the bottoms. The most obvious example is a still, or column. In the biox [biological-oxidation] plant, they take hydrolizer bottoms. The stuff they drive off the top in their reaction—the propylene oxide—is the stuff they want. The stuff in the bottom are by-products of the reaction, like polyglycols, that they don't want. Past practice was to simply flush these [into] the river. They built the biox plant when they realized it was no longer going to be accepted for them to run that stuff directly to the river. However, when I worked there, there was a three-way valve. It could either be closed, open to the river, or to the biox. When you first start up the plant, if you've been down for a while, you always went to the river, because you'd be making junk for a while, and you didn't want to feed the bugs bad stuff.

Management is able to reinforce the employees' sense of responsibility for polluting activities through disciplinary measures. These are usually applied when the leak or spill is caught. An employee is then blamed for the "accident." Environmental investigations are very much like health and safety procedures, except that, in the former, there is no union involvement (no joint committee, provided for by provincial legislation). Workers are made to feel that health and safety are their responsibility—that carelessness or negligence are the major causes of accidents. The false assumption here is that workers have equal authority to determine working conditions and the ways in which tasks will be carried out. This approach also assumes, wrongly, that workers and supervisors have equal knowledge about the chemicals they are working with and their potential risks. Often workers are told to do something without being informed of the risks. Finally, there is a pretense that there is no coercion involved—that workers are free to refuse any tasks or protest any working conditions they consider unsafe. The record of government vigilance in enforcing existing health and safety legislation is dismal; the legal rights won by workers are seldom sufficient to protect their jobs or their health. All of this is even more true for environmental conflicts at the point of production.

During the mercury controversy involving Dow Chemical in the late 1960s-early 1970s, management pinned a chlorine gas leak on its key opponent, local union president Ivan Hillier. In 1973, there was a major chlorine gas leak at Dow, which put eighty construction workers at the Suncor site in the hospital. The pipefitter on duty was blamed by the company. This was the incident which incited the Dow strike of 1973. Pretty described an arbitration case stemming from an incident which occurred not long after the blob controversy arose, and the company was particularly "environmentally sensitive."

> [T]he solvents unit at Dow Chemical shut down about noon (January 27, 1986), and there was an emission of chlorine to the atmosphere. The company then blamed the midnight shift operator, who came on at 7 PM on the 26th, and worked until 7 AM. They came down on him like a ton of bricks...to the extent of firing him, for something that happened five hours later—after he had completed his shift. It took me three days in arbitration and a day of argument to get that reversed.

Steven, a Dow process operator, had also been disciplined for an environmental incident. He claimed that someone else had left a valve open, allowing ethylene oxide to escape. He was new on the job; it was his first process job; and he had not been fully trained. Although he was not responsible for the spill, a letter of censure was added to his employee file.

Dow Chemical has an elaborate set of disciplinary procedures. There are five levels of disciplinary measures, including (from one to five): a verbal censure or warning; a letter which may be removed from the employee's file after one year (conditional on "good behaviour"); a "permanent" letter (record of infraction); suspension and threat of dismissal (probation); and dismissal.[83] Management (supervisors) also make "job performance reports" (JPRs) of employees on an ad hoc basis. According to one Dow employee, these are "often used for character slander rather than evaluations of your work... When a boss doesn't like you, that's when you see them."[84] This observation is confirmed by Michael's experience (described below).

Ironically, the Ontario government's introduction of the Spills Bill raised concerns among chemical workers that the proclivity of employers to shift the blame for environmental violations to the workforce would intensify. Pretty explained his conception of how the (Ontario) Environmental Protection Act would work:

> [The Ministry] now has the authority to walk into a plant at any time and say: "I want to talk to the guy who is the operator of that unit." And the guy who is the operator in that unit probably wants to co-operate, but he doesn't want to co-operate to the extent that he'll get himself in jail. Know what I mean? We have found situations where we would end up having our members charged under the Act, and then we have to...defend them.

Pretty believed that workers "have no protection under the Act, as [they do] under the Occupational Health and Safety Act."

> There's no rights in the EPA to secure the interests of the employee. We've had situations where the employer has not been charged, but the employee has. That's a reality that brings it home. It's a disincentive in trying to be honest and forthright...in letting the Ministry know what caused the spill.

In fact, Section 134B of the EPA gives the employee recourse to the Ontario Labour Relations Board in such a case (see chapter 3), but even the MOE admits that the employee's position—between employer and government authorities—is "a difficult one."[85] Indeed, in their advice to counsel for corporate defendants in EPA prosecutions, lawyers David Hunter and Michael W. Bader propose a "due diligence [on the part of the corporation] checklist" which includes a notable emphasis on the role of employees:

> (a) Identify the person or persons who supervise and have control over the operations.
> (b) Are there policy directives on environmental control? Have these directives been made available to workers?
> (c) Training manuals or specific published operating procedures.
> (d) Evidence of on-the-job training of employees, including any "classroom" training and distributed materials... It is also important to identify the chain of command in order to determine if the person or persons responsible for the occurrence were acting in response to orders or otherwise...[86]

Environmentalists and unions have called on the Ontario and federal governments to introduce an Environmental Bill of Rights which would strengthen provisions for the rights of workers who refuse to perform work which pollutes the environment.

Dan Ublansky, the legal counsel for the ECWU, admitted that the union could not effectively protect workers who refuse work which pollutes the environment.

> If the company disciplines them as a result of one of those [refuse to work] incidents, they'd get all the support in the world [from the union]. But I'm not sure that I would find that particularly comforting. If you're fired for an incident like that, it may take a year or more to resolve... [I]f I were in one of those plants, I'm not sure that would be good enough... At least [under the Occupational Health and Safety Act] a worker can file a complaint. The government will appoint an officer to investigate, and he will be able to put some pressure, informally, on the company to take a second look at what they've done. That doesn't always produce results, but it's better than nothing. On environmental issues, we don't really have that. So anybody that's sticking his neck out is taking a chance. I would have some difficulty being a very strong advocate that he should do that... And we're only talking about *organized* places.

Thus, internal company procedures and governmental legislation are sending conflicting directives to workers. They are expected to carry out work decisions over which they have minimal control, but are held responsible for the environmental consequences *as if they were free actors*. Moreover, in the event that some brave and principled employee should refuse, or report work which would pollute the environment, s/he would find little protection in either existing environmental or labour legislation, or in the grievance procedures agreed upon between employer and union.

In addition to the "blob-makers" whose daily work contributes to the environmental problem, workers are occasionally told to dump toxic wastes under more illicit circumstances. Michael witnessed such an incident, and his story provides many insights into the fate of a chemical worker who fights industrial pollution from within.[87]

"You Called the Wrong Pipefitter"

At the time of the "Dowtherm incident" (1980-81), Michael was a pipefitters' steward at Dow Chemical. His story illustrates the experience confronted by union militants who become involved with the environmental practices of their employers.

I caught a foreman and an operator who was doing what the foreman said, dumping Dowtherm down the sewer. [Dowtherm is the trade name for an oil that Dow uses as an insulator of pipes. At the styrene plant they use it for keeping the plastic [in a] fluid [state] until they get it piped to where they want it. There is a pipe within a pipe, with Dowtherm in the outer pipe.] I was working with my partner...on grating about 30 feet up. I looked down and saw [them dumping something from drums]. You could see something black and oozy going into the sewer. So I yelled down: "What the hell are you doing?!" They looked up, and went away. I was pipefitters' steward and the steward of that unit, too... I saw these other drums lined up, in various levels of full or empty... This was on a Thursday; Friday I was off, and they were going to have a family day on Saturday; they were going to bring the families in to see how nice the plant was. I believe that's why they were trying to get rid of these drums. So I went into the control room and told the operator: "Don't dump anything else down that sewer."

Michael determined that the sewer went to the river.[88] Then he went to the supervisor to report the incident and demand an investigation. This led to attempts to placate him (promises of an investigation, which were never acted on) and the warning, "Just do your job, Michael. Forget about all these other things." On Monday morning he was informed when he arrived at work that he was being moved to another unit. Two weeks later, he was told that he was not "productive enough." His supervisor wrote up a job performance evaluation report (JPR) on him. Although JPRs are supposed to be given on a yearly basis, Michael had had one only two months before. This one, and all his previous JPRs had been excellent. But the new one rated his work at the worst in every category. He demanded a grievance meeting to protest harassment. At the meeting, he was accused of a list of infractions, including "meddling in things that were none of [his] business," and safety infractions. Management showed him a photograph of a broken flange, which they accused him of breaking. He denied this.

The union charged the company with harassment and unfair labour practices. There were a lot of meetings. He was sent to yet another unit, where he was under constant surveillance by supervisors watching for a slip-up or infraction of rules to use against him. When he failed to provide this opportunity, he was assigned to what workers call the "boneyard" of the plant—the scrapyard. (Persons with disabilities are usually sent to the "boneyard.") Here he worked for four months with acetylene torch and sand-blasting equipment.

Michael said that he had seen a document from Dow's Oyster Creek plant on "How to break union militants," in the possession of a previous chief steward who had been harassed and eventually dismissed. The document outlined a strategy that involved putting the worker in a very visible job, and then giving him/her nothing to do, "so that he looks like a slacker." S/he becomes disoriented, bored, and starts to make mistakes. Michael could see that they were trying to do this to him, so he worked very hard: "I pretended to myself that every job I was given was the most critical job at Dow Chemical."

Meanwhile, the union lawyer tried to talk Michael out of pursuing his grievance. He had many meetings with the entire local executive, who wanted him to drop the complaint. His co-workers, however, backed him up, electing him chief steward during this period. This meant that he would become involved with all grievances. The previous chief steward, he claimed, had discouraged workers from filing grievances; the year Michael became chief steward, the number of grievances rose from about four to 120. The outcome of his grievance was that the company refused to admit that it had harassed Michael, but agreed not to do so in the future. He was moved back to the central maintenance shop.

On another occasion, Michael happened to be on shift when he discovered control room operators dumping perchloroethylene-contaminated acid and caustic soda (to neutralize the acid) into the sewer leading to the river. He calculated that they had been dumping 78,000 to 90,000 pounds of acid per hour for several days. They could have shut the plant down, but they had been instructed to empty the pipes. Michael called "an environmental control [department] person" to tell him to investigate. A half hour later, the unit superintendent sought him out and said in a menacing tone: "I hear you have a problem with what we're putting in the sewer." The dumping continued for five days; management did nothing. Michael said he did not call the Ministry of the Environment because "it would have been like signing your own death warrant. You can't trust them. They're worse than Dow."

Michael and others recount numerous incidents of unreported spills. Pipefitters know what goes into the river because they tend the pipes. Once Michael was asked to hook a sludge hose up to a pipe. When he found out that the funnel was running into the sewer to the river, he refused to hook it up. *"You called the wrong pipefitter,"* he said.

These examples show that the "guilt" or "complicity" aspect of workers distancing themselves from environmentalists has complex origins. Most workers prefer to accept management's explanations for the way work is directed; many internalize the "blame the victim" ideology of health and safety procedures and propaganda. That is, incidents which individuals could prevent are conflated with those arising from conditions over which workers have less control. Health and safety codes emphasize workers' responsibilities, while often downplaying the reality of dangerous industrial working conditions and management's role in directing the labour process. In addition, the macho attitude towards health and safety concerns is extended to (un)environmental practices.

Those who, like Michael, "cause trouble," have little protection from employer retaliation. Although still active in the union and in environmental issues when he was interviewed in 1986 and 1988, Michael admitted that the year of his grievance had worn him down. The risks and the stress of fighting the company under the circumstances were too great, especially for a worker with young children. Michael concluded that the only way to sustain activism is to "go at it like a priest, like Mother Theresa, or Stokely Carmichael." The same pressures were mentioned by a health and safety activist at Dow.

> We've been working on environmental issues within our own plant, and trying to control things for years, and [we're] always told ... it's none of [our] business. It's a lot of pressure to put on your family. You have to really believe in what you're doing. Through this health and safety [work] I'm always sticking my neck out with this company. Michael's job has been threatened. I had an ulcer the last time I was dealing with this issue... [89]

These statements say something about the isolated conditions in which rank-and-file activists struggle. While the union, when pressed, will seek to enforce their contractual rights, the overall structure of management-worker relations, as well as the attitudes cultivated by employers' campaigns in the broader community and by union officials' discourse, all function to dissuade workers from assuming responsibility for health, environmental, and other conditions.

Apathy

An explanation for workforce quietism commonly given by union officials is the "apathy" or ignorance of the rank and file. Some examples of such views are found in the following statements.

> There's a lot of complacency and these are difficult times... It's a very conservative community, politically and otherwise. It has been an affluent community, but the growth stopped, and rationalisation set in over the last four to five years. Those who are still receiving a good income become extremely complacent. They don't rush out to take on all social challenges... [T]here's a serious lack of participation in these community functions... [Dave Pretty]

> I don't think [workers] know what really happens [effects of dumping chemicals]. [T]he majority of [chemical workers] live in Sarnia. There are a few that live downriver, but not too many are directly affected by dumping stuff in the river. So they don't care that much about it. If something does happen, well, it goes downriver. Our beach, our fresh water [are fine]... [Ken Glassco]

> There's a sense that there should be something done about the environment, but we don't get a push that it should be the union doing it. And I think...there's an "out of sight, out of mind" mindset. [Stuart Sullivan]

In their study of the ideological perspectives of chemical workers at "Chem Co" in southern England, Huw Beynon and Theo Nichols regard union officials' complaints about rank-and-file "apathy" as "a strongly ideological view which should neither be taken at face value nor totally ignored."[90] Nichols and Beynon observe that the motivation and approval of these officials generally comes from "above," rather than below. The rank and file, on the other hand, view "the union" as a service organisation—a kind of bureaucracy over their heads, which periodically represents some of their immediate interests in negotiations with employers.[91] Indeed, "apathy" is rooted as much in workers' experience of *unionism* as it is in any experience of "affluence." (This is illustrated by "Peter's" observations, described below.)

Union Hierarchy

Naturally, this is not an explanation for union non-involvement in social issues which is given by full-time union officials. Rather, it emerges from the accounts of rank-and-file workers' experiences in trying to bring about workplace reforms or changes in union orientation. The problem of "the guys up there" is a very important element of the explanation for rank-and-file "apathy," militants' "burn-out," and union support for the status quo, and it is evident in the accounts of steelworkers and auto workers, as well as those of chemical workers.

When asked if the union (ECWU) should be participating in the St. Clair River International Citizens' Network, Peter offered these opinions:

> I think [what would have to happen for the union to get involved with environmentalists] is that [some workers] would have to do a lot of lobbying with the [management] at Dow and our union executive. Because unless you get a guy on the [ECWU Executive] Board who really believes in the issue...then we don't get any co-operation from the union executive, either. That would have to come right down from our national director. So you'd have to work from the top down... We're a rank and file union, and everything is supposed to go up, only, our union executives are in the middle. They're the people who control things, as far as what information gets across to people. For example, if we wanted to send Michael to a conference, it would have to go through the union executive. And if they have a letter from Reg [Basken, national union president] that [approves this], these guys will listen to that. But they're not going to listen to us [rank-and-file members]...

> I can't get [ECWU elected officials] real sympathetic towards the health and safety

issue, let alone the environmental issues. So it would take a lot of work. When we're talking about health and safety issues, we're talking about their dues-paying members; when you get into the environmental issues, you're talking about [what affects members as] citizens, and that's completely different... I can't get them sympathetic for our [health and safety] cause in a big way. They're like the company is a lot of times. They tell you, "yes, we're going to do this..." and then I can't get them to move on it. So there's a lot of lobbying on the part of guys like ourselves, who are down here and believe in what we're doing. But we've got to get everybody else on board with us... That's just as hard as dealing with the company.

Clearly, this account contradicts the statements of officials about the democratic, "rank-and-file" nature of their union (which they tend to contrast favourably with other industrial unions). Peter's comments also shed some light on the suspicions of citizens' groups regarding the sincerity and profundity of union concern for environmental issues. Rank-and-file chemical workers who are also environmental or health and safety activists (like Steven, Michael, and Peter) in fact share Kristina Lee's perception that they are representative of neither the workforce, nor the policies of the union hierarchy.

Job Insecurity

When asked if the ECWU was doing anything to prepare for the eventuality that environmental campaigns targeting the chemical industry would succeed (e.g., reduction of, or bans on certain plastic and chemical products), Peter replied:

I can see our members really having a problem with that. And I know our national director, Reg Basken, would have a problem with that. I can see that being a real concern with them, as far as, "Hey, you're taking our jobs away from us! You're taking the bread right out of our mouths!" What do we do about these multinational companies that say: "we can go to Venezuela"? And here's the government [of Canada] eliminating import [restrictions]... How are you going to control these big companies? We [the union] can't control them now. As soon as we give them a hard time they go elsewhere...

What is being acknowledged here is the essential powerlessness of the union—even acting in a nationally-coordinated way—to deal with multinational employers on equal terms. It is important to remember the characteristics of the petrochemical sector: internationalization; high degree of intra-firm integration; high capital-labour ratio; relatively small workforces per site; and, in Canada, relative freedom from trade and investment regulations. A strategy of international solidarity aimed at restricting the mobility of capital, is a precondition for effective environmental (or, for that matter, investment) regulation of these multinational firms. Yet, this strategy is difficult to envisage from the point of view of a rank- and-file activist for whom the most basic local reforms of working conditions at times seem hopeless. Restructuring had already brought about the loss of many jobs in the industry by 1988, as firms cut back on large-scale primary commodity production, relocated production, and installed labour-saving technology. Environmental regulation was viewed as yet another pressure to cut back or relocate production, at the same time offering no concrete alternatives for new products or jobs.

But the perceived weakness of the union is explained not only in relation to the strengths of employers or the political character of the environmental movement; it also has to do with the nature of union leadership and the relative isolation of chemical workers from potential allies in the other social movements. The union has carved out its territory in the economic realm, but as we have seen, its particular sector of the economy is dominated by free market principles and multinational corporations. On this turf, and

Toxic Chemical Pollution of the Chemical Valley 221

without politically forged alliances, it has few options but to play the game by the rules of employers.

NOTES

1. According to Gordon Taylor, a health and safety instructor for the CAW, interviewed in May 1988, as little as 5 ppb of TDI in the air can cause severe reactions and permanent sensitization. Short-term symptoms are similar to severe asthma. Persons exposed over a two-year period have lung function deterioration. These effects have been documented since the 1940s. TDI is also suspected as a carcinogen. See also the Chemical Hazard Summary for Toluene Diisocyanate (2,4-TDI and 2,6-TDI) produced by the Canadian Centre for Occupational Health and Safety (Hamilton, Ont.: CCOHS), updated regularly.
2. *Sarnia Observer*, May 30, 1979, p. 19.
3. *Sarnia Observer*, October 5, 1978, p. 7. In October 1978 Tricil's plant in Mississauga was fined $15,000 in provincial court after pleading guilty to five charges under the Ontario Environmental Protection Act.
4. John Jackson and Phil Weller, *Chemical Nightmare: The Unnecessary Legacy of Toxic Wastes* (Toronto: Between the Lines, 1982), pp. 54-55.
5. *Sarnia Observer*, February 3, 1981.
6. *Sarnia Observer*, August 24, 1985, p. 1. Predictably, an editorial in the February 28, 1986 issue of the paper supported Tricil's application and opposed the idea that disposal of hazardous wastes should be taken out of private sector hands. The writer(s) praised Tricil as "an example of how private business can successfully operate a waste disposal site for the benefit of the public and other industries."
7. MOE, *St. Clair River Pollution Investigation 1985-1986*, (Toronto: MOE, 1986), pp. 17, 20-21, 130-33.
8. Ibid., pp. 58-60. Octachlorodibenzodioxin was detected in the tap water of Sarnia, Wallaceburg, Mitchell's Bay and Windsor during November and December. Following announcement of the results, federal Environment Minister, McMillan, promised "the most broad-reaching, far-reaching environmental contaminants act anywhere in the western hemisphere." Bradley stated: "I don't think we can rule (the presence of dioxin and other toxins) out in any particular raw water or drinking water source in the province." See Jock Ferguson and Christopher Waddell, "New environment laws promised," *The Globe and Mail*, January 30, 1986.
9. Toby Vigod, "The Law and the 'Toxic Blob'," *Alternatives* vol. 13, no. 3 (Sept/Oct 1986), p. 25.
10. Testimony from a Dow employee at a Great Lakes United public hearing, held in Sarnia, October 9, 1986, revealed numerous occasions on which workers had reported suspected pollution offences to the Ministry office, only to be stonewalled. Even worse, the Ministry office told this worker's employer who the informant was. See also, Brian Fox, "Province orders shakeup," *Toronto Star*, November 1985; Jock Ferguson, "Ministry at odds with chemical industry," *The Globe and Mail*, November 5, 1985; Toby Vigod, "The law and the 'toxic blob'", p. 27.
11. In late January 1986, results of MOE testing showed that forms of dioxin were present in trace amounts in the water near Sarnia, Mitchell's Bay, Wallaceburg, and Windsor. See Jock Ferguson, "Sarnia awaits government commitments on pollution ills," *The Globe and Mail*, February 6, 1986, p. A19; Catherine Alpaugh and Trevor Price, "Windsor's Great Lakes Institute: the story behind the blob," *Windsor This Month*, March 1986. Further health concerns were raised by studies released in May 1986.
12. Mary Kehoe, "Dow jumps deadline for lockout: 600 non-union workers arrive at plant in convoy," *London Free Press*, April 25, 1988, pp. B1, B2.
13. Ibid.
14. "Dow counters strike threat with 600 non-union staff," *The Globe and Mail*, April 26, 1988.
15. This information was obtained from an interview with the employee in Sarnia, May 5, 1988. The names of rank-and-file ECWU members interviewed in Sarnia have been changed to protect them from possible employer harassment.
16. The MOE report *St. Clair River Pollution Investigation 1985-1986*, points out that MOE tests

taken in 1983, and Dow data from 1984 revealed that "the area in the vicinity of [Dow's] First Street sewer complex was severely contaminated" with hexachloroethane (HCE), hexachlorobutadiene (HCBD), pentachlorobenzene (QCB), hexachlorobenzene (HCB), and octachlorostyrene (OCS) (p. 78). Carbontetrachloride and hexes were among the compounds found in samples of the blob taken in 1985 (pp. 33-35). One lab technician reported results of up to 500 ppm of some hexes in the samples tested, levels similar to those detected in 1984, in samples of sediment near the First Street sewer. According to information available by May 1988, Dow lab technicians had found HCBD, HCE, and HCB in river sediments being dumped at LaSalle Road.

17. Minister Bradley, quoted in "Dow dumping toxics illegally, NDP critic says," *The Globe and Mail*, June 2, 1988. Dow was eventually charged by the MOE in July 1989.
18. Personal communication from Dow employee, July 27, 1988.
19. Author's notes from a SCRICN meeting, May 2, 1988, in Wallaceburg, where Dow's rotary kiln proposal was discussed. Dow news release on the rotary kiln, dated April 19, 1988 (Sarnia: Dow Chemical). Copy in author's possession.
20. The "hexes" story was told to the author a few days after this meeting, by chemical workers in Sarnia. At the time of the May 2 SCRICN meeting, none of the citizens knew about Dow's illegal dumping at the LaSalle landfill.
21. Author's notes from the GLU hearing, Sarnia, October 9, 1986.
22. Kristina Lee, interview by author, Wallaceburg, Ont., May 3, 1988.
23. In the March 23, 1985 issue of the *Sarnia Observer* ("Scope," p. 6B), Heath was quoted as saying: "The day of the bread-and-butter union which provides just benefits and dollars is gone. A union today has to be more socially responsible. Workers should have more input into the decision-making process and have more responsibility at work." In 1986 Heath enrolled at the University of Windsor to study labour politics.
24. This seems to reflect the link made with Pollution Probe more than a decade earlier. At that time, it was Pollution Probe that undertook a detailed investigation of the mercury problem.
25. Letter from Don Heath to James Bradley, November 20, 1985 (obtained from Don Heath).
26. *Take CAER, The Newsletter of the Lambton Community Awareness Emergency Response Organization* vol. 1, no. 1 (January 1988), p. 1.
27. Ibid., p. 2. (The president of CAER in January 1988 was a Dow Chemical executive, Dick Ford.)
28. Members of the St. Clair River International Citizens' Network attended this session, and subsequently raised concerns with the MOE regarding the chemicals being discharged into the St. Clair River. The MOE had given C-I-L an "emergency permit" to discharge more than 2 billion litres of treated waste water from its chemical fertilizer plant into the river. However, it turned out that the waste water contained the carcinogen dinitrotoluene. The permit was revoked in September, and C-I-L was required to build a storage pond on its site at Courtright. See David Israelson, "Ontario blocks company's plan to dump cancer-linked waste," *Toronto Star*, September 7, 1987.
29. LIS, "An Environmental Co-operative," *1985 Annual Report* (Sarnia, Ont.: Lambton Industrial Society, c. 1985), p. 24.
30. Ibid., p. 25.
31. Quoted in ibid., p. 2.
32. Meryl Davids, "Detoxing Dow's Reputation," *Public Relations Journal* (January 1987), p. 11.
33. Ibid.
34. Ibid. Naturally, Dow is not the only company engaged in such public relations campaigns. Between 1977 and 1982 DuPont and Monsanto spent over $8 million each year on "image advertizing." The chemical companies' theme was that they were honest corporate citizens, unfairly criticised by opponents using "sensationalist" tactics. However, as Larry George points out, the companies' "commitment to equal time in the market place of ideas ... has been a bit one-sided: when Central Michigan University permitted Jane Fonda to give a talk criticising Dow Chemical and other businesses, the company cut off all its gifts to the school." (Larry N. George, "Love Canal and the Politics of Corporate Terrorism," *Socialist Review* vol. 12, no. 6 (November/December 1982), p. 24.)
35. "One company's commitment to increasing organ donation," *Transplant Lifelines* vol. 2, no. 2 (May 1986), p. 2.

36. Quoted in ibid.
37. *Transplant Lifelines* vol. 1, issue 4 (Winter 1986), p. 2.
38. Dow Chemical, "Our Decision—Someone Else's Life," *Dow Canadian Dimensions* vol. 2, no. 2 (May 1986), p. 2.
39. Dow Chemical, "Where does the money go?" *Sarnia Division News* vol. 14, no. 10 (September 9, 1987), p. 4.
40. Ibid., p. 5.
41. Buzzelli and Saddy quoted in the *Sarnia Observer*, December 15, 1986, p. 1.
42. Charles C. Mann, "The Town of Dow," *Business Month* (December 1987), p. 59.
43. Andrew Walker, "Investing in the future," *Dow Canada Dimensions* (October/November 1987), p. 6.
44. Ibid., p. 7.
45. Ibid., p. 8.
46. *Sarnia Observer*, December 15, 1986, p. 1.
47. "Dow's eyes and ears in Ottawa," *Dow Canada Chemicals* (Oct/Nov. 1987), pp. 4-5.
48. Kristina Lee, interview, May 3, 1988.
49. Don Laprise, interview by author, Wallaceburg, Ont., May 7, 1988.
50. Letter from John Vincett, vice-president of Pat Delbridge Associates, to Rick Coronado, president of the Windsor and District Clean Water Alliance, dated April 4, 1988. Copy in author's possession.
51. According to the outline for the Community Advisory Panel of the CCPA: "The panel will have a close working relationship with the Director of Public Affairs for the CCPA, who will attend panel meetings. Reports will be made to the Director of Public Affairs summarizing the content of each meeting, but without identifying individual panel members (seemingly not necessary, as s/he would be at the meetings anyway). The Director of Public Affairs will make reports to the CCPA Board from time to time on the viewpoints expressed by the panels, and will report to the panel on a regular basis on the response from CCPA" (Ibid., p. 2).
52. Ibid., p. 1.
53. *Sarnia Observer*, October 16, 1986, p. 15.
54. This is Kristina Lee's version of the statement.
55. Lee, interview, May 2, 1988.
56. Note the similarity between these labels and the reaction to Greenpeace's actions in Sarnia. *The Sarnia Observer* and Conservative politicians' condemnation of Greenpeace, the NDP, and the Liberals used the same words, which found echoes downstream, even among some of the citizen activists.
57. *Sarnia Observer*, October 16, 1986, p. 15.
58. "Warning issued for Greenpeace" (editorial), *Sarnia Observer*, August 19, 1985.
59. Bradley, Sarnia MPP Andy Brandt, and Lambton MPP Dave Smith accompanied officials of the local MOE office and "business leaders" on a tour of the Tricil facilities near Brigden, and a cruise up the St. Clair River. (See Mary Jane Egan, "Environment Minister Tours Sarnia," *Sarnia Observer*, August 24, 1985, p. 1.)
60. "Group's scare tactics didn't work in Sarnia" (editorial), *Sarnia Observer*, August 26, 1985.
61. Gord Henderson, "Toxins worse than thought," and Brian Fox, "Province orders shakeup," *Windsor Star*, November 5, 1985, pp. A1, A2.
62. "Pollution: We've had enough!" (editorial), *Windsor Star*, November 1985 (no date). Note how both editorials end with statements of concern for the future health of children.
63. "More facts needed on river reports" (editorial), *Sarnia Observer*, November 6, 1985.
64. "Rae's media-circus only clouds issue" (editorial), *Sarnia Observer*, November 8, 1985.
65. Ibid. It is interesting how Andy Brandt's role is never depicted as partisan; he and his party are viewed as representatives of the industry's and—by extension—the community's interests.
66. Chris Vander Doelen and Ted Whipp, "Sarnia hates pollution talk," *Windsor Star*, November 7, 1985.
67. "Public debate needed on river pollution" (editorial), *Sarnia Observer*, December 6, 1985.
68. Mary Jane Egan, "Drinking water called safe," *Sarnia Observer*, December 9, 1985, p. A1.
69. Quoted by Joe Belanger, "Citizens' group forms to clean up lakes," *Windsor Star*, December 16, 1985.
70. Ibid. Immediately following the formation of the Clean Water Alliance, there were two "spills" from Polysar (containing isobutylene polymer and tertiary butyl alcohol). According to the company, a valve was "left open" and the computer which monitors waste water flow was "down for repairs," so the alarm did not sound. The chemicals are water soluble, so they were quickly

dispersed in the water and no clean-up was possible. This is the classic example of the industry's "spill" scenario.
71. Quoted by Linda McQuaig, "Publicity over blob in river irks many Sarnia residents," *The Globe and Mail*, February 7, 1986, p. A16.
72. Ibid.
73. Dow Chemical Canada, *Sarnia Division News* vol. 14, no. 10 (September 9, 1987), p. 5.
74. Quoted by McQuaig, "Publicity over blob."
75. James Hembree, quoted in the *Sarnia Observer*, February 8, 1986.
76. "$12 million to be spent by Dow in three-year program," Sarnia Observer, March 18, 1986, p. 13. (When Dow announced that it would spend $12 million over three years to improve pollution abatement at its Sarnia site [March 17, 1986], the news was billed in the *Observer* as "Environmental Concerns Top-Priority at Dow" [editorial, March 18, 1986].)
77. See Don Tschirhart, "Toxic vapour escapes near Port Huron," *Detroit News*, May 14, 1986; Dudley K. Pierson, "Canada's failure to disclose toxic leak angers state," *Detroit News*, May 15, 1986. Michigan authorities were angry about the incident, especially after six Dow chemical spills into the river since August 1985.
78. Mike Fisher, "Greenpeace seeks public involvement," *Sarnia Observer*, July 24, 1986, p. 1.
79. Mike Fisher, "No clear answers yet available about river's threat to health," *Sarnia Observer*, August 23, 1986.
80. Ron Denning, quoted by Mike Fisher, "Industry, government could clash over harsher pollution penalties," *Sarnia Observer*, August 27, 1986, p. 1.
81. Ibid.
82. Another example of workers' complicity in polluting practices is described in chapter 12, note 41.
83. Interview with Steven, December 3, 4, 1986, Sarnia.
84. Ibid.
85. These were the words of the Ministry official cited in chapter 3.
86. "The defence begins the day the discharge occurs—environmental prosecutions in Ontario,"in The Canadian Institute, *The Fundamentals of Environmental Law and Regulation* (Toronto: The Canadian Institute, 1994), p. 28.
87. "Michael" was interviewed in Sarnia December 4, 1986 and May 5,6, 1988.
88. Dowtherm was one of the substances detected in the blob in 1984-85.
89. "Peter," interviewed May 5, 1988, Sarnia.
90. Huw Beynon and Theo Nichols, eds., *Living with Capitalism*, (Boston: Routledge and Kegan Paul, 1977) p. 159. The "apathy" argument, also made by CAW union officials, is examined further in the next chapter.
91. This observation recalls Gramsci's characterisation of the relationship of rank-and-file workers to the union as an essentially passive one—like that of a voter who periodically casts a ballot in an election.

Part four

---

*Social Unionism and Social Movements:
The Canadian Autoworkers*

[12]

The CAW Environmental Policy

SOCIAL UNIONISM

The strategic perspectives discernible at different levels of the CAW leadership in the 1980s reflect the internal tensions created by the union's attempts to make links with other social movements, and to assert a more active influence in the politico-ideological sphere. The national leadership is concerned with effecting social and political changes. It has recognized the limitations of collective bargaining in the advancement of workers' needs and rights; and it has a sense of solidarity with other sections of the working class. Yet there is a tension between a democratic socialist direction, and a trade union structure and culture which are also characterised by social-democratic and hierarchical assumptions and practices.[1] The need to take positions on the issues raised by alternative social movements with considerable cultural and political influence (including on the conditions of trade union struggles) has led the union leadership to redefine (or reaffirm) its conception of unionism. This was also the case with the ECWU, which, for the most part, chose a direction in the 1980s which I have characterised as "elite-corporatist": that is, a strategy of negotiations among elites (union leaders, management, government) both at the level of bargaining and with regard to participation in corporatist consultative processes. This strategy is contrasted to one of rank-and-file education and mobilization, around an agenda of social and political reforms which extend beyond the corporate interests or identity of a particular group of workers.

The CAW, however, is the bearer of a different tradition of industrial unionism, which the union itself identifies as "social unionism."[2] The *Statement of Principles* in the Union's Constitution expresses a commitment to democratic unionism and to social unionism, defined in the following ways:

> [Democratic unionism] means a union which reflects the goals of its membership, allows the members full participation, and encourages workers to develop their own skills and understanding. Internal democracy also means we view each other as equals. Racial discrimination or sexual harassment violate our principles, undermine our solidarity and erode our strength. We not only oppose such responses but will actively work to overcome them...
>
> Unions are central to our society being democratic because: Unions bring a measure of democracy to the place of work, which is so central to people's lives. Unions act as partial counterweight to corporate power and the corporate agenda in society more generally.
>
> [Social unionism means that] our collective bargaining strength is based on our internal organization and mobilization, but it is also influenced by the more general climate around us: laws, policies, the economy, and social attitudes. Furthermore, our lives extend beyond collective bargaining and the workplace

and we must concern ourselves with issues like housing, taxation, education, medical services, the environment, the international economy.

Social unionism means unionism which is rooted in the workplace but understands the importance of participating in, and influencing, the general direction of society.[3]

Canadian political scientist Charlotte Yates has researched the origins of the CAW's "left-syndicalist tradition" and the "entrenchment of a union culture characterized by high rank-and-file participation and a strong commitment to internal union democracy" in the struggles of the 1940s, noting that this tradition was kept alive in certain core locals.[4] The struggles of the 1970s and 1980s then revitalized the collective identity and militant tradition of the UAW-Canadian Section. (The UAW-Canada broke away from the international union in 1985 to become the Canadian Auto Workers Union.)

In the 1970s struggles both inside the union and between the union, corporations and the federal government, cemented union members' commitment to their union as an agent of economic and political change. The growing influence of left-wing militants combined with the fact that the strategies employed in the 1970s were union-centred, rekindled the syndicalist ideological orientation of Canadian autoworkers. These developments, in conjunction with the success of mobilization strategies, expanded the Canadian UAW's perceived field of action as militancy now became a viable strategy for pursuing its objectives. In turn, organisational changes, such as the establishment of a Canadian research staff and a Canadian newspaper, enhanced the capacity of the Canadian UAW to successfully pursue its chosen strategy, independent of the International Union.[5]

These struggles, which cannot be described in detail here, included the winning of wage and benefit parity for Québec autoworkers with autoworkers in Ontario, the extension of French language services, union recognition of Québec as one of two founding nations in the Canadian confederation (the "two nations" position in Canadian constitutional politics), and a favourable position toward the Parti Québecois, which enjoyed growing support from francophone workers in Québec. These decisions avoided the breaking away of Québec autoworkers to form a Québec-based union, which, as Yates points out, would "destroy (the UAW's) monopolistic position in the auto industry and raise the possibility of union competition and variability on issues such as wages and benefits."[6] Also important were strikes, mass demonstrations, and the general strike organised in 1976 against the federal government's wage and price controls policy (1975-1978). The third factor discussed by Yates is the "series of violent and bitter strikes" in the 1970s, in which the union confronted massive police support for the companies, and which served to further cement solidarity among workers. In 1978, Robert White, associated with the "militant syndicalist tradition" of the UAW, was elected Director of the Canadian Region of the UAW. Yates shares the view of other observers of CAW leadership when she says that "the door to future militancy and independent action had been opened." [7]

Corporate restructuring in the 1980s gave the union cause to call on that tradition. In the early 1980s, the union responded to threatened plant closures by sit-down strikes, winning some important victories in terms of severance packages and government legislation. The corporations began demanding wage and benefit concessions, using the threat of lay-offs and plant closures. It is also important to note, as Yates does, that the corporations also initiated an ideological campaign "to mobilize workers and the UAW behind corporate strategy."

A new management discourse of team work, joint decision-making and "equality of sacrifice" accompanied corporate demands for concessions, heightened pressure for QWL programmes and the reorganisation of production. The auto corporations were intent upon allying workers and the UAW in corporate struggles to restore their competitiveness.[8]

The responses of the UAW international (US) leadership and those of the UAW-Canada leadership to these corporate demands have been much studied and compared.[9] In the view of the CAW's director of research, Sam Gindin, the capitulation of the UAW international leadership to concessions reflected "the refusal to fight," and the "rationalization of those defeats as 'victories.'"

In early 1982, the Canadians made the key decision—the one that launched the eventual breakaway from the Americans. The Canadian UAW chose to break ranks with the Americans and reject an early opening of the agreements with Ford and GM. Under the leadership of Bob White, the union saw the basic danger of concession bargaining: if the union consented to participate, it would collapse from internal conflicts and nullify its role as a social force within the Canadian labour movement and in Canadian society.[10]

Due to a complex set of factors, including the union's militant tradition, its education programme, its leadership, as well as differences in the economic and political situations of autoworkers in the United States and Canada, the Canadian autoworkers were successful in resisting concessions in the 1980s, and even in making breakthroughs in collective bargaining. These successes added to the confidence of the union members, especially in their capacity for national autonomy from the international union. They also transformed the CAW into the leading industrial union in the Canadian labour movement.

In the 1990s, the CAW has maintained its difference with respect to its response to management pressures to restructure work and reward systems along the lines of "lean production." Canadian analysts Pradeep Kumar and John Holmes describe the auto corporations' strategy in the 1990s, stemming from such concerns as the saturation of markets, the internationalization of production, and competition from Japanese firms, in the following terms:

> The Big Three have responded to this competitive crisis by revamping their production, supply and management systems to enhance efficiency, flexibility and product quality and by focusing on rationalization and cost-cutting. A key element of this "lean production" strategy is experimentation with Japanese style work organisation, human resource practices and enterprise unionism. Typically, the workplace changes sought by employers have included flexible work rules and work arrangements, fewer job classifications, variable compensation, team work, multi-tasking, and employee and union involvement in shopfloor decision-making to foster a "participatory" enterprise culture.
>
> These attempts by management to restructure work and reward systems, in line with the principles of lean production, have had numerous effects on workers and their unions including an increase in insecure and stressful jobs, the erosion of worker rights and union institutional security, and the breakdown of labour solidarity.[11]

As Kumar and Holmes' analysis of CAW responses shows, the union has maintained the position that union-management relations are fundamentally adversarial. This posi-

The CAW Environmental Policy

tion is contextualised by the discourse of the educational programme and union-sponsored campaigns, which seeks to create collective, working-class identity, and an implicitly Marxist understanding of capitalism. Thus, unlike the ECWU, the CAW leadership has unambiguously rejected the possibility of a "partnership"—implying equal powers—between workers and owners.

> This partnership and its promises are false. For all the talk about jointness and worker control, employers are certainly not putting equality between themselves and their employees on the agenda. Management will continue to jealously guard the management's rights clauses and to unilaterally decide when to modernize, how much to invest, what to produce, with what kind of technology and so on. The truth is that management's agenda is not about surrendering its power, but of finding sophisticated ways to extend it.[12]

However, rather than simply refusing to endorse management proposals, the union has drawn on the experiences of QWL experiments in the 1970s and work restructuring in the 1980s to develop a response which Kumar and Holmes describe as both "defensive and pro-active ...in the sense ...of taking the initiative, proposing alternatives, and negotiating for them," and reflecting "a culture of resistance and change within an adversarial framework of union-management relations."

> The key elements of the agenda include (1) challenging "the ideology of lean production, both in terms of its structures for partnership and its underlying logic of competitiveness," (2) a focus on the changes to jobs and production systems, and (3) responding to "new managerial techniques and workplace structures (teams, rotation, etc.)..." [The 1989 policy statement on work reorganisation] made clear that while "there is nothing inherently bad about working together and there may be some advantages," the union "will not support management attempts to use the team concepts or quality circles to manage the workplace by stress, to introduce speed up or to encourage workers to discipline each other."[13]

These positions are restated in the 1996 Collective Bargaining Programme of the CAW, which also refers to the union's culture of resistance, and identifies working conditions, workers' control over their time, and outsourcing of jobs as the key issues facing union members.[14] Educational brochures prepared by departments of the national union in recent years have also focused on the need to restrict overtime work (as a strategy to create employment) and to fight speed-up, connecting worker exhaustion to increased rates of accidents, injuries, and other problems.[15]

In his book *The Canadian Auto Workers: Birth and Transformation of a Union*, Sam Gindin discusses the importance of union educational efforts in creating this "culture of resistance" within a rapidly diversifying organisation which is also undergoing a crucial generational change (as the auto workers radicalized in the 1960s and 1970s are replaced by younger workers hired into "new management style" plants). The CAW's educational programme is paid for by employers' contributions, negotiated in collective bargaining, but administered completely by the union. Contributions per worker range between one and three cents per hour. The first Paid Education Leave (PEL) programme was negotiated in 1977, and, according to Sam Gindin, was "inspired by the educational work done within the Swedish trade union movement."

> The immediate drive to put the new programme in place came from the top. Union policy was that no staff rep could take it off the table without authorization from the Canadian director's office. Once negotiated, a committee that

includes the local and the education department chooses the students to attend the course. As of 1995, some 5,000 workers had gone through the four-week course... The PEL programme wasn't set up to provide bargaining and contract-administration skills but to contribute the background for using and developing such skills. PEL aims at providing working people with an understanding of capitalism, their place in this system, the role of unions as independent working class organisations, the history of workers and their organisations, and the principles and philosophy of the [CAW]. The program's goal is to develop future activists with a commitment to the union and to progressive change...

The "culture of resistance" that had developed in the union was rooted in a historical legacy and recent involvement in struggles. The role of education was to reinforce and consolidate that culture ("education" also included films, pamphlets, union newspapers, music, and even writing classes that encouraged workers to resist the dominant culture and tell their own stories). As a culture that permeated the union, it did not depend on or wait for leadership from "the top"...

When [Prime Minister] Mulroney announced his intention to move towards the FTA [Free Trade Agreement] with the United States in 1986, the CAW was there in opposition with its credibility and organisational/financial clout. Leadership meetings and forums were held in every community with a CAW base across the country. Bob White, as leader of the CAW, was generally viewed as a central leader and spokesperson for the anti-free trade coalition. Over one million pamphlets were distributed in the plants, to homes, at schools, and in malls. Full-page ads appeared in newspapers across the country when opposition to the agreement was flagging and in need of revitalization. And CAW activists across the country brought the issue into the plants and worked with others to introduce more Canadians to politics by way of the anti-FTA fight.[16]

The CAW's environmental policy since the mid-1980s allows us to examine both the potential and the limits of "social unionism" as a counter-hegemonic strategy of union leadership, entailing convergence with other social movements.

THE CAW ENVIRONMENTAL POLICY

In 1986 the national leadership of the CAW decided to "reactivate" the union's national and local environmental activities. Prior to the Canadian section's separation from the UAW, "recreation and conservation" standing committees were included in the union's constitution. These functioned mainly to organise sporting events and recreational activities like road trips and family days or picnics. The conservation side of this committee's mandate had largely fallen by the wayside. According to the Chairperson of the CAW Council Environment Committee at that time, Bill Van Gaal:

The reactivation of the CAW Environment Committee and Local Committees came as a result of a decision by the CAW that all Council Committees should be actively participating and [the CAW] made a number of appointments to the Committees. Prior to 1985 the Environment Committee of the Council had been inactive for about five years... Our new CAW-Canada Constitution spells out a separate Environmental Committee, with the result that as Standing Committee elections come about in many Locals, they are electing an Environmental Committee or Chairperson. The process is slow, but it is happening.[17]

In other words, prior to the separation from the UAW, the Recreation and

Conservation Committee had not been very active in environmental issues. The new constitution of the CAW provided for a separation of these areas of work. Locals would be encouraged to elect Recreation and Sports, and Environmental standing committees. The environmental committees were only beginning to get organised in the fall of 1986, when I made my first trip to Windsor. The CAW Canada Council Environmental Committee was formed in the summer of 1987. In my meetings with union officials and rank-and-file participants in the environmental committees, I tried to determine why the CAW national leadership had decided to elevate environmental concerns in the list of union priorities, and whether the decision reflected any pressure from rank-and-file members for such an extension of union activities. I also wanted to know why environmental committees had gotten off the ground where they had, i.e., in Windsor and St. Catharines, and not elsewhere.

It emerged from the interviews that the decision to associate the union more strongly with environmental concern stemmed from:
1. the perception by the national leadership that environmental issues were commanding considerable public attention (as evidenced by numerous polls and by the higher priority granted the environment by political parties), and that extra-parliamentary organizations were becoming increasingly influential in shaping public policy (including in the area of the economy);
2. the consensus among the higher levels of union officials and staff that the union should play a high profile political role in Ontario and nationally, in alliance with the NDP: the objective was to make the CAW a leader in the Canadian union movement. (Policies on sexual equality, anti-racism, and international solidarity have also undergone a "renewal" along with the new attention paid to the environment, and to the national debate over the Free Trade Agreement in 1987-88.)

Gary Parent, vice-president in 1986-88 of CAW Local 444 in Windsor, is one of many CAW officials who are also NDP members and who have run—or considered running—as NDP electoral candidates. Parent was a candidate for the NDP in the 1984 federal election. When asked about the timing of the CAW's decision to implement environmental committees, his answer was that "polls have shown that the environmental issue was near the top of the list in people's concerns [in the election]."[18] As part of a political strategy, the CAW's environmental policy had a success in 1988: Bob White was appointed to the Ontario Government's Round Table on Sustainable Development.

The "top down" nature of the environmental committee decision was confirmed by virtually all of the union officials and environment committee activists interviewed. Ken Gerard and Frank McAnally (Presidents of Locals 444 and 200 respectively) referred specifically to the leadership of Bob White, President of the CAW-Canada. According to Gerard, the push for more environmental involvement was "coming from the top, since 1985." He said, "Before that, there were certain local unions that had been interested [but] in the majority, I would say, there wasn't much interest. But there's a lot of pressure coming from the top."[19] McAnally described the CAW as a "pro-active union [about] things going on in the community and in the country." "I guess this is just another issue that we saw fit as the leadership of the CAW to get involved in." When asked about the timing of the decision, McAnally said, "It's the personality of Bob White that gives it more attention than it's ever gotten before. He's been more vocal on a number of issues than his predecessors."[20] Jack Ewart, Local 1973's representative on the CAW Canada Council, chairperson at the GM trim plant in Windsor, and member of the local's environmental committee, also attributed the new environmental emphasis to the foresight of Bob White: "Bob White, in my eyes [is] basically of the same mold as Walter Reuther. Everything is a number one priority to him. He found that the structure of [the] environment [committee—i.e., the Recreation and Conservation Committee] was basically a low-key, dying element that was not being brought out strongly enough."[21]

Thus in 1986 the CAW changed the bylaws of its national constitution to require every local to establish a standing committee on the environment. According to Ewart, in March 1987 the CAW Canada Council Environmental Standing Committee drafted a "structure" for the locals to follow. Gary St. Laurent, a plant chairperson (full time union official) in CAW Local 195, claimed that the environmental decision was "just a common sense decision that was made and brought out at the national level."[22] The editor of the Windsor area publication of the CAW, Tom Burton, said that the CAW was "probably more upfront" about environmental issues than any other union. "Our top leadership," he claimed, are committed to the environmental cause and this involvement is "filtering back down. The filtering-down effect is more prevalent in the CAW than in any other labour movement in Canada. That's indicative of the kind of leadership we have."[23] Rank-and-file environmental activists in the locals had the same impression of the origins of the decision to create environmental standing committees, although they were naturally more concerned with emphasizing the importance of what was happening locally.

There was no significant pressure from the rank and file for this restructuring of the standing committees or for the extension of the union's social activism regarding the environment. Indeed, the affirmative action and women's committee policies—which did have a mobilized base in the union and were also being implemented in 1986-1988— were meeting with some resistance. Local union officials already claimed a problem with rank-and-file "apathy," i.e., unconstituted or inactive standing committees, and could not envisage rank-and-file support for a new area of union involvement. Moreover, with major restructuring of the auto industry taking place, issues of job security, changing labour-management relations, protection of wages from concession demands and inflation, and so on, were the primary concerns of rank-and-file members and union officials. In these circumstances, the decision to create an environmental "department" in the CAW was really the project of the national staff and officials; it was taken up by a small number of rank-and-file activists who saw in the national decision an opportunity to pursue their particular environmental and political objectives. While the decision coincided with local developments in Windsor and St. Catharines, leading to the implementation of environmental committees in some locals, it did not originate with any groundswell of rank-and-file concern with environmental issues.[24]

FORMATION OF THE LOCAL ENVIRONMENTAL COMMITTEES: POLICY AND STRUCTURE

OFFICIAL AND ACTIVIST VIEWS

By September 1987 the national staff were aware of the existence of environmental committees in three locals: 444 (Chrysler-Windsor); 1973 (GM-Windsor); 199 (Amalgamated—15 plants—St. Catharines).[25] During a July-August 1987 trip to Windsor, I learned that two other locals in the Windsor area were taking positions on environmental issues and attempting to get environmental committees formed. Local 89 (General Chemical/Allied Signal)[26] in Amherstburg had a three-member environmental committee by August 1987, although it had not organised any activities.[27] Also, the plant chairperson at Kelsey Hayes, Gary St. Laurent, was acting as the representative of Local 195 (amalgamated-parts companies, covering 74 plants) on the Windsor and District Labour Council's Environment Committee in July 1987. By May 1988 Local 195 had an Environment Standing Committee, composed of St. Laurent and two other union officials.[28]

St. Catharines and Windsor, where the CAW represents large work forces,[29] have some of the most serious environmental problems in the country. Citizens of the St. Catharines area had been fighting a proposal by the Ontario Waste Management Corporation (OWMC) to build a toxic waste centre on 135 hectares of agricultural land in the township of West Lincoln. In November 1986 the West Lincoln Task Force Against Toxic Waste, claiming 1,000 members from Niagara-on-the-Lake, Peltham, Lincoln, and St. Catharines, held a People Power Convention, attended by about 1,500 people. The battle over the OWMC proposal was still on in 1988. In addition, various citizens' and environmental groups were involved in lobbying around the Canada-United States Niagara River Toxics Management Plan.

Developments in the Windsor area were described in the preceding chapter, dealing with toxic chemical pollution of the St. Clair and Detroit Rivers. The key issues from 1985 onward in this region included chemical industry pollution, industrial pollution of the Detroit River, the construction of a giant incinerator in Detroit,[30] problems at Detroit Edison's Fermi II nuclear reactor,[31] and various problems associated with the local auto industry (especially air emissions and disposal of hazardous wastes). Citizens' organisations involved in these issues included the Windsor and District Clean Water Alliance (CWA), People for Clean Air (which became the Evergreen Alliance), Citizens Concerned about Fermi II, and the St. Clair River International Citizens' Network.

The St. Catharines and Windsor cases have in common not only the context of severe industrial pollution problems, and the mobilization of large numbers of citizens concerned with these problems by the mid-1980s, but also the personal trajectories of their key activists. The leading member of the environmental committee of CAW Local 199 in St. Catharines, Catherine Murney, became involved in environmental politics as a result of the mobilization against the proposed toxic waste disposal site. She began attending environmental hearings and meetings, where she soon realized that "the corporations and governments were represented, but not labour."[32] Murney was also a member of the NDP, and a rank-and-file worker at the GM foundry in St. Catharines. When the CAW-Canada Council decision to implement environmental committees in the locals became known, she decided to try to use her union organisation as a vehicle for environmental work. Local 199's primary environmental concern was—as a result of the initial emphasis of its members—opposition to the toxic waste dump. The environment committee worked closely with Concerned Citizens, an organisation of "farmers and townspeople." With a base in the local's environment committee, Murney became a key rank-and-file spokesperson for the CAW on environmental issues in the region. She attended meetings of the Ontario Labour-Environment Co-ordinating Committee in 1987-88, and attempted to influence the direction of the CAW Canada Council Environment Committee.

The key activist in Local 444's environment committee (Windsor) was Rick Coronado. A line worker at the Chrysler van plant, Coronado was involved in the Windsor and District Clean Water Alliance, and through this group made connections with environmental organisations (GLU, Greenpeace, CELA, etc.), the Great Lakes Institute in Windsor, and area citizens' groups. He also had a left political perspective on this work, having been involved in radical politics and rank-and-file militancy in the 1960s and 1970s. When Coronado learned of the CAW Council decision to implement environmental committees, he immediately sought to combine his union and environmental objectives by organising an environmental committee in Local 444.[33]

Both Gordon Taylor of Local 1973 and Lynwood Martin of Local 89, key members of their locals' environment committees, had previously been active in occupational health and safety issues. They were also involved with Essex County Citizens Against Fermi II, and in other area environmental issues (e.g., the Detroit incinerator, water quality, Ford Foundry pollution). Their politicization about environmental problems developed through such citizens' campaigns, and they saw their environmental work within the union as an extension of occupational health and safety struggles.

In these four cases, the politicization of union activists about environmental issues originated in non-union led campaigns; the committees have continued their close links with these organisations, while attempting to use the organisational opportunities they see in the union structure. Although they had no part in the decision of the CAW Council to implement environment committees, the policy has opened up some space for these rank-and-file activists to pursue their political and environmental concerns within the union. Thus a key element in the explanation of why environment committees had been established by 1987 in Locals 199, 444, 1973, and 89 is the presence of a small number of rank-and-file activists, who were already involved in environmental politics. Of course (as the president of Local 444 pointed out), the larger locals have a greater membership pool to draw on in the formation of committees, and generally take a leading role in union affairs. However, the GM local in Oshawa, for example, is the largest in the union, but had no environment committee as of spring 1989. Environmental issues have not taken on the same local urgency and prominence in Oshawa as they have in Windsor and the Niagara Basin; in the latter areas there are vocal citizens' organisations which have achieved some influence with provincial and federal environmental authorities and the media, and have attracted the participation of some industrial workers.

The conclusion that the CAW's decision to create environmental standing committees did not emerge from rank-and-file pressure for a new area of union involvement is supported by the composition of the committees, and by the general nature of their activities. In addition, the results of surveys conducted between July 1987 and July 1988 (see appendix 1) show that, while workers overwhelmingly agreed that the union should be involved in environmental issues (88.8 percent), they did not see ways to participate within the existing union structures. In the first year of activity of the environment committees only 3.4 percent of workers surveyed said they had participated in activities of the committees (and these were likely accounted for by environment committee members or other union representatives). In a nutshell, the environment committees were formed like any other committees at the local or national levels—by the union staff and officials—and as representative rather than participatory bodies.

Local 444

There was unanimous agreement among my interviewees about the events leading to the formation of Local 444's environment committee (EC): it resulted from the initiative of Rick Coronado. The local president endorsed the initiative because of the desires to comply with the CAW Canada Council decision, and to demonstrate leadership in the new area. Gerard was pleased to have such a dedicated volunteer to carry out the environmental work of the local. According to Mike Longmoore, a rank-and-file member of the environment committee and a Local 444 delegate to the Windsor and District Labour Council, "Rick Coronado...went to the local and they ratified his chairmanship... Rick went to see people he knew...and co-opted them on to the committee."[34] Gary Parent, vice-president of Local 444 and president of the Labour Council, said, "Rick came to me and said he had heard about the Council decision; I said yes. I let him have a talk with Kenny [Gerard]... From that we formed our committee. Rick talked to me in [my capacity as president of the] Labour Council about an environmental committee; I said yes."

The first step for the activists was to win executive endorsement. Since this suited the interests of the executive very well, and they approved the individuals concerned, the

The CAW Environmental Policy

endorsement was forthcoming. The committee operated on an ad hoc basis until November 1987, when it became a standing committee. (The affirmative action and women's committees shared this situation.) In the interim, the EC's status was that of a sub-committee to the political action and occupational health and safety committees. With the election, Coronado continued as chairperson of the environment committee, and three other rank-and-file members were elected. Standing committee status entitles committee members to some paid leave of absence from their jobs, as well as the right to request money from the local's budget. All expenditures must, however, be authorized by the executive.

Local 444 has a high public profile in various areas of social activism in Windsor, including (since 1986) environmental issues; in 1986-89, its environment committee appeared to be the most active in the CAW. It is particularly notable, therefore, that this reputation was due largely to the work of one person, the committee chairperson. Mostly on his own time, and with very little recompense, he represented Local 444 at numerous meetings and events around the region. He continued, moreover, to act as the chairperson of the Windsor and District Clean Water Alliance (CWA), and as the delegate of Local 444 to the environmental committee of the Windsor and District Labour Council, as well as holding positions on the board of Great Lakes United.[35] As a representative of Local 444, Coronado attended the meetings of the Ontario Labour-Environment Co-ordinating Committee which were co-sponsored by the Ontario Environmental Network and the Ontario Federation of Labour (OFL), and held during 1987 and 1988. He also acted as a labour representative on the Public Advisory Committees appointed for the Detroit River and St. Clair River Remedial Action Plans (see chapter 7). In his capacity as chairperson of the CWA, he presented briefs to the Great Lakes United Citizens' Hearings on the Great Lakes Water Quality Agreement (October 1986), attended various government-sponsored and other meetings, and served on the Windsor-Essex County Water Quality Liaison Committee. He also acted as a liaison between the CWA and the St. Clair River International Citizens Network. He was involved in the attempt to create a Green Centre in Windsor in 1988. In short, there has not been an environmental cause in the region, virtually, in which Coronado has not had a hand since the mid-1980s. Practically everyone involved in environmental activities in the southwestern Ontario network knows Coronado as a key propelling force in labour-environment initiatives.

Naturally, all this reflects well on the leadership of Local 444. Local President Gerard took credit for recognizing the importance of the environmental issue, and for sponsoring the work of the committee. Comparing the CAW with the Energy and Chemical Workers' Union, Gerard said: "[Those] unions don't have the input from the top that they really should have… the leadership of [those] unions are not putting the attention that they ought to be putting in the question of the environment… [W]e don't have that problem in the CAW. We have active committees." Executive members also indicated that they were particularly impressed by the fact that Coronado put in long hours of work on his own time, and paid most of his expenses out of pocket; the environment committee—unlike some of the other, more established and traditional committees—offered few perks for its members. (Its 1987-1989 budget was, according to Coronado, nonexistent, and it was rare to have even travel expenses reimbursed.) Gary Parent, vice-president of Local 444, said: "I wish I had a quarter of the energy that Rick has…and, I mean, not ask for anything. He just does it because he feels that dedicated to the environmental cause. And we're very fortunate to have a person like that in our local." Indeed, both Parent and Gerard referred to the problem of people running for committee positions in order to get time off plant work, trips to conferences, and so on. Their views of such problems with the committees, like their views of the "apathy," self-interest, and conservatism of their membership, were the counterpart of perceptions of themselves as members of a progressive leadership. Gary Parent, for example, said: "Sometimes we get accused, quite frankly, even by our own membership, of getting involved in too much, but at the same time, we feel that it's needed, because the issues that we get involved in are social issues that do affect them, *even though they don't realize it at the time*... environmental issues, for example" (emphasis added).

The president of Local 1498 (clerical, office, professional workers at Chrysler), Jo-Anne Bawden,[36] expressed a much more critical opinion of the regular mode of operation and motivations of the union officials in Local 444. She said that committee positions are generally treated like "booty," hence the executives' surprise at Coronado's motivation and energy. When asked why Local 444 appeared to be leading on environmental issues, she expressed a view which was also voiced by various rank and file and non-union observers:

> There are two reasons. One is that it's the "in thing" to do... But [Ken Gerard] got lucky... He's got Rick Coronado... He's using Rick to further publicity for the local union on the environmental issues. It makes Kenny look good. Rick does [that work] all by himself... It doesn't have anything to do with the environment, sorry.[37]

Gerard was very close to the national leadership. Since 1985 he had been one of the five top officers of the CAW, as a National Executive Board member and the President of the Canadian Council. From 1982 to 1987 he was chairperson of the Chrysler- UAW/CAW Bargaining Council, and chairperson of the negotiating committee for all Chrysler workers in Canada. Like other executive officials, he was well established in the union bureaucracy; he had been a full-time union official since 1963, when he ran for the plant chairperson position at Chrysler's #3 assembly plant in Windsor. From there, he advanced up through the ranks. His periodic re-election as President of Local 444 was a foregone conclusion. When he and the entire executive were acclaimed in the March 1988 elections, Gerard interpreted this as an unparalleled vote of confidence and praise from the rank and file.[38] As president of Local 444 and a holder of various national union positions, Gerard wielded considerable powers of patronage, approval, and veto. This was apparent in the behaviour of lower-ranking officials toward him, and in the commonly made assumption that proposals or requests would require Gerard's endorsement before they might have any hope of implementation.[39]

Gerard was aware that "the national" had added the environment to the list of the union's social activism commitments. In addition, he was very proud of his local's leading role in the union. The existence of an active, high-profile environment committee certainly enhanced the leadership's prestige, and its standing with the national. Although the committee had not been given a budget, and was not considered as deserving of resources as the higher priority committees (and therefore could do little in the way of educating rank-and-file members) it did enhance the external image of the local very effectively.[40] Because of Coronado's connections with environmental and citizens' groups all over the region, and his willingness to devote virtually every non-working moment (he was still a worker in the van assembly plant) to environmental work, he was the ideal representative of the local and its leadership. From time to time Coronado would draft a letter for the executive officials to sign (e.g., expressing the union's opposition to the construction of the Detroit incinerator without state of the art pollution controls). He kept them informed about current issues, so that they could give comments to the media. He prepared briefs and attended meetings as the representative of the union. All of this created the impression of an environmentally informed and active workforce, but in essence, it remained the work of a few individuals. This is the way the standing committees typically work—as advisory committees for the executive, and as liaisons between the "represented" membership and the "outside" world. CAW Local 444, as mentioned above, had the most rank-and-file and activist committee; the stories of the other committees reveal an even more representational (as opposed to grassroots) model of union activism.

Local 1973

According to Jack Ewart, a full-time union official, the environment committee at Local 1973 (GM-Windsor) was established "almost immediately" after the national by-law change. From 1986 to 1987 Ewart was Local 1973's delegate to the CAW Canada Council, and a member of the Ontario Federation of Labour Energy, Conservation and Pollution Control Committee. He stated that he had been interested in environmental questions for many years, while a representative on the union recreation and conservation committee. Like Gerard, Ewart was a "career" union official; since at least 1975 he had held various positions which had taken him out of the trim plant. Between 1973 and 1982 he sat on all standing committees in the local, and in 1986 he was elected chairperson of the trim plant.

The other member of the environment committee in the 1986-89 period was Gordon Taylor. Taylor—as mentioned above—was a highly trained health and safety instructor as well as a skilled trades worker in the GM transmission plant. When he learned of the CAW Council decision to create environmental committees, he was interested because of his involvement in local environmental issues, and because he saw the new initiative as a natural extension of the union's health and safety concerns. Taylor said that he and Ewart recommended to the local executive that the standing committee on the environment include two representatives, one from the trim plant (about 3200 workers) and one from the transmission plant (about 2300 workers). The executive accepted this idea, the standing committee was created (by changes to the Local's bylaws), and Ewart and Taylor were duly elected to the two positions. (The term of office is three years.) From the outset, Taylor carried most of the load of the committee's activities; Ewart was occupied with other union functions and with his job as plant chairperson. When asked why the committee could not be enlarged, Taylor said that the bylaw would have to be changed. The suggestion that Ewart was monopolizing a position which he occupied in name only was also made in regard to his position on the OFL Committee. According to the rank-and-file activists, Ewart was among the officials who were resisting pressure from the activists for their inclusion in the OFL pollution committee's meetings.

Since 1986, Taylor had represented Local 1973 in the public participation process of the Canadian Environmental Protection Act review, in actions against the Detroit incinerator, in a campaign to prevent Peerless Cement from burning toxic waste in an incinerator, and on the Detroit River Remedial Action Plan. He told me in July 1987 that he was spending at least ten hours a week doing union work in addition to his 40-hour-a-week job at GM. He had also been involved (as an individual) in the Essex County Citizens Against Fermi II group and in a citizens' group protesting pollution from the Ford Foundry. One of the problems Taylor discussed when I interviewed him in May 1988 about developments with the committee, was getting authorization from the executive to pursue environmental activities on company time. Although he was the chairperson of the committee, every time he wanted to go to a meeting or an event, he had to go either to a general membership meeting or to a meeting of the executive board of the local to request the lost time. Unlike Rick Coronado, he was unwilling or unable to subsidize his union work out of his own wages. The executive board required him to present a letter from "the national" authorizing the leave. Taylor complained:

> I shouldn't have to call up to Toronto every damn time and say, "Send a letter down." For example, there may be a meeting I find out about [on short notice]; I won't be able to go. We [Rick and I] go to a tremendous number of meetings. I don't know how Rick does it—*he lives on about three days' pay a week.* He has to take all his time off; he's constantly being hassled by the company [for absenteeism]. And I don't think he's being supported enough by his local. I'm in the same position... I instruct in the plant. I'm responsible for the hazardous materials training, also... Plus we teach off-site, at locals 89, 195. That takes nights off. There's just so many nights you can do it. During the day, I can't be expected to take time off work... This is why we can't be as effective as we should be. We should be allowed this time off and paid for it by the National... I think that as long as I'm showing that I am responsible, I should be allowed to do these things... Sometimes it gets discouraging, it really does, when you have to answer to these guys [local executive members]... We have to have some kind of a mandate from Bob White's office [saying]: "Look, these guys have to function, and they're going to be given authority to do certain things. But they are accountable to the membership."

Taylor had become more aware of the various constraints on rank-and-file activists exercised by those in executive positions:

> Since becoming a member of this committee, I'm finding out all the stumbling blocks that are being thrown in your way. You can't be effective, because you're not given the authority to become effective. And they can control you any time they want. They can either turn it on or turn it off. We're not looking for handouts—we're trying to do something for the membership!

Taylor's complaints were echoed by a member of Local 444's environment committee: "I sometimes get frustrated by the fact that getting time off to go to workshops is very difficult. A lot of times we have to pay our own expenses to go out of town to attend workshops and seminars." This individual urged that the union give "priority consideration" to a full-time, qualified environmental representative.

Local 89

The central member of Local 89's environment committee, Lynwood Martin, was (like Gordon Taylor) a health and safety instructor with a long background in union health and safety issues. He had held various elected positions in the local since 1975, none of them executive positions. Prior to the CAW Council decision to implement environmental standing committees, Martin was active in the NDP and in Essex County Citizens Against Fermi II. Early in 1987 Local 89 created the standing committee and held elections; Martin was acclaimed as chairperson. Two other men were elected as well, but they seem to have had little involvement in environmental activities. He doubted whether the president of the local, Mickey Bertrand, was very informed, either. Indeed, an interview with Bertrand made it clear that—while he made the customary statements about the importance of the environment—he, too, saw the role of the environment committee as that of an advisory body to the executive. Martin had been delegated to handle the environmental area; the president had other priorities. Martin had concluded by 1988 that: "[I]t's the grassroots people like Rick and Gord Taylor and myself that are working on the environment issues. The plant chairpersons and presidents and on up don't seem to have a real feel for environmental issues." When I asked him why he thought these officials were not too interested in grassroots work on environmental issues, he said they were focused on "the same old thing...trying to make the union bigger, settle the contracts..." He also observed that the full-time officials were committed

The CAW Environmental Policy

to securing their positions in the hierarchy:

> Once you get there [into office] you want to do better. There's no sense in sitting there on that job and worrying about your membership. Let somebody else do that [while] you're fighting to get a better job—get to be an international rep, or whatever... Unless you can convince him [the official] that environmental issues are going to be of some benefit to him, then it goes nowhere.

Martin referred to Rick Coronado's position at Local 444: "all of the efforts Rick has put into it, and the union hasn't done anything." "The environmental committee would collapse in that plant," he said, if Rick were to leave.

Martin, like Coronado and Taylor, was conscious of being in a tenuous position between an executive whose approval he must retain (but who were pursuing their own career objectives), and a rank and file that showed little interest in his cause. He complained that he could not engender any support from rank-and-file members for meetings advertised in the plants: "There's no other person in my plant that attends any of the Fermi meetings. We had a big notice campaign for the meeting we had at the University of Windsor... If there was two people from my plant there...I'd be surprised." (This was in May 1988, after the environment committee had been in existence for over a year.)

There were a number of pollution issues in their own work places which Martin said they could not begin to address, because they were still making little headway on occupational health and safety issues. (Martin was a representative on both the occupational health and safety and environment committees during this period.) Among the pollution problems associated with General Chemical's and Allied Signal's plants were emissions of hydrogen flouride gas on a continual basis, which were damaging citizens' gardens and contaminating their water supplies.[41] When I asked him how the committee was progressing in 1988, he reported: "We haven't got anywhere with the environmental issues in the plant, or in Local 89 per se, at any of the plants. The other thing I see [is] that the CAW really hasn't done anything to try and promote [the environmental committees]." The only issue being discussed in the Local 89 environment committee was Fermi II (activities organised in conjunction with the Essex County Citizens Against Fermi II group). According to Martin: "We still have so many problems with health and safety in the plant that trying to get the membership behind us on environmental things is [impossible]."[42]

Martin won an award in February 1988 for his work in occupational health and safety and his involvement in the Fermi II group.[43] In the Local 89 *Report* (March 9, 1988) and the CAW *Guardian* (February 1988), various union officials congratulated Martin. His achievements were indeed significant, but they underline the fact that the environment committees were not reflective of a collective effort. Martin's environmental work had been carried out in virtual isolation from the base and with scant support from higher officials. (This was also true in the case of Ivan Hillier—described in chapter 10—who was given an OFL award for environmental stewardship for his work on Chemical Valley pollution.)

The union publications also exclude any reference to the personal costs of Martin's achievements. Although, as chairperson of the two committees he was entitled to some paid leave from his job, much of his time-off was not compensated. In 1988 he reported that:

> I lose three or four thousand a year by having this job... If I'm on a conference somewhere, I'll get my time [pay for regular work hours missed], but I may be missing out on overtime. I may miss out on a whole weekend [of overtime]. And if

your wife realizes this, then there's a lot of conflict at home... You'll see that everybody who is in a union position is either separated or divorced, or not married.

Local 195

This local did not have an environmental committee in 1987, but one of its elected officials, Gary St. Laurent, was very involved with various environmental issues and committees. In addition to being plant chairperson at Kelsey-Hayes (the Windsor company that makes wheel rims), he was on four Local 195 committees, and two Labour Council committees, including the environmental committee. He was the local's delegate to the Labour Council, and to the CAW Canada Council. St. Laurent described his main concerns as Fermi II, acid rain, water quality, industrial pollution, and recycling. He estimated that he was spending about three hours a week on environmental reading and committee meetings. In addition to his work as plant chairperson, he was attending three or four meetings a week.

Local 195 is an amalgamated local whose 74 different plant units encompassed in the late 1980s about 6,000 workers. Its union structure is therefore different from that of the other locals included in this study. Each plant elects delegates to a General Council of Local 195, according to the sizes of the workforces. Kelsey-Hayes, for example, elected seven or eight delegates to the General Council in 1987. The delegates represent their plants at monthly General Council meetings. Only these delegates elect members of the local's standing committees, although "members at large" may be appointed from the rank and file if such individuals come forward. St. Laurent explained how the standing committee positions are filled:

> The executive has a caucus first, to choose the persons [from the General Council delegates] that the top members of the local would like to see in there—people who are involved in things. Sometimes this caucus chooses the chairperson of the committee only; sometimes it chooses the whole committee. Then you go into the General Council on election night, for the committees, and the floor is open to anybody who wants to run. So, let's say, one person has gotten the nod from caucus; he says, O.K., he'll take the job. Then he goes into the General Council, and when they're holding nominations, that person's automatically got someone there to stand up and put his name in. But then the floor is open for the other three or four people that you need on the committee.[44]

Each standing committee has a chairperson, a financial secretary, and members at large. The chairperson is the spokesperson for the committee, and authorizes expenditures.

Union officials support this method of procedure. In their view, committee positions must be protected from abuse by individuals who would occupy them merely to "get out of work," to enjoy posh hotel rooms while playing hooky from conferences, and so on. The executives claim that they are looking for individuals who have demonstrated a commitment to unionism. Among the CAW executives I spoke with, another qualification was support for the NDP; active Liberal or Conservative Party supporters were vetoed. There are also, on occasion, individuals seen as troublemakers (e.g. critics of the executive) or personally undesirable, who are similarly vetoed.

By May 1988, Local 195 had formed an environmental committee. Its members included St. Laurent and the president of the local, Bruce Boyd. According to St. Laurent: "Boyd took it on because nobody else wanted it." Three other Local 195 members had become involved to some extent in the committee's activities. St. Laurent was still representing Local 195 on the Windsor and District Labour Council environment committee, and he had been appointed to the CAW Canada Council environment committee, which meets in Toronto. He was trying to remain active in the Clean Water Alliance, the Fermi II group, and the Disarmament Coalition. In addition, he had represented the Labour Council environment committee in supporting citizens opposed to the siting of a toxic waste disposal facility near Detroit. The Local 195 environment committee was involved in local efforts to prevent the barging of toxic waste from Detroit to Windsor.

Local 200

In August 1987 the absence of an environmental committee at Ford seemed in itself important.[45] The oldest Ford local in Canada, Local 200 encompassed in 1987 about 4,500 workers in three engine plants, a foundry, and an aluminum casting plant. Before the 1950s it had a militant history, but in the 1980s it was considered weak and defensive.[46]

The Ford local in Windsor was the auto industry workforce most directly confronted with a jobs-versus-the-environment conflict. The Ford Foundry on Drouillard Road had been a major air polluter for decades; by the 1980s, citizens in the area were pressuring Ford's management to implement pollution controls on the plant, with some success. The Foundry was at that time about sixty years old. The threat of closure had been imminent for years, but several union officials interviewed claimed that the Ford Foundry was very profitable; they did not view the threat too seriously.[47] (The problem of a polluting auto company, which was posed in both interviews and in the survey of rank-and-file auto workers, was drawn from the Ford Foundry conflict. In the interviews union representatives were asked: "What role do you think the environmental committee should play in a case where the union's plant is a polluter?" The survey described a hypothetical case of jobs-versus-the-environmental conflict, and asked respondents to select their preferred strategy of union response from among three options. (See appendix 1.)

The response of the local executive to the foundry issue is examined below in the discussion of the priorities of the environmental committees. While there is a difference of opinion over the extent to which the foundry problem might explain the slowness of the Ford local in creating an environmental committee, it does seem to be the case that environment concerns ranked low on the executive's list of priorities. It was the only large local in the area with no representation on the Labour Council environment committee, and with no official presence at the various environmental events taking place.[48] There was some informal representation at meetings of the citizens' group lobbying Ford. In an August 1987 interview, McAnally said that the local [executive] did plan to create a committee, but that there were other priorities: "We have been centering in on collective bargaining for this year, so we're waiting. Once our contract is behind us we'll have more time to put energy into starting the committee." The president had some doubts about whether they would have enough interest among rank-and-file members to form a committee.

Local 1498

Local 1498 (office, clerical, technical workers at Chrysler) did not have an environmental committee in July 1987 or May 1988 when I interviewed its president, Jo-Anne Bawden.[49] The reasons given for this were that the local membership is relatively small (only about 350 members), and that more "major" committees had only just been established. (The occupational health and safety committee was created in 1984-85.) Moreover, there had not been any initiatives from rank-and-file members requesting the executive to create an environmental standing committee.

Bawden was very concerned with occupational health and safety issues, and made little distinction between these and environmental issues. The local had not become officially involved in any of the area's environmental issues, although the president was aware of both the issues, and the involvement of other locals. She had a somewhat cynical attitude toward the high profile representation of other locals—especially Local 444—at environmental events, implying that underlying the appearance of commitment was a mixture of self-interest and compulsion by the national leadership of the union. As we have already noted, she claimed that the activist image of Local 444 in the environmental area was due mainly to the work of its committee chairperson, Rick Coronado. The normal state of affairs, she suggested, both in her own and other locals, was one of difficulty in forming committees, and little rank-and-file interest in union activities.

Views from the Rank and File

In my survey of auto workers (from CAW locals 444, 200, 89, 1498, and 1973, and of plant chairpersons from Local 195) I attempted to gather some information about what they thought about environmental issues, whether they thought their union ought to be involved in them, and how they perceived their own roles in the activities of the union. From discussions with union executive officials, one derives a picture of the rank and file as rather conservative, apathetic people who do not participate in union activities because they cannot be bothered or do not really approve of the executives' goals. While there is some truth in this, there is also evidence that auto workers have a very strong sense of the importance of environmental problems. In this section I examine some of the survey findings and their possible explanations.

The responses to the survey do not indicate that workers are particularly conservative in defining the parameters of union involvement. Eighty-eight percent of respondents said they thought the union should be involved in environmental issues. In no local was this percentage lower than 80.0 percent.[50] When the response was broken down into occupational groups, 86.7 percent of office workers and 85.5 percent of production workers said "yes" to union involvement, compared to 98.2 percent of skilled trades workers and 100.0 percent (12 in all) of full-time union representatives. Breakdowns by age groups and by years of employment showed that it was not the youngest workers, but those who were between 30 and 40, who were the most positive about union involvement in environmental issues. Approval declined with workers over 50, or with those who had been in the workforce for more than 30 years. However, large majorities in all categories favoured participation.[51]

The evidence also indicates considerable interest among workers in environmental issues. Ninety-four percent of the respondents said they would like to receive an environmental information sheet from their committees. Although only 3.4 percent indicated that they had participated in union-sponsored environmental activities, 15.2 percent said they thought they would participate in the future, and 61.0 percent said "maybe." The number who said they would like to participate in a non-union environmental group in the future was even higher (19.7 percent), and 61.4 percent said "maybe." The large number of "maybes" suggests an openness to participation, and raises the question: "What would have to happen for these individuals to be persuaded?" A closer look at who said yes (or no, or maybe), and at the responses to other questions provides some clues.

The sample was broken down into five age groups (21-30, 31-40, 41-50, 51-60, 61-64) and into two age groups (21-45, 46-64). Years of employment were also examined first in five-year groups and then in ten-year groups. The first method showed a decline in interest in the 41 to 50 age group.[52] However, the frequency distribution over the larger group of cells was too small to draw any strong conclusions. The second method showed that workers under 45 were more likely to say "yes" (16.3%) or "maybe" (61.4 %) to future participation than were workers over 45 years of age. But again, it is unwise to conclude too much on the basis of this arbitrary division, given the small cell sizes. Nor did cross-tabulation of years of employment with responses to the question of future participation in the union environment committee show a significant relationship.

Figures on male/female attitudes towards future participation in the environment

The CAW Environmental Policy   243

committees may indicate significant difference, although this is difficult to say with certainty, given the small number of women respondents in the sample (33 out of 267). While 16.5 percent of men said they would consider future participation, only 6.1 percent of women said they would. Women were also more negative (30.3 percent said they would not, compared to 22.6 percent of men), and more undecided. At the time the survey was conducted, there were no women in the environment committees in Windsor. (This difference is particularly interesting in light of the fact that outside the unions, in the citizens' environmental groups, women often predominate.) This difference might indicate a greater alienation of women from union structures in general. Women did not list lack of interest as a reason for non-participation more often than men did, so this does not seem to be the cause of their absence from the committees. More men listed lack of interest as a "very important reason" than women (24.8 compared to 12.1 percent). The "somewhat/ very important" categories combined were about the same for both sexes.

TABLE 20
POSITION IN UNION HIERARCHY VS. FUTURE PARTICIPATION IN A UNION ENVIRONMENT COMMITTEE.

Position	No answer		Yes		No		Maybe	
	no.	%	no.	%	no.	%	no.	%
none	2	1.1	24	13.0	43	23.4	115	62.5
elected, non executive	1	1.4	14	19.4	13	18.1	44	61.1
plant chairperson*			4	19.0	4	19.0	13	61.9
elected, plant executive			2	25.0	5	62.5	1	12.5

* This category includes the 21 plant chairpersons from all locals, including local 195.

Union members who had held an elected position were more likely to say they would participate in future than members who had never held any union position. However, rank-and-file members were just as likely to say "maybe" (table 20).

Respondents' ranking of priorities for the allocation of union resources indicated a consistently high concern for education (including environmental), and occupational health and safety, followed by (for production workers) the need for better contract enforcement (tables 21 and 22). There were significant differences between the views of production workers and the full-time executive officials on whether more resources should be allocated to contract enforcement and to executive expenses. Both the "rank-and-file" (no union position) and "production worker" categories registered much more concern for contract enforcement than union officials did. One interpretation of this is a difference of opinion over how satisfying working conditions are, including relations with management. A breakdown of the "executive expenses" category by union position showed a fairly wide gap between production and maintenance workers, on one hand, and full-time union officials, on the other. While about 34 percent of each of the first two groups said executive expenses should be decreased, 75 percent of the executive officials themselves said their expenses should remain the same. (The other officials did

TABLE 21
PRIORITIES FOR ALLOCATION OF UNION RESOURCES (FIVE LOCALS)

Category	More %	Less %	Same %	Don't know %
Education (including environment)	64.4	4.9	24.0	6.7
Research on economic issues	46.4	12.7	29.6	11.2
Contract negotiation	46.8	7.9	36.3	9.0
Contract enforcement	57.3	6.7	27.0	9.0
Occ. health & safety	63.7	3.7	25.8	6.7
Political action	33.7	26.6	31.1	8.6
Research staff	35.6	17.6	37.5	9.4
Executive expenses	16.5	33.3	38.6	11.6

TABLE 22
UNION PRIORITIES VS. OCCUPATIONAL GROUPS [FIVE LOCALS]
(PERCENT SUPPORTING MORE RESOURCES FOR EACH CATEGORY)

Category	Office workers	Maintenance/ Trades	Production workers	Full-time union
Education (including environmental)	53.3	67.2	65.9	58.3
Research on econ. issues	46.7	50.0	45.5	41.7
Contract negotiation	46.7	29.3	52.7	50.0
Contract enforcement	53.3	43.1	64.7	33.3
Occ. Health & Safety	53.3	62.1	67.1	50.0
Research staff	36.7	41.4	34.7	16.7
Executive expenses	13.3	12.1	17.4	33.3

not answer the question.)

Further examination of the education priority showed that the group most concerned with having more union resources allocated to education was composed of those who had held, or who currently held, non-executive elected positions. Of this group, 70.8 percent said more resources should be allocated to education, compared to 63.0 percent of rank-and-file members who had never held a union position, and 37.5 percent of executive officials. From these results, one might infer that many union members desire more participation in educational activities, and that an area for special attention would be occupational health and safety. These conclusions would support the perceptions of

The CAW Environmental Policy   245

| TABLE 23 |
| REASONS FOR NON-PARTICIPATION IN ENVIRONMENT COMMITTEES |

Responses	(Number of Times Selected)
Reasons listed as "very important"	
Did not know about the committee	104
Lack of information	98
Not enough time	71
Not interested in environmental issues	62
Other	6
Reasons listed as "somewhat important"	
Not enough time	63
Not interested in environmental issues	42
Lack of information	38
Did not know the committee existed	31
Other	5

rank-and-file activists that there is potential for more involvement, rather than the perceptions of executive officials that members are too apathetic to become more active in union campaigns.

Other reasons given by respondents for non-participation in the environment committees provide some alternative explanations to "apathy" and "conservatism." The question: "If you have not participated in any activities of the environment committee, why not?" produced the following results (table 23). From these rankings it appears that lack of time and information were at least as important as, and probably more important reasons for non-participation than, lack of interest.[53]

The workers who were most likely to cite lack of time as a very important reason for not participating were those under 30 years of age, or those over 50 (34.0 and 36.0 percent respectively). The group least concerned with this constraint was the 31- to 40-year-old workers, who again seem to be the most active stratum in the workforce (apart from the full-time and executive officials) with regard to union involvement. However, this factor was still listed as "somewhat" or "very" important by 45.9 percent of this age group. Interestingly, fewer women ranked lack of time as an important reason for non-participation than men (42.5 percent of women said this was a "somewhat" or "very" important reason, compared to 51.3 percent of men). This result contradicts the expectation that women would be more likely to lack time because of the double day they commonly work. (Perhaps they did have less time available for union activities, but did not consider this to the main reason for their non-participation.) The kinds of problems faced by women in the workplace, and in their relations with male union representatives, may be a more important explanation of their absence from union activities. These problems are illustrated by the experience of the women's committee in Local 200, which is described below.

The all-male union executive of Local 200 was quite frustrated by its experience with its women's committee. Its members had attempted to act as the representatives of other women on the shop floor, at times going directly to management or acting as intermediaries with male shop stewards. Women with concerns would approach their representatives on the women's committee, rather than approach a male union representative. As a result, a conflict developed with the male stewards, who complained that the women were usurping their functions. The executive blamed this on the women's naïveté about the way a union functions. The president of Local 200 described the problem this way:

> [A] lot of the women figured that if they were getting a women's committee, that they were going to have their own representatives and...that's not the purpose of the women's committee. The purpose is...to try and educate the women in terms of the trade union movement, which a lot of them don't know anything about. Some of them knew because they come from other, small [union] shops... but there's a lot of them, this is their first job in a factory, so they don't know anything about unions at all...
>
> They thought the people who got elected to the women's committee would be like their representatives in the plant; like, if they had a problem they wouldn't call the steward, they'd go to this woman, whoever she was, on the committee... [P]art of the problem was that some of the women who got elected viewed themselves as [representatives], which they shouldn't have... They'd get in trouble with the union reps in the plant, because [the women] would go, you know, sit there and lunch with some other girl who was complaining about a problem and then she'd go and talk to the steward. And the steward would say: "Why doesn't she call me? She's the one with the problem, not you!"

McAnally admitted that the women's previous experiences with male union representatives might be part of the problem, but, he said:

> ... what we view as the women's committee's role is to convince women that they have to go to that representative. He's there to protect you... [T]here was a few of the women who got elected who [saw] themselves as the representatives of the other women, and they'd stick their noses in where they didn't belong. And then they'd really get in trouble with the representative... And all they did was create animosity. Because we've never had women in the workplace there, when I wanted to start a women's committee [there was] animosity from the older guys. [They said]: "Why do the women need a committee? If they need a committee we'd better start one for the Italians."

(From this response one can begin to see why the women felt their grievances would get a better reception from members of the women's committee.) As a result of this conflict, the women's committee was, according to McAnally, "flopping around." The executive was awaiting the opportunity to replace its members with women more properly cognizant of the rules of the hierarchy. McAnally concluded:

> It'll take time... You've just got to get the right girl...at the top of the committee that knows what her role should be, to get the committee started... I'm sure eventually we'll get the right two or three women running the committee that know what a women's committee is all about and what they should be doing for women and with women.

Across the hall at Local 444's office, president Gerard complained that despite his efforts the local was still without a women's committee. He was concerned that this absence was creating an image problem for his local within the union. Local 444's executive had invited women members to a dinner, paid for by the union, in order to try to involve them in the union.[54] Gerard complained: "It's not that we're against women; we're in favour of them... But they don't come forward, so what the hell do you do?" When asked why he thought women were reluctant to become involved in the union, the reasons he gave were: "I would say, 50 percent of our women [don't participate] because the old man is telling them to stay at home—'I'll take care of the union's problems'... And the others would probably say that they are happy." The women, Gerard thought, would say (if asked): "Our local union is run by the leadership; we're happy with them; we got no complaints about them." However, Gerard was finding it impossible to take satisfaction in such happy members, because of pressure from the national office. The carrot approach had failed; women should be forewarned that there were costs for frustrating the objectives of the executive: "[I]f we're going to represent women, they've got to be part of our structures, sitting on our committees." He implied that the executive would only bargain for child care provisions if women became active in the union and carried this campaign themselves. If the women would form a committee, Gerard said, "Maybe I'd get off my ass a bit more on the question of women. It makes me upset to think I got 350 women and none of them are active."

Gerard's appearance of bewilderment over the non-participation of women was brushed aside by the female president of the Chrysler office workers' local. Bawden said:

> I'm not sure [the male union leaders] even see the problem. When you have a local that's full of 250 and 300 pound men, they have a tendency to be bullies. Most women don't voluntarily get into organizations where they have to frequently deal with bullies. They have better things to do with their time and energy than get into the political field with men who really don't want them there in the first place...
>
> Generally speaking, men in unions are like men everywhere else; they think women belong at home, out of their hair, or beside them at a party. The rest of the time they should keep quiet. However, that's not the position of the national union, and so they can't say that. They have to sit on their real feelings. But women are smart enough to understand that just because somebody says something, it doesn't mean that's what they mean.
>
> They are not going to get women to participate. There are many problems for women, only one of which is the bully syndrome. Another one is that, particularly for women who work in the factories, they have to work six days a week and have to go home and be a wife and a mother... While there are some changes in some of the younger men, the middle aged men and the older men still think the kitchen is a strictly female domain.

The problems at Ford and Chrysler suggest that the nature of gender relations in certain industrial workplaces (where the workforce and union officials are predominantly, and traditionally, male), may explain why women showed less willingness to participate in union structures, including the new environmental standing committees.

Finally, respondents were asked what changes, if any, would make it more convenient or attractive for them to participate in the environmental committees. Their suggestions are ranked in order of the number of times they were mentioned (table 24). Thus, of the 170 persons (64 percent of respondents) who answered this question, only twelve, or 7 percent said nothing would induce them to participate, 38 percent listed structural or organisational changes, 47 percent referred to problems getting information or service from their union representatives, and 10 percent mentioned other factors. These results do not indicate that lack of interest is the major problem facing the environmental and other committees of the union. Rather, they show that the reasons for non-participation are complex, predominantly related to the organisational practices of the union itself, and to the many restrictions on the time available to workers to develop non-wage labour activities.

TABLE 24
PROPOSED CHANGES TO ENCOURAGE PARTICIPATION

No suggestions		97
Better satisfaction from union reps/information		80
better information	76	
better satisfaction from union reps	4	
Structural/organizational		64
more paid time off for rank and file	34	
changes to the way cttees. are created	14	
change meeting times/problems with shift schedules	8	
all ideas listed on survey form	5	
enlarge the committees	3	
Other		14
more evidence of success	6	
more co-operation from employers	2	
other	6	
Nothing would make a difference		12
TOTAL		267

CONCLUSIONS

The executive officials' view of the environmental committees, and of the standing committees in general, was that they should function primarily as advisory bodies for the local executives, and to some extent as representatives of the union in relations with outside groups. Second, they were created because of a policy change at the national level. Local union officials saw this new area of "social unionism" as an opportunity to enhance their own reputations locally and nationally. Third, the committees were composed of a handful of rank-and-file activists who were exceptional in their ability and willingness to dedicate time to the work, and by full-time union officials who had filled in positions which attracted no rank-and-file interest, or who had monopolized these positions. In the Ford local, where a pollution problem directly concerned the workforce, no environmental committee had been created by 1988. The explanation for this is examined in greater detail in the section dealing with the Ford Foundry case. As for Local 1498, its "social unionism" standing seemed related to its executive's involvement in occupational health and safety and women's issues. Given the small size of the membership, leadership in the new area was not anticipated. Some of these points are examined in more detail below.

The frustrations of Taylor and Martin raise a number of important points about the constraints on rank-and-file activists, and the pressures which propel a few toward "career" unionism, while preventing the majority of rank-and-file workers from becoming active. First, it is necessary to understand that the most active individuals tend to have the fewest family commitments and/or restricted social lives. There is a kind of spectrum of positions—from the zealously dedicated existence of a Rick Coronado to people like Lynwood Martin or Mike Longmoore, who have spouses and young children, and who set certain limits to their union and other involvements. During the period of research, Coronado was the single parent of a son who was attending university. Ken

The CAW Environmental Policy

Gerard acknowledged his good luck in having such an activist in his ranks, saying: "It's tough to get volunteers, because [workers] like to stay with their families." Taylor, on the other hand, was married to a woman who was also working full-time. The only common day they had off was Sundays. While Taylor was critical of union representatives who "are not dedicated enough—they don't want to take their Sunday mornings, like I do," he admitted that: "I got to miss a lot of things. And my wife gets mad, too. Which I can't blame her, sometimes. We don't have that much time together." The same pressures were felt by the rank-and-file activists in the ECWU.

The standing committee structure cannot accommodate more than a small core of workers who might want to participate in union activities. All union activities are allocated among the standing committees; only through the executive can union resources be obtained for any educational, political, or social initiatives (rather than, say, a fund set aside to be allocated by the committee). The number of positions in a given standing committee is set in the local's bylaws, and rarely exceeds ten, even in a large local. The executive board of the local generally has to approve changes in the by-laws, including any increase in the number of positions on a standing committee. Rank-and-file members are not encouraged to attend standing committee meetings. The rationale for this is that a test of serious commitment is election—the willingness of an individual to attend monthly (or more frequent) meetings of the standing committee and to assume a representative function.

Unlike the citizens' groups, union meetings are not run like continually reassembled collectives with a circulation of tasks. The committees report to the general membership meetings, and that is where rank-and-file members may learn about the activities in which the union is involved (in addition to reading union publications). The problem is not that an elected committee meets regularly to plan activities, and so on (most large organisations have such committees). The problem is that standing committee meetings cannot involve more than a very small group. To broaden participation, the environmental standing committees would have to hold open meetings on various issues (at times which accommodate shiftwork), advertise joint actions with community groups, and find other ways to involve the workforce in thinking about environmental alternatives. This *mobilizing* function is, however, not the typical function of the standing committees, which is, rather, to represent union policies in the external environment, and to transmit national campaigns to the rank and file.

Moreover, candidates for standing committee positions are usually nominated by officials in the local, who have endorsed their candidacies. A rank-and-file worker who seeks to contest a position against an "official" candidate (usually an incumbent) rarely has a chance of winning. Executive officials interviewed gave the impression that they could "veto" a prospective candidate for a standing committee position if they disapproved of the individual for any reason.[55]

The representative structures of the union are, perhaps, no less democratic than, for example, the parliamentary system (a comparison made by Gary Parent, the vice-president of Local 444), but they are characterised by the same limitations: the inherent advantages of those who control information and allocate resources over those whose everyday experience excludes such opportunities. There is a certain way of doing things that the executive officials, having attained their positions, seek to enforce with the means available to them—primarily powers of exclusion or patronage. Rank-and-file activists are sensitive to the possible consequences of stepping outside these boundaries, by, for example, attempting to bypass the executive in communicating with the rank-and-file, employers, or outside groups. They also perceive advantages in attaining positions of some authority within the union structure; that is, they are drawn to the possibilities of using committee positions to obtain money for activities, access to union newsletters, and the (limited) right to represent the union.

From the perspective of a rank-and-file activist, there is a constant tension between the need to observe the implicit rules—acknowledgment of the hierarchy, of the authority of the executive—and the desire to mobilize other rank-and-file workers in a more profound way. However, these activists, too, are not certain how to do this, i.e., how to change the structures which are so deeply entrenched, and whose questioning entails a radically different conception of the functions and priorities of the union organisation itself. What is particularly interesting in the case of the environmental activists in the CAW is that they are dividing their energies between the union and outside organisations; they experience in the latter a less hierarchical and more grassroots oriented type of organisation. They are sometimes frustrated by both the lack of structure in these organisations, and the restrictive structures of the union.

The institutional functions of the union are not only implicit; they are also encoded in constitutions, collective agreements, and labour legislation. Both the union bureaucrats and management benefit from an entrenched representational structure. This is not to say that management will not attempt to exploit a rank-and-file initiative to discredit the union leadership, or to bypass union officials in order to undermine their legitimacy as representatives of the rank and file. This management strategy is sometimes raised by union officials in defence of the existing rules. During negotiations, for example, union officials exhort members to observe the collective bargaining agreement, and usually oppose wild-cat strikes or other actions which call into question the executive's ability to control the membership, upon which its institutionalized, intermediary position depends. Likewise, any attempts by rank-and-file workers to organise themselves, or to deal directly with management (bypassing union officials) are generally opposed.

The desire of union officials to retain control—to enforce the rules of the hierarchy—is demonstrated by the problem certain CAW executives were having with the formation of women's committees (a policy of some importance with the national leadership). There are lessons here regarding the constraints which may confront any committees which might try to establish more direct relations with the rank and file. The experience of the women's standing committees sheds some light on the power relationships within the union, and the motivations (at least at the local level) behind the implementation of progressive policies. Although the women's committees and policies like affirmative action do have a base within the rank and file—primarily women—they are also a response to the strength of the women's movement, as perceived by the union's leadership. Interestingly, the CAW negotiated with the Big Three in 1993, a Women's Advocate Program, in which rank-and-file women are trained to assist (on paid work time) other women who are experiencing harassment and sexism.[56] The environmental committees were essentially an imposition from the top, although there existed a small number of rank-and-file activists who were very dedicated to this cause. Both groups confronted the local bureaucracy's tight control over rank-and-file activists, limited means to mobilize their co-workers, tokenism, etc.

All of these factors act as disincentives for rank-and-file members to participate in the activities of the union. To play a part they must win the approval of the executive, run for election, and commit themselves to accepting considerable demands on their off-work time. There is no space within the union structures for individuals to participate on an informal, spontaneous or ad hoc basis.[57] A comment which appeared on the survey forms was that knowledge of union activities seemed to be the monopoly of a small elite of insiders.[58] As Martin's comments (above) indicate, the insiders are also perceived as becoming more concerned with moving into staff positions than with the day-to-day problems of the rank and file. It also became apparent from the survey that most rank-and-file workers—even those concerned with environmental issues—could see no way to participate in environmental committee activities. The question about this was simply irrelevant to their situation.

So the standing committees (including the environment committee) were relatively small and exclusive, with activities oriented towards representation, rather than mobilization, of the rank and file. It is also important to note that, while executive members complained about rank-and-file apathy, they were not making any effort to think about the structures—the institutional factors—that discourage participation. For example, they had not considered providing child care until women forced them to, and they were still not providing it as a matter of course at union meetings. They were not unhappy with the club atmosphere of their work; indeed, they were united in a certain sense of moral and intellectual superiority over the "less progressive" rank and file, and this provided a legitimating rationale for the exclusiveness of union structures.

The handful of committee members who, like Coronado and Taylor, take their work seriously, frequently suffer "burn out." Their only options are to reduce their political commitments or to seek more relief from wage labour. While Coronado had chosen to trade wages for time, and to limit his social life in order to pursue his activist goals, these solutions are either not feasible or not acceptable to most workers. Thus Taylor, Martin, and others were pushing for more union-sponsored autonomy from their company jobs. However, the creation of a few more full-time representatives is not a solution for the problem of rank-and-file participation. Not even the activists had many ideas about how to change union structures and bargaining priorities in order to facilitate participation.

It is important to distinguish in the locals studied, between the rank-and-file activists who may hold committee positions, and the full-time union representatives who, having left the shop floor, intend never to go back.[59] The first step does not always lead to the second; some committee representatives never seek executive offices, but continue to work from within the rank and file. However, almost invariably, the individuals who do attain a full-time position, become established in the union bureaucracy. There is a constant tension between the two groups, stemming from different perceptions of the goals of the union, of the rank and file, and so on. Some of these differences are described in the next chapter, which looks at the priorities of the environmental committees, and at how they suggest different conceptions of "social unionism."

NOTES

1. In his March 1989 brief to the NDP task force reviewing the party's federal election campaign, Bob White used socialism and social democracy interchangeably, adding to the confusion. Nevertheless, the brief presented a strong case for a more grass roots and "social movement" conception of the party and its goals. See Bob White, "From Defeat to Renewal: the NDP Tomorrow," reprinted in *This Magazine* vol. 23, no. 1 (May-June 1989), pp. 23-26.
2. There are now some very good historical accounts of the roots of industrial militancy in the CAW. See Charlotte Yates, *From Plant to Politics: The Autoworkers Union in Postwar Canada* (Philadelphia: Temple University Press, 1993); Charlotte Yates, "The Internal Dynamics of Union Power: Explaining Canadian Autoworkers' Militancy in the 1980s," in *Studies in Political Economy* 31 (Spring 1990), pp. 73-105, and Sam Gindin, *The Canadian Auto Workers: The Birth and Transformation of a Union* (Toronto: James Lorimer, 1995).
3. *Constitution of the National Automobile, Aerospace, Transportation and General Workers' Union of Canada*, (CAW-Canada), adopted at Québec City, Québec, August 1994, pp. 1-2.
4. Yates, "The Internal Dynamics of Union Power," pp. 79-81.

5. Ibid., p. 91.
6. Ibid., p. 88.
7. Ibid., p. 91.
8. Ibid., p. 93.
9. See, in particular: Pradeep Kumar and John Holmes, "Change, but in What Direction? Divergent Union Responses to Work Restructuring in the Integrated North American Auto Industry," in Frederic Deyo, ed. *Social Reconstructions of the World Automobile Industry: Competition, Power and Industrial Flexibility* (London: Macmillan Press (International Political Economy Series) and New York: St. Martin's Press, 1996), pp. 159-199; John Holmes and Pradeep Kumar, "Labour movement strategies in the era of free trade: The uneven transformation of industrial relations in the North American automobile industry," in Jane Jenson, Rianne Mahon, and Manfred Bienefeld, eds. *Production, Space, Identity* (Toronto: Canadian Scholars' Press, 1993); Charlotte Yates, "Public policy and Canadian and American autoworkers: Divergent fortunes," in Maureen Appel Molot, ed. *Driving Continentally: National Policies and the North American Auto Industry* (Ottawa: Carleton University Press, 1993); and Steve Babson, ed., *Lean Work: Empowerment and Exploitation in the Global Auto Industry* (Detroit: Wayne State University Press, 1995).
10. Gindin, *The Canadian Auto Workers*, pp. 185-186.
11. Kumar and Holmes, "Change, but in what direction?," p. 160.
12. Canadian Auto Workers, *CAW Statement on the Reorganization of Workers* (North York, Ont.: CAW, 1989), cited by Kumar and Holmes in "Change, but in What Direction?" p. 180.
13. Kumar and Holmes, "Change, but in what direction?," p. 181.
14. CAW, *False Solutions, Growing Protests: Recapturing the Agenda* (Report to the National Collective Bargaining and Political Action Convention (Toronto) June 4-7, 1996) (North York, Ont.: CAW, 1996), p. 22.
15. See, for example, the CAW publications: *Hard Times, New Times: Fighting for our Future*: Report to the National Collective Bargaining and Political Action Convention, Toronto, May 4-7, 1993 (North York, Ont.: CAW, 1993); *More time* (North York, Ont.: CAW, 1993); and *Fight Speed-up* (North York, Ont.: CAW,1995).
16. Gindin, *The Canadian Auto Workers*, pp. 188, 223.
17. Letter from Bill Van Gaal to the author, dated September 18, 1987.
18. Gary Parent, interviewed August 5, 1987, Windsor, Ont.
19. Ken Gerard, interviewed July 29, 1987, Windsor, Ont.
20. Frank McAnally, interviewed August 4, 1987, Windsor, Ont.
21. Jack Ewart, interviewed August 5, 1987, Windsor, Ont.
22. Gary St. Laurent, interviewed July 23, 1987, Windsor, Ont.
23. Tom Burton, interviewed July 29, 1987, Windsor, Ont.
24. This is not to say that rank-and-file auto workers have not generally become increasingly concerned with environmental problems, but that there is no evidence to suggest that they considered the union to be the obvious or appropriate vehicle to represent these concerns.
25. Letter to the author from Robert Chernecki, National Staff Representative and liaison for the Environmental Committee of the CAW Canadian Council, dated September 18, 1987.
26. Although the Amherstburg plant was a chemical plant, it was organised by the CAW rather than by the ECWU. Allied-Signal was formed in a merger of Allied Corporation and Signal corporation in September 1985. Based in Morristown, NJ, the company is a conglomerate operating businesses in aerospace, automotive, and chemical products. In 1991 it announced the closure of 10 plants in its "non-core" businesses. Its 15 plants in Canada were operating in the late 1980s under the subsidiaries Allied-Signal Chemical, Allied-Signal Aerospace, Garrett Canada and Bendix-Avelex Canada. Additional details on Allied-Signal's restructuring may be found in "Allied Signal to chop 5,000 jobs," *The Globe and Mail*, October 10, 1991, p. B9.
27. Interview with Lynwood Martin, chairperson of the Local 89 environmental committee, August 4, 1987.
28. Gary St. Laurent, interviewed by author, July 23, 1987 and May 9, 1988.
29. Local 199 (St. Catharines) encompassed at the time 8,600 members. The ten locals in Essex County comprised about 35,000 members. See CAW-Canada, *In Solidarity: A Family Album*

The CAW Environmental Policy 253

(North York, Ont.: CAW, April 1989); Ken Gerard, interview by author, July 29, 1987.
30. For a description of the opposition to the Detroit Incinerator, see L. Adkin and C. Alpaugh, "Labour, Ecology, and the Politics of Convergence in Canada," in *Social Movements and Social Change*, Frank Cunningham et al., eds. (Toronto: Between the Lines, 1988).
31. Detroit Edison has constructed two nuclear reactors in the area, known as Fermi I and Fermi II. There was a fuelling accident at Fermi I in 1966 and it was ordered closed in the early 1970s. Fermi II, located at Munroe, Michigan, has been under construction since 1968; its cost was originally estimated at $229 million, but by 1987 its cost had reached $3.65 billion. Although its nameplate capacity is 1,100 megawatts, it has never operated beyond 50 percent of this. Problems with Fermi II have included: inadequacy of emergency response procedures, malfunctioning detection instruments, improper handling of radioactive materials, poor employee training, inadequacy of radioactive waste disposal, problems with Safeteam (the company's safety programme to receive internal complaints), involving compromising of confidentiality and concerns not being addressed. Twenty-seven violations of plant procedures had been cited by the US Nuclear Regulatory Commission by May 1986, and approximately 2,000 complaints from Fermi II workers had been reported to Safeteam. In 1985 the reactor was started up "too soon." There was an accident that summer: during testing an atomic chain reaction was started. A few weeks later, the plant was shut down after a pump that provides water to cool the reactor stopped working during another test. Problems with Fermi II were continuing in 1988. Citizens of Amherstburg in Ontario are about 16 kms. from the plant. Groups opposed to the continued operation of Fermi II include: the Government Accountability Project (public interest law firm), Monroe chapter of the Safe Energy Coalition of Michigan, Servants of the Immaculate Heart of Mary (a teaching order of nuns, in Munroe), Union of Concerned Scientists, and citizens in Amherstburg, and Anderdon and Malden townships (Essex County Citizens Against Fermi II). See newspaper clippings compiled by the Great Lakes Institute, especially for the May 1986 period; *Detroit Free Press,* June 30, 1987; *The Globe and Mail,* January 7, 1988.
32. Murney, quoted by Art Kilgour, in "The Greening of the Union Movement," *National Union Magazine*, CAW-Canada, vol. 2, no. 5 (Winter 1987/88), p. 20.
33. I have had the benefit of numerous discussions with Mr. Coronado since 1986 about his background as a union militant, his experimentation with political tendencies since the 1960s, and his experiences in the environmental movement since the mid-1980s. His father was a well-known militant in the Chrysler local until his death.
34. Interview with Mike Longmoore, July 23, 1987. Longmoore was one of the persons "co-opted" on to the environment committee. He was elected a steward in March 1988.
35. Coronado was Treasurer of Great Lakes United in 1988, and a director-at-large in 1989.
36. Ms. Bawden changed her name to Jo-anne Johnson in 1988, after our initial interview. I refer to her as Jo-anne Bawden for the sake of consistency.
37. Jo-Anne Bawden, interview by author, May 12, 1988.
38. In his article entitled "Thank you for your confidence, as we continue to fight for your rights," (*444 News* no. 313, April 1988, p. 1), Gerard said: "Surely one of the highest compliments members of a union can bestow upon its leadership are acclamations for another term... No doubt it is in recognition of the gains we as members of our union have been able to achieve over the last several years."
39. It was made clear to me by everyone (rank-and-file activists, subordinate union officials, outside activists with contacts with the union) that if my survey of rank-and-file auto workers was to have any chance of implementation, I would first have to win Gerard's approval. Subsequently, I found it useful to refer to my meeting with Gerard, and his approval of my survey, in order to set up similar meetings with other union officials.
40. According to Gary Parent: "With all the other things we're involved in ...we've got to be pushed to [do] it, because ...our priorities are, with the amount of pressure we get, to do certain things... That's just the way we work. Like right now, the provincial election is up, but our negotiations are here, too. Now, where's our priority? It's got to be negotiations" (Gary Parent, interview by author, August 5, 1987).
41. An operator at Allied Signal, interviewed in 1987, and who asked to remain anonymous, reported: "We as operators in the plant pollute every day. We're either dumping oil in the sewers

or we're letting HF gas go off in the atmosphere." The operator also mentioned a problem with CFCs: "You know, Allied makes Freon. We call it Genatron, but it's the same product. You think they let a lot off in aerosol cans - that's nothing compared to what goes into the atmosphere every day [at Allied]. Tons of it. Bleeding lines, bleeding tanks...cylinders...to one-tonne [size]. When they come into the plant, we have to evacuate those—empty them out and refill them. That all goes out into the atmosphere." The Ontario Ministry of the Environment reported in October 1991 that it had found co..centrations of hydrogen flouride three times higher than allowed under provincial law in the air outside the plant. The minuscule *Globe and Mail* report on the story noted that flourides "have been linked to bone abnormalities in humans." (Cf. chapter 6, note 4 on the Akwesasne Mohawk Reserve.) See "Plant emissions exceed limits," *The Globe and Mail*, October 3, 1991. Note that the same month, Allied-Signal announced a massive corporate restructuring plan that included the elimination of 5,000 jobs.
42. Lynwood Martin, interviewed in May 1988.
43. The "Clifton Grant Award," sponsored by the Windsor Occupational Safety and Health Council and the Canadian Union of Public Employees, was created in 1982 to commemorate a carpenter who died at the age of 37 from asbestos-related cancer.
44. Gary St. Laurent, interviewed July 23, 1987, Windsor, Ont.
45. It was at this time that I interviewed Frank McAnally, president of the local at Ford. McAnally had been a full-time union official since around 1975. He became president of the local in 1984. In March 1987 he and most of the executive were re-elected for another three-year term. Like Gerard, McAnally described this as "an overwhelming vote of confidence," and said: "It really makes us feel good to know that you feel we are directing this local union in a manner in which you, the membership, totally agree with." (Local 200 President's Report, *The Guardian*, vol. 27 (May 1987), p. 13.)
46. On the Ford Windsor strike of 1945, which led to the Rand Formula decision, see David Moulton, "Ford Windsor 1945," in Irving Abella, ed., *On Strike: Six Key Labour Struggles in Canada, 1919-1949* (Toronto: James Lewis & Samuel, 1974).
47. Interviews with McAnally, Taylor and Longmoore. In 1970 Ford built a new foundry in Michigan to replace the Windsor Foundry, but found it unprofitably large; it was sold to Mazda and the site converted to auto assembly.
48. One exception to this is McAnally's official endorsement of the protest against the construction of the Detroit incinerator. Like the other CAW local presidents in the area, he signed a form letter (dated December 5, 1986) prepared by members of the Labour Council Environment Committee regarding this issue.
49. Bawden was, during the period of this study, a member of the CAW Council Women's Committee, and one of six Ontario NDP vice-presidents. These activities, in addition to her local's affairs, were her primary concerns.
50. Of the respondents from Local 89 (General and Allied Chemical) 80 percent said "yes" to union involvement, 5 percent said "no," and 10 percent (the largest "uncertain" group) said "don't know." The next lowest "yes" response was from Local 444 (84.9), which also had the largest group of "no's" (12.3). The Local 89 response may be due to its position as the only group of chemical workers in the CAW survey, but even in this case, the overwhelming majority of the workforce viewed union participation favourably.
51. Education and gender did not appear to affect the response to the question on union involvement in environmental issues.
52. This may be the same group which, selected by number of years in the workforce, corresponds to workers who had been employed for 26 to 35 years. The latter category of respondents also showed a decline in interest in union committee participation. It may be that workers in the 30 to 40 age group are most likely to participate in political/social activities, and that workers over 40 are less likely to do so, for reasons which have to do primarily with their life-cycle stages.
53. Perhaps as important as these alternative explanations is the fact that about a third of respondents chose not to rank these reasons at all. The percentages of non-response for the above reasons (in the order of the second list) were 40.8, 46.8, 41.6, 37.5, and 95.5 respectively. This was either because the question was too poorly constructed for easy comprehension, or because it was irrelevant to the experience of the respondents. i.e., they could see no likelihood of being

The CAW Environmental Policy

able to participate in the existing union structure for environmental activities.
54. According to Gerard, women numbered only 350 out of a total membership of about 7,100 in 1987.
55. In Local 444 the Executive Board has to approve any additions to the number of standing committee positions allowed in the by-laws. According to Gerard, "We are careful who we put on committees, because [some] talk, but never take action," or they may be trying to get in a position to "oppose all of the things you want to do." The vice-president of the local explained this last point in reference to an earlier, and potential, political division: "You don't want—say that you're in administration, as we are here—we don't want a hundred [members on a committee]... What happens if they [the Conservatives] have 75 and we [NDP] have 25?" Executive members generally have a lot of discretion to decide who gets what benefits of the union. McAnally described the selection process for applicants for the four-week paid education leave program: "Anyone interested applies to our education committee. Then the committee recommends [candidates] to Ray [financial secretary] and myself. We go over the selections with the chairman of the education committee and those names are forwarded to the national office." According to McAnally, the only criterion for selection is the expectation that the individual will become active in the union. (Education courses are specifically geared toward the mandates of the committees.)
56. See CAW, *False Solutions, Growing Protests: Recapturing the Agenda*, p. 82. The union had also, by 1996, developed "women activist leadership training, an annual women's conference and CAW Women's networks that are active in many areas and provide a structure where women can work together on bargaining, legislation and social action" (ibid., p. 85).
57. Initially I kept asking union officials why members could not just attend meetings of the environmental committees the way members of the citizens' groups do. It became apparent that they were committed to their mode of representative, restricted organisation, and that they feared losing control if the meetings (and structures) were opened. Thus Local 444's president insisted: "You got to be careful that you don't get too many on a committee—you can't get [anything] done."
58. One survey respondent said: "Only a handful of people make all the decisions, legislate and play politics... Then [decisions] are dictated to the membership that this is the way it is, because Mr. White said so." There were numerous complaints of lack of information about the existence and work of the committees. This is notwithstanding the likelihood that, because of the way the surveys were distributed in some locals, the sample group overall was fairly well disposed toward the union.
59. In the CAW, executive officials may or may not be full-time representatives, depending on the decisions made by local memberships. In many CAW locals the president and sometimes another officer are full-time officers. This was the case with the executive members and plant chairpersons who were interviewed in this study. See CAW, Education Dept., "You and Your Membership in the CAW" (North York, Ont.: CAW, August 1986), p. 7.

[13]

Two Strategies of Social Unionism

Implementation of the Environment Policy: Top and Base

In the formative stage of the development of the environmental committees (1986-1989), two parallel and at points conflicting roles for the committees developed.[1] These roles reflect the general strategic options available to unions, which I characterized in chapter 1 as "corporatist" and "counter-hegemonic," recognizing, of course, that these are "ideal types" and that actual union praxis almost necessarily manifests elements of both. Indeed, the most pervasive type of unionism in the Canadian case could be broadly characterized as "social democratic," a praxis which attempts to play both games at once. A counter-hegemonic conception of strategy has to some extent been expressed in the statements of the CAW's former president, Bob White, and in the objectives of some of the rank-and-file activists in the environmental committees. A second strategy, which reproduces the social democratic mode of politics and the bureaucratic organisation of the trade union movement, is found in the assumptions and practices of union officials at the local executive level, and thus is necessarily taken into account in the activists' decision-making. The external actors are the NDP and the extra-parliamentary citizens' and environmental organisations.

In various forums and statements the leadership of the CAW has related industrial pollution to corporations' pursuit of profit.[2] In speeches made to the Labour-Environmental Conference held in Hamilton in November 1986 (organised by the Ontario Environmental Network), and to the CAW Canadian Collective Bargaining and Legislative Convention in April 1987, President Bob White addressed the problem of job blackmail, i.e., of conflicts between workers' desire to protect their jobs, and corporate threats of plant closures or lay-offs in response to environmental pressures. In his November 1986 speech to an audience of Ontario labour representatives and environmentalists, White argued:

> First,...the real issue for us is not to choose between economic growth and the environment. We must organize society to achieve both because we must have both. The environment sustains and enriches us. Economic growth and technology are tools for helping us to develop as individuals and as a society. Second,... rejecting the false choice between economic progress and the environment requires putting these issues into a broader social context. It means recognizing that we don't have to take the world as given but can change it, that we don't have to be dominated by the priorities of the marketplace, but can challenge them and establish our own different priorities. And third,... if we do want to address such changes in society, we can only do it by articulating our own vision of what the world can be like, building alliances, and mobilizing amongst those who are likely to share our goals.[3]

This statement raises the question: "What kind of alliances should unions seek?" White's

Two Strategies of Social Unionism

arguments suggest that what he has in mind is a counter-hegemonic, politico-ideological project. The alliances this would entail are far more transformative than the short-term, tactical links between organisations that are typically made during electoral campaigns, or strikes, or regarding specific policies or issues.

As the CAW's environmental policy got off the ground, however, alliances were being formed primarily at the national and organisational levels. In June 1987 the Canadian Council voted to affiliate the CAW with Great Lakes United, a bi-national environmental organisation focusing on Great Lakes Basin pollution issues. According to the Chairperson of the CAW Council Environment Committee, the CAW was, by September 1987, "becoming active in, and taking out memberships in many environmental organizations, such as Canadian Coalition on Acid Rain, Greenpeace, Great Lakes United, Ontario and [the] Canadian Environmental Network, to name a few." He added that "labour people have presented briefs to many hearings and participate in some Environment Canada programs, such as the Environment Week Regional Advisory Committee."[4] The CAW Council Environment Committee endorsed NDP-sponsored legislation and policies (e.g., Ruth Grier's Environmental Bill of Rights, a private member's bill introduced in the Ontario Legislature). Moreover, public concern about the environment was viewed as a crucial element of the campaign against the Conservative government's proposed Free Trade Agreement.[5]

As the national CAW environment committee has found its feet, it has begun to evolve policies for transmission down to the local committees. This is the normal mode of operation of the standing committees. The local political action committees, for example, have been committees to elect the NDP, reflecting the (at least until the 1990s) close alliance between the national CAW leadership and the federal and Ontario NDP. Moreover, this is what the local activists expect—otherwise they do not know what they are "supposed" to be doing. A few environmental activists expressed concern that there was a lack of direction from the national about their work. In the meantime, they were doing what their local situations suggested was most important and possible, continually alert for signs of approval or disapproval from the local executives or "the national." Gordon Taylor (an environmental activist in Local 1973), said in an interview in July 1987: "We didn't have any guidelines to go on, so I wrote a letter to the CAW [National Office] asking for direction." He was worried at that time about having taken it upon himself to attend a public meeting at the City Hall on the draft Canadian Environmental Protection Act, because he had no instructions from the union to do so. He made suggestions for changes to the draft, and then sent them in writing to the National CAW committee, to see if they were "all right." Taylor received a reply from Basil Hargrove, then assistant to President White, in July 1987.[6] In it Hargrove apologized for "the lack of direction from our office," and said that "we have now taken steps to correct this." Specifically: "We have asked National Staff Representative Bob Chernecki to take the responsibility of working with the CAW Council environmental committee and working with this committee and the local unions on the environmental issues facing both our members and the communities in which they live." The CAW Council environment committee had just taken its resolutions in June 1987 to affiliate with Great Lakes United, and to support Ruth Grier's Environmental Bill of Rights,[7] and had not yet given much thought as to how the local committees would function.

When interviewed almost a year later, in May 1988, Taylor said he had not received any further correspondence from the national committee; nor had he been informed of the meetings in Toronto or their agenda. Lynwood Martin, of Local 89, had a similar story. When I interviewed him in August 1987, he had never heard of Bill Van Gaal, chairperson of the national committee, and knew nothing about the national committee's work. In

May 1988 the CAW Council Environment Committee's three members were (in addition to Chernecki, who was liaison with Bob White's office) Fraser Gillis, Local 444's delegate to the CAW Canada Council; Gary St. Laurent, Local 195's delegate to the CAW Canada Council; and Bill Van Gaal, Local 707's delegate to the Canada Council and committee chairperson. The normal practice is to appoint only elected executive-level officials to the CAW Canada Council committees; rank-and-file environmental activists are not "eligible."

The national environment committee was discussing the issue of industrial sewer discharges. One idea it was considering in May 1988 was to set up an environment workshop (focusing on sewer discharges and municipal policies to upgrade sewer systems and improve monitoring) at the next CAW conference on occupational health and safety. Council Environment Committee members had just participated in a full-day workshop on this issue at the national offices in Toronto. The purpose of the symposium, according to St. Laurent, would be to educate members of the local environment committees about the problems related to sewage, so that they could then monitor their own plants for illegal dumping into the sewers. These committees, in other words, would function like the occupational health and safety committees, attempting to enforce existing government legislation. If they failed to convince employers to stop their polluting practices, the next step would be to have members of the CAW Canada Council Environment Committee visit the offending plant management. Local environmental activists were interested in these ideas, and wanted to participate in the meetings of the national committee; however, they found that they were not invited, and concluded that the officials in the committee wanted to preserve policy-making for themselves. St. Laurent was more sympathetic to the frustration of these activists; they viewed him as a kind of liaison between themselves and the national level. In April 1988 members of the Local 444 and Local 199 environment committees requested a meeting with Chernecki, Van Gaal, Gillis, and St. Laurent "to discuss more input from the rank-and-file committees and try and give them some direction and suggestions on how to communicate better with rank-and-file committees and assist in developing local union environment committees."[8]

By mid-1988 the national committee was beginning to develop a framework for the work of the local committees: they would be encouraged to function in a parallel way to the occupational health and safety committees, only dealing with problems of plant pollution of the external environment; certain priorities and programmes would be developed at the national level and transmitted down to the locals through their environmental standing committees; committee members would participate in union courses on selected environmental problems, legislation, etc. This plan contained elements of both the strategies outlined above. On the one hand, building on parallels with occupational health and safety and focusing on workplace-based issues would provide a base for educating and involving rank-and-file workers. On the other hand, this involvement would be limited by the legislative focus and by the procedural aspects of a standing committee. As for the activists at the base, they seemed to be pursuing two strategies at once: trying to insert themselves into the decision-making bodies higher up the ladder, as rank-and-file representatives, and determining their own priorities at the local level, independent of policies being discussed by the national committee. (These activities are discussed in the following section.)

The nature of the alliances at the grassroots level envisaged by the national leadership was ambiguous. In his April 1987 speech to CAW union officials, White argued: "The labour movement has been showing that, given information and some workplace power, the work environment can be improved. We just similarly mobilize to show that the external environment can be protected."[9] The implication was that local unions would tackle environmental problems by incorporating such concerns into their bargaining relations with employers; environmental protection would be an extension of occupational health and safety struggles. This would require the mobilization not only of rank-and-file support, but of public pressure for legislative reforms. (For example, the union movement supports legislation modelled on occupational health and safety legislation which would give workers the right to refuse work which pollutes the environment.) Again, this seemed to indicate an approach which is concerned with involving rank-and-file workers. But was this happening at the local level?

ENVIRONMENTAL COMMITTEE PRIORITIES

While rank-and-file environmental activists interviewed between 1986 and 1988 saw many parallels between occupational and environmental health issues (especially with regard to job blackmail and employers' resistance), their priorities in this period were not employer-oriented. In the Windsor area, they were trying to establish the legitimacy of the environmental committees within their locals, to raise the awareness of union members about local environmental issues, and to form organisational-level alliances with environmental groups in the area. Their priorities in terms of issues reflected the agenda of the non-union organisations (e.g., the People for Clean Air/Evergreen Alliance, Clean Water Alliance, Citizens Concerned about Fermi II, Great Lakes United, etc.) rather than the agenda suggested by auto industry-related pollution (the Ford Foundry, auto plant emissions, recycling of auto industry scrap material, expanded public transportation, fuel-efficient vehicles, etc.). When asked to list environmental issues in which their union was involved, survey respondents most often mentioned (apart from issues of occupational health and safety) the Detroit incinerator, Fermi II, and general "air" or "water" pollution. Problems specific to CAW-organised plants (Chrysler plant paint fumes, the Ford Foundry, General Chemical's air emissions) were mentioned by only a very few members of the locals concerned (quite likely the environmental committee members, or other union representatives) (see table 25). No bargaining was going on over environmental issues between these locals and their employers.

TABLE 25
ENVIRONMENTAL ISSUES (NUMBER OF TIMES MENTIONED) VS. LOCAL NUMBER

	Local 444	Local 1973	Local 89	Local 200	Local 1498	Local 195	Total nn
Detroit incinerator	13	19		5	4	3	44
Fermi II	15	7	3	1	6	2	34
Air/Water	9	10	4	1	2	2	28
Ford Foundry				5			5
Clean Water Alliance	1	2		1			4
RAPS	2						2
Occ. Health & Safety	8	6		10	20		44
Chrysler		1					1
Other auto	1						1
Gen. Chemical			3				3
Barge	2					1	3
Landfill	1	4				1	6
Other local	7		1				8
Other big	3	1	1	3	2		10

During 1986 to 1987, the key concern of the environmental committees in Windsor was the campaign against the construction of the Detroit incinerator. The locals also made some presentations regarding the Great Lakes Water Quality Agreement and the draft Canadian Environmental Protection Act. The Fermi II nuclear reactor was another concern. All these were simultaneously at the top of the agenda of the area environmental and citizens' groups, and there was significant involvement of certain CAW activists in these organisations. Indeed, the base of these activists in the citizens' groups, and the growing influence of the latter vis-à-vis local media and the Ontario government, helped to establish the position of environmental activists within their locals. The leadership of the CAW locals perceived an opportunity to demonstrate social concern in alliance with the citizens' groups. At this juncture they could do so from a position of strength, without, that is, having to cede any autonomy or leadership, and without any perceived risks to the economic interests of their members.[10]

By contrast, the Detroit Incinerator controversy placed the United Auto Workers of America in Detroit in an awkward situation. Community activists urged the UAW to oppose the incinerator option because of concern for health—especially the health of the working class population of the Cass Corridor—and because of the job-intensive nature of an alternative "4Rs" (recycle, reuse, reduce, recover) waste handling strategy. However, the UAW had benefited in the past from a close relationship with Detroit's Democratic Mayor, Coleman Young, the incinerator's key proponent. The UAW avoided taking a position for months, before eventually deciding to support the incinerator, but to call on the federal government to subsidize better pollution technology. This stand was very disappointing to the citizens and environmental organisations grouped in the Evergreen Alliance. One Alliance member, Julia Beard, expressed the views of many in her group in an interview in May 1988. She felt that the UAW had acted mainly out of self-interest and was not a reliable ally in the environmental struggle.[11] However, the incinerator issue was a relatively "safe" one for the CAW; it entailed no immediate conflicts with the union's political allies. This was also the case for other issues pursued during the initial period of the existence of the environmental committees: CEPA, Great Lakes water quality, Fermi II, pesticides, the Peerless Cement issue, the barging of toxic waste across the Detroit River, and participation in the Detroit River Remedial Action Plan.

By 1988, a few of the committees (Locals 444, 195) were beginning to turn their attention to questions of workforce responses to employers' polluting activities, and to examine the ways in which some of their own employers were implicated. This development reflected the agenda of the national environment committee, which was becoming clearer by this stage. The emerging conception of the functions of the environmental standing committees paralleled the activities and structures of the occupational health and safety committees. This direction contained all kinds of ambiguities. On the one hand, the focus on "inward"-oriented activities seemed to hold more potential for a strategy which emphasizes rank-and-file mobilization, e.g., one could envisage campaigns to link polluting activities with other social costs of production for the purpose of profit, and actions to demonstrate workers' opposition to the socialisation of these costs, as well as solidarity with citizens "outside." On the other hand, if the environmental committees were to define their functions within the same parameters as existing occupational health and safety committees, the emphasis would more likely be on legislative lobbying and the training of workplace representatives to interpret legislation.

The national leadership's view of the appropriate direction for the environment committees was to some extent set out in the statements of Bob White and Gary St. Laurent quoted above. It included training for union environmental representatives who would attempt to enforce existing environmental legislation (through the Ministry of the

Environment) and to inform workers of their environmental rights. The environmental committees would also lobby governments for stronger environmental legislation. It was suggested that eventually there might be environment representatives in the plants, a situation which has been achieved for occupational health and safety through legislation and collective bargaining. By May 1989, the local committees were discussing the possibility of obtaining funding for environmental training courses for rank-and-file workers, along the lines of those in existence for occupational health and safety.[12] Several union representatives suggested that environmental concerns might eventually be included in the locals' collective bargaining agendas.[13]

At the same time, all the activists interviewed stressed education of rank-and-file members as a priority. They were not satisfied with the means available to them to do this, but they did not have concrete ideas about alternative union structures or procedures which would "activate" the membership. Nor did they have clear ideas about where they wanted to lead their co-workers. For Gordon Taylor and Lynwood Martin, education would itself resolve the conflicts facing workers—i.e., the problem was to convince workers and employers to change their ways. Rick Coronado and Mike Longmoore had more radical views of the conflict between profit and environmental protection—indeed, between profit and desirable social goals in general.

For Longmoore, radical change would require a very long term process of raising the political consciousness of workers, through their union organisations; he was committed to working from within this organisational base. The environment committee provided him with a toehold in the union structure. He defended the priorities of the unions (in particular job security) and was critical of the goals and tactics of environmental organisations like Greenpeace: "The labour movement has a different tactical perspective than, say, Greenpeace. I always saw Greenpeace in this way: …'We do this…outstanding action and the masses of the people immediately see the truth and the clarity of what happened.' [T]his is opposed to—polarized against—the concept that you have to organize the masses day by day, inch by inch… "[14] According to Longmoore, the priorities and goals of the environment committees should be:

> to engage in mass work in the plants…[We] have a great [opportunity], I mean, there are 7,000 people working in those plants, and they must have seventy thousand relatives all over the place… if you can influence those people to take some kind of action…offering them the service of the environment committee if they have a problem in their own community—building it up—that's where I see a major role: education, organization of the workforce, building a bridge between the general environmental movement and the labour movement, resolving contradictions within the labour movement on the question of the environment.

On the question of whether the means exist within the union structure to achieve these goals, and what might be changed to facilitate educational work, Longmoore had this answer:

> [T]he environment committees are…an important way to build unity in the work environment. But it requires… for the union to realize that the union is not just the bunch of lawyers sitting in the union office, like the stewards and committeemen getting people passes on Saturday night… It requires a change in the attitude of the workers and in the union office that the stewards and committeemen have got to be organizers—got to get in those plants. For instance, on the environment committees—make sure that people know what the environmental concerns are and how the environment committees will serve the needs of those

people. That's an educational ... organizational thing. You've got the organization there. The company's organized us very well into departments and plants and everything else, so all we've got to do is plug into that organization, and bring it to life in the interests of the environment committees and the union in general. The environment committees are part of the process of bringing this union to complete maturity.

More concretely, Longmoore added: "[If I were the president of the local], I would liberate some money. They're already spending thousands of dollars on their sports teams—they're in the red. I would spend money, and maybe begin to hold conferences ... to decide which way our local is going. How can we get people active and involved in their union? I would begin holding open meetings...in the union hall."

Longmoore's greatest concern regarding the future of the environmental committees was that they would become identified with the "outside" environmental movement and would thereby jeopardize their credibility with union officials. (His image of the environmental movement was one commonly held in the labour movement, i.e., that of a single-issue movement with no agenda for economic development.)

[We] have to be careful that the CAW environmental committees do not get captured by the outside environmental committees...that they begin to reflect the general environmental movement and no longer reflect the labour movement perspective on environmental concerns, which probably is different from the general environmental movement. The spectrum of the general environmental movement is probably this wide [gesture]—you've got everybody that wants to go back to nature, from one extreme to the other. Whereas the labour movement is concerned with job protection, a clean environment in the plant, the area around the plants—you know they've got all these concrete questions they have to address, whereas the general environmental movement sometimes...may not have the same focus. They may not be as concerned about jobs. They may say, "well, who cares about jobs? If this poisoning doesn't stop we're all going to be dead in 20 years." The labour movement can't have this perspective. So, if environmental committees are captured by the general environmental movement, then they might find themselves in conflict with the labour movement in general and at that point, the leadership of the CAW is going to squash them. If they see them as not furthering the goals of the labour movement whatever they might be... Like, our little organization could be squashed tomorrow.

While Longmoore's political views were in some ways more radical than those of Gordon Taylor, on the issue of the Ford Foundry, his approach was arguably the more conservative of the two. Longmoore said that the other CAW locals should be sensitive to the predicament of the Ford local, and not intervene. Taylor, on the other hand, condemned the Ford local for its failure to take a position on the pollution problem at its plants. Longmoore's strategy for achieving his objectives within the union structure was, in general, more cautious than Taylor's. When I asked Taylor what limits he thought he might come up against, vis-à-vis the union hierarchy and the "priority" concerns of the union, he said he did not know—that he would just keep going until he was stopped, and then he would think about what he would do. He was already getting negative reactions to his vocal position on the Ford Foundry.

THE FORD FOUNDRY CASE

The case of the Ford Foundry yields some insights into the differing strategic assumptions within the CAW regarding alliances with actors in the environmental movement. The Foundry case also suggests some of the limitations of the early stage of the CAW's environmental policy. Pressure on Ford to reduce air pollution from the old Foundry in Windsor began in the 1970s. The emissions have included dust and diamine compounds (which smell like decaying fish), iron, cadmium, chromium, copper, molybdenum, and sulphur gases. Ford management claimed that it had spent $8 million between 1970 and 1983 to control emissions. However, citizens in the area continued to complain of eye irritations, bronchial and sinus problems, and nausea. In late November 1983 more than 100 persons met to protest Ford Foundry pollution. A management representative told citizens that: "Unfortunately this is not a hospital, it is a foundry."[16] Nevertheless, Ford promised to spend another $400,000 by July 1984. The pollution control programme included the conversion of furnaces from coal to gas, installation of smokestack scrubbers, and taller stacks.

Despite Ford's claims that the problems were being remedied, area citizens continued to suffer from the odour, noise, and health effects of the Foundry.[17] A Citizens' Committee (for Ford) had formed by February 1985. Between 1986 and 1987 Ford implemented a number of measures to modernize the Foundry, which were presented as environmental expenditures. These included: a new baghouse collector for the basic oxygen furnace ($300,000), an improved 1E and 1W arc furnace baghouse ($100,000), a tipple separation system to purify recharge materials ($120,000), and new induction furnaces to replace five arc furnaces ($2 million).[18] There were citizens' meetings throughout 1986 and 1987; area members of parliament, Ford management, and union representatives were invited to participate.

The interviews with union members and the survey responses to the hypothetical case of a polluting employer indicate different perceptions of the choices available to the union in such a situation. On the one hand there is the "activist" approach of Gordon Taylor, which is echoed in general terms by various officials (e.g., Gerard). On the other hand, there is the cautious approach of Mike Longmoore, which is reflected in the passive behaviour of the Ford union executive.

By 1988, Taylor had been active for several years in the citizens' group protesting pollution from the Ford Foundry. He had in fact worked for ten years (until 1975) in the Foundry, before his jobs at Chrysler and General Motors. In addition to the external environmental problems caused by the Foundry, working conditions inside were considered poor. He had become involved in the citizens' group because he felt they could benefit from his experience inside the plant, and because he perceived that Ford's management was trying to deceive the citizens.

> I find that these people are going into meetings and they have to deal with Ford engineering personnel that snow them. Well, they're not going to snow me. I worked for Ford Motor Co. I worked in the Foundry and I'm fully aware of all the hazards in that environment, and what they're doing and what they're not doing. And I'm there to make sure that those people [know] that that's malarky. [Ford] *can* do it. Ford is upset because I speak out. I have executives telling me that they can't find the source of noise in the plant, or they can't find the source of the smell—which is a bunch of baloney. You might be able to tell a poor old woman on Drouillard Road that, but you're not going to tell me that.

In Taylor's view, the Ford local should have been taking a much more active role in the process, helping the citizens deal with Ford management. According to Taylor, the citizens' dealings were solely with management; the union had remained passive. Yet union officials, it seems, had complained about his outspoken participation in the citizens' group.

> I've been taking a lot of flak for [participating in the citizens' group]. I've even been approached by a former member of the [Ontario] legislature [who asked] me why—instead of complaining in the newspaper—I didn't approach the president of Local 200. I said, "Look, the president of Local 200 is fully aware that an environment committee is required by the constitution of the CAW. It's up to him to take the initiative to do it." Why he's not doing that, I don't know, but a lot of the problems at Ford could be solved, if they had an environment committee, because they could work from within to try and correct some of these problems... I told him [the M.P.]... "It's time the president of Local 200 ... implemented an environment committee ... and at least show [that] the workers are trying to do something. [If not], then take the flak in the newspaper, buddy. I don't care. This guy really bothered me, because we were at a health and safety conference and he said: "It's kind of embarrassing, you know—you got a labour guy on this committee, and he's squawking about pollution." I said, "Wait a minute, don't give me that—that it's not their fault. You haven't been there. If Local 200 is so concerned, tell them to come to the [citizens'] meetings and speak out."

It is evident from this statement that Taylor has a fairly clear idea of what the environmental committee should do—what its function should be in relation to its employer's environmental practices. In this case, it should side with the citizens in pressuring the company to clean up, and it should do so both from within the plant and publicly, in conjunction with the citizens' organisations.

When I suggested to Taylor that Ford workers might be reluctant to take these kinds of actions because of fear that the Foundry will close, he had two responses. The first was one of principle: "There's always been threats. That's what we have to live with every day. But my life and my community are more important than Ford Motor Company." The second was a denial of the existence of a real conflict. Taylor argued that the Foundry makes a lot of money, and therefore management's claim that pollution control is too costly is false. This argument implies, however, that the company's bluff will somehow be called, either by union or other independent research, or by government intervention. Even if such threats are mere bluffs in many or even most cases, there will be occasions when environmental demands do conflict with the profit goals of a corporation to the point that closure may be threatened. What is to be done in such a case? Ken Gerard's reply was:

> They ought to close 'em down...until the correct facilities are there to stop it. There's no other answer. Profits can't come over human beings... Corporations must be closed down when they pollute. They must be made to pay workers while they're down correcting that facility. They can't take away the livelihood of a person and it's their responsibility to do that correctly from day one. If they put more pressure...they would build in the necessary protection from day one. They escape it because of the cost. It goes to the lousy dollar bill—the buck. If you're going to put the protection of profit over people, then you're going to be a polluter... If the government was tough on them, there'd be no polluters.

A second approach, suggested by Mike Longmoore, is more cautious, that is, it places greater emphasis on the reality of job blackmail and on the union's responsibility to protect jobs. Longmoore saw Local 444 as a "strong" local, in terms of the size of its membership, the relative profitability of Chrysler's assembly plants in Windsor, and the politics of its leadership. He contrasted it to the Ford local, Local 200, which he saw as too weak to "take on the company." In this context, he concluded: "Local 200 is much softer on the pollution problem coming out of Ford's than I think they should be, but at the same time there's got to be a sensitivity within the environmental movement to each concrete situation. Each Local's got a different situation." Local 444, he said, should not involve itself in the affairs of Local 200 against the latter's wishes. Longmoore's views may also reflect his cautious approach to union alliances with environmental organisations, discussed above. In a case like the Ford Foundry, the workforce's concerns about job security should take precedence over the environmental concerns of area citizens or other "outside" groups; otherwise, the environmental committee risks isolation from the membership, thereby losing its potential base. The problem with this approach seems to be that it suggests no way out of the closed circle of union goals and functions. What is the environmental committee to do in the short and medium terms, to pose *alternatives* to the jobs/environment trade-off?

The local executive on the horns of this dilemma tried to downplay the existing conflict. When Local 200 President Frank McAnally was asked: "What role do you think the environmental committee should play in a case where the union's plant is a polluter?" his answer was: "Well, I think we've already done that [without an environmental committee]. We've had our Foundry committee started four or five years ago, in opposition to the pollution put into the air." He implied that the union had taken the initiative in forming a committee on this issue. When asked directly, however, whether this was the case, he admitted that it was a "community committee." It was headed by a woman whose name he could not remember, who invited the union and a local NDP Member of Parliament, Dave Cook, to participate. According to McAnally:

> There were several meetings held with the guy they appointed from Ford's—Max Jackson, the head engineer in the Foundry. They spent a lot of money in cleaning up the air. It's still not the best, but it's—I forget how many millions of dollars they spent as a result of this committee...and complaints from the community. So we took a very active role in participating in that committee. We attended the meetings and listened to the complaints... A lot of those complaints we were already lodging, in terms of the same kind of pollution in the plant. Maybe we were there to a certain extent for selfish reasons, because when things were done to clean up the pollutants...it affected [working conditions] inside the plant.

Opinions differed as to how "active" Local 200's participation in the citizens' committee was. Although McAnally said that the local's participation had been "official," and that he, as well as the union plant chairperson at the Foundry had attended, Gordon Taylor claimed that Local 200 had not participated, and Mike Longmoore had observed only "a couple of committeemen" at a meeting. He mentioned, moreover, that the citizens had been "pushing Local 200 to take a position" on Foundry pollution.[19] When I interviewed McAnally in August 1987, he did not know who the contact persons in the citizens' group were, or if the committee were still meeting. He emphasized, however, that Ford had spent "millions" to clean up the problem, implying that it had been taken care of, if not to the union's satisfaction, at least to a significant extent.

From these insights into the Ford Foundry case, several conclusions relevant to our analysis emerge. First, where the most developed conflict between citizens and an employer existed, the local union had not created an environmental committee to act as its representatives or as a special task force; local executive officers had acted to some extent as representatives at citizens' meetings, but there had been no real exchange of services or coordination of strategies. The union does not appear to have done any research on the economic costs or the technological alternatives available to reduce the pollution problem. (Nor does it seem to have been particularly successful in negotiating improvements in internal working conditions, prior to the additional pressure from the citizens outside.) Second, at no point was there any mobilization of rank-and-file members around the pollution issue, and all contact with the citizens occurred through union officials.

Third, a plant closure crisis has thus far been averted by the apparent profitability of the plant despite the expenditures on pollution control equipment and modernization. The possibility that demands for further investment in environmental improvement could eventually lead to a plant closure (or at least provide the pretext for one) seems to have been sufficient to limit the union's participation in the conflict. Local 200's executive had played its hand very cautiously, while warding off accusations that it had failed to be a "pro-active" union by downplaying the problem.

For Longmoore, this strategy was understandable and responsible, given that local's particular weaknesses. For Taylor (and at least rhetorically, Gerard), there was potential to push more. What leads some activists and officials in the CAW to be so confident that the jobs-versus-the-environment trade-off can be avoided? Their assumptions are examined below, in the section entitled "Social Unionism and Social Democracy." But before turning to this question, it is helpful to look first at the evidence on the way environmental issues, and the environmental committees, were seen by the rank and file, and how their views relate to the strategic priorities discussed above.

RANK-AND-FILE AWARENESS OF THE ENVIRONMENTAL POLICY

There was in general a low level of awareness among union members of the CAW's environmental policies and structures, and of the environmental activities of their union. Sixty percent said they were not aware of the environmental activities of their union, and this figure was probably low, for two reasons. First, when asked to list these issues, only 42 out of 267 (or 15.7 percent) could *name* one issue (compared to the 40 percent who said they were aware of them). Second, the sample overall probably represents a relatively more informed sub-group of the total union membership due to the method of questionnaire distribution.[20] Seventy-five percent said they were not aware of the CAW's decision to initiate environmental standing committees, and only 24 percent said that they were aware of the existence of an environmental committee in their local where one indeed existed. About 4 percent of respondents confused the environment committee with the occupational health and safety committee. (Most of these were in Local 1498, where little differentiation is made between the two by the executive.)

Cross-tabulation of union position with awareness of the existence of the committees showed that rank-and-file members who had held no union positions were the least aware of the existence of the committees (68 percent said they did not know the committees existed).[21] Members who had held an elected position claimed more knowledge (53 percent said they knew about the committees). Five out of eight members who had held executive office said they knew about the committees. Those who did know about the committees were asked to report how they had obtained this information. The two means most often listed (table 26) were: word of mouth/from a union representative and at a union meeting. This fits with the finding that members who had held union office (i.e., who were already integrated into the structures of the union, to varying extents) were more likely to know about the committees than rank-and-file members, whose main sources of information would be the local's bulletin or tabloid, and information posted in the workplace.[22]

I attempted to determine whether the environment committees were making a difference in raising awareness among rank-and-file members by cross-tabulating the

Two Strategies of Social Unionism 267

TABLE 26
MEANS OF INFORMATION ABOUT COMMITTEES LISTED BY RESPONDENTS
(NUMBER OF TIMES LISTED)

Word of mouth or union rep	23
Union meeting	20
Participation in OHS cttee.	6
Local paper	4
Other	4
Elections for environment committee	3
Information posted	3
Windsor media	3

responses to various questions with membership of the different locals. Locals 200 and 1498 did not have environment committees at the time their surveys were returned. Eleven out of eighteen of Local 195's forms were returned in 1987 before the local had an environmental standing committee. Local 89 had an environmental committee, but it had not organised any activities by the time the surveys were completed. Thus only Locals 444 and 1973 had active environmental committees in 1987, and therefore it might be expected that members of these locals would have higher levels of awareness than those in the other locals. The surveys from Local 444, moreover, were returned much later (March-July 1988) than those from the other locals, and thus these members had a longer period of exposure to the existence of the environment committee. (See appendix 1.)

Responses to the question "Are you aware of the environmental issues in which your union is involved?" (table 27) show that claimed awareness was indeed greater in Locals

TABLE 27
AWARENESS OF ENVIRONMENTAL ISSUES AMONG CAW LOCALS
(NUMBER AND PERCENT FOR EACH LOCAL)

Local no.	Aware No. (%)	Not aware No. (%)	No answer No. (%)	No. of respondents
1973	N=38 44.2	N=47 54.7	N=1 1.2	86
200	N=17 28.3	N=42 70.0	N=1 1.7	60
1498	N=12 46.2	N=13 50.0	N=1 3.8	26
89	N=5 25.0	N=13 65.0	N=2 10.0	20
444	N=31 42.5	N=41 56.2	N=1 1.4	73
Totals	N=103 38.6	N=158 59.2	N=6 2.2	N=267 100.0

TABLE 28
WILLINGNESS TO PARTICIPATE IN A LOCAL ENVIRONMENT COMMITTEE
(NUMBER AND PERCENT FOR EACH LOCAL)

Local no.	No Answer no. (%)	Yes no. (%)	No no. (%)	Maybe no. (%)	Row Total no. (%)
No local given				N=2 100.0	N=2 .7
1973	N=1 1.2	N=20 23.3	N=14 16.3	N=51 59.3	N=86 32.2
200	N=1 1.7	N=7 11.7	N=10 16.7	N=42 70.0	N=60 22.5
1498		N=3 11.5	N=11 42.3	N=12 46.2	N=26 9.7
89		N=2 10.0	N=8 40.0	N=10 50.0	N=20 7.5
444	N=1 1.4	N=8 11.0	N=20 27.4	N=44 60.3	N=73 27.3
Column Total	N=3 1.1	N=40 15.0	N=63 23.6	N=161 60.3	N=267 100.0

1973 and 444. Members of Local 1498 tended to equate their occupational health and safety issues with environmental issues, so the high (46.2 percent) "yes" response for this local overstates the level of awareness.

The Ford Local and Local 89 showed the lowest levels of awareness. However, the responses from 444 and 1973 in this case must be interpreted as reflecting in part the relatively large number of respondents in these groups who "had held" or "currently hold" elected union positions (23 and 36 percent respectively); this group, by virtue of its greater involvement in the union, tends to have better knowledge of its activities than rank-and-file members who have never held a union position. In addition, Local 444's survey forms—as noted above—were returned after several months of lobbying by the environmental and educational committees in that local. These factors also apply to the interpretation of the responses to the question: "Before reading this survey, were you aware of the CAW Canada Council's decision to establish environmental committees in all CAW locals?" (question #3). Thirty-four percent of Local 1973 respondents claimed to be aware of the decision, compared to 24.7 percent of Local 444 respondents, 15.0 percent from Local 200, 11.5 percent from Local 1498, and 20.0 percent from Local 89.

For the question: "Do you think you will participate in the environment committee of your local in the future?" Local 1973 showed a notably more positive response than the other locals (table 28). The most negative responses came from Locals 1498 and 89. Interestingly, a great many respondents from Local 200, where workers confront the Ford Foundry problem, said they would consider participating in future (70.0 percent). Indeed, combining the yes/maybe categories, the positive responses from Locals 1973 and 200 were about the same (82.0 percent).

Two Strategies of Social Unionism 269

TABLE 29
WILLINGNESS TO PARTICIPATE IN A NON-UNION ENVIRONMENT GROUP
(NUMBER AND PERCENT FOR EACH LOCAL)

Local No.	No answer No. (%)	Yes No. (%)	No No. (%)	Maybe No. (%)	Row Total No. (%)
No local given		N=1 50.0		N=1 50.0	N=2 .7
1973	N=1 1.2	N=23 26.7	N=12 14.0	N=50 58.1	N=86 32.2
200	N=1 1.7	N=11 18.3	N=9 15.0	N=39 65.0	N=60 22.5
1498		N=2 7.7	N=7 26.9	N=17 65.4	N=26 9.7
89		N=4 20.0	N=5 25.0	N=11 55.0	N=20 7.5
444	N=1 1.4	N=11 15.1	N=17 23.3	N=44 60.3	N=73 27.3
Column Total	N=3 1.1	N=52 19.5	N=50 18.7	N=162 60.3	N=267 100.0

Locals 1973 and 200 also showed the most openness to participation in *non-union* environmental groups (table 29), but there was no marked difference between the responses from Locals 1973 and 444 (the two locals which had had environmental committees in place the longest), and the others.

In order to see if a longer period of environment committee activity had affected responses to the question: "Should the union be involved in environmental issues?" responses to this question were cross-tabulated with Local number. The result showed no indication that a higher yes response was related to membership in Local 444 or 1973. (Indeed, the longer the period of environment committee activity, the more negative was the response. Ninety-two percent of those who completed the survey between August and September 1987 said "yes" to this question, compared with 84 percent of those who answered between March and July 1988.)

Finally, an analysis by Local number of those who could list at least one environmental issue in which their union was involved, showed a higher level of awareness in the three locals with environment committees (table 30). (Occupational health and safety issues were of greatest concern in Locals 200 and 1498—35.7 and 66.7 percent of respondents from these locals, respectively, listed occupational health and safety issues at least once, when asked to list environmental issues.)

To summarize, the survey data do not show an unambiguous relationship between the existence of an environmental committee and the level of rank-and-file awareness of the issues or the policy. There is some evidence that at least some of the campaigns undertaken by the committees in Locals 444 and 1973 were known to a considerable number of respondents from those locals. However, because the samples from these locals likely included individuals who had been "briefed" by their union representatives or committee

TABLE 30
CAW LOCAL ABILITY TO NAME ONE ENVIRONMENTAL ISSUE
(THOSE WHO LISTED AT LEAST ONE ISSUE THAT WAS NOT OCCUPATIONAL HEALTH AND SAFETY)

Local	Number	Percent
1973	27	31.4
200	9	15.0
1498	4	14.3
89	5	25.0
444	24	32.8

members, as well as a significant proportion of union representatives (past and present), it is not possible to draw general conclusions from the data about the local memberships' levels of awareness.[23] No doubt the survey itself had an impact on raising awareness about the existence and work of the environmental committees.

Subsequent surveys would probably show that even more union members had become aware of some of the environmental committees' activities than was the case in 1987 or 1988. However, it is important to remember that what we are measuring, essentially, is the "trickle down" effect of the campaigns undertaken by union representatives. The educational function of these committees is indeed important, and may increasingly influence the attitudes and beliefs of rank-and-file workers. What we cannot measure, at this stage, is changes in participation. If the goals of the union do not include creating and facilitating collective tasks for its members, then the educational goals of the environmental committees will face certain limitations. There will be little encouragement to develop—with the participation of workers and in alliance with citizens—alternatives to the existing forms and social objectives of production. Indeed, it will be easier for the committees to continue acting as "transmitters" of information from the top down, or as representatives of the base vis-à-vis external organisations, despite their sincere commitments to rank-and-file education.

SOCIAL UNIONISM AND SOCIAL DEMOCRACY

OBJECTIVES OF THE LOCAL EXECUTIVES

Underlying the seemingly radical views of many union officials (with regard to the priority of environmental and other social goals over profit) were almost invariably a set of assumptions about a division of labour between the union and its political party, the NDP; the necessary and desirable functions of the government; and the extent to which radical social change is necessary for such goals to be achieved. While the national-level leadership of the CAW expresses a democratic socialist orientation, at the lower levels of the hierarchy (at least in the locals studied) social-democratic ideology prevailed.

From the perspective of the local executives, the ultimate goal of the CAW's environmental policy is to bring about parliamentary reforms that will strengthen the regulatory and enforcement powers of the government vis-à-vis the private sector. The precondition for such reforms is the election of a pro-environment, pro-labour government. Once this is achieved, the jobs-versus-the-environment conflict will be "dissolved" in the corporatist logic of the social-democratic State. The labour movement, for the most part, has not envisaged ecological goals so radical as to require a more profound restructuring of the economy. The private sector can, within this limited vision of change, accommodate more stringent restrictions on activities which have undesirable social costs, e.g., pollution. This is, essentially, the "environmental management" or "sustainable development" approach of big capital.

Whenever I posed the question of a fundamental conflict between an economy based on profit-seeking, and ecological goals, union officials denied the existence of such a conflict. Or rather, they agreed that there was a conflict, but they believed that it could be resolved by more government intervention, in the forms of more regulation, better enforcement, subsidies to the private sector, or State compensation to redundant workers. The solutions, in other words, fell within the traditional parameters of the social-democratic State. The social-democratic perspective of the local-level union officials is illustrated by the following statements (made in the interviews):

Ken Gerard: As already noted, Gerard saw the problem as the government's failure to do the job it should do; the union is therefore obliged to try to bring pressure to bear on polluting employers. If plants must close, then the government must compensate workers.

Tom Burton: When asked how the environmental committees could generate interest among rank-and-file workers, and make "more activists," he immediately switched the focus of the problem from the union to the political sphere: "Effecting a political change in the province, over time, will make [environmental protection] a more priority item within the government... I think that's where it's got to come from. Because it's a tax problem; it's a cost problem to effect environmental change. The Liberals and Conservatives don't have the environment as a high priority item." When I noted that we had moved from a discussion of the rank and file to a discussion of the NDP, Burton replied: "That's right, I think we [make activists] by making them [workers] more astute to the political process—the legislative process." In response to a question about what the union should do when its employer is a polluter, and where there is a threat of job blackmail, Burton replied: "I think the governments have a responsibility to facilitate with grants, if a corporation truly can't justify their own expenditures, to assist them to clean up their environment and maintain the jobs."

Gary Parent: when asked how one would preserve unity in a coalition of environmentalists and workers, if job blackmail were used against unions, he replied:

> I think this is 1987, not 1937, and the companies today should be forced to adhere to the regulations that are set up, weak as they may be. If that means that that person loses his/her job...then the government had better live up to its responsibility...to stop that intimidation... On the other hand, where the company uses a threat that they will have to close down if they stop dumping...then I think the government has a responsibility to provide the means for that company to get rid of the waste... Subsidies, definitely. I mean there has to be responsibility by governments either to stop the people making these harmful chemicals, or to provide and subsidize a way of getting rid of [them].

Leading right in to the NDP, Parent continued: "But you have to have the political will. And we have not had governments as of [this] date that have had the political will."

Jack Ewart: When asked what the *union environment committee* should do in a case where the employer is polluting, Ewart replied: "I don't think the government should allow the companies to have that right to turn around and blackmail you and [me]—to pollute anywhere they want. We've taken a strong position that...to clean up our environment will create jobs."

Gary St. Laurent: This official also denied that there were any irresolvable conflicts between the unions' environmental and job security goals within the existing system. He gave the example of a company where, he claimed, the union had investigated and supervised the cleaning up of an occupational health and safety problem, making the plant more viable. In relation to the Ford Foundry, he was asked: "What kinds of tactics could the union take to avoid being forced to accept this trade-off between jobs and the environment?" His reply began with the need to educate the workforce and the management about the problem. Even employers, he said, "are human beings first and foremost," despite the profit motive, and if they understand what the consequences are, they will improve conditions. His preferred strategy would be to "work with the management to correct the problem, rather than just shut the plant down."

OBJECTIVES OF THE RANK-AND-FILE ACTIVISTS
Gordon Taylor: When asked the same question about job blackmail, Taylor took the example of Kimberly-Clark, the paper company whose pollution of Lake Superior was a current issue in Ontario.[24] He said that in his view environmental protection should be the first priority, even if it means plant closure. However, when pressed, he refused to accept that there was a real conflict between environmental protection and jobs for many workers. He said that the government may have to pay workers to be retrained, or given incomes while their plants are being "modernized." Regarding Kimberly-Clark, Taylor said: "If I were the Ministry of the Environment, I would go tomorrow and put a lock on that door. I'd pay every person in that town welfare, and I'd make the rest of the residents of Ontario and the corporation pay until that thing was cleaned up." (The people have to pay, he said, because they demand the products, like bleached paper. This argument was also made by Kristina Lee, and is fairly common amongst the citizens' base of the environmental movement.)

Rick Coronado: The social-democratic consensus is not supported by all activists. Coronado, for example, defined his goals for the environment committee in more radical terms than many of his co-activists. For him, environmental improvements entail radical social change—challenging the traditional prerogatives of the corporations and constantly pushing for greater democratization of economic decision-making. With one foot in each of the union and the Windsor and District Clean Water (citizens') Alliance, Coronado was trying to synthesize their organisational and ideological approaches—in his words, to "bring them together." He was committed to working at the grassroots, often finding himself in conflict with higher-ranking officials in the union bureaucracy over the allocation of union resources.

The democratic socialist agenda for the union and for the environmental movement, which Coronado had increasingly come to represent, was shared by a small minority of union activists. Another member of the environment committee of Local 444 expressed some of the themes of a socialist conception of convergence: "Unfortunately, labour has not put enough importance on environmental education to really do an appropriate environmental impact study. Hopefully, if done properly, the environmental committees can be used as a teaching aid, [and] to develop our own resources and research facilities." He emphasized that workers and their communities are inseparable.[25]

RANK-AND-FILE VIEWS OF THE ENVIRONMENT-JOBS TRADE-OFF
The questionnaire described a hypothetical situation of a conflict between short-term job security and eliminating a source of environmental pollution. It then listed three possible courses of action for the union, and asked respondents to choose (*a*) the most desirable,

and (*b*) the most effective for protecting jobs. The choices were constructed in such a way that the first (1) represented a narrowly corporatist response (union alliance with management to prevent closure at all costs); the second (2) represented a social-democratic variant of "social unionism" (in which the union's focus would be government lobbying); and the third (3) represented a more active and autonomous role for the union in proposing alternatives, thereby implying a rejection of the necessity for citizens or workers to pay the costs of private-sector pollution. One difficulty with the analysis of the responses is that the respondents interpreted (3) to mean two different strategies. The first (3*a*) was a union-management negotiated solution, exclusive of interaction with the citizens' groups or political alliance/lobbying. The second (3*b*) was more or less what I intended by (3) above. In many cases respondents did not explain their choice of (3), and I interpreted these responses to mean support for a more active union involvement in working out alternatives, although alliances are not specified—a more ambiguous response (3*c*). Options 3*a*, 3*b*, and 3*c* are all distinguished from (1)—the most conservative, corporatist response—by the respondents' explicit acknowledgment that (3) represented an option in which neither jobs nor the environment would be traded away by the union. The question was whether they believed that the conflict could be resolved through "reasonable" company-union negotiation alone, or would require external pressure (in the form of alliances with citizens' groups, environmentalists, and parliamentary actors). Option (1) was clearly viewed as a choice of jobs over the environment—an acceptance of the necessity of a trade-off.

Through a somewhat tortuous contextual coding of responses to question 13, taking into account the written comments, I was able to group responses into five categories of union strategy, described below.

1. *Conservative-corporatist*: a rejection of union involvement in social issues beyond the workplace; the argument that the union's first priority ought to be defending jobs at whatever cost; an acceptance of a necessary trade-off between jobs and environmental protection; a rejection of alliances with other social actors.
2. *Social-democratic*: a belief that State intervention is necessary and/or desirable in order to resolve the conflict; emphasis on the inability of the union to protect jobs through bargaining alone; the view that resolving such conflicts is appropriately the responsibility of the State, and not unions; a rejection of the necessity of a trade-off; a range of attitudes towards alliances with other social actors.
3. *Social-corporatist*: an emphasis on a strong, socially-conscious union which should take a more active role in developing alternatives to the trade-off; a belief that such a union could resolve the conflict through negotiations with employers, not necessitating any outside alliances.
4. *Social-corporatist or convergence*: an emphasis on a strong, socially-conscious union and union leadership which would take a more active role in developing alternatives to the trade-off (as above), but alliances unspecified; this group could tend either towards a corporatist strategy (union-employer negotiation) or a convergence strategy (alliances with other social actors, questioning of profit goal).
5. *Convergence*: an emphasis on strong union leadership (as in 3 or 4 above) in developing alternatives; a critique of the profit goal/recognition of a fundamental conflict with environmental goals; an openness to alliances with other social actors; the rejection of an opposition between workers and citizens.

The pattern of support for these strategies is shown in table 31.

It is clear from these results that the social-democratic strategy is that most widely endorsed by union members. Also striking is the fact that the most conservative option was chosen by a mere 1.5 percent of the total sample population. Although no rank-and-

TABLE 31
SUPPORT FOR UNION STRATEGIES (FIVE LOCALS)

Strategy	Value	Frequency	Percent
No answer	0	4	1.5
Conservative-corporatist	1	4	1.5
Social-democratic	2	138	51.7
Social-corporatist	3	31	11.6
Social-corporatist or convergence	4	46	17.2
Convergence	5	44	16.5
Total		267	100

file survey of energy and chemical workers was carried out, the analysis in part 3 suggests that the "conservative-corporatist" strategy would have had a larger following in this workforce. It is also noteworthy, however, that 47.3 percent of survey respondents opted for a strategy in which the role for the union goes beyond the traditional boundaries of social-democratic practice, i.e., they favoured a more interventionist role for the union (by choosing options 3, 4, or 5).

An analysis of the "strategy" responses by union position (table 32) shows that the group most likely to express views corresponding to the strategy I defined as "convergence" was comprised of those who had held or who currently held *elected, non-executive positions* (25 percent). Most of the plant chairpersons and executive level officials chose a social-democratic response, although there were too few respondents in this category to generalize from the survey results alone. While 51 percent of those who had never held union positions chose the social democratic option, 46 percent placed greater emphasis on a more active role for the union in developing its own alternatives to the trade-offs posed by capitalist ownership of the means of production (i.e., chose options 3, 4, or 5). The latter figure compares with 47 percent of elected, non-executive representatives, and 25 percent of executive officials.

Comments made by the respondents illustrate their reasoning about the choices available to workers faced with a jobs-environment conflict. Option (1) was clearly viewed by those who *rejected* it as a "cop out," or "selling out the environment." One respondent who preferred option (1) summed up his reasons in this way: "No job, no money." The "social corporatist" option typically corresponded to beliefs such as: "Companies and unions should work together for the benefit of all."

The social-democratic strategic choice was explained by such comments as:

"No company should be allowed to operate without pollution controls. The government should fine them heavily for doing so and also tell them that if they close because they don't want to fix it that they will be heavily fined (in excess of 2 million dollars) and all of their assets will be confiscated. Our lives are priceless. Their machines aren't."

"I chose #2 because so often a company will threaten closure instead of compliance with the changes needed. If the company closes, the parts will be made somewhere else. The pollutants will still be emitted. This is why I believe the government should be involved. I don't believe the union alone can force the company into compliance. But together along with legislation from government it's *possible*."

Table 32
Highest Union Position Held by Choice of Union Strategy (five locals)
(number and percent for each choice)

Position	No answer	Conservative-corporatist	Social democratic	Social corporatist	Social corporatist/ convergence	Convergence	Row total
None	2 1.1	3 1.6	94 51.1	26 14.1	33 17.9	26 14.1	184 68.9
Elected, non-executive	2 2.8	1 1.4	35 48.6	5 6.9	11 15.3	18 25.0	72 27.0
Plant chair-person			3 100.0				3 1.1
Elected, executive			6 75.0		2 25.0		8 3.0
Column Total	4 1.5	4 1.5	138 51.7	31 11.6	46 17.2	44 16.5	267 100.0

"The government should grant funding to improve environmental issues, to reduce costs to companies, to reduce plant closures, and save jobs."

"The government should get involved with the union and company and reach a solution to benefit everybody."

"Lobbying government reps to change environmental laws is the only way to turn around air pollution and also changing existing laws pertaining to plant closures will protect more jobs."

"[If the problem were dealt with] properly, the government would supplement money to resolve the problem jointly" (former executive member of Local 200).

"The union's job is not to find the answers; that's the government's job... If we had a responsible government the union wouldn't have to spend so much time and funds on this" (respondent was an NDP member).

"My union should react to proposals not make them" (respondent was an NDP member).

"The environmental specialist should know what would work and why, and the government has the power to protect jobs if they wish to do so."

"There will be no jobs lost if the government steps in and forces the company to obey the law."

Statements accompanying the "convergence" strategy included:

"The union would look to viable alternatives in a general way, whereas the company would only look at the profit margins when making their decisions."

"If the union analyzed the situation and proposed an alternative solution, the plant could continue operating, albeit at a lower profit margin."

"This is the avenue I believe the union should always have taken. Offering intelligent, creative and well-researched alternatives. However,...this has not been established practice."

"Naturally we are concerned about our jobs and we will have to continue the fight for plant closure legislation, but at the same time we have to be socially, economically, and environmentally responsible and put forward our solution."

"Industry seems more concerned about profit for owners and/or shareholders than human needs and do [sic] not put money towards environmental problems unless pressured into doing so, in most cases. Our tax dollars and our union dues should not have to be spent on environmental problems. Industries and corporations have made considerable profits over the years; they have not been held financially accountable for damage they have done to our environment and our health. For this reason some of our union dues must go towards educating our members so that we can inform others in the community and perhaps take an active part in being accountable if we are causing pollution or know of someone that is causing harm to our environment."

"Large profits have to be put aside to ensure a safe and clean environment for future generations. People who knowingly pollute or damage the environment or workers must pay for clean-up plus take the initiative to stop."

"Companies are profit-motivated and will move away if profits are threatened. Governments don't seem able or willing to do much about this, so people should work on alternatives themselves."

"I think it is the union's responsibility to do the rational thinking on the issues."

One respondent wrote an exceptionally long commentary which expresses very well the strategic choices facing his union:

> By their very nature unions are social movements. Their very foundation rests in the social and economic betterment of their fellow members and society as a whole. While the hypothesis given [hypothetical case in the questionnaire] is perhaps a valid...predicament, the unions should not trade or deal away the very concepts they were founded on... The efforts of the unions should be to apply these basic concepts, along with new ways, means, ideas, and avenues, to today's problems. I feel that if the unions can do this now, then future problems will be able to be dealt with concisely and expertly.
>
> Right now I feel that union members—ours, at least—are confused as to what a union is all about and [as] to where the union is heading in the future. Are we merely an organized negotiating group that concerns itself with its members' economic success only? Or are we more than that? Are we a social force that not only cares for our members' economic concerns but also their health and general life happiness? I say that we are a social phenomena [sic]! I say that our concerns are concerns that whole populations are involved with! I say that by our very nature we have no choice but to take the lead in social concerns and to educate the public about what we know and therefore what we know needs to be done to correct serious social problems. At the very least I feel that we should be involved in all areas of society, involved so that our intelligent and strong voice can be heard and respected and lent to possible solutions.[26]

Conclusions

What can we conclude from autoworkers' views about union strategy with regard to the larger question of the potential for a convergence with other progressive social movements? First, it seems clear that the predominant conception of appropriate union strategy in the 1980s and at the local level was social-democratic. While this approach does not exclude alliances with other social actors, such as environmental organisations or citizens' groups, it puts these in the context of tactical, single-issue coalitions. Moreover, it emphasizes a parliamentary political strategy, closely associated with electoral support for the NDP, rather than grassroots educational and organising activities. The latter observation applies to union efforts both with other organisations and with the union's own base.

Higher levels of the union structure (local executive members, plant chairpersons) were more committed to a social-democratic agenda than lower ranking union representatives and those who held no union positions. At these levels there was an equally strong rejection of business unionism, but a wider range of opinion about what kind of role the union should play in society. There was evidence of considerable support among rank-and-file workers for a much more active role for the union in the areas of education, research, bargaining around social issues (and occupational health and safety and working conditions), as well as political leadership.

The cultural bias in favour of a social-democratic strategy, along with the institutional functions of the union, largely explain the nature of the CAW environmental committees' priorities in the 1980s. These were government lobbying, the institutionalization of the status and functions of the committee within the union, and the negotiation of workplace environmental committees. A minority but potentially substantial tendency had a more radical and grassroots oriented agenda, but this was difficult—if not impossible—to implement within the existing structures of the union. These people were also ambivalent about the potential of the union to be a vehicle for the kind of politics they envisaged.

Thus the kind of convergence with the environmental movement implied by the CAW's strategy was one based on a social-democratic consensus. This, indeed, fit nicely with the social-democratic consensus underpinning much of the environmental movement in Canada. The more radical critique of and alternatives to the hegemonic model of development proposed by social ecologists, among others, remained on the margins of both movements. The CAW's involvement with environmental coalition-building was occurring mainly at the level of organisational elites. Sam Gindin, research director for the CAW, also drew this conclusion at a more general level in a February 1988 article:

> The coalitions labour is involved in do not generally reach the grassroots. It's an exaggeration to think that through them, labour is involved in a social movement. More commonly, labour participates in some meetings, and endorses positions, and that's good because it helps legitimize the cause. For example, through labour's participation, it's less likely that the peace movement will be red-baited. But it doesn't mean that anything is happening at the grassroots. Again, this is a place where socialists who understand the importance of building participation at the grassroots level can have a role.[27]

Yet the activities of a small cadre of activists, seeking to make links between workplace experience and broader social struggles were potentially important. First, the survey results indicate that there existed considerable openness among rank-and-file members toward a convergence strategy. There was evidence, moreover, that activists in the CAW environmental committees were gradually influencing the opinions of rank-and-file workers, through regular columns in union publications, and a focus on in-plant recycling and other campaigns which would involve workers. The environment committee in Local 1973 (GM), for example, organised an "environmental symposium" for members, held twice to accommodate both shifts, in September and October 1989. This was a significant attempt to provide an educational opportunity for the workforce. In addition, the environment committees were pushing the union as a whole to consider the implications of environmental problems for the economy, and for the interests of citizens-as-workers. The CAW in Windsor also encouraged the formation in 1989 of a "Tri-Council Environmental Group" encompassing the labour councils of the Windsor, Chatham, and Sarnia districts.[28] This initiative had the potential to involve the chemical workers in a coalition with more radical leadership. Also, through their participation in the SCRICN, and in the St. Clair and Detroit River RAPs' Public Advisory Committees, the CAW activists based in Windsor were providing a counterweight to the influence of the Chemical Valley employers.

The question to ask about the work of the activists, therefore, was not whether it was of any significance, given its institutional and political limitations, but how it might be facilitated, and the activist ranks expanded. In this regard, it is notable that Sam Gindin argued for more interaction between "outside socialists" and the union activists, in order to "create a significant cadre of socialists within the trade union movement."[29] However, a strategy of convergence between the labour and other social movements implies more than Gindin's wish to "put socialism on labour's agenda." While an analysis of the nature of capitalism is essential to understanding the origins of the contemporary environmental crisis, traditional socialist discourse does not provide a sufficient solution. In some respects, socialist discourse does not take us very far beyond the social democratic agenda of State regulation and public ownership—an agenda which does not necessarily challenge the values underlying production itself, or express a counter-cultural (and ecological) understanding of the conditions for happiness.[30] Contrary to the argument of socialist theorists, counter-hegemonic struggle does not mean simply reviving working class identity or consciousness, on the assumption that the vast majority of individuals can eventually be persuaded to adopt such an identity. It means, rather, rejecting the boundaries between subject positions such as workers and environmentalists, which (though their meanings are permanently contested) are deeply entrenched in bourgeois and modern understandings of the world through the construction of such binary oppositions. It means constructing new forms of identity (including conceptions of belonging to social communities and to places) which radically subvert the foundations of capitalism, patriarchy, white supremacy, extreme anthropocentrism, instrumental rationalism, and the domination of nature. Unions, as structures with educational, organisational, and economic capacities for changing the conditions of existence as well as the understandings of the individuals they represent, are potentially important actors within this more broadly conceived counter-hegemonic project.

NOTES

1. It is important to keep in mind that any analysis of this kind is limited by its static nature (as a "snapshot" of a particular period and terrain of struggle), since its objects are continually undergoing transformation.
2. Such statements were made in a letter to the author from Robert Chernecki, National Staff Representative,(September 18, 1987), in the presentation by Van Gaal to the GLU citizens' hearing in Windsor, October 1986, and in speeches by Bob White. This connection was also made by local-level officials in the union when I interviewed them.
3. Robert White, President, CAW-Canada, "Jobs and the Environment: Notes for a Speech," November 21, 1986, Hamilton, Ontario, pp. 14-15. Copy in the author's possession.
4. Letter to the author from Bill Van Gaal, dated September 18, 1987.
5. Bob White devoted a good part of his 1986 speech in Hamilton to the possible effects of the free trade agreement on the environment.
6. Letter from Basil "Buzz" Hargrove to Gordon Taylor, dated July 9, 1987.
7. Resolution # 1 and Resolution # 2, both submitted by Bill Van Gaal's Local 707 (Oakville) and passed June 6, 1987.
8. Letter from Rick Coronado to the author, dated April 17, 1988. By the summer of 1989, CAW Canada Council Environment members had become more willing to work with rank-and-file activists with environmental expertise; informal collaboration with the Windsor activists was developing.
9. Text of White's speech cited in letter to the author from Robert Chernecki, National Staff Representative, September 18, 1987.
10. Regarding the Detroit incinerator issue, the CAW locals and the Windsor and District Labour Council sent letters to the United States ambassador to Canada urging that the incinerator not be built without "best available technology." The position of the CAW was not substantially different

Two Strategies of Social Unionism

from that eventually taken by the UAW—both took a legalistic and technocratic approach to the resolution of the conflict. For an analysis of the mobilization against the Detroit incinerator, see Laurie Adkin and Catherine Alpaugh, "Labour, Ecology, and the Politics of Convergence in Canada," in *Social Movements/Social Change*, Frank Cunningham et al., eds. (Toronto: Between the Lines, 1988).

11. Interview with Julia and Derek Beard, May 12, 1988, Windsor.
12. Communication with Rick Coronado, May 9, 1989. Gordon Taylor proposed this in July 1987.
13. Interviews with Parent (August 5, 1987, Windsor), Taylor (July 27, 1987, Windsor),and Coronado (July 1987, various dates, Windsor).
14. This view of Greenpeace was echoed by Tom Burton: "I'm not sure whether Greenpeace is a help or a hindrance. When they climbed the Ambassador Bridge and stayed up there in a hammock touting the environment, people look at them as a bunch of nuts. And I think they do more harm than good when they do those kind of antics." (Interview by author, July 29, 1987, Windsor.)
15. Particulate emissions were reduced from 151 micrograms per cubic metre in 1972 to 69 micrograms in 1982, based on averages of monthly readings. See Paul McKeague, article on the Ford Foundry in the *Windsor Star*, November 9, 1983.
16. Ron Bright, Ford's director of environmental control and vehicle safety, quoted in the *Windsor Star*, November 28, 1983.
17. *Windsor Star*, February 18, 1985, p. A5. In 1986, Ford was twice charged by the Ontario Ministry of the Environment for violations (emissions of smoke and fumes, and an oil spill into the Detroit River) of the EPA, and was fined $16,750 for these offexnces. (MOE, Legal Services Branch, *Prosecution Report*, April 1, 1987 to March 31, 1988 (Toronto: MOE, 1988), pp. 6, 12, 13.)
18. Sources: Ford, "W.C.P. (Windsor Casting Plant) Pollution Abatement Action Plan," (presented to General Community Meeting, Holy Rosary Roman Catholic Church, Windsor, Sunday, June 7, 1987); Ford, Plant Engineering Dept., "Pollution Abatement Status Reports for Ford Community Pollution Meeting," September 21, 1986, and February 22, 1987; Ontario Ministry of Environment, Air Resources Branch, Phytotoxicology Section, "Results of the Phytotoxicology Section Assessment Survey in the Vicinity of the Ford Casting Plant, Windsor, on August 1, 1985"(Toronto, February 18, 1986).
19. Unfortunately, I was not able to interview anyone from the Ford Foundry citizens' committee; it would be interesting to hear their version of the relationship with the union.
20. In Local 444, the questionnaires were initially distributed according to a random numbering of the membership list. However, the returned questionnaires were lost by the union office, and the survey had to be readministered. This task was undertaken by the Environment Cttee, and the method of distribution could not be verified. It is possible that questionnaires were handed out on the shop floor, and that respondents were urged by E. Cttee members to return them. Cttee. members may have selected persons they thought would be most likely to take an interest in the survey in order to maximize the return. A detailed explanation of the survey methodology and analysis may be obtained from the author.
21. Interestingly, 53 percent of rank-and-file workers also listed lack of information as a very or somewhat important reason for not participating in the environment committees. Only one out of eight executive officials listed this as a reason.
22. As union officials often complain, most workers do not attend general membership meetings. Other meetings are relatively restricted, e.g., the standing committees.
23. See note 20.
24. See chapter 5, note 13.
25. Respondent #227 (39 year old male, member of 444's environment, political action, and elections committees, production worker with high school education).
26. Male production worker at General Motors, 28 years old, two years university education in social sciences, no union position.
27. Sam Gindin, "Putting Socialism on Labour's Agenda," *Canadian Dimension* vol. 22, no. 1 (February 1988), p. 45.
28. Letter from Ken Glassco, President of the Sarnia and District Labour Council, to the Windsor and Chatham District Labour Councils, dated February 28, 1989; Letter from Gary Parent, President

of the Windsor & District Labour Council, and Rick Coronado, Chairperson of the W & D Labour Council Environment Committee, to Ken Glassco, dated April 2, 1989.
29. Sam Gindin, "Putting Socialism on Labour's Agenda," p. 45.
30. See L. Adkin, "Environmental Politics, Political Economy, and Social Democracy in Canada," *Studies in Political Economy* 45 (Fall 1994).

[14]

Union-Environmental Movement Convergence

CAW AND ECWU STRATEGIES COMPARED

The CAW officials interviewed, and most of the CAW workforce surveyed in 1987-88, demonstrated considerable confidence that they would not have to pay the costs of pursuing environmental goals in a capitalist economy. In the worst case, they expected that governments would step in to provide compensation, subsidies, and retraining programs to ameliorate the costs to workers. This optimism—indeed, the whole "social unionism" thrust of the CAW—contrasts notably with the attitude of the chemical workers. How do we explain the differences in perspective?

First, it is significant that the CAW has had a different experience of the State's role in the economy than has the ECWU. While CAW officials confidently predicted that the State will act—or be compelled to act—in a social democratic fashion, the ECWU had few grounds for such faith. The Auto Pact, negotiated in 1965, was a key factor in enabling the Canadian auto industry to overcome the limits of a small domestic market, contributing to an era of growth in the sector which lasted until the late 1970s. In this agreement, tariffs were restructured to permit conditional (or "managed") free trade and greater integration of production between Canadian and US-based producers. United States-based multinational corporations (MNCs) were required to maintain certain levels of productive investment in Canada. The ECWU, by contrast, has operated in an economic sector where few restrictions have been placed on the operations of multinational corporations; such restrictions (e.g., the National Energy Programme [NEP]) have been fiercely and successfully resisted. The problem is not that petrochemicals production in Canada is dominated by foreign-based MNCs (or by MNCs *per se*), and the auto sector is not, for the auto industry is also characterized by highly concentrated ownership. Between 1966 and 1979 the largest four companies (General Motors, Ford, Chrysler, AMC) accounted for 73.4 percent of all value-added in the industry. General Motors, Ford and Chrysler accounted for 94 percent of all capital investment between 1978 and 1981.[1] Rather, the ECWU's relative weaknesses are explained by (among other factors) the different government policies toward regulation in each sector.

Second, the auto workers have exercised more political influence on government policies by virtue of the size of the workforce associated with the industry, its concentration in southern Ontario, and the importance of the sector in the economy overall. It is the largest manufacturing sector; in 1979 it employed approximately 110,000 workers directly. After restructuring from 1979 to 1984, the industry still employed over 100,000 persons and it was estimated that one in seven Canadian manufacturing jobs depended in some way on the auto industry.[2] In 1989 the CAW estimated its membership in the Big Three, Volvo, Suzuki, and the parts companies to amount to 95,000. Its total membership was put at over 160,000.[3] From 1974-1984, the auto sector contributed about 20 percent of Canada's merchandise exports and almost 60 percent of Canadian exports of manufactured end products. In 1987 the auto sector trade between the United States and Canada was valued at $70 billion.[4]

In the 1970s productivity gains in the Fordist manufacturing sectors began to stagnate. The crisis affecting the North American auto industry was intensified by the end of the decade by a saturated market for automobiles and competition from Japanese and European producers. Firms responded by centralizing, co-ordinating, and integrating production to reduce overcapacity. There was an increase in joint ventures, relocation of labour-intensive parts of the production process to low-wage zones, and investment in new (labour-saving) technology. There were also cuts in the workforce.[5] New capital investment in robotization and other automated forms of process control between 1980 and 1984 was on a massive scale. Ford (International), for example, invested $4 billion a year during this period.[6] General Motors invested more than $8 billion in new equipment and technology in Canada from 1980 to 1988.[7] In this context the large auto firms attempted to increase profits by bargaining for wage concessions, reduction of paid holidays, and the revision of work practices.[8] The greater resistance to such demands by the Canadian section of the UAW was one of the factors which led to its decision to separate from the international union in 1985.[9] In addition to these strategies, the auto companies began to try to apply some of the labour-management relations learned from the Japanese. These employers—like the chemical companies studied earlier—began to use language like: "Involvement and team work are our core values."[10] One outcome of this restructuring by 1984 was higher productivity. In 1983 labour productivity in manufacturing overall increased by 6.9 percent in Canada, while unit labour costs increased by only 0.5 percent.[11] However, while new technology and changes in the production process have succeeded in improving productivity gains, the industry has still not resolved the "overcapacity" problem.[12]

The CAW has responded to some of these employer initiatives in ways which reveal a marked difference from the ECWU's strategic response to restructuring. In general, the CAW has adopted a more militant stance towards collective bargaining, in conjunction with a more radical political response to the current restructuring goals of the multinational corporations and big capital based in Canada. The union took a leading role in the left-nationalist opposition to the Free Trade Agreement. Even earlier, the CAW's director of research, Sam Gindin, had argued against a social democratic incomes policy or acceptance of the neoconservative logic of "international competitiveness" at a meeting of New Democratic Party (NDP) strategists, socialist academics, and unionists in 1984.[13] Gindin's response to proposals for an incomes policy, endorsed by John Richards (NDP strategist) and Allan Blakeney (former NDP premier of Saskatchewan), rejected a corporatist strategy:

> The industrialized western economies are internationally engaged in intense competition. That has polarized policy alternatives, and created political crises.
>
> To solve these crises you have two choices. Either you strengthen the power of corporations to control resources or—what is a fairly radical choice!—you find an alternative to the corporation. Anything between, risks giving the worst of both: corporate shareholders will be angry, and the general public will not give wholehearted support. If there is to be a new social contract, you have to decide which of these two choices to pursue. If you opt for the first choice, to rely on private corporations and politically control labour, you cannot simultaneously promise social improvements. It's nice to talk about tax reform, for example, but if you increase taxes on profits—on the rich—then shareholders rebel; they go on strike. To undertake a regional policy that directs investments to the West or the

Maritimes requires that you bribe companies to relocate. And where do you get the money to bribe them? From the rest of us. If you reject the first choice, you have to come down very strongly on the side of labour. That means restricting the power of capital and extending the rights of organized labour...

If you don't want to accede to capital, you cannot avoid left wing policies: restricting capital flows, nationalizing the banks and other major corporations, planning foreign trade and the domestic economy...[14]

The CAW has taken a critical and cautious approach to the "new management agenda," which takes the form of various quality of work life schemes. Both at the shop floor[15] and leadership levels, there seems to be a determination to resist exploitative aspects of these schemes, while giving conditional support to those which meet union criteria.[16] The CAW's caution, to date, reflects an analysis of employers' objectives very similar to that of Stephen Wood, a political economist specializing in the study of labour relations in the auto industry. On the basis of a comprehensive overview of quality of worklife schemes implemented in the North American auto industry in the 1980s, Wood concluded that the programmes may to some extent increase workers' participation, but only in very limited ways, intended by management to increase product quality and production flexibility. His conclusion that enrichment of worklife is a goal subordinate to management control and profit maximization comes as no surprise to workers on the shop floor.[17]

A third aspect of restructuring has actually enhanced the bargaining power of the auto workers. Multi-sourcing of parts and the "just-in-time" delivery system have made the large firms more vulnerable to strike action. A strike of more than a few days' duration can lead to the temporary shutdown of plants throughout a firm's integrated system, affecting thousands of workers. For example, the 1987 strike by Canadian Chrysler workers in southern Ontario led to the laying off of 1,900 workers in the United States within days. (One US plant—in Belvidere, Illinois—used trim from the Ajax plant in Ontario. The stamping plant in Warren, Michigan, supplied parts to Windsor.)[18] When 32,500 Ford U. K. workers went on strike in February 1988, Ford was compelled to lay off 9,700 workers in Belgium and to reduce production at a West German plant within one day. By the end of the first week, production of Ford vehicles in Spain, Portugal, and other West German plants was also affected.[19] The energy and chemical workers have no such power. A comparison of the CAW's strike against Chrysler in the 1987 round of Big Three negotiations with the ECWU's strike against Dow Chemical in 1988—both negotiations had pension improvements as the union's priority demand—provides an example of the difference in the unions' bargaining strengths.

A fourth example of the different approaches of the two unions is derived from the area of occupational health and safety. The ECWU was in the 1980s still trying to accomplish some of the bargaining gains in this area that had already been achieved by the CAW. (The UAW-Canada won health and safety committees in 1973). The ECWU's focus was on lobbying government for reform of existing occupational health and safety legislation. Shop-floor activists complained when interviewed that neither the union nor most of the rank and file seemed willing to challenge management to enforce health and safety standards, although in certain cases workers had supported co-workers who had been, in their view, disciplined unfairly for infractions of safety rules. While to some extent the same problems exist in the CAW (activists complain that health and safety issues do not have the bargaining status they should have and several respondents to the survey wrote lengthy criticisms of the CAW's failures to deal with serious occupational health and safety problems at the Ford Foundry and at the Zalev Brothers' recycling and scrap plant[20]), various locals have defied employers and existing legislation in their struggles for safe workplaces, as evidenced by the mass work refusals at Boeing/de Havilland, McDonnell-Douglas, Spar Aerospace, and Woodbridge Foams. Moreover, strong voices in the CAW opposed the bipartite approach to the regulation of workplace occupational health and safety proposed by the Ontario Ministry of Labour in 1989 (i.e., the creation of a management-union Workplace Health and Safety Agency). These leaders and their members did not believe that the interests of workers and employers are equally represented within bipartite structures; and they were prepared to continue to use mass stop-work actions to protect their rights.[21]

In terms of bargaining for educational benefits, and the goals of education, the two unions also diverged significantly. The ECWU negotiated a Health, Safety, and Industrial Relations Training Fund in 1987-88 (see chapter 9). Employers have a say in its content, and its orientation is to promote better industrial relations. A two-day seminar financed by this fund was held in Benmiller, Ontario, in April 1989. According to the *ECWU Journal* report, the seminar:

> used the "Code of Conduct" as the framework for discussions and future plans for a better labour/management relationship. Participants included management personnel from employers in Sarnia, Ontario and Union executives from the Locals representing the Bargaining Units. The seminar concluded with the individual employers and the union executive making specific plans for action when they get home. In addition, the groups, as a whole, agreed to co-operate in counteracting the negative aspects of the chemical industry within their community (environment, pollution, etc.).[22]

By contrast, the CAW's education programme (outlined in chapter 12), which has been in place since 1977, has a labour-centred, socialist orientation. The curriculum includes labour history, effective speaking, racism and discrimination, labour economics, and "issues related to labour and society, including politics and international affairs."[23] By the early 1990s the CAW was putting together a paid education leave (PEL) course on environmental legislation and workers' and citizens' rights. These differences in bargaining priorities cannot be examined in detail here, but they do indicate the general tone, or orientation, of the two unions' relations to employers and conceptions of alliances with other social actors.

Finally, the CAW's national leadership has tried to assert a strong political voice for the union, albeit in alliance with the NDP. The CAW leadership is attempting to accumulate support for its democratic socialist agenda of reform through a strategy of alliances with other social actors. One of the reasons it has more confidence in the ability of the alternative movements to influence governments is that it grants more importance to their gains and social bases of support than the ECWU leadership did. Bob White, for example, acknowledged in his March 1989 (post-FTA election) brief to the NDP that:

> The grass-roots challenge to the business-Tory alliance gave the elite in this country a scare... The expansion of politics beyond Parliament was very significant. There is a widespread cynicism towards political parties and politicians. Politicians are often regarded as distant from our real concerns and full of opportunistic rhetoric and empty promises. The very fact that thousands of Canadians have chosen to act through single-issue coalitions, rather than through conventional political parties, reveals that it is not politics itself—the attempt to gain some collective control over our lives—that is being rejected, but the way in which politics is being conducted... [The NDP's] only strength lies in the energy it can generate to build a movement for social change.[24]

So the CAW, for reasons having to do with the development of the auto sector, as well as the political orientation of its leadership, has perceived itself to be in a position of strength from which to ally with other social movements. In the case of the environmental movement, the openness to alliance may also stem from several other factors which differentiate the position of the CAW from that of the ECWU. First, it is the chemical industry—not the auto industry—which has, until recently, been the target of environmental campaigns internationally. In response to this pressure, the chemical companies have evolved increasingly sophisticated strategies to shape public opinion, to foster divisions between its workers and "the public," and to secure company loyalty among employees either by persuasion and patronage or by threats. The industry has also succeeded, to some extent, in building a co-operative relationship with the national leadership of the ECWU, through the "continuing dialogue" programme, and various bipartite endeavours. Such alliances have proved useful in defending the industry (owners and workers) from environmental demands which threaten profits, investment freedom, and short-term job security.

As for the auto industry, the immense popularity of its product has so far prevented the environmental movement from making serious inroads.[25] Although the automobile and its infrastructure have had severely detrimental effects on the environment (aesthetically and physically) and on human health (deaths from accidents, air pollution and noise pollution), efforts to reduce production and restrict use have had little impact on the scale of production in North America. Other factors (competition in the North American market from off-shore producers, for example) have been far more significant. Moreover, the Canadian public does not yet strongly associate automobiles with threats to human health (although in other parts of the world, e.g., California, Mexico, major European cities, the problem is acknowledged as being severe).[26] Instead, the focuses of concern have been the chemical and—to a lesser extent—the nuclear industries. Nor has the industry found it difficult to comply with environmental regulations to date, such as restrictions on lead emissions, mufflers for noise, and exhaust filters. Environmental problems associated with production have likewise not received particular attention from the environmental movement or government regulators.

For all these reasons, the CAW was able to adopt a more active and alliance-oriented stance on environmental issues than the ECWU did during the same period. However, there is still the question of what the CAW's environmental policy amounts to in practice, and in regard to the potential for convergence with the environmental movement. Here it seems clear that, where the environmental committees had been established, they were imbedded in the social democratic and hierarchical nature of the union organisation and culture. Obstacles to increasing participation included sexism, the procedural formality and exclusiveness of the committee structure itself, the self-aggrandizing interests of some union officials (who wish to control access to union positions and to the rank and file by potential rivals), and the priorities in allocation of resources, stemming from the institutional *raison d'être* of the union in a capitalist market economy.

Analysis of the CAW environmental policy at the end of the 1980s confirmed that the potential for alliances with the environmental movement based on a social democratic consensus, and at an elite level certainly existed. However, without a change in the orientation of union practices to empower the educational and organisational nuclei within each local, and to permit real participation in union initiatives by the base, union representation in coalitions with environmentalists would remain largely formal. Confronted with real and increasingly difficult choices about the environmental and other conditions of economic restructuring, such coalitions would either remain largely tactical and unstable, or recognize the necessity to create the bases for a true convergence of counter-hegemonic struggles. Finally, the work of a dedicated cadre of rank-and-file activists to "bring together" union struggles and those of other social movements, as well as the openness of rank-and-file survey respondents to both their own involvement and greater union activism, were important sources of hope for the realization of an eventual convergence. The strategies adopted by environmentalists within such coalitions, of course, would certainly also play a part in determining their direction.

CAW ENVIRONMENTAL POLICY IN THE 1990S

Enormous and rapid changes in the political and economic environment of the Canadian labour and environmental movements as a whole, experienced particularly intensely in the traditional heartland of the CAW (southern Ontario), and accompanied by transformations in the composition of the union itself, provide the context in which major developments have occurred in the CAW's environmental policy in the 1990s. In a nutshell, the national union has developed policy statements on transportation and the environment, reduction of work time, and other issues crucial to political ecology. Local environment committees—including those working within the auto assembly and parts sector of the union—have undertaken educational work on alternative fuels, vehicles, and public transportation and urban planning strategies. In other words, the union has begun to address environmental issues linked to the core interests of its own membership, and which challenge management control over decisions regarding production and investment. CAW members have also taken the lead in participating in joint labour-environmentalist conferences, organisations, and coalitions such as the Green Work alliance in the Brampton, Ontario area, and the Windsor and District Labour-Environment Project. In addition, the union has been bargaining with employers for joint (management-union) environment committees, and other items related to environmentalism (an employer-funded Environment Fund, research into alternative vehicles) are under discussion. These developments are discussed in more detail in this section. We then turn to an assessment of their meaning in relation to the union's role as a counter-hegemonic actor, and to an analysis of the factors which explain the direction of CAW strategy.

NATIONAL UNION DIRECTION

The CAW national staff has developed a set of environmental policy statements in response to pressures from employers, government initiatives, and its rank-and-file activists. The Department responsible for Occupational Health and Safety and Workers' Compensation policy responses has taken on the additional task of providing research and direction on union environmental policy. Cathy Walker, the CAW's national Health and Safety director, also oversees environmental policy, and Nick de Carlo (the former president of the McDonnell-Douglas Local and a key figure in the Green Work Alliance), covers both environmental issues and Ontario Workers Compensation Board policy responses. Their lobbying at the national level has played an important role in raising the profile of environmental issues, and they have been the key links between the national leadership and the local-level environmental committees. The department is, of course, short-staffed and over-burdened, and environmental activists from a number of locals have argued that there should be a national representative solely concerned with environmental issues.

In response to requests for direction from the locals, the national office produced guidelines for setting up local union environment committees.[27] The advice to the local organisers included getting the local union executive and membership "on side," and getting executive approval for activities. In an interview, Walker acknowledged that local environment committees have had difficulty getting credibility with local executives, and suggested that in some cases this has to do with the gender dynamic between almost exclusively male executives, and committees which disproportionately attract female members (i.e., compared to other union standing committees).[28] Indeed, she agreed that there has been a gap between policies from the National on such issues as gender equity and the environment, and the attitudes of predominantly male local executives (the situation which I observed in the 1980s). Moreover, local environment committees remain dependent for funds on the approval of the local executives. Walker pointed out that local presidents may be even less inclined to fund environment committee activities when the committee is participating in a regional (CAW environmental) council. This might be because the committee is perceived to be functioning less as an advisory group to the local executive, and more autonomously from the executive in general. The activities of the environment committee might also be perceived as providing less recognition and prestige for the local executive when its activities are associated with a regional council or coalition.

Alex Keeney, the current President of Local 200 (Ford, Windsor), admitted that the environmental activists in his local had a "hard sell" convincing the executive that environmental issues were important, but that they had "persevered," eventually winning Keeney's support.[29] Thus the local activists see it as their task to educate not only the union membership, but also the local executive, about the connections between workplace and employment issues and environmental concerns. In these respects, local union activists must still deal with the necessity of demonstrating their utility to the local executive, in order to be able to function (have paid leave from work, get funds for activities, have access to local union newsletters, etc.) and to represent the local outside the workplace.

In other respects the National guidelines for the local union environment committees appear to address some of the limitations on rank-and-file participation which were noted in chapters 12 and 13. One of these was the restricted membership of the standing committee. While the National guidelines note that committee members must be either appointed by the chairperson or elected by the members, and states that "the local union executive should be consulted in making any standing committee appointments," they also state:

> A "paper committee" that does not work, is not a committee at all. If the committee is too small, it may not be representative of all the different ideas available. The size of the committee should be flexible so more good people can be added. There should be enough programs on a continuing basis so that all local union members can participate if they wish.[30]

Second, the strong interest in educational opportunities which was expressed by rank-and-file workers in the 1987 survey has been responded to within the framework of the Paid Education Leave (PEL) programme. The National has created both a one-week course on environmental issues and a weekend course which may be offered for a committee or a group of local environment committees. While these courses are intended for elected or appointed committee members, they do enhance the incentives as well as the opportunities for rank-and-file workers to become more involved in union activities. In addition to the National's *Health, Safety, and Environment Newsletter*, the local unions also produce newsletters in which the environmental committees may publish regular updates; in some cases, the committees or regional environment councils are producing their own publications for distribution in workplaces and in their communities (such as the Windsor Region Environment Council's *Global Guardian*).

The guidelines for the local environmental committees also encourage the latter to participate in coalitions with other unions as well as community groups. They state, however, that: "In any coalition work you should preserve your identity as the Local Union Environment Committee. Do your best to argue your position well in the coalition but if things take a completely wrong turn you may want to withdraw and work on the issue in a way you think makes sense." The specific identity of the Local Union Committee appears to refer to a discourse which addresses the jobs-versus-the-environment conflict. The guidelines state:

> You must always think of the impact of an environmental issue on jobs and do your best to secure the support of any workers who may be affected. You must analyze the situation carefully, especially company claims about possible job loss. These are often untrue or greatly exaggerated. You must carefully explain the correct position to get everyone on side...
>
> Nowhere is the jobs issue more sensitive than if it involves a workplace within your local. You must carefully analyze the issue and see how the issue may impact your membership. Many employers like to use scare tactics to frighten workers into supporting the employer position. Analyze the scare to see if it is a false threat...
>
> In many cases protecting the environment preserves or creates jobs...
>
> Conversion is an important concept we need to understand and popularize. We can make different products and provide different services which help to protect the environment...[31]

The National is in this way encouraging the local committees to take a position in coalitions which might be described as "eco-socialist," that is, one which links an analysis of economic priorities and alternatives (which capitalist employers attempt to obscure) to the interests of workers in security of subsistence as well as health and a clean environment. The health-environment connection is made through the observation that "protecting the environment is also about protecting the health of the workers who work in our workplaces." This linkage is also captured in the union's slogan: "Health and Safety: Environment with a fence around it." The guidelines encourage local unions to negotiate with management combined workplace health, safety, and environment committees, or separate joint environment committees for "very large workplaces where there is already enough work for the health and safety representatives." To assist in such efforts, the National has produced a Workplace Health, Safety, and Environment Committee Manual. The National produced a "Statement of Principles" on the Environment in 1991, and issues the *CAW Health, Safety, and Environment Newsletter* on a monthly basis, which updates members on environmental and health issues, legislative developments, union activities, and various events.

Following the 1991 Statement of Principles on the Environment, the National's Department of Health and Safety put together an important statement on transportation and the environment. This statement was included in the National Collective Bargaining and Political Action Convention programme of June 1996[32] and approved in principle by the National Executive Board. According to National Health and Safety Director, Cathy Walker, the key impetus behind the Statement on Transportation and the Environment was the leadership's desire to have pro-active, independent union positions on questions which were being posed by environmental regulation, initiatives from the corporations, and government-sponsored consultative bodies.[33] General Motors, for example, approached the union about possible co-operation on recycling and other issues, and it became apparent that without independent union research and strategic thinking, the agenda of environmental issues—which are, of course, inseparable from cost-reducing restructuring strategies in general—could soon be determined by the corporations, leaving the union in a reactive mode. Second, the CAW was represented on the Ontario

Round Table on the Economy and Environment, appointed by the NDP Government, and headed by an official from the Ministry of Transportation, Ken Ogilve. Since Ogilve wanted to develop a sustainable transportation policy, the CAW was compelled to engage with the issues of automobile production and use, public transportation, and so on.[34] These experiences prompted Walker to argue for the importance of the CAW developing its own transportation and environment policy. "We needed," she said, "to get our own house in order on the transportation and environment policy, because it directly concerns the products that our members produce."

Environmental activists who attended the CAW National Transportation and Environment Conference at Port Elgin in May 1995 (at which the key speaker was Amory Lovins) were also keen on the union developing positions on alternative transportation policies. The conference topics included: green vehicles, public transit, vehicle emissions (including the problems of smog and global warming), "our cities/our environment," transportation options, rail and the environment, the Fixed Link (the controversial bridge project connecting Prince Edward Island with New Brunswick), and van pooling for CAW workers. Environmental language for upcoming contract negotiations with the Big Three was also discussed. There is considerable interest among the environmental committees in such developments as the Solar Vehicle project at the University of Western Ontario, Canadian-made (Ballard) hydrogen fuel cell buses, and Lovins' designs for an ultralight hybrid vehicle.[35]

Another factor which cannot be overlooked in explaining the CAW's recent efforts to address transportation and environment issues is the growing environmental regulation of the auto industry. This is most advanced in the United States, where new standards are being adopted following a long period of opposition from automobile manufacturers.[36] Stricter standards have also been legislated by the NDP Government in British Columbia. The CAW Statement on Transportation and the Environment supports such regulation, as well as gradual conversion of production to zero emission vehicles.

> Over time, we need to replace the current fleet with vehicles that produce zero emissions and we need to insist that our members produce them. During the transitional period we need to see the fleet mix include some vehicles which produce zero emissions and others that produce lower emissions. Throughout this period we need to ensure that our members are trained to produce these new products and that our present workplaces are converted to produce these new products. In order to ensure there is a sufficient market to lower costs to the consumer, laws must drive these changes. We must support laws like the Clean Vehicles and Clean Fuels Regulations in B.C. These laws should be federal to apply to the entire country so that all Canadians are protected and vehicles suitable for all provinces are built in Canada. We cannot stand in the way of progressive technological change. We either get out in front and lead the technology in a way that benefits our membership or we try to retard new developments and see them push our members out the door.[37]

In committing itself to researching these issues, the union may also be responding to the saturation of consumer markets for private cars, which underpins the intense competition among the Big Three and other automobile manufacturers.

Thus CAW environmental policy has begun to take on the pollution issues which most directly affect the largest sector of the union's own membership. The CAW, however, is no longer only a union of auto assembly and parts workers. Following the mergers and membership drives of the 1985-1995 period (see table 33) the composition of the union, both in occupational and regional terms, has significantly changed. The union also represents rail, air, and road transport workers, as well as marine, mining, food, beverage and hospitality-sector workers, and fishers (see figure 3). Its transportation policy, therefore, needs to take into account the interests of its members in public as well as private transportation, and in creating a consensus around environmental stands that extends beyond the auto assembly and parts sector to include a membership which has become highly diverse.

As Bob White noted in his preface to the 1992 CAW Statement on Transportation:

> Structural changes within our union have led us to a very direct concern with transportation... [T]he CAW has emerged as the largest transportation union in the country. We now represent over 125,000 [now estimated at 145,000] transportation workers...
>
> Our concern with transportation does, of course, extend beyond this membership and union presence. Transportation shapes how we live. It affects the structure of our cities, the viability of communities and regions, the economic and social base of our country. When we talk about a "Canadian Transportation Policy," we inevitably address issues central to the broader national agenda: national unity, regional equity, jobs, the environment...
>
> The new diversity within our union naturally raises the question of potential conflicts over direction. For example, can workers in auto, aerospace, rail, or the airlines agree to any kind of common perspective on the future of public vs. private transit?[38]

In addition to the developments in National union leadership on labour-environment alliances outlined above, the National has joined the Canadian Environmental Network, is represented on the Ontario Environmental Network's (OEN) Labour Caucus, and has sponsored or co-sponsored various conferences. Among these is the biennial National Environment Conference held at Port Elgin (the CAW's residential educational centre), which was initiated in April 1991. The National also supports regional CAW Environment Conferences and meetings which have been held in London, Windsor, Greater Toronto, and lower mainland British Columbia. CAW National representative, Nick De Carlo, addressed the Democracy, Jobs, and the Environment Conference in Toronto in October 1992. The former President of the CAW, now President of the Canadian Labour Congress (CLC), Bob White, presided over a CLC Environment Conference held in January 1994, called "Organizing for Environmental Change." The OEN-Labour Caucus organised a conference held in September 1995, on the theme: "Jobs and the Environment beyond the year 2000." This conference, co-sponsored by the Ontario Ministry of the Environment, the CAW, and the Ontario Federation of Labour (OFL) drew eighty-three participants, with a "predominance of CAW people."[39] Nick De Carlo of the CAW National office led workshops on transportation and on the experience of the Green Work Alliance, and Mike Darnell of Local 444 and current chairperson of the CAW Council Environment Committee led a session on Green Communities.[40] The OEN Labour Caucus met in June 1996 to develop a statement on what workers and environmentalists have in common.

The CAW Council Environment Committee, established in 1987, has also been active in developing union environmental thinking, with input from the local activists. In March 1994 it presented an impressive policy paper to the CAW National Executive Board (NEB) Task Force, which begins with the statement:

TABLE 33
CAW MERGERS

Union	Members at Date of Merge	Effective Date
Canadian Association of Communication and Allied Workers (CACAW)	1,200	Feb. 17, 1995
Canadian Association of Smelter and Allied Workers (CASAW)	2,000	June 2, 1994
Canadian Brotherhood of Railway, Transport and General Workers (CBRT & GW)	33,437	June 1, 1994
Owen Sound Glass Workers (Local 248)	300	Nov. 22, 1993
Canadian Union of Mine, Mill and Smelter Workers	1,600	Aug. 20, 1993
United Electrical, Radio and Machine Workers of Canada (UE)	9,000	Nov. 30, 1992
Canadian Textile and Chemical Union (CTCU)	700	June 1, 1992
Canadian Association of Industrial Mechanical and Allied Workers (CAIMAW)	6,500	Jan. 1, 1992
TCU-Airline Division	3,500	May 24, 1990
The Brotherhood Railway Carmen of Canada	8,000	May 29, 1990
Great Lakes Fishermen and Allied Workers Union (CSAWU)	400	March 23, 1989
Canadian Seafood and Allied Workers Union (CSAWU)	3,000	May 30, 1989
Fishermen, Food and Allied Workers Union (FFAW)	24,000	Nov. 7, 1988
Canadian Glass Workers Union	800	Nov. 10, 1987
Canadian Association of Passenger Agents (CAPA)	800	Jan. 1, 1987
Canadian Air Line Employees' Association (CALEA)	4,100	July 1, 1985

SOURCE: Sam Gindin, *The Canadian Auto Workers* (Toronto: James Lorimer & Co., 1995), p. 228.

SECTORAL DISTRIBUTION
Of Dues-Paying Membership

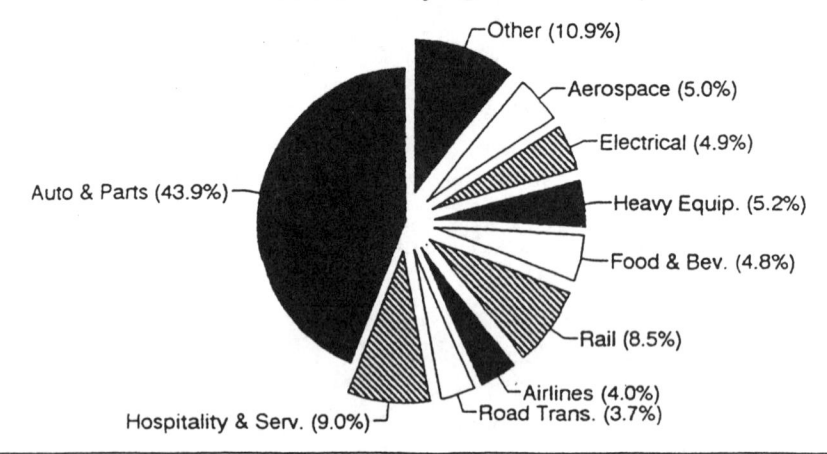

- Other (10.9%)
- Aerospace (5.0%)
- Electrical (4.9%)
- Heavy Equip. (5.2%)
- Food & Bev. (4.8%)
- Rail (8.5%)
- Airlines (4.0%)
- Road Trans. (3.7%)
- Hospitality & Serv. (9.0%)
- Auto & Parts (43.9%)

"AUTO AND PARTS" includes Assembly (18.1% of total membership), Captive Parts (9.7%), and Independent Parts (16.1%). "OTHER" includes Metal Fab. (3.0%), Mining (2.1%), Marine (1.4%), and Misc. "FOOD & BEV." includes FFAW members.

GEOGRAPHIC DISTRIBUTION
Of Dues-Paying Membership

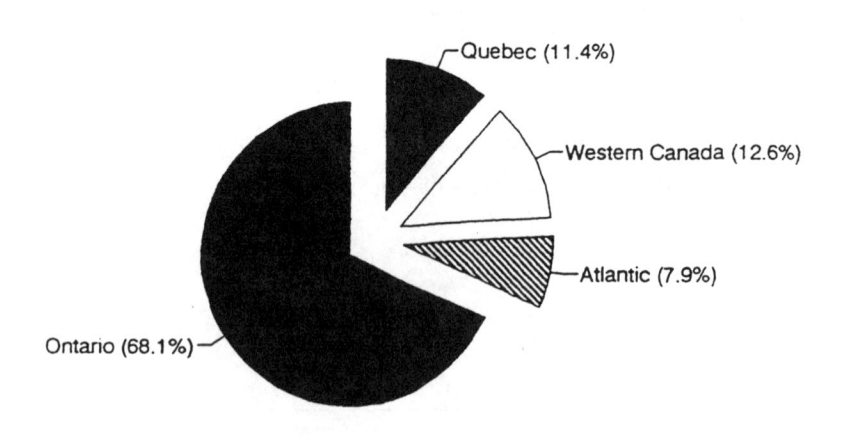

- Quebec (11.4%)
- Western Canada (12.6%)
- Atlantic (7.9%)
- Ontario (68.1%)

NOTE: These graphs include dues-paying members only.

SOURCE: *False Solutions, Growing Protests: Recapturing the Agenda* (National Collective Bargaining Programme) North York, Ont.: CAW, June 1996, p. iv.

> The reality is that the labour movement, including the CAW, has not fully integrated the environment into its activities much less into its basic program of action (bargaining or otherwise). In fact, increasingly the environment is losing its public profile due to the economic crisis... The pollution and destruction of the environment is not simply another issue. It is potentially the most fundamental crisis that humanity has ever faced. It is a crisis that primarily affects workers and those living in poverty...
>
> There are many reasons the union movement has not addressed the environmental crisis in a fundamental way. One of the most obvious is the fear of job loss. Another is that discussion of the environment and alternatives will be extremely complex and at times potentially divisive. Still another is that any attempt...will require a lot of expertise and resources that the labour movement simply has not committed at this time and is reluctant to commit as the economic squeeze intensifies. In other words the politics of the union, in so far as they force us to respond to short term concerns and turn away from long term implications, stand in the way of coming to grips with this crisis.[41]

This statement summarizes succinctly—in relation to the environmental movement—the nature of the institutional constraints on union practice that have been referred to in the previous discussion of union strategies. The document goes beyond both the social democratic and eco-socialist discourses of earlier CAW statements on labour-environment coalition building, expressing a conception of a social movement which is much closer to that which I have characterized as a transformative "convergence" of diverse counter-hegemonic struggles. Its authors grasp the argument of radical ecologists that the entire telos of production, as well as the (un)democratic nature of decision making regarding the priorities of social development, are at stake.

> Can we act to transform the environmental crisis into a positive factor in developing new forms of social and economic organization? Can the labour movement join with other social movements to transform our society's organization? If we fail to recognize the depth of the environmental crisis...we are missing an opportunity for developing a credible alternative agenda—for developing a powerful progressive social movement which will have the full support of workers.
>
> The reality is that any real solution to the pending environmental crisis will inevitably involve an entire reorganization of our society—economically, socially, and politically—of our way of thinking and acting. This need for transformation can be an opportunity—one that is consistent with the goals of labour and progressive organizations. In fact there is a tremendous amount of organizing already going on at the grass roots level of our union—organizing that is taking place largely without the support of the National level of the union but which has achieved a tremendous amount of support and respect at the community level.[42]

The submission to the NEB goes on to argue against both the eco-capitalist view that the market will take care of the environmental crisis, and the view held by many in the environmental movement that "green consumerism" will provide a solution.

> Though there will be environmental investment by business, in the end it is impossible to transform a world facing an environmental crisis without addressing the social goals and morals of society, and the relation [sic] of power in society. In order to address the environmental crisis and to transform the way society produces we have to introduce our own goals into the socio-economic system—goals which put the environment and humanity first—and new mechanisms—mechanisms which

either restrict and direct the market or provide alternatives to it. We cannot let corporations determine the agenda. We have to democratize the market.[43]

The CAW Council Environment Committee submission to the NEB also rejects the "tech-fix" approach to environmental destruction, and adopts the ecological principles of prudence and humility vis-à-vis knowledge and nature. It discusses sympathetically the view that natural experiences are essential to human spiritual well-being, as well as holistic approaches to mind/body wellness. In a section entitled "The Social Movement," the document argues:

> There is tremendous potential to build both worker support and social alliances for a program of action that unites the concern for the environment with a new outlook on the economy, on job creation, and on the politics and social organization of society... We have to build the alliance with organizations such as those that have fought against NAFTA [the North American Free Trade Agreement], medical reform groups, third world support groups, etc., etc. The social movement is a movement not just for the environment but for fundamental social transformation. The environmental fight, by its very nature, forces a re-evaluation of the economy and the unregulated market system as well as a re-evaluation of social values...
>
> But what type of social movement comes out of this alliance?... It has to be one that truly "empowers" the people of society—the workers and producers in society... It has to be a movement that brings together all the aspects of social need from employment, to housing, to education, to equality for citizens, to child care, etc...
>
> If the environmental movement is going to mean anything it must challenge and transform a power structure that makes decisions to suit the interests of those who control. It has to recognize that in fact an alternative power base has to be built that will be able to challenge the existing relations of power—power based on the control of money. It has to organize for genuine democratic control of society.[44]

The CAW's environmental activists have not missed the potential of environmentalism as a counter-hegemonic discourse, as not only various policy statements but also local organising activities (described below) demonstrate. The CAW Council Environment Committee followed up its submission to the NEB Task Force by proposing to Buzz Hargrove (President of the CAW) that he extend an invitation to the well-known Canadian environmentalist, Dr. David Suzuki, to address the CAW Council in December 1995. In his speech, described in the Windsor Region Environmental Council's publication, *The Global Guardian* (Fall 1995 issue), Suzuki argued that allocating social and economic decision-making to the market is both anti-ecological and anti-democratic.

While endorsing the steps taken by the National leadership outlined above, the CAW submission to the NEB recommended further initiatives:
1. an educational program (now in effect);
2. integration of environmental demands into collective bargaining;
3. development of environmental policy capacity within the union;
4. a dialogue with "the rest of the labour movement and with environmentalists and other allies (poverty groups, women's organizations, anti-NAFTA organizations, resident organizations, medical reform groups, third world support groups, etc.) on global policies on the environment and environmental solutions and alternative views of social and political organization";
5. research to develop "eco-economics."

To help carry out these tasks, the CAW Council Environment Committee called for the appointment of a full-time co-ordinator for the environment at the National Office. This resulted in Buzz Hargrove's decision to hire another person in the Health and Safety Department, Nick De Carlo, though (as mentioned above), his duties do not exclusively concern the environment. Items (3) through (5) are closely related, and will be examined in the context of grassroots organising in the next section.

Here I turn to a brief examination of the extent to which environmental demands have been included in collective bargaining agendas. The mobilization of rank-and-file workers which takes place around collective bargaining is an important opportunity for education, shaping of collective identity, and the formation of alliances with other social actors at community and other levels of society. The agenda of collective bargaining also provides a means to measure the importance attached to various demands, as well as the ways in which they are articulated to broader discourses about the social role of unionism.

In my interviews with union officials and activists in 1996 I asked them about the appropriateness of contract negotiations as a vehicle for bringing about changes in company decisions regarding investment in research and development. For example, could they envisage the day when unions would demand the adoption of technological changes to reduce vehicle emissions, or to increase fuel efficiency? Or, more radically, would they bargain for the conversion of production to "alternative" vehicles, or for company investment in research on such vehicles? The short statement on the position of the environment in collective-bargaining demands, included in the report to the 1996 CAW National Collective Bargaining and Political Action Convention, asserts that it is time for unions to try to determine the direction of technological innovation and decisions about production.

> The environment is affected by not just how we produce but by what we produce. If we produce, for example, tractors instead of tanks, we will reduce the harmful effects of war on the environment. If we produce zero emission vehicles powered by electricity or hydrogen rather than producing vehicles with gasoline powered engines, we prevent air pollution.
>
> But we as workers and unions don't decide what we produce; management does. Should unions put forward bargaining demands calling for more environmentally-friendly products? Of course we should. Why shouldn't we challenge management's "right" to tell us what we must make for them? Demands for more environmentally friendly products both protects the environment *and* our jobs since it is in our long term interests to produce products that consumers want and governments compel.[45]

It should be noted, of course, that the ecological argument about social alternatives does not stop at the questions "how we produce" and "what we produce." Producing zero-emission vehicles would reduce the quantities of particular harmful chemical substances, to be sure. However, since vehicles such as electric cars will increase demand on electricity generation, the effects of heavy use of private vehicles are in a sense merely displaced. The most desirable "transportation policy" is to reduce drastically the use of private vehicles. This entails not only a shift to various modes of public transportation, but the entire redesign of human settlements. For the auto workers, it also means the development of alternative employment and/or guaranteed income strategies, since an ecological approach—which is to reduce global entropy, particularly where consumption of energy is excessive—will ultimately mean the production of fewer cars. Not all of those who lose their jobs in the auto sector are likely to be reabsorbed by the transition (or conversion) to production of public transport. It is, however, significant that the CAW leadership and environmental activists are prepared to challenge management prerogatives as radically as the above statement suggests. Moreover, the "eco-economics" proposal (discussed below) does move in the direction of the broader ecological agenda.

Some CAW environmental activists also argued that the union, through collective bargaining gains, could push governments to legislate changes in environmental or economic policy.[46] Local 200's (Ford, Windsor) president, however, was of the view that unions should leave environmental regulation to governments. Alex Keeney viewed the CAW Statement on Transportation and the Environment as "a tool for trying to invoke *legislative* change. That's where it has to happen. It won't happen in the workplace. It won't happen bargaining with Ford, Chrysler, and General Motors."[47]

The 1996 Bargaining Convention report also called for the negotiation of "a work and environment fund" from employers.[48] This refers to a cents per hour fund to study and act on environmental issues (e.g., one minute's pay per employee, per month), which some were hoping to place on the agenda of 1996 contract negotiations with the Big Three. (The first agreement on an environment fund was won by Local 636, General Seating Unit, Woodstock, in July 1993.) Interestingly, CAW President Basil (Buzz) Hargrove said at the June 1996 bargaining convention that the environment would be a "priority" in the bargaining agenda.[49]

IMPLEMENTATION OF THE NATIONAL POLICY AND CAW ENVIRONMENTAL ACTIVISM AT THE LOCAL LEVEL

Collective Bargaining for Environmental Gains

The first national joint environment committee was agreed upon with Chrysler Canada in 1990—a demand that was particularly pushed by Local 444's president at the time, Larry Bauer.[50] However, the committee ceased to meet in 1994-95. According to the chairperson of Local 444's environment committee, Rob Sheehan, the CAW/Chrysler Environment Committee broke down because of disagreements over its mandate.[51] Chrysler management wanted the committee to have a solely advisory function, and its meetings to remain confidential. The union wanted the national committee to communicate with, and receive input from all Chrysler locals. The CAW environmental activists also wanted the committee to lobby the company to develop more environmentally-friendly products. They were hopeful that the Chrysler Council would include the reactivation of the committee in 1996 bargaining. In addition to the national committee, Sheehan would like to see the creation of in-plant recycling committees which would meet periodically and channel ideas to the national committee.

In the 1993 round of bargaining with Ford, the CAW negotiated language to have an annual joint meeting to discuss environmental concerns. This meeting is attended by union and company representatives from each Ford plant (six plants in Windsor, two in Oakville, one in St. Thomas, and one in Bramalea). Its agenda has focused on plant recycling, although invited speakers have addressed such questions as alternative fuels, and Ontario environmental regulations.[52] The Ford Council will be bargaining in 1996 for a full-time environment representative to pursue issues on behalf of all Ford locals. According to Alex Keeney and Herb John (of Ford Local 200), the environment representative's functions would be to "make sure that we're proceeding properly in the areas of waste management, recycling...not only with the corporation but with the community" as well as to "look at purchasing policies...buying from environmentally-friendly vendors... [and] issues like [the use of] environmentally-friendly cutting fluids instead of petroleum-based cutting fluids"...[53]

Ford Local 200's environment committee chairperson and local management set up in November 1992 a site-wide joint waste management committee which encourages the

"4Rs." The site-wide committee is chaired by Local 200's environment committee chairperson, Herb John. According to Local 200 president Alex Keeney and to Herb John, the main achievements of Ford-CAW co-operation so far have been the recycling of aluminum and foundry sand. These changes have made money for Ford, as well as helping to improve the company's corporate image. There are also "waste minimization" committees at plant level.[54]

The Local now has its own environment standing committee, which includes people from each of six plants in the local. Alex Keeney, who replaced Frank McAnally as President of Local 200, considers that the local has come a long way since 1989 (when the local's positions were last studied) on environmental issues. Regarding the problems of emissions from the Ford Foundry in Windsor, Keeney said: "They've cleaned that up tremendously... That was basically done with a lot of pushing from the Local 200 environment committee," working in conjunction with the Health and Safety Committee. He added that the cleanup is an "ongoing process," on which Ford has spent millions of dollars. Both Keeney and John viewed the Ford Foundry as more of an occupational health and safety issue than an environmental issue, and a matter for the in-plant elected union representatives. Asked about the health problems associated with the Foundry, Keeney replied: "We don't really know. There's never really been a study done on that... That's one of our demands—that the company pay for a mortality study in all plants. You can try and make links, but there's no concrete evidence there... So I don't think it's fair, really, for me to try and answer that."

When asked what the major environmental issues are facing Ford and the union, John talked about the environmental problems caused by cars, and the need to develop less-polluting technology. I asked if the union would take up an issue like research on electric cars with Ford. Keeney replied: "That wouldn't happen through a local committee. That would have to happen through the National." Echoing the social-democratic perspective of middle-level union officials interviewed in the 1980s, Keeney thought that it is the government's responsibility to legislate such requirements for companies. Moreover, Keeney did not think that his membership would support union demands for a transition to the production of less polluting vehicles. "I don't believe that they're educated to that degree about what the issues are with the automobile and the environment." Both Keeney and John pointed out that a switch to electric vehicles would result in a "tremendous job loss." Keeney:

> The environment is something we have to continually strive and work on, but I mean, if you go into the workplace and tell people, "Well, we're telling Ford we're not going to make this type of [internal combustion] engine any more..." and it's going to cut the workforce in half... The realism is that there's a job loss when you go the whole way... The people in the plant who are my age and older, who haven't had the environmental education that young people have today, it's pretty difficult to convince them the environment is unhealthy for them or that the cars they build are unhealthy for other people. So I don't think we'll see it today, anyway.

In contrast, Rob Sheehan of Local 444 (Chrysler, Windsor) had a more optimistic response to a similar question about the likely response of his membership to union support for zero emission automobiles:

> Half of the people would probably say "good"! A lot of our membership nowadays are very much educated... Our [local] was always notorious for that, and took pride in that. I think everybody knows that automobiles are a problem... but what stops people from adopting that type of policy is insecurity and fear...

Our local has always been able to pick up on concepts like this. We passed resolutions that we sent to the CAW Council and also to the Constitutional Convention [in 1994] calling for the use of zero-emission vehicles, and trying to get the government of Ontario to follow the governments of B.C. and California [even though] we make mini-vans. We're not afraid of controversy, but we'd rather be on the front of it than on the tail end.[55]

On the question of using collective bargaining to push companies toward different research and development priorities, Sheehan said: "We aren't going to tell them what to build, but we are going to help direct them... We're not going to tell them not to build cars. We're telling them to build clean cars."

A joint environment committee has been negotiated at the CAMI plant (GM/Suzuki) in Ingersoll, Ontario, by CAW Local 88. The 1992-1995 collective agreement established a committee comprised of two CAW representatives and two members of CAMI management, which would meet at least twice a year to discuss and to make recommendations regarding "issues involving the environment, recycling and energy conservation which are of concern to CAMI employees." The parties also agreed "that this committee and its functions should not in any way be adversarial and its clear purpose is to promote environmental awareness of all CAMI employees."[56] Management insisted, however, that statistics pertaining to CAMI were to remain confidential if so requested by any member. In addition, CAMI management agreed to co-operate in studying the possibility of van pooling to get employees to and from work. The 1995-1998 agreement also committed CAMI to providing training for union members of the (joint) Environmental Committee.

Cathy Austin, who co-chairs the union's environment committee, has identified a range of connections between automobile production in Ingersoll and environmental issues. These include: the quantity of packaging materials which becomes landfill waste; the use of water by the plant and the contamination of area wells by solvents; the higher energy costs of the just-in-time system of parts delivery which moved inputs from rail to highway transport; and the vehicles themselves. Local 88 participated in the CAW Southwest Ontario Environmental Conference held in Woodstock in November, 1994, at which "the importance of bargaining for environmentally sound production of vehicles" was discussed.[57] So far, however, the joint environment committee has focused on in-plant recycling and waste minimization. Such programmes, of course, complement company efforts to reduce costs. Austin provided an interesting account of difficulties encountered by the union members of the environment committee in overcoming the suspicions of both management and their co-workers, in a Japanese-management-style plant. The company initially viewed the environment committee with "extreme distrust," demonstrated by its decision to place on the committee the company lawyer and a management-employees relations person who had nothing to do with the operations of the plant. As a result, the committee was "completely ineffective" for the first few years. The committee now includes the head of facilities engineering and the person responsible for solid waste management, and has made more headway in recycling. The union also wants the joint committee to address energy and water conservation issues. Austin recognizes that these goals conform to the company's interest in reducing costs, but also points out the ways in which union objectives conflict with profit imperatives. For example, an injured worker was assigned the job of determining how workers could recycle materials in the few seconds permitted by the lean production system. The union is insisting that recycling be included in the production cycle, "so that every movement and time taken is included into the process time."[58]

The joint environment committee has also been viewed with suspicion by the workers, who see it as yet another way for the company to make money. When asked to recycle their soft drink containers, for example, they say: "So why should I help the company make more money?" What they would normally do at home (with the blue box system) as "good citizens" takes on a different meaning in the adversarial worker-boss relationship.[59] The union members have learned from this experience that it is important to maintain a distinct identity for the union's environmental standing committee.

Other CAW Locals in the region (notably, 707, 1973) also have active environment committees, although the activities of only a few can be sketched here. Local 636 (an amalgamated local in the Woodstock area, representing ten Units and 2200 members) has participated in various community coalitions, including Grassroots Woodstock (on the issue of water fluoridation), the Woodstock Environment Advisory Committee, the Oxford County Environment Committee, and a public forum on the NAFTA and all-candidates meetings on environmental issues. The Local 636 committee was also selected as a labour representative for an International Development Research Centre (IDRC) project on "global environment and education" in Costa Rica and Nicaragua. In addition, Local 636 established an Environment fund to support local environment initiatives. A particularly innovative educational initiative undertaken by the local is the production of a cable television program which seeks to link occupational health and environmental issues, discusses relevant legislation, and reports on CAW activities.[60] Local 1520 (St. Thomas) participates in the OEN Labour Caucus and played a key role in organising the September 1995 conference in London on "Jobs and the Environment beyond the year 2000."[61]

The above cases provide some examples of the kinds of priorities which the environmental committees have been able to pursue with employers to date. Waste reduction and conservation measures are clearly those which most closely coincide with management interests, as all the union representatives acknowledge. Areas which touch on other areas of management control—in particular, research and investment priorities—have not yet been seriously engaged by the union. Here, the union has not only to confront management, but also to mobilize membership support for such radical-seeming environmental demands, and in a context of considerable job insecurity. The major issues on the bargaining table with the Big Three in the 1996 negotiations were the out-sourcing of union jobs and intensifying workload/lean production. The union is, however, advocating the reduction of work time as a strategy to create employment, and is urging its members to stop working overtime. A strong stand on the reduction of work issue (combined with union research and coalition work on an alternative "eco-economy" agenda) will be a major contribution to the building of a social movement.[62]

The Union Environment Committees and Coalition-building

In 1987-1989 only a handful of CAW locals had established environmental standing committees. CAW officials estimate that today approximately 40 to 50 of the CAW's 364 locals have active environment committees.[63] These are mainly in the auto and auto-related sectors.[64] In addition, the most active environment committees remain those located in "CAW country"—Essex County, and these have become the models for the agendas and coalition-building initiatives of the more recently-formed committees in southwestern Ontario (e.g., Locals 636, 1520, 88). A brief survey of the activities of some of these local and regional CAW environmental organisations provides insights into their conception of the links between the workers' movement and the alternative social movements.

When describing CAW activism in Windsor, one hardly knows where to start, although the threads inevitably unravel to a handful of dedicated individuals, foremost among them, Rick Coronado. The key figure in Local 444's environmental committee in the 1987-1990 period, Coronado left the plant in 1991 to work full time on community-labour organising linking social justice and environmental issues. Since 1993 he has run the CAW Project Office at the University of Windsor, which houses the Windsor & Area Coalition for Social Justice (WACSJ). The WACSJ formed in 1992 to unite opposition against the North American Free Trade Agreement (NAFTA), and is connected to think-tanks on the left which are developing alternative economic strategy (including the Alternative Federal Budget group, Choices [Manitoba], the Canadian Centre for Policy Alternatives), and to the Action Canada Network (which formed initially to oppose the Free Trade Agreement in the 1980s).[65] According to Coronado, there are presently 28 social justice coalitions in Ontario.[66]

Coronado has also been closely involved with the CAW Windsor Regional Environmental Council (WREC), which was established in the early 1990s and is composed of representatives from eleven CAW Windsor and area union locals.[67] The WREC's statement of policy sets out a coalition-building project whose main objective is to "integrate the environmental movement socially, economically and politically."[68] In one sense, the WREC may be seen as an attempt by environmental and social activists within the CAW to create a more autonomous and influential base of operation vis-à-vis both their respective local executives, and citizens' environmental groups. In other words, the coalition-building orientation of the CAW environmental committee activists (observed in the study of the committees between 1987-1989) could not be "contained" by, or fully pursued within, the structure of the local union standing committee. While the WREC representatives are still accountable to, and dependent in various ways on the support of their respective union executives, by acting collectively the activists develop joint campaigns, share information, and generally exercise more influence and credibility vis-à-vis their executives. They can also call on support for their campaigns from the National office, using the existence of national policies to push forward local union agendas. At the same time, the WREC concentrates the CAW's presence and influence (its specifically labour-movement identity and analyses) vis-à-vis area coalitions. It is certainly clear from the agenda of goals set out in the WREC policy statement that the environmental committee activists have moved beyond the "legislative" definition of standing committee functions (interpretation and monitoring of government legislation and contractual undertakings related to environmental issues and workers' and employers' rights and obligations). They are, indeed, committed to defining and realizing an ecologically-sustainable, egalitarian regional development strategy. Their persistent theme, as expressed by Coronado and others in the WREC quarterly publication, *The Global Guardian*, is that "the environment can be shown to be a serious social justice issue."[69]

The WREC has pursued its objectives through a number of initiatives. Since January 1995 WREC has been offering an eco-socialist interpretation of environmental and economic problems, expressed consistently by the *Global Guardian*'s editor, Mark C. Parent. Parent argues, for example, that "the working class must exercise leadership in the monumental task concerning our environment," because environmentalists care too little for such problems as unemployment, and because corporations and governments must be compelled by collective bargaining and "progressive political action" to protect the environment. Moreover, Parent insists that environmental problems cannot be resolved solely through individual lifestyle choices; collective action is required to shift production decisions: "Labour is uniquely qualified to suggest sustainable solutions to the problem of toxic substances or waste management... The working class have all the components to effect and secure a safe and healthy environment for workers and our community. We must pool our efforts with all areas of academia, as mutual stakeholders of our future."[70]

Another initiative of these eco-socialist "organic intellectuals"[71] is the organisation, in conjunction with the Citizens' Environmental Alliance (CEA),[72] of annual "youth and the environment" conferences for high-school students in the Windsor area. These have been held in April 1995 and February 1996, each time drawing between 150 to 200 teenagers. They have been followed-up, moreover, by the formation of a student environmental network under the direction of Mark Parent (CAW Local 1973, GM, Windsor, environment committee member and editor of *The Global Guardian*). Among other themes, the 1996 conference examined the effects of the Ontario Conservative Government led by Premier Mike Harris on the environment, and mobilized student opposition to the Conservatives' (extremist neoliberal and neoconservative) agenda by making these connections.[73] The Southwest Ontario Environmental Council (Woodstock-London-Ingersoll) has also taken up the idea of organising a Youth and the Environment conference.[74] Local 88 (Ingersoll) made contact with local high school students in 1992, offering to share information with the students' environmental club. In general, the regional councils have a very strong educational focus which counters the activities of such business organisations as the Canadian Chemical Producers Association (see part 3) on the critical educational terrain of hegemonic struggle.

The educational efforts of the CAW local environmentalists also include adoption of the campaign to legalize the production of industrial hemp, which they identify as a key element of a regional sustainable development strategy for southwest Ontario. As a result of their campaign, which identifies low-THC hemp as a renewable and environmentally-friendly substitute for wood-based products and hydrocarbon-fuels, and as the basis for the creation of many new industries and jobs, the CAW regional environment councils succeeded in obtaining the legalization of hemp in June 1996.[75] The hemp campaign proposes an alternative to farmers who may need (or wish) to find a substitute for tobacco (a crop grown in this region of Ontario); to unemployed workers (including former auto workers); and to consumers who do not want to use paper products derived from the clear-cutting of forests, or fuels which are contributing to air pollution and global warming. (And high-school students find the campaign "cool" because hemp is associated with marijuana and rebellion against State authority!) The question: "Why isn't hemp production legal in Canada?" allowed the labour-environment activists to point to the interests of corporations in the forestry, energy, tobacco, and other industries in protecting their profits at the cost of environmental destruction, damage to human health, continuing unemployment, the bankruptcies of small farmers, and so on. In other words, the hemp campaign has provided an issue—an *alternative*—which makes connections among diverse social groups and interests, articulated via the theme of local, democratic control over decisions about the nature of social and economic development, as well as a critical discourse making visible the forms of power which oppose democratic, egalitarian, and ecological principles of development.

Under the Ontario NDP Government (1991-1995), the Windsor CAW labour-environment activists also got involved in another sustainable-development-oriented coalition. The NDP Government agreed to contribute funds to coalitions including small businesses and community organisations which were called "Green communities initiatives."[76] The coalition would hire individuals to go door-to-door in a community to explain how energy could be saved, household waste composted, and other such ideas. This would create a demand for retrofitting, and in turn create jobs in the environmental industry. To carry out this plan, the "partners" would form a committee, elect a board, select a work site, and train the neighbourhood canvassers. In Windsor, the CAW already had experience in co-operative housing, and had considerable influence in the community. So in this case (union participation in the Green Communities initiatives was rare elsewhere), the CAW was chosen to chair the Green Communities Initiative in the

Windsor area.[77] One of the projects they undertook was called "the Bounty of the County," and encouraged the processing of local produce for local markets. Its slogan was: "Buy the food your neighbours grow." The coalition was also beginning to grapple with the issues of a self-sufficiency-oriented local economy, when the Conservative Party replaced the NDP in government, and all of the Green Communities projects were cancelled. The Windsor coalition, however, is trying to find other sources of funding to continue its work.

Indeed, it appears that the radical measures of the Harris Government have deepened the sense of urgency around coalition-building on the part of many different social actors. The social justice coalitions, like the WACSJ, that formed initially to continue the struggle against the FTA and NAFTA, laid some of the groundwork through their critique of the consequences of turning more and more areas of societal decision making over to markets and their key players. The "inevitability" or necessity of sacrificing every solidaristic, egalitarian, or ecological concern to the goals of competitiveness and profits had become a much-frayed discourse by the time the Harris Government began to impose its version of market dictatorship. The social justice coalitions now confront the Harris Government's assault on workers, the environment (Omnibus Bill 26), health care, education, and social services, and their labour-environment activists have grasped as never before that all of these struggles are about the democratic rights of citizens to determine what kind of society they inhabit in the present and the future. The labour-movement activists have clearly understood the ways in which ecological critiques expose the antidemocratic nature of capitalism, and the seriously compromised, restricted nature of our liberal democratic institutions.

From Social Unionism to Movement Unionism: The Union Steps In

Three significant developments in the political economy of Canada and Ontario have challenged the labour movement to either take a more active role in shaping political discourse, or retreat to a corporate strategy of defence. The first is the 1980s fight against the FTA, in which (as discussed in chapter 13) the CAW took a leading role. The second is the rupture between the social democratic New Democratic Party (elected to government in Ontario in 1991) and the public sector unions brought about by the NDP's adoption of a neoliberal economic and social agenda dressed in neocorporatist rhetoric. The government tried to construct a labour-corporate "partnership" in a number of areas (including occupational health and safety),[78] and in 1993 imposed its "social contract" with public sector employees.[79] In the Ontario election of 1995, the NDP paid the price of alienating its grassroots support. Stephen McBride offers this assessment:

> A social democratic government has been tried in Ontario and found to be bankrupt of any ideas, save those espoused by its neo-conservative and post-Keynesian rivals. Because it lacked a social democratic alternative, the Rae government found itself a prisoner of the hegemonic ideas. The government's justification for its actions is essentially the same as that advanced in Mrs. Thatcher's famous line—"There is no alternative."[80]

Notably, in this polarisation of social forces, the CAW—alone among the industrial unions—sided with the public sector unions in withdrawing support for the NDP government.

The third development is the election of the Ontario Conservatives, led by Mike Harris, in 1995. The programme and ideological discourse of the Harris government cannot be described in detail here. Among its actions since taking office are massive budget cuts (on the order of 20 to 30 percent) in the areas of health, education, and social services, targeting the unemployed and the poor both economically and ideologically. It has also slashed funding for services of particular importance to women (e.g., shelters, co-op housing, daycare), opposes affirmative action employment policies, is attempting to remove legislative obstacles to privatization throughout the economy, and has repealed a number of the reforms to labour legislation made under the Rae government.

Thus, if ever there were circumstances calling for a phase of renewed mobilization by the labour movement—the historical pattern observed by Offe and Wiesenthal and discussed in chapter 1—they are present in the 1990s. However, some elements within the labour movement have grasped more clearly than others that social democratic management of the capitalist economy is no longer a solution for the economic and environmental crisis which confronts us at the end of the twentieth century. The repeated disappointments of NDP governments in office provincially have served to more sharply differentiate the supporters of an exhausted paradigm from the proponents of a new social project. The recent transition in the discourse of the CAW national leadership from "social unionism" (the theme of the 1980s) to "movement unionism" must be understood not only in the context of the offensive from the right, but in the context of social movements' *rejection* of social democratic management of the crisis. This rejection is a culmination of experiences like that of the Green Work Alliance, described below. This story is particularly interesting as an example of the failure, or refusal, of the NDP to assume the leadership of a truly alternative agenda of reforms. Rather, the leadership for such an agenda is coming from new middle class strata situated in the environmental, urban renewal, women's, and other movements, as well as from sectors of the labour movement.

In a section of its 1996 Collective Bargaining Convention report entitled "Missed Opportunities: The Failure of the Left," the CAW leadership summarizes its critique of social democratic government, arguing that the potential for mass mobilization around an alternative agenda of social change exists, but that the political leadership for such a project has been lacking. Expressing a very Gramscian understanding of counter-hegemonic strategy, the document states:

> In the understandable focus on electoral politics, we've missed out on the importance of organizing, *of building the solid and widespread base* that can really change things. We don't have the top-down power and resources of the corporations, so even if elected we find ourselves stymied—unless we've also affected the overall political climate in the country, mobilized people to act between elections, and created structures through which we can fight... This political insight has been grasped more clearly by the labour movement than by its political arm. As the labour movement searched for an effective response to the new corporate aggressiveness, a significant change occurred in its relationship to the NDP. It is no exaggeration to say that, over the past decade, the real political leadership within the left has shifted to the labour movement itself.[81]

It is significant that the social project being discussed here is identified with socialism. In this framework, what is being said is that it is the labour movement (or, more accurately, certain elements of leadership within it) which has taken on the role of the organic intellectuals of the working class, since the parliamentarist and intellectually bankrupt "political arm" of the working class has abdicated this role. The fundamental nature of social conflict is clearly presented in this document (as elsewhere in CAW literature) as a fight of workers (subsuming all other relationships of domination/subordination, or subject positions) against capitalism. And yet the problem posed is how to build a mass, oppositional movement against the capitalist monopolization of decision making about the kind of society we live in, and even this limited (because class-reductionist) conception of hegemonic power leads inevitably to a recognition of the importance of radical democratic discourse as the "cement" of such a movement. For it is through linkages with other social struggles (the women's movement, the environmental, peace, and anti-racist movements, anti-poverty coalitions, solidarity with these struggles globally, and others) which also express individual and social needs, and demand the democratic conditions for their fulfilment, that such a movement may ultimately be constructed. For the most part, CAW discourse about these "other" movements treats them as add-ons (as in collective bargaining priorities). The problem is presented as the creation of working class identity and collective action which is assumed to incorporate the totality of social struggles against various forms of oppression. However, real transformations of this discourse are occurring in the context of coalition-building, particularly at the grassroots level. Sam Gindin's definition of "movement unionism" seems pulled toward a conception of union/socialist leadership which brings to a social movement the important Marxist analysis of capitalism, but which is also open to a transformation of its own understanding of the nature of social conflict.

> [Movement unionism] means making the union into a vehicle through which its members can not only address their bargaining demands but actively lead the fight for everything that affects working people in their communities and the country. Movement unionism includes the shape of bargaining demands, the scope of union activities, the approach to issues of change, and above all, that sense of commitment to a larger movement that might suffer defeats, but can't be destroyed.
>
> The union movement has only recently begun discussing the issue in these terms, but concrete initiatives have emerged at various levels. In bargaining, the emphasis on reduced work-time was directly linked to creating job openings for others... In April 1995, a CAW conference in Windsor for young people interested in the environment led to the students' establishment of local environmental committees in their schools...[82]

Significantly, the penultimate section of Gindin's 1995 book is entitled "Democracy and Change." In it, he argues that the "goals of unions are rooted in democracy," and that the union organisation must, itself, be a model of egalitarian and participatory practices which empower members to become activists. In Gramscian terms, the union must not cultivate parliamentarism and passivity on the part of its membership, but encourage the formation of organic intellectuals of the counter-hegemonic movement. The CAW has succeeded in sustaining a culture which nourishes organic intellectuals of the working class (although Gindin does raise the issues of generational change and growing diversification of the membership, which will test the durability and the influence of this culture). The question now would seem to be, whether the shift from "social unionism" to "movement unionism" entails a transformation of the collective identity of the union's organic intellectuals—of their understanding of counter-hegemonic struggle. Certainly any observer of the union's praxis will concur with Gindin that the CAW confronts this challenge with "an impressive cadre of activists, staff, and leadership."[83]

An example of the impressive work of this cadre, and of the actual grassroots coalition-building which is transforming the strategic thinking of the CAW, is provided by the developments in Windsor, and by the experience of the Green Work Alliance, to which I now turn.

The Green Work Alliance

According to Nick De Carlo, who was a leading figure in the Green Work Alliance (GWA), a conjuncture of events gave rise to this initiative in the Brampton-Toronto region of Ontario.[84] The FTA had led to numerous plant closures, including the CAW-organised Brampton Caterpillar plant employing machinists and mechanics. In 1990-91 CAW workers had the opportunity to meet representatives of a workers' co-operative movement from Japan, and in the context of GWA meetings, also discussed the workers' proposals for the conversion of production at Lucas aerospace in England in the 1970s.[85] Another factor was the history of occupational health, safety, and disability grievances at local plants which, as Roger Keil notes in his account of the Green Work Alliance, "had long been issues for the CAW and other unions." Indeed, Nick De Carlo was, at the time, the President of CAW Local 1967 at Toronto's McDonnell-Douglas (aircraft) plant. Sam Gindin records that in the mid-1980s, there was renewed worker militancy over health and safety issues. In 1986 and 1987 "workers at de Havilland and McDonnell-Douglas staged the largest work refusals that had ever occurred for health and safety, shutting down production and making major gains in cleaning up the workplace, training and educating the workforce, and monitoring the health of workers."[86] In April 1991 workers took over the Caterpillar plant after the company announced a change in ownership.[87] There was thus a militant tradition of support for greater workers' control over production at these sites. Making the connections between the unhealthy environment of production and the need to transform the environmental conditions of economic development was also helped by the involvement in the GWA of Stan Gray, a long-time workers' occupational health and safety activist, who was at that time on staff with Greenpeace Canada.

Like the workers at Lucas Aerospace, the union locals involved in the GWA hoped that the existence of a social democratic government (in Britain in the 1975-1979 period the Labour Party was in government) would provide a supportive climate for their proposals.[88] Keil summarizes these as follows:

> The concrete project at hand was the demand for the re-opening of the Caterpillar plant as a site for green production. Various production models, technologies and products as well as ownership and financing alternatives were discussed. Yet it soon became clear that those who had formed the Green Work Alliance were on to something much more comprehensive. The opening of the plant with environmentally-friendly production was considered only one—albeit a central—element of a larger project. A "greenbelt not a rustbelt" was to emerge out of the region's battered economy.[89]

This "larger project," as described by De Carlo, was the subject of differing interpretations. However, one view was that workers' co-operatives would be limited and contained within the capitalist economy without linkage to a government-backed agenda of economic reforms. This included the creation of public corporations at the municipal, provincial and federal levels whose aim would be to convert plants to environmental production for regional markets. They would encourage the development of new technologies and products for international markets, as well. Workers would be represented on the boards of these corporations, as would community-based organisations, and environmentalists. In De Carlo's words, this project

> had tremendous support among workers because the idea of thinking about how to redesign things and being able to build alternatives really caught people's attention...For example, houses could be redone with solar water heating systems; retrofitting of low-energy windows; low energy appliances—all these things could be built locally. You could redo the production process *inside* of the workplaces so that workers could put their minds [to work] on how to redo the production systems.

By 1995, however, the Green Work Alliance had lost steam. According to De Carlo: "We lost the workers' support we had because there wasn't anything immediate to grab onto. There wasn't any immediate solution. So a lot of the activists involved dropped off." Now the GWA is comprised of a small number of persons who meet occasionally to discuss ideas. What happened to the energy and the momentum of the GWA between 1991-1995?

One of the obstacles mentioned by De Carlo was a lack of connections to scientists and engineers who could help in the development of proposals for new products, technology, work processes, and plant design. De Carlo makes a comparison here with the situation of Lucas Aerospace workers, who, as part of a general workers' federation which included such highly-trained people, had access to such assistance within the union movement. In Canada, the segregation (ideologically, organisationally, and professionally) of "professionals" in the science and engineering fields from the workers' movement (and other social movements) is a serious weakness of efforts to develop social and economic alternatives.[90]

A second problem has to do with the character of at least one sector of the 1990s urban environmental movement, which has tried to adapt to the market approach, i.e., finding profitable applications of pollution-abatement or energy conservation technology; using pricing and taxation mechanisms to orient corporate marketing and production decisions in more "energy efficient" directions; promoting "green" businesses (e.g., in development of technology, production of environmentally-friendly products and services, and consulting and marketing work), and green consumerism.[91] When the GWA unionists looked for help from environmentalists in developing alternatives, they encountered green entrepreneurs who wanted to draw up business plans. Again, in De Carlo's words:

> We didn't simply want to create one plant that would create something differently in the market place... That wasn't the concept. The concept was to develop a whole infrastructure—an alternative economy, in effect, or the basis for an alternative economy. That's why we wanted a public corporation that would be responsible for creating jobs outside of the normal market place—that wouldn't depend on competition in the market place, but more on creating its own market. For example, there was a massive housing project starting up in Brampton— 13,000 units. We thought that if we could get city council to agree to put low energy windows in, then we could start up a factory to produce those windows. All these things would fit together. That was why we would set up municipal [and] provincial corporations [to] work at different levels... [There would be] co-ordination and we would build what had to be built, not just [anything that would compete] in the market place.

The idea was also to employ local people to produce environmentally friendly, socially useful products for local markets—not to produce anything for any markets anywhere, taking jobs away from other groups of workers in those places, in the name of competition. The GWA was also sensitive to other dimensions of an alternative eco-economic strategy. For example, with regard to the production of low-energy windows, they wanted to ensure that the transportation of inputs and products to and from the plant would be environmentally sustainable. They wanted to have a work-process design that included child care. As De Carlo sums it up: "We began to see this as a political movement" whose theme became "jobs, environment, and democracy." "We couldn't solve the problems of jobs and the environment without dealing with the issue of who makes the decisions and who has control."

At this point, the GWA members concluded that they needed resources to do more research. They approached the Ontario government Ministries of the Environment and of Industry, Trade, and Development, to request funding to research the possibility of establishing a public corporation to promote worker and community-controlled production as well as demand for environmental products. This is where the response of the NDP government is most illuminating of its overall strategy of accommodation with the private sector. According to De Carlo, the government's response was: "if you had private venture capital then they would fund development of a business plan, but they didn't want to have anything to do with a public corporation." Fearing to antagonize a hostile business sector and to fuel its media campaigns against the government, the NDP put its eggs in the wrong basket.

De Carlo still believes that the GWA and other initiatives like it can be resurrected, and that the key is to win the creation of a public corporation of the kind outlined above. This requires the building of a political movement which will demand such reforms, and he thinks that the CAW can play a role in this effort. The main obstacle to this, in his view, is the limited resources of the union. But in addition, a priority like alternative community development is "straying far afield from what we are as a union... It is difficult to convince people of [its importance], and especially to organize." In other words, how much can a union do to develop alternative economic strategy for a region, a province, or a city, let alone a country? Is this not properly the task of a political party rooted in a mass movement, or, alternatively, of a broadly-based social coalition acting in conjunction with political representation? What are the limits of "movement unionism"?

CONCLUSIONS

The comparison of the responses of the ECWU and the CAW to the growing influence of the environmental movement culturally and in regard to State regulation, demonstrates that the explanations for their differences are complex, and that generalizations about the "inherent conservatism" or Fordist attachments of "the workers' movement" are best avoided. To explain the differences between the ECWU and the CAW we need to look not only at political and economic factors, but also at the ideological perspectives of the actors themselves, taking into account that these are by no means homogeneous. The problem, nevertheless, is to determine what the prevailing culture of the union is, vis-à-vis its collective identity and its conception of the social role of unionism. This culture—which is influenced by the discursive strategies of employers, political parties, and other collective actors (such as environmentalists), as well as by the internal practices and historical origins of the union organisation itself—turns out to be crucial to an appreciation of historical agency. Union strategy must therefore be understood as the continually changing outcome of a dynamic interaction between structural conditions and the strategic choices made by actors. Charlotte Yates came to a similar conclusion on the basis of her study of the explanation for CAW militancy in the 1980s: "External factors, such as the state of the economy, place limits on union choices and its capacity to effect chosen strategies. Within these limits, however, the internal dynamics of unions determine the course of action chosen."[92]

To take one example, it is pointed out that it is the energy and chemicals sectors which have been most besieged by citizens' environmental and health movements in North America, while the auto industry has managed to avoid the same degree of opposition to the production of its key commodities, and that these differences offer one explanation of the unions' different perceptions of their options. We see, however, that pressure for alternative transportation strategies and other forms of environmental regulation is intensifying in the 1990s and is likely to intensify further in the future, and that in this changing environment, the CAW is not adopting a more defensive strategy vis-à-vis the environmental movement. One might argue that this is because the heat is not yet hot enough to make rank-and-file workers feel insecure. However, the national leadership of the union has taken a proactive approach to *create* alternatives so that employers' job blackmail will not succeed. To understand this choice of direction, we need to look at the prevalent ideological perceptions of the union leadership and members.

Just as we cannot treat union "cultures" as homogeneous, we cannot theorize as if they are unchanging. The perspectives of the Chemical Valley membership of the ECWU, vis-à-vis the environmental movement, may well undergo significant change as a result of changes in their leadership's discourse, in the politico-economic context of union calculations, in the discourse of the environmental movement, and so on. The merger resulting in the CEP, along with generational change in union functionaries, presents a new mix of ideological influences. For example, the Paper and Pulp section of the union (in British Columbia), and the Pulp, Paper, and Woodworkers of Canada (PPWC) are viewed as having taken strong positions against pulp mill pollution. Moreover, one might expect that chemical and energy sector workers have now recognized that the "united front" with employers to improve the competitiveness (profitability) of the industry did not prevent job losses and plant closures. The union movement as a whole has been radicalized by the experiences of the 1980s and 1990s, and the CAW offers a pole of leadership for other industrial unions. A tentative sense of the direction of these changes is provided by the statement of the CEP representative before the International Joint Commission in the winter of 1993. The controversy at the heart of these meetings was the campaign to ban chlorine products, spear-headed by Greenpeace, endorsed by the IJC, and fiercely opposed by the chemical companies. While the tone of the CEP position is cautious and corporatist (seeing the resolution of the jobs-versus-the-environment conflict in co-operation and compromise among workers, business, environmentalists, and governments), it endorses a conception of sustainable development.[93]

A comparison of the CAW's labour-environment strategy in the periods from 1986-1989 and 1990-1996 allows us to observe, in another sense, the effect of changes in the "external environment" on union strategy. The complacency of the social democratic perspectives held by union officials interviewed in the earlier period has been disrupted by subsequent events. As Sam Gindin observes: "Social unionism emphasized the importance of electoral politics but the politics that emerged was in reality contracted out. Unions contributed bodies and money while party professionals determined the direction and strategy."[94] Forced to respond to the crisis of the social democratic paradigm, the CAW leadership has made steps toward a different kind of unionism.

The 1990s "convergence" approach of the national leadership vis-à-vis labour-environment relations, has also been "pushed" by the commitment of grassroots activists in the southwestern Ontario region to coalition-building. The 1994 submission to the CAW National Executive Board of the CAW Council Environment Committee acknowledges that the relatively low priority accorded to the integration of ecological discourse into the union's collective bargaining agenda and allocation of resources is out of step with the "tremendous amount of organising going on at the grassroots level of the union." At the same time, it must be remembered that the kind of coalition-building taking place in southwestern Ontario is exceptional because of the particularly militant, socialist culture of the CAW workforce in that region, as well as its influence vis-à-vis other social actors.

The recent political history of Ontario also plays an important role in explaining this sector of the union membership's exceptional role as "organic intellectuals" of a counter-hegemonic project of convergence. Workers in southern Ontario have experienced the brunt of industrial job losses following the implementation of the Free Trade Agreement in the late 1980s and have been both the objects and the subjects of intense politico-ideological contestation of the Tory government's "corporate agenda" (as CAW discourse labels it). They were then deeply antagonized and disillusioned by the capitulation of the Ontario NDP government to a corporatist version of the same project. Then came Harris' "common sense revolution," modelled very closely upon the so-called "Klein revolution" in the province of Alberta.[95] The national leadership has gone some way toward the adoption of an eco-socialist discourse, in response to pushing from elements within its traditionally "core" locals to which it is, moreover, sympathetic. The national leadership must also, however, avoid getting out of step with other sectors of a large, diverse membership. Indeed, as the activists in the southern Ontario region themselves admit, there is resistance even within the most historically militant locals to the more radical implications of ecological discourse (including to the reduction of work time). Finally, while green economics may be—as the activists and national staff representatives argue—a condition for the eventual cohesion of an alternative social movement (i.e., the concrete response to the neoliberal claim that "there is no alternative" to the market-driven organisation of societies), to assume the *leadership* of such a project is essentially to assume the role of a political party, and therefore poses the real problem of the limits of the union as a social movement.

NOTES

1. John Holmes, "The Contemporary Restructuring of Canadian Industry" (paper presented to The Workshop on Development in the 1980s: Canada in the Western Hemisphere, Queen's University, Kingston, May 10-13, 1984), p. 35.
2. Ibid., p. 33. The Automobile, Aerospace, and Agricultural Implement Workers of America (UAW) Canadian section reported memberships of 61,284, 119,211, and 118,440 in 1962, 1983, and 1984 respectively. Its Ontario membership in 1984 was 106,521. (Figures from Statistics Canada, *Corporations and Labour Unions Returns Act, Report for 1984*, Part II (Labour Unions) supplement, Statistics Canada, 1984.)
3. CAW, *In Solidarity: A Family Album* (North York, Ont.: CAW, April 1989), pp. 3, 12.
4. *Toronto Star*, March 8, 1987, pp. F1, F2.
5. At the Chrysler Pillette Road Truck Assembly Plant, there were in November 1986, 2,750 workers. In April 1988 this figure was 1,969. The truck plant on Tecumseh Rd. had 3,833 workers in April 1985, and 3,406 in April 1988. (*Windsor Star*, November 15, 1986, and November 29, 1986; *Local 444 News*, April 1988, p. 8.)
6. Holmes, "The Contemporary Restructuring of Canadian Industry," p. 40.
7. *The Globe and Mail*, February 18, 1988.
8. Ford management went even further. The President and CEO of Ford Canada, Kenneth Harrigan, supported the Free Trade Agreement and opposed Ontario laws regulating "overtime hours, pensions, workers' compensation, and workplace safety," because the latter "rob companies of needed flexibility" (*The Globe and Mail*, May 18, 1988).
9. The UAW and General Motors (US) agreed in 1984 on profit-sharing and lump-sum payments in lieu of negotiated wage increases. The Canadian Council of the UAW opposed the arrangement, and decided to strike for a higher wage increase for Canadian workers, as well as the return of nine paid holidays given up in 1982. While UAW leaders in the US were emphasizing "job security," the Canadian section was demanding that shorter work time, higher pensions, and substantial wage increases be made central bargaining goals for 1985-1986 contracts. (*The Globe and Mail*, June 25, 1984, pp. 1, 2.) On the CAW's separation from the UAW, see Sam Gindin, "Breaking Away: The Formation of the Canadian Auto Workers," *Studies in Political Economy* 29 (Summer 1989), esp. pp. 74-79.
10. See David Robertson and Jeff Wareham, "Technological Change in the Auto Industry (CAW Technology Report)," study funded by the Labour Canada Technology Impact Research Fund and supervised by the CAW research department and CAW Canada Council technology committee, April 1987 (North York: CAW, 1987), pp. 35-42.

11. *Statistics Canada Daily*, April 3, 1984, quoted by Holmes, "The Contemporary Restructuring of Canadian Industry," p. 16.
12. In November 1987, Chrysler temporarily shut down four plants in Canada, including the Pillette Road plant in Windsor, because of surplus inventory. Chrysler also closed a 5,500-employee assembly plant in Kenosha, Wisconsin, which it had just acquired from AMC. (James Dow, article in the *Toronto Star*, January 29, 1988.) The CAW negotiated twelve plant closures from January to May 1988, and six more were pending. (*The Globe and Mail*, May 4, 1988, p. B2.)
13. Gindin was a participant in a seminar held at the University of Alberta in May 1984. The proceedings were published in a book edited by John Richards and Don Kerr, called *Canada: What's Left?* (Edmonton: NeWest Publishers, 1986).
14. Ibid., pp. 85-87.
15. Although the Chrysler mini-van plant in Windsor is the site of a "motivational awareness program," this was considered one of the most militant locals in the region by union officials interviewed. This view is confirmed by Gindin in "Breaking Away: The Formation of the Canadian Auto Workers." One shop steward from the Chrysler plant objected at length to the publication of an article on environmental issues (written by the chairperson of the local's environment committee) in the *Chrysler Van News* (company newsletter for employees). He was concerned that this might be seen as a union endorsement of the "new management agenda" (Interview with Mike Longmoore, Local 444, July 23, 1987).
16. The negative aspects are listed as technology related job loss and displacement, high levels of insecurity, deskilling and downgrading, work intensification, increased management control, more rigid division of labour, isolation and polarisation, fractured workplaces and erosion of member support, impaired labour-management relations. The positive aspects are: reskilling and skill upgrading in some jobs, reduced physical workload and hazards, improved ergonomics, reduction of boring and repetitive jobs, enriched and enlarged jobs, improvement in working conditions, better social relations with peers and supervisors, more control, autonomy, and responsibility, increased worker involvement, greater job satisfaction and better treatment, better labour-management relations (Robertson and Wareham, "Technological Change," p. 54). The QWL guidelines appended to the *CAW's Master Agreement with General Motors*, 1987 (appendix F), also exemplify the union's caution and concern with stating its own criteria for such developments.
17. See Stephen Wood, "The Co-operative Labour Strategy in the U.S. Auto Industry," *Economic and Industrial Democracy* vol. 7 (1986), pp. 415-447.
18. Lorne Slotnick, "Effects of Chrysler Walkout quickly felt at U.S. plants," *The Globe and Mail*, September 16, 1987.
19. Edward Greenspon, "Cost-saving Ford strategy Achilles' heel in U.K. strike," *The Globe and Mail*, February 18, 1988.
20. Zalev Brothers has had dangerous working conditions, protested by its workers, according to one survey respondent who works there. The plant and scrap yard has also been charged on at least two occasions by the MOE. In October 1986 Zalev Brothers was charged under the EPA for emission of odour and particulate, and in September 1987 the firm was charged for allowing a fire to burn for several days, creating clouds of smoke which affected area residents. MOE, Legal Services Branch, *Prosecution Reports*, (Toronto: MOE, Legal Services Branch, 1987).
21. There was a debate within the union movement over whether new legislation represented an advance of workers' rights or a plan to integrate unions more fully into a system of industrial relations which benefits capital. See the analysis by Nick De Carlo, at the time the President of CAW Local 1967 (McDonnell-Douglas), "The Right to Refuse Bill 208," in *Our Times*, May 1989, pp. 9-11.
22. *ECWU Journal* no. 19 (April 1989), p. 9.
23. Wilfred List, "CAW wants more education pay," *The Globe and Mail*, February 29, 1988.
24. Robert White, "From Defeat to Renewal." *This Magazine*: 23, 1 (May-June 1989), p. 24.
25. In answer to the question "Why is the car treated like a sacred cow?" André Gorz argued that: "Mass motoring effects an absolute triumph of bourgeois ideology on the level of daily life. It gives and supports in everyone the illusion that each individual can seek his or her own benefit at the expense of everyone else." (See "The Social Ideology of the Motorcar," in *Ecology as Politics* (Montréal: Black Rose Press, 1980), p. 70.)
26. See for example, the articles by Murray Campbell in *The Globe and Mail*, October 10 and 11,

Union-Enivronmental Movement Convergence 311

1991, focusing on the severe air pollution problems facing Los Angeles. Campbell reported that vehicles account for two-thirds of the emissions that create Los Angeles' infamous smog ("Cleaning up, paying up," October 11, 1991, p. A11).
27. See CAW, "Local Union Environment Committees in the CAW" (North York, Ont.: CAW, n.d.).
28. Cathy Walker, interview by author, Toronto, June 5, 1996.
29. Alex Keeney, interview by author, Toronto, June 6, 1996.
30. CAW, "Local Union Environment Committees in the CAW," p. 4.
31. Ibid., pp. 6-7.
32. CAW, "CAW Statement on Transportation and the Environment," in *False Solutions, Growing Protests: Recapturing the Agenda*. Report to the National Collective Bargaining and Political Action Convention, Toronto, June 4-7, 1996 (North York, Willowdale, Ont.: CAW, 1996), pp. 138-141.
33. Walker, interview, June 5, 1996.
34. In Walker's view, the policy document produced by the Round Table was a considerable achievement. Notably, only the oil industry refused to sign on. See the "CAW Statement on Transportation", produced by the CAW Research and Communications depts. (North York, Ont.: CAW, 1992).
35. Environment committee members who attended the National Conference on Transportation and the Environment seem to have been very impressed by Lovins' presentation and by the information provided in the workshops, judging by their reports to their local members (see, e.g., the environment committee columns in the Local 1520 (St. Thomas, Ont..) and Local 88 (Ingersoll, Ont.) newsletters, and the *Global Guardian*), and by statements made in my interviews with activists in June 1996.
36. See Dennis J. Gayle, "Regulating the American automobile industry: Sources and consequences of US automobile air pollution standards," in Maureen Appel Molot, ed. *Driving Continentally* (Ottawa: Carleton University Press, 1993).
37. "CAW Statement on Transportation and the Environment," p. 139.
38. CAW, "CAW Statement on Transportation," pp. 1-2.
39. According to Local 1520's environment committee report, 13 CAW locals from the London area were represented, including: 27, 88, 127, 200, 222, 444, 636, 707, 1090, 1325, 1520, 1915, and 4451. Two CEP locals (672 and 848) also sent representatives.
40. See "Environment Committee Report," Local 1520 union newsletter (St. Thomas, Ont.: October 1995), p. 13.
41. CAW Council Environment Committee, "Submission to the CAW National Executive Board Task Force," March 29, 1994, p. 1.
42. Ibid., p. 3.
43. Ibid., p. 8.
44. Ibid., pp. 9-10.
45. Section entitled "Environment," in CAW, *False Solutions, Growing Protests*, p. 65.
46. Cathy Austin, co-chairperson of Local 88's environment committee, and Rob Sheehan, chairperson of Local 444's environment committee, expressed this view.
47. Keeney, interview, June 6, 1996.
48. CAW, *False Solutions, Growing Protests*, p. 65.
49. Author's notes from the session at which the environment section of the national bargaining programme was debated. The environment section was carried unanimously, after very little discussion from the floor. Only delegates from locals 200, 444, and 127 spoke to the issue—all in support of the section.
50. Chrysler was obliged by new government regulations to begin recycling materials formerly landfilled. Although the company is now making about $300,000 a year from recycling cardboard alone, management has admitted that the company probably would not have begun recycling had it not been for the new regulations.
51. Rob Sheehan, interviewed June 5-6, 1996, Toronto.
52. The CAW rep. at these meetings is National Health and Safety Co-ordinator for Ford Canada, Pat Dugal.
53. Both interviewed June 6, 1996, Toronto.

54. Ford has two aluminum casting plants which have begun to recycle aluminum previously landfilled. Sand from the foundry is now being used in road construction, mixed with asphalt. Herb John reported that the Ford plants in Essex County are now recycling 90-95 percent of all solid waste, including cardboard pallets, aluminum, blue-box items, oily rags, batteries, and wiring.
55. Rob Sheehan, interviewed June 5,6, 1996, Toronto.
56. Agreement between CAMI Automotive and CAW Local 88, effective October 19, 1992 to September 17, 1995, p. 93. Training for the union members of the committee and other minor changes were made to the joint environment committee section of the September 18, 1995-September 20, 1998 collective agreement. The second agreement also stipulated that the joint environment committee would meet at least four times per year.
57. Local 88 newsletter, (Ingersoll, Ont.: December 1994), p. 25.
58. Cathy Austin, written communication to author, September 3, 1996.
59. This is an interesting insight into the success of the union in inculcating an adversarial culture in a workforce that was selected by Suzuki management from the surrounding rural and small town population, and is for the most part a "first generation" of factory workers.
60. Information provided to the author by Doug Steele of Local 636, Woodstock, Ont.
61. Information provided to the author by Jim Mahon, Chairperson of Local 1520's Environment Committee.
62. I have made this argument elsewhere. See, especially, "Ecological politics in Canada: Elements of a strategy of collective action," in D. Bell, L. Fawcett, R. Keil, and P. Penz, eds. *Political Ecology: Global and Local Perspectives* (New York and London: Routledge, forthcoming).
63. June 5, 1996 interview by author with Mr. Van Gaal (Local 707 and a member of the CAW Council Environment Committee) and other members of the National Union, Toronto.
64. Union officials did not think that any active environment committees existed among the workforce inherited from the merger with the United Electrical Workers union in November 1992.
65. See the *Global Guardian* Spring 1996, p. 13. CAW Local 444 has contributed $30,000 to the operation of the CAW Project Office over a two-year period.
66. Personal communication with the author, July 23, 1996.
67. The CAW Regional Environmental Council idea has been adopted by locals in other areas. The first was the Lower Mainland British Columbia Regional Environmental Council, which has served as a model for the others in terms of structure. Other regional councils so far include: Woodstock-London-Ingersoll (the Southwest Ontario Environmental Council); and one now being formed in Winnipeg, Manitoba.
68. The WREC "policy statement" is appended to its Constitution, n.d., which is available from the CAW, WREC, 581 St. Pierre Street, Tecumseh, ON N8N 1Z2.
69. Rick Coronado, in "CAW Student Centre & Youth Environment Conference, a plus for everyone," the *Global Guardian* vol. 1, issue 1 (January 1995), p. 5.
70. Mark C. Parent, "Individual choices must become collective effort," and "Environment and the Labour Movement," in the *Global Guardian* vol. 1, issue 1 (January 1995), pp. 1, 3, 4.
71. For a definition of the term "organic intellectuals," see chapter 1, note 56.
72. The Citizens' Environmental Alliance of Southwestern Ontario grew out of the Clean Water Alliance (of Windsor) which was formed in response to the "Sarnia blob" in 1985 (see chapter 11). It has since broadened its mandate and grown in membership.
73. See the account of the conference in The *Global Guardian* vol. 2, issue 2 (Spring 1996).
74. A conference planned for May 1996 was ultimately cancelled because of disappointing enrollment, which may be an indication of the more conservative political terrain in which locals like 636 and 88 are operating. They plan to try again.
75. They argue, for example:

> more than 25,000 products can be made from industrial fibre hemp. Returning hemp to the Canadian farm would provide us with an endless supply of a renewable energy resource. Hemp can replace every fossil fuel energy product and is more environmentally benign. This would give Canadians numerous jobs, in a new labour intensive biomass fuel industry (conversion of plant matter to fuel). Hemp can produce 40-50 times more fuel per acre than its closest rival, corn. This would free up precious arable land required for food production. By

the way, this plant is also an excellent source of nutrition for both animals and humans... The hemp plant could provide us with pulp for paper that is stronger, more environmentally sound paper. Just one acre of this crop could produce as much pulp for paper as 4.1 acres of trees over a period of 20 years. Hemp paper can be recycled 7-8 times, compared with three times for wood pulp paper.

Source: C.A.W. Windsor Regional Environment Council, "Re-establish the hemp fibre industry in Canada," compilation of WREC articles on the subject, Winter 1996.

76. This account is based on information provided by Nick De Carlo, interviewed by the author, June 7, 1996, Toronto.
77. The fact that a union would lead a coalition of small businesses and community organisations indicates the exceptionally "hegemonic" role of the labour movement in Windsor.
78. For an illuminating criticism of the Rae government's attempt at labour-corporate "partnership," from the perspective of occupational health service workers, see Margaret Keith, "Common Non-Sense Revolution," the *Global Guardian* vol. 2, issue 1 (Winter 1996), pp. 16, 19. Keith cites a report authored by Ministry of Labour inspectors (who are OPSEU members), which states that between 1990 and 1995 there was "a dramatic rise in critical accidents and occupational illnesses which increased by 80% and 102% respectively." This trend is attributed to the NDP government's preference for "voluntary compliance" over inspections and enforcement actions. During its term, MOL inspections declined "by close to 50%, orders declined by an equal amount, and prosecutions declined by 69%" (Ibid., p. 16).
79. The government sought to eliminate $4 billion in expenditures, and demanded an additional $2 billion reduction in the wage bill, to be achieved either through pay cuts or lay-offs. One of the features of the social contract was a series of 5 percent wage cuts in each of three years to be achieved by workers taking 12 days of unpaid leave annually. These became known as the infamous "Rae days," named for the NDP Premier, Bob Rae. For an analysis of this conflict see Stephen McBride, "The continuing crisis of social democracy: Ontario's social contract in perspective," *Studies in Political Economy* 50 (Summer 1996).
80. McBride, "The continuing crisis of social democracy," p. 88.
81. CAW, *False Solutions, Growing Protests*, pp. 13-14.
82. Sam Gindin, *The Canadian Auto Workers: The Birth and Transformation of a Union* (Toronto: James Lorimer & Co.), p. 268.
83. Ibid., p. 281.
84. This account is based on an interview by the author with Nick De Carlo, June 7, 1996, Toronto. The Green Work Alliance is also the subject of an analysis by Roger Keil, who views it as an example of "working class environmentalism," in "Green Work Alliances: The Political Economy of Social Ecology," *Studies in Political Economy* 44 (Summer 1994). Keil was also a participant in the GWA.
85. According to De Carlo, a Toshiba plant scheduled for closure was occupied for eight years. Toshiba eventually transferred ownership to the workers, after a mobilization campaign that involved tens of thousands of people in demonstrations at all of Toshiba's plants in Japan. The workers are committed to making socially-useful products such as geiger-counters for citizens of the Ukraine and sound-systems for use by popular organisations. For accounts of the Lucas Aerospace experience, see: Hilary Wainwright and Dave Elliott, *The Lucas Plan: A New Trade Unionism in the Making* (London: Allison & Busby, 1982); Mike Cooley, *Architect or Bee?* (London: Slough: Langley Technical Services, 1987). In her book, *Arguments for a New Left*, Hilary Wainwright summarizes the experiment in these terms: "In the hope of bargaining support from the newly elected Labour government, the Lucas shop stewards drew up an imaginative plan, during two years of discussion and experimentation in Lucas factories across Britain, of socially useful products on which their supposedly 'redundant' skills and energies could be employed" (Oxford and Cambridge: Blackwell, 1984), p. 163.
86. Gindin, *The Canadian Auto Workers*, p. 224.
87. Ibid., p. 251.
88. See Wainwright, *Arguments for a New Left*, p. 163. The CAW locals involved in the GWA included: 1967 (McDonnell-Douglas), 1915 (Northern Telecom), 1285 (Chrysler-Bramalea), 584 (Ford warehouse depot), 673, and 112.

89. Roger Keil, "Green Work Alliances," pp. 19-20.
90. I have made this argument in more detail in the essay "Environmental politics, political economy, and social democracy in Canada," *Studies in Political Economy* 45 (Fall 1994).
91. In my 1992 essay, "Counter-hegemony and environmental politics in Canada," I described an "environmental management" approach, exemplified by Pollution Probe's "Profit from Pollution Prevention" and Green consumerism campaigns, and by Energy Probe's argument that elimination of government subsidies to electrical utilities will price nuclear energy out of the market. I also noted that there was a growing "environmental industry" which is quite compatible with an eco-capitalist construction of sustainable development. The extent to which the "environmental management" tendency now characterizes the urban environmental movement is a question which requires further investigation. (In *Organizing Dissent: Contemporary Social Movements in Theory and Practice*, William K. Carroll, ed. (Toronto: Garamond Press, 1992).)
92. Charlotte Yates, "The Internal Dynamics of Union Power: Explaining Canadian Autoworkers' Militancy in the 1980s." *Studies in Political Economy* 31 (Spring 1990), p. 75.
93. The CEP presentation, made by Brian Kohler, is published in full in GLU, *The Great Lakes United* vol. 8, no. 4 (Winter 1993/94), pp. 3-4.
94. Gindin, *The Canadian Auto Workers*, p. 270.
95. The Klein government's agenda is, in turn, modelled very closely on Thatcherite discourse and strategy. Left analyses of the so-called Klein revolution, named for the current Conservative Party premier of Alberta, Ralph Klein, have characterized the regime as authoritarian populist, neoliberal, patriarchal, and as exemplifying "postmodern fascism." For a sampling of such analyses, see Laurie E. Adkin, "Life in Kleinland: Democratic resistance to 'folksy fascism,'" *Canadian Dimension* vol. 29, no. 2 (April-May 1995); Lois Harder, "Depoliticizing insurgency: The politics of the family in Alberta," *Studies in Political Economy* vol. 50 (Summer 1996); Trevor Harrison and Gordon Laxer, eds. *The Trojan Horse: Alberta and the Future of Canada* (Montréal: Black Rose Books, 1995); and Malinda S. Smith, "A new folksy fascism in Alberta?: The ideology of the Klein 'Revolution'" (unpublished paper, Department of Political Science, University of Alberta, March 1995).

Conclusion

In chapter 1 I raised a number of questions about the nature of contemporary social change. What evidence do we find of counter-hegemonic elements in the discourse of citizen-environmentalists? Under what circumstances might unions take leading roles in counter-hegemonic politics? What are the themes of equivalence which might link the projects of workers, environmentalists, and other social actors in a broad counter-hegemonic movement?

COUNTER-HEGEMONY AND THE ENVIRONMENTAL MOVEMENT

The analysis of the discourse of actors engaged in struggles around environmental regulation in the 1980s led me to identify five variants of Canadian environmental discourse: 1) eco-capitalist/environmental management; 2) popular-democratic; 3) social-democratic/environmental management; 4) fundamentalist; and 5) eco-socialist.[1] Setting aside, for the moment, the "eco-capitalist" discourse, one finds in the environmental movement a number of counter-hegemonic themes. These include critiques of patriarchy, anthropocentrism, the devastating consequences for nature of the productivist logic of capitalist accumulation, and the undemocratic nature of economic and social decision-making.

The popular-democratic discourse of the citizens' groups defends "the people's" interests against corporate, technocratic, and bureaucratic interests, involving a conflict between, on one hand, social conceptions of property, access to resources, and the rights of future generations, and, on the other hand, the prerogatives of private ownership and appropriation of (social) resources and (socially-produced) wealth. "Popular interests" also refers to a fairly widespread critique among the citizens' groups of science and scientists, and of "experts," as agents of corporate and technocratic interests. The concerns of the citizens' groups give rise to demands for the democratization of institutions, the political system, and economic decision-making. These include demands for greater representation of communities and environmentalists in the governmental decision-making processes themselves (advisory committees, technical committees, monitoring bodies, round tables, and other multi-partite consultations involved in the drafting of legislation). They also demand the means to make such participation meaningful and more egalitarian, such as funding for the travel and other expenses of citizens to attend such bodies, for the hiring of technical or legal experts, and for educational activities.

The environmental and other new social movements have linked democratization to a philosophical view of the "good life" which includes social solidarity as well as personal freedom. Summarized, the themes which emerge from the demands and campaigns of the citizens' groups include: (1) the rejection of worker/citizen categories as a false and undesirable dichotomy; (2) the recognition that profit-motivated production and consumption are (in varying degrees) incompatible with the fulfillment of the legitimate needs of all members of society; (3) the rejection of the necessity of a trade-off between material security and quality of life; (4) an emphasis on social and individual responsibility for the future health of our children and our planet, which are viewed as a collective trust. These ethical positions are opposed to short-term corporate greed, the reckless exploitation of social resources, and "consumerism."

The remedial action plan citizens' committees went furthest in testing the flexibility of State institutions regarding the decentralization of decision-making power to local communities, and the realization of ecological conceptions of local development in opposition to the priorities of capitalist accumulation. Citizens' involvement in the RAPs, as well as in other environmental issues, transformed their understanding of what was at stake. For many, this entailed movement from a social-democratic faith in the possibility of reconciling environmental and business interests, to a critique of the fundamentally un-popular, un-democratic nature of the State, the economy, science, and technology. When efforts to lobby governments to bring about various policy changes proved ineffective, and evidence emerged of government-corporate sector collusion, the struggle shifted to one of democratizing the decision-making processes themselves, that is, of democratizing the State. *The stakes became the meaning of citizenship.* It is important to note, moreover, that this democratic struggle is inseparable from discursive struggles to determine the meaning of "sustainable development." The eco-capitalist (market-driven) and social-democratic (State-regulated) environmental discourses share a reliance on technological fixes, while neither calls into question the fundamentally anti-ecological and anti-democratic logic of the dominant model of development. Thus we see, in the case of the social-democratic New Democratic Party (NDP) government in Ontario, the ultimate inability of social democracy to accommodate the vision and the proposals advanced by grassroots initiatives like the GreenWork Alliance, and the lessons learned from this experience by the union and community activists.

A "fundamentalist" tendency, often associated with the environmental movement's "vanguard," expresses ecological and humanist ethics which (re)validate our relationships to our bodies, to nature, and to other species.[2] It affirms the desirability and possibility of non-exploitative and non-violent relationships both among humans and between humans and nature, a vision shared by many feminists. Derived from these ethics is opposition to growth for the sake of growth, or "progress" as commonly understood (viewed as a non-optimal and unsustainable path of development). Instead, ecologists envisage sustainable development as movement toward a dynamic equilibrium — not to be equated with stagnation. In this model the criteria for the production of goods and services include meeting needs in an egalitarian manner, maximizing leisure, autonomy and creativity, and minimizing harmful effects on the natural environment, resource depletion (reducing global entropy), as well as mentally and physically oppressive working and living conditions. This vision, however, may be only very vaguely attached to a theory of social change (the processes and actors which can bring it into being).

On the other hand, some environmentalists locate the explanation for disasters such as famines, war, and environmental devastation in a *fatally flawed human nature*, and thus hold pessimistic (even apocalyptic) ideas with regard to the possibilities for social change. This "human nature" explanation has been expressed by individuals within such organizations as Greenpeace and the Greens, as well as by leading environmentalists. It is also heard among the citizen-environmentalists, like Kristina Lee, who prefer a human nature explanation for environmental crisis over a structuralist-Marxist one. They agree about what needs to be changed (e.g., values, modes of consumption and production) but opt for the "individual conversions" approach rather than a strategy of collective action. Interestingly, the socialist discourse of the CAW environmental activists serves as a strong "corrective" to the "we are all equally responsible, as individuals, for the state of the environment" views

Conclusion

of many of the citizen-environmentalists. The CAW's *Global Guardian*, for example, argues that: "It is time for environmental sustainability to become a high priority component of our social and economic policy, as well as an individual choice."[3] Recall Rick Coronado's insistence that "the environment can be shown to be a serious social justice issue." The labour-environmentalists argue that capitalism is the main obstacle to a sustainable and egalitarian economy, and seek to identify the particular role for the labour movement in bringing about a transition to an alternative model of development.

Eco-socialists, whether located in the unions or in other milieux (social movement organizations, universities), do attempt to provide a theory of social change which identifies the bases for alliances among social actors. They are aware that, without convincing alternatives to the eco-capitalist project, the environmental movement cannot attract the support of people whose livelihoods are presently dependent on the growth of what Václav Havel has called "some monstrously huge, noisy, and stinking machine, whose real meaning is not clear to anyone."[4] The priority for eco-socialists is to link the alternative movements to the traditional social movement (organized labour) by way of a renewed socialist theory and practice. It is also important to note here that individuals like Rick Coronado, Nick De Carlo, and Cathy Austin, among others, are the organic intellectuals of this eco-socialist convergence, bridging the two movements through democratic discourse.

The citizens' groups which form the grassroots base of the environmental, peace, international solidarity, urban quality of life, anti-poverty, anti-free trade and other networks, are, in a sense, the "laboratories" of the radical democratic project. They are the sites of intense conflict among competing discourses, which seek to interpret, politically, the particular issues and values espoused by the members of these groups. The issues they confront involve relationships of subordination/domination which may become problematized by a radical democratic discourse. Questions are raised which — at least implicitly — challenge the traditional prerogatives of capitalists to control economic development, or of bureaucrats and technocrats to take decisions affecting various excluded collectivities. Questions about the *purpose and the meaning* of the model of development make alternatives thinkable.

This is not to say, of course, that because the alternative movements place on the political agenda questions which are not allowed, a radical discourse has achieved predominant influence within these movements. Many in the environmental movement, like the labour movement, continue to have faith in social-democratic solutions to the environmental and economic crises, although this faith has been badly shaken by the experience of neo-corporatist NDP governments. And there are "fundamentalist" and "socialist" elements of the Canadian environmental movement which have not yet transcended the "red versus green" debate[5] sufficiently to adopt a radical and pluralist democratic discourse. In the latter conception of counter-hegemonic politics, no one subject position — be it defined by class, race, gender, or any other relation — forms a centre which gives to all other forms of oppression their essential meaning. Subject positions are constructed by practices of articulation, as are the relations of equivalence or difference among them. Radical and pluralist democracy, therefore, expresses a project which is capable of articulating to one another the themes and struggles of the alternative movements and the workers' movement without insisting on the privileging of one identity or struggle over another. It is such a privileging which the term "eco-socialist" suggests, and which is at the centre of the debate between "ecologists" and "socialists". Certain socialist theorists have dismissed the NSMs as single-issue-oriented, apolitical, scatterings of groups, with no direct interests in the concerns of citizens-as-workers or conflicts with capital. It is true that socialist discourse has served to radicalize the politics of environmentalists, feminists, and workers. Yet radical ecology, radical feminism, anti-racism, and other social movements have also rejected socialism's western, androcentric, modernizing world-view. Thus, as I argued in chapter 1, it bears emphasising that what is at stake is not making socialism the hegemonic discourse of ecology, but constructing a more truly radical critique of the nature of power and domination, along with an alternative vision for the next century.

We thus find different articulations of the environmental to the social within the environmental movement, many of which contribute elements of counter-hegemonic discourse. At the same time, business associations are actively seeking to articulate "the environment" or "sustainable development" to an eco-capitalist project on the grounds that the market, along with technological change, can resolve even the most serious manifestions of ecological crisis. The ideological hegemony of neo-liberalism since the 1980s has indeed succeeded in diverting a portion of the environmental movement in such directions as green enterprises, green marketing, green consumerism, and environmental consulting, all seeking to achieve minimal environmental reforms within the framework of corporate profitability. The linkage of ecology with social justice and egalitarianism is thereby subordinated to the objective of a cleaner, greener capitalism, regardless of the social conditions in which this environmental modernization is achieved. We cannot, therefore, say that the environmental movement is inherently anti-capitalist, or feminist, or anti-racist, only that the potential exists for linkages to be made with radical critiques of capitalism, patriarchy, and white supremacy. Moreover, the analysis of the actual discourse of social actors in the environmental movement suggests that the key to linking these counter-hegemonic critiques and visions is a discourse of radical democratization.

Finally, the environmental movement, like other social movements in Canada and in the other advanced capitalist societies, has been subjected to atomizing pressures during the neo-liberal regime. The inability to secure positions within State decision-making processes (as exemplified by the RAPs experience), along with the transferral of more and more areas of decision-making to the realm of the market (and hence to private sector actors), have shifted the balance of forces in the citizens' prolonged war of position. Environmental issues have been placed on the back burner by all governments (except rhetorically, and with the arguable exception of the Harcourt NDP Government of British Columbia, where there is a particularly strong environmental movement). Pressure from the private sector is building for deregulation and voluntary compliance (discussed in part 2) which will weaken federal standards and enforcement. Simultaneously, the social opportunity structures of the new middle class radicals have been severely eroded, particularly in the public sector and human service professions. The universities and government research centres where scientific and social research is carried out relating to environmental problems have lost staff and research funding, and are being restructured to more closely conform to demands emanating from the private sector.

On the other hand, the announcement of one neo-liberal measure after another which will worsen the environmental crisis (deregulation of polluters, privatisation of parks, removal of limits on resource exploitation, etc.) makes ever more clear the environmental movement's need for a humanist, ecological, and democratic critique of global capitalism. In the absence of a credible social democratic or Green party in Canada, the movement finds itself at an unknown crossroads facing the dual dangers of isolation (of its radical elements) and deradicalization (the environmental management tendency). Thus its choices now appear to be: (i) professionalization, or the "greening" of capitalism; (ii) social-movement-building with other actors. With regard to the second option, the leadership for a radical *sortie* from the current impasse of the environmental movement will have different origins depending upon the constellation of social forces particular to each region (British Columbia, for example, is not Ontario, and each case requires a specific analysis). In the region which is the subject of this study (i.e., southern Ontario), it is notable that, while in the 1980s radical ecological themes were advanced almost solely by citizens and environmental organizations, in the mid-1990s significant leadership for a counter-hegemonic political ecology movement is emerging also from the environmental activists of the CAW, who have sustained an organizational base for grassroots coalition-building, and who are the bearers of an anti-capitalist discourse. Let us therefore turn to the question of the role of unions in counter-hegemonic politics.

COUNTER-HEGEMONY AND THE LABOUR MOVEMENT

I argued in chapter 1 that leeway exists for union leadership to take counter-hegemonic rather than conservative or corporatist directions, even in normal times. Indeed, the ECWU and CAW cases show that there were always choices of *direction, principles, and objectives*, notwithstanding structural constraints, if one thinks of strategy in gradualist terms. Moreover, in a period of extended crisis, social polarisation, inability of the bourgeoisie to resolve the social crisis for a significant portion of the population, and repressive measures against the labour movement, union leaders are compelled — minimally — to defend the institutional framework which authorizes their existence and functions in capitalist society. This entails appealing to the arguments and values that underpinned the formation of the unions, i.e., their *raison d'être* as defenders of workers' rights against *capitalisme sauvage*. However, it is not possible to generalize about what discourse all union leaders will adopt in these circumstances. There are complex factors to take into account in explaining the differences among union responses to deepening economic and social crisis, including their views of alliances with other social actors. It is also important to keep in mind that the union-environmental movement interface is only one part of the larger picture. A comprehensive analysis of union strategies (in these cases or others) would have to examine as well the unions' interfaces with the anti-nuclear, peace, women's, anti-racist, anti-poverty, and other movements. The labour-environmental interface does, however, suggest the broad outlines of the strategic orientations of union actors in relation to the prospects for counter-hegemonic convergence.

Generally, we find evidence for the NSM theorists' view that unions have not originated the counter-cultural critiques of modernization's negative aspects, as exemplified by the environmental crisis. Both the ECWU and the CAW members and leaders have been strongly committed to a social democratic conception of economic development, full employment, environmental management, and a party/union division of labour. Rather, it is the radical ecologists and others who have been most critical of the social democratic model of industrial capitalist development. However, we also find evidence that — in the context of a thoroughly discredited social democratic paradigm, and an aggressive resurgence of *capitalisme sauvage*, as well as the presence in the "universe of discourse" of the radical NSM critiques — certain elements within the labour movement are capable of transcending their previously-defined institutional roles to assume a leadership role in the building of a new social movement. The significant differences of orientation between these two industrial trade unions suggest that generalizations such as the attachment of the old social movement to the stakes of the industrial era are overly-schematic. Likewise, classical Marxist and elite-theory views of the unions as inevitably bureaucratic and conservative organizations are contradicted by historical exceptions. Industrial and other workers are not actors frozen in time; nor are they immune to all of the surrounding influences of competing discourses. Neither are union organizations internally homogeneous; rather, they are characterized by tensions on a number of axes. Numerically, the industrial working class has shrunk in the West, and its composition has changed along with its conditions of work. We may not, however, derive its political positioning, in reductionist manner, solely from such structural changes. Rather, these changes have obliged the labour movement as a whole to redefine its *raison d'être*. The important questions thus become what options are available, and what factors will determine the directions taken by these social actors?

In chapter 14 I identified the factors which explain the differences between the "elite-corporatist" strategy adopted by the ECWU toward its employers and toward the environmental movement, and the CAW's more militant, socialist strategy of "social unionism." These factors include the political economy of their respective sectors (including corporate strategies, State policies), and the cultural-ideological perspectives of union leaders and rank-and-file members, as well as the strategies adopted by other social actors and their implications for the unions. For the ECWU, faced with a severe industry recession in the early 1980s, the only alternative to endorsing employers' demands (including a reduction in government royalties and taxes on feedstocks, measures to promote petrochemical exports, government subsidies for corporate modernization, elimination of the two-price system for oil and gas, wage concessions) was to fight for a radically different model of development for the energy sector (including a priority of conservation of resources, domestic self-sufficiency and reduction of petrochemical exports, investment in labour-intensive "soft energy" and renewable energy sources and technologies, State compensation for displaced workers, Canadianization of the industry, etc.). The latter path appeared to entail greater short-term risks for union members; the potential for alliances with other social actors around such an agenda as well as the political environment needed to be calculated. The absence of a strong and cohesive ecology movement — or of a broadly-based political movement with a left-environmental agenda — making more likely the realization of an eventual victory, was no doubt an important factor in the ECWU's alliance strategy at this point. Instead, the union opted for an alliance with employers which offered the promise of more investment and jobs in the short-to-medium terms. In so doing, it shifted the long-term balance of forces in favour of capital, because the agreement reached between employers, union, and the State (the post-1984 deregulation and other measures of the Conservative Government) reinforced the country's reliance on production and trade based on an ever-increasing exploitation of non-renewable resources, and accepted the rule of the market in this sector.

Even in the case of energy policy, where one might view the political and economic odds against the success of an alternative strategy to have been overwhelming, these factors do not entirely explain the corporatist path of the union leadership. It is conceivable that different leaders might have chosen to build on the 1978-1980 positions of the union, which emphasized conservation, national self-sufficiency, and social ownership, i.e., to fight the political battle in the belief that this was the only way to achieve the long-term interests of workers (in secure and meaningful employment, in quality of life, etc.). Admittedly, such leadership would have been exceptional. However, the ideological orientation of the leadership and the "culture" of specific workforces appear to take on even greater importance as explanatory factors in light of the ECWU's responses to other environmental issues (e.g., the industrial pollution of the Chemical Valley during periods of relative prosperity, or the union's stance on the lead issue). It is not altogether clear that, even in the presence of a stronger environmental movement, the ECWU leadership would have chosen a "social unionism" path, although there may well have been more internal debate and division over union strategy, particularly at the rank-and-file level.

To explain the choices of union leaders and workers, we also need to understand, in addition to the political and economic factors, the ideological aspects of their interpretations

Conclusion 321

of the options available to them. In the case of the ECWU, a factor working against union alliance with environmentalists was the elite-corporatist *culture* promoted by employers and reinforced by certain policies of the national leadership. The chemical companies use sophisticated strategies to create favourable images of their products (demonstrating their social usefulness, their indispensability to downstream industry and to consumers) and to convince the public that they are good corporate citizens, i.e., that they are concerned about the environment, the quality of life, and the community (e.g., the slogan of the chemical companies in Sarnia: "We live here, too!"). At the same time there is an "internal" corporate ideology directed toward "employees" (a term which suggests a higher status than that of an hourly wage-worker). The gist of this is that they are valuable, indispensable, highly-skilled, and equally members of the heroic enterprise. They are made to feel like a unique group, set apart from the "lay persons" (citizens/consumers) outside the plant who are both dependent on their knowledge and skills for these products, and ignorant of the complex processes which go into their making. The corporatist ideology is played up when the company is seen to be under siege, either by competitors or by government regulatory initiatives.

This corporatist culture is of course contradicted by the day-to-day experience of workers in these plants. They may be creating more value-added than any other manufacturing workers, but their work is still tied to the monotonous, repetitive tasks of continuous process, operated by shifts. They have no "creative autonomy," despite the claims made by management for the quality of work life and other programs which have been introduced since the late 1970s. The corporate ideology enters into crisis during a strike, when power relations are stripped of their corporatist fancy dress. However, in other circumstances, chemical workers have employed a version of this ideology in defence of their perceived interests. When confronted with the demands of citizens' and environmental groups, they have adopted the identity of highly skilled "employees," privileged with special knowledge, to legitimate a dismissive attitude towards those who would threaten their jobs. The attitude of some union officials toward the St. Clair River International Citizens' Network was that these people did not know what they were talking about — that they were exaggerating the real risks associated with chemicals. When it was suggested to union officials that the environmental campaigns, along with a series of new environmental laws and government initiatives (CEPA, Spills Bill, MISA, RAPs) would increasingly require a response from chemical workers, and that an attempt to work out environmentally acceptable economic alternatives with environmental groups might be in their interests, the response was: "It's up to the environmentalists to make a move, because we've got something they want and they need. They need us more than we need them."[6]

The division of chemical workers (and other groups of male industrial workers) from citizens/laypersons (outsiders) is also effected by gender ideologies and identities. The masculine gender stereotype includes the idea that concern for one's person/body/physical security is unmanly. According to one health and safety activist at Dow Chemical, interviewed in 1988, workers were resisting his efforts to reduce the dangers of working with asbestos. Ivan Hillier did not succeed in mobilizing active rank and file support for his efforts to eliminate mercury vapours in the workplace twenty years earlier. In other cases — as with the steel and coke oven workers in Sydney, Nova Scotia — the toleration of dangerous working conditions over decades is explained not only by the economic or structural weakness of the union as a bargaining agent, but also by a male industrial working-class culture which lends little support to the militants who demand changes. Indeed, at SYSCO, the latter were treated as rivals for authority by union officials, or simply as persons who did not know their place and might jeopardize the security of others by their actions.[7] The ridicule and dismissal, however, could take the form of criticizing a "sissy," i.e., someone not manly enough to suffer like all the rest. The citizen-environmentalists' concern with public health is trivialized and even ridiculed by many workers; in effect, their concerns are "feminized" — characterized as alarmist, hysterical, or gullible, and contrasted with the rational, scientific, "objective" knowledge of the technical workers. The feminization of environmental concerns is strengthened by the fact that women are very active in the citizens' groups, often acting as media spokespersons.

Macho attitudes disguise (and perhaps help to compensate for) the reality of workplace hierarchies. Feelings of powerlessness vis-à-vis management generate an anger which may be turned not against employers, but against those people outside who are not exposed to the same risks, and who will not applaud workers' masculine fortitude. "Those people," they say, "seem to think their lives are more valuable than ours." Yet in reality it is the workers themselves, and their employers, who value workers' lives and health too little. Gender ideology also comes into play in constructing a bread-winner role for the male wage-earner, who is responsible for a dependent family. This role is, of course, threatened by the presence of women in the work force. The bread-winner responsibility also undermines the male worker's determination to fight employers if this entails the real or potential loss of wages. Assumptions about appropriate gender roles also help to legitimate the sacrifices (e.g., industrial illnesses) made in the name of the family.[8] Some employer strategies exploit gender ideologies rather overtly, such as the practices of giving hiring preference to married men with families, and sponsoring family-oriented company activities and benefits (e.g., scholarships for children of employees, family days at the plants, organized sports and social activities). In Sarnia, this paternal relationship was indeed extended to the whole community, as the companies were the benefactors of various charitable, recreational, and cultural activities.

Another interpretation of chemical workers' passive-dismissive response toward environmentalists is simply the wish not to offend the actor perceived as being a more powerful decider of workers' fate, i.e., employers. Chemical workers perceive that they have a better chance of securing jobs by not transgressing the established norms of industrial relations. The counterpart of this is a perception of the citizens' groups and environmental movement as lacking sufficient power as allies — as being as yet unable to offer any comparable security, for example, by influencing the State to intervene in a jobs-versus-the-environment conflict to protect the interests of citizens-as-workers. This last factor is compounded by the tendency of some union officials to value the private influence they may win with employers more greatly than the public influence they might have in the context of a popular coalition. Indeed, there is a perception that alliance with the citizens' and environmental groups would jeopardize the intermediary position of union officials, and that their "autonomy" or "neutrality" must therefore be preserved (e.g., the concern of the Sarnia chemical workers to distance themselves from Greenpeace and their reluctance to become involved in the SCRICN). This is a necessary condition for maintaining their private, "managerial" relationship with employers, promoted through such programs as "continuing dialogue." The professional image sought by the national leadership is associated with participation in corporatist consultation processes, and is at odds with the grassroots politics of the environmental movement.

The CAW, too, has faced certain trade-offs created by industry restructuring. However, its decision to implement an aggressive bargaining campaign rather than to continue to make concessions, and its high-profile public role in the 1980s reflect — in contrast to the ECWU — not only a confident view of the union's bargaining power and political influence, but also the greater weight attached to popular alliances by its leadership, and the greater openness of rank-and-file auto workers to a socially active role for their union. With the worsening of the external environment for union bargaining in the

Conclusion 323

1990s, moreover, the CAW strategy has entered a phase of radicalization rather than retreat. Thus, at least in light of the available evidence, the "culture" of the CAW is notably different from that of the ECWU.

The factors mentioned above, therefore, may predispose unions either to maintain a kind of social neutrality — or even hostility — vis-à-vis other social movements, or to participate in coalitions. Are there, however, limitations to such participation, and to what extent can the institutional concerns of the union organization (to maintain its authority vis-à-vis membership and employers, to prevent the erosion of membership through lay-offs or attrition, to enforce collective bargaining agreements, etc.) be maintained in the context of coalition-building? Some answers to these questions were suggested by an examination of the "strong case" of social unionism — the CAW's environmental policy.

CHANGING UNION STRATEGY: THE CASE OF THE CAW

The environmental committees which got off the ground in 1986 were initially characterized by the social movement versus institutional-legal choices of direction and priorities that are described in chapters 12 and 13. By the early 1990s, this tension had not disappeared, but had largely been resolved by the predominance of the institutional-legal definition of the functions of the committees. Environmental committee members had come to see their main responsibilities to be developing expertise about environmental regulations affecting their industry and workers' rights., educating members about such questions, and contributing to the development of union positions on regulatory initiatives. Some efforts have been made to develop model contract language for employer-union cooperation on environmental issues, but these have so far mainly taken the form of measures which enhance profitability (e.g., plant recycling of materials). Environmental issues in general have not been a priority of the national leadership or the membership as a whole. Nor have environmental issues become "strikable" issues, i.e., priority items in collective bargaining. Thus, environmental committee mandates have followed the path of the occupational health and safety committees, while not yet achieving comparable status as aspects of "worker's rights" or as bargaining objectives.

The appearance of considerable union involvement in environmental issues is really the product of the work of a small core of activists and executive and staff officials. As Sam Gindin predicted, there has been little mobilization of, and few means of participation for the rank and file membership.[9] This may be attributed to the representative, parliamentary functions of the organization which preclude more direct participatory democratic practices. Moreover, the representative functions of the environment committees are quite compatible with the predominantly social-democratic ideological perspective of most of the middle-level unison officials interviewed in the 1980s, insofar as the latter entails a political/economic division of labour between the NDP and the union, and a reliance upon the State to mediate capital-labour conflict. In the locals studied, union leaders viewed their primary political task as delivering electoral support to the NDP (this was also the case for the ECWU); independent union research and educational work directed toward the development of alternative economic, social, and environmental policies, in conjunction with other unions and with extra-parliamentary organizations, was not considered a core task of the union.

Yet the "activist" role envisaged by many rank and file workers for their union (to judge by the survey of CAW locals in the Windsor area) does encompass a more "preemptive" role in the areas of research, planning, and coalition-building.[10] The evidence of divergent perceptions among executive-level officials, rank and file activists, and the rank and file membership supports the view that potential for a greater mobilization of workers, and for alliances with other social actors, existed at this time. However, lack of information about union activities, the small size and constitutional formality of the standing committee, as well as shift work and overtime, made the environmental committees poor vehicles for participation for all but the most committed activists.

Apart from the lack of means for participation within the union organization, there is the question of the ends of mobilization. Current structures and functions of the union are oriented toward tactical mobilizations in support of collective bargaining demands, or occasional demonstrations of support for other workers or social causes. The more radical and far-reaching goals of social-ecological change require the involvement of producers in technological, economic and other areas of planning. The orientation of the CAW environmental committees toward work-place monitoring and legal enforcement of workers' rights (e.g., to refuse work which pollutes the environment), has the important aspect of connecting work place knowledge and control to a larger social interest. However, problems beyond pollution regulation and legal enforcement — beyond the management mandate of the social-democratic State — were not on the agenda in the 1980s (e.g., the necessity for massive private consumption of automobiles, given the harmful environmental consequences).

By the mid-1990s it was being acknowledged at the national level of the union and by the local environmental committees that restrictions on private automobile use and the development of more efficient and accessible public transportation, among other campaigns, will require auto workers to choose between a defensive strategy and a pre-emptive one. The saturation of the North American market for automobiles may also push auto workers toward participation in planning for the development of public transportation systems, alternative employment, conversion of redundant plant capacity, and so on. This kind of planning implies cooperation with environmentalists and others engaged in such work. It will also provide an opportunity for the direct and sustained involvement of rank and file workers in the development of alternatives. However, such involvement will require that workplace relations be democratized in a number of ways. Indeed, as the Green Work Alliance was beginning to envisage, a union commitment to radical ecological and social change would entail the widespread involvement of citizens-as-workers in various activities connected to their work experience and knowledge (research and data collection related to plant, firm, and sectoral-level planning) and organized in conjunction with other social actors (e.g., in joint working groups). The transformation of the workplace organization would be based on the goals of facilitating participation and empowerment of individuals in union-organized activities (through changes in interpersonal relations, provision of child care, open meetings, and the involvement of workers' skills and knowledge). These goals would be connected to collective bargaining demands (e.g., reduced work time, access to company information, more paid leave of absence for education), as well as to political struggles for reforms which will enhance workers' rights in the workplace and create more "space for affordable dissent"[11] (socialized child care, more accessible higher education, environmental and occupational health legislation to protect workers, greater government direction of investment and control over capital mobility, etc.).

What developments have made such changes in union priorities more likely? With respect to the "external environment," unions — particularly the public sector unions — have had to develop political responses to the policies of the post-Keynesian State. Public sector workers have generally been on the front lines of the neoliberal offensive, and have led the political opposition to the deregulation, privatization agenda. The private sector unions have been somewhat slower to mobilize politically, and the industrial unions have

Conclusion

been most committed to support for the social-democratic paradigm and most resistant to integrating the issues advanced by the NSMs. The exception, in the Canadian case, is the auto workers, who sided with the public sector unions against the NDP government in Ontario, and have implemented campaigns and educational programmes on racism, sexism, human rights, and the environment.

The growing strength of the new social movements in the 1970s-1980s also exerted a certain *pull* on the unions. The women's movement caused the unions to include gender equality issues in their bargaining agendas, and to support changes in social policies, partly by bringing about changes in social values and goals from which the labour movement was not immune, and partly by supporting the struggles of women workers within the unions. The environmental movement has become an economic player, insofar as its demands have immediate as well as far-reaching implications for the terms of investment, production, and consumption. Its successes in mobilizing citizens around numerous issues have increasingly necessitated some response from the workers affected. However, to date, the environmental movement in Canada has made only very sporadic and tactical links with citizens-as-workers; the normal practice of environmental organizations, indeed, is to bypass workers in their dealings with employers and governments. Whether citizens-as-workers will be drawn toward the ethics and goals of the environmental movement will depend largely on the costs (in terms of material deprivation and insecurity) and the attractiveness of the alternatives to the status quo.

The global capitalist restructuring of the 1990s has also made environmental thinking relevant to the union movement in a new way, which we see in the case of the CAW. The CAW has become a leader in the opposition to the entire agenda of the neoliberal regime. At the national level, the leadership has supported the government-legislated reduction of work time, income redistribution, and the use of fiscal and monetary regulation to restore full employment and to reduce social inequalities. CAW locals are active in coalition-building not only against neoliberal governments, but *for* an alternative strategy of social and economic development. It is in the development of *alternatives* that political ecological thought may be seen to have influenced the discourse of the CAW and created the potential for new coalitions. Thus one finds CAW members involved in "greenwork" alliances, the drafting of a "Green economy for Ontario" (in opposition to the Harris Government), the Futurework Network (an electronic network of researchers working on sustainable development alternatives), as well as many initiatives at the local level. Ecological (or "sustainable") development has become both an objective of, and an argument for, alternatives to authoritarian liberal-productivism. Labour activists have found ecological positions to be another entry point into community coalitions, one which allows them to go beyond a defensive or "sectionalist" stance ("jobs for auto workers") toward an agenda of alternatives based on arguments about individual and societal needs and the democratization which is the precondition for their realization.

The "sectionalism" option is also blocked in the case of the CAW by the changes in its internal composition since the 1970s. The membership is no longer predominantly located in the automobile industry (although the automobile industry remains one of the most important sectors of the Canadian economy, and is relatively concentrated geographically). Only one in four members of the CAW today is an autoworker; the CAW also represents public transport workers (including in the airline industry), office workers, fish plant workers, and many other groups. Thus, on a question like the private use of automobiles versus the promotion of public transport (a growing ecological concern), the CAW needs to represent the views and interests of a broad spectrum of Canadian society.

"Green" thinking has also played a role in distinguishing the "social movement" orientation of the CAW from the more parliamentarist, social democratic orientation of the other leading industrial unions (e.g., the United Steelworkers of America, the CEP). As the crisis has deepened, and NDP provincial governments have converted to the monotheism of neoliberal economists and corporations, the labour movement has increasingly divided over the question of continuing support for the NDP. The split is now very sharply defined in Ontario, following the one-term NDP government led by Bob Rae. The CAW leadership and militants were deeply disappointed by (or confirmed in their expectations of) the Rae government's "social contract" policy, its elitism, and its view that the role of unions is to discipline their members and to procure rank and file agreement to policies of the NDP. The CAW is now channelling its energies into coalition-building at various levels. It has withdrawn active support for the NDP as a vehicle for effective opposition or meaningful social change. The current conjuncture has indeed compelled the CAW to choose more clearly than ever before between a "social movement" direction (construction of a counter-hegemonic historical bloc) and a corporatist direction (cooperation with capital mediated by the social democratic State). Ecological thought has helped to construct the alternatives available to the CAW and to reinforce the position of those militants within the membership who support the social movement path.

With the transition from social unionism to movement unionism, the CAW has entered an intensified phase of political struggle and has assumed a key leadership role in Ontario as well as nationally. In doing so, the leadership has gambled that broad social mobilization (which it will help to create) will prevent the union's isolation. In chapter 14 I identified some of the factors which explain the present direction of the CAW's leadership. What is important to emphasize here, is that the social-movement-building project which the leadership has assumed, contains inherent tensions. First, as I argued in chapter 1, the building of a social movement involves the rearticulation of interests and identities in new ways; none of the elements can remain unchanged, their differences left intact, their interpretations of the nature of the struggle left untouched. To link the women's movement, anti-racist struggles, youth, the unemployed (in other words, a host of inter-related subject positions) in opposition to a multi-faceted hegemonic order is an enormously complex task. It requires a philosophy of human needs and of the good life sufficiently pluralistic to speak to different experiences of subordination and to allow the co-existence of different visions. Socialist discourse will not suffice for these purposes, although its analysis of capitalism will be an essential element of a more inclusive counter-hegemonic discourse. The socialist militants of the CAW are therefore moving into partially unknown terrain, where interaction with other radical discourses will require not only that they lead, but that they rethink the nature of power, "the enemy," and their own positions in relation to other subjects.

Second, there is the possibility of an increasing gap between the union movement's organic intellectuals of convergence and the rank-and-file membership. This gap is already evident with regard to the question of work hours,[12] and willingness to endanger job security through the pursuit of environmental objectives, as well as in the limited participation of union members in political activism (not a problem unique to the CAW, or to unions, by any means). The union leadership must avoid getting too far "out in front" of the prevalent world-view of its members, while at the same time attempting to transform this world-view.

Third, the CAW as a union is constrained in the ways it can function as a political party, and one senses at times the underlying wish of the union leadership that the NDP would resurrect itself and relieve the union of a heavy burden.[13] One of the keys to the CAW's political influence (as well as its militant, confident, internal culture) has been its collective bargaining strength; if organizational work is neglected, or if rank-and-file support for the leadership's direction is compromised, the union may find itself isolated and on the defensive in both economic and political spheres.

Lastly, what can we conclude on the basis of the foregoing analysis, regarding the roles

Conclusion 327

of NSMs and union actors as historical agents of social change? The comparative examination of the strategies and discourses of two industrial unions and one "new social movement" leads us to reject the ahistorical, homogenizing, and overly abstract generalizations made by both orthodox Marxist and some NSM theorists with regard to historical agency. We can no more safely generalize about the decline or ascendance of the industrial working class as a social movement than we can about the historical mission of the new mid class. The social opportunity structures and counter-cultural traditions of the new middle class are equally prone to change; what modernization processes create they may as easily undermine or restructure. Just as we may identify significantly different political discourses among unions within one country, or among union movements in different countries, we find variations of environmental discourse within movements and cross-culturally. Thus we can never definitively say which social actors will take the lead in counter-hegemonic struggle. We can, however, ask what causes particular actors to take the lead when and where they do, and what are the limits or radical possibilities of the discourses they adopt? In this respect, I would suggest that any such theorization of social change would be incomplete without an examination of the conditions which explain the formation (or the absence) of the organic intellectuals of counter-hegemonic projects.

THE POSSIBILITIES OF CONVERGENCE

I have described the radical democratic elements of the citizen-environmentalists' discourse. Their struggles also express ethical positions regarding the good and just society as well as arguments about human needs and the conditions for happiness. The same elements are found in the discourse of the labour-environmentalists, which has increasingly linked security of livelihood, health, and the right to enjoyment of a clean environment to the problem of democracy. Recall Nick De Carlo's description of the development of the GreenWork Alliance: "We began to see this as a political movement [whose theme was] 'jobs, environment, and democracy.' We couldn't solve the problems of jobs and the environment without dealing with the issue of who makes the decisions and who has control." Rick Coronado and other grassroots activists emphasize the ways in which green economics have provided an alternative agenda for coalition-building in which workers can play an important role. Moreover, in the vacuum left by the collapse of social democracy, the building of social movements appears to be the only path available to radical ecologists, unions, and other groups to pursue their goals of social change.

However, barriers remain between environmentalists and organized labour. Many environmentalists remain wary of the motives behind union participation in joint bodies, government consultation processes, and coalitions. An example of this suspicion that unions bring a "defence of the status quo" or purely sectional interests to the table is provided by one experience related by Cathy Austin. The environmental committee at Austin's CAW Local 88 learned about a conference in Toronto on "better transportation" and decided to send one of its members. When the conference participants were invited to introduce themselves, the room full of environmentalists froze at the Local 88 member's statement that she represented a local of the Canadian Auto Workers Union. So certain were they that she would obstruct their critical discussions of the automobile that they asked her to leave. Fortunately for both sides, Local 88's representative insisted on staying. According to Austin, she informed the gathering: "No, this is why we want to be here. We don't like producing vehicles that kill our children with respiratory problems. But we need a job. We would like to produce something that doesn't harm the environment."[14] So she was allowed to stay at the meeting, and subsequently the "better transportation" group and the union have developed an ongoing dialogue.

There are also many suspicions on the part of unionists towards environmentalists, as demonstrated by the statements made by various union activists and officials. They referred, for example, to "pure" environmentalists or "extreme" environmentalists who do not recognize the importance of employment concerns. Indeed, this concern serves to differentiate the union's position in coalitions from those of environmental organizations or citizen's groups. This "unique labour perspective" is reiterated in the publications of the CAW National as well as in the newsletters of the locals and their environmental committees.

Initiatives like the joint labour-environment conferences are helping to establish a sense of trust and common purpose between environmentalists and unions, while the neoliberal assault on both environmental and labour rights makes such alliance efforts ever more urgent. Joint attempts to put together the outlines of an alternative agenda (the Labour Caucus of the OEN, the conferences, the GreenWork Alliance, the Windsor initiatives) have been tentative and partial.[15] Inasmuch as the neoliberal *blitzkrieg* creates the conditions for new linkages among diverse social actors who are victimized by the regime, it also intensifies the pressure on each organization to defend its own constituents. Their participation in coalitions is therefore continually braked by the demands and limited resources of their respective constituencies.

It is also important to reiterate that the CAW (along with public sector unions) constitutes one pole of the labour movement today. Other unions may or may not follow the "movement unionism" lead of the CAW in relation to non-union social actors. The CAW case demonstrates the *possibility* of convergence — even insofar as the future of the automobile itself is at stake. Its exceptionalism among the industrial unions calls attention to the importance of leadership in determining the path of union strategy.

Meanwhile, corporations and their associations have not been idle in seeking to attach environmentalism to their own modernization project. This study examined the strategies of the chemical producers and other business associations to weaken or prevent environmental regulation, over a period of decades, often in the name of environmental concern. In these struggles, which seek to define the meaning of sustainable development, as well as what constitutes authoritative science/knowledge, the private sector has made full use of all the advantages at its disposal, including the means of mass communication, legal and technical expertise, and the dependence of the State on private investment in the economy. They have also adopted their own, corporate discourse of "citizenship," in which the corporation is personified as one citizen among others, and its rights are equated with the individual rights said to underpin liberal democratic society. This strategy is used to oppose the conceptions of social rights and responsibilities advanced by the citizen's groups. On the one hand, the corporations attempt to assert the dependence of "democracy" and material well-being upon the freedom of capital and markets. On the other hand, the citizen's critiques make visible the inequalities and harms which result from such "freedoms."

In the Chemical Valley case, we saw how a chemical company succeeded in dividing its opposition in one town by adopting an aggressive environmental public relations campaign. In this case, the companies were aided by two other factors. First, the socio-ideological differences between some citizen-environmentalists (the Wallaceburg Clean Water Committee) and industrial workers created barriers on both sides to an alliance. While individuals with middle-class education, occupations, and perspectives could not bring themselves to link an environmental issue to a capital-labour conflict, partly for fear of losing their public image of "impartiality" and their influence with employers, union officials viewed the citizens as outsiders with irrational (and potentially threatening) concerns.[16] Second, the citizens lacked confidence that the union or the chemical workforce would provide committed allies — they perceived the union as an organization primarily concerned with the protection of its members' economic position, and unwilling to take a significant part in a broader social conflict.

Other sociological factors also help to explain the problems facing a strategy of labour-environmental convergence. The active base of the environmental movement is very different from that of the predominantly male, traditional industrial workforce and its leaders. Environmental activists tend to make "quality of life" choices over "security" choices. This confidence may be a function of the relative youth and security in other respects (education, political and social skills). While the environmental activist might be working part time in order to have more time free for family, skiing or hiking trips, or volunteer work, or may be working in a low-paid "movement" job, an admittedly shrinking category of industrial worker puts in as much overtime as possible to pay for the mortgage, children's university education, the yearly holiday, and retirement savings. The new social movements are also populated in large number by women, and tend to be characterized by less hierarchical structures and norms. Contrast this with the more authoritarian, sexist and homophobic culture of the male industrial workforce. These factors certainly serve as disincentives on both sides to working together. Environmentalists (typically young, educated, computer-literate, employed in the educational, government or semi-institutional spheres) do not necessarily have any sympathy toward the predicament of industrial or resource-sector workers, although some of them do. Many have had their fingers burned in attempts to make alliances, or have been involved in conflicts where unions sided with employers and against environmentalists. The conclusions derived from such experiences are often untempered by a real appreciation of the dilemma their actions create for workers, particularly in declining industrial sectors. And it is precisely between young environmental activists and older, male industrial workers that the cultural and social divide is greatest.

On the other hand, there is some overlap between environmental and other NSM activists and the "new type of proletariat" described by Marc Lesage in *Les Vagabonds du Rêve*. In his work for the Québec Confédération des Syndicats nationaux in the 1980s, Lesage observed that the regular, permanent worker was being succeeded by "a multitude of new faces": part-time workers, temporary or casual workers, volunteer labour, illegal workers, involuntary household workers, as well as the unemployed, the socially assisted, and those getting money by some means (e.g., students). "At the heart of advanced capitalism, there are today several dozen million persons who are finding themselves on the paths of marginalization ... In search for something other than the repetitive and brutalizing metro-work-zombie grind, these dream-seekers constitute a new type of proletariat."[17]

The motives which guide the choices of the middle-class activist are not so different from those which cause some workers to give up their jobs and material security for another kind of life, one more marginal, but more free. The attitudes of both groups (new middle class and new proletariat) toward work, self-development, and many other things are quite different from those of older, skilled, full-time industrial workers. The unions are finding it difficult to respond to the interests of this "new proletariat." Continuing high unemployment among youth and growing alienation from work for those who have it, create potential bases of support for a "liberation from work" component of an alternative ecological-economic agenda.[18] Having made the above observations, however, I hasten to reiterate that the political orientations of various groups defined in sociological terms cannot simply be derived from these socioeconomic positions. Rather, the ways in which individuals make sense of their life experiences are determined by discursive practices, and these, indeed, are behind the very existence of such social identities as "environmentalist" or "worker," or the contested meanings of citizenship and sustainable development.

Finally, some have asked whether the conditions presently exist to advance political ecology as an alternative strategy of development. In other words, have social movements and the labour movement already been so disorganized, weakened, and isolated that a long-term structural and ideological shift (in favour of capital) has been effected, implying a long war of position against *la pensée unique*? Or, have we arrived, in Canada, at a critical stage of confrontation where resistance on the part of a majority of citizens to the social values and consequences of authoritarian liberal-productivism is gathering cohesion, unity and strength? These questions call for specific contextual analyses, yet even the best of these will not allow us to predict the outcome of these conflicts. History, as Philip Abrams has argued, is the outcome of "the way social action and social structure create and contain one another." The method of historical sociology is "necessarily dialectical, reflecting the endlessly moving interplay of fact and meaning that constitutes, decomposes and reconstitutes social experience."[19] Any analysis like that attempted in this book can but capture momentary constellations in a universe of discourse which suggest possible futures. Ultimately, it is actors who, as they make meaning of experience, determine the course of history. One may take heart in the knowledge that many of the actors within the unions, the environmental movement, and other social movements, have grasped Gramsci's point that: "Given that whatever one does one is always playing somebody's game, the important thing is to seek in every way to play one's own game with success."[20] A democratic, ecological project is the answer to the liberal-productivist proclamation that "there is no alternative," and the sooner we start playing our own game, the better.

NOTES

1. These categories are derived not only from the regulatory battles examined in this book, but also from analysis of the discourses of a broader range of environmental organizations and issues in Canada. For a more detailed discussion of these tendencies, see Laurie E. Adkin, "Counter-hegemony and environmental politics in Canada," in William K. Carroll, ed., *Organizing Dissent: Contemporary Social Movements in Theory and Practice* (Toronto: Garamond Press, 1992), pp. 135-156.
2. It is important to distinguish here between the kind of "fundamentalism" associated with, for example, the "fundos" in the German and other European green movements, whose discourse is both ecological and humanist, and the "Earth First" variant. Certain groups of environmentalists in the United States, as well as factions within the Green movements generally described as the "right wing" espouse neo-Malthusian, neo-Hobbesian, or national-populist views.
3. Mark C. Parent, "Individual choices must become collective effort," *The Global Guardian* vol. 1, no. 1 (January 1995), p. 3.
4. "New Year's Address" (January 1990), delivered on Czech and Slovak Radio and Television, New Year's Day. Trans. in *The Spectator*, January 27, 1990, and reprinted in Václav Havel, *Open Letters: Selected Writings 1965-1990*, selected and edited by Paul Wilson (New York: Alfred A. Knopf, 1991), pp. 390-396.
5. This debate, which penetrated Canadian left intellectual circles in the 1980s, is preoccupied with Marxism's relationship to the concerns of ecology.
6. Dan Ublansky, Legislative Director and Health and Safety Co-ordinator, ECWU, London, May 1988.
7. Interview with Joe Legge, former coke oven worker at SYSCO, November 4, 1987, Sydney, Nova Scotia.
8. The ideology of sacrifice and internalization of traditional gender roles are important to explaining the long history of unhealthy and unsafe working conditions at the Sydney Steel Company, and the community's toleration of the pollution created by the steel mill, coke ovens, and tar ponds.
9. This reference is to the statement by Sam Gindin quoted in chapter 13.

Conclusion 331

10. Forty-six percent of rank-and-file workers who had never held union positions chose strategic options entailing a more pre-emptive role for their union.
11. Raymond Williams uses this phrase in *Towards 2000*: "All the decisive pressures of a capitalist social order are exerted at very short range and in the very short term. There is a job that has to be kept, a debt that has to be repaid, a family that has to be supported ... The significance of a predominantly middle-class leadership or membership of the new movements and campaigns is not to be found in some reductive analysis of the determined agencies of change. It is, first, in the fact of some available social distance, an area for affordable dissent" (p. 255).
12. Many auto workers in the big plants are resisting the national leadership's advocacy of the reduction of overtime work as an employment/solidarity strategy. Not knowing how long they will have their relatively well-paying jobs, they want to work as many hours as they can. CAW leadership has observed not only that this response is ultimately self-defeating as a strategy to protect material security, but also enervates the union in the area of political activism. People working overtime are unavailable for participation in community coalitions, educational programmes, and anti-government protests.
13. This desire seemed to underpin the CAW leadership's readiness to endorse the electoral campaign of NDP leader Glen Clark in the 1996 provincial election in British Columbia. Clark presented himself as a "workers'" candidate and campaigned forcefully against the debt and deficit reduction platform of the Liberal and Reform parties.
14. Cathy Austin, interview by author, Toronto, June 7, 1996.
15. For example, the involvement of CAW locals in Great Lakes United became strained in the 1990s, due to management-staff conflicts at GLU (in which the unionists sided with the staff) and to what the unionists perceived as the increasing orientation of GLU toward government lobbying and consultative work, and away from grassroots organizing. These differences led to several of the CAW locals choosing not to renew their memberships in GLU. In this context, GLU relocated its Canadian office from Windsor to Montreal.
16. Although they would deny this, it is likely that the union officials were also concerned that an alliance with an environmental organization would jeopardize their bargaining relations with employers.
17. Marc Lesage, *Les Vagabonds du Rêve: Vers une société de marginaux?* (Montréal: Boreal Express, 1986), from the avant-propos, my translation.
18. I have developed this argument further in "Ecological politics in Canada: Elements of a strategy of collective action," in *Political Ecology: Global and Local Perspectives*, David V. J. Bell, Lisa Fawcett, Roger Keil, and Peter Penz, eds. (New York and London: Routledge, forthcoming, 1998).
19. *Historical Sociology* (Somerset, England: Open Books Publishing, 1982), p. 108.
20. Gramsci, *Selections from the Prison Notebooks*, p. 154.

[Appendix 1]

SURVEY OF *CAW* MEMBERS IN THE WINDSOR AREA ON LABOUR-ENVIRONMENTAL ISSUES, JULY-AUGUST 1987

Please note:

Your name has been randomly selected by computer from a list of all the members of your local. The results of this survey will contribute to research on labour and environmental politics being conducted by a doctoral student in Political Studies at Queen's University. Names of the respondents will not be included in the survey results and will remain strictly confidential. This research is intended to contribute to the advance of the labour movement, and your participation is greatly appreciated. Seal the completed questionnaire in the accompanying envelope, and write your local number on the envelope. Return it to a designated union representative or to a collection box in your work place. Please take time to complete the survey and return it no later than September 4, 1987. Survey results will be obtainable from the Windsor and District Labour Council Environment Committee.

Personal Data

Age: _____

Sex: male ( )   female ( )

Education completed or ongoing: High school ( ) University ( ) Vocational institution ( )
( ) other (please specify): _____

CAW Local number: _____

Years of employment at:
  ____ Ford
  ____ Chrysler
  ____ General Motors
  ____ other (please specify): _____

Occupation   ( ) office worker   ( ) production work
              ( ) maintenance   ( ) full-time union rep.

Union positions you have held or currently hold:
_____

1. Do you think that the union should be involved in environmental issues?
   ( ) yes   ( ) no   ( ) don't know
2. Are you aware of the environmental issues or campaigns in which the union is involved in your area?   ( ) yes   ( ) no
   a) If yes, please list these:_____
   _____
   _____

Appendix 333

3. Before reading this survey, were you aware:
   a) of the CAW Canada Council's decision to establish environmental committees in all CAW locals? ( ) yes ( ) no
   b) that an environmental committee exists, or is being formed, in your local?
      ( ) yes ( ) no ( ) no committee is being formed yet

4. If the answer to question 3 (b) is *yes*, how did you find out about the committee's existence?_____
   _____

5. Have you participated in any of the activities of the environmental committee since it was established?
   ( ) yes ( ) no ( ) no environmental committee yet

   a) *If no*, why not? Please rate each of the following reasons on a scale of one (1) = not important; two (2) = somewhat important; three (3) = very important.
   (Circle one number for each item.)

1	2	3	not interested in environmental issues
1	2	3	not enough time
1	2	3	lack of information about the committee's work
1	2	3	didn't know the committee existed
1	2	3	other (please specify):_____

6. Are there any changes which would make it more convenient or attractive for you to participate in the environmental committees (e.g., changes to the time, length, or location of meetings, more paid time off for union-related activities, better information about committee work, changes to the structure of the meetings, changes to the way committees are created in your local, etc.)?
   _____
   _____

7. Environmental problems sometimes appear to pose trade-offs between different social goals. Would you say that improving the quality of the environment is *more important than* (1), *less important than* (2), or *equally as important* as (3), the following goals? Please circle *one* number for each item.

1	2	3	improving work place occupational health and safety
1	2	3	improving the economic security of the work force
1	2	3	improving the standard of living of the work force
1	2	3	increasing industrial production
1	2	3	increasing agricultural production

Additional comments:
_____
_____

8. How would you like to see union resources allocated to the following areas? (1) *more*, (2) *less*, or (3) *the same* (as presently) (Please circle *one* number for each item.)

1	2	3	educational activities (including environment-related)
1	2	3	research on occupational health and safety issues
1	2	3	political action
1	2	3	research on jobs-related economic issues
1	2	3	contract negotiation
1	2	3	contract enforcement
1	2	3	research staff and facilities
1	2	3	executive expenses
1	2	3	other (please specify):_____

9. Are you active in any social or political group or issue outside the workplace? (Please specify the general nature of the activity, e.g., community sports or recreation, nature club, charity work, political party, etc.)

   _____

10. Do you think that you will participate in the environment committee of your local in the future?
    ( ) yes   ( ) no   ( ) maybe

11. Would you like to have the environmental committee distribute a brief information sheet on a regular basis, to all members?
    ( ) yes   ( ) no

12. Do you think that you will participate in an environmental organization or citizens' group concerned with environmental issues in the future?
    ( ) yes   ( ) no   ( ) maybe

13. Finally, please consider this hypothetical situation: An industrial firm located in your community is producing airborne emissions containing toxic chemicals. These emissions include known carcinogens, as well as particulate matter linked to sinus and respiratory problems. The plant needs modernizing in order to be as productive as others in the industry. In response to pressure from environmental and citizens' groups, the firm's management has claimed inability to implement pollution control equipment because of the cost, and has made public statements about the possibility of closing the plant. The plant's union is faced with a number of possible courses of action:

    (1) The union should ally with company management to prevent closure at all costs.
    (2) The union should support the demands of the environmental and citizens' groups, while lobbying government officials and MPs to prevent a plant closure.
    (3) The union should analyze the economic and environmental status of the firm and propose its own plan for eliminating pollution and providing employment for any union members affected.

    Which of the above options do you believe to be the most *desirable*?
    (Circle one)   1   2   3

Which of these options do you believe to be the *most effective* for protecting jobs?
(Circle one) 1 2 3

Please explain your choices:

14. Please add any comments you would like to make about the environmental committees or about any of the above questions.

SURVEY SAMPLE SIZE AND RESPONSE RATE

Excluding Local 195, the total population from which I attempted to sample one percent was approximately 19, 081 workers. My questionnaires covered about four percent of this population, and given a response of 267 out of 771, or 35 percent, the percentage of the total population "represented" by the survey responses is 1.4 percent. In Local 195, only plant chairpersons were surveyed, and these questionnaires are not included in the "rank-and-file" category.

TABLE 34
DATA ON SURVEY DISTRIBUTION AND RESPONSE

Local No.	Number of Surveys Distributed	Number of Surveys Received	Date Surveys Received	Percent Received
444	300	36	March 1988	
		37	July 1988	24.0
195	74	11	Aug-Sept/87	
		7	May 1988	24.0
200	180	60	Aug-Sept/87	33.0
89	36	20	Aug-Sept/87	55.5
1498	35	28	Aug-Sept/87	80.0
1973	220	86	Aug-Sept/87	39.0
TOTAL	845	285		34.0*

Excluding Local 195, the rate of return on the survey was 35.0 percent.

Selected Bibliography

Abella, Irving, ed. *On Strike: Six Key Labour Struggles in Canada, 1919-1949.* Toronto: James Lewis & Samuel Pubs., 1974.
Abrams, Philip. *Historical Sociology.* Somerset, England: Open Books Publishing Ltd., 1982.
Adhesives and Sealants Manufacturers Assoc. of Canada. "Comments of the ASMAC on the Proposed Environmental Protection Act." Brief submitted to Environment Canada, February 17, 1987.
Adkin, Laurie E. "Ecological Politics in Canada: Elements of a Strategy of Collective Action." In *Political Ecology: Global and Local Perspectives.* Edited by D. Bell, L. Fawcett, R. Keil, and P. Penz. New York and London: Routledge, forthcoming.
———. "Life in Kleinland: Democratic Resistance to 'Folksy Fascism'." *Canadian Dimension*: 29, 2 (April-May 1995).
———. "Environmental Politics, Political Economy, and Social Democracy in Canada." *Studies in Political Economy*: 45 (Fall 1994).
———. "Ecology and Labour: Towards a New Societal Paradigm." In *Culture and Social Change.* Edited by Colin Leys and Marguerite Mendell. Montréal: Black Rose Books, 1992.
———. "Counter-Hegemony and Environmental Politics in Canada." In *Organizing Dissent: Contemporary Social Movements in Theory and Practice.* Edited by William K. Carroll. Toronto: Garamond Press, 1992.
Adkin, Laurie E., and Catherine Alpaugh. "Labour, Ecology, and the Politics of Convergence in Canada." In *Social Movements/ Social Change: The Politics and Practice of Organizing [Socialist Studies*: 4 (1988)]. Edited by F. Cunningham, et al. Toronto: Socialist Studies Society/Between the Lines, 1988.
Adkin, Laurie E. "A Labour-Ecology Programme for Social Change." *Our Times.* (February 1987).
Aglietta, Michel. *A Theory of Capitalist Regulation: The U.S. Experience.* London: New Left Books, 1979.
Alaluf, Mateo. "Work and the Working Class." *Socialist Register* (1985/86).
Alpaugh, Catherine, and Trevor Price. "Windsor's Great Lakes Institute: The Story Behind the Blob." *Windsor This Month* (March 1986).
Alpaugh, Catherine, and Lynn Sabean. "The Politics of PCBs in the 1980s." *International Journal of Environmental Studies* (1987).
Aronowitz, Stanley. *Science as Power: Discourse and Ideology in Modern Society.* Minneapolis: Univ. of Minnesota Press, 1988.
Ashworth, William. *The Late, Great Lakes: An Environmental History.* 1st ed. New York: Knopf/Random House, 1986.
Babson, Steve, ed. *Lean Work: Empowerment and Exploitation in the Global Auto Industry.* Detroit: Wayne State University Press, 1995.
Bannerji, Himani. "But Who Speaks for Us? Experience and Agency in Conventional Feminist Paradigms." In *Unsettling Relations: The University as a Site of Feminist Struggles*, Himani Bannerji, Linda Carty, Kari Delhi, Susan Heald, and Kate McKenna. Toronto: The Women's Press, 1991.
Berger, John. J. *Restoring the Earth.* New York: Alfred A. Knopf, 1985.
Berman, Daniel. *Death on the Job: Occupational Health and Safety Struggles in the United States.* New York: Monthly Review Press, 1978.

Bero, Kathy. "RAP Study: Tell Us What's Going On!" *Great Lakes United* (Winter 1993/94).
Beynon, Huw and Theo Nichols. *Living with Capitalism: Class Relations and the Modern Factory.* London, Henley, and Boston: Routledge and Kegan Paul, 1977.
Blackler, F. H. M., and C. A. Brown. *Whatever Happened to Shell's New Philosophy of Management?* Farnborough, Hants, UK: Teakfield Ltd., 1980.
Boggs, Carl. *Gramsci's Marxism.* London: Pluto Press, 1976.
———. *The Two Revolutions: Gramsci and the Dilemmas of Western Marxism.* Boston: South End Press, 1984.
British Columbia Forest Products, Ltd., G. G. Flater, President, "Submission to the Hon. Tom McMillan and The Hon. Jake Epp Regarding the Proposed Environmental Protection Act." April 27, 1987.
Brown, Michael. *Laying Waste: The Poisoning of America by Toxic Chemicals.* New York: Pantheon, 1980.
Canada. Dept. of Environment and the Ontario Ministry of the Environment. *Public Meetings on the Review of the 1978 Great Lakes Water Quality Agreement.* A report submitted to the Review Board for the Canada-Ontario Agreement Respecting Great Lakes Water Quality. Prepared by the Canadian Environmental Law Research Foundation. Toronto: December 1987.
———. Dept. of Environment. *Summary of Public Hearings on the Proposed Environmental Protection Act.* Ottawa: Environment Canada, March 31, 1987.
———. Dept. of Environment. *Questions and Answers on the Proposed Environmental Protection Act.* Ottawa: Environment Canada, December 1986.
———. Dept. of Environment. *State of the Environment Report for Canada.* Written by Peter M. Bird, David J. Rapport. Ottawa: Environment Canada, 1986.
———. Dept. of Environment. Inland Waters Directorate. *Public Perceptions of Water Quality in the Great Lakes.* Ottawa: Environment Canada, 1981.
———. Dept. of National Health and Welfare. *Human Exposure to Environmental Lead.* Ottawa: Health and Welfare Canada, November 1982.
———. Minister of the Environment, Tom McMillan. "The Right to a Healthy Environment: An Overview of the Proposed Environmental Protection Act." Ottawa: Environment Canada, 1987.
———. Minister of the Environment. *Proposed Environmental Protection Act.* Ottawa: Environment Canada, December 1986.
———. *Minutes and Proceedings and Evidence of the Legislative Committee on Bill C-74, an Act respecting the protection of the environment and human life and health.* Issue no. 6 (15-16 December 1987 and 21 January 1988).
———. National Research Council. Associate Committee on Scientific Criteria for Environmental Quality. *Effects of Lead in the Environment—1978—Quantitative Aspects.* Ottawa, 1979.
———. *Response of the Federal Government to the Recommendations of the Consultative Task Force on the Canadian Petrochemical Industry.* Ottawa: May 1979. GOV. DOC. CA1 TI823 79R27.
———. Statistics Canada. *Corporations and Labour Unions.* Ottawa, 1985.
———. Statistics Canada. *Corporations and Labour Unions Returns Act, Report for 1985.* Part II: Labour Unions, supplement. Ottawa, 1985.
———. Statistics Canada. *Employment Earnings and Hours:* 60 (December 1982).
Canadian Association of Industrial, Mechanical, and Allied Workers. "Brief to Environment Canada on the Proposed Environmental Protection Act." March 1987.
Canadian Auto Workers. *False Solutions, Growing Protests: Recapturing the Agenda.* Report to the National Collective Bargaining and Political Action Convention. Toronto, June 4-7, 1996. North York, Ont.: CAW, 1986.
———. *Fight Speed-up.* North York, Ont.: CAW, 1995.
———. *Constitution of the National Automobile, Aerospace, Transportation and General Workers' Union of Canada (CAW-Canada).* Adopted at Quebec City, Quebec, August 1994. North York, Ont.: CAW, 1994.
———. *Hard Times, New Times: Fighting for our Future.* Report to the National Collective Bargaining and Political Action Convention, Toronto, May 4-7, 1993. North York, Ont.: CAW, 1993.
———. *More time.* North York, Ont.: CAW, 1993.
———. *CAW Statement on the Reorganization of Workers.* North York, Ont.: CAW, 1989.
———. *In Solidarity: A Family Album.* North York, Ont.: CAW, April 1989.
———. *You and Your Membership in the CAW.* North York, Ont.: CAW, August 1986.
Canadian Chemical Producers Association. "The Key Role of the Chemical Industry in Canada's

Economy." Submission to the MacDonald Royal Commission on the Economy. June 1983.
———. "Submission to Environment Canada on the Proposed Environmental Protection Act." March 1987.
Canadian Environmental Law Association. "Submission to Environment Canada on the Proposed Federal Environmental Protection Act." Prepared by Toby Vigod and Marcia Valiante. Toronto: CELA, March 1987.
Canadian Institute. *The Fundamentals of Environmental Law and Regulation.* Toronto: The Canadian Institute, 1994.
Canadian Labour Congress. "Submission on Proposals for Amendments to the Environmental Contaminants Act." Ottawa: CLC, August 1985.
———. "Energy Policy Statement." Document No. 19, 17th Constitutional Convention, May 9-13, 1988. Ottawa: CLC, 1988.
Canadian Manufacturers Association. "Submission to the Minister of the Environment. The Hon. Thomas McMillan, on the Draft Environmental Protection Act." Toronto: March 1987.
Citizens' Coalition for Clean Water. "Submission to Environment Canada Regarding the Newly Proposed Environmental Protection Act." Wallaceburg, Ont.: CCCW, March 7, 1987.
City of Toronto. Public Health Dept., and the Ontario Cancer Treatment and Research Foundation. *Junction Triangle Historical Cohort Cancer Study: A Study of Cancer Incidence in an Urban Neighbourhood.* Toronto: City of Toronto, Dept. of Public Health, 1986.
———. Public Health Dept. *Human Exposure Routes to Selected Persistent Toxic Chemicals in the Great Lakes Basin: A Case Study.* By Katherine Davies and Joan Campbell. Toronto: City of Toronto, Dept. of Public Health, May 1986.
———. Planning Board. *Neighbourhood Plan Proposals: Junction Triangle.* Toronto: Planning Board, May 1979.
Confédération des Syndicats nationaux. "Memoire de la Confédération des Syndicats nationaux, présenté au Ministère de l'environnement du Canada, sur l'avant-projet de Loi sur la protection de l'environnement." Montréal, March 10, 1987.
Cooley, Mike. *Architect or Bee: The Human Price of Technology.*Compiled and edited by Shirley Cooley. London: Slough: Langley Technical Services, 1987.
Cooper, Kathy, et. al. *The Citizen's Guide to Lead in Ontario.* Toronto: New Canada Press, 1986.
Creet, Mario. "The Quiescence of the Chemical Worker." Unpublished paper, Queen's University, Kingston, April 1985.
Crozier, Michel, Samuel Huntington, et al. *The Crisis of Democracy* (Report on the Governability of Democracies to the Trilateral Commission). New York: New York University Press, 1975.
Davids, Meryl. "Detoxing Dow's Reputation." *Public Relations Journal* (January 1987).
De Carlo, Nick. "The Right to Refuse Bill 208." *Our Times* [Toronto, Canada] (May 1989).
Dorman, Peter. "Environmental Protection, Employment, and Profit: The Politics of Public Interest in the Tacoma (Washington)/ ASARCO Dispute." *Review of Radical Political Economics*: 16, 4 (1984).
Dow Chemical Canada. "Submission to the Royal Commission on the Economic Union and Development Prospects for Canada." November 1983. "Additional comments in response to the discussion paper 'Challenges and Choices.'"Sarnia, Ont.: Dow Chemical Canada Inc., July 1984.
———. "Remarks to the Standing Senate Committee on Energy and Natural Resources Review of the National Energy Program." Sarnia, Ont.: Dow Chemical Canada Inc., May 8, 1984.
———. *Dow Canadian Dimensions* (October/November 1987; May 1986).
———. *1984 Annual Report.*
———. "Free Trade: A Closing Window of Opportunity." Speech by William McCagherty, Vice President of Hydrocarbons and Materials Management, Dow Chemical Canada Inc. Presented to the Sarnia Rotary Club, August 17, 1987.
———. "A Profile." In *The Blue Book of Canadian Business.* Toronto: Canadian Newspaper Services International Ltd., 1987.
———. Public Relations Dept. "Our Commitment to a Clean Environment at Dow's Sarnia Division." Sarnia: Dow Chemical, 1986.
———. "Where does the money go?" *Sarnia Division News*: 14, 10 (September 9, 1987).
———. "Comments on the Draft Environmental Protection Act." By George T. Marshall, Manager, Government Affairs, Western Canada Division, February 20, 1987.

———. Dow Chemical Canada Inc., Submission on the Proposed Environmental Protection Act." Sarnia, Ont.: Dow Chemical Canada Inc., March 4, 1987.

———. "Dow's eyes and ears in Ottawa," *Dow Canada Chemicals* (October/November 1987).

Drimmie, Patricia. *A History of Labour in Sarnia and Lambton County*. Sarnia: Sarnia and District Labour Council,1978.

Duplé, N., ed. *Le Droit à la Qualité de l'Environnement*. Montréal: Québec Amérique, 1988.

DuPont Canada Inc. J. A. Walsh, V.P. Corporate Affairs. "Comments on the Proposed New Environmental Protection Act." March 2, 1987.

Dunlap, Riley E. "Polls, Pollution, and Politics Revisited: Public Opinion on the Environment in the Reagan Era." *Environment*: 29, 6 (July/August 1987).

Eder, Klaus. *The New Politics of Class: Social Movements and Cultural Dynamics in Advanced Societies*. London: Sage, 1993.

Energy and Chemical Workers Union. *Constitutional Convention Proceedings* 1984, 1986, 1988.

———. "Energy Policy Statement" (1980) in Proceedings of ECWU Founding and Merger Convention, June 1980. Edmonton, Alta.: ECWU, 1981.

———. *ECWU Journal*. Issues 1980-1989.(Edmonton, Alta.)

———. "The Energy and Chemical Workers' Union: A United Voice for 35,000 Employees in Canada's Resource Sector." Edmonton, Alta.: ECWU, c. 1983.

———. "Human Exposure to Environmental Lead" (Comments submitted by the Energy and Chemical Workers Union on the report prepared by the Dept. of National Health and Welfare for the Dept. of the Environment), May 1983.

Environmental Contaminants Act Amendments Consultative Committee. *Final Report*. Ottawa: October 1986.

Fiberglass Canada Inc. T.S. Munro, Manager, Industrial Hygiene and Environmental Services. "Submission to Environment Canada on the Proposed Environmental Protection Act." Sarnia, Ont.: March 18, 1987.

Field, Diane. "Beyond Male Bias in Occupational Health." *Healthsharing* (Summer 1985).

Flanagan, S., and R. Dalton. "Parties under Stress: Realignment and Dealignment in Advanced Industrial Societies." *West European Politics*: 7, 1 (1984).

Ford, R. W. *A History of the Chemical Industry in Lambton County*. Canadian Society for Chemical Engineering, 1976.

Forrest, Anne. "History of Unionism in the Petro-Chemicals Industry." Unpublished paper, September 1979.

Fox Keller, Evelyn. *Reflections on Gender and Science*. New Haven: Yale Univ. Press, 1985.

Franklin, Ursula. *The Real World of Technology*. CBC Massey Lecture Series. Toronto: CBC Enterprises, 1990.

Gayle, Dennis J. "Regulating the American Automobile Industry: Sources and Consequences of US Automobile Air Pollution Standards." In *Driving Continentally*. Edited by Maureen Appel Molot. Ottawa: Carleton University Press, 1993.

George, Larry N. "Love Canal and the Politics of Corporate Terrorism." *Socialist Review*: 12, 6 (November/December 1982).

Geras, Norman. "Post-Marxism?" *New Left Review*: 163 (May/June 1987).

Gindin, Sam. *The Canadian Auto Workers: The Birth and Transformation of a Union*. Toronto: James Lorimer & Co., 1995.

———. "Breaking Away: The Formation of the Canadian Auto Workers." *Studies in Political Economy*: 29 (Summer 1989).

———. "Putting Socialism on Labour's Agenda." *Canadian Dimension*: 22, 1 (February 1988).

Goldenberg, Naomi. "Resurrecting the Body: An Agenda for Feminist Theory." In *Women and Men: Interdisciplinary Writings on Gender*. Edited by Greta Hofmann Nemiroff. Montréal: Fitzhenry & Whiteside, 1987.

Gorz, André. *Farewell to the Working Class: An Essay on Post-Industrial Socialism*. Trans., Michael Sonenscher. London: Pluto Press, 1982.

———. *Ecology as Politics*. Trans., P. Vigderman and J. Cloud. Montréal: Black Rose Books, 1980.

Gramsci, Antonio. *Selections from the Prison Notebooks*. Edited and translated by Quintin Hoare and Geoffrey Nowell Smith. New York: International Publishers, 1971.

———. *Ecrits Politiques* Vol. II (1921-1922) and Vol. III (1923-1926). Edited by Robert Paris. Trans., M.

Martin-Gistucci, G. Moget, and R. Paris. Paris: Editions Gallimard, 1975.
———. *Selections from the Political Writings, 1910-1920.* Edited by Quintin Hoare. Trans., John Mathews. New York: International Publishers, 1977.
———. *Selections from Political Writings, 1921-1926.* Edited and translated by Quintin Hoare. London: Lawrence & Wishart, 1978.
Gray, Stan. "Sharing the Shop Floor." In *Women and Men.* Edited by Greta Hofmann Nemiroff. Montréal: Fitzhenry and Whiteside, 1987.
Great Lakes United. *Unfulfilled Promises: A Citizens' Review of the International Great Lakes Quality Agreement.* Buffalo, NY: GLU Water Quality Task Force, February 1987.
———. *Citizen Action in Developing Clean-Up Plans for the 42 Great Lakes Toxic Hot-Spots.* Report from a Remedial Action Plan Workshop for Citizens and Community Leaders, Buffalo, NY, September 11-13, 1987. Buffalo, NY: GLU, 1987.
———. *Great Lakes United* (issues 1986-1996).
Halle, David. *America's Working Man.* Chicago and London: The University of Chicago Press, 1984.
Halpern, Norman. "Strategies for Dealing with Forces Acting on the Process of Organization Change in a Unionized Setting: A Case Study." PhD diss. Ed.D. Dept. of Education, Adult and Continuing, University of Toronto, 1983.
Harder, Lois. "Depoliticizing Insurgency: The Politics of the Family in Alberta." *Studies in Political Economy:* 50 (Summer 1996).
Harding, Sandra. *The Science Question and Feminism.* Ithaca: Cornell Univ. Press, 1986.
Harding, S. and Jean F. O'Barr, eds. *Sex and Scientific Inquiry.* Chicago: Univ. of Chicago Press, 1985.
Harrison, Kathryn, George Hoberg, and Gregory Hein. *Risk, Science, and Politics.* Montréal: McGill-Queen's University Press, 1994.
Harrison, Trevor, and Gordon Laxer, eds. *The Trojan Horse: Alberta and the Future of Canada.* Montréal: Black Rose Books, 1995.
Heckscher, C. *The New Unionism.* New York: Basic Books, 1988.
Hirsch, Joachim. "The Crisis of Fordism, Transformations of the 'Keynesian' Security State, and New Social Movements." *Research in Social Movements, Conflicts and Change:* 10 (1988).
Holmes, John. "The Contemporary Restructuring of Canadian Industry." Paper presented to the Workshop on Development in the 1980s: Canada in the Western Hemisphere. Queen's University, Kingston, Ont., May 10-13, 1984.
Holmes, John, and Pradeep Kumar. "Labour Movement Strategies in the Era of Free Trade: The Uneven Transformation of Industrial Relations in the North American Automobile Industry." In *Production, Space, Identity.* Edited by Jane Jenson, Rianne Mahon, and Manfred Bienefeld. Toronto: Canadian Scholars' Press, 1993.
Hughes, Elaine L. "Civil Rights to Environmental Quality." In *Environmental Law and Policy.* Edited by E. Hughes, A. Lucas, and W. Tilleman II. Toronto: Emond Montgomery Pubs. Ltd., 1993.
Hyman, Richard. *Strikes.* 3rd ed. Fontana, 1984.
Illich, Ivan. *Tools for Conviviality.* 1st ed. New York: Harper & Row, 1973.
Inglehart, Ronald. *Culture Shift.* Princeton, NJ: Princeton University Press, 1990.
———. *The Silent Revolution.* Princeton, NJ: Princeton University Press, 1977.
International Joint Commission. Water Quality Board. *Summary of the Forum for Remedial Action Plan Co-ordinators* (Windsor, Ont., October 20-21, 1986). Windsor, Ont.: IJC, 1986.
———. Water Quality Board. *1985 Report on Great Lakes Water Quality.* Windsor, Ont.: IJC, 1985.
———. Water Quality Board. *Summary of the Second Remedial Action Plan Forum* (Toledo, Ohio, November 19-20, 1987). Windsor, Ont.: IJC, 1987.
———. Water Quality Board. *1987 Report on Great Lakes Water Quality.* Windsor, Ont.: IJC, 1987.
Jackson, John. "The Spread of 'Regulatory Voluntarism': Abandonment of the Goal of Zero Discharge." *Great Lakes United* vol. 9, no. 2 (Fall 1994).
———. "RAPs: Will There be Money for Actual Cleanup?" *Great Lakes United* vol. 9, no. 4 (Summer 1995).
———. "If Not RAPs, What?" *Great Lakes United* vol. 10, no. 2 (Winter 1995-96).
———. "Ontario and Environment: Galloping Backwards." *Great Lakes United* vol. 10, no. 3 (Spring 1996).
Jackson, John, and Phillip Weller. *Chemical Nightmare: The Unnecessary Legacy of Toxic Wastes.* Toronto: Between the Lines, 1982.

Jacques, Martin and Francis Mulhern, eds., *The Forward March of Labour Halted?* London: NLB, in assoc. with *Marxism Today*, 1981.

Jenson, Jane, and George Ross. "Post-War Class Struggles and the Crisis of Left Politics." *Socialist Register* (1985/86).

Jolley, Linda. "Regulating a Toxic Substance: The Impact on Workers." Paper presented to the Conference on Jobs and the Environment, Hamilton, Ont., November 21-23, 1986.

Keating, Michael. *To the Last Drop.* Toronto: Macmillan, 1986.

Keil, Roger. "Green Work Alliances: The Political Economy of Social Ecology." *Studies in Political Economy*: 44 (Summer 1994).

Kelly, John. *Trade Unions and Socialist Politics.* London: Verso Books, 1988.

Kilgour, Art. "The Greening of the Union Movement." *National Union Magazine*: 2, 5 (Winter 1987/88). [CAW-Canada].

Kirchheimer, Otto. "The Transformation of the Western European Party Systems." In *Political Parties and Political Development*. Edited by J. Lapalombara and W. Weiner. Princeton, NJ: Princeton University Press, 1966.

Kitching, Gavin. *Rethinking Socialism.* London and New York: Methuen, 1983.

Kumar, Pradeep, and John Holmes. "Change, but in what Direction? Divergent Union Responses to Work Restructuring in the Integrated North American Auto Industry." In *Social Reconstructions of the World Automobile Industry: Competition, Power, and Industrial Flexibility*. Edited by Frederic Deyo. London: Macmillan (International Political Economy Series)and New York: St. Martin's Press, 1996.

Lambton Industrial Society. *1985 Annual Report.* Sarnia, Ont.: Lambton Industrial Society, c. 1985.

Lees, David. "Club Lead." *Toronto Life Magazine* (December 1986).

Leighton, Rebecca. "Developing a Remedial Action Plan: The Green Bay Experience." *Great Lakes United* (Fall 1986).

———. "Lessons from Green Bay: How to Make a RAP Work." *Great Lakes United* (Spring 1989).

Lerner, Sally. "Environmental Constituency-Building: Local Initiatives and Volunteer Stewardship." *Alternatives*: 13, 3 (September/October 1986).

Lesage, Marc. *Les Vagabonds du Rêve* (Vers une société de marginaux?). Montréal: Boreal Express, 1986.

Lipietz, Alain. *Towards a New Economic Order: Postfordism, Ecology, and Democracy.* Oxford: Polity Press, 1992.

———. "Reflections on a Tale: The Marxist Foundations of the Concepts of Regulation and Accumulation." Trans., Jane Jenson and Marguerite Mendell. *Studies in Political Economy*: 26 (Summer 1988).

———. *Mirages and Miracles: The Crisis of Global Fordism.* Trans., David Macey. London: Verso Books, 1987.

———. "How Monetarism Choked Third World Industrialisation." *New Left Review*: 145 (May-June 1984).

———. "Towards Global Fordism?" *New Left Review*: 132 (March-April 1982).

Mann, Charles C. "The Town of Dow." *Business Month* (December 1987).

Martel, Elie. *Still Not Healthy, Still Not Safe. Report of the Ontario New Democratic Caucus Second Task Force on Occupational Health and Safety.* Toronto: Ontario NDP, July 1986.

Mayor of Toronto. "Action Task Force on Chemical Spills and Air Emissions in the Junction Triangle" (Report). Toronto, 1982.

McBride, Stephen. "The Continuing Crisis of Social Democracy: Ontario's Social Contract in Perspective." *Studies in Political Economy*: 50 (Summer 1996).

Miliband, Ralph, and Marcel Liebman. "Beyond Social Democracy." *Socialist Register* (1985/86).

Mineau, P., et al. "Using the herring gull to monitor levels and effects of organo chlorine contamination in the Canadian Great Lakes." In *Toxic Contaminants in the Great Lakes*. Edited by Jerome O. Nriagu and Milagros S. Simmons. New York: John Wiley & Sons, 1984.

Mining Association of Canada. C. George Miller, Managing Director, "Submission to Environment Canada on the New Environmental Protection Act." Ottawa, April 3, 1987.

Mol, Arthur P. J. *The Refinement of Production: Ecological Modernization Theory and the Chemical Industry.* Utrecht: Van Arkel, 1995.

Mouffe, Chantal. *The Return of the Political.* London: Verso, 1993.

Bibliography

———. "Radical democracy or liberal democracy?" *Socialist Review*: 20, 2 (April-June, 1990).
———. "Hegemony and new political subjects: toward a new concept of democracy." In *Marxism and the Interpretation of Culture*. Edited by C. Nelson and L. Grossberg. Chicago: University of Illinois Press, 1988.
———. "Working Class Hegemony and the Struggle for Socialism." *Studies in Political Economy*: 12 (Fall 1983).
———. "Hegemony and Ideology in Gramsci." In *Gramsci and Marxist Theory*. London and NY: Routledge and Kegan Paul, 1979.
Mouffe, Chantal, and Ernesto Laclau. "Reply to Norman Geras." *New Left Review*: 164 (1987).
———. *Hegemony and Socialist Strategy: Towards a Radical Democratic Politics*. London: Verso Books, 1985.
———. "Recasting Marxism: Hegemony and New Political Movements." *Socialist Review*: 12, 6 (November-December 1982).
Moulton, David. "Ford Windsor 1945." In *On Strike: Six Key Labour Struggles in Canada, 1919-1949*. Edited by Irving Abella. Toronto: James Lewis & Samuel Pubs., 1974.
National Research Council (US), and Royal Society of Canada. *The Great Lakes Water Quality Agreement: An Evolving Instrument for Ecosystem Management*. Washington, DC: National Academy Press, 1985.
Nguyen, Y-Lang. "Governments Abandoning Hotspot Cleanup Plans." *Great Lakes United* vol. 10, no. 2 (Winter 1995-96).
Nichols, Theo, et al. *Workers Divided*. Glasgow: William Collins Sons & Co., Ltd., 1976.
Niedringhaus Davis, Lee. *The Corporate Alchemists: Profit Takers and Problem Makers in the Chemical Industry*. New York: William Morrow and Co., 1984.
O'Sullivan, Dermot. "Earnings of Canadian Chemical Firms Improved Last Year," *Chemical and Engineering News* (February 23, 1987).
OECD. *Petrochemical Industry: Energy Aspects of Structural Change*. Paris: OECD, 1985.
———. *The Petrochemical Industry: Trends in Production and Investment to 1985*. Paris: OECD, 1979.
———. Environmental Directorate. *Economic Aspects of International Chemicals Control*. Paris: OECD, 1983.
Offe, Claus. "New Social Movements: Challenging the Boundaries of Institutional Politics." *Social Research*: 52, 4 (Winter 1985).
———. *Contradictions of the Welfare State*. Edited by John Keane. Cambridge, MA: The MIT Press, 1984.
Offe, Claus, and Hans Wiesenthal. "Two Logics of Collective Action." In *Disorganized Capitalism*. Oxford: Polity Press, 1985.
Ontario. Legislative Assembly. *Journals*: CXII (1978), 31st Parliament, 2nd Session.
———. Ministry of the Environment. *MISA Issue Resolution Process: Final Report*. Toronto: MOE, September 1991.
———. Ministry of the Environment. *MISA Issues Resolution Process: Issue Resolution Committee Reports*. Toronto: MOE, June 1990.
———. Ministry of the Environment. *MISA Issues Resolution Process: Background*. Toronto: MOE, February 1990.
———. Ministry of the Environment. Legal Services Branch. *Prosecution Activity Reports*. Toronto: MOE, (April 1977 to October 1988).
———. Ministry of the Environment. *Lead Concentrations in Soil on Residential, Public, and Publicly Accessible Commercial Properties in the Vicinity of Toronto Refiners and Smelters Ltd., Toronto, 1985-1987*. Toronto: MOE, June 1988.
———. Ministry of the Environment. *Environmental Review, Toronto Refiners and Smelters Ltd*. Toronto: MOE, September 1987.
———. Ministry of the Environment. Intergovernmental Relations Office. "Public Consultation Process for Remedial Action Plans." Toronto: MOE, March 1987.
———. Ministry of the Environment. *The Public Review of the MISA White Paper and the MOE's Response to it*. Toronto: MOE, January 1987.
———. Ministry of the Environment. *St. Clair River Pollution Investigation, 1985-1986*. Toronto: MOE, 1986.
———. Ministry of the Environment. *Municipal-Industrial Strategy of Abatement (MISA). A Policy*

and *Program Statement of the Government of Ontario on Controlling Municipal and Industrial Discharges into Surface Waters.* Toronto: MOE, June 1986.
Palloix, Christian. "The Labour Process: From Fordism to neo-Fordism." In *The Labour Process and Class Strategies.* London: CSE Books, 1976.
Panitch, Leo. "Founding the UAW in Canada: Reflections on the Working Class." *Canadian Dimension:* 19, 5 (December 1985).
———. "The Impasse of Social Democratic Politics." *Socialist Register* (1985/86).
Petroleum Association for the Conservation of the Canadian Environment (PACE). "PACE Submission on the proposed Environmental Protection Act." Ottawa, March 2, 1987.
Petrochemical Industry Consultative Task Force. *Report of the Consultative Task Force on Petrochemicals.* June 1978. GOV. DOC. CA1 TI823 78R21.
Petroleum Assoc. for Conservation of the Canadian Environment. *PACE Submission on the Proposed Environmental Protection Act.* March 2, 1987.
Poulantzas, Nicos. *Classes in Contemporary Capitalism.* Trans., David Fernbach. London: New Left Books, 1978.
Pratt, Larry. "Energy: The Roots of National Policy," *Studies in Political Economy:* 7 (Winter 1982).
Rankin, Tom. *New Forms of Work Organization: the Challenge for North American Unions.* Toronto: University of Toronto Press, 1990.
Review Board of the Canada-Ontario Agreement respecting Great Lakes Water Quality. *Summary of Discussion at the Workshop on the Great Lakes Water Quality Agreement, July 16-17, 1987, Burlington, Ontario.* Prepared by the Canadian Environmental Law Research Foundation, December 1987.
Richards, John, and Don Kerr. *Canada: What's Left?* Edmonton: NeWest Publishers Ltd., 1986.
Roberts, Wayne. *Cracking the Canadian Formula: The Making of the Energy and Chemical Workers Union.* Toronto: Between the Lines, 1990.
Robertson, David, and Jeff Wareham. *Technological Change in the Auto Industry.* CAW Technology Report. North York, Ont.: CAW, April 1987.
Rothbaum, Melvin. *The Government of the Oil and Chemical Workers of America.* New York and London: Institute of Labor and Industrial Relations, University of Illinois and John Wiley & Sons, Inc., 1962.
Schrecker, Ted. "Class Conflict, Technology and Health: The Hidden Agendas of 'Risk Management'." *Alternatives* [Canada]: 11, 3-4 (Summer/Fall 1983).
———. "The Mobilization of Bias in Closed Systems: Environmental Regulation in Canada." *Journal of Business Administration:* 15 (1984/85).
———. "Resisting Regulation: Environmental Policy and Corporate Power." *Alternatives* [Canada]: 13, 1 (December 1985).
Sentes, Ray. "Asbestos, Jobs and Health," *The Facts [CUPE]:* 8, 6 (November/December 1986).
Shragge, Eric, R. Babin, and J. Vaillancourt eds. *Roots of Peace.* Toronto: Between the Lines, 1986.
Smyth, Donna. "Finding Out—the Rise of Citizen Science." Narr. Lister Sinclair. Writer Donna Smyth. CBC Radio, "Ideas." January 8-22, 1985.
Snow, Duart. "The Holmes Foundry Strike of March 1937: 'We'll give their jobs to white men!'" *Ontario History.* Ontario Historical Society, 1977.
Spengler, Robert F. "Water Contamination by Toxic Chemicals a Challenge to Cancer Registries in Assessing Population Risks." *Focus on Great Lakes Water Quality:* 7, 2 (IJC Great Lakes Regional Office, Windsor, Ont.).
Smith, Malinda S. "On 'Folksy Fascism': The Ideology of the Klein Revolution." Unpublished paper, Department of Political Science, University of Alberta, March 1995.
Spitzer, Walter O. "A Study of the Health Status of Residents of the Junction Triangle, Toronto, Final Report." Toronto: City of Toronto, Public Health Dept., April 1984.
St. Clair River International Citizens' Network. "Submission to the Ministry of the Environment on the MISA White Paper." September 1986.
State of Michigan. Office of the Great Lakes. *St. Clair River Situation Report.* July 1986.
Stuart-Harle, M. "Dirty Pool." *Canadian Research:* 20, 2 (February 1987).
Task Force on the Management of Chemicals. *From Cradle-to-Grave: A Management Approach to Chemicals.* Ottawa: Environment Canada and Health and Welfare Canada, September 1986.

Task Force on the Petrochemical Industry. *Petrochemical Industry Task Force Report*. Report of the Petrochemical Industry Task Force to the Hon. Edward C. Lumley, Minister of Regional Industrial Expansion and the Hon. Jean Chretien, Minister of Energy, Mines and Resources. February 1984. GOV. DOC. CA1 RI800 84P23.

Taylor, Graham D., and Patricia E. Sudnik. *DuPont and the International Chemical Industry*. Boston: Twayne Publishers, 1984.

Thompson, Barbara. *Mercury in our Environment (with special reference to the St. Clair River system)*. Sarnia: Sarnia Pollution Probe, 1971.

Touraine, Alain, M. Wieviorka, and F. Dubet. *The Workers' Movement*. Trans., Ian Patterson. Cambridge: Cambridge University Press, 1987.

Touraine, Alain, et al. *Anti-Nuclear Protest: The Opposition to Nuclear Energy in France*. Cambridge University Press, 1983. Originally published as *La Prophétie Anti-Nucléaire* (Paris: Editions du Seuil, 1980).

———. *The Voice and the Eye: An Analysis of Social Movements*. Cambridge: Cambridge Univ. Press, and Editions de La Maison des Sciences de l'Homme, 1981. Originally published as *La Voix et le Regard* (Paris: Editions du Seuil, 1978).

Trost, Cathy. *Elements of Risk*. New York: Times Books, 1984.

Union Carbide Canada. "Submission to Environment Canada on the Proposed Environmental Protect Act." (Toronto) February 19, 1987.

United Nations. WCED. *Our Common Future. Report of the World Commission on Environment and Development*. Oxford: Oxford University Press, 1987.

Vergara, Walter, and Donald Brown. "The New Face of the World Petrochemical Sector: Implications for Developing Countries." World Bank Technical Paper No. 84, Industry and Energy Series. Washington, DC: The World Bank, 1988.

Vigod, Toby. "The Law and the Toxic Blob." *Alternatives* [Canada] 13, 3 (September/October 1986).

———. "Overview of federal law, regulation, and policy." In Canadian Institute, *The Fundamentals of Environmental Law and Regulation*. Toronto: The Canadian Institute, 1994.

Wainwright, Hilary. *Arguments for a New Left*. Oxford and Cambridge: Blackwell, 1994.

Wainwright, Hilary, and Dave Elliott. *The Lucas Plan: A New Trade Unionism in the Making*. London: Allison & Busby, 1982.

Walker, Andrew. "Investing in the future." *Dow Canada Dimensions* (October/November 1987).

Weber, Arnold R. "Competitive Unionism in the Chemical Industry." *Industrial and Labor Research Review* (October 1959).

Weber, Max. *The Methodology of the Social Sciences*. Translated and edited by E. Shils and F. Finch. New York: Free Press, 1949.

White, Robert. "From Defeat to Renewal." *This Magazine*: 23, 1 (May-June 1989).

———. "Jobs and the Environment: Notes for a Speech by Robert White, President, CAW-Canada." Jobs and Environment Conference, Hamilton, Ont., November 21, 1986.

Williams, Bob. "Toting familiar demands, OCAW faces uphill fight in negotiations." *Oil and Gas Journal*: 85, 51 (21 December 1987).

Williams, Raymond. *Resources of Hope: Culture, Democracy, and Socialism*. Edited by Robin Gable. London: Verso Books, 1989.

———. *Towards 2000*. London: Hogarth Press, 1983.

———. "Problems in the Coming Period." *New Left Review*: 140 (July-August 1983).

Windsor & District Clean Water Alliance. "Comment on the Municipal-Industrial Strategy of Abatement." September 12, 1986.

Windsor-Essex Water Quality Liaison Committee. "Comments on the Ontario Ministry of the Environment's Municipal-Industrial Strategy of Abatement." August 28, 1986.

Winfield, Mark, and John Swaigen. "Water." In *Environment on Trial: A Guide to Ontario Environmental Law and Policy*. 3rd ed. Edited by David Estrin and John Swaigen. Toronto: Emond Montgomery Publications Ltd., 1993.

Wood, Ellen Meiksins. *Retreat from Class*. London: Verso Books, 1986.

———. and Peter Meiksins. "Beyond Class: A Reply to Chantal Mouffe." *Studies in Political Economy*: 17 (Summer 1985).

———. "Marxism Without Class Struggle?" *Socialist Register* (1983).

Wood, Stephen. "The Co-operative Labour Strategy in the U.S. Auto Industry." *Economic and Industrial Democracy*: 7 (1986), pp. 415-447.

Yates, Charlotte. *From Plant to Politics: The Autoworkers Union in Postwar Canada*. Philadelphia: Temple University Press, 1993.

———. "Public Policy and Canadian and American Autoworkers: Divergent Fortunes." In *Driving Continentally: National Policies and the North American Auto Industry*. Edited by Maureen Appel Molot. Ottawa: Carleton University Press, 1993.

———. "The Internal Dynamics of Union Power: Explaining Canadian Autoworkers' Militancy in the 1980s." *Studies in Political Economy*: 31 (Spring 1990).